THE
ROOTS OF THE WAR

A NON-TECHNICAL HISTORY
OF EUROPE 1870-1914 A.D.

BY

WILLIAM STEARNS DAVIS, Ph.D.

IN COLLABORATION WITH

WILLIAM ANDERSON, Ph.D.
AND
MASON W. TYLER, Ph.D.
OF THE FACULTY OF THE UNIVERSITY OF MINNESOTA

NEW YORK
THE CENTURY CO.
1918

Reprinted, September, 1918
Reprinted, October, 1918

TO

THE GREAT HOST OF YOUNG MEN

WHO HAVE GONE FORTH FROM THE CLASSROOMS
OF THE
UNIVERSITY OF MINNESOTA
TO IMPERIL THEIR LIVES
THAT RIGHTEOUSNESS MAY NOT PERISH
BEFORE AUTOCRACY

INTRODUCTION

This history has been written during the stressful period since the United States became a participant in the great World War. It is not, however, merely a "war book." It is an attempt to relate in a non-technical fashion the history of the development of the various forces that led up to the catastrophe of 1914. The leader of the American Republic, himself a historian as well as a statesman, has stated that "you can explain most wars very simply, but the explanation of this war is not so simple. Its roots run deep into all the obscure soils of history." [1] It is to discover some of these roots and their fateful growths that this book is written.

By general consent the period of history which ended in 1914 saw its beginning in 1870 when the Prussian militarists won their original triumph over France, thereby establishing a precedent for the use of armed force as a wise supplement to flagging diplomacy, a precedent that was to be applied with incalculable effect upon a much greater field of action forty-four years later. During this interval many national and international forces were at work simultaneously, which all together helped to produce the climax of Armageddon. Of course, however, not all the factors that were very prominent in the history of the period contributed directly to this terrific end. For example, socialism, potent as it was, does not seem to have helped to bring about the final war, except indirectly, by making the junker lords of Prussia fearful at its progress and therefore the more willing to try desperate remedies to wean the German people from the new heresy by the counter-excitements and joys of a great military victory. The many colonial and domestic questions of Great Britain also, although of large historical importance, did little *directly* to hasten the war, save by making the Pan-Germans believe that their island rivals were so beset with internal

[1] President Wilson, address at Buffalo, November 12, 1917.

issues that Britons would probably let the Teutonic empires crush France and Russia unhindered, leaving the British Empire to be devoured a little later.

Many things, therefore, that would have an honored place in any comprehensive general history can be wisely omitted from this: nor has there been any attempt at formal discussion of the interests of the United States in Old World affairs before 1914. But in the opinion of the writers of this book there were three dominant factors in the international relations of the last forty years that enabled the Pan-German conspirators to bring on the great calamity in the precise form in which it finally inflicted itself upon the world. These were:

I. The old hate between France and Germany, nourished by the unhealed and unforgetable Alsace-Lorraine question.

II. The newer hate between Britain and Germany, caused partly by commercial rivalry, but much more by the overweening jealousy of the Pan-Germans of the British colonial empire, and by the antipathy inevitable between two great nations, one essentially liberal and non-militaristic, the other precisely the reverse.

III. The eternal Balkan question, the problem of the disposition of the dying Turkish Empire and the straining anxiety of Russia on the one hand and Germany and Austria on the other to become the preferred heirs to the "Sick Man of Europe."

These three factors came to play simultaneously into the hands of the Pan-German schemers, master-financiers and manufacturers, doctrinaire professors, irresponsible journalists, highly-titled officers, princely and royal "Serenities" and "Highnesses," and above these finally, it would seem, the "All-Highest" himself, in *their deliberate conspiracy to achieve at one or, at most, two or three ruthless and gigantic strokes of the sword, the establishment of a world empire, an Empire of Teutonia, indescribably vaster, richer, more irresistible, more universal than that of imperial Rome.*

This book undertakes to outline the circumstances that made this inconceivably daring attempt seem possible.

AUTHORS' NOTE

The majority of the chapters of this book have been written by Mr. William Stearns Davis. Chapters VII, VIII, and XVI have been written by Mr. William Anderson, and chapters XIV, XIX, and XXI by Mr. Mason W. Tyler. Each collaborator is responsible for the final form of his statements, although in every case his two friends have given careful scrutiny to his work. The maps and statistical tables have been prepared by the kindness of Mr. Paul S. Smith, assistant in history in this university.

The authors have felt keenly the difficulty of handling highly controversial subjects in a scientific spirit during this time of great public stress. They have sometimes expressed robust opinions and have not hesitated to call a spade a spade. They have made a faithful effort, however, to write with a due sense of historical as well as patriotic responsibility, and to record nothing that they would, as scholars, be ashamed to review after peace and normal councils have returned. They are all three absolutely persuaded of the justice of the great cause in behalf of which this book is written, and their spirit was well expressed by a British scholar, Mr. J. W. Headlam, when he wrote in the preface of his "History of Twelve Days," published in 1915: "It would be foolish to claim the merit of impartiality. Impartiality means indifference to the results of investigation, and to us the results are of vital moment. I will say this [however]. . . . I have written nothing which I do not believe to be true. Had I found in the course of the work that the result would be unfavorable to the justice and honesty of the cause [of the foes of Germany], I should have adopted the only possible course and kept silent until the war was over."

W. S. D.
W. A.
M. W. T.

The University of Minnesota:
Minneapolis, Minnesota.
March, 1918.

CONTENTS

CONTENTS

LIST OF MAPS

THE ROOTS OF THE WAR

THE GENIUS OF PRUSSIANISM

"The decision on these principles [of liberty against monarchy] will not come by parliamentary debates, nor by majorities of eleven votes. Sooner or later the God who directs the battle will cast His iron dice." (Bismarck, in the Prussian assembly, March 22, 1849.)

"I look for Prussian honor in Prussia's abstinence from any shameful union with democracy." (Bismarck, speaking in 1850.)

> "Thor stood at the mid-night end of the world,
>   His battle-mace flew from his hand:
> 'So far as my clangorous hammer I 've hurled
>   Mine are the sea and the land!'
> And onward hurtled the mighty sledge
>   O'er the wide, wide earth to fall
> At last on the Southland's furthest edge
>   In token that *his* was all.—
> Since then 'tis the joyous German right
>   With the hammer lands to win.
> *We mean to inherit world-wide might*
>   *As the Hammer-God's kith and kin.*"
>   (Felix Dahn, in 1878.) [1]

"I hope that to Germany it will be granted . . . to become in the future as closely united, as powerful, and as authoritative *as was once the Roman Empire.*" (Emperor William II, speaking in 1900.)

THE FRUITAGE OF PRUSSIANISM

"The object of this war [against Germany] is to deliver the free peoples of the world from the menace and actual power of a vast military establishment controlled by an irresponsible government which, having secretly planned to dominate the world, proceeded to carry out the plan without regard either to the sacred obligations of treaty or the long established practices of international action and honor: which chose its own time for the war: delivered its blow fiercely and suddenly: stopped at no barrier either of law or of mercy: [and] swept a whole continent within a tide of blood—not the blood of soldiers only, but the blood of innocent women and children also and of the helpless poor." (President Wilson to Pope Benedict XV, August 27, 1917.)

[1] By kind permission of Doubleday, Page and Company.

THE ROOTS OF THE WAR

CHAPTER I

THE GREAT WAR WHICH BRED A GREATER

ON the evening of July 13, 1870, three high-born gentlemen found themselves around a dining-table in Berlin. The first of these was Otto von Bismarck, minister-president of Prussia: the second was Hellmuth von Moltke, chief of staff of the Prussian army: the third was Albrecht von Roon, Prussian minister of war.

While they discussed the international situation, a telegram was brought in to Bismarck, and the others watched him anxiously. The wire was from their king, William I of Prussia, who was at the watering-place of Ems, and related to an interview he had had with the French ambassador, Benedetti, relative to the proposed candidacy of a Hohenzollern prince for the vacant throne of Spain. Foolish speeches against "Prussian aggressions" and ambitions in Spain had been uttered in Paris, and the French ambassador had been unduly importunate in demanding of the king not merely that he discourage his kinsman, the Prince of Hohenzollern, from seeking the Spanish throne at that time, but that he also pledge the same policy for all the future. King William I, however, was a kind-hearted and moderate man, and although he refused the French requests, he had parted with Benedetti in a manner that left an honorable retreat open to the Paris cabinet and to its emperor, Napoleon III. In France there were, indeed, headstrong fire-eaters, but there were also sensible statesmen who were quite willing to meet the king halfway and not let a petty incident provoke a great war. Therefore King William had sent a fair and non-irritating account of what had taken place in Ems, and had left to Bismarck, his minister, the task of deciding whether or not to communicate the facts to the public.

But Bismarck's heart was not set on peace, nor was that of Moltke, nor that of Roon. The prime-minister who a few years earlier had publicly avowed that German national unity could be won only by "blood and iron," and who in behalf of that unity had provoked two easily avoidable wars, first with Denmark in 1864 and then with Austria in 1866, had now come to believe that France would never be a contented neighbor to a consolidated Germany, that war with her was inevitable, and that such a war would bring into the union led by Prussia those South German states that had refused to enter the North German Confederation founded by Bismarck after the defeat of Austria in 1866.

He had been filled with wrath at what seemed the too yielding attitude of his king toward France, and his feelings were completely shared by Moltke and by Roon. They saw the opportunity for precipitating a war with France slipping away, and were depressed and melancholy at the whole prospect. Perhaps at some later day, when France had modernized her army and had secured an abler leader than the semi-invalid Napoleon III, they would have to fight at greater military disadvantage. Also the desired inclusion of Baden, Würtemberg, and Bavaria under Prussian leadership might have to wait a few years longer. These three high-born gentlemen, therefore, had been sitting over their Rhenish, silent and moody; but now Bismarck, studying the telegram, suddenly realized that the fates were playing into his hands. The king had given him permission to decide what kind of an abstract of his message to give to the papers, and the man who had crushed Denmark and Austria would use all his power.

The minister-president therefore strode into the next room and, bending over a table, with ready pencil "edited" the royal despatch. By striking out a clause here, by rendering a shade harsher a phrase there, and by generally excluding all expressions of conciliation and kindliness, Bismarck transformed what had been a studiously moderate document into what seemed a deliberate challenge to war. William was made to treat the French envoy with almost incredible brusk- ness and discourtesy, and finally to have "shown him the door"; as at least all Paris soon furiously asserted.

The revised despatch was read to Moltke and Roon amid their warmly expressed approval.

"Before it sounded like a parley," declared Moltke; "now it is a defiance."

Bismarck asked a few questions about the state of the army. Roon assured him that all was ready. Moltke declared that nothing could be absolutely certain in a great war, but that he looked on the future with calm anticipation. So the min- ister and the two generals spent a merry social hour, confi- dent now that all chances of peace were gone and that two mighty nations were headed straight toward bloodshed, and thanking their "good old German God" who had brought it all to pass.

Soon another messenger was summoned. Bismarck gave him the new despatch, to be published under the inaccurate date-line of "Ems" in every German newspaper, and to be wired to every Prussian embassy. The next morning all the world was reading how the King of Prussia had "turned his back" on the French ambassador. "There is little doubt," says an authoritative historian, peculiarly favorable to the German cause, "that had this telegram been worded differ- ently, the Franco-German struggle might have been avoided." [1] The responsibility for deluging two great nations with blood and, incidentally, for sowing very many of the dragon's teeth that were to spring up for a fearful harvest in 1914 must, therefore, rest largely with Otto von Bismarck and his two jovial friends.

This does not save the ministers of Napoleon III from the charge of criminal folly and recklessness in forcing the quarrel about the "Spanish candidacy" to a point where Bismarck could catch them in the terrible dilemma of either

[1] Henderson, "Short History of Germany," II, p. 419.

submitting to national humiliation or declaring a war for which they were grievously unprepared.

The foreign minister, Gramont, afterward plaintively excused himself by saying that he would never have pressed the issue had not the military men grossly misled him as to the state of the French army. Bismarck, however, bears all the responsibility of a calm, intelligent man who deliberately eggs on an excited, ignorant one to begin a bloody quarrel.

The great minister in later years was to boast of his act and to expatiate upon the details. The facts are undeniable, and in after days German statesmen, to whom the example of Bismarck loomed as that of a second Jupiter, were taught to consider robust deeds like these to be the very essence of wise patriotism. The Ems despatch was in the mind of every officer and diplomat who met around the council table of the grandson of William I, when that grandson summoned his mighty men to Potsdam late in July, 1914, to consider declaring war on Russia and France and violating the neutrality of Belgium.

"Nothing succeeds like success." This is an American saying, probably of slight ethical value. During the next decades, however, it made Bismarck seem the king of all statesmen. There had been a strong peace party at Paris, despite much jealousy and dislike toward Prussia. The "Spanish-candidature" episode had seemed on the point of being happily lived down, despite high words and newspaper froth. Then, like a bolt from the blue, came the outrageous Bismarckian version of the king's interview with Benedetti. The warm summer weather had filled the Paris boulevards, and the light-headed irresponsible mob simply thundered its cries for war, "To Berlin!" French honor, the honor of the most sensitive people in Europe, had been insulted before all the world. The last arguments for peace were stifled in the French cabinet. Napoleon III, the great adventurer, was none too secure upon his throne. To have refused this challenge to arms would have ruined his prestige with the two elements which then held the rulers of France in the hollow of their hands, the army and the populace of Paris. The

French Chamber of Deputies was in a white heat. Ollivier, the premier, almost a pacifist in his former tendencies, uplifted his voice for action. "If ever a war was necessary," he cried, "it is this war to which Prussia drives us. We continued to negotiate [for a peaceful issue], and in the meantime they announce to Europe that they have shown our envoy the door." The chamber voted for war by two hundred and forty-six, against only ten for peace. The streets of Paris rang with cheers and patriotic music, while men stood about telling tales of Jena and of the first Napoleon's victorious march through Prussia, followed by the glorious peace of Tilsit. In a few days the opposing diplomats had closed their embassies in Berlin and Paris, exchanged declarations of war, and had bowed their respective farewells "with the highest personal consideration," while the two greatest nations of continental Europe rang with the turmoil of mobilization. Bismarck and Moltke were to have their wish.

The story of the months that followed should have been writ large in the school history-books of every American who had grown up imagining that successful armies could be created in a day. It was because the fearful facts developed in 1870 were not forgotten by the French nation that the world did not fall promptly under Teutonic dominion in 1914, when an even greater struggle was loosed upon the earth. Recent events have amply demonstrated, even to their foes, that the French are, at the very least, as brave, as valorous, and as capable of patriotic effort and sacrifice as any of their rivals, and are past-masters in the modern science of war. But the contest of 1870 gave a perfect illustration of the futility of mere bravery and patriotism, when without proper preparation or leadership it is required to cope with a scientifically constructed war-machine controlled by a competent general staff.

The army of Prussia and of the South German allied states (Bavaria, Würtemberg, and Baden) was essentially the same type of army as that which in 1914 went across Belgium and which was halted only at the Marne. Between 1870 and the later date it had, of course, become larger, with more up-to-

date weapons and other military appliances, and with some
improvements in organization. But, in the main, in 1914 it
was still essentially the developed creation of Moltke and of
Roon, perpetuated, but not case-hardened.

The army of France in 1870 was absolutely different from
that second fighting machine which, mobilizing a little more
slowly in 1914 than its rival and swept back at first, turned,
nevertheless, and saved Paris, France, and the world for
democracy in those great September days one short month
after the beginning of Armageddon. The soldier of Napoleon III was just as skilful, brave, and patriotic as his grand-
sire under Napoleon the Great, or his son under Joffre, but the
lack of scientific preparation and capable leadership doomed
him to fight with one hand tied behind his back. The result
was the abject humiliation of France.

Napoleon III, the purple-clad adventurer "condemned to
be brilliant," who had vainly tried to persuade the world
that he was a worthy successor of his mighty uncle, had gained
his throne by too devious methods to be able to place the best
talent of France in charge of his armies. Many of his generals were superannuated and incapable; others were downright soldiers of fortune, more loyal to their own interests
than to their nation. Universal military training had been
introduced into France very imperfectly. A large part of
the population had been exempted from conscription. The
reserves for the regular professional army were inadequate.
The railways were ill-arranged for mobilization. Many articles for equipping the troops were missing. The field-artillery
guns were notoriously inferior to the German. Above all, a
competent commander-in-chief was soon discovered to be utterly lacking. Everything, in short, was amiss, except the
bravery and patriotism of the private and field officers, and
in the circumstances these were to be miserably sacrificed.
It was a case where a nation, proud, courageous, and poten-
tially containing the best fighting material in the world, but
acting under an overwhelming handicap, was to be pitted
against Moltke's relentless fighting-machine.

When the French armies began to mobilize around their

great frontier towns of Metz and Strassburg, the confusion
of their system would have been ludicrous, had not the price
of the laugh been the ruin of the nation. The officers sent to
defend the boundary telegraphed back that they had no maps
of France, although they had many of Germany "soon to be
invaded." An artillery general reported that out of eight
hundred horse-collars sent him, five hundred were too tight
for his horses. A brigadier-general wired Paris: "I have
not found my brigade or my superior commander. What
shall I do? Don't know the whereabouts of my regiments."
Yet all the time Moltke's mobilization was proceeding like
clock-work, so much so that, according to a popular tale, when
the final declaration of war had been handed the general late
one night, he had simply turned to his orderly, saying, "Go
to my desk and telegraph file No. ——," and had peacefully
retired to bed. All had been prearranged. Prussian and
South German mobilization had proceeded without the slightest hitch or hindrance, and speedily vast hosts were pouring
down to the Rhinelands, ready to burst over the frontiers.

When actual hostilities began, Moltke disposed of nearly
five hundred thousand men, besides ample reserves. Napoleon III, if certain paper projects had been executed, should
have had nearly seven hundred and fifty thousand, but the
French program had been only nominally executed. In fact,
the very year that the war broke out a scheme for reducing
the size of the army had been agitated by the pacifists of 1870.
Napoleon III had not assembled many more than three hundred and fifty thousand men before he ceased to be emperor.
Some of these troops were grievously ill-equipped, and not
one of the major armies was properly concentrated. The
only real chance the French had for victory was by a quick
dash into southern Germany, where the alliances between the
local governments and Prussia were still new, and very possibly, in case of defeats, unstable. A blow there, before Prussian mobilization was completed, might have produced great
results, but this chance was entirely thrown away by the
delay in assembling the French armies. Napoleon III, therefore, seemed able only to string out his men in rather isolated

detachments along the frontiers and await the Prussian thunderbolt. The initiative had thus passed at the outset to Germany, and to secure the initiative in war involves winning half the battle. In Paris, meanwhile, the crowds, deceived by a mendacious censorship and assured by the imperial ministers that "the army was ready down to the last gaiter-lacing," complained angrily because no great victories were as yet reported.

Napoleon III had one really capable general, Marshal MacMahon, but he was not in command at Metz, where the main French Army was mustering. The emperor, sick, distracted by silly counsels, and beset with fears for his political future, tried for a while to play the commander-in-chief himself. MacMahon was put in charge of the forces in Alsace, the second theater of war, where he was isolated from his supports and inferior in numbers to the Germans concentrating against him. On August 6, Prince Frederick Charles, leader of the Prussian advance, fell upon him at the heights of Wörth. The French cavalry scouting had been very poor, and they did not realize how they were outnumbered, or they might not have risked a battle. As it was, forty thousand Frenchmen tried to halt the progress of eighty thousand Teutons. MacMahon beat off all frontal attacks, until superior numbers turned his flank and made his case hopeless. The French did all that brave men well could, but presently they left the field in what was little better than a rout. Moltke's machine had struck its first blow.

On this same day there had been a second battle in Lorraine, at Spicheren, where another German army collided with General Frossard's corps. At first the French had superior numbers and superior chances. But by a fatality Frossard himself was absent from the field when the fight began, telegraphing to his superiors at Metz. No subordinate dared order a grand charge. Still the French held their own, and did even better until almost evening, when Frossard, who had returned to find his opportunity gone, began to fear lest German reinforcements were getting near his line of retreat, and ordered a complete retirement. The French had almost won the day, and yet they lost the battle. The soldiers were becoming sullen and were beginning to lose confidence in their leaders, who obviously were without ability as organizers, strategists, or tacticians.

After these two blows there was still greater demoralization and almost despair at the imperial headquarters in Metz. The Germans were pressing forward relentlessly; nevertheless the main French Army was still unbeaten. Under a good commander it could have made a successful stand, but Napoleon III and his parasites were losing their grip on the situation. After wasting time in senselessly marching and counter-marching much of the army, the emperor resigned the actual command at Metz to Marshal Bazaine. The latter was a bluff, high-speaking officer, with a considerable reputation founded on easy successes in Mexico, but he also had a tendency to play the politician as well as the soldier. The position at Metz was so bad that Bazaine quickly resolved to retreat across the Moselle and put his army under the forts of Verdun. But now intervened more procrastination and irresolution, and the Prussians came still closer at his heels. On the fourteenth of August, while Bazaine was trying to march out of Metz to the west, the German advance-guard attacked his rear from the east. The French flung back this force, but it was no real victory. Bazaine's retreat had been halted at a time when every hour had become precious. On the fifteenth the German cavalry was over the Moselle, south of Metz, and threatened to cut the roads to Verdun. On the sixteenth there was infantry with the cavalry, and the battle of Mars-la-Tour, or Vionville, was fought.

The next day Bazaine pretended that he had won a success. Actually he had sustained a disastrous defeat. One hundred and thirty thousand French troops were on the scene and only half as many Prussians; yet the Teutons throughout kept the offensive, and their foes had one exhibition after another of the bungling of their own commanders. When some French divisions won ground, there came no reinforcements, because Bazaine worried more about keeping open the road in his rear, toward Metz, than the one to safety, toward Verdun.

On the seventeenth the great main French Army ignominiously fell back on Metz for ammunition and supplies, while
the steady advance of King William's legions over the Moselle
bridges brought nearer the next act in the tragedy.

On the eighteenth of August, Moltke attacked Bazaine before Metz. His aim was to drive the French back under the
fortress's guns, block their roads of retreat west and north,
and so pen up the whole army. This battle is commonly
called Gravelotte, from one of the small villages around which
the tempest raged. The German victory was complete.
Moltke had now about two hundred thousand men against
only one hundred and forty thousand Frenchmen. But if
Bazaine had been a great leader he need not have lost. He
was, in fact, only a small man overwhelmed by a tremendous
situation. Many of his corps held their own admirably
against all attacks, but his right wing, where the German
assault proved fiercest, received no reinforcements, although
within a few miles of the danger-point lay ample reserves.
Bazaine was holding these back, because he was foolishly in
terror for his left wing, where there was not the slightest real
danger. The French right was thus crumpled up, and their
whole line being outflanked, they fell back hastily upon the
strong fortress of Metz.

The main French army was, therefore, mewed up around
Metz. Speedily it became evident that Bazaine lacked both
energy and power to cut his way through to safety. The
railroad and telegraph were, of course, soon severed by the
enemy, and he could only communicate occasionally with the
emperor by means of disguised messengers. It is needless to
say that he called lustily for help.

A semblance of an army was still left to Napoleon III,
however. MacMahon, after escaping from Wörth, had been
reorganizing his beaten forces, plus some reinforcements and
some unreliable reserve divisions at Châlons. This array was
so obviously inferior to the host that Moltke could detach
from the siege of Metz and aim straight toward Paris, that
MacMahon considered it futile to risk another pitched battle.
Sorely as it hurt his French pride, the marshal realized that

there was only one really wise thing to do, to retire from Châlons toward Paris, fighting delaying actions and, for a while at least, leaving Bazaine to his fate. The latter had supplies to hold out for two months and by drawing the Germans far from their base and by allowing time to organize the great resources of France, MacMahon could hope to turn and rend the invader. This was an intelligent program. It was very like Joffre's scheme in 1914, when after the first efforts to hold the lines in Belgium had failed, that doughty Frenchman retreated to the Marne and under better conditions won a terrific battle. But MacMahon was far less fortunate than his successor. Behind Joffre was a Government brave and willing to trust France. Behind MacMahon was a coterie of self-seeking adventurers and sordid politicians who constituted the court and cabinet of "Napoleon the Little." Already Paris was growling because no victories had been reported and because the invader was on French soil. The emperor was vainly telegraphing "all can be recovered," and his ministers were now reduced to the shifts of issuing lying bulletins, pretending that it was only for high strategic reasons that they did not give out news which would cause the capital "to be illuminated." At the Tuileries, in fact, there was much more fear of the Paris mob than of the advancing Prussians. Base politics had left France unprepared for war; baser politics were now to destroy her last chance of averting defeat.

When MacMahon announced that he intended to retire from Châlons toward Paris, consternation reigned in the imperial ministry. Comte de Palikao, the incapable minister of war, telegraphed that if he abandoned Bazaine, there would be "the gravest consequences [that is, a revolution] in Paris." Napoleon III, who had slipped away from Metz in the nick of time, had not dared to return to his capital with only reports of disasters. He was with MacMahon, not in direct command, but not giving his general the proper moral support to withstand the protests from Paris. MacMahon's heart was heavy, but he dared not disobey Palikao, more especially as vague messages were being smuggled through from Bazaine conveying the idea that he intended to break out of Metz toward the north and hoped that MacMahon would arrange to join him. That marshal, therefore, ordered his poorly organized one hundred and fifty thousand men to march not toward Paris, but toward the Meuse, headed somewhere between Verdun and Sedan, on the desperate chance that he could get into direct touch with Bazaine.

This new movement was so contrary to all rules of sound strategy that for a few days the Prussian general staff could not believe the French would uncover the road to their capital and despatch their only remaining free army on a wild-goose chase. After their cavalry scouts had confirmed the rumors, however, an overwhelming body of German troops was sent after MacMahon. Had the French been a picked force, well provided with cavalry scouts and with good transport service, they might have got safely across the Meuse and worked into contact with Bazaine. But many of the brigades were composed of raw, soft men, and the baggage-train was pitifully inadequate. The columns merely crawled forward, and later the approach of the Prussians made the French hustle in confusion from one place to another, seeking some temporary refuge. On the twenty-eighth of August the state of affairs was so bad that MacMahon for the last time resolved to order a retreat, but Palikao telegraphed him again, "If you desert Bazaine, there will be a revolution in Paris," and the luckless general preferred to face the strong chances of defeat and capture if he held on, to slander and disgrace if he fell back.

On the thirtieth of August MacMahon found himself across the Meuse, indeed, but with his whole army piled upon Sedan, a little town wedged between the river and the Belgian frontier. On the thirty-first the weary French waited carelessly, uncertain of their own plans and ignorant of their imminent danger, but on the afternoon of that day they suddenly found the Germans closing in on them from all sides. The next morning the trap was sprung.

September 1, 1870, saw the climax. The French were outnumbered almost two to one, lacked confidence in their leaders, and were in a veritable pocket between hills and river, where the Germans could seize all the heights commanding the valley and rake it with their cannon. The resistance was gallant and desperate. The French "marine infantry" repeatedly forced back the attackers. The cavalry, which had failed utterly in its proper task of scouting, now flung away its lives recklessly in heroic, though vain, charges upon the Prussian guns. By afternoon the last avenue of escape had been closed, and the French were being forced back into the small fortress of Sedan, now subjected from every side to a terrible converging fire. MacMahon had been wounded, and there was a disgraceful contention among the other generals as to who was next in command. At last Napoleon III, realizing that further resistance meant slaughter, ordered the white flag to be raised and sent this memorable letter to King William:

Monsieur, my brother: Not having been able to die in the midst of my troops, it only remains for me to place my sword in the hands of your Majesty. I am your Majesty's good brother,

NAPOLEON.

Moltke was adamant to the pleas of the French leaders for better terms than absolute surrender. Bismarck declared bluntly that the French were an envious and jealous people on whose gratitude it was useless to count, and that magnanimity, therefore, was quite out of place. There was no possible escape for the trapped army, and eighty-one thousand men— including, as the German despatches gleefully reported, "one emperor,"—gave themselves up on September 2. Earlier in the battle over thirty-seven thousand men had been killed, wounded, or taken prisoner. There had almost never been a like overthrow in all history.

Bazaine already had made a blundering attempt on the thirty-first of August to cut his way out of Metz. It had failed completely. One French army was therefore firmly blockaded; the second had been captured outright. There was no effective force between the Germans and Paris.

By September 19, Moltke had drawn his lines around Paris and was pressing against the forts that encircled that city, but it was not the old government of the Second Empire which now resisted him. Late on the third of September tidings of the disaster at Sedan began to leak out in the great anxious capital. Soon crowds were parading the streets, shouting, "Down with the empire, long live the republic!" The Empress-Regent Eugénie, and her minister, Palikao, were powerless. General Trochu, commander of the garrison, gave them little aid. By the fourth the upheaval had taken an organized form. Prominent Liberals and old Republican leaders, enemies of the Bonaparte dynasty, seized the helm of state with the prompt consent of garrison and populace. A Republican Government of National Defense sprang into being and was accepted everywhere, thanks to the fearful emergency. Eugénie, her young son, the luckless 'Prince Imperial,' and their adherents fled precipitantly to England. On the sixth, Jules Favre, the new foreign minister, could proclaim that "the revolution of September fourth had taken place without the shedding of a drop of blood or the loss of liberty to a single person."

This new Government remained nominally in Paris during the ensuing siege, but a delegation from it left before the Prussians closed around, and undertook to rouse France against the invader. During the two weeks' interval between the revolution and the coming of the Prussians great energy was exerted to improve the defenses of the capital; forts were strengthened, provisions rushed in, and useless mouths sent out. The city defended itself much longer than Moltke and Roon had estimated. The Republican leaders talked, indeed, of peace:—the Bonapartists had made the war: the new régime was not responsible for it. On the nineteenth of September Favre had an interview with Bismarck to see if the invasion could be stopped. The French might have paid an indemnity, but when the Germans demanded Alsace, Favre's proud reply was, "Not an inch of our land, not a stone of our fortresses." After that there could only be war to the bitter end.

The rest of the struggle, however, although it had many heroic chapters, could only have one outcome. The French were without a single field-army of trained and organized troops wherewith to raise the siege of Paris, and within the city only a small proportion of the large garrison was made up of experienced men fit to be pitted against the Teutonic veterans. Nevertheless, for a few weeks there seemed a chance to save the city, for the Germans were now deep in a hostile land, with an extremely long line of communication.

On October 7, Léon Gambetta escaped from Paris. It was before the days of aëroplanes, but he made use of a balloon and landed safely outside the hostile lines. During the siege sixty-four balloons are said to have left Paris, of which five were captured and two lost at sea. Three hundred and sixty-three carrier-pigeons were sent out, and fifty-seven came in. The Germans were on the alert to shoot the birds, but they did not get all of them.

Gambetta was a man of abounding energy and extraordinary capacity for organization. In a short time his enthusiasm was evoking large armies from central and southern France and was preparing to hurl them against the German lines around the capital. These new forces had bravery and patriotism, but they were composed of raw recruits hastily thrown together under inexperienced leaders. Still, they might have succeeded, had not Bazaine done his afflicted country one last disservice. On October 27 he surrendered at Metz, with nearly one hundred and eighty thousand officers and men and about thirteen hundred and forty cannon. Assuredly he was terribly straitened for provisions, but since Sedan he had shown almost no initiative in trying to escape from his besiegers. Probably he had expected some kind of peace would be patched up, and that then his army would be released to restore the emperor to Paris. Certain it is that Bismarck duped him by pretended negotiations, spun along until supplies were at an end. But the French were never satisfied that Bazaine had resisted to the uttermost, or that he could not have held out a little longer, even if his men were almost starving. If it is sometimes the duty of a soldier to die for his country, he ought also sometimes to be willing to exist for it on pitifully short rations. Bazaine was condemned after the war as a traitor, and although his life was

spared and he escaped into Spain, he was to die in ignominious exile, shunned like a kind of Benedict Arnold. Traitor,
coward, or incompetent, his surrender in any case sealed the
doom of France. The two hundred thousand odd Germans
who had been employed in blockading Metz could now be
hurried up to thwart the relief of Paris, and against such
reinforcements Gambetta's improvised militia could only beat
themselves in vain.

The French won some minor successes, but they were never
able to win a general battle or break the ring around Paris.
For one hundred and thirty days the great city held out
courageously, despite growing scarcity of food, while rats and
cats were served in the boulevard restaurants and infants
died for lack of milk. There were several brave sorties, but
none penetrated the German lines far enough to get in touch
with Gambetta's armies beyond. The Germans bombarded
the city with heavy guns and wrought much damage, although
not enough to force a surrender. The end came late in January, when the last sortie had failed and there was no longer
bread enough in Paris for even a scanty ration. The Government of National Defense had not been able to save the capital,
but it had certainly saved French national honor. A winter
of unparalleled severity had increased the demoralization of
the new armies; every attempt to get foreign alliances or intervention from England, Austria, Russia, or Italy, had met with
polite refusals, and flesh and blood could hold out no longer.

On January 28, Paris capitulated on condition that her
garrison give itself up,—all save twelve thousand men retained to preserve order,—and that she pay a special war
contribution of forty million dollars [two hundred million
francs]. On the same day an armistice was arranged to allow
the election of a French National Assembly to discuss terms of
peace.

These terms of peace the French well knew were likely to
be very hard. Gambetta protested vainly against any truce
and desired to continue the war, but the responsible generals
told him the case was hopeless, and the French peasantry were
unwilling to make further vain sacrifices. The newly elected

National Assembly met in February at Bordeaux, and on February 24, Louis Adolphe Thiers, the veteran Liberal statesman, whom the assembly had named as provisional "head of the executive power,"—they had not yet organized the new government—went to Versailles to get the best conditions he could from Bismarck. It was a pathetic and humiliating task —the representative of a proud and hitherto mighty nation forced to go to the triumphant foe and plead for mercy for his country. Thiers acquitted himself bravely and not without some success.

Bismarck bluntly stated the required pound of flesh. He demanded a war indemnity of six billion francs—one billion two hundred million dollars—and the cession of part of Lorraine, all of Alsace, and the fortress city of Belfort near the Franco-Swiss frontier.

When her rulers foolishly rushed her into war, France, if victorious, no doubt had intended to demand the cession of lands in Rhenish Germany. This would have been a wrong, but the world has never acceded to the evil doctrine that two sets of wrongs create a status of right. Alsace-Lorraine had been a part of the debatable lands which had lain between Germany and France in the Middle Ages. They had certainly once belonged to the Medieval Holy Roman Empire wherein Germany had been the main factor. But France had acquired Strassburg, the capital of Alsace, in 1681. She had, however, acquired Metz, the chief town in Lorraine, in 1552. The possession of these lands had been confirmed to France by the great European peace congress at Vienna in 1815, although that congress had been dominated by her victorious foes. As to mere historical claims of possession, there are surely limits to the right to assert them, or Holland might justly be claiming the State of New York, because she held the Hudson Valley up to 1664. A statute of international limitations must some time run out; otherwise there would be no honest peace for the world.

Germans admitted that the Alsatians were contented and civilized under French dominion. Their entire loyalty went to Paris and not to Berlin. They had supplied France with

many of her most distinguished generals and statesmen. A
certain amount of mongrel German was spoken in their villages, but this did not affect the sympathies of the region. If
the question of annexation to Germany had been submitted
to popular vote, the proposition would have been buried under
an enormous adverse majority.

Nevertheless, Prussia demanded Alsace-Lorraine. The
country had been overrun by her armies. German sentiment
demanded that as much of the old "Imperial Land" as possible should be returned to the newly consolidated empire, and
King William had just assumed the title of German Emperor.
Strassburg in French hands always presented great strategic
opportunities for an invasion of Baden and Würtemberg,
while Metz in German hands offered corresponding military
chances for a great thrust into the heart of France. The
wishes of the fifteen hundred thousand Alsace-Lorrainers,
as cultivated, industrious, and honorable folk as existed in
Europe, were the last thing the victors chose to consider.

Nevertheless, Bismarck was too shrewd not to realize that
it would be a serious matter to absorb into the new German
Empire too many Frenchmen. Early in 1871 he talked of
taking only Alsace and Strassburg, but of leaving Metz to
the vanquished, and of using a part of the indemnity to build
a huge fortress a few miles back to cover the frontier. "I do
not like so many Frenchmen being in our house against their
will," he said. "The military men, however, will not be
willing to let Metz slip, and perhaps they are right." Moltke,
for his part, declared that the possession of Metz was worth
one hundred thousand men at the opening of a campaign, and
he easily talked over King William,—now also emperor—who
was first and last a soldier rather than a statesman.

In 1866, Bismarck had deliberately argued that easy terms
must be granted to defeated Austria, because Austria would
some day be valuable as a friend; but he showed no such
merciful wisdom now in dealing with France. As for the
indemnity, it seemed so huge a sum that the victors coldly
calculated that the French would be economically crippled

for many decades in their effort to pay it, and consequently would be incapable of a blow for "revenge."

In behalf of Alsace-Lorraine, Thiers exhausted all his resources; but he found the German leader hard as adamant. In the matter of the indemnity, however, he beat down the claim to five billion francs—one billion dollars,—thanks, possibly, to the aid of British influences which did not care to see the financial world demoralized by the bankruptcy of France. Also to save Belfort Thiers made a resolute stand. Belfort alone of all the great French fortresses had made a brave and successful defense. Its commandant had been no Bazaine. The Germans had been unable to capture it. Now when the Teutons demanded a city which was purely French and which had specially endeared itself to the hearts of all Frenchmen, Thiers turned desperately at bay.

"These negotiations are nothing but a sham!" he cried. "Make war, then! Ravage our provinces, burn our houses, slaughter the inoffensive inhabitants, complete your work! We will fight you to our last breath. We may be defeated, but at least we will not be dishonored."

Bismarck was moved. He could not be sure if Thiers was in earnest, but he did know that the other nations in Europe were growing anxious at the sudden and tremendous growth of German power, and that if war were resumed, France might suddenly find a formidable friend. He retired to consult Emperor William and Moltke. On returning, he said that the French might retain Belfort, provided that Paris would consent to a triumphal march of the Prussians through her gates, something excluded by the original capitulation. This blow to French pride destroyed all the advantages of magnanimity, but Paris submitted to the parade of her enemies, and Belfort was saved. When, in 1914, this fortress became an invaluable bulwark against German invasion from Alsace, no doubt many Teutonic officers cursed the weakness of Bismarck in allowing himself to be overborne by Thiers.

So, by the final treaty—completed in detail at Frankfort, May 10, 1871—France had to pay the enormous sum of one

ars and see a German army occupy her provinces
debt was paid, and was also forcibly deprived of
thousand square miles of territory, with one million
red thousand inhabitants. Vainly some thirty-five
of the doomed lands protested before the French National Assembly against this treaty which tore them away from
France. "Alsace and Lorraine," they proclaimed, "refuse
to be alienated; with one voice the citizens at their fire-sides,
the soldiers under arms, the former by voting, the latter by
fighting, proclaim to Germany and to the world at large *their
immutable will to remain French.*" But nothing could be
done for them. France herself was helpless. England, Russia, Italy, and Austria did not stir. The treaty was ratified.

Thus ended the Franco-Prussian War, provoked by Bismarck for his ulterior ends and precipitated by the incompetent statesmen of Napoleon III, the Germans' unconscious
puppets. Its main consequences were four-fold.

I. It certainly aided to hasten the unification of the German
nation into the new empire. This, however, would have come
to pass within a few years in any event.

II. It weakened France, dethroned her as "first power in
Europe," and put Germany in her place.

III. It gave the rulers of the new Germany unbounded confidence in their military machine, and became a guiding precedent for the unscrupulous but successful use of the same
in wars provoked for aggrandizement.

IV. It fixed a deep gulf of enmity between France and
Germany, and by the creation of the never-ending "Alsace-
Lorraine problem" made it impossible to bridge this chasm
for forty-three years.

To no small extent, therefore, the consequences of this war
produced the greater war of 1914, in which, during 1917, the
United States of America was engulfed despite its ardent love
for peace.

On January 5, 1918, Mr. Lloyd George, Prime-Minister
of Great Britain, spoke of the need of "a reconsideration of
the great wrong of 1871, when Alsace-Lorraine was torn
away from them [the French]. *This sore has poisoned the*

peace of Europe for half a century, and until it is cured, healthy conditions cannot be restored.''

Three days later President Wilson declared to the American Congress that ''the wrong done to France by Prussia in 1871 in the matter of Alsace-Lorraine has unsettled the peace of the world for nearly fifty years.''

CHAPTER II

IN 1871, when the treaty of Frankfort closed the Franco-Prussian War, the map of Europe presented almost the same aspect as in July 1914, saving only the Balkan peninsula, where were to occur eventful changes. In the interval, indeed, Norway was to secede peacefully from her union with Sweden under a common king; and Luxemburg was to become an independent principality, no longer under the king of the Netherlands; but these things were only locally important.

In many respects not shown by the map, the world of 1871 also presented "modern aspects" which made the transition to the twentieth century not very abrupt. The telegraph was in familiar existence, although not as yet the telephone. Gaslights were in the cities, although electric-light so far was hardly practical. The nations already were covered by a considerable network of railways. Iron screw-steamships were plying the ocean, and the first cable was working to America. The recent war had been fought with breech-loading rifles on both sides, and the French had used a type of machine-gun, albeit imperfect and unsatisfactory. In the scientific field Darwin was announcing his epoch-making theories, and modern medicine was advancing to its great discoveries. It had achieved the use of anesthetics, although not yet that of antiseptics. Modern industrialism and commerce, also, were fairly embarked along those lines of development which they were to follow down to 1914.

In political life most of the monarchs of Europe had reluctantly concluded that constitutions, or similar charters of liberties, were unavoidable perquisites of their subjects, and, outside of Russia and Turkey, there were at least the forms of law-making parliaments, popular elections, and political agitation. There were already some people who were classified as socialists, and these were making an organized attack on the privileges of capital and property. The old battle for religious toleration had been won almost everywhere, save in Russia; and Catholics, Protestants, and Jews were usually equal before the law, although often subject to local stigma and social persecution.

The forty-three years which followed, therefore, were not marked in the majority of nations by those bloody struggles for liberty, political or religious, which have made up the history of past ages. As for the claims of socialism and its demand for a new order in society, however vigorous its growth during this time, it did not result in any wars or successful revolutions. Thus in many respects the entire period from 1871 to 1914 lacks the dramatic events and the spectacular heroisms which bulk so large in human annals.

Nevertheless, this whole period was one of the most significant and, it is fair to say, most decisively important in the whole history of mankind. It was the era during which the great peoples of Europe, most of whom had been in a process of consolidation and violent flux since at least 1848, found themselves as nations, solved many of their local problems, suppressed their internal woes and enmities, grew rich and strong and self-confident, and began to look outward. This whole process of looking outward brought them into constant contact,—a contact often jealous and unfriendly,—with their equally forward-thrusting neighbors. For a time, however, the resources of diplomacy sufficed to bridge over the difficulties. No great general war resulted. There were almost annual threats and "crises," but no actual appeal to the cannon. Men accounted wise and honest assured the world that, thanks to the growing spirit of brotherhood and humanity among all peoples, the scientific demonstrations of the folly of war, the absence of many of the causes of quarrel which had formerly set nations by the ears, and the development of the use of courts of arbitration and "peace tribunals" for solving international troubles, a great European war would never come. This confidence grew, rather than diminished, despite sundry ominous warnings from passing events, down to the last days of July, 1914.

And then, suddenly, "the windows of heaven were opened" to pour down not rain, but a deluge of blood. Mankind awoke from its infatuation to discover that all the time it had been merrily trading, traveling, manufacturing, conducting scientific investigations, or agitating schemes for social betterment, another set of forces—whose serious existence it had often ignored, or even denied—had been making all things ready for a carnival of death and devastation such as had not been since intelligent beings walked this planet.

Between 1871 and 1914 there had been slowly collected for action a quantity of international explosives of terrific power. Year by year this fearful magazine grew larger. Year by year the interlocking of human interests made it more certain that very obscure deeds and occasions could produce terrible results. Year by year new scientific inventions also made it certain that the great war—when it came—would be unprecedentedly devilish and would almost unavoidably involve innocent and neutral peoples.[1] Down to the end, however, the falsely optimistic pacifist prophets continued their cry of "Peace, peace!" where there was to be no peace. Then came twelve days of acute stress and agony, from the presentation of the fateful Serbian note by Austria to the final declaration of war upon Germany by Great Britain, and at length the world realized that it had been living in a fools' paradise.

Many things which a few years ago were very obscure, or which could not be spoken of bluntly, are quite clear now and demand plain speaking. To tell the whole story of the decades before 1914, however, it will be needful to wait many years,—till private memoirs have been written and confidential state papers are published. Nevertheless, the great

[1] Before the days of aëroplanes and Zeppelins it would have been impossible to kill women and children in towns hundreds of miles from the war zone. Before the invention of submarines it would have been almost impossible, even for a government as reckless as that of Germany in 1914–17, to indulge in a naval policy which could work such bloody havoc to neutrals as to make the offending country an outlaw among the nations.

facts stand out unmistakably. Curious points will be cleared up later; minor errors will be corrected; but the main chapters can be accurately written.

In 1871 there were, as to-day, six great powers in Europe—Great Britain, France, Germany (the successor to victorious Prussia), Russia, Austria, and Italy. The last named was the smallest, weakest, and newest claimant for major honors. Her position remained somewhat equivocal. Outside of Europe there seemed to be no formidable nations. The United States of America was recognized as a huge body of people who had succeeded in preserving their unity after the great Civil War. It seemed an utterly remote country, however, with many curious problems which few Europeans understood; its navy was small and its army still smaller. Americans took even less interest in European affairs than Europeans did in American problems. Europe also was too busy with her own troubles just then to care to consider whether the Monroe Doctrine was worth violating.[1] That America should actually intervene in Old World problems and diplomatic conferences seemed about the least probable thing imaginable.

As for what is now the eighth great power in the world, Japan, she was barely emerging from the chrysalis of isolation that had imprisoned her for centuries, and she was just beginning to cultivate relations with the Western World. A serious war between the Mikado and his feudal dynasts had been racking her. Japan was regarded in Europe as a second China, only smaller and even less formidable.

One great capital event was startling the world in 1871—the dethronement of France as "first power" in Continental Europe. No nation in modern times ever had so fearful and sudden a humiliation as that which had come to France in the Metz-Sedan campaign. For nearly two hundred years England had, indeed, been mistress of the seas. Her commerce and colonies had grown apace. But for over two hundred years France had been the center of the military, social, and

[1] Napoleon III's experiment in Mexico (1863–67) had been a disastrous failure and a clear warning against similar adventures.

diplomatic life of Europe. She had not succeeded in defeating England upon the ocean, partly at least because so much of her energies had been consumed upon land; but as a witty Parisian had said, "Though England may blockade Havre, the Paris boulevards will remain very pleasant just the same."

Frenchmen liked to call themselves citizens of "the Grand Nation." They could repeat with seeming justice the old boast of their kings: "The ruler of France *without* allies can go to war with whomsoever he will; but the greatest king elsewhere dare not go to war with France, except he have many allies." France had been beaten in great wars. Louis XIV had been defeated; Napoleon I had been defeated. But these defeats were compliments to the greatness of France. Practically all Europe had been obliged in each case to unite against her to prevent her from conquering the wide continent, and even after her defeat she had been left with sufficient power and prestige to make her neighbors shiver at the threat of her anger. Under Napoleon III, vain "man of destiny" as he proved to be, the old prestige of the nation seemed to have returned. His armies had defeated the Russians in the Crimean War and the Austrians in the War for the Liberation of Italy. The axis of European life seemed to revolve in Paris. "France is happy," Napoleon III had arrogantly asserted in 1851, "Europe may live in peace." The French language, French ideas, French books, French manners, French clothes, and French products went everywhere—to the Levant, to the heart of Russia, to South America, to almost every land not strictly dominated by Anglo-Saxons, and when the phrase "European civilization" was used, the speaker, whatever his nationality, probably unconsciously thought of the types and examples of Paris.

Now all was changed in a twinkling. France was not merely defeated in battle. The fearfulness of her disaster seemed to imply that her whole culture and attitude toward life was bad. The world assumed that no nation could undergo so terrible a catastrophe and not be rotten to the core. Men dwelt on certain undoubted defects in the French character and exaggerated the glittering vices that had been purveyed to foreign visitors in Paris; while in such nations as Russia and England, both of which had formerly dreaded French rivalry or invasion, there was ill-concealed satisfaction at her downfall. France was no longer the greatest power in Europe. She was, at best, only a second-class power. There were plenty to argue that she was not a power at all, but a decadent, dwindling nation, now in the evening of her history and without the hope of a national dawn.

All that France lost by the war of 1870–71, Germany gained. And more, too. She was now undoubtedly the "first power" on the Continent. "Europe," it was wittily said, "had lost a mistress and gained a master." The perfection of Moltke's war machine was such that no military nation would have ventured to measure strength with it, unless supported by several formidable allies. But an alliance against Germany seemed one of the last things probable. Italy was still a decidedly weak and unconsolidated nation. Austria had not actually forgotten how Prussia had defeated her in 1866; but Bismarck had taken good care not to humiliate her in the treaty of that year, and he was already making it plain that if the Vienna government would only let German affairs alone and turn its face toward the Balkans, it would meet with no hostility, but probably with decided helpfulness from its neighbor at Berlin.

Russia was extremely friendly to Germany. In 1870 the Czar had virtually served notice on Austria that if the latter came to the rescue of France, Russia would balance matters by aiding Prussia. In return for this, Bismarck had aided the Czar to set aside the old treaty of 1856, which bound him not to keep warships on the Black Sea. This proceeding made England scowl and grumble, but she did not prepare to fight.

With England Bismarck's relations were, indeed, somewhat cold. He was on bad personal terms with the Crown Princess Frederick (wife of the later Emperor Frederick) who, as eldest daughter of Queen Victoria, was accused of conducting a kind of pro-English propaganda at the Berlin court. But England was, on the whole, decidedly friendly to the new order of things in Europe. She had disliked and distrusted Napoleon

III. Prussia had seemed, perhaps, rather too drastic in her penalizing of France, but it was hard to arouse much sympathy for a nation which Englishmen had been taught to glory over—with due memories of Agincourt, Trafalgar, and Waterloo—and to regard as their "natural enemy."

Germany also had another great asset in English eyes. She was not a naval power. France had always possessed a fleet strong enough to give the British Admiralty serious anxiety. Germany had only a few coast-defense iron-clads and gunboats. She had no colonies, and her merchant marine was small. Englishmen did not worry because threats from Berlin caused consternation in Paris and Vienna. Moltke's legions could not fly across or swim the Channel. The average Briton probably would have indorsed Thomas Carlyle's view "that Germany is to stand on her feet henceforth, and not be dismembered on the highway, but face all manner of Napoleons and hungry, springing dogs, with clear steel and honest purpose in her heart,—this seems to me the best news we or Europe has had for the last forty years or more."[1]

Germany therefore could confront the future without great fear of her neighbors. France was helpless. Italy seemed weak and not unfriendly. Austria was forgetting her old grudges. Czar Alexander II and Kaiser William I were warm personal friends. England looked on benevolently while Germany made progress. And so all the great powers were accounted for.

The military success of Germany, of course, enabled her genius to find an outlet in hundreds of peaceful ways. The moral rebound from her victory promptly stimulated her universities, her laboratories, and her printing presses. The wealth which was to pour in upon her from the great indemnity coming out of France gave her financiers and manufacturers for the first time the opportunity to undertake huge commercial and industrial enterprises such as had hitherto centered mainly in England.

The deeds of the German armies made all the world take

---

[1] Carlyle actually said this in 1866, after the defeat of Austria, but it remained good for the British attitude in 1870–71.

notice of those less martial deeds of the preceding century which had shown how versatile were the national capacities. As has been well said, "during the last hundred years the Germans had gained fresh distinction in many fields of national endeavor. German literature could show names which rivalled any in the literature of England or France; German music had surpassed the glory of the Italian; German philosophy, with its cluster of celebrities of the first rank, had not been equalled since the days of Greece; German science had already come to be regarded as second to none; German universities, as the models of learning and advanced thought, were attracting students from all over the civilized world." [1]

There is no prompter advertisement for a nation, however, than that of a military triumph. For the next thirty years all mankind seemed going to school in Germany. The excellence of her science, philosophy, educational, business, and practical efficiency systems made people lose interest in other questions, such as whether her political institutions were keeping pace with the remaining sides of her progress and whether the unscrupulous spirit which had provoked three wars in behalf of German unity might not some day provoke another war in behalf of German imperialism and arrogant expansion. So long as the empire, however, remained under the control of its founder, there was relatively little danger of its launching on a policy of raw aggrandizement. Bismarck in 1871 looked on the new German Federation as a structure altogether too young and uncertain to be subject to fresh risks and chances. Practical in all things, he knew how to draw the wise line between boldness and rashness. He believed that Germany now had territories enough, and that any new annexations would mean danger. He did not see any necessity for imitating England and seeking colonies. He looked on a fleet as a useless expense and luxury, more likely to involve the nation in trouble than to defend its interest. He dreaded the lasting anger of France, and believed that after Sedan and Alsace-Lorraine it was useless to expect that Berlin and Paris could preserve more than official friendship. But France, fighting

[1] Coolidge, "Origins of the Triple Alliance," p. 23.

alone, seemed now too crippled to constitute a serious danger. Bismarck therefore did his best to patch up old feuds with Austria, and particularly tried not to anger either England or Russia. Unless one of these two powers joined with France, Germany seemed safe; and the standing difficulties France had with England and Russia seemed to make the Iron Chancellor's task easy. So long as France was isolated, Germany was secure; so long as Germany was secure, Bismarck was an ardent lover of peace.

All Europe recognized the commanding position and the great personal genius of Bismarck, even while his foes cursed the checkmate he gave to their policies. Not since Napoleon I has any other man ever cast his shadow so impressively over nations not his own. Here is a fair sketch of his character: "His dominant personality, his gift of caustic expression, his apparent frankness, nay, the very brutality of his utterances, fascinated and subjugated those with whom he came in contact. Born for strife, he passionately resented opposition, and was a good hater who seldom forgot an injury. He was infinitely resourceful in detail, keeping open various possibilities and ready to change on the instant, if need be, from one cause of action to another, and constantly bewildering his opponents; but at bottom his aims and ambitions were not complicated." [1] As has been said, his object now was to strengthen Germany and to put her in a position to weather future storms.

Bismarck was now chancellor of the new German Empire. Nominally, he was merely the agent and mouth-piece of his sovereign, Emperor William I. But that worthy old gentleman was not a person of sufficiently acute intelligence and strength of character to hold his own against the demands of the redoubtable minister, to whom, as he understood well enough, he owed his imperial throne and his glory. Also, in fairness be it said, the personal relations of the two men were those of intimate and sincere friendship. Bismarck was therefore really an autocrat. He had been the opponent of liberal and parliamentary institutions in his youth, and he

[1] Coolidge; Ibid, p. 27.

made only the most grudging concessions to the spirit of liberalism in his later days. To him the test of government was prompt efficiency, and prompt efficiency seemed to him to come best in a hereditary monarchy, where the monarch was wise enough to intrust all his vast power to a few energetic, capable ministers, or, better still, to a *single* arch-minister (such as Otto von Bismarck!) who would provide for the public good out of the plenitude of his wisdom, unhampered by sordid political considerations and the tug of parties.

Bismarck could not quite dispense with parliamentary forms; but he accepted their machinery and limitations just as hesitantly as possible. Government, for him, was to be prompt, severe, impersonal, scientific, and therefore efficient. He would willingly have indorsed the adage of the eighteenth century despots, "everything for the people; nothing by the people." There is no evidence, I believe, that he ever read Lincoln's "Gettysburg Address," but undoubtedly he would have declared, if candid, that its ideals of popular sovereignty "of the people, by the people, for the people" was disproved by all historic experience, and threatened extreme disaster for the government which followed and tested it.

Bismarck's political methods and ideas became a standard for the rulers of Prussia and Germany long after his death in 1898. Their fruition came in July, 1914, when a small body of real or alleged military and diplomatic "experts," sitting around the imperial council table at Potsdam, hurried the German Empire into war without giving the nation one fair chance to consider the necessity thereof, and when the well-disciplined German people, on its part, enthusiastically accepted the fearful decision which its lauded and trusted experts had made for it.

In short, the following statement can fairly stand in history:—Between 1871 and 1914 the democratic ideal and its applied political methods made rapid progress in almost every civilized land *save in Germany;* but in Germany, as will be explained later, autocracy and privilege seemed to be making a successful stand. Nay more, by their very efficiency, by the wealth, glory, and creature comforts, and by the glittering hopes extended for the national future, hopes which they presented to the people they dominated, the Prussian militarists and officials seemed to give the lie to the claims of democracy. If their "intelligent monarchy," with its powerful sovereign, officer caste, and its tentacles of civil officialdom, was to prove a lasting success, there would be a setback for democracy throughout the entire world, for democracy would have to be branded as incapable of governing the most formidable, intellectual, and progressive nation of Europe. For this renewed lease of life to monarchism and the things that go with it, the foes of democracy must undoubtedly thank the genius of Otto von Bismarck.

In 1871 Bismarck had achieved no small success as a civil administrator, however rough his methods. He had put down the demands of the Prussian Liberals for a "responsible" government, dependent not upon the will of the prince, but upon a parliamentary majority. He had secured national unity and military glory in a manner that silenced his erstwhile critics and made it impossible for liberalism to get enough hearing in the empire to resume a successful political campaign.

But Bismarck's main triumphs had really been as a diplomat, as a master-player upon the fears, interests, and personal frailties of the rulers of other nations. Indeed, except for his success as a diplomat, he could never have won that prestige for the Prussian throne which saved its domestic power. Bismarck took the international world as he found it, used its methods, and, it must be said, did nothing to improve them. He did not believe in "pitiless publicity," in general arbitration treaties, or in allowing any kind of popular opinion, much less popular clamor, to mold the policies which he conceived (out of his superior wisdom) to be for the interest of the Prussian State. When he actually made a treaty, he executed it faithfully,[1] though by no means overliberally; but

[1] It is impossible to believe that Bismarck could not have realized how the violation of Belgium would have produced consequences outweighing almost any resulting military gains, and would have prevented the German staff from taking the action it did in 1914. He was

when he made a less formal private agreement, his performance thereof often made the statesmen opposed to him curse
themselves as his dupes, misled by glozing words and half-
promises. His methods were those of the private cabinet
and cipher-correspondence. He used innumerable "private-
agents" and downright spies in the foreign capitals, and often
the accredited ambassadors of Prussia were ignorant of their
master's real policy and were allowed to make statements and
engage in actions which Bismarck himself could promptly
repudiate, if such a turn pleased him. Thus, in 1870 the
Prussian Ambassador at Paris ingenuously worked for peace
with Napoleon III, at the very moment that his superior was
pulling every wire in order to bring about war.

In private life the chancellor was undoubtedly a man of
keen personal honor and was not without most of the tokens of
a high-minded gentleman, but in behalf of prince and fatherland he often selected curious standards. Sometimes his
duplicity was so brazen as to have caused the ruin of any
diplomat less astute and without a formidable military state
behind him to make cross-examination perilous. Thus, in
1871 he met the Austrian statesman Beust and disclaimed to
him any intention of trying to acquire the German-speaking
provinces of Austria. "I would rather," asserted the chancellor, "annex Holland to Germany." A little later, however, Beust went to London as ambassador for his government.
Here he met the new Dutch envoy, an old diplomatic friend,
who had earlier been accredited to Berlin. "The first thing
he told me," recounts Beust in his memoirs, "was that Bismarck had reassured him as to the rumor that Germany
wished to annex Holland, by saying that he (Bismarck) would
greatly prefer to annex the German provinces of Austria." [1]

Such methods appear so outrageous as to be likely to produce
their own punishment. But Bismarck had many factors in
his favor. In the first place, Napoleon III, the ruler whom he

unscrupulous, but not blind to the practical disadvantages of immorality
in many cases.

[1] Coolidge; "Origins of the Triple Alliance," p. 31, note quoting
Beust's memoirs.

befooled the most, met so utter a downfall that he could never take vengeance. In the next place, the mighty Teuton did not overdo the game of duplicity. Very frequently he bluntly spoke the truth, threw all finesse to the winds, and went straight to the point of his desires. It was far more dangerous to assume that he was lying than that he was sincere. In the third place, oblique methods in diplomacy were no monopoly of his. They had been inherited from the long line of red- or purple-robed prevaricators, whereof the leaders had been such Olympians as Richelieu, Frederick the Great, and (more recently) the Austrian Metternich. Diplomacy, the game of kings, with cities as pawns and provinces as the greater pieces, had long been reckoned a refined combat of wits in which the least guileful was the surest loser. All must be done dexterously, smoothly, politely, remembering well that the penalty for loss of temper at a detected intrigue or falsehood might well be a very disastrous war. You lied to your neighbor because he was presumably lying to you; and Bismarck had probably a much cleaner record in these matters than many of the hopelessly mediocre French, Austrian, and Russian diplomats with whom he contended.

Theoretically, the standards of European diplomacy were more honorable in 1871 than they had been, let us say, a hundred years earlier. Honesty was being recognized as usually the best policy. Wars were becoming so terrible that they were not entered upon save for some presentable public end. But while, even in Prussia and Russia, governments had come to hesitate over imposing a new tax or a new civil reform, without at least taking public opinion into account; and while in most other lands any internal change was impossible without free public discussion and legislation in a parliament; yet *diplomacy,* i. e., the settling of questions of peace and war and matters touching the lives and happiness of millions, usually was handled by a small cabinet of ministers, if not by only *one* minister alone with his prince. And if there was a parliament, it was only convened to give perfunctory assent to an accomplished fact, or perhaps to vote the money-credits for a war already declared.

Diplomacy, in short, had not become democratized to any large extent. It still continued suave, private, and often immoral. In the name of the public weal, things innumerable could be done behind the curtain, and a clever writer has thus parodied the diplomatic records of days, alas, not too far departed. He makes a hypothetical ambassador report: "His Excellency, the foreign minister, received me with the uttermost cordiality. He assured me that his Government had sent no letter to the 'Panjandrum' and had never entertained the idea of sending any. As I had myself read the letter which His Excellency had sent, I thought it best to express the uttermost gratification at his Excellency's assurance, and said that my Government had been guided by the same principles. I do not think he detected my knowledge, or suspected that *I had written* to the 'Panjandrum' *first!*" [1]

France, Russia, Austria, England, as well as Germany, had been doing these things for centuries. But the world was getting sick of such methods. They were no longer proving absolutely necessary to success. Cavour, the great Italian, seems to have been able to unite his country territorially, without making public and personal honor pitifully separate. Other leaders in other lands were trying to uphold better standards. But Bismarck preferred, on the whole, the old way, a way which was to become increasingly revolting to men of the twentieth century. The "secret service fund," the elaborate spy-system, the corrupted foreign official, the intercepted mail-packet, the confidential half-promise and understanding —these he did not despise. He used them successfully. His lieutenants, who grew into his power, used them. Their standards were not changed. At last came the catastrophe of 1914.

To sum up, then, the achievements of Bismarck. He consummated the federation of all the German states (minus the Austrian lands) into one empire; he made that empire the most formidable power in Europe; he put the German people in a position to give free rein to their remarkable abilities for

[1] Murray; "Foreign Policy of Sir Edward Grey," p. 42.

intellectual, scientific, and commercial conquests; but he did not give them a free government; and he did not introduce into diplomacy any new ideals corresponding with the world's developments in science, personal ethics, and humanity. He used the old tools of statecraft, now becoming rusty in other hands, and he gave them new credit by wielding them with incomparable skill. The Germans did well to honor him as a supremely great man; but they did grievously ill not to recognize how much of clay was mingled with his iron.

CHAPTER III

HAVING conquered his main foes, Bismarck desired for the remainder of his career to preserve the public peace.[1] This, as already explained, was not so difficult a task as it became after his death. In 1871 almost all the great powers of Europe were winding up a series of experiments in the way of internal reforms or changes, and until the results of those changes were evident, none of them was very anxious to seek trouble by schemes against its neighbors. In the Balkans, to be sure, the extreme feebleness of the Turkish Empire and the oppression of the Christian populations therein by their Moslem masters were creating a problem which gave intense interest, especially to Russia, England, and Austria. But in the main, international conditions after 1871 were fairly static.

To understand these conditions in Europe it is needful, therefore, to say something about these internal problems, because even if a story deals primarily with wars and diplomacy, the interior politics of a nation often react seriously upon its whole attitude toward a foreign question. Fear of an economic setback has kept many a country at peace when its hotheads have cried for war, and there is also ample room for the contention that finally, in 1914, the German ruling classes desired war, to a large extent because the pressure for liberal reforms (especially in favor of the hated socialists) was becoming so serious that it could not well be resisted, unless all domestic questions were dropped from sight amid the uproar of a great international conflict.

In 1871 the six great powers had each a set of internal problems sufficiently serious to tax the best energies of their respective statesmen. Two of these nations—France and Ger-

[1] Whether, by exception, he desired war with France in 1875 will be taken up elsewhere.

many—had such important questions to solve that they are
best handled in separate chapters, but an explanation may be
made of the status in which each of the other four nations
found themselves.

By far the greatest power in Europe outside of Germany
and possibly including Germany, was Great Britain. Her
army was small and sent no tremors through the war department at Berlin, but Bismarck, though he disliked the English,
never committed the folly of despising them. His relations
with England, though sometimes cold, were always correct,
and usually they were outwardly friendly. England, he realized, by her fleet could blockade any coast; by her wealth she
could finance many poorer powers with large armies; and by
her vast network of commercial and economic interests she
could exert her influence all over the globe. Thus he saw she
was a nation which it would be folly to provoke without the
gravest possible cause.

England had possibly reached the zenith of her career in
1815, but she had hardly declined. No European power pretended to rival her navy, and it was long before there was
serious rivalry to her merchant marine, her commerce, and her
manufactures. In the sixties the American Civil War and the
substitution of steel for wooden vessels had enabled her to
escape from the competition of American shipping which for a
while had been becoming formidable. Her colonial empire
did not cover as much of Africa as it does to-day; but she
already held in her grasp India, Canada, Australia, and innumerable isles. Resting secure behind her "oaken walls"
(now, with the change in ship-building, becoming no less formidable "walls of steel"), she had been able to keep clear of
most of the rivalries and wars of the Continent. She entered
into no permanent alliances. She threw her mighty influence
usually on the side of peace, and always on the side of that
party which was striving to preserve the status quo and to prevent the alteration of the "balance of power,"—in other
words, the sudden uprising of some Continental Empire which
would overshadow all others and ultimately become a menace

to England. Since Bismarck had put a happy stop to French schemes against Britain, and himself seemed quite content with the gains of 1871, England reciprocated his desire for friendly relations, although by no means indorsing all his deeds and methods.

In 1871 England most decidedly was not looking beyond herself, but was concerned with internal questions. Her constitution and institutions were entering upon a new period of growth and peaceful development. In 1867 she had adopted a new system of choosing members of Parliament, by which the vote was open not merely to the middle, but also to the great industrial working classes. This change was bound to undermine the former control of English politics by the nobility and high-bred gentlemen, and to put the country gradually upon a democratic basis, with the king more than ever allowed ''to reign, but not to govern.'' However, the management of English policy was still mainly in the hands of men with genealogies, who wore long black coats and who could quote university Latin. It was clear, nevertheless, that the old order was passing. In 1868 Mr. Gladstone became prime minister and remained in office until 1874. To him and to his fellow Liberals aggressive war and an ambitious foreign policy was one of the last things possible. They were not ultra pacifists, but they were so intent upon a long program of internal reforms—for the benefit of the working classes, for the relief of the undoubted woes of Ireland, for the termination of some of the absurdities still retained by the established Church of England—that they restricted their foreign interests to a minimum. The great colonial empire was an inconvenience, something possibly to be gotten rid of. ''Little Englanders,'' so their Conservative foes sarcastically called them. And whatever their faults, certainly a willingness to rush the British nation into war was not to be reckoned among them. They allowed France to be crushed in 1871 and never raised a finger; and they had no pet projects in foreign parts which awakened the anxiety of Continental statesmen.

In 1871 England seemed a mighty power, yet more than ever she appeared to be *in* the European system, but not *of* it.

Thanks to this detached position behind "the inviolate sea," Englishmen boasted that they had no need for the great conscript armies which all the Continental nations were adopting in imitation of Germany. The British army was made up of professional soldiers. The officers were usually younger sons of the nobility and gentry, who entered the army as a career in lieu of the church or the law. The rank and file came from such of the lower classes as had been unsuccessful or were dissatisfied in civil life. The average enlistment was long, and the army was never part of the nation, as in France or Germany. The British army was reputed very brave, and had won many victories over African and Asiatic barbarians, but critics claimed that its valor was more heroic than scientific. In the Crimean War (1853-56) it had not seemed on the whole to have fought so well as its French allies. That Britain was a purely naval power, and could not be expected to make a formidable diversion in a European land war, was something regarded as almost axiomatic down to 1914, and this fact entered into all the calculations of Continental statesmen, much as they dreaded England's wealth and navy.

If England was the richest, most sedate, and secure of the great European states, Italy was the poorest, most recently consolidated, and most uncertain as to her future.

Until 1859 Italy had been only a mass of petty principalities and kingdoms, backward, despot-ridden, poverty-stricken, and very unhappy. "Italy is merely a geographical expression," Metternich, the one-time prime minister of Austria, is said to have remarked. In 1859-61, however, thanks to the genius of Cavour, the great minister of Victor Emmanuel, king of Sardinia-Piedmont, and to the intervention of the French armies of Napoleon III, Austrian influence had been largely destroyed in the peninsula, and the process of territorial unification had been completed by the winning of Venetia in 1866 and of Rome in 1870.

The domestic problems of this new great power are treated elsewhere. They were sore enough to give the statesmen of the reigning house of Savoy scope for all their energies, without looking beyond their borders. Nevertheless, after the first years of reconstruction Italy began to discover that she had hopes and policies that took her beyond her boundaries of 1870. These ambitions were somewhat three-fold:

I. The problem of *Italia Irredenta* (Unredeemed Italy), which concerned the Italian-speaking lands at or near the head of the Adriatic. Here there was a great question which in 1915 was to set the nation again on fire, but its details are discussed in another place.

II. Across the Mediterranean, in North Africa, France had already annexed Algeria and was making a fair beginning toward a vast colonial empire. Italians, however, were even then casting longing eyes on Tunis (directly opposite Sicily), and on Tripoli, which lay more to the east. In ancient days the Mediterranean had been an Italian lake. Might it not be so again? The Italians were too weak and undeveloped at first, nevertheless, to prevent France from seizing Tunis. Much later, however, they were themselves to stir up the diplomats by their seizure of Tripoli, one of the main acts in the drama directly preliminary to the outbreak of the Great War.

III. In addition to North Africa, the Italians presently discovered an interest in a country nearer home. Directly across the Adriatic lay Albania, a misruled province of the crumbling Turkish Empire. If Italy held the ports of Albania, she would control the exits to the Adriatic, a position of enormous strategic advantage. So long as "Turkey in Europe" retained its grip on Albania, Italy did not stir, but her interest therein was long known. When, in 1912, during the first Balkan War, the Turk was obliged to turn Albania loose, the Italian interest therein was instantly manifest; and it was partly through fear lest Austria gain control of the Adriatic that Italy entered the Great War in 1915.

In 1871, however, the main concern of Italy was to keep herself together. Besides the clerical opposition, her leaders faced numerous agitators for a socialistic republic and gangs of downright revolutionists with hankerings for anarchy. The extreme poverty of the country made an ambitious foreign policy almost impossible, and German military critics sneered cynically at the alleged fighting qualities of the Italian army. Nevertheless, for the sake of national prestige, Victor Emmanuel's ministers claimed for their country the honors and prerogatives of a Great Power, and her neighbors were compelled rather grudgingly to make room for her.

Between 1871 and 1914 Italy was to grow steadily in internal strength and international consideration. Very possibly it was her refusal in 1914 to side with Germany, and her decision in 1915 to fight against her, which largely determined the later tendencies of the Great War.

The old foe and present neighbor of Italy was the Austro-Hungarian monarchy, or more popularly Austria.[1]

Austria was not a nation; it was a conglomerate of peoples under the Hapsburg dynasty. That it existed for centuries, and even expanded its bulk sometimes, was due to an amazing amount of good luck, eked out frequently by the great personal abilities of its rulers. Down to 1804 the rulers of the divergent "Austrian lands" had usually claimed leadership in the shadowy Holy Roman Empire, which was merely a loose confederation of the states of Germany. They had actually called themselves "Cæsars" and "Roman Emperors," as if heirs of Charlemagne and Augustus. This absurdity had gone on for centuries. But the Holy Roman Empire, which long before its dissolution had become a pitiful pretence to greatness, had finally evaporated amid the cannon smoke of Napoleon I. The ruler of Vienna dropped the pretentious title and took the sounder one of Emperor of Austria, based on the ample lands he held in his own right.

To state all the countries over which the Hapsburg kaisers claimed personal lordship was a geographical exercise. Some of the lands had been gained by conquest, some by marriage treaties, and some by recovery from the Turks of Christian territories where the infidels had destroyed the native dynasties.[2] Each district had its own institutions, nobility, privi-

---

[1] Austria will be ordinarily used hereafter as the convenient name for this government, including that of Hungary.

[2] This was the main basis for Austrian claims to Hungary.

leges, and often its own special race and language. Even if loyal to the person of the emperor, the various nationalities hated nearly all their neighbors under the same ruler. It was this state of mutual antipathy which made some kind of central authority indispensable, lest the whole region dissolve in local wars and anarchy. This really kept the empire alive through many crises which almost destroyed it.

In 1870 the Austrian kaiser was Franz-Joseph, who had begun to reign in 1849 and who died a very old man during the Great War (1916). In 1848 a revolution had racked the empire. The then ruler, Ferdinand, had been constrained to take solemn oath to respect the new constitution granted to Hungary. Soon, however, the reactionaries, getting the upper hand, wished to annul this charter. Ferdinand's oath stood in their way, and they persuaded the emperor to abdicate in favor of his nephew, Franz-Joseph (1849). The new ruler was bound by no personal pledges, and therefore felt free to violate the constitution. War blazed up. The outraged Hungarians defended themselves valiantly, but the czar hastened to the support of his fellow-autocrat. The liberal movement, both in Austria proper and also in Hungary, had ended in the blood or exile of its champions. Franz-Joseph thus began his reign with a broken promise and a victory over his own subjects.

This was not an auspicious beginning for a reign, and later events, in their turn, had not been fortunate. In 1859 this kaiser had been defeated by the French and by Sardinia-Piedmont and was forced to cede Milan to the Italians. In 1866 Bismarck had entangled him in war with Prussia and Italy. Austria, at least on the northern side, again had been roundly beaten. She had to make peace by surrendering Venetia to Victor Emmanuel, and even more humiliating was her promise to withdraw from all her old interests in Germany and to leave Bismarck free to organize first the North German Confederation, and next the mighty German Empire. In 1871 Austria was by no means so large nor so formidable a power as she had seemed when Franz-Joseph began his government. Nevertheless, he did not lose his throne. The political situation within his dominions was so complex, with so many cross-currents and contending races and interests, that responsible men shuddered at the prospect of deposing their kaiser and launching forth on the waves of revolution. Each people within the empire desired a preferred position for itself, but most of them were willing to acknowledge Franz-Joseph as their personal sovereign, rather than experiment with an upstart local dynasty.

History will probably have trouble in deciding whether this ruler, who lived and reigned for almost sixty-seven years, was a great statesman or merely a clever politician. His personal life was not blameless. The story of his estrangement from his noble empress, Elizabeth, makes very unpleasant gossip. Under his influence the court at Vienna had more than the ordinary amount of scandal among the archdukes and archduchesses—morganatic marriages, divorces, elopements, duels, and downright murders. As a public character, it may also be said that Franz-Joseph healed very few of the grievous sores and evils which existed in his empire when his reign began. Certainly, too, he possessed no constructive genius. But if he did few great things, he surely did many clever things, and he kept the "Dual Monarchy" together as a formidable power, despite constant predictions of disaster and dissolution.

To have organized this ruler's empire into a compact, unified nation would have exceeded the abilities of Julius Cæsar. Omitting smaller races, like the Jews and Gipsies, at least nine considerable peoples jostled one another within the confines of the monarchy. In the west, centering around Vienna, were the Germans, who liked to consider themselves the ruling class for the entire dominion. In Bohemia were the Slavic Czechs; in Galicia (the Austrian share of dismembered Poland) were the equally Slavic Poles, while along the shores of the Adriatic and in the Tyrolian land, the "Trentino," the speech and race was Italian. However, within the dominions of the old "Crown of St. Stephen," in other words Hungary, the ruling folk (though not the majority of the whole population) were the lordly Magyars, who lived on cold terms with their Slavic neighbors, the Croatians, the Slovenes, Ruthenians, etc., and their "Latin" neighbors in the eastern districts, the Rumanians. Although the Germans and the Magyars, taken altogether, were in a minority when opposed to the various Slavs and Latins, nevertheless these two races were in a position of such advantage through long possession of the government, superior wealth, social influence, and the like that they could ordinarily manage the entire empire, provided they were able to work together. Unfortunately, however, for the stability of the races, in 1848–49 the imperial government had fallen out utterly with the Magyars, and this produced a schism in the empire, which spelled confusion. Therefore, after being beaten by France in 1859, Franz-Joseph had tried to consolidate and popularize his régime by granting a constitution, with only limited popular rights, to be sure, which attempted to organize all the races into a single empire on a decidedly consolidated system. This was the "Constitution of 1860," modified in 1861.

The attempt broke down, partly because the new government was not sufficiently liberal in its theories, but mainly because its success would have put the administration almost exclusively in the hands of the German element which controlled the court, the army, and the capital. All the lesser races boiled with anger, but the Magyars most of all. They did not recognize Franz-Joseph's right to make over their beloved native institutions, and their Diet refused to address him as "Emperor," but only as its "Most Gracious Lord." By 1865 it was evident that this scheme for a united Austrian monarchy was a failure. Then, in 1866, came the disastrous war with Prussia, and Franz-Joseph was driven to still further concessions to mollify his subjects.

The battle of Sadowa that year did more than deprive Austria of her right to meddle in strictly German affairs; it compelled her to become a semi-eastern state. She had now been booted out of Italy and also from Germany. Her Hapsburg emperors of strictly German lineage no longer reckoned more than twenty per cent. of their subjects as of the same race as themselves. They had just lost nearly all their grip

on Italy. They had no hopes of expansion toward the west.
If their monarchy was to have any future, it must be by expanding eastward, by cultivating its non-German elements,
and by trying to vie with Russia as one of the preferred heirs
of the moribund Turkish Empire. The obvious thing to do,
therefore, was to make the powerful Magyars happy within the
Hapsburg dominions, and the Vienna kaiser promptly made
the needful concessions.

The emperor at this stage intrusted his policy mainly to the
guidance of a former Saxon nobleman, von Beust, who had
entered Austrian service and who was able to take a fairly
detached view of the claims of the contending races. Von
Beust saw clearly that the only hope of preserving the monarchy was by uniting the two predominant races—the Germans and the Magyars—against the numerous lesser races—
especially the Czechs, Poles, and Croats. In 1867 the empire
was completely reorganized along certain main lines. These
were preserved, despite much friction, down to 1914. The
Hapsburg dominions were deliberately cut in twain, except
for certain essential purposes. The sovereign took the title
of *Emperor* of Austria when he was in Vienna, but the *King*
of Hungary when he was in Budapest. Hungary, with
Croatia, Slavonia, and Transylvania, was set off as a separate
monarchy, with its internal institutions so arranged that the
masterful Magyars were practically sure to control its politics.
Austria, i. e., all the rest of the Hapsburg dominions extending in an irregular semicircle from Rumanian Bukowina on
the east to the Italian lands on the southwest, was somewhat
less surely dominated by the Germans centering around
Vienna. Von Beust was quite frank in his attitude toward
the various lesser peoples, remarking cynically to the new
Hungarian ministry, "Do you take care of *your* barbarians;
we will take care of ours!"

Each of these states of the Dual Monarchy had its parliament, with ministries which were to a certain extent dependent upon the good-will of the majority of the deputies, and it
also had its own complete internal autonomy. The coins of
each country circulated in its neighbor, but the legends on one

set were Hungarian, and on the other were Austrian. Foreign affairs, the army and navy, and certain finances connected with common expenses, the two states shared together. When there was need for adjusting these problems delegations from the two parliaments, equal in number, convened separately, and after exchanging opinions in writing, if they could not reach an agreement, met jointly not to debate, but only to vote. A bare majority of this united body settled the issue. In almost every respect the equality of the two realms seemed complete, but the Magyars showed their political skill and willingness to take advantage of Franz-Joseph's need for harmonious action by driving a hard bargain financially. They took over only thirty per cent. of the old imperial public debt, although Hungary probably contained much more than that proportion of the whole wealth of the empire; and since 1867 it has often been complained that the Magyars exercised more than fifty per cent. of the influence in the Dual Monarchy, but bore less than one third of the economic burden.

In 1870 this experiment of a twin state was very young and defied classification by political theorists. Its bloody dissolution was frequently predicted. All the lesser peoples were more or less dissatisfied, and some were speedily working themselves into an ugly mood. If the Magyars could make equal terms with the Germans, why not the various branches of Slavs? But the lesser races, it was to develop, were too weak singly and too disunited collectively to make great headway. In Bohemia the agitation of the Czechs for a separate "kingdom" at Prague, just as there was now a "kingdom" at Budapest, became bitter and resulted in many riots, with the virtual exclusion of the German language from many quarters of the region. Like hopes and antipathies also arose in Croatia under the Magyar supremacy. But Franz-Joseph proved a master-politician in playing one angry group against another and in fending off any actual rebellion. To keep the Czechs from getting allies, the German-Austrians, in their turn, made friends with the unfortunate Poles of Galicia. This fragment of the old Polish kingdom had nothing to expect in the way of independent existence, unless Russia and

Prussia should disgorge their Polish seizures. The Galicians therefore were quite willing to work happily with the Germans in exchange for fair local treatment Within Hungary, also, the skill of the Magyar minority kept the non-Magyar majority completely divided. The Rumanians in Transylvania had nothing in common with the Slavs in Croatia, except a certain dislike for their common masters, and a moderate amount of skill prevented them from *all* agitating too fiercely at the same time for official recognition of their native languages (a frequent point at issue) or for other special privileges. A clever juggling of elections usually made the Hungarian parliament consist largely of Magyars. The lesser peoples were noisily angry, but physically helpless.

Thus Austria's main problems in 1871 seemed to be strictly internal. What object in seeking new territories, when the old ones seemed worse compacted than those of any other power in Europe? But the Hapsburgs were an old and proud dynasty, with a long record of ambitious wars and acquisitions. If they resigned all hopes of expansion, were they not doomed to wither and perish? Besides, have not foreign broils and wars, assuming they bring glory, been a standard remedy with old-line statesmen for internal discontents? Likewise, it should be noticed that Franz-Joseph's reign had so far not been very fortunate. He had lost his grip alike on Italy and Germany, although one of the favorite titles of the princes of his line had been "augmenter of the realm," and he could only vindicate himself by new annexations. Finally, it should be said, Austria, taken as a whole, lacked an adequate sea-coast. She was not so landlocked as Russia; she had, in fact, several good harbors on the Adriatic and an efficient navy which had defeated the Italians in 1866. Nevertheless, the eyes of Vienna and Budapest statesmen turned greedily toward Saloniki, that great city on the Ægean which is the natural outlet for two thirds of the Balkan peninsula, if they did not turn toward Constantinople itself. While Russia felt herself the predestined heir to the Turkish Empire, Austria was hardly less conscious of this same destiny. After 1866, with her losses in Italy and Germany, the location of all her hopes and aspirations was violently shifted toward the east, and down to 1914 her statesmen never ceased to look on the Balkan Peninsula as containing the lands which some day would recompense them for the losses of 1859 and 1866.

Austria had a large army recruited by universal conscription, as was now, indeed, the custom of practically the entire continent. Her troops were reputed brave and skilful, despite defeats by France and Prussia. Her industrial life was not very highly developed, but her commerce was considerable, and the great estates on the plains of Hungary, the possessions of the lordly Magyar magnates, represented a huge agricultural interest. Taken all together, Austria seemed a far more powerful and wealthy empire, for one cannot say nation, than Italy, although she was considerably overshadowed by her mighty neighbors, Germany and Russia.

Russia, like England, was in Europe, but hardly of it. Napoleon had said, "Scratch a Russian and find a Tartar''; and while this sweeping generalization was possibly unfair, it was undoubtedly true that the Russians had far more in common with Asiatics than any of their western neighbors.

Nearly two centuries had elapsed, in 1871, since Peter the Great (1682–1725) had begun the introduction of foreign customs and refinements into his utterly backward empire. It was nearly a century since the mightiest of his successors, Catherine the Great, had driven the Turks from the northern side of the Black Sea and begun to intrude Russian influence into the politics and policies of Western Europe. Russia was still an enigma, however, to her foreign contemporaries; and it is proper to say that she was also an enigma to herself. The czars claimed for their people full status as a civilized race and the right to participate in the general life of the world. Yet of their hundred million-odd subjects, only a very small percentage were in a position to enjoy that general civilization which Germans, French, Italians, Englishmen, and Americans seemed to possess in common. The reason for this, of course, was that western ideas and manners had not grown up in Russia spontaneously; they had been imposed by authority from above. Peter the Great, by the sheer force of his personality and the ruthless use of the despotic powers of the czars, but with the direct sympathy of only a minute fraction of his subjects, had compelled the Russian *boyars* to indulge in such elementary refinements as trimming their outrageous beards and allowing their women to escape from a seclusion almost as strict as that of Turkish harems. He had also imposed on Russia a taxation system based on western models, an army system organized somewhat after the principles of Prince Eugene and the Duke of Marlborough, and a scheme of administrative ministries and government bureaus not unlike those of Louis XIV of France. He had contended with a vast amount of national inertia and a certain amount of downright rebellion; but the more obnoxious malcontents had quickly lost their heads. The great czar had lived long enough to put his impress upon his entire country, and things never reverted to their old medieval stagnation.

Late in the eighteenth century, at the court of Catherine the Great (1762–1796), could have been seen a company of fine ladies and gentlemen, talking French, dabbling in French philosophy, affecting the theories of French humanitarianism, and wearing Paris-cut garments. The administration, army, and the life of the Russian upper classes had by this time received a distinct veneer of the glittering culture which characterized the old régime just before 1789 and the French revolution. But these philosophizing lords and ladies did little that was effective in lifting the level of the doltish peasantry under them. The serfs in the innumerable villages still dragged out life in hovels and kennels, tilled the soil in dense ignorance of all wise systems of agriculture, and groveled before the local orthodox priest and his dirty icons. At the empress's court it was entirely agreed that the serfs *ought* to be freed; but no one could hit on a proper method of doing it. There were no really large cities in the empire, save only St. Petersburg [1] and Moscow, and consequently there was little of that intellectual progress which comes from an active, urban

[1] Since the term Petrograd was only ordained in 1914, it has seemed best in an historical work to keep the old-style spelling.

life. Industries and commerce were backward. The empire lacked harbors, save on the Black Sea (where the exits were controlled by the Turks) and on the Baltic and White Seas, where the ice halted navigation for six months each year. There was a Russian navy, but many of the officers had been Englishmen, Dutchmen, and the like, and it was, on the whole, the sovereign's expensive toy and luxury. Roads were bad, and communication between province and province was incredibly slow. The government disposed of a host of officials who could, in theory, have provided a highly centralized administration. In practice few of these officials took their duties seriously, and their salaries were so scanty that it was freely understood that they might eke them out with pickings and stealings, provided they kept their extortions within reasonable amounts. Russia about the year 1800 was, in short, a country that claimed to be Europeanized, but where the contrasts between pretensions and performance were grotesque.

Between 1800 and 1871 there had been considerable change for the better. Alexander I, who reigned in Napoleon's time and who saw that conqueror slink back from Moscow, had been a man of liberal and fertile ideas, until the fear of revolution had driven him into reaction. He had executed sundry reforms which promised a better day. Above all, various young Russian officers had begun dreaming dreams of a free constitution along Franco-British lines. Had their schemes succeeded, the result would have been chaos, for no Christian country was then less prepared for parliamentary institutions than Russia. Shortly after Alexander's death (1825) they inspired two regiments at St. Petersburg to begin an insurrection, nominally in favor of a certain popular prince Constantine who had claims to the throne. The soldiers were taught to cry "Long live Constantine and the Constitution!" and the men did so promptly, innocently believing that "Constitution" was Constantine's wife! The revolt, of course, failed and the ring-leaders were executed.

Nicholas I, who was now czar (1825–55), a man devoted to Old Russian ideals and an extreme conservative, spent his whole life painfully and conscientiously combating new ideas and preserving the unlimited power of his monarchy. Censorship, secret police, the spy system, arbitrary arrest, sudden exiling to Siberia—all were never before or since quite what they became under this implacable emperor. He believed that he was summoned by God to defend Holy Russia against western corruption, misrule, and infidelity. For a generation this grim despot terrorized his land and cast his malignant influence over Europe; but in 1855 he died during the disastrous Crimean War, which had grievously shaken his prestige.

His son, Alexander II (1855–81), was a far more humane and intelligent man. Despite all his father's efforts, liberal ideas, secret propaganda, smuggled books, surreptitiously published pamphlets, and the penetrations of Westernism through the universities had not been really prevented. Russia was becoming caught in world-movements, and the new czar for a while drifted with the current. The proportion of really educated persons in his empire was still pitifully small, but these "intelligentzias," or, as their native critics sometimes called them, the "Westerners," were now numerous enough to have a real influence upon the state. The first fruit of their efforts was the abolition of serfdom. Nearly all the peasantry had been serfs, bound to the soil and with about the legal rights of dogs, as against often brutal and extortionate masters. Many of the nobles had, of course, treated their human cattle with fair liberality, but the system had long been recognized as outrageous. On February 19, 1861, by an imperial *ukase*, serfdom was abolished in the czar's dominions. Nominally, the masses of Russia became freemen and were entitled to a share in their communal affairs. They were given in full ownership a part of the lands they had once held from their masters, but if they wished the entire farm they had once cultivated as serfs, a compensation was due the nobleman, and the state made loans to the peasantry to help them discharge this expense.

The reform was a great and noble one. Its ultimate results proved incalculable, but the immediate consequences were disappointing. The peasants often could not understand why they should pay anything for lands their fathers had tilled, and they often found their new freedom of little practical use, provided their old masters had been of the humane class. Very many of the nobles, in turn, with their estates destroyed or compromised, faced bankruptcy. Peasants quit the lands and began to drift to towns. There, presently, they began to engage in crude industries. All this, of course, upset society and commerce, and produced general discontent. The first results of the reform were therefore disquieting.

After 1861 the liberals had expected the czar to give them a constitution. Alexander II did not have the courage or imagination to risk this decisive step, and an insurrection (ill-organized and soon suppressed) in his Polish provinces in 1863 diverted his energies. As a sop to rising sentiment he established *zemstvos,* local assemblies in the districts, and higher zemstvos for the provinces, to act upon ''matters connected with the economic interests and needs of the people.'' The method of electing deputies to these bodies put the main influence in the hands of the nobles and city folks, although the peasants had a form of representation. Some reforms were also made in the courts so as to grant juries in criminal cases and to give other precautions for justice to all classes. These innovations did not satisfy the rising demands of the liberals, but they were all that Alexander II could be induced to concede, and soon after 1871 there intruded foreign problems to complicate the home situation.

In 1871 Russia already presented the situation which she still presented in 1914—an enormous empire without a single, good, ice-free port, save only Odessa, which in its turn could be locked up at the will of the Sultan controlling the Straits of Constantinople.

The right of a great nation to reasonable access to the sea would seem, at least according to abstract ethics, to be a fundamental one, and the denial of this right proved a menace to the peace of the world. Ever since Peter the Great's time (about 1700) Russia had been consciously reaching forth for an outlet upon the open ocean. She had gained in the interval great blocks of territory in Europe and Asia—Finland, the bulk of Poland, and wide reaches of mountain, prairie, and desert in Turkestan, the heart of Asia. She also had a grasp upon coasts along the Pacific, but again only on ice-bound waters—the gloomy isle of Sakhalin, the Sea of Okhotsk, and Behring Sea. All these did not solve her problem. During the next generation a large part of the history of the world was to turn on the efforts of Russia to break through the ring of land or ice about her *somewhere* and thus enter on the just inheritance of every great nation. In at least three directions the Russians made a conscious effort.

I. The czar's followers reached forth their hands across Turkestan and dreamed of reaching the Indian Ocean by absorbing Afghanistan, expelling the English from India and conquering the weak dominions of the Shah of Persia. Here, of course, the chances of serious friction or a great war with England were considerable. But from the Russian standpoint this route was the hardest to follow. It involved crossing the almost unpassable Hindoo-Kush and Himalaya mountains and undertaking to absorb the millions of India. These physical difficulties, as well as the certainty of a life-and-death duel with England, kept the peace far better than many hours of frantic telegraphing by the diplomats.

II. The Russians also sought an outlet on the Pacific, just north of China. In 1871 this was only a vague project. The trans-Siberian railway was only a vision. The distances seemed enormous. But the military task seemed far easier than that against India. China appeared to be a helpless jellyfish. Japan was barely emerging from isolation. Early in the twentieth century this idea of Russian domination along the Japan and Yellow Seas, and embracing at least Korea, Manchuria, and Northern China, was to come close enough to reality to awaken the grave concern of the entire world. This scheme, however, was blasted by the rise of Japan as a great military power and the disastrous Russo-Japanese War of 1904-5; but between 1871 and the later date the eyes of Russians were fixed on the Far East to an astonishing extent.

III. The Russians, finally and preferably, were seeking to

gain a warm-water port by obtaining access to the Mediterranean after the violent death of the Turkish Empire. The two preceding projects had been desperate expedients, but this third aspiration became part of an enduring national policy. The Russians traced their religion and, very largely, their civilization to the "Christian Empire of Constantinople" (Byzantium), destroyed by the Turks in 1453. To expel the Ottomans from their usurped dominions seemed to orthodox Muscovites not merely a national advantage, but almost a religious crusade. The Turks had been thrust out of their old holdings north of the Black Sea. Thanks mostly to Russian valor, their grip on the Christian peoples of the Balkans had been already seriously shaken. In 1853 Russia had declared war on Turkey, with the obvious intention of putting the "sick man of Europe" out of his long misery. But England and France had declared war on behalf of the sultan. Austria had seemed ready to join them. Russia had been defeated in the Crimean War. She had lost prestige and even some territory. Very galling to her pride had been the proviso in the Treaty of Paris (1856) that she was not to keep ships-of-war on the Black Sea. In 1870, however, a sharp turn ended this handicap. The czar had been friendly to Prussia, and Bismarck understood how to reward the "benevolent neutrality" that had warned back Austria from becoming an ally of France. He certainly approved in advance the action of Prince Gortschakoff, Alexander's prime minister, when, in October, 1870, the latter sent to all the European powers a note stating that Russia intended to resume her "sovereign rights" upon the Black Sea, because (as if anticipating Teutonic acts and words in 1914) "of infringements to which most European transactions have been latterly exposed, and in the face of which it would be difficult to maintain that the written law . . . retains the moral validity which it may have possessed at other times."

England was furious at this stroke, which seemed to destroy most of the fruits of the Crimean War. Lord Granville spoke angrily about this "arbitrary repudiation of a solemn engagement." Count Beust of Austria was "painfully affected" and could not "conceal his extreme astonishment." But no war followed. Prussia had France by the throat. Austria dared not fight without an ally. England was wrathful, but she was not willing to kindle a world-war without a greater interest at stake. Russia was therefore permitted to come to a solemn conference convened at London in December, where the interested powers agreed that she should be allowed to abrogate the obnoxious clauses of the Treaty of Paris. Thus in *form* the treaty had been merely revised, not broken; though in fact, all the world knew that the czar had first broken the treaty, and then had asked permission to do so. It was another application of Bismarckian methods, if not a direct act of that master-statesman.

By 1871, therefore, it was clear enough that Russia was looking again toward Constantinople. Here was her best outlet upon the ocean, her greatest reward for a mighty national effort. The conditions within the Turkish Empire were exceedingly promising for a new attempt to gratify the darling ambition of the czars. Elsewhere in Europe conditions pointed at least temporarily toward peace. England was intent on internal reform; France was healing her wounds; Italy was consolidating her nationality; Austria was developing her dual system; and Germany was digesting her recent gains and testing her new organization. Russia, however, by stress of many circumstances, was decidedly looking outward, and the lines of least resistance turned her toward the south.

How weak internally the Czar's régime really was, how unequal it was to the strain of a prolonged modern war, and how the lack of enlightenment among the lower classes would leave them the victims of every outrageous revolutionary theory the instant the old autocratic authority was removed,— these were circumstances rarely suspected by even the harshest critics of the vast and imposing Russian Empire.

CHAPTER IV

THE OTTOMAN TURKS AND THEIR BALKAN SUBJECTS

WITHIN five years after the close of the Franco-Prussian War the peace of Europe was menaced again. This time it was by a recrudescence of the miseries and misdoings of the Ottoman Turks and of their subjects. Writing in 1875, a distinguished English diplomat, who knew the Eastern problem well, summed up the case thus: "That Turkey is weak, fanatical, and misgoverned no one can honestly deny. . . . The chief powers of Christendom have all more or less an interest in the fortunes of an Empire which from being systematically aggressive has become a tottering and untoward neighbor." [1] These words would probably have been true twenty years before they were written, and they continued to be true forty years after they were written. The great war of 1914 had many causes, but one of the most obvious was that the liquidation of the Turkish Empire was by no means complete. It was still in existence, and even lands emancipated from its tyranny had by no means "found themselves," either as to their appropriate boundaries or as to their relations to their own people or their neighbors. In no case was the old-style diplomacy of which Bismarck was the chief exponent (although in this case he had only limited responsibility) more bankrupt in its results than in its long attempts to deal with the Eastern Question. All Christian Europe was united in the belief that the Turks were bloody interlopers upon the Continent, and despite the undoubted fighting ability of the sultan's armies, any one of the Great Powers could have conquered his entire empire, had the invader been sure of no interference from Christian rivals. But over the fate of the Ottoman dominions innumerable diplomats brooded long, yet

[1] Lord Stratford de Redcliffe.

produced nothing but national jealousies, internal intrigues, costly and indecisive wars, and a new lease of life for the Moslem offender.

In truth, it might have been pleaded that the complete disposition of the Turkish Empire would have taxed the skill of a heaven-sent disposing angel. The Ottoman Turks—an Asiatic race of Finnish and Tartar connection—had entered Europe about 1353, and in 1453 they had taken Constantinople. For the next two centuries they had dominated not merely the Balkan peninsula, but had even lorded it over the greater part of Hungary. A Turkish pasha ruled in Budapest during most of the seventeenth century. In 1683 only by a mighty effort had the forces of the "Padishah" been flung back from Vienna; but after that the strength of the Ottomans had waned rapidly before Austria and Russia. Long before Napoleon's day it had been recognized that either one of these powers probably could make the Turkish Empire its spoil, provided it were permitted to throw all of its strength into the contest. But the moment the weakness of the sultans became visible, that moment saw a veritable apple of discord cast before the clamorous "heirs" of the declining rulers of Constantinople. Napoleon himself had a keen ambition to make the Turkish territories part of his ever-swelling French Empire, and one of the reasons he broke with Czar Alexander I and started on his disastrous Moscow campaign in 1812 was because he was unwilling to give the czar a free hand in overrunning Turkey in the interests of Russia.

The Congress of Vienna (1815), which wound up the affairs of Europe after the fall of Napoleon, left the lands of the sultans practically intact and gave their decrepit government a new chance to reform and repair itself. But the opportunity was poorly used. If it is hard for a Westerner to alter the ways of Orientals, it is still harder for Orientals to alter their own ways. Misrule increased, instead of diminishing. In 1853 Czar Nicholas I stated the case bluntly to the English ambassador, Sir Hamilton Seymour. "Turkey," he asserted, "is in a critical state . . . the country seems falling to pieces . . . we have on our hands a sick man, a very sick man; it will be, I tell you frankly, a great misfortune if, one of these days, he should slip away from us before all necessary arrangements are made." The czar, therefore, advanced schemes for carving up the real estate of the "sick man" for the joint benefit of Russia and Great Britain. England, however, did not accede kindly to suggestions that the downfall of the Turkish Empire should be taken for granted. Her statesmen saw visions of Cossack regiments forcing their way nearer the great highroads to India. France, with important interests in the Levant, also took umbrage, and Napoleon III, who had just gained power, needed a victorious war to increase his prestige. The Crimean War (1853–6) followed, England and France aiding Turkey against Russia, who claimed to be fighting as the champion of civilization and to save the Christian people under the sultan from grievous oppression. Russia was defeated and obliged to postpone her schemes, but the war brought little save glory to the victors. It was a wholly avoidable war and could have been shunned by a little conciliatoriness on *either* side. The Treaty of Paris (1856) deliberately gave the Turks another lease of life, and the great contracting powers solemnly "guaranteed the integrity of the Ottoman Empire." Within twenty years, however, even many Englishmen were ready to admit that the Crimean War, with all its storied valor and suffering, had been, if not a crime, at least a great blunder. "The only perfectly useless modern war that has been waged," wrote Sir Robert Morier in 1870, and about 1890 Lord Salisbury, then prime minister, declared bluntly that "England put her money on the wrong horse."

Without wasting time on this question, it is fair to say that if England and France had frankly accepted the czar's suggestion in 1853 and had made arrangements for the deliberate dismemberment of Turkey, they would have given the last blow to an empire that had forfeited any ordinary claim to existence and would have surely avoided at least four later wars, as well as the extension of the Great War of 1914 to the East. Indeed, if the Ottoman Question had been wisely handled earlier, Armageddon for Europe and America could never have come upon the world in exactly the manner that it did.

But Turkey was spared in 1856, and if her rulers had been capable men, they would have accepted the respite and made honest use of it. Yet only a great sultan could have redeemed Turkey. The governing class labored under two handicaps, both so serious that the problem was practically hopeless. (I) They were Turks; and the Turkish race, although able to produce admirable fighters and even generals, has never been able to produce civil administrators of decent ability. Turkish civil rulers had been so scarce, even in the days of their widest empire, that many of the non-military posts had been filled by supple, clever Greeks or Armenians, who, if willing to become Mohammedans, were often able to rise to be grand viziers and stand on the footsteps of the throne. (II) They were Mohammedans, and this meant that they were tied hand and foot by the rigid law and tradition of the prophet, whose precepts were possibly suitable for Arabian desert tribes, but became grotesque for a modern civilized empire. Any attempt at reform was met by the passive resistance of all the *ulemas* (the religious-legal class), by denunciation of "heresy," and by downright rebellion.[1] The mandate of Mohammed to his followers to fight against Christians and Jews until they paid tribute and submitted themselves as inferiors, made it practically impossible for the sultans to place their Moslem and non-Moslem subjects really upon terms of equality. The official religion of Turkey was therefore an almost impenetrable barrier to any real attempt to sweep away the standard abuses of medieval Oriental despotism.

There had been, indeed, some perfunctory and well-meant

[1] An American resident in Constantinople in 1875 relates that even as late as that date good Mohammedan Turks would not take the small ferry-steamers across the Bosphorus, but left them to "Christian *giaours.*" The reason was that "if the Prophet had intended true believers to use steam-boats, he would have mentioned them in the Koran!" The orthodox Turks therefore crossed slowly and painfully in hired row-boats.

efforts by the sultans to remedy the worst abuses. In 1856 a solemn document, the once famous "Hatti-Humayoun," had promised a long string of paper reforms, especially to the Christian subjects of the empire. They were to have complete personal and religious liberty, equality before the law, eligibility to public office, equality in taxation, etc. But this went the way of countless other equally solemn documents. Practically nothing came of it. In the provinces the pashas and the *begs* continued to decree justice at their own sweet will, a mere sweep of the hand often being sufficient sign for the executioner. In the sultan's palace at Constantinople the whim of the reigning Circassian slave-girl in the harem, or more likely of the chief black eunuch who had purchased this slave-girl for his lord, the *padishah*, frequently carried more weight than the remonstrances of some partly-Europeanized grand vizier, who hoped to turn promised reforms into realities, or the protests of the British ambassador, who naturally felt anxious about the conduct of the government that his nation had aided to rescue from Russia.

In 1861 Sultan Abdul-Medjid had drunk himself into the grave, and Abdul-Aziz reigned in his stead. Things were then so bad in Syria that the British ministry warned the sultan that they could not prevent "the signal punishment of a government which would permit such atrocities [as in Syria] to continue." In later years came further warnings, but they were all flung to the winds. Abdul-Aziz was not personally so bloodthirsty as many Eastern tyrants, but he was weak, irresponsible, and extravagant. To satisfy the demands of the hordes of luxurious women and eunuchs who swarmed in his harem, the treasury was sucked dry, public works were neglected, and even well-intentioned pashas were obliged to squeeze extra taxes out of their luckless provinces. As for the administration of justice under this régime, the case was pithily summed up in the report of a British consul: "I do not hesitate to say that of all cases of justice, whether between Mussulmen solely, or Turks and Christians, ninety out of one hundred are settled by bribery alone." In a word, the Turkish Empire was not merely an Oriental despotism; it was *a peculiarly abominable and degenerate type of Oriental despotism,* and it showed no signs of becoming better.

To expect that under these circumstances Austrians would forget their longings for expansion toward Saloniki and the Ægean, and still more that Russians would put aside old hopes for a warm-water port and the straits of Constantinople, was something contrary to human nature. The weakness of the Turkish Empire became more evident day by day, and the striving of the Christian races in the Balkan Peninsula to escape from an intolerable yoke supplied to Czar Alexander II a pretext, perhaps it would be fairer to say a very justifiable reason, for intervening in the affairs of Turkey.

It is an axiom of history that serious wars usually spring from one of two sovereign causes: the ambitions of strong empires, or the internal miseries of weak ones. When the two cases are simultaneous, the powder and the match almost invariably come together. It was so in 1877–78.

The Balkan peninsula is the dumping-ground for more races than any other similar region on the planet. This is probably because it forms the bridge connecting Europe with Asia, and also because it was the first block of land into which emigrant tribes could turn south, when in early barbaric times they rolled across the steppes of Russia, headed toward that blue, open water and the delightful warm countries beside it, whereof they had heard by rumor. The Danube River and the Balkan Mountains are formidable barriers, but they are not unsurmountable by an enterprising horde of barbarians. By 1871, of course, the period of migrations had long ceased. For better or worse there were at least six different races in the peninsula—Turks, Greeks, Albanians, South-Slavs (usually divided into Bosnians and Serbians), Bulgarians, and Rumanians. One cannot understand the mazes of that devil's dance called the Eastern Question without knowing a little of the characteristics, annals, and ambitions of each of these six races.

The Turks, of course, were the ruling race. Outside of

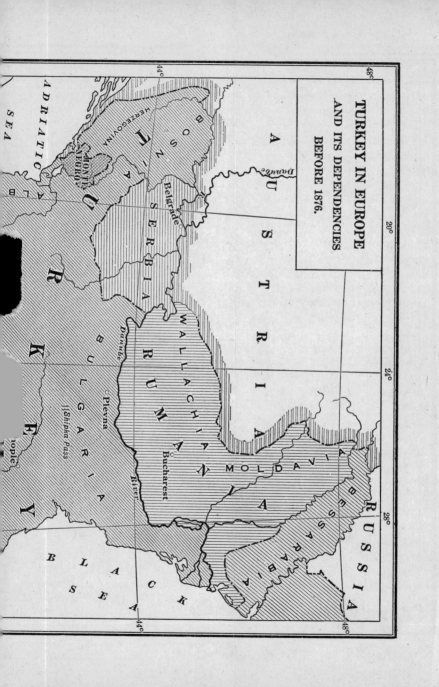

TURKEY IN EUROPE

AND ITS DEPENDENCIES

BEFORE 1876.

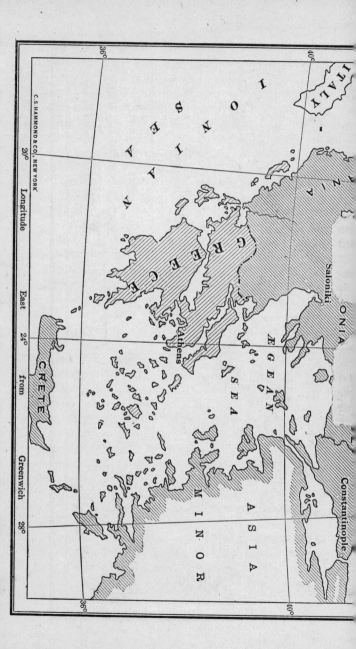

ITALY

IONIAN

IONIAN SEA

GREECE

Athens

CRETE

ÆGEAN SEA

ASIA MINOR

Saloniki

ONIA

Constantinople

C.S. HAMMOND & CO., NEW YORK

Longitude   East   from   Greenwich

20°   24°   28°

36°   40°

36°   40°

Constantinople they were decidedly a minority all over the peninsula, although stronger in certain districts than others, with especial strength in Thrace. Little need be said of them, because the sultan's government then extended clear to the Danube, with formal suzerainty over Rumania to the north. In discussing the fate of the Turkish Empire we necessarily discuss the Turks. They were, of course, all Mohammedans, such a thing as a Christian Turk being practically an impossibility.

The Greeks, occupying Old Hellas, the coasts of the Ægean, and having sizable colonies in Constantinople and in various Asiatic cities, claimed to be the descendants of the heroes of the Trojan War and of the Battle of Marathon. Down to 1453 they had undoubtedly been the predominant race in the Levant, and after the fall of Constantinople the Turks had found them useful in helping to govern other conquered Christian races. The Greeks had never been quite so oppressed as the other miserable 'rayahs,' the non-Moslem subjects of the sultans. Practically all the Christians of the Balkans belonged to the orthodox church, which did not acknowledge the supremacy of the Pope, and until well into the nineteenth century the Greeks had controlled that church, supplying the supreme "patriarch of Constantinople" and otherwise lording it over their fellow-believers. The Greeks were a supple, clever race, who usually circumvented their Turkish tyrants by a liberal use of smoothness and sharp wits, and they won remarkable success in commerce and seafaring enterprise. Their enemies charged them with many slippery vices. The answer was that only by devious means was it possible to escape from infidel oppression.

In 1871, however, only a part of the Greeks were still under Turkish tyranny. Since the taking of Constantinople and the fall of the old Christian empire centered there, the race had long seemed sunk in helpless lethargy. The old Greek language had long become so corrupted with Italian, Slavic, and Albanian words that it appeared a mere jargon, compared with the tongue of Plato. The very race, it was alleged, had intermarried so freely with all the other Levantine folk, and especially with the Slavs and Albanians, as to make any claim to classical ancestry absurd. But about the time the French Revolution came to stir the souls and imaginations of all Europe there was an awakening of the old national Greek spirit. The language was purified and gradually brought back closer to ancient models. Merchants and travelers who had visited Western lands kindled an extreme discontent against Turkish despotism. French and Russian agents and agitators from time to time stirred up similar feelings and excited hopes of foreign intervention, in order to create trouble for the sultan among his own subjects. In 1821 this feeling had blown into flame. The Greek War for Independence began. It was an inchoate, desperate struggle. The Greeks were without organized armies, and their fleets were mostly armed merchantmen; but their mountains swarmed with *klephts* ("brigands" to-day, "heroes of freedom" to-morrow), admirable for conducting guerilla warfare, and their daring seamen of the Ægean, with their corsair barks and fireships, spread terror among the sultan's armadas. The Greeks, too, received much unofficial sympathy from Europe. "Phil-hellenes," classical scholars who hailed the revival of the old glories of Greece, sent them money and cannon, as well as good will. Lord Byron, the most distinguished poet of his day, went to Greece, joined the insurgents, and died trying to aid them. The great powers, fearful of anything which would disturb the peace of the world, had at first given the insurgents scanty official sympathy, but gradually public opinion forced France, England, and Russia to act. In 1827, after horrible massacres by the Turks had outraged Europe, the fleets of these three powers annihilated a Turkish armada in the harbor of Navarino. In 1829, following a land war between Turkey and Russia, the sultan was compelled to acknowledge the independence of his revolted subject, and the new Kingdom of Greece was born.

This kingdom was for long very small, disorderly, and unhappy. For fear of disintegrating Turkey, the powers had only given it narrow boundaries—practically nothing north of the famous Pass of Thermopylæ and only a small part of the numerous Ægean islands. Fully half of the Greek-speaking peoples were still under the Ottoman yoke. But even within the new kingdom, there was for long only one spasm of disorder after another. A Levantine people, crushed down by centuries of despotism, but naturally quick, liberal, and democratic in its genius, was now painfully trying to learn how to govern itself. In 1833 the great powers sent out as king, Otto, a son of the king of Bavaria. He was a well-intentioned, but heavy and tactless man, who was forced by an uprising in 1843 to grant a constitution to his subjects. Even thus, however, he did not become popular enough to keep his throne after another insurrection in 1862. He was compelled to abdicate, and the Greek National Assembly offered the crown to Prince Alfred, second son of Queen Victoria. England, however, dared not offend Russia by appearing to make this great extension of her influence in the Levant. The proffer was politely declined. An undignified canvassing of all the eligible cadets of royal houses and other highnesses and serenities in Europe followed, until at last a son of the King of Denmark was proclaimed George I in 1863. He was destined to reign till 1913.

King George had a thankless task and often undutiful subjects. The resources of his little kingdom were scanty, but his turbulent people were full of constant visions of recovering the districts still enslaved by the Turks, or even of restoring the Christian Empire of Constantinople. Frequent threats and coercion by the great powers seemed necessary to keep the Greeks from flying into wars with Turkey, and so destroying the general "tranquility of the East." The Greeks themselves were entirely democratic, without an aristocracy, and so treated their king with almost an American lack of ceremony. At Athens one ministry would succeed another in the hot personal strife of fierce parties and factions. Only very gradually did the nation come to understand that before it could make a good case for wider boundaries and an honored place among the earth's peoples, it must develop its peaceful industries, pay its debts, and substitute law and order for picturesque lawlessness. In 1863 the Greeks had, indeed, been given the Ionian Isles (Corfu, Zante, etc.) off their western coast by Great Britain, which had found their "protection" somewhat expensive and unprofitable, but the Greek kingdom was still one great hothouse for unsatisfied national aspirations. Athens was reputed to have a more strenuous political life and to have more journalists with strident party "organs" than many other far more populous capitals. Too many of her young men were also handicapped by such christenings as Agamemnon or Odysseus, with the implied obligation to live up to the greatness of their names. And yet all the while outrageous acts of brigandage were taking place within a dozen miles of the royal palace.[1]

Nevertheless, all these discouraging circumstances were no more than to be expected in a nation barely emerging from many centuries of Roman, Byzantine, and finally Turkish despotism. The Greeks were a people of undoubted capacity, and had a fair claim to be awarded the entire inheritance of the retiring Turks, had there not been other heirs equally importunate and often more powerful.

The Albanians require far less attention than the Greeks. They were a very old race, quite as old as their Greek neighbors who dwelt to the south of them. Their grandfathers had been the Illyrians of Greco-Roman times, brave, hardy barbarians who had kept their speech and native customs, little spoiled by the "civilization" about them, all through the ages. The Albanians had resisted the Turks valiantly, but at last had partially succumbed. A large fraction of the nation had become Mohammedan, although very many remained staunchly Christian.[2]

The Turks had embodied Albania nominally into their em-

---

[1] In 1870 a party of titled Englishmen and an Italian nobleman, while returning from a visit to Athens from the battlefield of Marathon, were carried off by brigands and, when ransom was refused and rescue attempted, murdered by their captors.

[2] These Christians are divided between Catholics and Orthodox, betwixt whom there is a painful lack of charity. The religious issue in Albania is therefore not two-sided, but three-sided, to the great affliction of the country.

pire, but the authority of the sultan was never taken seriously along its jagged hills and valleys. The Albanians were brave soldiers and supplied the padishahs with admirable regiments and generals. When, however, taxes were proposed for them, all the mountains blazed up in rebellion. No region of Europe was so uncivilized and backward as that which lay directly across the Adriatic from southern Italy. Travelers found it almost equal to a voyage to Africa to try penetrating the Albanian hinterland. As a nation, Albania was too barbarous and too divided religiously to have general aspirations. All it asked was to be let alone by the Turkish fiscal oppressors and to be ignored by all modern "improvements." Tribal government was the order of the day. In 1871 nobody gave Albania serious consideration, or believed that in her aspirations lay a European problem.

This statement could hardly be made of the Albanians' northern neighbors, the Serbs. A more proper name for this race would have been South Slavs. In the nineteenth century this region was split into three rather distinct fragments —Serbia proper, Montenegro, and Bosnia. These all dated from a migration of a branch of the great Slavic race into the Balkan peninsula in the sixth and seventh centuries A. D. The history of this settlement had been sufficiently troubled. The Slavic invaders had been sometimes subject to, sometimes at bitter war with, the Christian emperors of Constantinople. The people had become for the most part Orthodox Christians. In the fourteenth century, under a great king, Stephen Duchan, they had seemed on the point of actually taking Constantinople and of becoming lords of the entire Balkan region. But these days of power were brief. Speedily the Turks came, and in 1389 the famous battle of Kossova saw the end of the independence of Serbia proper. Bosnia, a separate principality, held out after a fashion until the fifteenth century, when it also went the way of slavery. But in the rugged hills along the Adriatic the Slavs of the "Black Mountain," Montenegro, had kept the Turks at bay. In their few bleak mountain-pockets these valorous hillsmen, almost alone in southeastern Europe, flung back the Ottomans. They were never really conquered, but continued under their independent and very militant prince-bishops, until in the nineteenth century the sultans gave up the impossible task of trying to subdue them. Then they gradually assumed the status of an independent power, the smallest in Europe, except, of course, such pocket-handkerchief states as Liechtenstein, Andorra, San Marino, and Monaco.

Montenegro contained in its narrow limits only a small fraction of the South Slavs. In Bosnia and the companion district of Herzegovina the bulk of the nobility had apostatized and become Moslem, although the peasantry remained Christian. These Bosnian nobles became notorious alike for their oppression of their inferiors, and also for the scant obedience they rendered their nominal lord, the sultan. The pashalik of Bosnia had, therefore, one of the most turbulent, misruled provinces in the whole afflicted empire. The Slavs of Serbia proper, however, had remained on the whole staunchly Christian. Turkish oppression destroyed the native nobility and thus society was brought down to a common level and became strictly democratic. Life was very primitive in the Serbian country. The natives were nearly all farmers or graziers, or very frequently were raisers of swine; and to be a successful pig-merchant was a kind of token of respectability. The Turks had left the village life of the Serbs fairly intact, and the nation had continued sound at heart, if very unsophisticated. Between 1804 and 1817 there had been revolts against the oppressor, which had terminated in a partial success. A principality of Serbia came into being which, thanks to Russian intervention, was officially recognized by the sultan in 1830 as an autonomous state, although in theory subject to Constantinople and with Turkish garrisons still in certain fortresses. In 1867, after many clashes between Serb and Ottoman, these garrisons were withdrawn, and Serbia was independent in about all but name.

This Serbian principality was even weaker and more distracted than the kingdom of Greece. There were no traditions of civil liberty or of fixed institutions. Belgrade, the

capital, was only a small, ill-built, and very muddy city situated in the extreme north of the country, and there were no
other towns of size. Orderly government was handicapped
by the existence of two rival "princely" houses, sprung from
two leaders in the struggle for independence. The Kara-
georgevic dynasty had supplied Prince Alexander I, who
reigned from 1842 to 1859, being then tumultuously deposed
by a popular uprising and chased into exile. In his stead
reigned Milosh of the Obrenovic line, who held power only
until 1860. He was a very old man, and on his death his son,
Michael, succeeded him. The new prince was a person of
considerable moderation and ability, and he induced the European powers to aid him in expelling the Turkish garrisons.
But he was unable to reconcile himself to large factions of
his unruly subjects, both those who adhered to the rival house
and those who entertained an utterly premature vision of an
expanded Serbia spreading over the whole of the Balkan peninsula, of course at the expense of the Turks. Michael thus
became unpopular, and the Balkan countries, like Central
American republics, had developed abrupt and ungenteel political methods. In 1868, as Michael walked in the palace
park at Belgrade with his betrothed wife and her mother,
three men rushed from the shrubbery and fired several shots.
Michael fell dead, as did the older woman. There was not the
least doubt that these assassins (who were later caught and
executed) were the tools of more influential persons, probably
the exiled Karageorgevics. The plot, however, was really a
failure. Michael's friends kept their hold on the government,
and Milan I, his cousin and the next heir, was seated as
prince. As a stop-gap to popular discontent, Milan proclaimed a constitution in 1869, which, however, retained great
powers for the crown.

In 1871 Serbia was a small, weak country, decidedly in the
making. The great powers hardly took seriously her brave
claims, based on her one-time boundaries in the fourteenth
century, to a large share of the Balkans. She looked to Russia, the "great brother" of all the Slavs, as her friend and
protector. Yet economically, thanks to her absolutely back-

ward agricultural and industrial state and the absence of any
seaport for her commerce, she was almost a satrapy of Austria. In Bosnia a great number of kindred Slavs were still
under the heel of Turkish oppression, and the Serbs naturally
dreamed of the day when they could unite their entire people
under one flag; but the statesmen at Vienna smiled at these
high expectations.

Across the mountains in the eastern Balkans dwelt a race
essentially different from the Serbians—the Bulgars. In no
other part of their European empire had the Turks laid a
heavier hand or crushed out native liberties more completely.
The Bulgars were not Slavs. They were originally a Finnish-
Turanian-Tartar race, with a distant kinship to the Turks
themselves. They had entered the Balkan peninsula in the
seventh and eighth centuries and had founded what had been
for the nonce a pretentious kingdom. Their religion and type
of culture had come from the Greeks of Constantinople, but
contact with the Slavs had modified their language so that it
seemed almost like a regular Slavic tongue. Along with so
many other races, they had been conquered by the Turks and
reduced to the status of mere peasants, at the same time absorbing so much Slavic blood as to change largely the original
condition of their race. They were without any types of native aristocracy, and even the control of their orthodox church
had been grasped by the Greeks, whom the Turks regularly
sustained as the most useful branch of their Christian subjects.
So completely did the identity of the Bulgarian nation seem
lost, that foreign travelers in the region spoke of them as a
kind of Greeks, and down to about the time of the Crimean
War any Bulgar lucky enough to claim wealth and education
was likely to describe himself as a "Greek." Then in the
nineteenth century Bulgarian nationality, like so many other
half-extinguished nationalities, reasserted itself. Russian
diplomacy came to realize the value of encouraging a people
who might well pass as Slavs and who could possibly be kindled
to appeal to the czar to protect them against Islam. A considerable movement for Bulgarian schools and the use of the

native tongue in churches began, and in 1860 the Bulgarian
Christians announced that they would recognize the authority
of the patriarch of Constantinople no longer. The sultan possibly had not enjoyed this assertion. The patriarch had been
his convenient tool.[1] But in 1870 Russian pressure had compelled him to set up an "exarch" in Bulgaria, to rule the
local Christians. This gave the awakening nation a center
and an official rallying-point. The next step might be toward
secular, as well as religious, independence. Nevertheless, in
1871 Europe hardly realized that there was a Bulgarian nation, much less a Bulgarian problem. The mountains in the
eastern Balkans were still Turkish *pashaliks*, and no outsider
bothered about them. Then suddenly, as by the wave of a
magician's wand, in 1876 the name of Bulgaria was to be on
every man's lips.

One other Balkan population had been under Ottoman lordship. North of the Danube lay what had long been called
The Principalities, i.e., Wallachia and Moldavia. In 1859,
decidedly against the judgment of the great powers, the people of these districts had insisted on uniting themselves into
the single principality of Rumania. The Rumanians had a
very ancient and honorable history. About 104 A. D. the Roman emperor Trajan had conquered the region (Old Dacia)
and filled it with Latinized settlers. About 270 A. D., at the
advance of the barbarians, the Roman government had evacuated the country, and seemingly it lapsed back to the uncouth
Goths, Huns, Avars, and other despoilers of the dying empire. But the Latin-speaking settlers had not retired with
the legions. In the Carpathian mountain valleys, in the great
plains between the Pruth and the Danube, they had lived on,
maintaining a speech which, on the whole, was closer to the
tongue of old Rome than any other in Europe.[2] The great

[1] There is a possibility, however, that at this time the patriarchs were
getting out of hand, and the sultans were not wholly averse to a convenient Bulgarian make-weight.

[2] A good Latin student can derive much profit and amusement by
reading a Bucharest newspaper, just as a Greek student can derive the
same by reading a periodical from modern Athens.

invasions and the passage of conquering races did not seem to destroy them. They have a native proverb which time has made good: "The Rumanian never dies." When modern history dawned, the two principalities of Wallachia and Moldavia, together with considerable overflow into lands presently absorbed by Russia and Austria, were found to contain a race that traced its speech and traditions back to imperial Rome, however much the blood of the first settlers may have been diluted by later infusions.

The Turks had overrun the country, but they had never completely conquered it. The natives kept their local institutions, including a decidedly influential nobility and the right to have Christian *hospodars* to rule each principality. After 1815, thanks to increasing Russian intervention and pressure, the suzerainty of the sultan became little more than a name, but both Austria and Russia watched the Rumanians with a jealous eye, with a view to absorption the moment the general European situation favored the respective ambitions of Vienna or St. Petersburg.

But during the nineteenth century the Rumanians also awoke to full race consciousness. In 1859 they succeeded in uniting their two principalities under a single government, and the general condition of the world was too precarious then for Austria and Russia to intervene. From 1859 to 1866 the new consolidated principality was ruled by Prince Alexander Cousa, a native nobleman of good abilities. He founded universities and schools, broke up the unnecessary number of monasteries which had absorbed an absurd proportion of the land, and, greatest stroke of all, abolished serfdom among the peasantry. But Cousa's methods were those of the familiar "strong man," who rides down all opposition by setting aside paper constitutions. He made numerous enemies. In 1866 a bloodless revolution deposed and banished him.

In 1866 the Rumanians offered their throne to Prince Carol of a side-branch of the Hohenzollern family, who was also, however, connected through his mother with the dynasty of Napoleon. Austria and Russia were not enthusiastic over seeing a Hohenzollern reigning at Bucharest, but Bismarck saw the chance to put a friend of Prussia in the Balkans and urged the young prince to accept. "Even if you fail," said the great minister, "you will always remember with pleasure an adventure which can never be a reproach to you." Through fear of being halted by Austria, the prince traveled down the Danube disguised as a second-class passenger, until at Turnu-Severin, on Rumanian soil, he left the boat and was greeted by his future prime minister. Austria fumed and might have taken action, but her great war with Prussia was about to break out and she soon had more grievous troubles. The other powers declined to intervene, and the sultan, the prince's nominal suzerain, confirmed the new ruler. Thus Prince Carol kept his throne.

In 1871 Rumania, therefore, was a country much more completely "made" than Greece, Serbia, and, of course, Bulgaria. She had a rich agricultural territory, great landowners, and— a far more doubtful asset—hordes of poverty-stricken peasantry. She had laws and institutions of fairly long standing, and a reasonably well-organized army, but her problems were still many. She had not a mile of railway and very few good roads. Bucharest was a pitiful pretense for a capital, and the prince on his arrival "could scarcely believe that a one-storied building, looking out upon a dirty square, was the 'palace.'"

There were many wealthy Jews in Rumania. Their relations with their Christian neighbors were deplorable. The latter accused the Jews of taking gross financial advantage of the ignorant peasantry, and retaliated by frequent riots, rabblings, and burning of synagogues, as well as by denying the Jews the rights of citizenship. The great *boyars* were likewise charged with extreme oppression of the petty farmers. The finances of the principality were also in the usual Balkan tangle.

Prince Carol, however, in the early 'seventies was already showing himself a capable and tactful administrator. The native parliaments were becoming less turbulent and more responsible. The economic condition of the country was gradually improving. When, in 1877, the great storm broke over the Balkan peninsula, Rumania was better prepared than any other of the minor countries to play an honorable part.

Such, then, were the principal actors in the new drama about to begin in the Near East. Turkey hopelessly corrupt, medieval, and dying by inches; Greece and Serbia both crude, restless, and seeking expansion far beyond their powers; Albania and Bulgaria seemingly mere districts of the Turkish Empire, and ignored by the outside world. Rumania alone was obviously in a fairly honorable and recognized position. As for the great powers of Europe, Austria and Russia were ready for any chance that would open for them the door to Constantinople, and were equally ready to bar it in the face of a rival. France was too perplexed at home and too helpless, and Italy was too newly consolidated as a great power to become active factors. The statesmen of England, however, were still obsessed by their old notion that any advance of Russia toward a warm-water port meant peril to their own road to India, and therefore that, despite its obvious sins, "the integrity of the Ottoman Empire must be preserved." The sixth great power of Europe, curiously enough, seemed without interest in the Balkan problems. Bismarck considered that Germany had tasks nearer home, in strengthening her new federal empire. It was during this period that he remarked, "I never take the trouble to open the mail-bag from Constantinople," and again, "The whole of the Balkans is not worth the bones of a single Pomeranian grenadier." That German policy should ever seem to revolve around the sultan's palace, was a thing that apparently never entered the head of the cool, practical, and eminently conservative founder of the Hohenzollerns' empire.

CHAPTER V

THE SICK MAN OF EUROPE AND HIS SURGEONS

IN 1875 the peasants of Herzegovina, a district of Bosnia, infuriated by the taxes imposed by the Turkish officials and also by the demands for forced labor by their own Mohammedanized nobles, rose against their oppressors and defeated a small Turkish army. Instantly their Slavic brethren in Serbia, Montenegro, and even in the Austrian province of Dalmatia, flocked in as volunteers. Serious fighting set in, and diplomats began to spend anxious evenings and did much telegraphing. There is good reason to believe that both Austrian and Russian agents had been stirring up discontent in the province, for neither Czar Alexander II nor Kaiser Franz-Joseph were men unwilling to fish in suitably troubled waters.

The case, nevertheless, soon became so dangerous that the European consuls in Bosnia had to stir themselves to end the disturbances. The insurgents, however, were tired of Turkish promises and of mollifying speeches from Christian peoples more fortunate than themselves. They demanded what amounted to autonomy. The sultan responded with pledges of glittering reforms. These did not end the insurrection, and on top of this the Turkish government was obliged to display its evil state to all the world by announcing that it could not pay the full interest on its public debt. Such an act, of course, forced the issue. Many millions' worth of Turkish bonds were held throughout Europe. The bondholders were far more influential and their outcries carried much further than the wretched Bosnian peasants. The first fruits of their clamors was the formation of a common program by the three great imperial powers, Germany, Austria, and Russia, which were then loosely allied together in what was known as the "League of the Three Emperors." With the consent of the other two empires, Count Andrassy, chancellor of Austria, addressed a solemn admonition to the sultan, reciting the sins of his government and specifying certain reforms which seemed indispensable. The Ottomans received this Andrassy Note in January, 1876, with the nominal acceptance of most of its clauses; but the Bosnian insurgents were not willing to lay down their arms merely because the Austrian consuls now told them that the sultan had promised to be good; and the Turks retaliated by saying they could not institute reforms in taxation, fair treatment of the peasantry, the administration of justice, etc., while their subjects were still in arms against them. The insurrection thus grew, instead of ending. Serbia and Montenegro seemed on the point of declaring a regular war in behalf of their brethren in Bosnia, and Mohammedan fanaticism in turn became kindled. In May, 1876, a fierce Moslem mob attacked and murdered the German and French consuls in the city of Saloniki. There were riots in Constantinople. The several thousand *softas,* or Turkish theological students, rose, crying out against the grand vizier as being too friendly to Russia, and the weak sultan was compelled to dismiss him. All this, of course, showed that the situation was getting out of control.

Already the "three emperors' league" was considering another attempt to calm the rising tempest. In May, 1876, appeared the Berlin Memorandum, a document prepared after conference with Prince Bismarck by the Russian and Austrian prime-ministers. It demanded an armistice with the Bosnians and the appointment of a mixed commission of natives, with a Christian president to arrange the affairs of their country. The insurgents were to be allowed to remain in arms until the sultan's promises became a reality. To this note France and Italy assented; but there was one power which did not assent, namely, Great Britain.

Many Englishmen since 1876 have considered this action by their government as a crowning blunder. The prime-minister of Great Britain at this time was Mr. Disraeli, soon to be known as the Earl of Beaconsfield. This brilliant and versatile leader of the Conservative party may fairly be called the founder of modern British imperialism. To him England was not a "tight little island," with a thriving commerce which was increased by the chance that she possessed divers colonies; she was the center of an enormous empire embracing manifold lands and races, many in species but one in loyalty and abiding principles, and making the oceans her highway to bind her mighty members together. In compliance with this ideal, Disraeli caused Queen Victoria to be proclaimed "Empress of India," and otherwise indicated his belief in the imperial nature of Britain and her possessions.

Disraeli, however, carried with this zeal to extend the power and limits of Britain another passion, less fortunate, it proved, even for selfish British interests. All English statesmen in the later nineteenth century were bred in the belief that Russia was irrevocably their foe; and every move in the world's politics which seemed to Russia's advantage appeared a direct stab at the interests of their own empire. This feeling Disraeli possessed, even beyond the run of his peers. He was anything but a pacifist in his theories, and repeatedly he seems to have been quite willing to force diplomatic action with Russia to the breaking point, and then to welcome the bloody issue. His colleagues in the ministry could usually restrain him, but to the end of his career he remained the distrustful foe of *anything* satisfactory to the czar. Disraeli, also, was of Jewish ancestry, although a member of the English established church. His enemies taunted him with an undue willingness to see good in Mohammedanism, and in any case he became an extreme apologist for the dark doings of the sultans and a strenuous defender of the "integrity of the Ottoman Empire." It is necessary to understand this viewpoint and these personal peculiarities of the prime minister of England to interpret the things which followed.

Great Britain refused to concur in the Berlin Memorandum. There is no doubt that Disraeli felt justly piqued because the ministers of the three emperors proceeded to formulate common demands on the Ottomans without consulting England in advance. The "Concert of Europe" had been decidedly wrenched by the action. Nevertheless, the consequences of

British refusal to support the demands of the other powers on the sultan spelled misery for the innocent, and also caused a bloody war. The Turks had been accustomed to play one Christian empire against another, and then to snap their fingers. They now reckoned that Germany, France, and Italy would never go beyond diplomatic protests; Russia and Austria they also felt sure could not unite in a firm alliance; while England, for so Disraeli's attitude seemed to indicate, would probably give them military and naval aid against the czar.

In May, 1876, the Berlin Note was presented, and almost simultaneously Great Britain, as if to show her friendship for the Turks, ordered a squadron to Besika Bay. In Constantinople matters were moving briskly. The reigning sultan, Abdul-Aziz, had disgusted all responsible Turks by his extravagance and gross incapacity. There was a fairly intelligent faction in Constantinople which saw the empire drifting to calamity for lack of efficient leadership. This party secured the *fetvah* (solemn decree) of the Sheik-ul-Islam (the head of the Turkish branch of Islam), authorizing the removal of the *Padishah* whose government was bringing ruin to the faithful. The guards about the palace were tampered with. Abdul-Aziz was easily overpowered and deposed, and his nephew, Murad V, was set upon the throne of Mohammed the Conqueror. Four days later it was announced that Abdul-Aziz had committed suicide by means of a pair of scissors, loaned him for trimming his beard.[1] Murad, however, soon proved to be either "feeble minded," or possibly was not sufficiently pliable for the *pashas* who had put him in power. In August, he in turn was deposed, and in his place reigned his brother, Abdul-Hamid II, who was at first too inexperienced to have a will of his own, although later he was to develop into one of the shrewdest and most bloody of all the Ottoman line.

While this national party among the *begs* and *pashas* was

[1] Improbable as this story seems, in view of the usual fate of deposed Oriental monarchs, it is by no means certain that Abdul-Aziz was murdered.

trying to introduce a modest degree of efficiency into the Constantinople government, to shake off foreign influence, and to rally the nation to the cry of "Turkey for the Turks," officers in their army were making it impossible for Great Britain to give their country the expected aid against Russia. The Bosnian revolt had spread elsewhere in the Balkans. The Bulgarian villages had become restless. There was a feeble insurrection in their region. About one hundred Turks were killed by the Bulgar insurgents. The answer came when the government sent an army of regular troops and a still larger horde of Bashi-Bazouks, irregular soldiers under the laxest kind of discipline, into the Bulgarian Mountains. The slaughter of the defenseless peasantry was terrible. In the town of Batak only two thousand of the seven thousand inhabitants escaped cold-blooded murder. The whole number of Christians thus massacred was probably over twelve thousand. Sex or age had not been spared, and a British commissioner, sent to investigate the rumors of horror, reported the whole deed as "perhaps the most heinous crime that has stained the history of the present century." [1] Achmet Aga, the leader of this murderous crew, was, however, decorated by his government for his brave services, and for an instant the Disraeli government committed the blunder of trying to minimize this deed of their announced protégés. But the English Liberal papers soon ran down the facts. Mr. Gladstone, former and future prime minister, and Disraeli's chief political opponent, left his theological studies on "Future Retribution" to write a famous and utterly damning pamphlet entitled "The Bulgarian Horrors." The conscience of England was stirred by his speeches and publications. It asserted to his stern dictum, "Let the Turks now carry away their abuses in the only possible manner, namely, *by carrying away themselves*. . . . One and all, bag and baggage, [they] shall, I hope, clear out of the province they have desolated and profaned."

[1] On the highroad from Sophia to Ruschuk, used by the Bashi-Bazouks, even to-day the towns are not built along the general way, but are concealed in the valleys and gorges. Thither the wretched Bulgar peasants fled in 1876, and all of them have never come down again.

It was folly for the Disraeli government to invite repudiation at home by giving further countenance to a government which could work deeds like these. "Even if Russia were to declare war against the Porte [1] (sultan)," wrote Lord Derby to Constantinople, "Her Majesty's government would find it practically impossible to interfere."

War between Russia and Turkey was becoming every day more of a certainty. While the Bulgarian massacres were proceeding, Serbia and Montenegro had declared war (June, 1876) upon the sultan. Their zeal to rescue their oppressed fellow-Slavs in Bosnia was excellent, but a good cause does not always spell victory. The Montenegrins won some successes, but the more ambitious Serbian campaign speedily came to grief. Once more, as so often has happened, it was disclosed that, grievously as the Turks had degenerated, they were still first-class fighting men. The sultan's ministers had not been too corrupt and inefficient to fail to obtain a good supply of breech-loading rifles. The Serbian army, despite large reënforcements by Russian volunteers, was speedily defeated, and Prince Milan called lustily for an armistice. But the powers were unable to arrange a satisfactory accommodation between the contending parties. Every day that the quarrel continued promised new perils for the peace of the world, and the English, in turn, began to give their Ottoman protégés frank advice about reforms and pacification. It was not English admonition, however, but Russian action, which brought a momentary respite. On the thirtieth of October General Ignatieff, the special ambassador of the czar to Constantinople, gave the Turks forty-eight hours to conclude an armistice with Serbia. With this pistol at his head, the sultan halted. Fighting ceased. The diplomats once more resumed their weary efforts, making a last desperate attempt to save the sultan from his sins.

In December, 1876, a conference of the powers met at Constantinople for the purpose of giving Abdul-Hamid II sage advice. Even as their excellencies the ambassadors were in

[1] The Sublime Porte is the ordinary official title for the Turkish government.

session, sudden salvos of artillery distracted their august deliberations. Prompt questions were raised, and a sleek and smiling pasha announced that the *Padishah*, out of his vast love for his people, had bestowed upon them a liberal constitution, a constitution, in fact, more liberal on paper than that of Russia, Germany, or possibly even that of Austria. A nominated senate, an elected chamber of deputies, a responsible ministry, freedom of meeting and of the press, compulsory education, etc., etc.,—all these blessings, by one stroke of the pen, were to come to the fortunate subjects of the successor of the kalifs and the sultans. The diplomats, however, were too hard-headed to be imposed upon by any such farce. Even the British delegates refused to take the new liberty seriously, and the Russian ambassador soon quit Constantinople in wrath.

But the Turks used their new constitution with some adroitness as a scheme for further delay. How could the powers continue to demand reforms when all possible reforms were going to be voted and put into effect—just as soon, of course, as the new parliament could be convened and pass the necessary measures? And, in the meantime, how could the *Padishah*, as a "constitutional sovereign," enact legislation by his mere fiat? As for other matters, the Turks proved themselves to the ambassadors to be incorrigible. When the question of Bulgaria was raised, the sultan's ministers at first solemnly averred "they did not know what the word meant." They permitted themselves to remember that it might be a "geographical term for the region north of the Balkans," but that was all. In short, these slippery barbarians, "who wore tight clothes and chattered French," but who seemed to have neither honesty nor intelligence under their red fezzes, alienated their last friends and drove even England to wash her hands of them. Lord Salisbury, going home in despair, declared that "all had tried to save Turkey, but she would not allow them to save her." Thus the year 1877 opened with war between the czar and sultan all but certain, and England looking on as a neutral.

Czar Alexander II was probably an honest lover of peace,

but despotic as were the institutions of Russia, he could not be indifferent to public opinion.[1] The Muscovite empire had lately been stirred by a strong Pan-Slavic movement, an agitation for the union of all Slavdom in one confederacy, of course under the hegemony of Russia. So far as this affected the Slavs ruled by Austria, such an ambition had to be checked by the government, or it would have led to interminable wars; but the rescue and vindication of the South Slavs of Bosnia and Serbia was a different affair. Likewise, the outraged Bulgars were counted Slavs, too; and their woes had produced a great impression at St. Petersburg and Moscow. Also, to the Muscovites, with their passionate loyalty to the orthodox church, the summons to rescue their fellow-Christians from Turkish tyranny came as a call to a crusade; and Russians, imperfect as had long been their own liberty, have repeatedly shown the idealism which carried them on to make sacrifices for the liberties of others. Finally, and of still keener national interest, was the fact that in marching as the champion of Christian civilization against the sultan, Russia was also taking another step toward that outlet upon warm, blue water which was a necessity for her empire. All in all, Alexander II drew the sword in 1877 with a great national enthusiasm impelling him forward. The war was popular for the time in Russia. A private understanding with Austria had assured the czar against interference from Franz-Joseph, and the military course therefore seemed very plain.

On April 10, 1877, the Turks in a spirit of incredible folly rejected the London Protocol, a last despairing proposal for reform which had been flung at them by the concert of the powers. Down to the last the sultan and his grand vizier had hugged the delusion that England would somehow fight for them. Lord Salisbury had vainly telegraphed to London from the Constantinople conference, ''The grand vizier be-

---

[1] By Russian "public opinion" is meant of course that of the small but influential educated upper classes. The ignorant lower classes were then probably without any ideas about foreign policy save possibly a vague notion that it was always well to rescue Christians from the infidel.

lieves that he can count on the assistance of Lord Derby and Lord Beaconsfield.'' Yet the British cabinet had nevertheless failed to make it plain to Abdul-Hamid that it could never stand between him and the wrath of Russia, as he had now provoked it. The Turkish ''free parliament,'' although duly ''elected'' and opened with some pomp in March, 1877, had instantly exhibited itself as nothing but a comically useless tool for the purposes of despotism. Its members were mere dummies for the government,[1] and were speedily nicknamed the ''Yes, Sirs'' (*Evet Effendim*), from their willingness to ratify every suggestion from above. On April 24 the czar took the long expected action and declared war.

The Russian navy on the Black Sea had not been rebuilt sufficiently since 1871 to cope with the Turkish fleet which contained several formidable ironclads. The way to Constantinople, therefore, lay across Rumania. There were divided councils at Bucharest as to permitting the Russians to go through, but the sultan committed the blunder not merely of calling on ''his vassal'' to preserve neutrality, but of summoning Prince Carol to take up arms against the enemies of his suzerain. The prince was naturally anxious to become an independent sovereign, and speedily made a treaty with Russia for full alliance, although Gortchakoff, the czar's prime minister, arrogantly told him at first, ''Russia has no need for the assistance of the Rumanian army.'' The legions of Alexander II, therefore, streamed across Wallachia, while the prince issued a formal proclamation of Rumanian independence.

The Russians had entered into the war with enthusiasm and confidence that the odds were so entirely on their side that, if Western Europe would but give them fair play, they could easily crush the infidel. Their difficulties, however, were great. The Turkish navy prevented the use of transports on the Black Sea and the railroads through Southern Russia were few and in Rumania still fewer. The hindrances to moving

[1] When once it was evident that the new "constitution" would serve no purpose, it was duly suspended (1878), and without being formally abolished, remained in innocuous desuetude until 1908, when it was very curiously revived. (See chap. XIII.)

huge armies at a vast distance from their base thus proved almost unsurmountable. The czar's forces also suffered, as in the
Great War some four decades later, from rascally contractors
and grievously imperfect munitions and supplies. Alexander,
too, at first had trouble in finding highly competent generals.
Nevertheless, the incapacity of the Turkish commanders was,
on the whole, so great that only the offsetting excellence of
the Turkish infantrymen seemed likely to make the war at
all equal. In the summer of 1877 the Russians forced their
way over the Danube, penetrated Bulgaria, took Tirnova, the
old capital of that afflicted country, and, to crown all, seized
Shipka Pass, the best defile over the Balkan Mountains.
There was panic in Constantinople, and a hasty shifting of
posts took place among the excited pashas. Then came a long
respite. The Turks had found a really able general—one
of those admirable fighters who often come out of the Orient—
Osman Pasha, who was able to inflict on the czar and his
grand dukes anxious nights, heavy losses, and a humiliating
delay.

In their sudden advance through Bulgaria the Russians had
neglected to occupy the small town of Plevna, located most
strategically at the intersection of the main roads along which
the invaders must pass. With some forty-five thousand men
Osman Pasha flung himself into Plevna, and suddenly the
Russians found their whole line of advance menaced. On
July 20, not realizing the strength of their enemies, they as-
saulted with inadequate forces and met a bloody repulse.
Ten days later a more powerful attack met a still greater
disaster. There was nothing for it but the Grand Duke
Nicholas must needs telegraph to Prince Carol to bring up
his despised Rumanian allies to aid in the siege. The prince
proudly required (and obtained) that he should be appointed
commander-in-chief of the entire besieging force. On September 11 there was a third and still more desperate assault.
The Rumanians covered themselves with glory before the
bloody Turkish breastworks, but the pasha's inner lines could
not be carried. The only option was to bring up reënforcements, hem Osman in, and slowly starve him out. This last

stage of the siege lasted till December 10. In the meantime
the whole Russian plan of campaign lagged, and if there had
been real capacity at Constantinople, something might have
been done to save the Ottoman Empire from overthrow. But
Osman was unique in his tenacity and skill among the Turkish
commanders. In Asia, in the Caucasus region, where, of
course, an independent campaign could be conducted, the
Turks had been driven from post to post, and on November 18
they lost the great fortress of Kars. At last, in December,
the stout Osman was at the end of his resources. He served
out his last biscuits and ammunition to his men and made
a despairing attempt to cut his way through the besiegers.
The effort failed, and he surrendered with forty thousand
half-starved troops. The Russians treated him honorably as
a doughty foe, and well they might. He had cost them twenty-
one thousand men (sixteen thousand Russians and five thousand Rumanians) and five months of valuable time. But the
roads through Bulgaria had been opened at last!

The surrender of Osman was followed by the speedy rout
of the remaining Turkish armies. The czar's service had
now developed two redoubtable generals, Gurko and Skobe-
leff. The first of these took Sofia and utterly defeated the
army of Suleiman Pasha near Philippopolis; the second re-
opened Shipka Pass, which had been almost rewon by the
Turks during the siege of Plevna. Serbia, too, was again in
arms; likewise little Montenegro; while from every other
quarter messengers of calamity hastened in toward Abdul-
Hamid's palace. The Cossacks raged and raided through
the Mohammedan regions around Adrianople in a manner that
indicated that Christians also understood the arts of massacre. Adrianople itself fell in January, 1878, and so far as
the sultan's own strength was concerned, the Turkish power
was at an end. There was nothing for it but to negotiate.
With a noose about their necks the Ottomans accepted an
armistice on January 31, to be followed by the more definitive
Treaty of San Stefano, signed on March 3, 1878.

San Stefano is a small village on the outskirts of Constantinople, the Russians having thus advanced almost to the goal

of their ambition. The Muscovites were in great anxiety to tie their defeated foes by a hard and fast treaty and confront Europe with an "accomplished deed" before the other great powers, and especially England, could intervene. The czar's ministers knew that not merely England, but Austria would fight to the death rather than see them occupy Constantinople, and they did not attempt it; but otherwise the changes they dictated were sweeping enough. Montenegro and Serbia were to receive appreciable increases of territory. Bosnia was to be "reformed" not by promises only, but under the joint control of Austria and Russia. Other reforms were to be granted the oppressed Armenians in Asia Minor, in which region a considerable strip of territory (including Kars) was to be ceded outright to Russia. As for Rumania, she was to be set up as a strictly independent nation, but she was to cede Bessarabia [1] to Russia and receive in return (at the expense of Turkey) the Dobrudja, the miasmic marshy delta of the Danube. But the most striking clause was that relating to the creation of an entirely new unit in modern Europe—Bulgaria. According to the terms of this treaty a huge Bulgaria would have sprung into existence. Constantinople and its hinterland back to Adrianople, Saloniki and the territory around it, and part of Albania would have been left to the sultan; otherwise he would have been expelled from Europe. The lost dominions were to be formed into "an autonomous tributary principality, with a Christian governor and a national militia." Abdul-Hamid's pride might be salved a little by saying that the new country was merely to be a vassal-region of the Ottoman Empire. The fact, of course, was evident to all men that practically the vassalage consisted in a certain amount of tribute money, likely to cease some fine day. By their own sins and follies the Ottomans had had themselves pushed to the outermost corner of Europe.

As the Russians advanced, and, still more, as the full tenor of their demands became evident, a large percentage of the

[1] This strip of country was inhabited by Rumanians, but it had been held by Russia prior to the Treaty of Paris (1856), when the czar had been forced to surrender it.

English public took ever-increasing alarm. The memory of the Bulgarian massacres was already fading; the fear of the Muscovites advancing along the road to India by way of Constantinople began again to grip the British heart. It was claimed, with some show of justice, that the czar was anxious to impose a peace, as if the quarrel were between him and the sultan alone, to the total ignoring of legitimate British interests. Within the London cabinet there was much difference of opinion. Disraeli himself said whimsically that "there were six parties in the ministry. The first party wanted immediate war with Russia; the second was for war in order to save Constantinople; the third was for peace at any price; the fourth would let the Russians take Constantinople and *then* turn them out; the fifth wanted to plant the cross on the dome of St. Sophia; and then there was the Prime Minister and the Chancellor of the Exchequer [Northcote] who desired to see something done, but did n't know exactly what!" [1]   It is fairly certain, however, that Disraeli was quite ready to go to war, if Russia did not knuckle under, and only the resistance of his colleagues prevented more drastic action being taken by England than actually eventuated.

Thus for some weeks the Muscovites and Turks confronted one another grimly at the very gates of Constantinople, while a British fleet rode in the Sea of Marmora inside the Dardanelles, ready to land men at Constantinople itself, in case the invaders showed signs of attacking the city. The whole situation was ticklish for the peace of Europe. The least untoward incident would have set the Russians and British at one another's throats, despite the fact that unless England had found a land ally, the struggle would have been, as Bismarck sarcastically declared, "a fight between an elephant and a whale."

Under these circumstances war would surely have followed, had not Russia been willing to consider the question of the revision of the Treaty of San Stefano. There were plenty of hot-headed officers around the czar and plenty of ardent Pan-Slavists in the rear quite ready to urge flinging defiance at

[1] Quoted in Rose's "Development of European Nations," Vol. I, p. 267.

Disraeli and tempting his government to do its worst. But
Russia's hand was forced by the threatening attitude of Austria. Despite the fact that Franz-Joseph had given some
kind of assurances of neutrality when the attack on Turkey
began, Austrian troops now began to mobilize in the Carpathians in a position to make a deadly flank attack upon the
Russians, strung out as they were in a long line of communication through Rumania and Bulgaria to the gates of Constantinople. The fear lest the proposed Bulgarian state would
be a satrapy of Russia in all but name had entered the hearts
of the leaders at Vienna no less than at London. It would
have been tempting destruction to have fought both England
and Austria simultaneously, and, as a consequence, even before
the final signing of the Treaty of San Stefano, the czar began giving tokens of a willingness to compromise. Nevertheless, ere Alexander II could be induced to lay the settlement
of the Balkans before a general congress of the powers, there
were tense moments and renewed threats of war.

During this period of stress, when London was tossed by
a patriotic fervor, the famous phrase "jingoism" seems to
have been coined. It probably originated from a popular
music-hall effusion by an unofficial poet-laureate, which ran
thus:

> We don't want to fight,
> But, *by jingo*, if we do,
> We 've got the ships, we 've got the men,
> And we 've got the money, too!

On April 1, 1878, Disraeli gave notice that the reserves of
the British army and navy would be called out. Fifteen days
later, to advertise to the world the solidarity of the queen's
empire, he ordered eight regiments of Indian Sepoy troops
to Malta. This sign of resolution brought the czar's ministers to a more tractable mood, and they agreed to such concessions concerning the boundaries of Bulgaria, etc., as to
make it likely that peace could be maintained. But meantime Disraeli was proving to the Turks that he was not cham-
pioning their integrity out of pure disinterested friendship.
By letting them believe that Russia was likely to renew the

war, and that English aid would be indispensable, the sultan was induced to promise that if Russia retained her conquests in Asia Minor (as it was perfectly certain she would do) and was likely to push her conquests further, England would give armed aid to the sultan, but to enable England to defend these territories the Ottomans gave her the occupation and administration of Cyprus.[1] The sultan also promised to introduce the "necessary reforms" for the protection of the Armenian Christians. The peculiar execution of these reforms and England's part therein were destined to play a very ignoble part in later history.

Russia was thus forced to submit her entire scheme for the reconstruction of the Balkans to a congress of the powers. This congress presently assembled (June 13 to July 13, 1878) at Berlin, and was undoubtedly the most distinguished diplomatic gathering since the Congress of Vienna (1814–15).

That Bismarck, the acknowledged center of the public life of Europe, should preside over this assembly was, of course, only natural. He had invited the diplomats to accept the hospitality of his emperor on the ground that Germany had no selfish interests to pursue in the Balkans, was partner in no quarrels, and was intensely anxious to keep the general peace. He openly proclaimed himself as sure to be an "honest broker" for all his distinguished friends and clients. Nevertheless, the Russians went to Berlin with the firm expectation that the "Iron Chancellor" would prove their potent advocate and even their champion. The services Russia rendered Germany in 1870, when a broad hint from the czar prevented Austria from going to the aid of France, were admittedly very great. William I, himself, had written to Alexander II, "Prussia will never forget that she owes it to you that the war (with France) did not assume the most extreme dimensions; may God bless you for it."[2] Now,

[1] The innocent Turks did know that Britain and Russia had reached a working agreement five days before the Cyprus Convention was signed (June 4, 1878). They had bartered away a rich island for a promise to fight in behalf of the Ottomans, which England knew she would not have to redeem!

[2] Coolidge; "Origins of the Triple Alliance." p. 156.

surely, was the time for active gratitude, for the exertion of all Bismarck's tremendous influence to see to it that the arrangements of San Stefano were modified as little as possible!

The Russians went to Berlin in at least partial innocency. They found themselves utterly deceived. The "Iron Chancellor" afterward said he in no wise deserved their wrath, but rather that he ought to have been decorated by the czar for his very friendly services. Russian public opinion, however, laughed his protestations to scorn. It could point to the undeniable fact that at the congress of powers Bismarck had swung all his influence over to the side of England and Austria, and had permitted the Treaty of San Stefano to be rewritten radically and that, too, in a manner to Russia's great hurt. The motives Bismarck had for this change of policy are explained elsewhere, but the accomplished results were blazoned before all Europe. In 1878 it became perfectly evident that between Berlin and St. Petersburg warm friendship had ceased.

Aside from Bismarck himself, the gathering at Berlin was notable. Seldom have more premiers or foreign ministers of mighty nations sat around one table. France and Italy were represented, although France was still too crushed by the events of 1870 to have much influence, and Italy was hardly as yet counted a great power, except by courtesy. Austria sent her prime minister, the astute Count Andrassy, Russia her chancellor, Prince Gortchakoff, a man of considerable ability, but on bad personal terms with Bismarck and therefore not a fortunate delegate to win the favor of the grim president of the congress; and England was represented by her capable foreign secretary, Lord Salisbury, and last but not least by Disraeli himself, now elevated by his countrymen to the peerage as the Earl of Beaconsfield. The proceedings of the congress were, of course, after the bad type of the old-style diplomacy, where the formal sessions and official protocols were only half to disclose and confirm what had been determined in private conferences and "deals."

Bismarck and the strong Austrian influence were so decidedly on Beaconsfield's side that he had little difficulty in forcing the Russians to assent to almost any terms which were not too humiliating. In fact, Beaconsfield personally seemed to dominate the entire gathering. "The old Jew—*he* is the man!" remarked Bismarck pithily; and the English prime minister himself was quite aware of his hour of triumph. It is recorded that the Russo-Polish Princess Radziwill met him at a brilliant reception the night that the news of the Cyprus convention was made public. As he wandered among the throng of buzzing, criticizing, yet admiring generals and diplomats, the princess asked the prime minister, "What are you thinking of?" "I am not *thinking* at all," replied Beaconsfield magnificently, "I am merely *enjoying* myself."

The czar's ministers, in short, were soon aware that they could not fight England with Austria as her ally, and with the sinister hands of Bismarck behind Austria. There was nothing for it but to save out of the wreck of the San Stefano project whatever part they could. The sultan, of course, had his direct advocates, Katheodri Pasha and Mehemet Ali Pasha, respectively a Greek and a German adventurer, who had entered the service of Abdul-Hamid and pleaded his cause more skilfully than any native Ottoman. The Greeks, Serbs, and Rumanians also had their delegates to press their national claims and grievances, but the real results of the conference came from four men—Beaconsfield, Bismarck, Andrassy, and Gortchakoff.

Substantially speaking, the Treaty of San Stefano was attacked on the ground that the Great Bulgaria, proposed by it, denied the claims of Serbia and Greece to expansion and unduly curtailed the Turkish dominions in Europe; for the sultan, so urged his apologists, must surely be left enough land west of the Bosphorus still to be able to pass for an European power. But the readjustments were made very unskilfully, with far greater care on the part of the opponents of Russia to prevent the wide extension of her power than to make any redistribution of the Balkan lands that would meet the reasonable demands of national hopes and international justice. The principal points in the Treaty of Berlin can best be stated in summary:

I. Some extensions were given to Serbia and Montenegro, but not so great as by the San Stefano scheme; and between the two South Slav countries was left wedged the "Sanjak of Novi-Bazar," a miserable little district now handed back to Turkey.

II. Bosnia and Herzegovina were assigned to Austria, to be "occupied and administered" by her pending the restoration of their peace and prosperity. Theoretically, they were still part of Turkey. The Serbs and their kinsmen, the Bosnians, were angered at this evidence that Bosnia was not to escape from the moribund sultan into the hands of Serbia, but was to become a spoil of lusty Austria. Still, the new arrangement was on paper and "temporary," and the South Slavs were to live in vain hopes for thirty years, until Austria destroyed the illusion by downright annexation.

III. Greece was given a promise of an extension of her northern borders, a promise which the sultan was slow to fulfill. It was only reluctantly and partially executed in 1881 after severe pressure from the powers. However, for the great Island of Crete, with its large Hellenic population, Greece pleaded in vain. It was left for thirty-four years more of misrule and bondage. .

IV. In Asia Minor Russia was compelled to disgorge part of her conquests, although she retained the strong fortress of Kars. The sultan also solemnly engaged "to carry out, without further delay, the ameliorations and reforms demanded in the provinces (of) the Armenians, and to guarantee their security against the Circassians and Kurds." How Abdul-Hamid executed this binding promise will be told in a bloody sequel.

V. The Great Bulgaria of San Stefano was flung into the scrap-heap. England would have none of it; the proposed new state, in her opinion, would become merely a Russian satrapy. The proposed unit was therefore cut into three parts, each with a different fate: (a) The southern region, especially Macedonia, was handed back to the sultan, to be oppressed by his myrmidons and its own factions until 1912, with a history miserable and bloody even beyond the run of Turkish provinces. (b) The northern regions, a "Small Bulgaria," were formed into an "autonomous and tributary principality," practically clear of the sultan save for an annual tribute, to have a prince and constitution of its own. (c) Between Bulgaria and the Turkish dominions was to be an "autonomous province under the direct political and military authority of the sultan," but with a Christian governor named every five years. This new unit was Eastern Rumelia. It was a wholly artificial creation, its inhabitants being almost entirely Bulgars. Common sense, which often evades great diplomats, should have indicated that it could hardly exist long.

VI. As a sop to Russia and as a reward to the czar's people for their sacrifices in a victorious war, it was confirmed that Bessarabia should be detached from Rumania and given to the Muscovites. The desolate Dobrudja seemed a poor enough recompense for this loss of a land inhabited almost strictly by Rumanians, and Prince Carol's ministers pleaded in vain against the change. To no purpose they invoked the memories of their faithful service at Plevna. Gortchakoff was inexorable, and Beaconsfield was not willing to risk a great war merely in behalf of an angry and outraged East European people. The weaker power gloomily submitted, one of her statesmen uttering the naked truth that "it was not vanquished Turkey which paid Russia for the expenses of the war, but Rumania." Doubtless Alexander II was in sore need of some tangible annexations to satisfy Russian public opinion for the great sacrifices made in the conflict, but it was pitiful that the gain of Russia had to be her faithful ally's loss. This ungenerous act almost drove the Rumanians into a standing alliance with Germany and Austria.

With these results, then, the great Congress of Berlin adjourned, and Beaconsfield returned to London in fine feather, bringing, he told his applauding countrymen, "peace with honor," and also cynically asserting that he had "consolidated the Turkish Empire."² He had consolidated it by allowing Turkey to be two thirds expelled from Europe and by causing England herself to bag Cyprus! The diplomatic wiseacres declared "peace and happiness were now assured to the Balkans." On the contrary, forty years' retrospect shows that few human arrangements were more short-sighted and transitory than this much-lauded Treaty of Berlin, when Beaconsfield and Bismarck had made pawns of the peoples of Southeastern Europe. The unhappy results that presently developed were these:

I. The Bosnian Question, which was thrust upon Serbia and Austria, became pregnant with almost certain war.

II. Bulgaria was bound to reach out for Eastern Rumelia and then for an outlet upon the open sea—the Ægean.

III. The failure to award Crete to Greece promised hot friction and probably a war between Greece and Turkey.

IV. The return of Macedonia to the Turks implied that the miseries of that unhappy land should presently make it a veritable gunpowder factory for all Europe and indirectly for all the world.

V. The action of Bismarck in favoring England and Austria at the expense of Russia was to erect a barrier between Germany and Russia that was soon to develop into an enmity which, in its own turn, was likely to breed a world war.

VI. By exacting Cyprus from Turkey as a reward for "protection," England destroyed the claims of gratitude she might have had upon the sultan. Abdul-Hamid clearly understood that Great Britain had come to his rescue from no disinterested affection. From this time onward the diplomatic influence of Great Britain at Constantinople waned.

VII. By helping to secure the return of Macedonia and other regions to the Ottomans, by other friendly acts, and by exacting no territorial concessions in return, Germany convinced the Turks that in *her* there was a really powerful and unselfish friend. This was the beginning of a German influence at Constantinople which twenty years later was to develop into mighty things.

To sum up the story of the Berlin settlement: it was no

settlement at all, merely a *modus vivendi* and armistice before the resumption of intrigues and battle. Russia was bound to resume her thrust southward for access to open water; Turkey was bound to give another exhibition of her unfitness to exist as a ruler of civilized men; Austrian ambition was in no wise sated by the occupation of Bosnia; and Greece, Rumania, Serbia, and Bulgaria were each left with unsatisfactory boundaries and a particular burden of woe. Nobody left Berlin really satisfied, save Beaconsfield, and he was to die in 1881— too soon to realize the imperfection of his vaunted achievement. History will say of him that he had an imperial vision for Britain and that he was a master politician, but not that he was a world statesman.

It is told that on the morrow of the signature of the treaty of Berlin, Bismarck sent for the Turkish representatives and said: "Well, gentlemen, you ought to be very much pleased. We have secured you a respite of twenty years. You have that period of grace in which to put your house in order. It is probably the last chance the Ottoman Empire will get, and of one thing I am pretty sure, *you won't take it.*" [1]

Part of the seeds of the calamity of 1914 had been sown in 1871, when Germany dictated an unjust treaty of peace to France. Another very large part, however, was sown in 1878, when Beaconsfield and Bismarck imposed on the Near East not a real peace, but a most unsatisfactory truce.

[1] Marriot's "The Eastern Question," p. 346. The story may be apocryphal, but falls in well with probabilities.

CHAPTER VI

IN November, 1869, there was a great celebration in the bor-
der-land between Egypt and Palestine. The Suez Canal
had been opened. It had been built by the skill, persistence,
and energy of a great French engineer, Ferdinand de Lesseps,
who had coaxed the money out of the financiers of Europe and
overcome countless difficulties while conducting a vast enterprise in an almost waterless desert-country. The fêtes at the
opening of the canal were magnificent. It was just before
the Franco-Prussian War and the fall of the Second Empire.
Napoleon III was still in power, but he was unable to leave
France. He sent, however, his glittering Empress Eugénie,
and there came, likewise, the Emperor of Austria, the Crown
Prince of Prussia, and a Russian Grand Duke. The host of
the occasion was the Khedive of Egypt, Ismaïl Pasha.

The khedive was nominally only the viceroy of the Turkish
sultan; actually he was an hereditary semi-independent prince.
Ismaïl may have been Oriental enough in his personal habits,
but he imitated his European guests in the magnificence of
his hospitality. Nothing was too extreme for him, when it
came to meeting the whims of his crowned visitors. The Empress Eugénie expressed a desire to visit the pyramids of
Gizeh. Almost instantly her host ordered ten thousand peasants, driven by the lash to forced labor under the broiling
heat, to build a suitable road from Cairo seven miles out to
the pyramids. The visitors, especially the French, were
charmed by his hospitality, and if Napoleon III had remained
in power, Ismaïl might have found a firm patron and protector
in the Second Empire. Unfortunately, however, the next
year Bismarck and Moltke sent Eugénie and Napoleon III fleeing into exile. Ismaïl, therefore, had only his expenditures
for his pains.

Egypt, about 1870, appeared to be a land with certain superficial Western improvements. There were European quarters in Cairo and Alexandria, a few European officials and "advisers" in the khedival service, and the beginnings of railroads, with sundry steamers on the Nile. The army wore tight uniforms of the Western type and carried Western rifles. There was a great deal of bad French and Italian chattered in the larger towns, but otherwise Egypt was still a decidedly unspoiled oriental Islamic country. The population was sunk in Eastern unprogressiveness and squalor; the system of government was practically that of Turkey, with the average Egyptian official a little more tyrannous and rapacious possibly than the average Ottoman official. Bribery was so common in the courts that a *muftee* who failed to grow rich by taking fees for his decisions was looked upon as an extraordinary man. Torture, *bastinado,* the clipping of ears, or other mutilations were standard penalties for petty offenses. The ruling classes rejoiced in the name of Turks, though they were often of native origin. There was a considerable number of Copts, native Christians, who by superior intelligence maintained a tolerable position. The great bulk of the population, however, were wretched *fellahs,* the most abject, downtrodden peasantry in the near East, direct descendants of the bondsmen of the ancient Pharaohs, with little but their religion altered and possibly subjected to the heaviest taxes anywhere in the world. Living in filthy mud-villages, ruled by the rhinoceros-whip of the khedive's tax-gatherers, dragged off frequently to forced labor on the Nile dikes, the roads, or other government works, they endured a lot beside which that of the late serf in Russia was enviable.

Most execrable of all was the method of recruiting the khedive's army. Peasants were shackled together like convicts, dragged away from their villages by policemen, and shipped off to distant garrisons where they could not mutiny. There they were given guns and taught the forms of soldiering. They were seldom paid, were miserably fed, and very few ever saw their homes again. It is needless to say that this army was one of the most cowardly in all the world.

In short, Egypt was a country in which the veneer of civilization was very thin indeed.

England watched Egypt with anxious interest. It controlled the route to India. English statesmen had beheld the development of French influence in the country with great anxiety and felt still greater anxiety because French capital and energy had directed the building of the Suez Canal. If there had been no Franco-Prussian War to ruin France, Frenchman and Briton might have clashed over Egypt; as it turned out, France was weak, and England was content to leave Ismaïl in quasi-independence so long as he kept up the outward forms of orderly government, despite much grievous oppression.

Ismaïl, however, with all the blood-money he extracted from his subjects, was fain to spend gold like a Crœsus. All kinds of financial harpies and adventurers, such as abounded in the Levant, had fastened upon him. They filled his head with grandiose schemes for public works, whereon the money was squandered and nothing was accomplished. The khedive, too, had a harem of enormous proportions. The various houris thereof were one and all importunate for Paris costumes, costly porcelain, precious jewels, elaborate furniture, and every other trickery which the West could foist upon the East. The khedive was as a child concerning European methods, but a horde of "bankers"—French, German, and Jewish—assured him he was a Solomon in money-matters and got him to sign one authorization after another for a new issue of Egyptian bonds. Naturally, every person at the Cairo court had his hand in the treasury, and this régime was delightfully popular to the favored circle. Often the plundering was open and gross; and of Ismaïl it was well written that "he always contrived to obtain *the least possible value* for his expenditure."

In 1875 it was evident that the khedive's financial exploits were nearing their climax. He then disposed of his last great asset, four million pounds' worth of shares in the new Suez Canal. The astute English prime minister, Disraeli, got wind of the fact that Ismaïl was trying to negotiate these shares in

the Paris money-market, and before the French government
or any other power could intervene he bought the whole block
on his own authority for England and then got Parliament to
ratify his act. Three English directors henceforth sat on
the board of the canal company. Paris grumbled, but was
helpless. England was tightening her grip on the all-important road to India.

This sale, however, did Ismaïl little good. He was at the
end of his financial rope. In 1876 came a time when he could
no longer borrow, even at most ruinous rates of usury. The
result was that interest on the Egyptian debt was suspended.
At first England refused to intervene, but when it became
clear that France intended to force a thorough overhauling
of the khedive's affairs, Britain decided to join with her. In
1878, therefore, the pressure from the great powers led to the
appointment of ministers who were directly under European
influence and who could be relied upon to stop the financial
disorder. But Ismaïl was not anxious thus to be allowed to
reign, indeed, but no longer to govern. Early in 1879 he
stirred up a mutiny in his own army, with the main object of
compelling Nubar Pasha, a very enlightened Armenian, to
resign as his prime minister. Ismaïl reckoned that France
and England were too jealous of one another ever to agree on
a scheme of actual coercion, but he failed to reckon on Germany.

Bismarck's real motives are not very clear, but the chancellor
speedily announced that the interests of certain German
creditors made intervention necessary. The Turkish sultan
took the hint. He was only too glad to show that, in name at
least, the khedive was only a viceroy. On June 26, 1879, came
a telegram from Constantinople to "Ismaïl Pasha, *late*
Khedive of Egypt," informing his highness that his son ruled
in his stead.

Ismaïl did not struggle with destiny. He salaamed to
Tewfik, his son and successor, and only stipulated that he
should be allowed to depart to Naples with *part* of his harem.
He was accommodated to the extent of being allowed to take
some three hundred of his ladies with him. The tale is that

the unlucky and angered consorts who were *not* selected to depart with their lord from Cairo, wrecked all the china, furniture, and draperies in the palace before he could depart with his chosen retinue.

Ismaïl left Naples in 1887 and went to Constantinople, but there Abdul-Hamid shrewdly held him as a kind of prisoner until his death in 1895, lest he escape back to Egypt and stir up a revolt.

Tewfik thus "succeeded to a bankrupt state, an undisciplined army, and a discontented people." France and England agreed on a scheme for dual control of the finances to pay off the vast debt, each of the two guardian powers naming some of the fiscal managers who were to try to introduce order into Ismaïl's financial confusion. But the sight of Europeans taking virtual charge of Egyptian affairs kindled the anger of various native elements. There is not the slightest evidence that the despairing peasantry, on whom the burden of taxation almost entirely fell, were anything but glad at any change which promised a little relief. Sundry army officers, however, saw their fat posts in danger. In 1881 the regiments began to mutiny and to demand the dismissal of unpopular ministers, and in February, 1881, a certain Colonel Arabi, an upstart adventurer, by almost training guns upon the palace, forced the khedive to appoint him as war minister.

If England and France could have agreed upon joint action to rid the khedive of this mutinous dictatorship, all might have been well. They did, indeed, send a joint note to Egypt, warning the native rulers that the mutineers were playing with fire and that a country dominating the Suez Canal could not be suffered to fall into anarchy. Each nation also sent a fleet to Alexandria, but France was very distrustful of England and feared to be made a cat's paw by her old rival; also at this moment there was a cabinet crisis in Paris and home politics made the French government weak and unwilling to embark on anything like war.

Arabi and his irresponsible "Egypt for Egyptians" party soon forced the issue and compelled England to take action alone. On June 11, 1882, there was a serious massacre of

Christians in Alexandria and the case for all the Europeans in Egypt became so threatening that a few days later over fourteen thousand of them fled the country, while many others anxiously awaited steamers. Arabi, who now felt very confident, next committed the blunder of beginning to build batteries wherewith to drive the British fleet from the harbor of Alexandria. This was too much for the British admiral. The French ships refused to assist him, but on July 11, 1882, his eight iron-clads opened fire. Ships against forts are proverbially at a disadvantage, but Arabi's gunners were wretched, and although the ships had some slight losses, they presently silenced all the batteries. The next day British troops and marines landed in the city, to stop the looting and murder by the mutineers.

Arabi, however, remained still defiant. He had managed to keep the obedience and loyalty of his men, and by holding the khedive in semi-captivity pretended to retain the forms of lawful authority. In England there was a Liberal cabinet, headed by Mr. Gladstone. The ministry was very loath to let itself be diverted from its long program of domestic reforms by any kind of foreign adventure. But Arabi was now in a mood to make a drive at the Suez Canal and to menace the precious route to India. Besides, his rule in Egypt promised nothing but outrage and anarchy. France was still too hesitant and too fearful of a sudden thrust from Germany to be willing to send an army. Italy sent good wishes, but did not care to do any fighting. There was nothing for it but for England either to present Egypt to Arabi or to drive him out, and the Gladstone ministry was not pacifistic enough to refuse a plain national duty.

Early in September the British, led by the queen's ablest general, Lord Wolseley, landed a small army of their best old-style professional troops at Ismailia on the Suez Canal. Arabi had been expecting an attack near Alexandria, but now he assembled his forces, somewhat skilfully, to meet the invaders. There was only one battle—at Tel-el-Kebir. At dawn on September 13, thirteen thousand British regulars struck twice as many Egyptians supported by seventy cannon. There was a volley or two, and some hard fighting on the summit of the Egyptian intrenchments; then the miserable *fellah* infantry broke and ran. The British cavalry chased them furiously, merrily slapping the runaways from behind with the flat of their sabres and soon transforming the whole native army into a flying rabble. All the Egyptian guns were taken. There had never been a more complete victory. Sundry tales of this battle have a comic-opera flavor. It is said that many of Arabi's officers and men stripped off their uniforms and strove to escape capture by working in the fields as peaceful agriculturalists; or that they endeavored to pile into a railway train standing ready in their rear, but were all captured when a single British trooper rode up and shot the engineer, since no Egyptian had skill enough to start the locomotive.

The last courage oozed out of the khedival army, and when the next day five hundred English horsemen, after a furious ride, appeared before Cairo, eleven thousand native troops, with a strong citadel, surrendered after hardly a shot. On September 19 the "Official Journal" of Cairo appeared with a laconic decree of the khedive, "The Egyptian army is disbanded"—a significant story in few words. England was fairly grasping Egypt, the key to the East and to India.

No enemy of Britain would believe the statement, but nevertheless it was a fact that the island empire was not anxious to retain possession of this old land of Rameses and Cleopatra. The Gladstone cabinet contained a large element that was almost fanatically opposed to anything like conquest and aggressive war. John Bright, the great radical leader, had resigned from it in July, 1882, rather than seem to give consent to Lord Wolseley's expedition. Less extreme Englishmen realized that to retain their grip on Egypt meant to enrage France, which, since Napoleon Bonaparte's invasion, had regarded the country as in one sense her own. It would also seem a direct slap at Russia in her pressure southward, and would estrange the Turks, who still considered Egypt as an outlying *pashalik*. Italy and Austria, likewise, as hopeful Mediterranean powers, would hardly be pleased. Only Germany, curiously enough, seemed wholly quiescent. Bismarck's shrewd lips hardly concealed his satisfaction at a turn which seemed to set France and England permanently asunder.

Nevertheless, it was soon perfectly clear that, after seizing the Egyptian bunch of nettles, to drop it would be hard. In Cairo the bulk of the natives did not hide their delight at the coming of the British troops, and two thousand six hundred European residents of Alexandria signed a petition in favor of permanent occupation. Lord Granville, the statesman in charge, announced, indeed, that "he contemplated shortly commencing the withdrawal of the British troops from Egypt," but when attempts were made to untangle the situation and to put Tewfik in a position to rule firmly and progressively, the case seemed almost hopeless. There was really no effective native element to fall back upon. Arabi was tried for treason and banished to Ceylon, but what was to prevent another adventurer from doing his bloody work all over again? The vast debt accumulated by Ismaïl was still unpaid. It was needful to put Egyptian finances under a competent British expert, Sir Auckland Colvin. This of course was followed by the discovery that the whole internal administration of the country was hopelessly rotten. The canal system and the control of irrigation from the Nile had been allowed to run down, so that much arable land was reverting to desert, thus, of course, reducing the whole food supply of the country. The khedive, therefore, had to receive the authoritative "advice" to put his four important departments of irrigation, army, justice, and police under the charge of British agents. He was also told to prohibit the *bastinado* for extorting confessions in the courts, hitherto an indispensable part of about every Egyptian trial. On top of these changes, the cholera broke out to claim its thousands, and the British medical men found themselves helpless to check the scourge, so long as native officials stubbornly refused to carry out their suggestions. There was nothing for it, despite much talk of an early withdrawal, but to defer the announced evacuation. Sir Evelyn Baring (later Lord Cromer), an administrator of remarkable tact and ability, was stationed at Cairo in 1883 as "agent" and consul-general. At convenient call there was a small but reliable body of British troops, usually some six thousand men. Baring's position nominally was only that of adviser and next friend to His Highness the Khedive; actually, his advice was of a kind that it would have cost Tewfik his vicegeral throne to have disobeyed. Baring thus took his post in September, 1883. He left it in 1907. The evacuation of Egypt, despite the scowls and even the menaces of France, was seemingly to take place at "the Greek kalends," which is to say, never.

Hardly were the British in full possession of Cairo than a new factor arose to plague them and to render evacuation difficult. Ismaïl and his predecessors had conquered in a partial, haphazard way a huge province south of Egypt along the upper Nile, and were reaching into the heart of Africa almost to the great Nyanza lakes, whence issues the mighty river. This Equatoria was a most ill-compacted territory of half-naked head-hunters, uncouth desert tribes, negroes, "Arabs" (i. e., partly negroid Mohammedans), etc. Its government was utterly feeble; its commerce was almost exclusively in slaves and ivory. Only at the capital, Khartoum, was there something like a civilized community, a collection of Levantine traders, a few government buildings, and fairly regular communications with the north. The cataracts in the Nile, however, made through traffic by steamer impossible, and there was as yet no railway system. Equatoria, in short, was a misgoverned, inchoate block on the map, containing mostly savages, hippopotami, and desert or jungle. It added nothing to the strength and glory of its nominal master, the khedive.

When Tewfik's power began to be shaken in the north by Arabi, and when the empty treasury made it almost impossible to pay the Egyptian garrisons, the khedive's power in this vast "province" quickly evaporated. A *mahdi* (messiah) arose in 1881. His methods were obviously an imitation of those of Mohammed, but he declared war impartially on Moslems and Christians.[1] He would conquer all Egypt, then

[1] Mahdism seems to have borne about the same crude resemblance to Islam that Mormonism presented to Christianity.

Constantinople, then the rest of the world, and finally enforce a new religion. The tribes of the Sudan followed him by the thousands. He was able to inspire his converts with the implicit conviction that those who fell fighting in his cause sped straight to paradise. The result was that they rushed into battle swinging their scimitars with all the fanaticism of the first converts to Islam.

The dissolution of authority in Egypt in 1882 left the Mahdi free to make headway in Equatoria. In 1883 the slowly reorganizing Egyptian government tried to do something to check him, but England refused to send troops. Equatoria, declared Lord Granville, was no concern of Britain's. As a consequence, an Egyptian army, described as a "worthless rabble of Nile *fellahs*," was sent against the messiah. The general was Hicks Pasha, a brave Englishman in the khedival service, but very few reliable men followed him. Hicks's forces wandered into the desert until almost crazed by thirst, and then were attacked and massacred nearly to a man by the Mahdi.

Soon all that was left of Equatoria were a few hard-pressed garrisons and especially the town of Khartoum. The English ministers were resolved to evacuate the Sudan, for to hold it was beyond the power of the khedive, and they had no ambition to station a British army in the heart of Africa. But the loyal garrisons had to be rescued, and in 1884 General Charles George Gordon, a British soldier of fortune of a remarkably attractive personal type, was sent out to the Sudan with orders to bring the garrison and foreigners away in safety. Gordon had caught the imagination of England by his surprisingly winsome character and by his robust faith in Christianity. He had been before in the Sudan in the khedival service, and the natives loved and trusted him. It was supposed he was to arrange promptly for the evacuation of Khartoum, but there is no doubt that he was made to feel that very much was left to his discretion. Certain, he was treated when he left England as if he had carte blanche to untangle a perplexing situation. "Lord Granville took the general's ticket; Lord Wolseley carried his hand-bag; the Duke of Cambridge

held open the door of the railway carriage.'' Gordon reached
Cairo in January, 1884, and proceeded to Khartoum. Very
soon it appeared that he was unable to arrange promptly for
the evacuation.

To this day it is a moot question just why Gordon failed to
get away from Khartoum. Since he perished there, his own
detailed story was never told, although he managed to send
through his despatches from time to time explaining his position. The probability is that, once on the ground, he felt it
outrageous to abandon a great region, and especially many
native tribes who were friendly to Egypt and the Europeans,
to the cruel mercies of their foe, the Mahdi. Presently it became evident that Gordon could not himself leave Khartoum,
even if he would. He was closely besieged in the city, with a
small loyal garrison and a few Europeans and friendly natives, by a horde of fanatics thirsting for his blood, and the
English advisers in Cairo began bombarding London with
telegrams urging a prompt expedition up the Nile to save him
from destruction.

A Nile expedition was one of the last things the pacifist
Gladstone ministry desired. It implied a further dip into the
unwelcome Egyptian adventure. There was a strong disposition to believe that Gordon could escape if he only wished
to, and therefore to leave him to his fate. But Gordon was a
hero to half of England. Countless voices were raised in his
behalf. His case entered politics. Very reluctantly, therefore, Mr. Gladstone's cabinet ordered an expedition under
Lord Wolseley to ascend the river and rescue Khartoum. It
was a difficult advance, now across the desert, now portaging
boats around the boiling cataracts. A contingent of Canadian *voyageurs* was used to navigate the Nile rapids. At last
the final dash was made. On January 28, 1885, the head of the
expedition came in sight of Khartoum. Their steamers were
then met with a heavy fire. The whole town was evidently in
the hands of armed barbarians. Two days earlier Gordon,
who had held out until his garrison had been fed on crushed
palm-fiber and gum, had been overpowered and slain. Thus
the entire Sudan had passed into the power of the Mahdi.

There was nothing for it but to retire. Wolseley's force was too small to break the Mahdi's power and avenge Gordon, but great was the sorrow of England. It was felt, and not unjustly, that the Gladstone ministry had almost deliberately sacrificed the heroic general by its cold-blooded procrastination in not sending the relief expedition until it was too late. In the next parliamentary elections this dissatisfaction over the casting away of Gordon was a large factor in the balloting which drove Mr. Gladstone from power.[1]

The new Conservative (Salisbury) ministry, which took the reins in 1885, had too many problems, however, to undertake to crush the Mahdi merely for the sentimental satisfaction of avenging Gordon. A garrison was placed on the southern confines of Egypt, and it was not hard to keep the fanatics from penetrating north. The Sudan relapsed temporarily to degenerate barbarism.

But if the Sudan was thus abandoned, Egypt could not be abandoned. Only the inveterate foes of England have been able to deny that to have returned the country to its native rulers would have been to blast the chances of the miserable peasantry ever seeing better days. If England had withdrawn, some other power would have cheerfully assumed at least *this* part of "the white man's burden"; and no British government was able to permit a rival nation to camp itself on the route to India. In general, the English did not abolish the native administration. At the elbow of the khedive was the all-powerful consul-general and "Adviser," whose word was law to the Cairo garrison and therefore to His Highness himself. Behind each one of the khedival ministers were yet other British advisers, whose suggestions usually amounted to mandates. The country was terribly poor. The French, angry enough at the English occupation, insisted on the scrupulous discharge of the huge debt. Only by a great effort and a most skilful piece of financiering was the country rescued from bankruptcy and a little surplus accumulated for

[1] The Liberals had styled their leader the "G. O. M.," i. e., the "Grand Old Man." Their Conservative opponents declared the letters meant "Gordon's Only Murderer." The parody stuck long.

public works and reforms. In 1888, for the first time, the treasury books balanced, and then came steady improvement. The cruel *corvés* (forced labor system) for keeping up the Nile canals were abolished, and decent wages were paid to the toiling *fellahs*. The irrigation and agricultural systems were improved, something like efficient schools were introduced, and peasants capable of enterprise and thrift learned that they were not to be ruinously taxed and plundered by a rapacious government, just as soon as they displayed a little prosperity. Justice could no longer be purchased in the courts. Wise supervision trebled the cotton crop and the sugar crop. A railway was built along the Nile, and last, but not least, by means of certain great dams and reservoirs, especially the magnificent dam at Assouan at the southern end of Egypt proper, it was made possible to increase enormously the amount of land irrigated by the Nile, and so to reclaim millions of acres of arable fields from the desert.

Another reform of a very different kind was that of the native army. The old-line khedival troops were probably as inefficient wretches as ever disgraced a uniform. Now, under British auspices, soldiers were no longer collected by dragging them off in chain-gangs; but a small contingent was more peaceably enlisted and the men "to their astonishment found themselves well fed, well clothed, unbeaten, paid punctually, and even allowed furloughs to visit their families." These new troops proved reliable against the Sudanese dervishes, and gradually their force was increased and army service became popular. By 1897 the reformed Egyptian army had reached such efficiency and the treasury was so well prepared to stand an extra strain that, with a little help from England,[1] it was determined to try to reconquer the Sudan.

The Mahdi, the self-appointed messiah, had long since perished. In 1885 he had wronged a woman, who took vengeance by administering to the prophet a lingering poison from which he expired after eight days of prolonged agony. Supersti-

[1] The British Government loaned Egypt eight hundred thousand pounds at only two and three-quarters per cent., also a sufficient force of British regulars to give a good stiffening to the army.

tions, however, died hard in the land of fanatics. A favorite lieutenant of the Mahdi now proclaimed himself "Khalifa" (successor) in his stead, and he speedily gained complete ascendency over the semi-negroes of the Sudan. Tens of thousands of swarthy dervishes, convinced that death in the holy war opened the portals of paradise, obeyed his summons.[1] His chieftains were men of a good deal of military ability. An attack upon his power was nothing to be attempted lightly.

In 1897 there was preliminary fighting, preparation, and clearing of the frontier posts. In 1898 the real advance on Khartoum began. The expedition was supposed to be conducted jointly by the British and the Egyptian governments, under the common command of the "Sirdar" (general-in-chief), Sir Herbert Kitchener, a British leader who had already won a marked reputation. The whole expeditionary force amounted to about twenty-three thousand, with ten gunboats and five transport-steamers on the Nile. A great part of the difficulty lay in getting around the cataracts and in building railways across several short-cuts through the desert where the river made a great detour. At last, on September 1, 1898, the army had worked close to Omdurman itself, only two miles north of Khartoum, and there it met the host of the Khalifa, all in battle-array.

It was a picturesque, hideously spectacular battle, a battle between aggressive civilization and embattled barbarism, such as when Cortes flung his strange and terrible horsemen upon the redoubtable Aztecs. The dervishes far outnumbered their enemies. They formed a crescent around the Anglo-Egyptians, then charged in solid battalions, roaring their pious invocations to Allah and bent on sweeping the invaders back into the Nile. The Sirdar's cannon tore gaps in them, but they came forward, "never slackening their advance, except when

[1] The khalifa would regale his followers with tales such as that in a vision the late Mahdi had given him "an oblong-shaped light" which, in turn, had been transmitted by the Angel Gabriel directly from God Almighty. Hearers who did not believe such sayings were promptly silenced by torture or death. A pretentious mosque was erected at Omdurman over the Mahdi's grave, and miracles were claimed to be worked at it.

groups halted to discharge their muskets at impossible ranges. Waving their flags and intoning their prayers, the dervishes charged on in utter scorn of death, but when their ranks came within range of musketry fire, they went down like grass under the scythe.'' Here and there the dervishes almost came to grips with their foes, but nowhere was their headlong valor able to get them through the zone of death made by the magazine-rifles. By eleven o'clock Kitchener could order a general advance. The remnants of the fanatics now broke and fled. The Khalifa, doubting his own pledges of paradise, escaped on a swift dromedary. About ten thousand of his followers had perished outright. Very many more died of their wounds. The remnant of the army was scattered. Kitchener entered triumphantly into Omdurman and then Khartoum, and there, opposite the ruins of the palace where Gordon had met his doom, the British regiments paraded, a chaplain read the funeral service, and the assembly sang the fallen hero's hymn, "Abide With Me." Thirteen years had gone by, but Gordon had been well avenged.

The Khalifa was destined to wander, a discredited fugitive, for nearly a year before he was cut off and slain with his band, but his power had ended with the battle. Equatoria, or more properly now the Sudan, had been restored to civilized influences and "peaceful penetration," nominally under the joint administration of Egypt and Britain. By 1914 Khartoum had become a fairly sanitary and sophisticated community, with a railway, hotels, and shops, and was regularly included in the Cook tourist system. Such is the prosaic anticlimax of the Battle of Omdurman.

The Sudan, however, came near being the occasion of a far greater war than that with the Khalifa. Hardly was Kitchener fairly in possession of Khartoum than he learned with astonishment that six white men and one hundred African troops were in possession of Fashoda, a village on the White Nile, three hundred miles to the south. The Sirdar hastened down in person. He found there the French major, Marchand, who, with a very small force, had been for two years heroically battling his way across deserts, swamps, mountains, and rapids from the French west coast of Africa to these headwaters of the Nile. There he expected to plant the flag of France permanently, and to hold it against Britain and all the world. Had the Anglo-Egyptian expedition been a little later, very possibly he might have succeeded.

As it was, however, although Marchand stoutly refused to haul down the French flag at Kitchener's orders and said he would die first at his post, both officers had the common sense not to come to blows, but to refer the case to London and Paris. Lord Salisbury's government at once took a stiff attitude. The victory of Omdurman, it announced, had put them in control of the whole Nile Valley and had given them all the lands claimed by the Khalifa, including Fashoda. The French were angry, and if they could have persuaded themselves that their navy was a match for England's, they might have refused to recall Marchand and so have forced the fighting. But with their smaller fleet they felt helpless, especially as Franco-German relations at the time were bad. Marchand returned to Paris, to be praised, lionized, and fêted. He was a brave and resourceful man who just missed winning a great reward.

This Fashoda incident, needless to say, was intensely humiliating to France, and for several years made her relations with England very bitter. No person reading the Paris or London papers of October, 1898, could have imagined that 1914 would see Gaul and Briton in hearty alliance. So much could the common dread of Germany avail to suppress old grudges!

By 1914, Egypt, thanks to English supervision, had become a transformed country. It was prosperous, progressive, and, for an Oriental land, reasonably clean. To the great Sir Evelyn Baring (later Lord Cromer), Egypt owed a large part of the success of the new régime. Cromer deserves to rank among the very wisest and best of the British proconsuls. The bulk of Egypt's people were contented with the new régime and recognized its benefits. There was, indeed, a party of Egyptian Nationalists which clamored noisily for the withdrawal of the English and for large political rights. They represented only a number of semi-educated natives who hungered for public office. The majority of the people took absolutely no interest in politics and were content with any government, so long as it was beneficent, and a beginning had already been made of setting up a council of native representatives.

The political condition of the country was anomalous, however. Theoretically, the British occupation was only temporary, the khedive being the vassal not of George V, but of the Turkish sultan, since the British "advisers" were mere sojourners who might at any moment depart. Practically, however, everybody knew that England had come to stay. Since 1904 France had formally agreed not to urge her old rival to fix a date for quitting the country. However, the great empire which was ever more intent upon becoming England's successor to world power had fastened eager eyes upon Egypt. In scores of writings the Pan-Germans indicated their belief that Egypt was Britain's "Achilles's heel," the capture whereof would topple over her entire dominion. Therefore a cardinal part of their program was to cultivate friendship with the Turk, as being, among other things, the master of the land route in attacking Egypt; and another part of their plotting was to stimulate disaffection and even rebellion among the Egyptian nationalists.

CHAPTER VII

THE year 1913 and the first half of the year 1914 found the world entertaining the most discouraging opinions concerning the French people and their republic. France seemed to be getting deeper and deeper into a miry rut. The casual newspaper reader was aware that ministries in the French government were as unstable as ever. Every ministry had clearly stamped upon it from its very beginning the symptoms of discord and disintegration. Corruption, too, was charged as frequently as ever before, while scandal seemed in France to be inseparable from things political. At this time it happened to be the Caillaux trial which filled the newspapers, but this scandal differed from others in French republican history only in details. Behind the sharp, sinister lines in the foreground of this picture, those persons who traveled abroad and were better read were able to fill in a background of hazy, gray details. Everywhere there was incompetence and inefficiency in administration; there were too many officers to do a little work, and always too much red tape. The industrial progress of France was slow compared to that of her neighbors; her population, due to a declining birth-rate, was practically stationary. Freakish tendencies in French art pointed almost to mental degeneracy, while the great production of cheap French novels, available in every city in the world, proved to many a prudish traveler that the licentiousness of the Parisian demi-monde was infecting the very sources of literary production in France.

Viewed as a whole, the picture was a gloomy one, and most people had accepted for it the easiest explanation. The French, they said, were a decadent nation. Indeed, the phrase "decadent France" was to be found very commonly in books and in magazines, being often used even by people of information and judgment. Just what was meant by decadent was not entirely clear. Some interpreted it as meaning that France had run her course in history, that her people were "played out," and that as a consequence France would be of ever-diminishing importance in world affairs. Others seem to have thought of it as meaning that the French had become a godless and immoral people. No doubt other meanings were possible. It became habitual for writers, even among the best friends of France, to speak of the "decay" or the "decline" of this and that in France, instead of thinking of the rise of its opposite. Thus Mr. J. E. C. Bodley, himself no believer in the idea that France was decadent, allowed himself to entitle an excellent essay, "The Decay of Idealism in France," a title which suggested more than he meant. He was thinking of the changes in the direction of hedonism and realism brought about in France by the mechanical age, changes which were paralleled in England at an earlier age and in Germany at about the same time as in France. The industrial revolution had, indeed, changed letters and thinking and social customs in England no less than it was doing more slowly in France.

Howbeit, France was in 1914 "decadent France," and in 1916, if not slightly earlier, "splendid France." This is the paradox which must be solved. In the course of two years the world almost completely changed its opinion about the French. Now the way in which this change in our thinking was brought about is clear to all who have really lived during the past three years. The German war-machine, held up for a few precious days in August, 1914, near the Belgian boundary, soon broke away and began to roll down upon France. Apparently the French military authorities had really expected Germany to respect her treaty concerning Belgium, and were not prepared for the thrust through that country. But the machine rolled on. Brussels fell, and later Antwerp. Soon the German columns were crossing the French frontier with apparently irresistible force. The French and English together were unable to check the movement. An appalling quiet seemed to have settled upon France. The few items of news which filtered out were not reassuring. As the Germans drew near Paris, the seat of the government was hastily removed to Bordeaux. Paris, yes, France itself, seemed doomed. Another débâcle like that of 1870 was imminent, to be followed by a peace made on French soil with the victorious invader.

Then came that miracle of modern warfare, the Battle of the Marne. The French armies, defeated and flung back upon their own soil, turned and defeated the invader, driving him back toward Belgium. Whether or not German military mistakes were partly responsible for this defeat, certain it is that the glory due France cannot be overstated. Then it was that the world began to change its mind about the French and to speak some words of commendation. We began to look somewhat below the surface, and as we did, we saw things long unsuspected. France, caught unprepared for war, compelled by the perfidy of the enemy to change her whole plan of defensive campaign, had in the course of a few weeks, with great courage and orderliness, accepted early defeats and retreat, had continued to gather more troops and to place them quietly where they could be most effectively used, and then, on the darkest day, had put in operation a plan of battle which in a few days drove the enemy far from his objective. But it was perhaps not so much of the Battle of the Marne as Verdun which finally changed our opinion of the French. The undying heroism of the French troops in those awful days remade France in our eyes. Germany undertook to bleed France white in that battle, and the French accepted the challenge. The end we know. France held Verdun, and when the time came she regained in a few short, decisive battles all that German arms had taken from her at such terrible cost.

However, to state the paradox is not to explain it. Why was the world so deceived in France before 1914? If France was *not* really decadent, why did that idea get abroad, and how explain some of the phenomena which seem to justify that conclusion? The answer is that phenomena must be explained according to their time, their place, and the accompanying circumstances, not always taken at their face value. Furthermore, they must be studied with sympathy for the subject, not with hostility. The following short but sympathetic account of France under the Third Republic may be of value to an understanding of France as she really is.

The Third French Republic dates from September 4, 1870. It has enjoyed a life far longer than any previous régime in France since 1789. From 1852 until his overthrow in 1870 Napoleon III had ruled over France as head of the Second Empire. He began his reign by destroying the republic established in 1848, and for the first ten years of his rule he evinced little regard for the rights and wishes of the people. Beginning, however, in 1860 he was compelled more and more to seek their support—a sure sign of decline in an autocrat. In 1859 and 1860 he alienated the affections of a large part of the clerical party in France by the aid he had given in driving Austria from Italy and incidentally in undermining the temporal power of the pope. In order not to lose this support entirely, he despatched to Rome a French guard to sustain the papal authority there. In 1866 Prussia defeated Austria and made herself head of the German Confederation, while Italy was able to annex Venetia and Venice. In the next year came the final failure of the Mexican expedition. Thus, while France stood still or went backward, Germany and Italy were consolidating and expanding their powers. The comparison was exceedingly painful to Frenchmen, who were not a little jealous of both their neighboring rivals. The splendors of the Universal Exposition in Paris, 1867, though dazzling, did not blind the French nation to the facts.

The republican party, though small during the middle years of the Second Empire, had never forgiven Napoleon the *coup d'état* whereby he overturned the republic. As his government grew weaker and less successful in the late 'sixties, they took advantage of his rising unpopularity to come out openly in condemnation of him. Léon Gambetta, French citizen but the son of an Italian grocer of Cahors, was most outspoken of them all. He publicly declared that the *coup d'état* would be revenged.

To silence criticism, several courses of action short of abdication were open to Napoleon.   He might use stern repressive measures, or he might liberalize his rule, or he might win back the people's confidence by a successful war, for, after all, the chief objection to him, outside of the small group of republicans, was his failure to hold up France's head among the nations.   Repression might have led to rebellion and civil war. He chose the second expedient first, and in the course of the years 1867–70 he had enacted the laws creating the so-called "Liberal Empire."   This sign of yielding, far from satisfying the growing republican party, made their demonstrations even bolder than before.   The next expedient was war, and France soon learned that Napoleon was not averse to trying it.

This is no place to speak of the suicidal war of the Second Empire with Prussia.   The fatal reverse of Sedan came on September 2, 1870, and the news reached Paris late the next day.   That night the legislative body held a meeting just long enough to receive the evil news.   The army caught at Sedan had been compelled to surrender to the enemy, and the emperor with them.   Jules Favre took a few minutes to propose the dissolution of the empire and the establishment of a temporary government, but the *Corps Législatif* adjourned till the day following.   When it met on that memorable Sunday, the fourth of September, the excited Paris crowd filled the halls and galleries.   In irresistible tones it demanded the establishment of a republic.   The government leaders, henchmen of Napoleon, were confused and at a loss what to do.   Gambetta and Jules Favre, popular idols both, tried to quiet the people so that business might proceed, but all in vain.   At last, when stubbornness was no longer a virtue, they yielded, Gambetta first, then Favre, both crying, "Yes, long live the Republic!" Soon after they appeared at the *Hôtel de Ville*, heading a motley throng, to proclaim the dissolution of the empire and the establishment of a republic.   This was revolution, nothing less, affecting the lives of millions of Frenchmen, but brought about by a few thousand Parisians.   It was a quiet and easy revolution, comparatively, and without immediate bloodshed. The republic then and thus proclaimed lives to this day.

During the following months Paris was besieged, while Gambetta vainly but valiantly organized opposition in the south. At last the city capitulated and further resistance became useless. A National Assembly, chosen almost without any official pressure, was called together at Bordeaux to ratify the terms of peace, which were being worked out by Thiers for the French government, and the Prussian leaders. Having finished this bitter task, and having heard the heartbreaking final farewell of the members from the relinquished departments of Alsace and Lorraine, the National Assembly continued to sit for the purpose of reorganizing the shattered finances and for rehabilitating the economic and political life of the republic.

For, be it remembered, in the years following 1870 France continued to be a republic not by common consent but because no party was strong enough to overthrow it. Few tried to reëstablish the empire, and but few thought seriously of it. Yet, while the form was republican and Thiers was soon made the first president, a large majority of the National Assembly were in favor of another form, namely, monarchy. It was sometimes called a "Republic without Republicans." Thiers himself, an old man who had served under the July monarchy, which was overthrown in 1848, at first favored the monarchical form. Herein lay great danger for France. Swayed by the brilliant speeches of Gambetta and a few other republican leaders, who went about their propaganda with tireless zeal, thousands of Frenchmen were daily coming around to republican views. The National Assembly, however, which showed no signs of a desire to dissolve and hold a new election, was monarchist in its leanings. Had the monarchists been able to agree on a candidate, France might have been changed once more into a monarchy. But the candidates for the crown were two, representing different branches of the ancient ruling house, and between them the monarchists in the Assembly were fairly evenly divided. The negotiations for an agreement between the rival pretenders were at first conducted successfully, but the more eligible of the two, the Comte de Chambord, showed an exceeding vanity. He thought himself so indispensable to France that it would take him on any terms. He insisted, even, that France should accept the white flag of the old monarchy, abolishing the beloved tricolor of the Revolution. Such conditions were, of course, impossible, and when at last the Assembly could delay no longer to establish a permanent régime for France, enough monarchists had been converted to a republic, or were at least willing to swallow their pride and stifle their scruples, to give a majority to the so-called "constitutional laws" of 1875.

To the passage of these laws both Gambetta and Thiers contributed in different ways. The republic which the monarchists mainly feared was the "red republic," governed by the rabble and the socialists, the republic in which life and property were without protection. They bethought themselves with trembling of the "Reign of Terror" and of the Commune of 1871. But Gambetta himself was of the bourgeois class, the middle class of professional men and small merchants, and he daily gave evidence that he was not a convinced and inflexible radical, impervious to argument and reason, but rather an opportunist who was even willing to accept some monarchical features with his republic. Thiers, on the other hand, soon saw that the monarchists were hopelessly divided, while if either faction should win, it would merely mean a prolongation of strife in France. He came out, therefore, for a republic, as the form which "divides us least." Indeed, thoughout his short term as president he proved to France that republics, too, can respect property and suppress disorder without mercy. Thus there came about a gradual meeting of minds. The republic was, indeed, confirmed by the National Assembly without enthusiasm, but it was necessary to France and it had to come.

The present republican constitution of France is grounded firmly in the principle of popular sovereignty. The Chamber of Deputies of the French parliament is chosen by manhood suffrage, and so is every important district and municipal council in the republic. To Gambetta, indeed, universal suffrage was a sort of political first principle. Give the people the suffrage, he reasoned, and all other good things would follow. Furthermore, it was final. Monarchs and emperors can abdicate, and are always in danger of being overthrown. But "universal suffrage cannot abdicate," and therefore when the republic arrived, it came to stay.

Upon this foundation of manhood suffrage the constitution-makers of 1875 reared a republican form of government corresponding as closely as possible to the English limited monarchy. The Chamber of Deputies is a large body, elected directly by the voters. The Senate is a smaller body, elected for longer terms from the various "departments" by colleges of electors, themselves chosen directly by the people.[1] The President of the Republic, a dignitary who, it has been flippantly said, "neither reigns nor rules," is chosen for seven years by the two chambers together.

The constitutional laws went into effect in 1875, and the next year occurred the first elections to the Chamber of Deputies. Though there were no real parties or party organizations, as in an American election, those who favored the continuance of the republic made every effort to defeat the monarchists and to have republicans elected in their places. They were inspired to do this by fear lest the monarchists overthrow the republic. The National Assembly in 1873 had elected a monarchist, Marshal MacMahon, to be president of the republic, and had confirmed his authority for seven years from that date. It was well known that some of that party, seeing that a monarchy was not immediately possible, hoped that in the course of the "Septennate" under MacMahon an opportunity would come to destroy the republic and to reëstablish the throne in France. The republicans intended to be prepared for all eventualities, and fortunately succeeded in capturing a large majority of the seats in the Chamber of Deputies. The Senate, however, was monarchist in complexion, and it was suspected that the disgruntled monarchist party would not stop short of violence to regain control of the government.

Here were materials prepared for an explosion, and it was not long in coming. The clerical party had been conducting for several years a propaganda which was endangering the

---

[1] At first, many of the senators were named for life.

peace of the republic. It wished to see France embark on a policy of hostility to Italy, desiring to see the temporal power of the pope restored; in effect, it preached war on Italy. It was hostile to Germany, also. The liberal ministry, urged on by Gambetta and the Chamber of Deputies, accepted a resolution denouncing the clericals for their dangerous agitation. The ministry continued to have the full confidence of the Chamber, but MacMahon, incensed at its yielding and himself egged on by the clericals and monarchists, dismissed the ministry as no longer having his confidence. This was, of course, entirely contrary to the parliamentary principle that a ministry is entitled to remain in office as long as it has the confidence of parliament. MacMahon quickly found it impossible to get a new ministry which could work in harmony with the Chamber of Deputies, and thereupon, with the consent of the Senate, he dissolved the Chamber and provided for new elections.

The campaign which followed (1877) was an extremely heated one. The republicans felt that the republic itself was at stake. Opposed to them was the full strength of both clerical and monarchist parties. *"Clericalism, that is the enemy!"* said Gambetta, and that became the issue of the election. He even went so far as to say that when the decision had been rendered at the polls, MacMahon must either submit to it or resign. Despite governmental influence at the polls, the republicans won again. They were jubilant, for to them it seemed that the republic had been saved. MacMahon wisely submitted to the decision, and as his position became increasingly uncomfortable, he resigned before the end of his term, in 1879.

The new régime had thus weathered its first great storm. The Septennate had passed without the monarchists having been able to destroy the republic. Nevertheless, the danger was by no means over. Frenchmen, and it seems especially true in politics, cling tenaciously to their ideas. Contrary majorities are no argument to *them*. The monarchists, being Frenchmen, continued to be monarchists and Frenchmen, even under the republic. Time and again in French history after

1877, there appeared this same sinister coalition of monarchists and clericalists, threatening the very existence of the republic. Once, in the Boulanger incident, they had with them much of the army, the greatest single organization in France, and also the chauvinists. At a somewhat later day they mustered to their cause a still larger part of the army, as well as all the anti-Semites; this was during the Dreyfus incident. In both cases the republic rocked and trembled, but it withstood the storm.

It is a curious but significant commentary on the Third French Republic that most of the histories of it devote a considerable portion of their pages to a series of apparently disconnected, meaningless, and unprofitable "incidents." The sixteenth of May, 1877,—for to Frenchmen a mere date is often the full, sufficient, and sometimes the only name they have for an event, great or small—the Wilson scandal and the Boulanger affair in the 'eighties, the Panama scandal and the Dreyfus incident in the 'nineties, and to many the Caillaux incident of the new century—all receive much attention. The number of these per decade seems, happily, to be growing smaller, but on the other hand it is a mistake to consider them meaningless. Men who did not know Dreyfus, who would perhaps have been repulsed rather than attracted by him, and who had not the slightest interest in him personally, fought as stoutly upon his side as his personal friends and his relatives. In each of the more important of these incidents,—the sixteenth of May, Boulangism, and the Dreyfus case,—the struggle soon became one for an ideal, and the alinement of parties in all three was almost identical. Each became a struggle of the anti-clerical, anti-militaristic republicans against the reactionary and disruptive forces within the republic—the monarchists, the clericals, and the military party. That in each of these cases the struggle took on this character is just as much the fault of the republicans as it is that of their opponents. Each party hates just as bitterly and forgives as reluctantly as the other. Neither seems ever to forget. Incidents which in England or America would be settled in an orderly way in six months and forgotten in a year become in France the occasion of the most violent strife and scurrilous attack. Incidents are idealized, if we may so use the word. To republicans, the Dreyfus conviction did not mean the chance miscarriage of justice in the case of an otherwise insignificant young Jewish army officer. It meant that a coalition of reactionaries and clericals, always the enemies of the republic and now strong in the army, with the anti-Semites, were trying to ride roughshod over the rights of the people, and therefore over the republic itself. That thought girded them to endure continuous strife and sacrifice, until the wrong had been righted and "the principle of the thing" established, as we say. Let any American compare this attitude with our own easy consciences during the notorious Frank case of a few years ago, and he will see wherein the difference consists.

In politics and government the sixteenth of May incident had other important results. The right of the government to dissolve parliament whenever it clearly no longer represents the people or when there is grave doubt as to the people's wishes is essential to the proper working of every parliamentary system. If it is not used, then every parliament is, upon election, definitely assured of its four- or five-year term, and during that period it is absolutely irresponsible and all powerful. If, on the other hand, the government can hold the threat of an appeal to the people over the head of parliament as a club, responsibility can be enforced. Members think twice before risking the expense and fatigue and uncertainty of a new election. But because it was a monarchist president, MacMahon, who first used the right of dissolution in France, and because his act was considered an attempt to overthrow the republic in favor of a monarchy, no president since his day has used the power to dissolve parliament, for fear that his act would be similarly interpreted. This is not the only reason, indeed, but the fact is that there has been no dissolution of a parliament in France since 1877. The result of this, and of a pernicious committee system recently slightly reformed, and of the inexplicable suspicion which French parliaments evince toward their leaders in the cabinet, is that *parliament has all the power and no responsibility, while the cabinet has all the responsibility, but almost no power.*

Another factor, too, should be mentioned here. France has no parties in the American or English sense, but only many small factions. Republicanism is the only enduring issue in France, and almost the entire parliamentary membership is republican. For that reason factions differ little from each other; they are to a considerable extent based on personal leadership. But no cabinet can take office until it has combined enough of these factions to make up a majority in parliament. Now the approved way to combine factions is to give cabinet places to those who lead the factions, and thus every cabinet contains the leaders of at least three or four of these small groups. The result can be nothing but quick disintegration, and that, indeed, is what happens. In the forty years from 1875 to 1915, France had *fifty* cabinets, or about one every ten months. Although some served as much as two years or more, some lasted only a few weeks or months. Cabinets flit by like straws in the breeze, and often with no more effect. But of course the members are not entirely changed from one cabinet to the next. Some of the same names often appear in one cabinet after another, and then reappear again after a lapse of time. Moreover, the mere fact that the cabinet has changed does not stop important legislation; that is mainly controlled by the Chambers themselves and by their committees, and it goes on in happy ignorance of shiftings in the ministry.

Because of this constant procession of weak and short-lived ministries; because, through constant changes, their character remains always the same; because of the corruption and inefficiency which seem to be ineradicable from French politics; because of the personal vituperation, the unbridled scurrility which attends all elections; and because of other contributing factors, politics in France has fallen into the control of a class of men who are far from being the best that the "Grand Nation" can show. The same may be true in other countries, but it is strikingly the case in France. The industrious, tem-

perate, thrifty, and often pious man of toil or small business is
unrepresented in parliament. The leaders in business, in art,
in letters, are also strangers within its walls. The former
class, very large, displays nothing but an imperturbable indifference to politics. The latter classes, small but able,
though without power in the field of politics, assume the pes-
simistic attitude toward the republic which has become typical
of them.

Does all this mean that France is incapable of self-government? Far from it; but it certainly *does* mean that parliamentary institutions are not adapted to the political conditions existing in France. The parliamentary system grew
up in England, and its growth was the result of conditions
there existing. These conditions are apparently the *sine qua
non* of a parliamentary system: a two party system, a trusted
titular head of the government who can act as umpire between
the parties, and absolute confidence on all sides that both parties and the king himself are completely loyal to the constitution. France has none of these conditions, and for that
reason the parliamentary system has not worked well. France
may sooner or later have to change the form of her government, but the basic principles—republicanism or popular
sovereignty, and manhood or universal suffrage—must remain,
for the French will continue to be a democratic, self-governing
people.

The rise and fall of ministries in England and the quad-
rennial election of presidents in the United States form convenient and often important landmarks in the histories of
these respective countries. Since the resignation of MacMahon in 1879, every president of France has been a republican
and a moderate, but though a man were a leader when he
became president, upon his elevation to that post he ceases to
have any tangible influence on affairs. For that reason the
presidential term in France, though of convenient length, is
a wholly impertinent division of historical time. On the
other hand, the duration of a ministry is too uncertain and,
as a rule, too ephemeral to make it of real importance in an

all-too-brief survey of the history of the republic. Indeed, the history of the republic is itself so short that its further subdivision into periods of time is not very useful. The best method of attack is to take up the leading great "incidents" already mentioned and the great problems which have continued throughout the history of the republic. And in a history like this, which attempts to trace the origins of the Great War back to about 1870, the great problems of Alsace-Lorraine and *Revanche*, and military competition with Germany, deserve special treatment. The more exclusively diplomatic problems are dealt with in separate chapters, while domestic scandal must be ignored.

Both Alsace and Lorraine lie on the west bank of the Rhine. They constitute a part of that neutral language zone stretching from Belgium south and east through Luxemburg, along the upper Rhine valley, through Switzerland, and thence along the Italian "Irredenta," a zone where the Germanic languages and those of Latin origin are spoken in about equal degree. To the east of this nameless zone lie the German-speaking Hollanders, Germans, and Austrians; to the west the Romance-speaking Belgians, French, and Italians. Through centuries the zone has hardly changed, but the government of the territory involved has been one of the most bitterly contested issues in European history.

Alsace and Lorraine were, undoubtedly, during the middle and early modern ages part of the so-called "Holy Roman Empire," that vast fiction which pretended to be the successor of the real Roman Empire, and which was "neither holy, nor Roman, nor an empire." It claimed dominion over most of the German peoples of the Middle Ages, but did not really govern them. At the beginning of the modern age, while France was the greatest power on the continent, German national feeling was so weak that the "Holy Roman Empire" rapidly fell to pieces. Then it was that France extended her control over Lorraine and Alsace, acquiring the former in the sixteenth and the latter in the seventeenth century. Throughout the eighteenth century and the years of the Revolution and the Napoleonic era, they remained French, and in 1815 they were confirmed to France by the Congress of Vienna, in which Austria and Prussia took leading parts. During these years, and also after 1815, the people in both districts shared equally with all other parts of France in governmental affairs, in the Revolution, and in the Napoleonic wars. That there was among them any material dissatisfaction with their government or their French allegiance has not been proved. During the seventeenth and eighteenth centuries the French language and French culture spread rapidly among them, but so did it throughout Germany proper in the days when even a Prussian king (Frederick the Great,) preferred the French language to his own.

But the nineteenth century beheld a most remarkable outburst of German national feeling, an effervescence which resulted presently in the creation of a new German Empire, based upon the principle of nationality. Before the empire was created, however, Prussia had first torn away territory from Denmark and then ousted Austria from German leadership by a short, sharp conflict in 1866. Even yet the work could not be completed. The new confederation, headed by Prussia, had first to humble France, the greatest single power on the Continent, before the southern German states could be induced to enter the federation. This was the work of the war of 1870. Upon the solid basis of military power, as proved by the defeat of France, was to be founded the new national empire under Prussian hegemony. The war was fought, and with a success which must have surprised even the Prussians. So great, indeed, was the victory, that Germany could have asked almost *any* terms from the victim, France.

In 1866 Prussia had been lenient with Austria. What would her terms to France be? That the rulers of Prussia had already outlined the main points on which they would insist in case of overwhelming victory, we cannot doubt. But that even well-informed Germans outside government circles did not know what the terms would be, and had not specifically formulated any demand for annexation of territory, is indubitable. While the war was still going on, Heinrich

von Treitschke, an influential historian, published on the spur
of the moment a pointed and bombastic article entitled,
"What We Demand from France." [1] Germany was already
sure of victory, and King William had promised the people
"that the peace shall be worthy of our sacrifices." Much
was still dark as to conditions in France, the writer confessed.
"But one task remains for our press—to bring out the un
uttered and half-formed hopes which move in every breast
into clear consciousness, so that, on the conclusion of peace,
a firm and intelligent national pride may rise in enthusiasm
behind our statesmen. . . . The thought, however, which, after
first knocking timidly at our doors as a shamefaced wish, has,
in four swift weeks, grown to be the mighty war-cry of the
nation, is no other than this: 'Restore what you stole from
us long ago; give back Alsace and Lorraine.' "

Thus, among the first fruits of German nationalism was a
sort of "irredentist" doctrine, distinguishable in almost no
particular from the Italian desire to "recover" the Trentino
and Trieste and the present French desire to recover Alsace
and Lorraine. But it seems to make a difference whose ox is
gored! "During the last two centuries, from the earliest
beginnings of the Prussian state," continues Treitschke, "we
have been struggling to liberate the lost German lands from
foreign domination." Having said that, he threw out this
somewhat unflattering remark concerning the people in the
lost German lands concerned: "We cannot permit a German people, thoroughly degraded and debased, to serve against
Germany, before our eyes, as the vassal of a foreign power."
He offered other reasons, too, why Alsace and Lorraine should
be annexed to Germany; among them principally the military
argument. Germany needed to control these lands for her
own defense. "The sense of justice to Germany demands
the lessening of France." "Our military organization has
no meaning without secure boundaries." And then, prophetic
premise, but misguided conclusion, comes a typical bit of

[1] Heinrich von Treitschke; "Germany, France, Russia, and Islam,"
translated into English, with a foreword by George Haven Putnam,
1915, pp. 96–179.

German reasoning: *"The distracted world already foresees a whole brood of wars springing out of the bloody seed of this.* We owe it some guarantee of permanent peace among the nations, and we shall only give it, so far as human strength can, when German guns frown from the fortified passes of the Vosges on the territories of the Gaulish race, when our armies can sweep into the plains of Champagne in a few days' march, when the teeth of the wild beast are broken, and weakened France can no longer venture to attack us."

The mere fact that Alsatians and Lorrainers of 1871 did not want to be annexed to Germany bore no meaning to this writer. Upon the declaration of war an "anxious cry rang through Alsace and Lorraine, 'The dice are to be thrown to settle the destiny of our provinces!'" But "in view of our obligation to secure the peace of the world, who will venture to object that the people of Alsace and Lorraine do not want to belong to us? The doctrine of the right of all the branches of the German race to decide on their own destinies, the plausible solution of demagogues without a fatherland, shiver to pieces in the presence of the sacred necessity of these great days. These territories are ours by the right of the sword, and we shall dispose of them in virtue of a higher right—the right of the German nation which will not permit its lost children to remain strangers to the German Empire. We Germans, who know Germany and France, know better than these unfortunates themselves what is good for the people of Alsace, who have remained under the misleading influence of their French connection outside the sympathies of new Germany. Against their will we shall restore them to their true selves."

But quotations from Treitschke can easily be overdone, and they probably do not represent the thoughts of the entire people. What did the French think when they had to give up the whole of Alsace and a large part of Lorraine to the conqueror still encamped upon their own soil? The members from the severed districts themselves presented to the National Assembly on February 16, 1871, a declaration against the dismemberment so burning in its terms that it seres itself into the heart even now, almost fifty years later. They denied that France, or even Europe itself, could ratify the act of the aggressor in tearing them from France in such a way as to make the deed binding on them.[1] But if France could not sanction the treaty in such a way as to bind the victims, it had to endure the blow. *De facto,* the cession was made.

In the seventeenth and eighteenth centuries France had been "the mistress of Europe." Her culture, her literature, her language, had swept almost everything before them. The Revolution had not materially dimmed her luster, nor had the defeat inflicted upon Napoleon by the great European coalition really deprived her of her proud position as the strongest single power in Europe. Despite frequent changes in her government during the early nineteenth century, the fiction of her leadership still remained. Frenchmen were not only reverently and righteously proud of their history, but they also loved their land as did few other peoples in the world. These are some of the reasons why the forced cession of Alsace and Lorraine was so bitter, so unforgivable and unforgetable a blow.

Despite the "decline of idealism" in France already mentioned, the French are neither hedonists nor realists. They continue to this day to idealize things and events. The idea which has become associated in their minds with the wresting from them of these beautiful portions of their land, is that it proves their national decadence and impotence. It is a blot on the scutcheon, or, as it were, a symbol of their decline. Until the blot is wiped out, France continues to be a second-rate power, or less.

There have been many explanations of the deadening pessimism which fell upon the more well-to-do and educated classes in France after the Franco-Prussian War, spreading even into other strata of society. Among the causes which contributed to that feeling, none was more potent than this idealization of the loss of Alsace and Lorraine. Of the meta-

---

[1] "Declaration of Bordeaux," 1871. It will be found reprinted in the "New York Times Current History," August, 1917, pp. 264–65.

phors which the French used to describe their loss, that which styled it "an open sore in the side of France" was most expressive and most strangely true. It was not that France was literally bleeding to death through this wound. France lives not so much by the blood in her veins, as by the thoughts, emotions, and ideals centering about her glorious national history. It was these which trickled from her through the gaping hole in the northeast, and in their place grew up a soul-stifling pessimism.

Nevertheless, her material recovery from the great defeat was quick,—astoundingly so. The debt was paid back with a celerity which opened the eyes of Germany. The nation which was to have been "lessened" for many decades became prosperous again in less than one. As early as 1875 Germany showed fear that, instead of insuring peace for herself, she had indeed sowed the seeds of another war. From that day down to 1914 every outburst in France of popular feeling against Germany, every change in the military preparation of that country, has caused the German rulers not only annoyance, but downright apprehension. War scares have come again and again. Bismarck, desiring no colonies for Germany, tried to divert French attention and energies away from "revenge" for Alsace-Lorraine to distant colonial enterprises. This policy he varied at times by attempts to embroil France with her neighbors, especially Italy.[1] These expedients failed in every way. France had energy enough to carry out large colonization projects and at the same time to prepare against the day of another Franco-German war. It was impossible to keep France and Italy constantly at loggerheads. Later on Germany herself desired colonies, and then especially was revealed Bismarck's short-sightedness in encouraging French colonial schemes.

Hatred of Germany, the desire for *revanche*, burned on unquenched in France. Gambetta, who had organized defense against the Prussians in the south during 1871 and who signed the Bordeaux Declaration, was to most Germans the personifi-

[1] In 1878 he urged both governments at the same time to seize Tunis. For the Tunisian affair and its results, see pp. 316–18.

cation of the *revanche* idea. When he died on the last day of 1882, Germany heaved a sigh of relief. As a matter of fact, however, Gambetta had generally suppressed his desire to preach revenge, by which the French mean the retaking of Alsace and Lorraine. It was his most bitter opponents, the monarchists and clericalists, who caused the war scare of 1875, and during the next two years he led in the attempt to curb these elements. To him, clericalism was always the enemy. After his death the revenge idea was aroused again by Boulanger, with a resultant war scare in 1887. But the propaganda cannot be connected with the names of any persons or any party. It was all-pervasive, until the various socialist groups and parties appeared in the field. They have generally discouraged it.

The fuels to keep the fire burning have been supplied, however, rather by Prussian misgovernment in Alsace-Lorraine, than by the French desire for revenge. Had Germany really been able to satisfy the Alsatians, especially, it is doubtful whether France would have clung so tenaciously to the idea of retaking that which was stolen from her. This is a side of the question which is handled elsewhere. The Alsatians and Lorrainers have desired real self-government and have clamored for it year in and year out. Always they have been met with rebuffs. Despairing, especially since 1910, of getting reform from Germany, they have kept alive the hope of restoration to France, a hope that since 1914 many have thought possible of realization. German authors and German newspapers, too, have continued to fan the flames, taunting the French constantly with a desire for revenge, a challenge which French newspapers have not been slow to accept.

So far it has seemed impossible for French and German minds really to meet on the question. Germany says that the settlement of 1870 was final, and that France should have accepted it as such. The French retort that the settlement of 1681, which gave the provinces to France, was reopened by the Prussian War nearly two centuries later. Germany alleges that the lands are typically and historically German. France replies that the people of both provinces were happy when a part of France, that they resented the forced separation, and that they have continued to desire reannexation to France. Germany alleges that she has a right to hold the provinces, because she has a right to protection against France. France justly rejoins that the danger of German attack on France is just as great as the danger of a French attack on Germany; that a people of forty million is not very likely to attack unjustly one of seventy million; and that France has just as much right to protection against Germany as Germany has against France. So the debate runs, with many more arguments. The usual German apologist, unable to think back to the days before 1870, when the situation was nearly reversed, condemns France without measure for refusing to accept the Treaty of Frankfort, 1871, as a final settlement. The ordinary American finds it difficult not to accept the French view, and all he needs to confirm him in this view, ordinarily, is to read some German argument to the contrary. What however was to be the final solution was placed "in the lap of the gods," when the Great War broke out in 1914.

Did the French desire to retake Alsace and Lorraine bring on the present war? The charge was commonly made by German writers and statesmen at the beginning of the conflict. Suffice it to say, however, that other parts of this book will show that the causes of the war lay elsewhere. But, certainly, the constant French apprehension of a new war with Germany forced her into an unnatural alliance with the Russian autocracy, an alliance which, having once been completed, kept alive French hopes of a successful war some day against Germany.

The history of France as a military power begins far back in almost forgotten centuries, but never before in time of peace did her armies represent so large a proportion of her population as in the years before the Great War. It is a common assertion in Germany that the French armies during this time were being organized for aggression upon the empire of Bismarck. Competent and impartial observers, while as-

tounded at the spectacle of a democracy yielding up all her
sons for military training, have scouted this idea. It was
not an aggressive, war-loving spirit which was dominating
France. It was *dread*, simply common dread. The Franco-
Prussian War taught France her great lesson. The fear of
another Teutonic invasion, with the white and black flags of
Prussia being carried once more in triumph through the
streets of Paris, steeled even the hearts of the French republicans to prepare against this day of disaster. To this end
no sacrifice seemed too great, no burden too heavy.

France had had tastes of universal compulsory service before, but the policy became fixed in 1872. At first the laws
were loose, many exemptions being allowed and service being
nominally for three years. Then, in 1905, while the term
of service was cut to two years, all exemptions, save for
physical disability, were abolished. For a time this sufficed.
But always the attempt had been to keep up with Germany,—
a thing which was becoming rapidly impossible. France's
population was nearly stationary, while Germany advanced
with giant strides. France had long been compelled to train
all her young men, while Germany was annually able to
reject many. Even so, France was unable to maintain the
pace. In 1910 Germany's effective forces were 620,000 men,
while those of France were 552,000, of which some were
Algerians and Tunisians stationed in Africa, plus a native
colonial army of little training. Besides this discrepancy in
land forces, France had for some years been inferior to Germany in naval power, and she was rapidly growing, in proportion to Germany, still weaker upon the seas.

Beginning, perhaps, with Italy's war on Turkey in Tripoli
in 1911, the tension in the European diplomatic situation grew
greater daily. The agitation expressed itself in Germany
during 1911, 1912, and 1913, in extraordinary increases in
military expenditures and effective forces. The forts were
strengthened especially along the French border in Alsace-
Lorraine, and the garrisons there were increased. Secret military advices reached France, both in 1912 and 1913, indicating a pending early attack on France. The German officers

responsible for the proposed increases made, in their unofficial capacities, no secret of the purpose of the increases. French authorities were thrown into a flutter of anxiety. On the two-year service basis France had already reached the limit of her military strength. There was only one thing left to do—increase the period of service to three years, and thus have three classes always under arms. Acting under a power apparently given by the law of 1905, the minister of war ordered that the class of 1910 be held during 1913, making its third year of service. This action was later ratified by a substantial majority in parliament, despite a violent campaign conducted by socialists, syndicalists, and anarchists. Up to this time France had been able to keep fairly close behind Germany in her preparations. The three-year law of 1913 seemed now to meet the new exigency, the recently elected president of the republic, M. Poincairé, himself speaking in high praise of the arrangements. From the summer of 1913 on, however, it became increasingly evident that the army was woefully unprepared and poorly equipped. Investigation proved that the apparent increase of strength was a sheer delusion, due to mismanagement. The authorities proceeded at once to set their house in order, but the war in 1914 found them still in the midst of their preparations.

Despite many distractions and a heavy military burden, France has, under the Third Republic, notably expanded her colonial dominions and improved the conditions of her people.

In the seventeenth century the French monarchy was able to lay claim to territories in America, Africa, and Asia, but the wars of the eighteenth century up to 1763 left her deprived of most of her American domain. Not until the acquisition of a claim to Algeria in 1830 did her colonial activities permanently revive. Then for about thirty years France made extensive explorations in Asia, Africa, and Oceania, laying hands on some territories and establishing claims to others. America was, of course, closed to her after 1823 by the Monroe Doctrine.

The next twenty years, though not a period of quiescence, brought no fruits into her lap. The most recent and most productive period of colonial acquisition was inaugurated in 1881 by the declaration of a protectorate over Tunis. During the following fifteen years Tonking, Annam, and Laos in Asia, Congo, Upper Senegal and Niger, Dahomey, and Mauritania became French colonies in quick succession. In the same period France also made good certain ancient claims to a number of Oceanic Islands, Madagascar, and Senegal. Sahara and Morocco have since been brought definitely within her sphere.

Thus, in the last thirty years France has tremendously increased her colonial holdings. The area of the African colonies alone exceeds that of the United States and Alaska, but it is unprofitable to compare Sahara sands with Alaskan ice-fields or fertile American plains. French colonies lie in every quarter of the globe, but are principally equatorial, and have a population, mainly African and Asiatic, in excess of forty millions. Unfortunately, Frenchmen are not good colonizers. They are attached by strong bonds to their native soil. Very few, indeed, leave their beloved villages for foreign lands, even for French colonies. It is deplorable, too, that the French colonial policy has been dictated mainly by a desire to promote the commercial interests of France. Nevertheless, French colonies are in the main well administered, while recent changes in policy, looking toward the self-administration of the colonies for the colonies, are extremely promising.

Social progress in France is a fact not generally heralded from the housetops. Germany undoubtedly led and still leads France, as she leads England and the United States, in provision for the amelioration of the condition of the poor. Whether or not the German system of social-welfare legislation was, as has been recently alleged, a sop to appease the German workman for his unfortunate political status, Germany should still be given full credit for working out the laws.

In France the acts have been passed by the representatives of the sovereign people at the people's behest. These laws include a workman's compensation act, in effect since 1898, an old age and invalidity pension law, effective since 1907, and an old age insurance law, which is partly compulsory, in effect since 1910. Still more recent laws make special provision for women in factories and legalize allowances for mothers. Eleven hours of labor per day, with a rest day on Sunday, has been made the legal limit for all workers. A special department of labor, with a seat in the ministry, has existed since 1906. These laws, it should be said, are mainly the result of the rapid advance to power of the various socialist and radical groups in parliament, to whom most of the credit it due. As a result of the operation of the acts, together with the slow increase of population, the remarkable thrift of the people, and a host of other factors, the state of popular well-being in France compares favorably with that of any country in the world.

The "Grand Nation" of the eighteenth and earlier centuries has in more modern times revealed undoubted faults. She has to some extent resigned herself to a weakening passion for revenge, forgetting Bacon's saying that "in taking revenge, a man is but even with his enemy; but in passing over it, he is superior." She has looked too much abroad for her models, many of her own people coming to believe that merely because France could not keep up with Germany and England in population figures and in the growth of industry, she therefore must be decadent. She has suffered from much bad government and public inefficiency. A small scandal-breeding class in Paris, largely foreign or under foreign influence, by gaining notoriety for itself, has served to soil the very name of France in the thought of a captious but uninformed world. Much more could be written in this vein, but when all is said, France stands in our minds to-day the France of Verdun. Under the stress of events, even her government has been materially improved, while all the quiet virtues of the people, —their thrift, their orderliness, their sense of duty to France, their heroism, yes, even their natural, deep piety,—have come to the fore in the united effort of the nation to drive the arrogant invader from French soil.

CHAPTER VIII

FREE ITALY AND ITS CONSOLIDATION

NAPOLEON is generally credited with having kindled in the hearts of Italians the desire for national unity, and from his day to this the fires have never gone out. Having conquered the peninsula he gave it uniform laws, notably a civil code and a system of administration. He created in northern Italy a new Kingdom of Italy, of which in 1805 he took the crown. He made other disposition of the south. Thereby he destroyed, almost at a blow, many old boundaries and old institutions, and gave Italians to see that across the limits their neighbors were even as they were themselves.

With the defeat and exile of Napoleon, Italy was in 1815 divided once more according to the previous boundaries. Austrians were put on some thrones, restored Bourbons on others, while the pope retained his estates at the center. The Austrian influence was everywhere. Yet things were not as they had been. Italians had seen their unity, and now when the tyrants began to govern according to the methods of Machiavelli, but without the moderation he really advised, they found themselves opposed not by single communities, but by the rising surge of national feeling. Though cruelly suppressed, the outbreaks became numerous in the thirties and forties, and they assumed more and more the character of a national movement for liberation. National unity became to Italians not only a coveted end in itself, but also a means of liberating Italians, of redeeming Italy, from the oppression of the foreigner. The revolutionary spirit was abroad, and it soon took the form of a movement to make Italy one state, Italians one people, and to give them one government, and that their own.

Fortunately there were leaders in Italy, clever, strong,

imaginative, daring, unselfish men who caught the vision of a great Italy rousing herself and rising to a high place among the nations, and who were not afraid to risk all in the struggle. The rulers of Piedmont, a noble and ancient house, soon put themselves in the van. King Charles Albert, and after him his son Victor Emmanuel II, led in the movement which was destined to change them from the almost absolute rulers of Piedmont to the constitutional monarchs of a united Italy. The desired end was a free and united nation. For this Mazzini agitated and conspired, Garibaldi fought, and Count Camillo Cavour negotiated and planned. The year 1848 saw Charles Albert grant to the Piedmontese a liberal constitution, and soon after saw him lead the half-organized Italian national forces against the Austrians. At first the Italians enjoyed a little success, but they were ill-united, and the White Coats were too strong. Terrible defeats followed at Custozza in 1848 and at Novara in 1849. In the latter year Charles Albert resigned his throne rather than accept the oppressive terms of the Austrians. The national movement seemed crushed. The reaction under Austrian leadership was terrible. Gladstone visited Italy at this time, and described what he saw in Naples during the persecution of the liberals there by the king of the "Two Sicilies" as "an outrage upon religion, upon civilization, upon humanity, and upon decency," . . . "the negation of God erected into a system of government."

But the leaders had not yet lost hope. Charles Albert was succeeded by his far more able son, Victor Emmanuel II, who remained loyal to the liberal constitution of 1848 despite strong and tempting inducements to overthrow it, inasmuch as Austria feared the existence of a liberal government anywhere in Italy. Soon after, Cavour became head of the ministry of Piedmont, and Piedmont, alone in Italy, began immediately to enjoy constitutional liberty and progressive liberal legislation. But always Cavour looked ahead, to the time when he could do for all Italy what he was then doing simply for Piedmont. Incidentally he prepared Piedmont and its army for leadership in the coming struggle with

Austria. He seized every opportunity to raise Piedmont to a high place in international affairs, even taking what seemed a rash part in the Crimean War. He played upon Napoleon III, Emperor of France, winning him to the Italian cause as against Austria. He advertised to the world the tyrannies of the Austrians and inspired Italians to believe that Piedmont would lead them to liberty. At last when the time was ripe, he goaded Austria on to the rashness of declaring war, and the die was cast. Napoleon III came to the aid of Piedmont. In 1859 Austria was defeated at Magenta and Solferino, but before the Austrian armies had been driven entirely out of Italy, Napoleon made a hasty peace with the enemy. There was nothing for Piedmont to do but accept the terms. Venetia, in the northeast, remained Austrian territory, but Lombardy was ceded by Austria to Napoleon and by him to Piedmont. At the same time the way was cleared for the union of the northern Italian states with Piedmont, while Garibaldi and "the thousand" brought the Kingdom of the Two Sicilies, that is Sicily and southern Italy, also into line. Thus in the year 1860 Parma, Modena, Romagna, Tuscany, Umbria, the Marches, and the Kingdom of the Two Sicilies were able to accept the constitution of Piedmont and Victor Emmanuel as their king. In 1861 there was convened at Turin the first Italian parliament. With the exceptions of the Trentino, Venetia, Trieste and Istria on the north and east, and Rome, where French troops maintained the last vestige of the temporal power of the pope, Italy was now united under one government, and freed from the Austrian yoke.

It is little wonder, therefore, that Italians like to think of the year 1861—a year fateful to us because it nearly meant the end of our union—as the year of their national unification. In this year the whole of Italy territorially, save Rome and Venetia, had a national government,—one king and one constitution. These had, moreover, not been forced upon the people, but chosen by and from among themselves. We say nearly all of Italy and almost all the Italians were now under one government, but unfortunately we cannot say all. There were some Italian lands and some Italian people "unredeemed" as yet, and the problem of bringing them also into the new kingdom has come back to plague Italy again and again, even to this present day.

It was, perhaps, Italy's greatest mistake to think of 1861 not as a year of beginnings, but as a day of the fulfilment of her desires—a sort of millennium. She believed herself unified, and to her that meant that she was now able and entitled to play a great rôle among the nations. But national unity is a thing of many parts and not to be attained in a day, as the United States has well learned. It requires that there shall be a common national government, that all the nation and the national territory shall be under this one government, and no parts still under foreign control. It involves giving all classes within the nation more or less a part in the government and equal opportunity for sharing in the national heritage, for otherwise there will be internal divisions. It requires, finally, that the nation, the territory, the government, shall together constitute as a matter of fact a self-standing, independent unit, free from the control of any foreign power. If it becomes commercially, politically, or in any other way the mere appanage of another power, it is not itself a national unity, but merely part of a larger unit.

Now, Italy in 1861 was not a national-state in several of these particulars, and was doomed in the following fifty years to go through new struggles for unity, and yet to find herself in 1911, her jubilee year, still forced to speak of an "unredeemed" portion of her territory and her people, and to recognize that certain internal divisions and dissensions still existed. Four years later, in 1915, she awoke to find that even while she had been struggling for internal unity, an arrogant foreign power had so spread its influence in the land that the foreigner looked upon Italy almost as a mere dependency. The history of Italy since 1861 is not, therefore, a history of a truly "united" Italy, as some would have it, but a history of the sometimes enlightened, though often blind, striving after the substance of independence and unity.

Of all the great national states formed during the 18th and 19th centuries, none has had more difficult problems to solve than has Italy. Among these problems, however, there has *not* been that of establishing a liberal constitutional régime.

The *Statuto,* which is to-day the constitution of united Italy, was drawn up in 1848 for Piedmont alone. It made no provision for future amendments and in fact the text of the instrument has not been formally changed in any particular to this day. Nevertheless the principle has slowly developed that all necessary adaptations of the constitution and laws to the needs of the country and the people can be made by the king and parliament, and in this way several minor features of the constitution have really been overruled. Whether or not the monarchical principle, or the parliamentary system of government, could be changed by ordinary act is a question which has not arisen in any practical way and is at present unlikely to arise. For this there are several reasons.

In the first place, the kings from Charles Albert down to the present monarch, Victor Emmanuel III, have been loyal to the constitutional principle. They have not at any time tried to force their ideas upon an unwilling parliament, but have always governed in strict accord with the constitution. It is true that when one ministry has lost its control of parliament, the king has a fairly wide range of choice in selecting another, for Italy does not have two leading parties which alternate in control of the government. But in the exercise of this choice the king has not been arbitrary. Thus the ruling house of Italy has endeared itself to most of the people, and in spite of a long continued agitation by certain groups of radicals for the adoption of a republican form of government, Italy continues a limited monarchy. It required only the assassination of King Humbert in 1900 by an ignorant nihilist to unite the whole nation against the republicans. The present monarch leans so far toward democracy that he has declared it his "intention to govern with the people for the people." To this principle he adheres. Instead of using every effort to suppress the socialists, as was done by Emperor William II of Germany up to the present war, he has introduced socialists into his cabinets. He is, indeed, living up to Crispi's ideal, when he said "The King is only the head of the nation, the Prince chosen by the people; with us there is no sovereign but the nation." [1]

On the other hand, the people have been so long accustomed to parliamentary forms, and the elections to parliament have been put in recent years upon so broad a popular basis, that this feature also of the constitution is free from the danger of hasty change.

The continued stability of the form of government, coupled with its real ease of amendment, has been no small factor in furthering the unification of Italy. The stability of institutions is especially tried in years of great shifts in party control, when the losing party is inclined to believe that the incoming government is subversive of the constitution. In France the great shift in the control of the government from the conservative, monarchical parties to the republicans in 1876 caused dangerous disturbances and nearly resulted shortly thereafter in a *coup d'état*. Not so in Italy, where the great transfer of power from the conservative "right" to the liberal and radical "left" occurred in the same year without a hitch.

The "left" which came into power can hardly be called a party. Indeed, the "right" had so completely lost in the elections that it had almost disappeared, while the "left" had such a tremendous majority as to be embarrassed by its own strength. It quickly broke up into groups, each following its personal leader and all being equally without definite political principles. Under such circumstances there is only one way of getting a majority, and that is by forming coalitions of several groups. Such coalitions, being never based upon principle, but rather upon some unsavory bargain among the personal leaders of the units concerned, tend to be unstable. Thus it has come to pass that since 1876 cabinets have come and gone in Italy with almost as great frequency as in France. Out of this constant shifting among

[1] F. M. Underwood, "United Italy," 1912, pp. 225–226.

the groups there has been developed a new type of parliamentary leader, one who knows and cares little about the needs of the country and the elements of statesmanship; but who is especially skilled in the strategy of combining groups into a majority *bloc*. Leaders like Giolitti have brought this art to its highest perfection, contriving to keep themselves in office year after year despite cabinet changes, and using the power thus gained to control elections, by fair means or foul, to return a majority favorable to the government.

Under this malign political system, the government of Italy presents to the outsider all the evil aspects of the French. Indeed, the picture is even darker for Italy than for France. There is open and known corruption at elections, with not a little rioting and bloodshed.[1] Italians themselves profess to see a steady improvement in the conduct of elections, and that the politicians do not entirely control the people was proved by certain events in 1915. In fact, it must be said that as in France, so in Italy, the virtues of the people far surpass those of their politicians and government. At home the Italian is normally hard-working, frugal, honest, and hospitable, and he who judges the Italian people by their parliamentary institutions does them a gross injustice.

It should also be remembered, that while politics and government under the "left" are odiously bad, the general trend of legislation since 1876 has been in the direction of democracy and the further unification of the people. When the "left" took office the suffrage was limited to literate persons who paid a fairly high direct tax, and to tradesmen and manufacturers who owned property of a certain value. Under this law only about two and one-half per cent. of the people could vote. By a law of 1882 passed by the "left" the number of voters was almost tripled, and in 1912–13 a complete new suffrage law extended the right to vote to a larger proportion of the

[1] There seem also to have been municipal scandals of a type all too familiar to Americans. A few years ago Naples was favored with a municipal house-cleaning during which there were exposed more varieties of corruption than Tammany Hall could have boasted in its palmiest days.

people than is the case in many American states. By this act the vote was given to all literate male Italians over twenty-one, to all illiterate males over thirty, and to all who have served in the army or navy, even though not twenty-one years old. The change has more than doubled the electorate, which now becomes considerably over twenty per cent. of the population. By these successive steps, dangerous though they be, one section of the people after another has been brought into closer touch with the government, and serious groups for disaffection have been removed.[1]

The unification of 1861 was merely political and was not complete even in that sphere. Socially and economically, Italy was not then, nor has it yet become, completely one nation. This fact is the more surprising when we recall that Italy is a small country, in area no larger than the state of Nevada. Considerable parts of this small area are mountainous and scarcely habitable, while the inhabited portions are separated from each other by very formidable mountain barriers and present great differences in arability and climate. Since the fall of the Roman Empire these various parts have had dissimilar histories which are still evidenced in differences in dialect, architecture, and mode of life. Thus in the long, narrow "peninsula of peninsulas," which stretches full 700 miles from Aosta in the northwest to the Straits of Messina, are to be found social and economic diversities as great as any existing in the United States, and perhaps greater, while those which *do* exist are the results of centuries of localized development.

Broadly speaking, there is a "north" and a "south" in Italy, and the questions which this fact raises bristle with difficulties. Besides speaking a slightly different dialect, the north is more prosperous, more generally literate, more highly developed commercially and industrially than the south. Its upper classes are more individualistic than those in the south, its working classes more intelligent and more

[1] Cf. Amos S. Hershey, "The Recent Italian Elections," in "The American Political Science Review," February, 1914, VIII, 50–56.

open to the appeals of the Socialist party. Its schools are better, its people more law-abiding, its politics cleaner.

The south, on the other hand, is oppressed by poverty and illiteracy. These evils, it is to be understood, exist throughout Italy, but are most virulent in the south. Workmen who received as little as twelve cents a day were not unknown in southern Italy just before the Great War began, while women worked for less. The diet of the poor is almost exclusively vegetarian and often of the coarsest. Once born in poverty, they are kept there by ignorance and illiteracy. To be sure before the war thousands went annually to the United States, and from that haven they sent each year millions of dollars, thus doubly relieving the pressure at home; yet even this did not suffice. The communes, mainly rural and agricultural in the south, were unable to maintain schools; while the state had little money to give. Thus illiteracy still stood, in 1911, at 69 per cent. of the entire population over six years old in Calabria, whereas in Piedmont the illiterates were only 11 per cent. of the people.

Another evil, too, has long oppressed the south. Through centuries of cruel and tyrannical government, the people of Naples and Sicily especially had learned to distrust all government. To them government had come to mean not order but violence, not justice but oppression. In the course of time, and it seems especially under the hated Austrian, they had taken the law into their own hands much after the fashion of certain mountain communities in our own South. It was not mob rule and lynch law, which results from sudden outbursts of popular passion. It was instead the orderly organization of secret societies, Mafia and Camorra, whose decisions were absolute law to their members, superseding not only the laws of the state but even those of common morality. These societies defied the authorities of the state, dealing out rewards to friends and punishments to enemies which did not stop short of the most cruel death penalty—a wild and rough sort of justice, but very effective.

This problem of north and south has not by any means been solved. There are explanations enough, some of which are worth repeating. In the first place the debt incurred in the wars of liberation and in creating a united Italy was extremely onerous to a poverty-stricken country. For many years in succession there were deficits, and never a surplus which could be used to promote education, to improve agriculture, or to ameliorate social conditions. Then, with the growth in prosperity, Italy must needs create a large army and navy, and later on dabble in doubtful colonial exploits, which always seemed to be considered before all other things, while the taking over of the railways added large amounts of necessary annual expense. Certain people in the north lay the whole blame on the south for not suppressing crime, supporting schools, and improving the condition of the poor. To this the south retorts that it had a later start and smaller resources than the north, while its problem was far graver, and it adds that the north is itself partly to blame, for while it has controlled the national government almost continuously since 1861 it has done almost nothing to help the south to solve its difficulties.

The problem is indeed a thorny one, and the explanations merely serve to show that it is very real. As long as there is a "north" and a "south" in Italy, the Italians are not really a united nation. Unfortunately, too, the trend is not all toward unity, for there are those who talk of home rule for Sicily, to which a few non-thinking people in the north retort that it would be good riddance.

If the people are divided between north and south, they are everywhere sundered on the great question of church and state. Even the present war finds this problem pressing and unsolved.

Briefly stated, the recent history of the controversy between the papacy and "united Italy" is this. The unification of 1859-61 deprived the church of all its "temporal estates" except Rome and its immediate surroundings. Before that time the pope had ruled a number of contiguous territories extending northeastward across the peninsula. The revolts of 1848 and 1849, and those of ten years later, were in part directed against the pope, and the last ones succeeded. The revolted church estates in north central Italy became, in 1860, part of the new kingdom of united Italy, but Pope Pius IX did not cease to protest at having been thus robbed of his dominions. His expostulations were all in vain. The best he could do, and that with the aid of French bayonets, was to maintain his power in Rome itself.

In the following ten years the radical "left" in the newly created Italian parliament clamored oft and loudly for immediate and drastic action to oust the pope from Rome also. There was every reason to believe that an attack by Italy on Rome at this time would have meant war with France. For this reason the more conservative "right" which was still in power, held back and waited a better day. The opportunity came at last in 1870, when Napoleon III fell before the Prussians, and the French guard in Rome was recalled to meet the Teutonic invader. Then, with little bloodshed, but against the protests of the pope, the Italian arms breached the walls of Rome and entered the city by the Porta Pia. Once there, there was no going back. "We are in Rome, and here we shall remain," said Victor Emmanuel on making his triumphal entry in 1871. The overwhelmingly favorable vote of the people of Rome themselves only strengthened the monarchy in this determination.

The question of the status of the church and especially of the pope had yet to be settled. Few Italians wished the complete withdrawal of the papacy from Italy; rather the contrary. Not only did it increase Italy's prestige in the world to be the seat and home of the church, but the Italians themselves were overwhelmingly Roman Catholic. It is said that an Italian is Roman Catholic or nothing, and indeed the number of Protestants in Italy is almost insignificant. The danger of foreign intervention on behalf of the papacy was also always to be feared. Thus a peaceful settlement to keep the papacy at Rome was dictated by circumstances.

In 1870, therefore, the government proceeded to pass the so-called Law of the Papal Guaranties, which became effective in May, 1871. In the debates preceding the passage of this act were revived the various earlier projects for settlement of the church question, and especially Cavour's plan of a "free church in a free state." The law passed assumed that there was a clear and known line of demarcation between temporal and spiritual affairs, a wholly unwarranted assumption as it now appears, at least for Italy, and proceeded to guarantee the pope sufficient income and liberty "to fulfil all the functions of his spiritual ministry," not neglecting even to assure him of very definite temporal rights also. He was guaranteed from state revenues an income of over $600,-000 annually, equal to what his estates had been bringing him, together with entire control of the Vatican and Lateran palaces with their grounds and appurtenances. His person was declared sacred and inviolable; his rights, when anywhere in the kingdom, were to be those of a visiting sovereign. His correspondence and his telegraphic communications were to be free from molestation by officers of the state. The government specifically renounced the right to appoint bishops, but the law reserved to the king his existing right to appoint to other benefices which were part of the royal patronage. With the exception of acts affecting appointments or the property of the Church, no ecclesiastical acts were henceforth to require government sanction. Thus the church was made entirely free as to its teachings and doctrine, and even as to its punishment of ecclesiastical offenses, though no act or punishment could become legal which was against the laws of the state. The state in concluding promised to pass a law for the reorganization and administration of church property in Italy.

That the law of the guaranties was passed in a sincere effort to settle fairly the entire question cannot now be doubted. That its terms could have been much improved by more careful consideration at the time is also hardly open to dispute. But its chief weakness lay in the fact that it was made by the conqueror for the conquered. The Pope was unable to bring himself to the point of accepting its terms. The act spoke of him as free in the spiritual realm and made his person inviolable, incapable of arrest, detention, or penalty. Incapable of being imprisoned, he took prison walls unto himself, proclaiming to loyal Catholics throughout the world that he was being kept in duress in the Vatican. The law gave him a legal claim to a large annuity from the state treasury in lieu of the income he formerly had from his estates. This money he has refused to claim, for he still denies the validity of the acts which deprived him of his domains; and therefore he cannot without recognizing the "robber's right" receive as a gift any part of the "ill-gotten spoils."

Thus from its very inception, the Pope's hostility to the law has prevented its proper enforcement. In the course of over forty years, numerous points have arisen for interpretation, and few have been settled. The government, being the authority to enforce the law, has been subjected to constant criticism by the Church, which has assumed consistently the attitude of a weak and persecuted society. That the government merits much criticism is undoubtedly true. It has been, perhaps, too slow in giving up its control of the appointment of clergy, and seems at times to have used the power for political purposes. It still controls much ecclesiastical property and distributes to the Church in return less revenue than the clergy had expected. The questions of civil marriage and religious education are still unsolved and grievous.

The government and the anti-Catholics, on the other hand, have reason to be exceedingly bitter against the Church. They feel that in trying to be upright they have positively leaned ever backwards, endangering the very stability of the state in the attempt to be fair to the Church, while the popes have traitorously connived to bring about foreign intervention. For thirty years after the settlement of 1870, a strong but dwindling Catholic party in France openly endeavored to induce the French government to restore the papal estates, to make the Pope once more a Pope-King. This movement the papacy did not discourage. At one time Pope Leo XIII prevented Emperor Franz-Joseph from visiting King Humbert in Rome, saying that it would be an insult to the Catholic Church. To weaken Italy, and to make possible the restoration of the temporal power, Leo XIII would perhaps have wrecked the Triple Alliance had opportunity offered.[1]

These charges, which can be substantiated, clearly show that the Vatican has not accepted in good faith either the unification of Italy or the *fait accompli* of 1870–1871. It has instead used its influence to embroil Italy with foreign powers. But it has gone even further, for it has attempted to weaken Italy by causing dissensions at home. The principal effort in this direction has been to discourage Catholics from voting or from recognizing the government of united Italy by co-operation in any way. As early as 1883 Catholics were told that it was "inexpedient" to vote in parliamentary elections, though municipal elections were not to be similarly shunned. From that day until the momentous election of 1904 the Vatican maintained its attitude, and the mère fact that Catholics were generally too wise, patriotic, and independent to obey the injunction does not absolve the Vatican from blame.

Thus has the papacy worked against the perfection of the unity of Italy, and not without some success. Clearly the problem of Church and state relations was one which could not be avoided and just as clearly it is as yet unsolved. No pope has yet fully and unequivocally renounced all thought of restoring the temporal power.

The revocation of the *non expedit*, forced on the papacy by the extraordinary conditions in Italy following the general strike of 1904, was only partial, while one result has been to raise the issue of clericalism again in Italy.

During the present war, the clericals have failed to take a strong pro-Italian stand, and may, indeed, have some difficulty in clearing themselves of the charges of pro-Germanism, and assistance to the enemy, now becoming current even in very responsibly written books.[2] The slow but steady movement since about 1900 toward a more conciliatory policy on both sides probably received a complete check when, at the beginning of the war, the Pope showed an entire inability to stand

[1] Bolton King, and Thomas Okey, "Italy To-day," 1913 Ed., p. 45.
[2] Cf. William Kay Wallace, "Greater Italy," 1917, 175–178; cf. also E. J. Dillon, "From the Triple to the Quadruple Alliance," 1915, 178–184.

out against the destruction of Belgium and Poland or even
to comprehend, much less to sympathize with, the national
aspirations of Italy.

Directly related to the difficulties between Italy and the
papacy was the extreme unhappiness which existed from
1860 almost down to 1900 in the relations of Italy and France.
Some distrust of France went back, of course, to the days
of 1859 and 1860, when Napoleon III suddenly dropped the
campaign against Austria before driving her completely out
of Italy, and yet insisted upon the cession of Savoy to France
before the unification of Italy began. Napoleon had found
indeed that he had overreached himself. In warring on
Austrian domination of Italy, he had encouraged the revolt
of the Papal States also, and thus had struck a blow at the
temporal power. Turning to view the results of this act, he
seems to have observed that he was alienating the necessary
support of the Catholics at home. Therefore, as if to restore himself in the good graces of his own people, he sent
French troops to Rome to support the papacy in its claims
of temporal authority over this, its last stronghold. For
ten years, then, Italy was restrained by French arms from
making Rome the capital. For ten years every Italian movement against Rome risked a war between France and Italy.
With the cry "Rome or death" upon his lips the popular
hero Garibaldi twice tried to make Rome the capital of Italy.
On the second occasion, he was defeated by French arms
at Mentana (1867), a defeat which Italians never forgave.

The withdrawal of the French garrison in 1870 during the
Franco-Prussian War did not soften the hatred of the Italian
republicans and anti-clericals for France, though Rome was
made the capital at last. There began at once in France a
movement among the Catholics to restore the temporal power.
Had Italy but known it, Gambetta and the republicans in
France were themselves during the seventies to wage a successful if not final fight against clericalism. But the republicans were still a minority in France. Thiers, who then

headed the provisional government, had definite clerical leanings, and it was from France that the papacy looked for
succor. For thirty years the clerical party in France showed
great vitality. French pilgrims to Rome on several occasions
irritated the Italians by indiscreet utterances concerning the
restoration of the Pope-King. Almost down to 1900 Italy
feared and the papacy hoped to see French bayonets once
more in Rome.

A distrust thus engendered was doomed to find other suspicions on which to feed, other reasons for its continuance.
In 1881 France occupied Tunis, just across from Sicily. Bismarck suggested it, desiring to keep France busy abroad, while
England offered no objections. France had fairly good pre-
texts, but Italy was aroused and indignant. She had had
some designs on Tunis also, and certainly did not relish the
thought of France controlling the whole northern coast of
Africa. Thus Italy, which would have been far more comfortable in an alliance with France, was repelled from that
measure and forced either to go forward alone, risking a war
with France if the latter should determine to restore the
temporal power, or to ally herself with the eastern enemy
Austria, and Prussia. The latter step was the one taken.
The Dual Alliance became the Triple Alliance in 1882. Italy
may have thought it a great stroke. In some ways the move
was inevitable. But Italy had to sacrifice ''her most sacred
aspiration'' while in the alliance, namely, her desire for
the unredeemed parts of Italy, and she awoke years later to
a knowledge that she had been a makeweight rather than a full
participating member of the alliance.[1]

Relations with France were destined to become even worse
before they became better. In 1887 Italy adopted a high
protective tariff and in 1888 the treaty of commerce with
France was broken. Then followed a short tariff war, in
which Italian trade both in manufactures and agricultural
products suffered grievously. From 1889 trade was pos-

[1] See speech of Premier Salandra to Chamber of Deputies, May 20,
1915; Baron Sonnino's public note of May 23, 1915.

sible on somewhat better terms but was little revived. Rather it sought new directions and not until 1898 was a new and liberal French commercial treaty made.

By this time French-Italian relations were reaching a better understanding. The papacy had almost ceased to hope for restoration of the temporal power by force of French arms, and in 1905, with the separation of church and state in France, the possibility of such action passed away forever. But already the evil results of the fear and hatred of France were manifest and not to be recalled. Italy had sacrificed her independence of action, her national aspirations, and in a sense a part of her duty, by the forced alliance with Austria and Germany. Not until she denounced the alliance in 1915 did she assume once more that free and independent position among the nations of the world to which she was entitled.

It was especially her desire to incorporate "unredeemed" portions of Italian territory that Italy had to give up while in the "unholy" Triple Alliance. The problem of the Irredenta has long been interesting to Italians. The whole struggle of the Italian-speaking people from the days of the first uprisings against Austria down to 1870 was a struggle to redeem Italy from the sword and oppression of the foreign tyrant. Mazzini would have included even Corsica as an Italian territory to be redeemed.

Suffice it to say that the task of redemption was far from complete in 1861. The Trentino in the north center, Italian-speaking and located on the Italian Adige River, was still Austrian. Venice and Venetia, with all the Italian-speaking land north, east, and south to Trieste, were also under the Hapsburgs. Rome itself was still denied to Italy.

In 1866 Prussia, desirous of ending Austrian predominance in German affairs, and of placing herself at the head of the Germanic federation, made war upon Austria in alliance with Italy. Though it was not accomplished by the force of Italian arms, Austria was quickly defeated. The Italians, failing in their part of the campaign, won no battles; but the Prussians had profited much by the Italian alliance, since Austria had been compelled to divide her forces. Quickly forced to sue for peace, Austria was astounded at the lenience of the Prussian terms. Prussia first, in violation of her treaty with Italy, made a separate treaty with Austria, and then refused to back up Italy in her demands. The latter, in claiming the Trentino, undoubtedly went beyond what she was entitled to by the treaty with Prussia, but Prussia clearly was playing to mollify Austria rather than to support Italy. Venetia was at last ceded to Italy,[1] but it was Venetia bounded by the Judrio River on the east, leaving the bridge-head of Gorizia, and the important passes in the hands of Austria.

Beyond the political boundaries fixed for Italy in 1859 and 1867 lay at that time much territory called Italian and many purely Italian-speaking communities, mainly in Austria. These constituted the *Irredenta*. The passage of fifty years has made little change in the situation, save that the proportion of non-Italian-speaking people has risen considerably in parts of the Trieste district owing to the immigration of Slavs. The Trentino proper contains over 330,000 Italians and less than 10,000 of other races. The upper Adige valley, however, is preponderantly German-speaking, but as its population is smaller the balance throughout the entire Trentino region is distinctly on the Italian side—about two to one in a population of under 600,000.

Farther east Italy makes no claims until Gorizia and Eastern Friuli are reached. Here the Germans are very few, but the Italians are slightly overbalanced by Slavs, many of recent immigration. In Trieste, also claimed as a part of the *Irredenta*, a city of over 200,000, over 70 per cent. are Italian. In Istria the Slavs again outnumber the Italians who form about 40 per cent. or 160,000 in a total population of 400,000. In Dalmatia the Italians are, however, far outnumbered by Slavs and others. Indeed, the rural districts almost everywhere at the head of the Adriatic are predominantly non-Italian.

[1] The terms of the treaty of cession of 1866 were very hastily drafted, and the boundaries of Venetia most carelessly delimited, with Austria being left in control of most of the strategic points in the Julian Alps.

The Italian claims to the *Irredenta* are principally three. The weakest is the historical. There was no Italy before 1860, save in a geographical sense, and to argue that Trieste, for example, should belong to Italy because it was once controlled by Venice, is trivial. Wisely enough, the *Irredentists* put little stress on the historical argument. The second claim is geographic. The northern and eastern boundaries of Italy are mainly purely arbitrary and correspond to no true geographic divisions. From a military point of view, too, they are unfair, since Austria has been left in control of all the strong passes. It is characteristic that Austria controls the headwaters of many streams which are mainly Italian. Austria controls the upper reaches and Italy the lower of some of the same valleys.

The final argument is that of racial, social, and linguistic affinity. The people in the *Irredenta* are largely, in some places almost exclusively Italian, with a passionate attachment to Italy. Wherever other races preponderate, it is due to active efforts on the part of Austria to suppress the Italian language and Italian schools, and to import large numbers of other people, especially Slavs. Against this oppression the Italians in the "unredeemed" territories have fought successfully for fifty years.

Before Italy entered the Triple Alliance (1882) there had been several outbursts of popular feeling in favor of conquering the *Irredenta*. Garibaldi fought in vain for the Trentino in 1866. In 1878 and 1879 there were organized popular demonstrations, when Austria had been made protector of Bosnia, to oust her from "unredeemed Italy." A few years later the signing of the Triple Alliance imposed on the Italian government the necessity of suppressing *Irredentismo*. In the nineties Crispi uttered strong words of warning, and for a time the movement received a quietus under his repressive measures. The movement would not down entirely, and when, from about 1900 onwards, the fact became more and more clear that Austria's Balkan policy was against the vital interests of Italy, the agitation revived. The annexation of Bosnia and Herzegovina by Austria in

1908, finally proving to Italy that her ally could not be trusted, was the signal for the old movement to take on a new life.

Finally, in 1914 the movement to annex the *Irredenta* was adopted by the Italian government as its own policy. The negotiations with Austria to this end failed completely. Italy was at last compelled to break the Triple Alliance and to take up the gage of battle to protect her vital interests. When so doing, in a circular letter to the powers, she denounced the persistence with which the Austro-Hungarian government had tried to destroy all vestige of Italian nationality and civilization in the Eastern Adriatic, as indicating the "deep rooted sentiment of hostility and aversion for Italy" prevailing among influential classes in Austria-Hungary.[1]

While these and other urgent questions perplexed the young kingdom, a new peril was creeping upon it unseen and unsuspected. It was the sinister influence of Germany, gained by peaceful penetration, which for a while in 1914 and 1915 almost paralyzed the kingdom, depriving it of a will of its own.

The evidences of this penetration are only beginning to come to us in America, but the origin seems to have been financial. When Italy joined the Triple Alliance, aiming thus at France, France was naturally displeased. The dislike became greater when, a few years later, the commercial treaty was denounced. A brief tariff war then ensued, followed presently (1893) by France's dumping on the market a large amount of Italian securities, apparently owing to a trivial war-scare. A panic ensued in Italy, and she was practically forced into the arms of the bankers of Germany, her chief ally. The next year German capital founded the Italian Commercial Bank (*Banca Commerciale Italiana*) at Milan, and the process of penetration was begun.

As the bank grew in resources it grew in influence, and its next step was to control commerce and industry as a branch of its banking business. German students and trade-spies

[1] "Italy's Green Book," 1915, Baron Sonnino's note of May 23, 1915.

were employed in increasing numbers to seek out means of extending German business in Italy. Italian business men who received credit from the bank, were given to understand that they must buy some or all of their goods in Germany. Certain industries, such as the electric power business, fell completely under German domination.

From financial and industrial control, the German influence began to extend itself into the field of public opinion and politics. Financially needy or purchasable newspapers began to fall under Teutonic control. Soon there was the use of money also to swing elections and the process of making Italy a mere appanage of Germany was on its way to completion. Other less important factors, such as the close proximity of Italy to Germany, some international marriages, and the education of young Italians, especially army men, in Germany, were supporting causes of the great influence which Germany exercised in Italy in the stressful days of 1914 and 1915.

When the war began Germany used every effort to keep Italy from going into it. Italy's interests were so clearly opposed to Austria in the latter's Balkan policy, that the best German leaders really hoped for was to keep Italy neutral. The pro-Germans in Italy assumed at once the name of neutralists. The papal-clerical party seemed to be mainly of that stamp. So too was the powerful popular leader Giolitti; so were many senators and deputies. A former German Imperial Chancellor, Prince von Bülow, was sent to Rome to direct the campaign to keep Italy on the sidelines.

For weeks and months Italy was unable to see things as they really were. Popular sympathy was with France, Belgium, and England, but the pressure to stay neutral was heavy, while the issues were not entirely clear. But a few outstanding leaders, among them Baron Sydney Sonnino, Minister of Foreign Affairs, kept their heads clear and their minds upon the interests of the kingdom. They were able to control affairs despite the German propaganda until the people were ready to listen to reason and patriotism. Then the bandages were quickly removed from Italy's eyes. She saw how the Triple Alliance had bound her, absolutely stopping the process of unification, how the treaty had been disregarded by the other participants, especially Austria, with impunity, and how under its cover Germany had established her commercial and political power within Italy itself. From the Austrian oppressor of the days before 1860 the Italians seemed to have freed themselves only to find a new master in Germany.

It was then that Italy asserted her "sacred egoism," her unity and independence, her right and her ability to stand alone. In a memorable speech in the Italian capitol on June 2, 1915, Premier Salandra proclaimed, amid the plaudits of his countrymen, "No vassalage, no protectorate under any one." This was Italy's declaration of independence.

CHAPTER IX

THE NEW GERMAN EMPIRE AND ITS GENIUS

O N January 18, 1871, while yet the cannon were booming around starving and defiant Paris, there was a remarkable state spectacle at Versailles, the old residence town of Louis XIV, then occupied by the besieging Teutonic armies. Before a brilliant assemblage of German princes and generals in the famous "Hall of Mirrors," with the Grand Duke of Baden to lead the *"Hochs"* and *"Vivats,"* William I, King of Prussia, was proclaimed "German Emperor" in token of the fact that he had been accepted by all the other sovereigns and free cities of Germany as the hereditary president of the newly founded German Empire. From that day to this the interest and power of Prussia have largely merged in the greater interests and power of this imperial state which Bismarck and his sovereign had founded. For the next forty-three years the newly created Empire remained the great salient fact for Europe and almost for the entire world. In the place of the old disjointed Germanic Federation, distracted by innumerable forms of particularism, the battle-ground for foreign armies, without colonies, merchant marine or fleet, and economically far behind England or France, there was to be an enormous state more populous than France, with the most formidable army in the world, consolidated and controlled by a remarkably efficient and energetic government, and speedily able to build merchant and battle-ships, to seize colonies, to meddle in the affairs of Turkey, Morocco, Oceania and China, and compete with Great Britain in almost every form of economic enterprise. All this transformation was wrought between 1862, when Bismarck assumed the charge of Prussian affairs, and 1871—the year of French defeat and German unity and triumph. There have been few greater overturns in the history of the world.

Fortunately for the peace of Europe, Bismarck wisely and sincerely believed that after the conquest of Alsace-Lorraine Germany was "satiated," and that what she needed was not more of victorious war, but peaceful consolidation and internal development. To be sure he kept up the strength of the army and took every precaution to protect himself against Russia and France. But the great chancellor seized every opportunity also to proclaim that German greatness was no menace to the world's peace—and on the whole the world believed him. This was true down to 1890—the year of his downfall; and what sane American in 1890 could possibly have said that his own country would ever be involved in an indescribably expensive and bloody war with Germany, over an issue that nominally started over a quarrel between Vienna and St. Petersburg, about the right of the Czar to protect Serbia from the wrath of Austria? Yet twenty-seven years after Bismarck quitted power the unthinkable had become reality. Unconsciously in part, he and his generation in Germany had sown the wind. The next generation was to reap the whirlwind. To understand the causes of the débâcle of 1914, one must also understand the genius of Prussia which in 1871 gained the mastery of the German people.

This people of Germany was admittedly one of the predominant units of the human race. In almost every form of cultural achievement it had either surpassed or crowded the other leaders hard. Music, art, philosophy, theology, the sciences, whether applied or theoretical—it competed or triumphed in all. But *in one great form of human endeavor the Germans had not triumphed—they had never played their due part in the human struggle for political liberty.* It is possible to find historical reasons for this: the failure of the Medieval Empire and the friction between the multifarious petty princes. But the fact remained. England had written very many chapters in the "Golden Book of Liberty." So had the city republics of mediæval Italy, and the mountain cantons of Switzerland, likewise the stout burgher-communities of Holland and Flanders. Even in France under the absolute monarchy the memory of the mediæval "States Gen-

eral" had never been forgotten, and was to revive magically in that year of wonder, 1789. Germany had added no chapters to the story. Her heroes had been either valorous paladins and princes like Frederick Barbarossa, or scholars and master-theologians like Martin Luther. The numerous "free cities" of her later Middle Ages had been only "free" as respected the control of some outside elector or duke. Within they had been usually governed by a privileged class of burghers or "patricians," with little enough share at most times for the common people.

It might have been imagined that the Protestant Reformation with its accent on the right of the individual to select his own view of religious truth would have given a great impetus to the development of political liberty also. It did really the reverse. Luther was intensely interested in the triumph of his religious cause. He cared little for political considerations and he greatly needed firm helpers against the Pope. He therefore threw his whole enormous influence in favor of strengthening the power of the German princes. The new Lutheran church was on the whole far more dependent on the government than the old Catholic church had been. Indeed after Luther's death and the loss of the original impulses of his movement the Lutheran clergy (it is not unfair to say) became very convenient instruments in the hands of the average prince, for keeping his subjects in order. Certain familiar Bible texts have been worn threadbare in German Protestant pulpits—"Fear God, honor the king," "Render unto Cæsar the things that are Cæsar's," and the like. Church and state thus made an extremely close alliance. It is needless to say that the state was not the loser by the bargain.[1]

About one-third of Germany proper indeed remained Catholic, but this fact did not help to promote political liberty. Outside of the Austrian lands and Bavaria almost all the

[1] The absence of bishops, with their claims to secular consideration and social prestige, in the Lutheran Church, and the substitution for them of mere official superintendents, controlled completely by the prince, of course increased the grip of the governments upon German Protestantism.

German Catholics were subject to "Prince-Bishops" (e. g. of Mainz, Köln, Würzburg, etc.) narrow-minded, petty, essentially secular despots, who were only too glad to use their spiritual authority to eke out their ordinary civil power. Thus both the old church and the new worked against the development of any kind of democracy.

In all German history down to 1848 there was never any well-matured uprising of a great mass of the people to secure political rights, although there had been some frantic and desperate revolts of the ignorant peasantry (as e. g. in Martin Luther's time) to secure redress from brutal oppression by the petty nobles. These beast-like revolts had been quieted in blood, and some of the princes had been wise enough to remedy the grosser evils, but there had been serfage, accompanied by outrageous privileges for the nobility in Germany down to Napoleon's conquests. The subjects of a German prince had been often not much better than biped cattle, such as were the miserable Hessians whose ruler shipped them for a price to America, when George III of England found it hard to get his own self-respecting subjects to enlist to coerce George Washington and his fellow "rebels."

The chief curse of Germany in the seventeenth and eighteenth centuries had been, of course, her ruinous sub-division into innumerable states. When Napoleon I went through the land, wrecking old institutions like a human whirlwind, there had been nearly three hundred principalities, little and great, "free cities," etc., all pretending to be part of the now disintegrating Holy Roman Empire. Some of these "states" had been comically small, as, e. g., that of Count William of Buckeburg who had dominions that could be crossed by a single old-style cannon shot, but who solemnly built a pretentious fortress to defend "a range of wooden huts, an observatory, and a potato field." Some of the states, on the other hand, were respectable small countries—e. g., Saxony, Bavaria and Würtemberg. There was one, however, which was still larger and had been growing between 1648 and 1800, to the great alarm of its neighbors—the most eastern large state of Germany—Prussia.

Prussia had been the creation of a line of remarkable princes, who had seemed able to provide one fairly capable sovereign after another. In the seventeenth century the "Great Elector," Frederick William, had made his state of Brandenburg-Prussia, though it was still poor, and territorially disjointed, into a fairly formidable military monarchy. Early in the seventeenth century this one-time "electorate" had become the "Kingdom of Prussia." [1] Between 1713 and 1740 had reigned King Frederick William I, a hard, tyrannous, coarse and crabbed man, but one who (after his lights) had labored with remarkable efficiency and success for the benefit of his subjects. "Salvation is of the Lord. All else is in *my* province!" he had asserted; and he had lived up to the dictum. He left a large and well-organized army and the nucleus of a powerful state to his remarkably able son, Frederick the Great.

Frederick the Great (1740–1786) made Prussia one of the great powers of Europe. In two sustained and terrible wars he defeated Austria, France, and Russia, now singly and now with them all allied against him. He won a name as one of the great captains of history—worthy of a pedestal only a little lower than Napoleon's. Many of his traits were admirable. He not only won battles but he wrought great things for the cultural advancement of his people. He was the model for "enlightened despots," but his methods were such as to constitute an evil example for his successors. International law (even as then known) and likewise treaties he violated most brazenly. He gained a name for bad faith which would have been his ruin had he not been a military genius. In 1740, without warning, he attacked Austria and seized Silesia—to which his claims were very flimsy—almost solely because Austria was in dynastic troubles and could not defend the coveted province. In 1756 he began the "Seven Years'

[1] It was called "Prussia" and not "Brandenburg" (the other half of the original state) because the province of Prussia was not strictly part of the old Germanic Empire, and its ruler might therefore claim royal honors without seeming to lord it too much over the other German princes who were still nominally subject to the "Emperor" at Vienna.

War" by being the aggressor against Austria and France as soon as he believed conflict "inevitable"; and since he needed the helpless neutral country of Saxony for strategic reasons, he entered, violated and exploited that perfectly innocent land, as if it had been in league with his enemies.[1] He cynically confessed to a public immorality which most of his contemporaries had the decency at least to disavow. "The question of right is an affair of the ministers," he once wrote, ". . . it is time to consider it in secret, for the orders to the troops have been given."—"Take what you can," he wrote again, "You are never wrong unless you are obliged to give back." This man, then, was what Macaulay called him, a tyrant "without fear, without faith and without mercy." Yet his success was so great: his creative qualities enabled him to lift so high the fabric of Prussian greatness, that to his successors he seemed like a demi-god. It was a species of treason to suggest that a given practice was wrong provided Frederick the Great had sanctioned it:—and very many of Frederick's usages were to be revived in 1914.

After this king, Prussia fell on evil days. Napoleon defeated her and maltreated her worse than almost any other of his national victims. But at least the overrunning of practically all of Germany by the French brought the destruction of many old abuses. Of the three hundred odd "princes" and free cities before 1800, nearly all the weaker ones were destroyed and absorbed by the larger states. There were only thirty-five reigning "Majesties, Highnesses, and Serenities" left in 1817, and four free cities. Better still, serfdom was abolished even in ultra-conservative Prussia. Other modernizing reforms came to pass under the French whip and spur. In short, things were never as bad after 1814 when Napoleon departed for Elba, as they had been before the Corsican's shadow crossed the Teutonic lands.

[1] The violation of Saxony by Frederick undoubtedly seemed a decisive and happy precedent for the German high command in 1914 when it decided on the quite similar violation of Belgium. Bernhardi, the Pan-German author, in 1911 took pains to commend the examples set by Frederick, especially the manner in which he struck boldly, and began his wars the moment they seemed useful to his policy.

Napoleon was driven back over the Rhine by a great alliance of the nations, but the Germans played a noble part therein. Made frantic by the outrageous oppression of the invaders, the Prussian people for the first time really asserted themselves. They almost coerced their timid king, Frederick William III, into drawing the sword; and they were the backbone of the coalition (with Austria, Russia and England) which defeated Napoleon at Leipzig (1813) in the terrific "Battle of the Nations" and ultimately hurled him from his throne. There had been a strong hope among the leaders of this patriotic movement that as reward for the expulsion of the foreign enemy there would come the granting of a free constitution to Prussia. Frederick William III did indeed in 1814 and again in 1815 solemnly promise to his subjects a constitution; but the instant there ceased to be any need of conciliating them to get common action against the French, the king fell under ultra-conservative and reactionary influences. He lived till 1840, without redeeming this promise. In some of the lesser states of Germany, constitutions (often not very liberal) were granted; but already Prussia embraced almost 50 per cent. of the German people—omitting the Austrians. So the first great opportunity for establishing a free system of government for the Fatherland was lost.

In 1840 began the reign of Frederick William IV of Prussia, a brilliant, unstable, exceedingly opinionated man who was destined presently to become insane and to die in 1861 after four years of confinement. This king met the rising demands of his subjects for a constitution with an angry negation. In 1843 he publicly asserted that he would never allow "to come between Almighty God and this land a blotted parchment (i. e., a constitution) to rule us with paragraphs, and to replace the ancient sacred bond of loyalty."

But the liberal movement in Germany was swelling to a point where it seemed likely to burst every barrier. Nearly all the intelligent elements of the nation were crying out for a real federal constitution for all Germany to replace the miserably weak "confederation" which had been founded in 1815 under the domination of Austria; also in each separate state, but especially in Prussia, they demanded a local constitution securing the essentials of freedom. The revolution of 1848 in France and the temporary establishment of a French republic had its tremendous echoes beyond the Rhine. Popular uprisings shook every German throne and especially that of Frederick William IV. There was fighting in the streets of Berlin. This king and the lesser princes bowed before the blast. A national parliament was convoked at Frankfort to give a constitution to all Germany, and its members were chosen by popular vote. For an instant it seemed as if the Fatherland was about to become a "free country" in the best sense of the term.

Then followed one of the greatest misfortunes in history. The 586 deputies were men without experience in debate or law-making. There were very many professors of political science, each man full of fine theories which differed widely from those of his colleagues. There were very few practical men of accepted leadership. Upon a certain problem there were "nine projects and 189 orators." A dangerous amount of time was wasted over fine questions about "the bill of rights." There were radical Republicans who tried to declare a republic upon the spot and to send the princes to the scrapheap. So the days crept by, ardor cooled, dissensions thickened, and it became increasingly evident that Austria would never consent (unless after a war) to any scheme which excluded her from the leadership of a revivified German Empire. This the German patriots could not grant.[1] They at last prepared a constitution for a federal empire of a pretty liberal type, and offered the imperial crown to Frederick William IV. (1849.)

That unstable prince had grown disgusted with the whole popular movement. He wanted, indeed, an imperial crown, not by gift of the people but by gift of the lesser princes—the

[1] The chief objection to Austria was of course that she was only "German" in a minor fraction of her dominions. The Frankfort parliament was not anxious to see the new Empire controlled by a state wherein the Magyars, Czechs, Croats, Slovenes, Poles, etc., were the largest element.

only rulers whose rights he recognized. He rejected the proffer by the parliament of what he contemptuously called "a crown of mud and wood." "If any one is to award the crown of the German nation," he asserted, "it is myself and my equals who should give it." His action, the hostile attitude of Austria, which was very loath to let go of her general supervision over German affairs, and the jealousy of many of the minor princes towards any scheme to advance Prussia, made the whole project break down. The parliament sorrowfully dispersed. A few radical leaders induced some Baden regiments to obey them and started an insurrection in South Germany to establish a republic. A Prussian army put down this brave but impracticable adventure. Many Republicans fled to France, Switzerland or America. Those who tarried were arrested, and some of them were shot. These were the days when Carl Schurz and many another of the best blood of Germany escaped into Transatlantic exile. Great numbers of other Teutons, profoundly discouraged at the failure of their patriotic hopes and the miserable plight of their country, emigrated more voluntarily. In Prussia itself Frederick William IV was canceling his promised reforms and proclaiming the grievously illiberal constitution of 1850. It was a time of pessimism and anguish for every freedom-loving man in Germany.

There are times when great calamities befall nations, calamities the true seriousness whereof cannot be appreciated until long years afterward. If the American war for Independence had failed, if the Bourbon monarchy had crushed the French Revolution, if Abraham Lincoln had failed to preserve the North American Union—the results of the disaster would have remained to curse America and France respectively—and other nations too—for many decades. And so it was with the abortive German Revolution of 1848–49. For a few happy months it had seemed as if without prolonged bloodshed, with the acquiescence of the princes, and by the joyous agreement of the people of all parts of Germany, a liberal federative Empire was about to be established, uniting the Fatherland but with due preservation of local antonomy and local interests. The success of this movement would have established the doctrine of the sovereignty of the people, and of the subordination of the princes to the popular will. Germany would thus have become a great united free nation *without* invoking militarism. If, however, she had wished for colonial expansion, there was still in the 1850's and '60's plenty of available territories in Africa, Asia, and Oceania, unappropriated by France, England, or any other civilized power, and easy for the new Germany to annex.

Now all hopes of a liberal German Empire had for the moment gone glimmering. The failure had not merely disappointed the aspirations of the liberals. It had apparently been caused by the sheer political incapacity of the liberals themselves. Hereafter the conservatives could openly assert that monarchy was the only government possible for Germans, because, as an ex-chancellor (Von Bülow) wrote in 1913, "despite the abundance of merits and the great qualities with which the German nation is endowed, *political talent has been denied it.*" [1] Every future champion of liberalism had the pitiful failure of 1848–49 cast in his face. Not merely was the coming of genuine liberty to Germany postponed but the chance for expansion beyond seas was lost. It was to be well after 1880 before the empire which Bismarck founded gained sufficient stability to pursue a colonial policy. By that time England and France had preëmpted the best parts of the African field and Japan was growing strong in Asia. If the Fatherland then desired really useful and promising colonies they must be won by the sword.

After a period of anxious discouragement, liberalism lifted its head again, especially in Prussia. Grievously monarchical and oligarchic as was the constitution which in 1850 Frederick William IV had grudgingly conceded to his people (see p. 182), it was better than nothing. The liberal impulse was

---

[1] Considering the very honorable record in American political life of many Germans, or Americans of pure Germanic ancestry, this statement may be flatly declared to be untrue. The home conditions of the Teutonic race were, however, very ill suited for developing efficient political instincts.

so strong that despite a franchise which peculiarly favored the wealthy and the noble the Prussian Chamber of Deputies became a mouth-piece for protest and agitation. The majority of the members stood for greater popular liberties and drastic general reforms. In 1858 Frederick William IV's mind gave way. He ended his days in pitiful confinement. His brother and heir, Prince William (soon King William I) was proclaimed regent. The new ruler was primarily a military man. He had (as will be seen) many personal virtues, but he had an intense dislike of liberalism. When he took over the government he proclaimed publicly, "what has already been promised shall be performed, what has not been promised will be withheld." There was little hope for a free Prussia in those words!

By 1860 it was clear enough that there were two things the great majority of Germans wanted: I. The union of all the land in a single effective federal empire, so that the Germanic folk might become a true nation: not a loose "bund" of contending states, always bullied by Austria and sometimes kicked by France. II. The establishment of a liberal political system both in the new central government and the several federated states. However much the majority of the junker Prussian aristocracy (champions of extreme monarchism) and even the royal house of Prussia itself, were in favor of the first proposition, they were utterly out of sympathy with the second. A kind of working hypothesis seems therefore to have possessed the Prussian aristocracy and the whole Hohenzollern governmental machine in the years which followed. They must secure unity for the German nation:—this would be for their own glory, because they intended to dominate the new Empire. By thus giving the people *half* of what they were craving: by giving them to boot a government which should flatter national pride by great victories, should increase the national wealth, raise the standard of living, fulfil in fact almost every material ideal except that of political liberty,—the German people could be satisfied. They would drop their demand for free constitutions because the Hohenzollerns and their Prussian army nobles were giving them better things than a liberal régime could give. Autocracy in other words must survive—because it was so very efficient.

No "junker" statesman ever avowed this precise program, but Bismarck and his lieutenants certainly lived up to the spirit of it most consistently. Thanks to the execution of the policy, in 1914, William II had a much firmer grip on the government than his grand-father possessed in 1858: and this fact caused much history to be written.

In 1861 William I and his advisers, to assure themselves that if Germany were consolidated it should be under Prussian and not Austrian leadership, began a radical strengthening of their army. The Prussian Chamber of Deputies, disliking the autocratic tendencies of the government, refused to vote the needful money. The king, however, refused to drop his military projects. He appointed as prime minister an approved and devoted champion of the rights of absolute monarchy—Otto von Bismarck, a genuine Prussian junker. Popular wrath was rising. The king was afraid for his throne and even for his head: but Bismarck offered to hold office despite hostile votes in parliament, and to collect taxes without authority of law (1862). So long as the army did not actually mutiny he was willing to snap his fingers at resolutions of censure. It was at this time that Bismarck bluntly asserted, "It is not Prussia's liberalism which Germany looks to but her military power": and again his famous dictum, "The unity of Germany is not to be brought about by speeches, nor by votes of majorities, but by *blood and iron.*" And he held on his way. Protests by the parliament were not even received by the king. Liberal newspapers were censored or suppressed. Municipal councils presented petitions to the sovereign: they were fined for their action. Public meetings were broken up. Feeling against the king and his despotic minister ran high, but Bismarck continued unfaltering, while his master, though often with fears, tenaciously supported him.

It seems strange indeed, but from 1862 to 1866 the ruler who was later acclaimed as Kaiser Wilhelm "der Grosse," and his minister who became the national hero of Germany, were intensely unpopular among their own subjects. All the best intelligence of Prussia,—journalists, university professors, great capitalists, etc., seemed to be execrating them. Even Frederick, the Crown Prince (later Emperor Frederick III, and father of William II) bitterly denounced Bismarck for endangering the dynasty by his excessively arbitrary methods. But there was one element that stood stoutly by— the junker lords; they supplied the army officers and kept the troops loyal to the autocratic régime. Once more Hohenzollernism and junkerdom displayed their indissoluble alliance— and all the time Von Moltke and Von Roon, a great general and a great war minister respectively, continued their reforms and the enlargement of the army, until it was ready to astonish the world.

In 1864 Bismarck struck his first blow. He inveigled Austria into making an alliance with Prussia and expelled the Danes from Schleswig-Holstein, alleging that King Frederick VIII of Denmark was trying to "Danize" a nominally German land.[1] In 1866 he was ready for his greater blow. Germany could never be united under the leadership of Prussia until Austria had suffered complete military overthrow. Bismarck's government was extremely unpopular in South Germany. Even in his own Prussia the liberals had little enthusiasm when he sounded the call to arms. He heeded this not. The new army was loyal, fit, and ready. On the 14th of June, 1866, Prussia broke with Austria and with nearly all the lesser German states. She had, however, Italy for an ally. On July 2nd, Moltke's new military machine blasted the power of Austria completely at the battle of Sadowa. "Your Majesty," reported the victorious general to his king, "you have won not merely the battle but the campaign." On the 23rd of July Austria was so humbled that she asked for an armistice to save herself from seeing the Prussian army in Vienna, and a treaty of peace soon followed. Austria was to quit Germany altogether. She was to leave the South German states (Hesse-Darmstadt, Baden, Würtemberg and Ba-

[1] For the later Schleswig-Holstein problem, see p. 228.

varia) independent, and to let Prussia organize the rest of Germany into the "North German Confederation."

The new German Empire was *almost* made by this victory of 1866. Prussia hastened to round out her dominions by absorbing several of the smaller northern states which had failed to bolster up her policies. Schleswig-Holstein she now annexed outright, likewise the free city of Frankfort, the principalities of Hesse-Cassel and Nassau and especially the kingdom of Hanover. The wishes of the communities were in no wise consulted. Prussia completed her deed through mere arbitrary might.[1] Bismarck then, with great haste, organized his new "North German Confederation." At the time it embraced about 70 per cent. of all the population of Germany. The South Germans were still hesitant and distrustful. He could not bring them in, but he deliberately arranged that the constitution of the Confederation should be capable, with a few modifications, of being expanded to embrace these southern states also. This constitution of 1866 was therefore in essential points the constitution of the actual German Empire (see p. 182).

But Bismarck had achieved more than the humiliation of Austria by Moltke's victory. Austria had been defeated and so had the Prussian liberals. They had watched him begin the war with intense misgiving, but now the glory of the victory, the enthusiasm over the partial unification of the Fatherland, swept them off their feet. After all—had not "blood and iron" been the means to success? They could protest no longer. Many of Bismarck's old foes became his admirers. The army was immensely popular. It was impossible to brand as despots and usurpers the ministers who had won such an amazing success. Political theories must go down!

In the 1866 elections in Prussia the liberals lost seats right and left, and nearly all the gain was by the "Conservatives,"

[1] Of course this was the annexation of German communities to people of their own kin—not like that of the Danes, Poles and Alsatians. Nevertheless, the expulsion of the old kings was resented long and bitterly in Hanover. In Hesse-Cassel, where the prince had been tyrannical and unpopular, the change was accepted more readily.

the deputies for the extreme monarchists and junkers. Bismarck then boldly went before the Prussian parliament and asked for a bill of indemnity for having collected taxes without authority. It was voted 230 to 75, many of the liberals concurring. *By this act the Prussian liberals cut their own throats.* They said in substance that a minister was sometimes quite justified in defying law and constitutional rights if only he thought his own ends were good. The old Prussian Liberal party, deprived of a common principle for which to battle, speedily went to pieces. There were still some protesting radicals, but a great number proclaimed themselves "National Liberals," declaring that they would "sustain the government fully in its foreign policy" though "maintaining in home matters the position of a watchful and loyal opposition." From such an "opposition" Bismarck had nothing to fear.

In 1849 German liberalism had sustained its first terrible defeat,—despite an excellent opportunity, it had failed to unify the nation. In 1866 it had met its second overthrow —it had seen the nation almost unified, not by its efforts but despite them; and it had been forced to condone the utter defiance of its principles. After Sadowa the Hohenzollerns and the junkers had no reason to tremble for their power. They were giving to German people half of what it wanted, and felt safe in withholding the other half.

In 1870 (p. 1) Bismarck completed the work by precipitating the war with France. He believed that the common victory would sweep the South German states into the new federation,[1] and give to this young creation of his all the strength and enthusiasm for the future which might come with a great success. In this he was entirely right.

After Sedan there had been many negotiations between Prussia and the South German states. The latter had feared decidedly their great northern neighbor and her masterful ways. Their people were more democratic than the Prussians, and some of their princes were not anxious to be over-

[1] The South German states were already in military alliance with Prussia and gave her effective help from the beginning of the war with France.

shadowed by their "brother" at Berlin. But the Grand Duke of Baden was strongly pro-Prussian, and at last King Louis of Bavaria (the most prominent ruler in the southern group) outwardly took the initiative.

This king was an eccentric man who spent his days in feuds with his ministers and family, largely because of his insistence upon squandering every *gröschen* of his income on extravagant and useless palaces. He was ultimately to be declared insane and to perish (1886) by drowning himself in the Starnberger Lake near his castle of Berg. In 1871 he was reputed to have hated Bismarck and the Prussians cordially, but circumstances were too much for him. He was finally induced to send to the other South German princes a letter suggesting union under Prussia, a letter which had undoubtedly been drafted by Bismarck himself. Rumor asserts on grounds not lightly to be dismissed that the opposition of King Louis was not withdrawn until the Bavarian court favorite, Count Holstein, came to Versailles, and left it not merely with Bismarck's letter, but also with a considerable sum of money for his royal master and himself.[1] Certain it is that the great chancellor was never squeamish as to his methods when it was a question of persuading non-Prussian statesmen to accept his views. Here again he set an example for less adroit successors to his power, suggesting certain strange ways utilized for influencing the government of the United States and other neutral organs of authority during the years 1914–17.

Bismarck had had the practical wisdom, when he induced the Southern states to come in, to grant special privileges within the new Empire to Bavaria and, to a less extent, Würtemberg. Bavaria was to keep the control of her army in peace-time, of her post and telegraphs, and much of her taxation. Nevertheless, in any case, the practical effect of the

---

[1] J. H. Rose, "The Development of European Nations," I, p. 155–6. This very responsible English historian wrote his statement in 1905, long before his own country and Germany were at war, or even dangerously unfriendly. Mr. Rose heartily admired many things about Bismarck's policy.

Bismarckian régime was to tie the remainder of Germany firmly and effectually to Prussia. The south German states were still to preserve local autonomy: they were still to hold at arm's length the immediate pressure of junkerdom: they were to enjoy state constitutions and popular rights which were (compared with Prussia) "liberal," but notwithstanding all this they were to contribute their economic and military strength to the glorification of the house of Hohenzollern, and to the advancement presently of the schemes of the Pan-Germans who (under the Hohenzollern aegis) were to bring about a world war in their efforts to dominate the planet. Therefore Bismarck could afford to be conciliatory. The "New Empire" of 1871 really meant the complete subordination of the remainder of Germany to the iron hand of Prussia. It was wise to case that hand in a velvet glove.

An ex-chancellor of Germany in 1913 commended Bismarck because when securing imperial unity "with incomparable audacity and constructive statesmanship . . . he left out of play the political capacities of the Germans, in which they had never excelled, while he called into action their fighting powers which have always been their strongest point." [1] In other words, it was to be arranged that all the Germans should be rendered available to fight the new Kaiser's battles, but they were not to have any large extension of political rights. For this end the constitution of the four-year-old North German Confederation was easily expanded a little, and its head given a prouder title. Sedan was merely completing the work of Sadowa.

From 1871 down to the outbreak of the Great War Germany was governed essentially upon the following system. The King of Prussia became ipso facto "German Emperor." [2] Since the offices of King and Emperor were inseparable and Prussia was an hereditary monarchy, the "Kaisership" was also hereditary. The Emperor could declare offensive war

[1] Von Bülow, "Imperial Germany," p. 12.

[2] Bismarck shunned the title of "Emperor of Germany" to avoid implying that the Prussian king exercised direct sovereign power over Bavaria and the other "touchy" lesser states.

only after consulting the "Federal Council," but *defensive* war he could declare on his own personal fiat. Since no modern government has ever admitted that any war it has had to wage was other than "defensive," the Emperor thus really held the supreme issues in his own hands. He controlled foreign affairs, and the army and navy. Under him was one arch-minister, the chancellor—his factotum and representative in everything, and holding office at the sole will of his imperial master, to whom he was "responsible" for the government of the Empire. There were lesser ministers of state, but they were really only the chancellor's high clerks and handy assistants. They were responsible to the chancellor only and not to any parliamentary body.

Under the Emperor was the *form* of a free legislature. The lower house of this parliament, the *Reichstag,* consisted of 397 members elected by pretty complete manhood suffrage. Bismarck was no lover of parliaments, but he understood the need of affecting to conciliate the liberal elements in his hour of triumph; he also understood the great value of a large "talking" body—to voice public opinion and to let off explosive ideas in a harmless manner:—in short of an imperial safety valve. He took ample precautions that the powers of the Reichstag should be so limited that it was not a great deal better than a pretentious official debating club, although in theory it had the right to amend the budget and originate laws.

The real governing body (and in truth Bismarck's masterpiece) was not the Reichstag, but the "Federal Council" (*Bundesrat*). Its functions were often executive and judicial as well as merely legislative. Its meetings were private. It initiated nearly all the legislation presented to the Reichstag, and its consent was needful to validate any bill the Reichstag might have managed to pass. The Bundesrat was, in short, the mainspring of the whole Bismarckian régime. It was not responsible to the people, nor elected by the people, but was a council of 61 members [1] *representing very strictly the princes*

[1] Originally only 58, but three were added for Alsace-Lorraine in 1911. These, however, practically were controlled by Prussia.

of Germany. Prussia had 17 of these votes, Bavaria six, some of the lesser states two, three or four, and fourteen of the lesser "sovereigns," like the starving little prince of Schaumberg-Lippe, had only one apiece, as did the three "free cities" (Hamburg, Bremen and Lübeck).

These 61 "Excellencies" in the Bundesrat were mere dummies, or perhaps it were more respectful to say instructed ambassadors for their royal, ducal, or princely masters, appointed and removed at the respective august pleasures of said masters. They were obliged to vote the way their rulers ordered, no matter what arguments might come up in debate. Since Prussia now supplied over 60 per cent. of both the area and the population of the Empire it seemed a gracious concession for her King to be content with only seventeen votes—fourteen less than a majority.[1] But the fact was that the Prussian government with its great influence could almost invariably win over by means of very small favors enough of the lesser princes to command a sure majority. With a little tact in the Bundesrat, Prussia could always have her way; and thus by means of this monarchic, non-parliamentary, *secret,* and utterly un-democratic Federal Council the King of Prussia could place an absolute veto on all legislation, could hem in the Reichstag, and, since the Bundesrat had large duties of administration and acted often as a court of high appeal, affect a great part of the official machinery throughout the land. The Bundesrat was content to exclude the public from its debates and leave the noisy Reichstag in the lime-light. None the less it was the mainspring of the whole Bismarckian régime.

The Reichstag undoubtedly served its prime end as "a debating club and a debating club that had no power of seeing its will carried out." It was indeed required to pass on appropriations, and upon new taxes and forms of proposed legislation. Usually for the sake of peace the chancellor

[1] Also it requires only 14 votes to defeat any change in the Federal Constitution, while changes in the army and navy laws and in the most important tax laws are specifically made subject to the *absolute* veto of the Kaiser.

would refrain from forcing upon it very unwelcome fiscal
proposals, and would allow minor amendments. But on great
serious issues the government did not hesitate to defy the
Reichstag, and by implied threats and official pressure compel
it to eat its words; and by dissolving it and seeking a new
election, it could always get a more subservient body. The
Reischtag knew that it was in the last analysis powerless.
Therefore, its members, being irresponsible and reckless—
split also into many groups and factions,—gave vent to crude
speeches, and generally acted as men will who are told to
criticize but not to act:—all of which confirmed the monarchists in the opinion that "Germans are not a political people."

Bismarck and all his successors repeatedly told the Reichstag the
chancellors were responsible to the Kaiser, not to it. Bismarck declared that the Reichstag could not even stop the payment of his salary,
—if it refused the vote he would merely go to law and collect it. Bethmann-Hollweg in a famous speech said bluntly, "Gentlemen, I do not
serve parliament"; and another time, referring to the ministerial responsibility existing in France, "I know full well that there are those
who are striving to establish similar institutions here. I shall oppose
them with all my force."

Later a very serious new grievance arose. Originally the districts for
members of the Reichstag had been distributed on the basis of one for
about every 100,000 inhabitants. As time advanced, and especially as
certain great cities grew and as rural districts declined, the districts
became exceedingly unequal. The government refused to allow a new
distribution,—it feared the increased votes that would come to the
Socialists in the Reichstag, thanks to the remarkable increase of the
city populations. The result was that about 1914 in conservative East
Prussia the average deputy represented about 24,000 voters. In Socialistic Berlin he represented about 125,000 voters. Every attempt to
remedy this glaring injustice was abruptly defeated.

In January, 1914, just on the eve of Armageddon, Friedrich Naumann, an intelligent and moderate liberal in the
Reichstag, uttered these bitter words, "The man who compared this house to a hall of echoes was not far wrong. . . .
When one asks the question, 'What part has the Reichstag
in German history as a whole?' it will be seen that the part
is a very limited one."

The Hohenzollerns and their devoted servants, therefore, between the powers of the imperial office direct and the grip Prussia had upon the Bundesrat, controlled the whole imperial government.

But of course under the Bismarckian system a very large part of the business of government was reserved for the different states:[1] and the welfare of all the 40,0000,000-odd Prussians in 1914 was quite as much affected by the doings of their Landtag as by the deliberations of the more pretentious imperial parliament.

If the Hohenzollern ministers had a firm grip on the central government, upon the affairs of Prussia they had a stranglehold. Prussia was governed, down to the Great War, by the sham constitution awarded by Frederick William IV in 1850, and every attempt to modify it essentially had failed. In fact, although the royal ministers themselves, rendered anxious by the popular clamor, had sometimes suggested liberalizing amendments, the noble "junkers" who controlled the majority in both houses had headed off every effort to weaken the old régime which served the aristocracy so well.

This constitution had been "granted" by the King, as if out of his loving favor. There was nothing to indicate that he might not withdraw or alter it at will. Popular sovereignty was nowhere admitted. The king gave, the king might take away; blessed be the name of the king! Statesmen and jurists were agreed that such might be the case.

The king of course had an absolute veto upon all laws. He named the Prussian ministers and dismissed them at his good pleasure. In the words of a famous legal commentator, "Everything which is decided or carried out in the state takes place in the name of the King. *He is the personified power of the state.*" (Schulze.) In short he could perform almost

[1] Roughly speaking the division of powers between the German states and the central government is somewhat the same as in the United States, although the imperial government can legislate on a wider range of matters than the American Congress. On the other hand, many more of the Federal laws are entrusted to enforcement by the local authorities than with us.

any conceivable act except where, by the constitution, he had tentatively agreed not to do it.[1]

The upper house of parliament (*Herrenhaus*—"House of Lords") was composed of princes, some very high nobles, and a large number of lesser nobles and magnates all appointed for life by the King. Needless to say, no man unwelcome to the royal government had this honor thrust upon him. If ever this body had ventured to defy the King, he could promptly swamp the hostile majority by creating new "lords." But such an amazing accident never happened, and the Herrenhaus was of course always the ardent champion of "the altar and the throne"—of the church and the government, each in its most conservative form.

However, there was a lower house (*Abgeordnetenhaus* —"House of Representatives") which gave a semblance of popular representation. No better system of confirming privileges, under a few of the forms of democracy, was ever presented than by this creation of the degenerating brain of Frederick William IV. The districts were, in the first place, allotted on a basis not really revised since 1860, with a few changes in 1906. Up to that time the great city of Berlin had returned only nine members, then it was graciously allowed to have twelve out of the total of 443.

[1] The terms which Prussian court etiquette and usage insisted should be used in addressing the Emperor-King indicate sufficiently the position he occupied in the minds of his loyal subjects. Non-Teutonic persons might have imagined them borrowed from the annals of Sennacherib, Xerxes, Harun-al-Raschid or other departed Oriental despots.

Thus, e. g., Von Arnim (a very distinguished Prussian nobleman) addressing a petition to William I, appealed to the "Most illustrious, very powerful Emperor and King, Gracious Emperor, King and Sovereign." Prince Henry of Prussia publicly addresses his brother William II "most august Emperor, most high and mighty King and Lord, illustrious brother," and then proceeds to thank him for his favor "out of his faithful, fraternal and most obedient heart."

A standing official term for the Emperor-King was "the All-Highest." In loyal circles frequently it was not proper to refer to the Emperor's actions directly: many things were spoken of as ordered or initiated "from Above." This did not imply an act of Divine Providence but of William I or II of Hohenzollern.

Furthermore, the system of voting was deliberately calculated to keep the masses of the people just as completely out of power as possible. The deputies were not chosen directly, but by means of "sub-district electors" who were themselves elected by the people, and next all the electors from the sub-districts, meeting in a common body to represent the larger "district," proceeded to choose the local worthy to go to the Landtag. This process of course gave the government a chance to bring much personal pressure on the very controllable groups of electors. But "pressure" was not very often needed. The original voters in every sub-district were carefully grouped into three classes—each choosing one-third of its "electors." This three-class system was the keystone of the Prussian edifice. In the first class were put the largest tax contributors, who paid one-third of the tax-quotas of the districts, in the second class the tax payers who contributed the second third of the taxes, in the third group all the rest of the "Kaiser und König's" loving subjects. The "electors" from these three groups were on terms of absolute equality in numbers and influence when they met to choose the district representative, and a bare majority of their electoral ballots always prevailed. Considering the extreme inequality in the distribution of wealth in Prussia the main result was predetermined from the first.

Shortly before 1914 there were 2,214 "sub-electoral-districts" in Prussia where one-third of the taxes were paid by *a single man,* who *therefore cast the entire vote* for the first-class electors in his entire precinct. There were 1,703 precincts where there were only *two* first-class voters, "high-born" gentlemen, usually in happy harmony. The voting was open. Every citizen had to announce his favorite candidate. If a peasant or workman voted for a radical condemned as "dangerous" by his landlord or employer the poor man had to take the possible consequences. Under those circumstances it is amazing that any considerable radical vote was polled at all. It profited little if a third-class voter took his economic life in his hands, however, and voted "for the Left" (i.e., against the Government). In 1907 this remarkable system saw about 3% of the electorate belonging to the first class, 9.5% to the second, 87.5% to the third—and *all three of precisely the same influence!* It was a cold strange day when the lordly "first-classer" could not find enough pliable or socially aspiring "second-classers" to join with him and give him the majority. In 1903 it was said that a total of only 324,000 votes actually elected 143 conservative representatives, while 314,000 Social Democrat votes did not yield the party a single member. In 1908 by a great effort the Social Democrats *did* elect seven members out of the 443. They had to cast about 24% of the total number of votes to accomplish this. Considering the fruits of this system and the method of balloting [1] there was grim humor in Bethmann-Hollweg's remarks in 1910, when he said, "We are opposed to secret balloting because . . . it favors the *terrorism* which Socialists exercise over the burgher-class voters!"

As a matter of fact, under this system many men felt it was useless to go to the polls. In 1903 only 23.6% of the total number of Prussian voters cast ballots in their *Landtag* election: but in that same year when there was a more genuine contest for the *Reichstag* about 75% voted:—a sufficient comment on the Prussian system.

This arrangement, of course, for two generations had awakened the wrath of a great part of Germany. Even Bismarck had damned it as "the most miserable and absurd election law that had ever been formulated in any country." The iron chancellor had been indeed no lover of popular liberty, but he had a keen sense of absurdities and understood how unwelcome agitators could be controlled by subtler methods. Every attempt, however, to remedy this system failed. The Prussian ministry, responsible for the contentment of the

[1] It is easy to heap up statistics which illustrate the gross injustice of this system of balloting. In 1908 there were in all Prussia 293,000, 1st class voters, 1,065,240, 2nd class and 6,324,000, 3rd class. In the rich city of Köln there were 370 1st class, 2,584 2nd class and 22,324, 3rd class. In Saärbrucken, Baron von Sturm, the only 1st class voter, blandly announced "that he did not suffer from isolation." In one of the iniquitously large Berlin districts, a worthy Herr Hefte, a manufacturer of sausages, covered the entire first-class vote with his own hat.

land and anxious to conciliate liberal opinion in South Germany, were not averse to certain concessions. Indeed sometimes they found the thick-headed opposition of the Conservatives to all kinds of reforms a great hindrance to the chief glory of the Hohenzollern régime—systematized efficiency. They had, however, created an engine they could not control. Several times, notably in 1910, there were great public demonstrations in Berlin and elsewhere, and even gatherings approaching riots to indicate popular wrath at the "three classes." The government repeatedly introduced measures calculated at least to throw a sop to the Cerberus of general discontent: but the Conservatives in the House of Representatives, aided sometimes by their allies in the House of Peers, voted down even the most innocent reforms. Prussia was still under the three-class system when the final earthquake shook Europe.

So in all the numerous matters reserved to the German states, the 40,000,000 people of Prussia were subject to a régime where a king, autocratic in practically every matter of administration, shared his legislative power with a parliament controlled by the worst kind of an aristocracy—an aristocracy based on wealth rather than merit. In most of the rest of Germany somewhat more liberal conditions prevailed. In Bavaria, Würtemberg and Baden there was equal male suffrage; in Saxony there was the secret ballot and *five* classes of voters, although here some of the extra privileges went to men of superior education or professional ability, and also to men aged over fifty. The great free-city of Hamburg had a House of Burgesses in choosing which the wealthy and highly placed had special privileges; while the wretched little principality of Lippe imitated mighty Prussia with a three-class system.

Government in the smaller principalities was of course often paternal and very personal, irrespective of the forms of the local constitution. In the Mecklenburgs there was no constitution at all,—only a survival of a mediaeval system of privileged "estates."

The ruler of a small principality was not likely to be a grim warlord, but an urbane, kindly gentleman, who walked out in the park of his little "residence-city," bowed politely to the courtesying women he met, and stopped to pat the heads of their smiling children. If he offended public sentiment he did not have to wait for a protest from his parliament to teach him his error. Some years ago His Grand Ducal Highness of Saxe-Weimar-Eisenach, having become a widower, visited at Eisenach the grave of his late wife, on the anniversary of her death. He went to the grave in an automobile (then rather uncommon in Germany) and not in a horse-drawn carriage. This unconventionality and insult to the departed shook the principality, and produced spontaneously "such respectful but emphatic protests" from all ages, classes and sexes of his subjects that His Highness promised not to offend against the proprieties again.—All of which goes to illustrate that the spirit of Prussia is not always the true spirit of the whole of Germany!

However, the hand of Prussian junkers affected even the liberal South Germans in a sinister way. Besides the fact that his own Prussian aristocrats were likely to have more influence on the Emperor than Bavarians or Badeners, the imperial chancellor was also minister-president—head of the state cabinet—of Prussia. He must govern the empire and the great kingdom simultaneously. In the Empire he might indeed control the Bundesrat through the great influence of the Prussian crown; he could divide the factions of the Reichstag and defy them; but in Prussia he had to reckon with the solid and perpetual conservative majority in both houses of parliament. The Conservatives exercised the prerogatives of loyal friends of the crown;—they were more royal than the Emperor-King. As a mocking epigram said, *"They wished for an absolute Kaiser, if he would do only the things they wanted."* They knew perfectly well that the government could not defy them—otherwise it would be driven into the arms of the hated liberals. The junkers provided the heads of the great civil bureaucracy, the diplomatic service, and above all nearly the whole officers' corps in the army. In the last analysis they had the Hohenzollerns at their mercy. Therefore an imperial chancellor always faced this peril; if he advocated any quasi-liberal measures in the *imperial* government the Conservatives were furious. They did not have a majority in the Reichstag nor in the Bundesrat; [1] but they

[1] The votes of Prussia in the Bundesrat would be of course cast the way the King of Prussia personally directed.

could trade out their spleen in retaliation by making life miserable for the minister-president (alias chancellor) in both houses of the *Prussian* parliament which they absolutely controlled. A Hohenzollern chief minister therefore was obliged to walk a conservative path in the Reichstag, lest he come utterly to grief in the decidedly important Landtag. Thus the three-class system really placed the grip of the wealthy and "well-born" upon the entire nation.

This undemocratic Prussian government between 1871 and 1914 was to exhibit almost uncanny efficiency—else it could never have strengthened its grasp upon the Empire and reached out a giant hand for the mastery of the world. Under the system of districting, the majority of the Prussian Landtag was elected from the level agricultural lands east of the Elbe, and there converging on Poland lay the strongholds of the mighty Junkers and the original seats of their old masters the Hohenzollerns. The junkers (i.e., "young lords"—squires) had the virtues of a country aristocracy— they were brave, hard-hitting, with a keen sense of personal honor, an extreme devotion to duty as they saw it, and an intense loyalty to their king. They were (as a class) honorably exempt from the more sordid forms of the pursuit of money. They were devout Lutherans after a very conservative type of theology. They had also an intense caste pride, despising alike the professional classes, the merchants of the towns and the artisans of the factories no less than the tow-headed peasants who were still (despite the laws formally conferring personal "freedom") not very much better than serfs upon the great estates.

A typical junker was the owner of a great landed property with a picturesque and uncomfortable ancient *schloss* for his residence, dominating a village or two where peasant children scrambled with the pigs and the chickens in the great dung-heaps before the doors of the houses. He might indeed come to enjoy city life, the excitements of a visit to Berlin and such modern luxuries as his means would afford. He might improve his agricultural methods and be glad to invest his surplus income in factories (genteelly conducted indirectly, through a manager) or to dabble in foreign investments. None the less he remained heart and soul a *country* aristocrat, with all the prejudices of a squierarchy;—accustomed to curse his inferiors, to cane his servants, to despise all who lived by "trade" and to bend only to the King.

The eldest son of such a "junker" would of course ordinarily be the heir to the *schloss;* but the rights of primogeniture were not as strict in Prussia as in England, and all the sons of a nobleman wore the "von" (the prefix of nobility) or the countly or baronial title. Only by exception would they look forward to any kind of productive career other than the always gentlemanly task of the remote over-sight of farm-labor. Some would enter the Emperor-King's civil service, some would be his diplomats, but the career par excellence for a Prussian squire was the army. To enter a military school, to struggle through the "glittering misery" of the rank of sub-lieutenant, by hard and faithful work to win approval and rise to the higher grades of the army; to reinforce one's income by marriage with the daughter of a wealthy "merchant," whose *mit-gift* (dowry) would offset her lack of pedigree, and to end up as an "Excellenz"—the lieutenant-general of an army corps, that was the career through which many young Prussians, "poor but noble," elected to struggle. The army and the landed aristocracy never lost touch; and they were both absolutely essential to the crown. They literally made the Hohenzollern régime possible, and the "All-highest" was never allowed to forget the fact.

The pay of Prussian junior rank officers was pitifully small. A second lieutenant was paid about $367 annually against $1,700 in the United States army. How to "live like a man of honor" upon that sum has been a problem to very many young officers whose families could not give them a large allowance. But the practice of giving the social preëminence to the military, made it often easy for an officer to marry the daughter of some rich burgher who would feel flattered to have a member of the ruling class for his son-in-law. Before a young officer married, he had to submit the qualifications of the bride to the scrutiny of a committee of his senior officers to see whether the young lady were acceptable personally in military circles, and also whether her dowry or allowance would make her husband able to maintain a proper establishment.   Once married the wife of a sub-lieutenant would have the social entrée ahead of her mother, who might be the wife of a wealthy captain of industry or banker, a world-renowned university professor, or a scientist credited with epoch-making discoveries.

This *payment by means of social honor* instead of by salaries was of course part of the efficient Prussian system of getting the greatest possible results for the minimum public expenditure.   It helped to enable the Hohenzollerns to keep up a huge army on a relatively small military budget.

The Prussian aristocracy therefore had many virtues and many marked limitations.   Its members desired to see Germany powerful, expanding and (in a material way) progressive.   They were not opposed to exploiting all the fruits of modern natural science.   Like the eighteenth century enlightened despots they were abounding in good will towards the less favored population committed to their charge.   They took their duties very seriously, and they were never idle or venal. They were also able to inspire the great mass of their subordinates—drill sergeants, police officers, tax-collectors, public inspectors, etc.—with a profound sense of loyalty and zeal for executing their system.

The German people, naturally law-abiding and cheerful under reasonable authority, were not irked by such rulers (the masses indeed having always been without considerable "rights") except where the arm of the government became especially heavy.   It has been alleged that the Prussian aristocracy, arising in the extreme east of Germany, was really more Polish and Wendish than Teutonic in its ancestry; but its whole spirit fell in well indeed with the German tendency to analyze, systematize and regulate all things down to the minutest detail.   The Prussian régime being essentially military, the military spirit was carried out into the civilian population by a system of minute police commands and prohibitions such as was unknown in any other clime or age.[1]   The cult of the infallibility of the government became a prime element

[1] The obedience of the civilian population was of course expedited by the fact that the greater part of the German youth passed years of their life under a compulsory military system, where they were subjected to a

in secular education and religion. The elaborate school system was carefully adjusted to make every lesson in history a lesson in loyalty to the house of Hohenzollern; and, as has been seen, the Lutheran church was a bulwark of the throne.

The zealous government, through its hierarchy of officials, provided for the regulation of its subjects from the cradle to the grave. The park benches of a Prussian city were carefully labeled with the classes and sexes of the public entitled to sit on each bench. The hours for piano playing were subject to police control: also the number of pedestrians that might walk abreast on the city streets. The size of the beer-mug, the sidewalks permissible for an infant's perambulator, the location of flower pots on a window sill, these are random matters which a paternal government regulated for its people. Most of the regulations were indeed theoretically wise, but the Prussian genius never grasped the fact that nine-tenths of them were superfluous and tended to make their victims automata rather than responsible men.[1]

Had this absolutely inquisitorial and military régime been senseless and inefficient it would have spelled its own ruin. On the contrary, it was directed by men who were within their limitations intelligent, patriotic, self-sacrificing and if anything far too logical. Autocracy and privilege, on the defensive everywhere else in the world, half-consciously were trying in Prussianized Germany to show how much greater happiness and success they could bring to their nation than the easy-going, blundering, semi-efficient and sometimes even corrupt and non-progressive liberalism of England, France, America and other lands. The alliance between the Hohenzollern dynasty and the military aristocracy was absolute. The military caste hated the thought that the monarch should choose his ministers at the behest of a popularly made parlia-

decidedly more severe discipline and taught a far more abject subservience to their officers than in any other West European army. It was quite easy to transfer their habits of implicit military obedience to civil life.

[1] See note at end of chapter.

ment. This was not from any fine-spun political theory, but because the Hohenzollerns could not have two masters, the officers and the people. "The dearest wish of every Prussian," said Bethmann-Hollweg, in January, 1914, "is to see the King's army completely under the control of the King, and not becoming the army of the parliament." A little earlier a typical junker, Herr von Oldenburg, had stated this view of the case even more bluntly on the floor of the Imperial Diet itself. "The Kaiser should be in a position to say at any moment to a lieutenant: *Take ten men and shut up the Reichstag!*"

After 1871 this spirit of Prussian junkerdom was to enter into closer alliance with the monarchy than ever before and to hold back the rising wave of liberalism by giving the German nation almost everything a proud people could desire save only political liberty. The German folk were to enjoy the memories of a victorious past, the satisfaction of a prosperous present, and before them was to be dangled the hope of a yet more golden future. Thereby all but a minority were to be drugged. It was even as Harden, the noted journalist, said: *"In order to be strong, Germany has rejected the great modern comfort of democracy."* [1]

So long as this alliance of modern material progress and medieval political privilege was to affect only Germany, the rest of mankind could simply look on in bewilderment: at length came the time when it was to affect the whole world. [1]

AN EXAMPLE OF PRUSSIAN THOROUGHNESS

The following story, illustrative of the intense scrutiny of minutiae prevalent among Prussian officialdom, came directly to the author while in Germany, and he believes it to be quite true.

In Breslau, Silesia, there is a government hospital, likewise an arsenal. Some time ago both institutions were asked to send to Berlin a detailed inventory of the public property in each, also an estimate for its upkeep during the ensuing year. Each institution dutifully reported in its inventory "one cat," and the hospital also reported a request for 20 pfennigs per day for "milk and meat for said cat." The

---

[1] It was complained that although men of non-noble birth sometimes got into the lower grades of the Prussian officers, very few ever were promoted to high command.

arsenal made no such request. Presently the director of each establishment received an official envelope from Berlin requesting an answer to the following dilemma:—"Why did the hospital require upkeep money for its cat, while the arsenal made no corresponding requisition? Was the hospital wasting the 'Kaiser und König's' funds? Or was the arsenal failing to feed its cat properly and therefore allowing the public livestock to deteriorate?"

The two "highly well-born" directors held a meeting and framed a respectful answer. They explained that in the hospital the supply of mice, rats, etc., was so small, a maintenance fund for the cat was absolutely necessary; in the arsenal, however, the local cat enjoyed such opportunities for private foraging that there was no need of a demand on His Majesty's treasury. This explanation proved satisfactory in Berlin and the papers in the case were peacefully filed.

As another somewhat dissimilar instance of the zeal for excessive regulation characteristic of the new German régime, may be noticed the usage in various cities, notably Leipzig (Saxon indeed, but under Prussian influence), of posting in each trolley-car the cost to a passenger should he break one of the windows, the expense varying according to the size of the glass. It was alleged that students would sometimes compute the cost of thus smashing up the entire car, make up the necessary purse, and then proceed to execute their learned project; when the process was finished paying over the required sum to the grinning official with perfect good humor on both sides.

CHAPTER X

BETWEEN 1871 and 1914 the newly created German Empire enjoyed a material and economic expansion which astonished the world. Only the United States of America seemed growing faster in population, wealth and prosperity; and in some respects German expansion (based as it was on an exhausted, limited soil) surpassed that of the Western Republic with its virgin continent and enormous area. Great as were the Prussian military achievements in 1866 and 1870 they seemed less startling than the Prussian economic achievements in the next generation.

Statistics are often repellent impersonal things, but they can tell a long and significant story in a very few words. In 1871 the population of the German Empire had been barely 41,000,000. In 1890 it was 49,400,000. In 1900 it was 56,360,000. In 1913 it was estimated at the very least at 66,000,000. The Empire, in other words, was increasing more rapidly than any other country in Europe save prolific but backward Russia. This great increase in population, however, was being met by such industrial expansion, such opportunities for gainful employment that Germans were not constrained in great numbers to emigrate beyond seas. After the disappointments of 1848, tens of thousands of virile Germans had come to America, partly for political reasons, but a greater number had emigrated solely to better their personal fortunes. This emigration had not ceased in 1871. Between e.g. 1880 and 1892 no less than 1,700,000 children of the Fatherland departed from their native soil for the United States alone. Others went in large numbers to Brazil, Argentina and Canada. But this was before the new imperial régime had caught its full stride. As the opportunities for successful industry increased at home, the stream of emigration sank to a mere trickle. In 1905 only about 28,000 Germans quitted the Empire for good,—26,000 of them for the United States. Just before the great war the numbers were even less (25,800 in all in 1913). These figures are eloquent witnesses to two important facts: I. The domestic prosperity of Germany had become so great that as a rule only the "black sheep," and the chronically unsuccessful were anxious to emigrate; II. There was little justification for the demand for great colonies to absorb the surplus population and keep it still under the Kaiser's banner—because, in fact, there was no surplus population to send away.

Until rather shortly before the unification of the nation by Bismarck, Germany had ranked as a decidedly poor land mainly given to agriculture. Her wealth could not compare with that of England, France, or (considering respective sizes) Belgium and Holland. Amsterdam was for a long time a much more important financial center than Berlin.

In 1842 a German professor discussing the rise of socialism in other countries declared that Germany had nothing to fear from such a movement, because the country was so completely given over to agriculture that it did not possess any regular artisan industrial class. Between his time, however, and 1871 a great deal had been accomplished. Railways were built, many kinds of manufactures were initiated, and a class of city toilers, as against mere peasants, had developed. The greatest change, however, was to take place during the forty years after the victory over France. The great war indemnity ($1,000,000,000) was indeed a very doubtful benefit to some of the conquerors. It supplied the German financiers with a capital larger than they were prepared for and so opened the door to an era of reckless speculation, stock-jobbing and downright rascality which had its natural climax in a great business panic in the seventies. Nevertheless the indemnity *did* provide the German nation with enough capital and credit to get itself industrially and economically fully upon its feet.

What followed can again best be summed up in figures. In 1882 the number of Germans kept busy by manufactures

and commerce was about 20,000,000. In 1910 it was 35,000,-
000. In 1885 less than 4,000,000 tons of pig iron were smelted
in Germany; in 1913 about 15,000,000. In 1891, 73,000,000
tons of coal sufficed for the nation; in 1913, 185,000,000 tons
were needed and supplied; and to complete the story as late
as 1890 the export trade of Germany was worth only about
$875,000,000. In 1913 it was quite $2,500,000,000. In short,
the Empire founded by Bismarck was second in its manufactures only to Great Britain, "the workshop of the world."
German technical skill, coupled with admirable methods of
seeking trade, advancing credits and retaining the good will
of foreign customers, the cheapness and usually the utility
of German manufactures of every kind, the adroitness with
which the imperial government used its great diplomatic influence to back up its merchant and commercial travelers:—
these combined factors accounted for most of the triumph.
The demands of the manufacturer of course implied a corresponding exploitation of the nation's coal and iron mines,
natural advantages with which Germany is almost as much
favored as England. The great commerce also implied the
development of a correspondingly great merchant marine.
Unlike the United States, which was endeavoring to build up
a world trade carried almost exclusively on foreign bottoms,
the statesmen of the Empire regarded the German merchant
ship as the indispensable ally of the German merchant. Some
steamship lines were subsidized outright; others received less
direct but nevertheless very genuine official encouragement.
It was commonly reported that the imperial family had invested much of its private fortunes in the Hamburg-American
and the North German Lloyd companies, the two greatest
steamship corporations in the world.[1] In 1871 the German
merchant marine had been insignificant; in 1913 it was the
second greatest on the planet and was giving its British rival
sore anxiety as regards supremacy in the carrying trade.

[1] Herr Ballin, the head of the Hamburg-American Line, was so intimate with William II that he was frequently called, after the medieval
usage, the "Emperor's Jew"—i.e., official money-lender—by captious
German Anti-Semites.

Naturally, since the extent of German arable land was fixed by the boundary stones, there had been no corresponding expansion in the nation's agriculture. The great landed interests of Prussia, however, insisted on wringing every possible favor out of the government, and they were never frankly abandoned (as in free trade England) to the competition of American, Argentinian and Australian wheat. But it seemed impossible for Germany to feed herself completely. She had to import about 4,500,000 tons of cereals per year to cover her home deficiencies. This did not seem to be a serious danger, however. The Empire was not on an island. If she were at war with Russia (a great wheat country) she could still import from overseas. If she were blockaded by the naval might of England she could still draw abundant supplies from Russia. That Russia and England would *both* unite in warfare against Germany, seemed in view of the diplomatic situation, grossly improbable—at least until a very few years before Armageddon.

Everywhere in the Empire the cities grew by leaps and bounds—even as in the American Western States. In 1870 Hamburg possessed barely 350,000 inhabitants; in 1910 nearly 1,000,000. In 1870 Berlin boasted only 820,000; in 1910 over 2,000,000. As for the expansion of such "iron" towns as Essen, the seat of the famous Krupp works, it had been simply phenomenal. From about 50,000 in 1870, it had swollen to about 300,000 on the eve of the great war. Such were the outward evidences, to be read by all men, of the mighty change that had come over the most powerful nation in Europe.

It was inevitable that a physical transformation as complete and dramatic as this should be followed by a more subtle, but none the less significant, *change in the whole mood and temper of the German people.* In the ages before Bismarck the nation certainly had suffered grievously from an excess of what might be called "other-worldliness." In the 18th century an ill-natured Frenchman, Voltaire, had said that France had elected to rule the land, England the sea, and Germany the clouds. There was a germ of truth in this un-

fair sarcasm. For example, the supreme national hero for
two-thirds of Germany was not a general, a law-giver, or even
a poet, but a theologian—Martin Luther. The Fatherland
had produced many giants in learning, letters and art, but
almost none of them, save the philosopher Kant,[1] had come
from the original provinces of Prussia. Lessing. Fichte, Luther and Wagner were Saxons, Holbein and Dürer Bavarians,
Goethe from Frankfort, Wieland, Schiller and Hegel were
Swabians, Beethoven a Rhinelander and Bach a Thuringian.
Prussia and its spirit had therefore never been the guide of
Germany in matters intellectual.

The average Teuton of the age preceding Bismarck con-
trasted absolutely in temper, ambitions and methods with his
hard, efficient, practical grandsons of 1914 and their intense
pursuit of the material forms of success. Germans themselves, writing shortly before the great war, stated this change
very frankly. Said one (Fuchs), "The German of a hundred years ago was poor, despised, ridiculed and defrauded.
He was the uncomplaining slave of others: his fields were
their battle ground, and the goods which he had inherited
from his fathers were trodden under foot and dispersed. He
shed his blood heroically without asking why. He never troubled when the riches of the outside world were divided without regard to him. [Nevertheless] as he sat in his little bare
room high under the roof, in simple coat and clumsy shoes,
his heart was full of sweet dreams and uplifted by the chords
of Beethoven to a rapture which threatened to rend his breast.
. . . The happiness of his longing consumed him, and as he
listened to Schubert's song his soul became one with the soul
of the universe."

Professor Rein of Jena University wrote bluntly, "Have we
Germans kept a harmonious balance between the economic
and moral side of our development? . . . Not so: . . . in the
nation as in the individual we see with the increase of wealth
the decrease of moral power."

Other candid students of the nation's tendencies deplored
the growing unwillingness to keep up the old German inter-

[1] He was, it is worth noting, of Scottish ancestry.

est in philosophy and all other non-utilitarian sciences and the demonstrable fact that the nation of "poets and thinkers" was becoming a nation of soldiers, factory magnates and commercial adventurers. Doubtless Germany had lived in the clouds too long; a reasonable return to Mother Earth was very desirable; but what took place under the new Empire was not so much a reaction as a revolution: a revolution that was to affect the entire world.

But whatever the criticisms, the new régime in Germany certainly produced an astonishing outward success. For the first time since the Middle Ages the Teutonic genius for practical achievement was to get full scope for its energies. The nation seemed politically united if not politically free; its rulers might be autocrats but they committed none of the clumsy blunders of traditional despotism. School, church, factory, army, diplomatic service, university—all were articulated in the great disciplined Prussian machine working together to make the Fatherland rich and glorious. The reward came naturally as the result of the effort. In 1914 not merely was Prussianized Germany leading all the nations in very many forms of cultural and economic achievement, she was making open-minded foreign students doubt whether (in view of the relative success of the two systems) the democracies of England, France and America were all that was claimed for them. Democracy was on the defensive and on trial all over the world in 1914—and Prussia seemed the real prosecutor at the bar.

Nevertheless, public life in the strengthened Fatherland had been by no means entirely overshadowed by economic activity between 1871 and 1914. It ran in its own peculiar channels; it certainly avoided those bewildering changes which mark the annals of countries ruled by parliamentary or popular majorities. The Prussian theory required that the government should be "above all parties," listening to their complaints and suggestions with paternal indulgence, but reserving the final decision for its own wisdom. A "government," however, is after all a human institution. Between 1871 and 1914 it may be fairly said that two men successively constituted the disposing force in the "government" of Germany: from 1871 to 1890 Otto von Bismarck; from 1890 to 1914 William II of Hohenzollern. To trace the deeds and policies of the twain is to trace the history of the Empire.

William I of course was the Emperor and King down to his death in 1888. He was a kindly moderate man of limited talent and vision, and an understanding almost entirely confined to things military. But he was a man of keen personal honor, genuinely religious and anxious for the best good of his people—as he comprehended it,—and he had two enormous assets:—he was entirely conscious of his own lack of genius, and he was able to select certain very great ministers—Bismarck, Moltke, and Roon—to hold them in office despite popular clamor, to grant them a free rein for their policies, and to give them honest moral support in all they decided to do. As Bismarck said of him, "When anything of importance was going on, he usually began by taking the wrong road: but in the end he always allowed himself to be put straight again." This willingness to hearken to and to support good counsel brought him a magnificent reward. The reign of this plain unassuming soldier ended amid a galaxy of glory; as "Kaiser Wilhelm de Grosse" he passed into official history, being thus put on the level of Alexander and Charlemagne by his enthusiastic grandson.[1]

Between Bismarck and his Emperor the relations were of the uttermost friendship; not merely those of sovereign and minister. Several times the two men did not see eye to eye: then the chancellor would coerce the monarch by suggesting that he had better resign. "Never!" was always the emphatic answer; and the monarch gracefully yielded and all went on as before. So long as William I lived, any displacement of Bismarck was inconceivable. He was virtually the dictator of Germany, and undoubtedly the most potent man in all Europe.

Bismarck and his sovereign were alike persons of moderation who did not let a great victory turn their heads. The

[1] A more just title for "William the Great" would have been "William the Victorious."

chancellor, more fortunate than his contemporaries Cavour and Lincoln, who died in the hour of their triumphs, had the great privilege of living twenty-seven years after the unification of Germany, and of seeing his creation grow from strength to strength. He looked on Germany as a "satiated state." It needed no new European conquests. He was not even enthusiastic about acquiring foreign colonies. He saw no requirement for a great navy. In the nineteen years during which he remained Chancellor after 1871 his main effort, therefore, was to preserve peace and to promote internal prosperity. He accomplished the former by creating the Triple Alliance, the formation of which is described elsewhere (p. 318. He promoted internal prosperity and public stability by a series of social and economic measures, mostly adroit but some merely repressive, of which many details have no place in this story.

In 1873 Bismarck came to loggerheads with the Catholic Church over the question of the right of the government to control education. The contest was a bitter one, because the chancellor had set his heart on making all the clergy of Germany, Protestant and Catholic, the convenient agents of the state. Catholic priests were not to be allowed to exercise their functions in Prussia, unless they had spent three years in a university under government control, and had received a government certificate. Priests and bishops who did not fall in with this program were subject to suspension from office and even to fines and imprisonment. Of course the Catholic clergy resisted with all the power at their disposal, and the Pope encouraged them. In this "Kultur-Kampf" ("War in defense of Civilization") Bismarck persisted until 1878, when he found the rise of the socialists much more dangerous than the Catholics; then he gradually withdrew most of the obnoxious laws and made a friendly treaty with the Vatican. The net result of the struggle was, however, not advantageous to Bismarck. In self-defense the Catholics had formed a solid political party, the so-called "Center" (Centrum). This soon had many seats in the Reichstag and did not dissolve when the Kultur-Kampf was over. The Centrum was to remain a great factor in the Reichstag down to 1914, oscillating now to the Conservatives, now to the Liberals, and always demanding a high price for supporting the government on critical measures. Bismarck's first contest in the new Empire consequently was hardly fortunate.

He did not prosper much better in his second contest. The socialists were coming rapidly to the front, now that Germany was industrializing itself. Karl Marx (1818–1883) had begun to publish in 1867 his great work *Das Kapital* ("Capital"), sometimes styled "the working man's Bible." The socialist movement was taking a definite form in Germany, and showing itself as a formidable political agitation. The socialists were of course ultra-radicals. They wished not merely a liberal political régime but an economic revolution. They were outspoken in their hopes for a republic in place of Hohenzollernism. Bismarck undertook to fight them the instant their propaganda seemed serious. Two unsuccessful attempts to murder William I, which the chancellor imputed, probably unjustly, to socialistic conspiracies, enabled him to carry an extremely severe law in 1878, prohibiting publications, meetings and associations having for their purpose "the subversion of the social order," and authorizing the government to proclaim martial law in any city threatened with labor disturbances. These laws were to have effect for twelve years, and the zealous German police understood excellently how to enforce them. The movement, however, though driven into hiding, was not checked. Secret societies and papers smuggled in from Switzerland continued to spread the obnoxious doctrines. There was an increased socialist vote at each election.

Bismarck's attack on the socialists was not, however, purely negative. He undertook to pass a number of measures to improve the lot of the working classes, frankly confessing that he was throwing a sop to the proletariat to make them contented with the Prussian régime. "Give the workingman the right to work as long as he is healthy," he said in 1884, "assure him care when he is sick and maintenance when he is old . . . *then* if the State will show a little more Christian solicitude for the workingman, the socialists will sing their song in vain.''

In 1885 laws for accident and sickness insurance for the industrial classes were put into effect. In 1889 there followed a law for insurance for the aged and the incapacitated. These laws were much discussed in England and America, and considered worthy of partial imitation. They undoubtedly wrought considerable good in Germany. A portion of the expense for the pensions was paid by the employers of the laborers, and part also by the state—but a very large fraction had to be deducted from the wages of the laboring man himself. There was much complaint at the enforced contribution by many who could not hope (for various reasons) to enjoy the final benefit. Many fraudulent cases of disablement and sickness were reported, and investigators claimed that the responsibility and initiative of many workingmen were stunted. The chief complaint, however, was that this insurance legislation appeared in every case as a benefaction from ''above,'' not as a gain for the brotherhood of men. The laws were not a decided failure, but the workingmen were dissatisfied and were not turned away from socialism.

Bismarck was more successful with his protective tariff. Before 1879 Germany had been partially on a low tariff basis. In that year the chancellor frankly espoused protection and put through a high tariff bill. The theoretical question of free trade vs. protection need not be discussed here; but it is fair to say that Bismarck's high tariff gave a favorable impulse to German industries then just getting on their feet, and helped to keep alive native agriculture struggling against American and Russian wheat. The manufacturers and the great landed proprietors of Germany were ready for years, therefore, to rise up before the chancellor and call him blessed.

Bismarck saw another thing accomplished in the 1880's —albeit without enthusiasm on his part. There were strong commercial impulses in Germany calling for the acquisition of colonies, and the possession of a chain of colonies around the world, after the fashion of those of England, France or little Holland, would certainly flatter the pride of the people of the strongest monarchy of Europe. Unfortunately, however, Germany had come on the field as a great power very late. There were not many unclaimed and sparsely populated or barbarous lands available. India was preëmpted; as also of course was Australia. South America was under the aegis of the Monroe Doctrine and much of Africa was already divided. However, public pressure forced Bismarck to accede to the demands that certain "claims" established in Africa and Oceania by German private merchants and adventurers be transformed into downright annexations as colonies. In this way in Africa Germany acquired Togoland, Kamerun, German Southwest Africa and German East Africa,—dominions great in extent, but for the most part roaring wildernesses or jungles and by no means equal to the African holdings of England, France or even to the new Congo Free State under Belgian protection. In the Pacific, too, German traders were allowed to hoist the Kaiser's flag over parts of New Guinea and the adjacent "Solomon" isles and to establish a claim to Samoa which was ultimately settled (after grievous friction with America) by a division of that small archipelego between Germany and the United States.[1]

These were significant things for Bismarck's home administration, but of course they lacked the dramatic interest of the days between 1862 and 1871 when he first fought the Prussian Liberals in behalf of the royal prerogative, and then "made Germany" by the three scientifically provoked wars of 1864, 1866 and 1870. In truth, Bismarck was greater as a diplomat than as a civil statesman. The secluded office where, around the table-head, a few diplomats could meet— and where he, by a marvelous mingling of cajollery, flattery, brusqueness, blunt threatening and insinuating suggestions, could induce them to put their signatures upon some secret treaty which was to settle the fate of empires—*that* was his true kingdom. In him (as has already been said) the old style diplomacy found its incarnate genius.

So long as William I, his bosom friend, sat on the throne, Bismarck's position was inviolable. He seemed one of the

[1] For a table of the German colonies in 1914 see appendix to volume.

fixtures of Europe and an indispensable prop of the Hohenzollerns. By his system of alliances (see p. 318) he had isolated France and made it impossible for her to execute schemes
for "revenge," he had assured himself of the good will of
Russia, he had also maintained official cordiality with England and he had almost convinced the world that the enormous
German army was—as he always proclaimed it—an engine
solely to ensure peace. In March, 1888, however, the Emperor-King, a hoary veteran of ninety-one, slept with his fathers. His character, military, but kindly and unpretending,
has already been described. In his death Bismarck lost not
merely his grateful sovereign but his best personal friend.

William I was succeeded by his son Frederick III, who
had married Victoria, Princess Royal of England and eldest
daughter of Victoria the great queen. He had been on bad
terms with Bismarck earlier, but for long they had been reconciled. Frederick, however, did not share the political views
of his father. There is no reason for presuming that he would
have proved a radical or a democrat, but he undoubtedly
stood for a much more liberal parliamentary régime in Germany than had existed. Had fortune given him a twenty-
year reign, he might well have so changed the institutions
of the Empire that the catastrophe of 1914 would never have
been possible; but the fate which let Julius Cæsar be stricken
down just as he was about to reform the world was unfriendly
to this monarch also. Fell disease was upon him when his
father died. He was proclaimed Emperor on March 9th,
1888. Already there had been a major operation for a malignant growth in his throat. The case was hopeless. Frederick could hardly take up the reins of power. He lived
long enough to hold a few sorrowful reviews of his guard.
"Hail, soldiers:—I about to die salute you!"—is the old
Roman gladiatorial chant the dying Cæsar is said to have uttered to his troops. One or two ultra-bureaucratic ministers
were dismissed by his orders. Then on June 15th this ninety-
six-day reign ended. There was great grief in Germany.
The liberals had expected great things when Frederick came
to the throne: he was a man of sufficient force and kindliness

to have handled Bismarck with discretion and to have introduced reasonable changes.

For the second time in one year the army of Prussia took oath to a new "Kaiser und König." William I had died a very old man. Frederick III also was not youthful; but now the imperial power passed to a young man of twenty-nine years, with all the temper, ardor and restless enthusiasm of the new, aggressive and materialistic Hohenzollern régime. William II had been brought up to reverence the abilities of Bismarck, but the two men were of such temperaments that it was impossible for the one to wait until death should remove the great minister to whom he owed his imperial crown; or for the other to efface himself before the imperious young master so unlike his kindly grandfather.[1] During 1889, while William II was getting into the saddle, there was no outward break, but the great chancellor found that his power was being undermined and that the Emperor was open to other advisers. Then followed friction about the question of renewing the laws against the socialists, and the final catastrophe came over the issue of maintaining the regular usage that the Prussian ministers should report directly to the Chancellor (as Minister-President of Prussia) and not to the Emperor-King. William II was determined to take into his own hands all the control of the Prussian departments and so to strip the Chancellor of half of his powers. In March, 1890, there was a famous interview in Berlin at the imperial *Schloss*. The Emperor explained his intention of making the change. The Chancellor objected. The Emperor was insistent that his will must be carried out, "if not by Bismarck, then by another." Flint struck steel: *"Then I am to understand, your Majesty,"* spoke the man who had saved Hohenzollernism [2] and made the German Empire, *"that I am in your way?"* *"Yes!"* came the firm retort of the young man before him.

[1] William II in abundant speeches lauded and even deified the character of "his sainted grandfather," but he never imitated his qualities of modesty, self-distrust and gratitude.

[2] Considering the impetus to Liberalism in Prussia between 1859 and 1866, any missteps or faltering of Bismarck as minister then would have undoubtedly ruined the whole Hohenzollern dynasty.

Bismarck bowed his head, took prompt leave, and departed to his residence where he drew up a letter of resignation. He wished to take pains with the document and did not hurry it to the palace as the Emperor wished. William sent verbally, urging its prompt despatch. It came not, and the next morning the Emperor drove out in haste and caused Bismarck to be aroused from bed to meet his angry sovereign. William had heard that Windthorst (a politician he detested) had lately called upon Bismarck. He now told the chancellor he did not wish his ministers to meet parliamentary leaders without his permission. Bismarck denied that there had been any political discussion, and said he could not allow any supervision over the guests he invited to his own house.

"Not if I order it as your sovereign?" demanded the kaiser.

"No," spoke back the seventy-four-year-old man who had given his visitor everything. "The commands of my King cease in my wife's drawing-room."

After that no reconciliation was possible. The resignation of the chancellor produced an enormous sensation, and won the Emperor for the nonce great unpopularity. In vain William showered all manner of titles and decorations on the man he had declared superfluous. "The dog's kick-out" Bismarck angrily called them, likening his new title of "Duke of Lauenburg" (which he would not accept) to the boot-thrust with which the Prussian squires were wont to repel the too eager attentions of devoted hounds.[1]

---

[1] Bismarck retired to his residence at Friedrichsruh, where for some years he was visited by admiring delegations from all parts of Germany. His relations with the court were such that, had he been any lesser man, probably William II would have prosecuted him. A Hamburg newspaper became the regular organ for his bitter criticisms of the government and, by very clear implication, of the Emperor himself. The government retaliated by affecting to place his family under a kind of ostracism. However, in 1894, there was a formal reconciliation, although it may be questioned whether his relations with the Emperor were ever in the least cordial. Bismarck died July 30th, 1898. No doubt his dominant personality made him a very difficult personage for a much more conciliatory monarch than William II to get along with, but the circumstances of his dismissal were a foretaste of the things the new ruler had waiting for all the world.

And so, as a famous English cartoonist captioned his picture, William II "unshipped the pilot." Henceforth, whatever the Emperor's fortunes, they were at least of his own making. From 1890 down to 1914 the third ruler of the new German Empire, far beyond the wont of most monarchs, did that which seemed right in his own eyes.

William II of Hohenzollern is not at this writing a personage of whom it is easy for an American to write impartially. Before 1914 Transatlantic opinion was, like that of all the rest of the world, bewildered at his versatile performances and his kaleidoscopic moods of utterance; but despite his obvious lack of sympathy for democratic institutions and many performances that seemed to savor of crass medievalism, he was not without many ardent admirers in the United States, and criticism of him was for the most part playful and insignificant.[1] The same was somewhat true in Great Britain, even as the relations of Britain and Germany became strained. There were not a few Frenchmen also who entertained a covert admiration for this grandson of the conqueror of Alsace-Lorraine. Since 1914 his name has become anathema in every non-Teutonized land. What is here written is written with an honest attempt to speak soberly, accurately and in a manner which will not bring regret to the author if he is suffered to re-read his words years later.

William II was born in 1859. He was the son of the then Crown Prince Frederick and of the Princess Royal Victoria of England. He received that systematic and severe discipline in things military and administrative which the Hohenzollern princes always received to fit them for their great office, idleness and levity never having been among the Prussian sins. His relations with his father were not very cordial, with his mother even worse; but chilliness towards one's

---

[1] Part of the good favor in which William II was held in America doubtless was part of the result of the world-wide German propaganda. I have heard of a case in which the agents for a school text-book urged its author to insert matter commendatory of the Emperor, as "likely to help the book in German-American communities." Probably these publishers (a very old and honorable firm) were perfectly unconscious that they were being indirectly "worked" by foreign influences.

parents seems to be a prerogative of Prussian crown princes,[1] and he was the apple of the eye of old Emperor William I, who gave him many personal lessons on the powers and responsibilities which hedge about a throne. William II was never weary of singing the praises of his grandfather on countless public occasions, although he gave his father's honorable memory no more attention than the situation barely required. He was twenty-nine when he came to the throne. When he was only twenty-three, Bismarck, who had watched him shrewdly from under his shaggy old eyebrows, is reputed to have said, "He wishes to take the government into his own hands, he is energetic and determined, not at all disposed to put up with parliamentary co-regents, a regular guardsman. Perhaps some day, however, he may develop into the 'rock of bronze' of which we stand in need." A little later the young Prince sent the chancellor his own picture with the ominous Latin words written beneath it: "*Cave! adsum*" ("Take care: I am here"). However, when William II was proclaimed, he was supposed to be on excellent terms with his chancellor. How the breach came has already been described.

In 1888 William II began to reign. In 1890 he began to govern. From that time onward *Germany was subjected more strictly to a personal government than almost any other great country in modern times.* Bismarck was the first and last of his prime ministers who really dared to pursue an independent policy and tell him blunt truths to his face. None of the later chancellors were more than "handy men" to take the brunt of public criticism, to work out the laborious details of a selected policy, to dress up the Emperor's ideas with smooth phrases and finally to be dismissed promptly when they ceased to please their master or when public dissent with the government became too warm. In 1901 a favor-mongering though distinguished professor (Lamprecht) wrote a sketch of the

[1] Notably in the case of Frederick the Great and his father Frederick William II. Of course William II was destined to be on very bad terms with his own heir, the Crown Prince Frederick William, whom, it is rumored, the most violent Pan-Germans talked of setting in his father's stead in case the Emperor declined to fall in with their schemes for a "necessary war in 1914."

Kaiser which was dutifully submitted to William II for his direct approval. The All-Highest graciously allowed the following sentence to stand and be published: "When one listens to the [sovereign's] ministers one is again and again amazed at the extent to which *they merely repeat the Emperor's ideas,* and whoever has seen opponents coming from an interview with him must be struck equally at the way in which they were dominated by the charm of his personality." And freely it must be admitted that often the eloquence, affability and undeniable magnetism of the Kaiser genuinely supplemented that power of persuasion which a great office can give even to a very mediocre man.

It may be agreed at the outset that William II was a person of noteworthy abilities. In the Middle Ages he would have won fame like the versatile Frederick II, "the wonder of the world." As a wealthy private citizen under a republic he would probably have developed high powers of leadership— not merely in politics, but in the field of education, philanthropy and the encouragement of letters and art. He was also an honestly religious man. His frequent and seemingly patronizing references to the Deity as his constant associate in all worthy endeavor were probably perfectly sincere. It may be left to the theologians to settle whether his "God" was the God of Christianity or some survival of a tribal deity; but it is only just to say that his belief was probably without the least conscious hypocrisy. He delighted in playing the virtuoso, in giving authoritative hints to authors of grand operas and symphonies, and also to artists and sculptors, especially if their creations seemed to perpetuate the great deeds of the Hohenzollern dynasty. He took a keen interest in the development of modern education, and in 1903 he publicly accepted the interpretations of the Bible according to the radical "Higher Criticism" as propounded by the learned lectures of Professor Delitzch. He had a real eloquence, and at patriotic assemblages, the launching of war-ships and the commemoration of great battles was able to carry his audience with him in genuine flights of oratory. He understood also the history of the past, especially of his own house, in detail and was able to sprinkle his speeches with superabundant, but usually very apt, historical allusions. To distinguished foreign visitors he could be graciousness and affability incarnate; fond of friendly interviews, charming "indiscretions" of frank speech, and of hospitality without insulting condescension. More than one professor from a great American university seems to have been sent home rendered a convinced advocate of the cause of Prussianism by the cheap bribe of an invitation to an informal luncheon at Potsdam and a few banal and harmless words from the man before whom all Germany stood in trembling awe. The Emperor too was a mighty traveler and yachtsman. He knew the fjords of Norway, the isles of Greece and the British coast, especially the Isle of Wight in regatta week. His frequent wanderings were not merely for political effect, but because of a keen interest in men and things. *Der Reise-Kaiser* ("the Traveler-Emperor") his subjects sometimes called him, because he was so often away from them. Indeed he was probably quite sincere in his statement that he wished he could see his way clear to visit America. In short, here was a man sent upon earth with vast powers for good or for mischief; and very many of his qualities seemed noble and high.

But William II was born under the shadow of Prussianism and the traditions of the House of Hohenzollern had steeped his soul. He had been brought up in a military atmosphere, and after his twentieth year was almost divorced from civil life until the crown was thrust upon him. In 1885 he was appointed colonel of the Hussar-guard. His teachers and companions were old Prussian officers who had surrounded Von Moltke, and young Prussian noblemen who longed for the summons to battle. Everything around him taught him or told him two things—first, that the sovereign of Prussianized Germany ruled by the grace of God and that it was the duty of all honest subjects to obey him; second, that under a kindly applauding Providence, he owed throne, honors, and all else to the Prussian army, without whose loyal support he would be instantly reduced to impotence. When he took power his first act was to make an address to "his army"; [1] only three days later did he issue a statement to "his people," and repeatedly during his reign he voiced the fateful sentiment, "The soldier and the army, not parliamentary majorities, have welded the German Empire together. *My confidence is placed on the army.*"

Whether, assuming he had found no Reichstag and no Prussian Constitution (lame as it was), he would have allowed them to be created, is a question without an answer. Doubtless he found it useful that his subjects had some orderly means for periodic ebullitions on political subjects, and a recognized method of presenting their petitions for his august consideration. In a long series of famous utterances, however, he made plain his conviction that since he ruled by the express summons and commission of God, therefore in the last analysis his own will was the highest earthly law. As early as March, 1890, he made the famous statement, "Every one who is against me I shall crush!"

Since His Imperial and Royal Majesty spoke frequently on the subject of his own supreme office, a list of even his most notable sayings thereon would be lengthy. Here are a few very familiar ones, extremely hackneyed to-day, but which seem likely to be long remembered in history:

"One shall be the master, even I!"

"The will of the king is the highest law." (*Suprema lex regis voluntas*—a sentiment written in the "Golden Book of Munich" in liberal Bavaria.)

To some army recruits about to be sworn in: "In the presence of the socialist agitation it may happen—though God forefend—that I shall order you to shoot down your

---

[1] In this address to the army, William II declared, "I swear to remember that the eyes of my ancestors look down on me from the other world, and that I shall one day have to render account to them for the honor and glory of the army."

At the time it was recalled that his father had first addressed the people, and then the army; but it was to be inferred that the second William was to be a Frederick the Great, and not a "Citizen-Emperor" as the liberal Frederick III had longed to be known.

relatives, brothers, yes, even parents; but you must obey my commands without murmuring.''

Some of his claims to divine commission and consequent autocracy were of inconceivable bluntness: thus e. g., ''The Hohenzollern house is imbued with a feeling of duty resting upon the knowledge that it has been set up by God and has to render only to Him and to its own conscience an account of what it does for the good of its land.''

Again: ''Just as the first King of Prussia said, 'I have created my own crown' . . . so, like my imperial grandfather, I represent monarchy by the grace of God.''

''(The office of monarch) is fraught with a terrible responsibilty to God alone—from which no man, no minister, no Parliament, can relieve the princes.''

And finally: *''Considering myself as the instrument of the Lord, I go on my way . . . and so I am indifferent to the views and the opinions of the moment.''*

In the seventeenth century Louis XIV, at the time he was threatening to dominate the world through France, is alleged to have made the famous statement, ''I am the state''—and the world trembled and armed herself to resist him. In the twentieth century William II made statements equally blunt and crude—and England and America were only mildly amused, the words seemed so grotesquely medieval. But there was nothing medieval about the German war-machine which this elocutionary monarch controlled.

This Emperor, as stated, could have useful servants, the indispensable viziers to his power, but he could have no real ministers to add their strength to his own. ''A good minister,'' Bismarck once said, ''should not trouble about his sovereign's favor, but speak his mind freely.'' Bismarck had acted on that theory and had lost his position for his pains. After him had come Caprivi (1890–94), who labored industriously and honestly to serve his master and the country, but succeeded in neither. He was beset by the junkers on one side, for their loyalty always made them hungry for government favor, and by the liberals on the other. His master grew tired of him and in 1894 threw him over. He was the first of several chancellors who were mere shadows in the former chair of the welder of German unity.

After Caprivi came Prince Hohenlohe (1894–1900), an elderly man of considerable ability, and one who had kept on fairly friendly terms with Bismarck. He also soon found out that "a number of politicians and high placed busybodies were doing their best to discredit me with His Majesty." He bought the support of the Conservatives by passing laws favoring the agricultural interests, but in the end the Kaiser wearied of him. Feeling that his power was slipping away, he resigned in 1900. He put it in his memoirs that William II was actually waiting for his resignation, and already had chosen his successor.

The next vizier to the All-Highest was Prince von Bülow, "a diplomat and polished man of the world, gifted with a happy disposition, which never deserted him, even in the most difficult situations." Bismarck had declared in a famous speech, "We Germans fear God and nothing else in the world"; and a political wag asserted, "Bülow fears the junkers and nothing else in the world." For a time he got on excellently, knowing how to bend the Kaiser's personal whims and yet to retain something of his own personality. He managed for long to carry the government's measures through the Reichstag by means of compromises with the Catholic "Centrum" and the Conservatives. But in 1909 the Conservatives, before whom he had kow-towed, deserted him, and held up his legislation. Already the Kaiser was tiring of him. He had tried haltingly to check his sovereign's habit of making very indiscreet speeches, although William had broken over the traces once and again. "You do not know how much I prevent!" Bülow said when reproved for failing to prevent a peculiar unwise utterance. Now the Emperor threw him over. Bethmann-Hollweg occupied his chair.

This last chancellor before the mighty storm was known mainly as a quiet, fairly adroit politician and as a clever orator. He showed himself a good diplomat in the Balkan crisis of 1912–13, and even in retrospect he may be called, in the main, a lover of peace. But Bethmann-Hollweg was destined to a more lasting place in history than any chancellor since Bismarck, for in August, 1914, he was to make the famous speech wherein he said that Belgium must be violated, even wrongfully, "because necessity knows no law"; and he was to describe a solemn treaty with England as a "scrap of paper."

Concerning all these chancellors as well as the lesser ministers their helpers, a German writer left a clear-cut judgment shortly before the outbreak of the great war, "Our ministers are fairly capable officials (for ordinary routine duty) . . . But the idea of representing to the Emperor independent opinions, plans or criticism, or of opposing him from a sense of duty—*that* would savor to them of sacrilege." Yet all the while that the chancellors were thus failing in this plainest duty of a minister to a monarch, sycophants and parasites were pouring flatteries into the ears of William of Hohenzollern, which daily confirmed his ideas of his own greatness. One courtier is even reported to have told him unabashed, "Your Majesty becomes every day more like Frederick the Great—but without his defects." Some of the Emperor's noble friends were doubtless men of parts and insight; others were personages over whose private lives it is best to draw a veil. In 1907 the famous editor Maximilian Harden in his *Zukunft* began a series of revelations as to the habits of certain individuals near and presumably dear to His Imperial and Royal Majesty. Long-drawn legal proceedings followed. The character of the Emperor himself was left unstained, but the personal morals of his confidants Prince Philip Eulenburg and Count Kuno Moltke were left blasted before the world. The net result of the prosecutions was good. The Emperor emancipated himself from at least part of the very unsavory clique that had surrounded him. He also allowed a relaxation in the outrageous press-laws which had permitted frequent prosecutions for *lèse-majesté* for very innocent references to the doings and intentions of the ruler and his family and ministers.

During the reign of William II there was very little

domestic legislation which calls for extended comment. The chief task of the average chancellor, from 1895 onward, had been to induce the often recalcitrant Reichstags to vote the increasingly huge naval bills on which the Emperor had set his heart, and (less contentiously as a rule) to provide for the steady increase of the army. The Conservatives with all their professed love for the throne and zeal for the army, were, as a class, by no means anxious to pay heavy taxes for a fleet; [1] and it was necessary to buy their support by constant concessions to the agrarian interests, as well as to conciliate the Catholic "Centrum" by legislation favorable to the church. The making of the new German navy, however, is a story for another chapter, as are all other questions of imperial foreign policy.

The extremely severe laws of 1878 enacted by Bismarck against the socialists had not been renewed when they expired in 1890; nevertheless the Prussian police had abundant weapons in their arsenal wherewith to fight against a movement which the Emperor and all the junker element regarded with indescribable anger. In 1895 the police used a law of 1850 for dissolving the socialist organization in Berlin, and at every possible turn the whole power of the government was used against the unwelcome propaganda. Yet despite imprisonments, fines, social ostracism and intimidation the socialist vote grew steadily. The radical leaders were extremely skillful in keeping within the letter of the law and avoiding its spirit, in filling their newspapers with easily interpreted innuendo, and in using the privileges of the Reichstag to the fullest extent possible for a parliamentary body that was allowed to *talk* fairly freely, even if not really to govern.

Since 1881, when the vote for the socialist candidates in a general Reichstag election were 311,961, their number of ballots increased on each dissolution of the parliament until

[1] Many junkers, whose families regarded the army posts almost as hereditary perquisites, were not enthusiastic about the proposition to create a rival naval service which could hardly share the aristocratic traditions of the military department.

1912, when it had swelled to the menacing number of about 4,250,000. Twice, by the unjust manner in which seats were gerrymandered, they lost in their membership in the Reichstag even though their popular vote was swelled. Thus in 1907 they lost 38 seats at Berlin although their whole vote was increased by over 500,000; but in 1912 they added alike 750,-000 votes to their total, and won 63 new seats in the Reichstag. They had thus in all 110 seats, making them the largest single party in Germany, and so forcing the government to win the favor of nearly all the other disjointed and irresponsible parties, Conservatives, "Centrum," National Liberals, Progressives, etc., to be able to carry through its measures.

This great expansion of the socialist vote, however, did not imply that a large fraction of all the German nation was in favor of an ultra-socialistic Marxian régime. The socialists themselves were seriously divided between the old-line theorists who wished for an abrupt revolution and a complete change in the ordinary methods of holding capital and property, and the newer element which aimed to bring a happier day by agitating for moderate practical reforms, while hoping for a general economic change through peaceful evolution. The organization of the socialist party was very perfect; its clubs, circles, officials, etc., were evidences of that same militaristic efficiency system, which its members denounced. However, great numbers of Germans, who had no real sympathy with even a denatured form of socialism, "voted with the Left" (i. e., against the government), to voice their general dislike of many features of the Hohenzollern régime. The balloting for the Reichstag was secret; the temptation to register a silent protest against the arrogance of the junkers and the maintenance of the three-class system in nearly all local elections, was very great. Had by any chance the socialists found themselves possessed of the government, and abruptly tried to put their extreme economic theories into practice they would probably have been deserted promptly by very many of their nominal followers. It is irresponsibility, and a desire to register a general protest, that often makes men feel "radical" when they approach the ballot-box.[1]

Theoretically the socialists professed themselves utterly opposed to militarism, and their members voted against almost every increase of the army or fleet when the question came up in the Reichstag.   Their opponents taunted them regularly upon their lack of patriotism, and in foreign lands many hopes were founded by ardent pacifists on the suggestions that in event of war the German socialists would refuse the summons to arms against "their brothers," the toilers of France, Russia and England. In the Reichstag and elsewhere, however, the socialist orators, although deprecating schemes for aggrandizement, always professed that if the Fatherland were really attacked they would "put their rifles to their shoulders as readily as their middle-class countrymen." It was for the Emperor and his Prussian lords to see to it that every German believed the Fatherland had been "attacked," when the call came to arms in 1914.

The socialists were in any case an anti-militarist and an anti-absolutist force.   They represented the rising opposition of a great and very intelligent nation to the régime founded by Bismarck and perpetuated by William II.   It was very probably the steady increase of their apparent influence which led the imperialists and Pan-Germans to feel the more ready for one great throw of the dice in 1914;—for if they won the victory they would be alike masters of the domestic and of the international world, and the hurrahs of conquest would stifle radicalism at home.   Bismarck and Moltke had defeated Liberalism by humiliating first Austria and then France. The heirs to these giants would stifle socialism by bringing home the trophies of a defeated world.   This was not the sole cause of Armageddon—but it was a contributing factor.

In 1913 occurred an incident which brought the hostility between the military caste and the civilian element into dangerous relief, and taught many a German how com-

---

[1] Just as in American elections, very often citizens vote for a candidate they know is unworthy, merely to rebuke the iniquitous "party in power" of which they are weary.

pletely visionary was his claim to be the citizen of a free nation. In the opinion of a shrewd official observer this affair decided the "system"—i. e., the military autocracy—upon a speedy war.[1] It certainly was a serious warning to the militarists that their power was in danger, and that radical measures were necessary to rehabilitate their prestige. This famous incident has passed into history as *the Zabern affair*.

Zabern was a pleasant little city in Alsace, and the fact that the trouble arose in the much-disputed "Reichsland" added nothing to the ease of smoothing out the quarrel. In its garrison was the 91st Prussian infantry, and among the officers thereof was a youthful lieutenant of the true junker school, a certain noble Baron von Forstner of some twenty years of age, who took his honors very seriously. School children and factory lads seem to have called names at him, and he, in addressing his men, seems to have retaliated by styling the Alsatian recruits *Wackes*, a local title of derogation. There was another story that he had promised his men a ten-mark piece if one of them brought down a Social Democrat provided it came to shooting. The reports of von Forstner's crude remarks spread; the town papers grew caustic and the colonel of the garrison, von Reuter, warned the local civil magistrate, Director Mahler, to restore order (there having been small demonstrations) or he would do so himself. On November 29, 1913, Mahler having refused to object to lawful proceedings, when a civilian crowd gathered in front of the barracks, von Reuter directed a subaltern to order it to go home. The angry burghers refused, whereupon the military charged out and arrested some fifteen civilians, including three high judges and the state prosecuting attorney himself who chanced to get caught in the throng. These four dignitaries were speedily released; the other civilians were held in durance vile over night and then released.

This clash of burgher and soldier produced wrath throughout Germany; von Reuter was already hated by the liberals as an exponent of extreme junker theories. He was tried for violating the law which forbade the soldiery to interfere

[1] James W. Gerard, "My Four Years in Germany," p. 75.

in civilian matters, but was promptly acquitted by his military court on a technicality. The wrath of the liberals was great, and it was shared by many level-headed conservatives. The Governor-General of Alsace himself felt constrained to resign as a protest at this usurpation of civilian functions—but an order from the Emperor commanding the military henceforth to keep within their authority caused him to withdraw his action.

Very quickly, however, Zabern and the noble lieutenant Baron von Forstner again gave business for the telegraph. This highborn gentleman had not been wisely withdrawn to another garrison town less acquainted with his mannerisms. He fell into an undignified altercation with a lame shoemaker of the neighborhood. Very probably the clown presumed upon his physical weakness and made unflattering remarks. Von Forstner, not feeling that his opponent's infirmity should be any protection, drew his saber and wounded the cripple. Once more there was uproar. Von Forstner was promptly tried by court martial. In a lower court he was convicted and sentenced to one year in custody; a higher tribunal, however, promptly took up the case on appeal and acquitted the lieutenant "for self-defense"! [1]

Von Forstner had thus vindicated his "honor," so dear to every Prussian officer, by repaying revilings with a blow from the noble's weapon, but in the Reichstag civilian wrath boiled over. The defense of the government advanced by Bethmann-Hollweg was feeble and evasive; and oil was poured on the flames by the arrogance of the war-minister, who spoke also, and said bluntly that von Forstner might have been over-anxious to protect himself, but that such a "courageous young officer" was an asset to the nation. The chancellor was of course not so much to blame as the military officials, and behind them the Kaiser their chief, who had allowed the folly of a subaltern workman, and the "lewd fellows of the baser sort" in an Alsatian town, to make a great

[1] The crippled shoemaker was held by two soldiers while their lieutenant slashed him. *Afterwards* a pocket knife was discovered in the civilian's pocket. It was against this that the officer defended himself.

national issue. But it was easier to bait Bethmann-Hollweg than William of Hohenzollern and the War Office. The Reichstag, on the 6th of December, 1913, passed a vote of censure upon the government, 393 to 54, only the ever-faithful Conservatives voting in behalf of the military.

Had this vote of censure been carried in almost any other European parliament, the Prime Minister and all his subordinates would have resigned immediately. As it was, Bethmann-Hollweg, holding his office not by parliamentary majorities but by the good favor of the Kaiser and the military, smiled blandly and continued with the next items on the government program. Only the socialists were bold enough to insist that he should quit office. The "National Liberals" and the "Centrum," although they had voted for the censure, were unwilling to force the issue. The Reichstag had simply expressed the opinion of a pretentious, officially recognized debating club.

Nevertheless the incident had sent panic through the junkers and the princely gentlemen in the Potsdam palaces. Doubtless they cursed von Forstner and von Reuter roundly in private as "blockheads" and "asses" even while they publicly defended them. The rift between the civilians and the military had been advertised too clearly. If the Reichstag factions had been a little bolder, had really dared to hold up essential legislation in order to force Bethmann-Hollweg out, then one of three things must have happened:— (I) The Chancellor must have resigned and been replaced by a man agreeable to the majority of the Reichstag. This would possibly have been the substitution of a liberal parliamentary system for Bismarckism: (II) The Kaiser must have dissolved the Reichstag and ordered a new election: but in the inflamed state of public opinion it was likely that a new Reichstag would be more radical and less pliable than the old one: (III) The government must have collected taxes and paid out money without the Reichstag's authorization, but this would have been a wanton violation of even the circumscribed privileges granted by the Hohenzollern régime. It would have been revolutionary and probably would have provoked a counter-revolution.

The Zabern incident, in other words, taught the junkers, the Pan-German propagandists, and their allies the great manufacturers who were clutching at world trade, that despite the great material prosperity they had brought the Empire, despite the careful drilling of public opinion their position was getting precarious. It doubtless had its effect upon their august personal head, the God-crowned Emperor and King. Its whole effect surely was to get them all to quicken their efforts, already promising fearful success, to ease the home situation by a foreign war.

However, even without the affair at Zabern, the attitude of Germany in foreign affairs was no longer that of Bismarck's "satiated" state, seeking only for inward development and peace. She was building a great navy, she was increasing her already mighty army, she was reaching out hungrily for colonies, she was giving foreign statesmen anxious nights when they brooded on her aggressive policy. A great host of skillful pamphleteers and propagandists was carrying out to the nation the peace-destroying gospel that Germany needed new opportunities for riches, power and expansion and that *all these good things could be wisely and speedily won by the sword*. As for William II, a diplomat who saw him often just before the débâcle, gives this summary of his probable attitude: "He must have said to himself then that the first part of his task was over, and the second about to begin. He had launched his people upon a career of prosperity and progress in which it could no longer cry halt, and a new war, so far from checking this marvelous economic advance, would only act as a fresh stimulus. Germany, having trebled her commerce and almost doubled her population, with millions of workers who no longer left their country to seek a living elsewhere, needed new fields for expansion, and thirsted for an unquestioned supremacy in every sphere. It would be the glory of William, while still in the full vigor of his years, to realize these splendid ambitions." [1]

[1] Baron Beyens, "Germany Before the War," p. 29. Beyens was Belgian minister to Berlin in 1914. Despite the wrongs done to his country he writes with moderation and relative lack of prejudice, as well as

On November 22nd, 1913, at the time the Zabern "incident" was at its height, Jules Cambon, Ambassador for France at Berlin, sent a confidential communication to his government. He reported how a fortnight earlier King Albert of Belgium had visited Potsdam and had been at a banquet with the Emperor and General von Moltke,[1] the chief of staff. The King was grievously distressed at the tone of the conversation, over the walnuts and wine. War seemed in the air. The Emperor's influence was no longer exerted, as "on so many critical occasions, in support of peace." The General talked even more openly of how *war was necessary and inevitable.* By war of course was meant a great European war against a coalition of great powers. Jules Cambon, a sage diplomat, sent the report in to Paris with this solemn observation: "The Emperor is becoming used to an order of ideas [making for war] which were formerly repugnant to him, and, to borrow from him a phrase he likes to use, 'we must keep our powder dry'!"[2]

The ambassador soon found justification for his warning.

PRUSSIAN MILITARY COURTS AND DUELLING

One of the prerogatives of German army officers is to be tried by their fellow officers and not suffer the indignity of making their defence before a tribunal of civilians.

The "honor," assumed to be inherent in each Prussian officer, compelled him to avenge every insult to his personal dignity, not by legal process, but by his good right arm. In altercations with his equals an officer was obliged to fight a duel if a "court of honor" (usually composed of his senior officers) decided that this was necessary to atone for the insult. The duel might be with heavy sabers (far more deadly than the student's weapon) or in extreme cases with pistols. Many Prussian military duels seem to have ended fatally.

In deference to civilian protests there were certain regulations discouraging duelling, but they were never strictly enforced. It was said

with much insight and sincere effort to understand the German side of the case.

[1] Nephew of the famous Moltke who died in 1891.

[2] French "Diplomatic Correspondence respecting the War," document 6. It is commonly supposed that Monsieur Cambon got his information about this imperial supper-party from King Albert himself or at least from Baron Beyens.

that only the Emperor himself could stop duelling in the army, by a stern personal mandate—but this he was unwilling to issue. If a German officer was convicted of an offence, he would commonly be sentenced only to mild imprisonment in a "fortress," a penalty that carried no social taint, and not have to commingle with the common herd in an ordinary prison. In the winter of 1916–17 a German military officer, having been convicted in this country of gross offences against the United States neutrality laws, is alleged to have demanded that America, no less than Germany, should let him serve out his term of confinement in some place more honorable and comfortable than the regular penitentiary provided for the run of base-born Yankee offenders. —The American court does not seem to have been able to comply with the worthy officer's wish.

CHAPTER XI

THE UNHAPPY FRONTIER LANDS OF THE HOHENZOLLERNS

GREAT and certain of a glorious history appeared the Empire of the Hohenzollerns in 1914, despite its conservative junkers in Prussia, its arrogant officer caste, its rapacious great capitalists, and its muttering, disruptive and impractical socialists. Of course its statesmen were facing the usual number of problems in finance and social reform, common to every civilized state. They were also holding at arm's length a very disagreeable demand for greater political liberties. Yet the material success of the Empire was so great, and so marked was the ability of the Hohenzollern dynasts to justify its power by the efficient government, physical well-being, economic expansion and national prestige which it had brought their subjects, that one could fairly say that the system which Bismarck had initiated in 1871 seemed in little danger of serious modification forty-three years later. Intolerable blundering, gross oppression, unsuccessful wars, famines, general calamity—these are the things which usually provoke dangerous wrath and revolution within a nation, not theoretical claims for a better scheme of government; and the German imperial system had suffered from none of these disasters. In 1914 it was confidently lauded by its champions as an unmitigated success, while the people committed to its fostering care were advancing economically from strength to strength. Even outside the Empire, in the democratic lands of France, England and America, it was regarded with a kind of bewildered admiration—this system that appeared such a contradiction to all the theories of democracies, and which nevertheless seemed more efficient than they. How much better were the Germans' commercial methods than the English, or their army mobilization schemes than the French, or their city governments than the American! For the solution of almost every material public problem, Germany presented herself as the schoolhouse of the world. A foreign community almost automatically sent "a commission to Germany," to learn its approved methods, whether the question were that of establishing a municipal piggery or a college of music.

Nevertheless there was certainly *one* matter in which the Fatherland gave no lessons to the rest of humanity. Along its northern, eastern, and western frontiers there were large and populous districts whereof the inhabitants were bitterly resentful of Berlin rule, and if a great war should break out they could by no means be relied upon to pray for German victory.

It is a nice question for political theorists to settle when a barbarous or imperfectly civilized people has reached such a stage in its upward development that the tutelage of a civilized power should cease, and the subordinate people be left more or less to walk upon its own feet. All great nations, excluding Austria, but including America, had colonies in the tropics calling for considerable "administration" of the natives. But it is only a dealer in quiddities who claims that there is ordinarily the same resentfulness of outside political control in a Malay as in an Anglo-Saxon. In 1914 it was at least not supposed to be the proper thing for white men to deny large rights of self-government to other white men. It is true this theory was often imperfectly developed. In Austria there was a regular complex of "minor races," jangling with the predominant Germans and Magyars, and crying out lustily against real or alleged deeds of oppression. But Austria was not a nation but a conglomerate. There could be no real hope, despite German and Magyar ambitions, of reducing all her peoples to one fixed type and mould. The friction between her races was only the inevitable heat engendered by the painful process of finding some system of federation which would be reasonably just and satisfactory to all parties. There was also the great fraction of Poland and the whole of Finland, grasped in the clutch of Russian Czardom, and often brutally threatened with violent "Russification." But this again was merely one phase of that whole outrageous system of "despotism tempered by inefficiency" that was paving the way for the Russian Revolution of 1917. The Poles and Finns suffered differently, but hardly more grievously than did all the liberal elements of native Russians who felt the heavy weight of Nicholas II's blundering machine. Once more, there was the case of Ireland, which certainly had been sorely tormented by its British rulers in the past, and now was clamoring for deliverance. But British public opinion had already resolved on extending to Ireland every kind of good gift and favor, even to the point of almost complete self-government: the only real difficulty had been that 25 per cent. of Ireland (Ulster) had angrily refused the boon which the other 75 per cent. demanded, and threatened civil war if "home rule" were thrust upon it.[1] None of these cases constituted a serious refutation to the general proposition that no European nation had the right to oppress the people of another European nation. As for France and Italy, there were no dwellers in those countries who did not wish to be counted Frenchmen or Italians; although just over their respective borders there were less happy districts that would probably have been very glad to transfer their allegiance to Paris or Rome. But incorporated within the German Empire were no less than three populous areas, inhabited by civilized Europeans, who detested the German rule and wished heartily for some different political connection. The Berlin government had tried cajoling these people into becoming "good Germans"—and it had failed. It had tried coercing them—it had still more completely failed. At least two of these national groups were seemingly less loyal and happy in their relations to Germany in 1914 than they had been, let us say, in 1884. This was a very serious problem, for it affected the physical integrity of the Hohenzollerns' Empire. The inabil-

[1] In any case the Irish did not desire to be annexed to some outside, non-British power. Dublin may have hated the rule of London, but it did not wish to substitute that of Paris or Berlin. There is therefore no parallel between the case of Ireland and that e. g. of Alsace-Lorraine.

ity of the Kaiser's ministers to solve it was a proof that all the Prussian science, discipline, system and efficiency could not meet very vital human questions.

The three regions that looked angrily away from the rest of Germany were: I. Schleswig-Holstein: II. The Polish Provinces on the east: III. Alsace-Lorraine. It is best to begin with the first because it was the least important.

In 1864 Prussia in alliance with Austria had taken from the King of Denmark the duchies of Schleswig-Holstein, which had formerly been united by a kind of personal union with the Danish crown. In 1866 Bismarck, having defeated his late ally Austria in war, caused these countries to be annexed entirely to Prussia. Holstein had been an almost purely German land. Danish rule had not been popular. The region soon settled down under its new government. But the case of Schleswig was very different. The population contained no less than 200,000 Danes occupying nearly all the northern sections of the province. They had not the least desire to become Germans and were proud of their northern language and robust type of civilization. In 1866, when after Sadowa Austria agreed to retire from all activity in German affairs, her statesmen had the grace to require that a clause be put in the treaty with Prussia specifically providing that "the population of the northern district of Schleswig, when by a popular vote it shall have expressed its wish to be incorporated with Denmark, shall be surrendered to that country."

This clause never remained more than a pious wish. There was strong feeling in Germany at the time that the forcible incorporation of the Danes was by no means advisable. "It would be a wise and statesmanlike act to renounce North Schleswig voluntarily," declared the *Kölnische Zeitung*, one of the most influential papers in Prussia, in 1866. But Bismarck seldom relaxed his grip on anything. In his speeches he said that the treaty must be fulfilled, but that the vote must only come after time enough had elapsed to make sure the Schleswigers really wanted to secede, and that their action was "independent and voluntary." But this happy time, when the region could be trusted to settle its own destinies, never arrived. In 1878 Austria and Germany were negotiating over Balkan issues, and Bismarck (for favors granted elsewhere) easily induced Franz Joseph's statesmen to "revise" this clause about Schleswig by formally declaring it "null and void." (*Ausser Gültigkeit gesetz.*) So the Schleswigers were left to their Prussian masters.

The Danes, as a people, had far more in common with their conquerors than the Poles and the Franco-Alsatians: and yet fifty years of most unhappy local history have demonstrated the inability of Prussian officialdom, with all its system and mechanical efficiency, to card-catalog and bring under control the soul of a people. The issue turned very largely around the use of the Danish language. Nearly twelve million Prussian subjects had spoken Low German, a form of speech almost as different from the official and literary "High German" as was Danish, and no one had questioned their loyalty to *Kaiser und König:* but against Danish the Berlin ministers now set themselves as against a tongue of sedition. After various half measures, German was not merely introduced in 1889 into all the Schleswig schools, but it was forbidden to teach Danish under any circumstances whatever. No family could engage a Danish tutor, and even parents who undertook to teach Danish systematically to their children were liable to prosecution. Still another regulation forbade parents to send their children to school in Denmark.

If government mandates from Berlin could have solved the Schleswig problem it would have vanished speedily. A ministerial order commanded all school children in the region to learn by heart twenty songs from the official song book. Of these twelve were German national or war songs, and one of them was the famous *Preussenlied,* with its refrain "*Ich bin ein Preusse.*" As for local history, schoolmasters were forbidden to teach their charges anything of the annals of Denmark, or even anything of those of Schleswig prior to 1864 (the date of the conquest). Only strictly German history prior to that time could be taught, and that too in text-books wherein the rulers of Prussia were extolled as patriotic demi-gods whose sole end was the good of their people, and who had rescued poor Schleswig from the tyrannous clutches of Denmark. Where the text-book failed the school-master's rod theoretically completed the process. Children who spoke Danish in the school or on its playground were subject to punishment. At Aabenraa for a time there was devised a system of fines for every Danish word a school-child uttered, but this proved unsatisfactory and a system of making the youthful malefactors "stay in" was substituted. Some of the tyrants of the birch became notorious, as e.g., the redoubtable Herr Blohm of Haderslev, a mighty school master of the eighties.

By such means no doubt outward obedience was often maintained, but the stolid unbending northern farmers continued proof against this type of petty persecution. They were without hope of rescue by weak Denmark, and the Prussian juggernaut might grind over them, suppress their papers, silence or banish their native pastors, flog their children, but it could not make them Prussians or make them wish to be Prussians. At election after election one or two Schleswig deputies would be returned to the Reichstag to uplift their voices vainly but bravely against this process of crushing out the habits and language of a liberty-loving, intelligent people. And in 1905 by unimpeachable German statistics there were 162,000 persons in Schleswig whom all the bullying and cajoling of the Berlin Ministry of Education could not induce to call themselves Germans but still were reckoned "Danes." The situation was hardly better in 1914. When the great war began, a district only a little north of the Kiel Canal and extending from the Baltic to the North Sea was held by people whom fifty years of Prussian occupation could not make ardent soldiers for the Kaiser.[1]

The Danish problem was bad: but after all the Schleswig malcontents reckoned barely 0.25 per cent. of the whole popu-

---

[1] A prominent Schleswiger who emigrated to America thus expressed the feelings of his people, in an interview in the American press in 1917: "I was born in Schleswig-Holstein and know what it means to live under German iron rule. Every one who spoke a Danish word,

lation of Germany. It was quite different with the Polish problem. On the eve of the Great War over 3,800,000 subjects of William II called themselves Poles instead of Prussians, and the question of their Germanization and loyalty was one of the weighty questions for the Fatherland. The third and last partition of Poland had taken place in 1795. In 1815 there had been a redistribution of the divided land between the three spoilers, Prussia, Russia, and Austria, but no restoration of the Polish kingdom. The joint crime of Frederick the Great, Catherine of Russia and Maria Theresa [1] and her descendants had never been punished. It is true that Poland had, during its independent days, been afflicted by one of the craziest and most unworkable systems of "government" ever possessed by a so-called civilized country: an elective kingship with only nominal powers for the ruler and with an unlimited opportunity for lawless nobles to do that which was right in their own eyes. True again, the oppressions of the peasantry by their noble lords had been so great that when the foreign conquerors entered the land, the patriotic upper classes could not get enough support from the lower classes to make Kosciusko's last resistance more than brave but hopeless heroism. True likewise, that economic and agricultural conditions in independent Poland had been utterly primitive, as bad as in medieval Russia,—few towns, fewer roads, squalor, poverty and superstition everywhere. Nevertheless the forcible dismemberment of Poland late in the 18th century had been one of those great crimes against the justice of history that surely will return and plague the offending empires. It certainly returned to plague Prussia.

sang a Danish song, or bought a cap with a Danish flag upon it was immediately arrested by the German authorities and expelled from the country without mercy. Therefore I came to America."

Even allowing for prejudice and exaggeration, this is a pungent comment on the abilities of Prussia to deal with non-Prussians.

[1] In fairness to Maria Theresa it should be said that the original plot to dismember Poland originated with her mighty "brother" and "sister" and she entered only reluctantly upon their schemes for spoliation.

Shortly before 1914 there were about 21,000,000 persons
speaking Polish, and all of them willing candidates for citizenship in a revived Polish kingdom. Of these about 3,800,000
were in Germany, 5,000,000 in Austria, and some 12,000,000
in Russia. The Czar thus grasped the largest fraction of the
unhappy race as well as Warsaw, its old capital. The Poles
did not love their Russian masters. They were Catholics;
the Russians were "Orthodox," and were not at all tender
in the means whereby they propagated their type of Christianity. The Czars, especially since the abortive revolution
of 1863, had stamped out almost the last vestige of local
liberty for the Poles, had exiled and imprisoned their leaders
right and left, had induced Russian adventurers to settle in
the land and given them office and preferment, had discouraged the Polish language,—in short, had generally played the
irresponsible tyrants. The condition of the Russian Poles
was therefore bad. But it was not hopeless. They lay on
the edge of Russia, and were only on paper an integral part
thereof. Russian officialdom was often brutal, stupid and
corrupt; but it was usually also inefficient. It was a long
way sometimes from publishing a Czar's ukase to enforcing
its harsh details in a Polish village.[1] The better type of Russian officials were more urbane, tactful and more complaisant
than their companions just across the Prussian border. Above
all, every intelligent Pole knew that the old régime in Russia
could not last forever. When it went down, the Russian
liberals could not belie themselves by refusing decent justice
to Poland. The Russian fraction of the Poles therefore often
lived most uncomfortably, but they lived in hope.

Likewise the Austrian Poles had their consolations. They
were subject indeed to the government at Vienna. But in the
distracted Dual Monarchy, where every possible helper was
needed to aid the Germans and Magyars to hold their own
against the jealous lesser peoples, the Poles were able to get
a good price for a steady support of Franz Josef's ministers.

[1] The very corruptibility of many Russian imperial officials made it
possible often to abate the workings of the severest mandates by a little
well placed bribe-money.

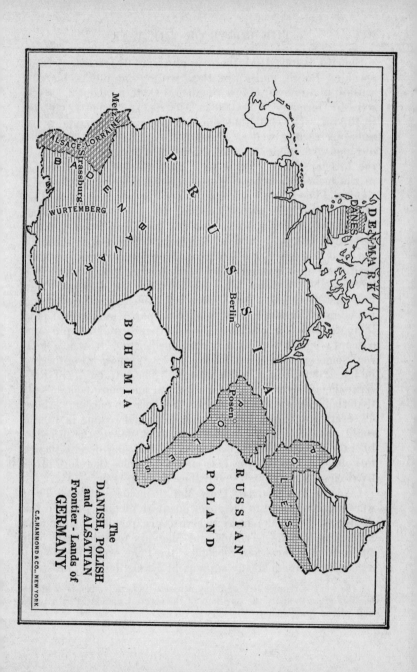

The
DANISH, POLISH
and ALSATIAN
Frontier - Lands of
GERMANY

C.S.HAMMOND & CO., NEW YORK

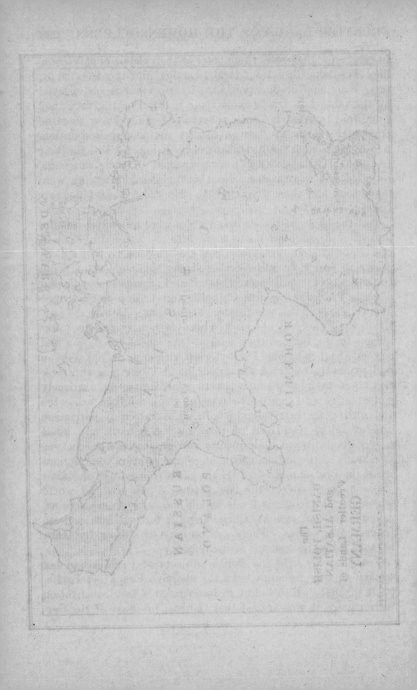

In return for the pro-German votes of their deputies at Vienna, they were able to extract local liberties, and the free use of their language in education, etc., to an extent never enjoyed by the other two fractions of their race. For the time they submitted to Austria fairly cheerfully. They knew that the Hapsburg monarchy was an utterly artificial consolidation. At any moment it might transform itself and leave them their freedom. Till then they were respected in their language, religion and institutions. No thoroughgoing attempts were made to render them "Germans." They also could bide their time.

But the hopes of the Prussian Poles were much less certain, and their present lot much more bitter. After all, Russian and Pole had one great common tie—they were both Slavs. Austrian and Pole at least shared the common lot of being Catholics. Prussian and Pole found themselves opposed alike as Protestant against Catholic, and Teuton against Slav. The religious chasm was in any case serious. Before the partition the Poles had not always been extremely zealous Catholics. In the 16th century a large fraction of the nation had seemed about to become Presbyterian, although the old religion had presently regained the upper hand. But now the mere fact that their Prussian masters represented an extremely conservative and aggressive type of Protestantism made the Poles cling to their religion both as a matter of patriotism and of faith. Deprived of their own governors and kings they rallied around their priests and archbishops as the visible heads of the nation. This of course aroused the religious ire of the Protestants. In 1914 the eastern provinces of Kaiser Wilhelm were one of the few places in the civilized world where the old religious feuds which had once everywhere arrayed Christian against Christian still burned hot, and intruded into politics. There was no hope of stilling the issue, because it had become one of race loyalty.

Yet down to 1870 the Polish subjects of Prussia had not seemed so very unhappy. In the abortive Frankfort Parliament of 1848, which ought to have given a free constitution to Germany, it was argued that the real interests of the German people required that Poland should be restored. The poet Herwegh declaimed then in favor of a war against Russia in behalf of oppressed Poland, crying out that "there could be no free Germany without a free Poland, and no free Poland without a free Germany!" All these chivalrous projects failed, of course, with the failure of the Frankfort parliament: but in 1866 and 1870 the Poles of the Prussian provinces fought bravely for William I and did nothing to hamper his government during its times of sore ordeal. It was after 1871, when the Empire was consolidating, when the official bureaucracy was completing its systematizing and regulating of every practice and every individual in the realm, that the Poles first realized the full weight of the task-master.

In truth the Prussians, for their part, were becoming somewhat alarmed at the situation upon their whole eastern frontier and especially in the important province of Posen. For example, in 1886 it was discovered that in the preceding twenty-five years the Poles there had increased by two hundred thousand and the Germans by only four thousand. The Prussian government had imagined that contact with the superior *Kultur* of its native citizens, the introduction of German peasants into Polish communities and the like would produce a gradual Teutonization of these "Eastern Marches." Precisely the reverse happened. The German peasant had many robust virtues, but he often succumbed rapidly to the local influences, good or bad, of any new home assigned him. In the present case the government awoke to the fact that the German settlers were becoming Poles. In 1886 there were 759 children with German names in the primary schools of Posen in whose families nothing but Polish was spoken. The Poles were exceedingly prolific and easily distanced the Germans in the size of their households. "They multiply like rabbits!" angrily cried one Prussian statesman. In short, in this year 1886 the situation seemed so menacing that Bismarck and his associates decided on radical remedies.

The Iron Chancellor set himself like flint against any proposition to restore Polish independence. "Any arrangement," he wrote, "likely to satisfy Poland is impossible without the breaking up and decomposing of Prussia.'' The proposed remedy was therefore to gradually grind down and Germanize the Poles by a wholesale introduction of Teutonic colonists for whom lands were to be provided by the public exchequer. A land commission was set up. Small farms were to be purchased and parceled out to German colonists on extremely convenient terms. It was relatively easy for Bismarck to get his scheme for an eastern land commission and a liberal appropriation through the Prussian parliament. It was entirely another matter actually to get the land itself. The Poles, who had hitherto been somewhat dormant in their patriotism, now rallied generally to meet the common danger. Against the government subsidies and grants they pitted their private loan and self-help societies and banks, in which great Slavic noblemen invested liberally, to enable their peasantry to hold their own. The Pole who sold land to the Prussian land commission had to face the anathema of the parish priest and the boycott of all his neighbors. What land the commission *could* buy usually came from great German estate holders in the region who, getting anxious and disgusted at the situation, were glad to sell out and move away. The Polish private land societies took advantage of this condition to buy German land themselves in districts next to their own, thus extending the holdings of the Polish peasants. Only about 30 per cent. of the land the government commission was able to purchase came from Poles: the rest came from Germans—it had been robbing Peter to pay Paul! In 1911 it was estimated that the whole result of this competition up to date had been the net *gain by the Poles* of some 240,000 acres which had enjoyed German ownership prior to 1896 or earlier.

The struggle was intensified in 1902 when Chancellor von Bülow introduced a bill in Prussia to give teeth to the powers of the land commission, by the *compulsory expropriation* of the lands of the Polish peasants. The results, however, were still unsatisfactory. Even Prussian officialdom could not coerce German farmers to quit comfortable estates elsewhere in the Empire and settle in a land where they were at sword's points with all their neighbors, were without con-

genial associates and sometimes needed police protection
The Polish villagers clung in desperation to their traits and
their language, and their unwelcome guests had perforce to
assimilate themselves to have the least companionship. While
Bethmann-Hollweg was Prussian Minister of the Interior he
visited one of the new "colonies" and asked a German settler,
"How do you like your new home?" "All right," came the
answer, "except that we cannot yet understand the Poles
well enough. But" (reassuringly) "never mind, *we shall
learn Polish yet!*"

Against this tenacious use of their native vernacular, the
Prussian régime fought with the same soldiery it had mobilized in Schleswig—the school-masters. Up to 1872 Polish
studies had not been entirely taboo in the annexed provinces,
but in that year German was made the sole language in the
elementary schools, save only that instruction in "religion" [1]
was at first permitted, at least in the lower grades, in the
native vernacular. But speedily even this privilege began to
be curtailed. As fast as children learned enough German
in the lower grade secular studies they were transferred to
the German "religion classes." Inasmuch as religion and
national patriotism, to a Polish mind, were closely intertwined,
this measure was calculated to produce the maximum of resentment. The clergy sided with the people against requiring the children "to learn the sacred religion in the hateful
German language." It was branded as merely a clumsy attempt to inculcate Protestantism. The lot of the German-
speaking priest commissioned to teach the most precise kind
of Catholicism, but in the hated tongue, was no happy one.
His authority was constantly defied in every possible manner.

At last in 1906 came the famous school-strike. In over
1000 schools in Posen and West Prussia some 60,000 scholars,
under instructions from their parents, refused to answer questions in German on the catechism or to learn German hymns.
The Polish press and clergy egged them on and applauded.
The enforced use of German was styled "a sinful desecration

[1] That is, of course, the rudiments of the Catholic faith taught by a
priest, albeit under government license and supervision.

of the Catholic religion" and "a tyranny over the conscience in which only the devil in the gorge of hell and the Prussian government could find satisfaction." The children, under such pious urgings, greeted their unlucky "religious teacher" with Polish songs and execrations, or strewed the roadside with fragments of their German catechisms. The Prussian government of course retaliated by every means in its power. Children who proved non-pliable were "kept back" and refused promotion. Parents who encouraged them openly were fined: if they took them away from school outright the parents were sent to prison. But as a most effective measure of all the government appointed additional teachers to the staffs in malcontent villages. The salaries of these extra instructors of course fell directly on the little communities. These increased taxes broke the back of the mutiny. By Easter, 1907, it was ended—but leaving a heritage of hatred in all the Poles of the rising generation. It was a decidedly Pyrrhic victory for Prussia.[1]

Of course the details in this long story of friction between two races, one superior and hectoring, the other very angrily on the defensive, concern only strictly local history. The Poles fought tooth and nail against the discouragement of their language. The Prussian police retaliated by suppressing all kinds of Polish open-air meetings and keeping every indoor meeting under strict surveillance; by frequently forbidding Polish theatrical performances; by refusing to allow Poles to plead their cases in the courts in their mother tongue, even in districts where this had been the language for a millenium; and by actually trying to give a Germanized form to Polish family names whenever they had to be officially recorded. Of course no genuine Pole was welcome in the German civil or military service. The judgeships, the postal service, the great body of railway officials, all the other thousand and one positions which drew the government pay were closed to them. A few great nobles indeed had made their peace with Prussia and won high positions in the diplomatic

[1] For an interesting description of this "strike" see R. H. Fife, "The German Empire between two Wars," pp. 258–59.

service: but they were considered almost apostates to their own people. The Poles in their turn remained a separate political party, returning twelve members to the Prussian Parliament (Landtag) in 1913 and increasing the number of small irresponsible, discontented factions which were the curse of German public life.

Under the stress of Prussian coercion the German fraction of the Poles had come together as a people as they had never done in the days of their turbulent independence. The peasantry, who had seen their nation die without any worthy effort to help their nobility to save her, were in 1914 joining secret societies and giving ear to a propaganda which spelled nothing but trouble for their century-long masters. A few years before the outbreak of the great war, the vigilant Prussian police had seized a vernacular prayer-book circulated among the Polish laborers who had been induced to work in the coal mines of Westphalia. Some of the invocations were these:

Mother of God, Queen of the Poles, save Poland! . . .
From the Muscovite and Prussian bondage free us, O Lord!
By the Martyrdom of the soldiers murdered by the Prussians at Fischau, free us, O Lord!
For death on the battlefield we beseech thee, O Lord!
For the re-possession of the Polish Fatherland, we beseech thee, O Lord!
For an early universal call "To arms," we beseech thee, O Lord!

And yet Poland had been officially declared dead and buried in 1796.

It was clear that here at least German science had been unable to accomplish what Americans have styled the "benevolent assimilation" of a fraction of a people, which, whatever its undoubted faults, was gallant, talented, artistic and under right conditions worthy of the best.

It was no favorable commentary on the achievements of Bismarck and his successors that in 1914, when for obvious reasons both Russia and Germany were bidding for Polish support, the best wishes of the Poles, whatever their masters, seemed to go with the blundering autocracy of Nicholas II.

The Polish problem, therefore, was much like the Schleswig problem only larger, more bitter and much more dangerous. But still more dangerous was that of Alsace-Lorraine. Schleswig had only a very weak country to sympathize with its troubles and to dream of its rescue. Prussian Poland had no friend among the independent nations at all, all its brethren were in other houses of bondage: but Alsace-Lorraine had a mighty friend, close at hand, who never let the story of its troubles sleep.

Gambetta had adjured his French countrymen, concerning the loss of the two provinces, "Think of it often, speak of it never!" But an injunction to such heroic silence was not always obeyed by a great but sometimes voluble nation. Every 14th of July, the "Bastile" national holiday, a solemn procession moved through Paris to place a wreath of mourning on the statue personifying the genius of Strassburg. The remembrance of the disaster of 1870–71 was kept alive by every veteran of Sedan and of the great siege. It was hard sometimes for responsible statesmen to keep expressions of national resentment within bounds and to prevent a serious affront to Germany: for French military men knew perfectly well the excellence of the Kaiser's war-machine and that in any new duel in which France fought without allies her cause might seem good but her case would be desperate. As time went on, as material prosperity returned to France, as a new generation with new interests arose, the memory of the original loss did indeed become a little less keen. Indeed shortly before 1914 there were those who argued that sensible Frenchmen realized that the lost provinces were lost forever, and had only an academic interest in their problems. However, the instant war was declared that year, it was plain as day that the Alsace-Lorraine question was one of the very first issues in the Great Debate.

Possibly if the lost provinces had seemed reasonably contented and happy under their new rulers, Frenchmen would not have been reminded of their disaster so often. But to provide tactful masters did not lie in the German genius.

In 1914 Alsace-Lorraine was barely if any more reconciled to its fate, than in 1871, when the tearful deputies of the two regions quitted the despairing National Assembly at Bordeaux which had voted them away. The poet Schiller, whose precepts have been called oracles by his countrymen, once asserted, *"The noblest sign of culture (Bildung) is respect for other peoples' liberty."* Such a sign of culture was never given by Prussian *Kultur*.

Of course the annexation was a direct act of physical violence by the victor. Bismarck, as has been explained (p. 20), had hesitated about taking all the land which Von Moltke and the military camarilla demanded. "As you see, we are keeping Metz," he told an English journalist, "but I confess I do not like that part of the arrangement. Strassburg is German in speech, and will be so in heart ten years hence. Metz, however, is French, and will be a hot-bed of disaffection for a long time to come." [1] Bismarck was right about Metz. He was grievously wrong about Strassburg. In 1914 the Germans had to take almost as many precautions against sedition in one city as the other.

The German conquerors realized, of course, that at the outset they would be unpopular, but their hearts teemed with good intentions towards the unlucky folk who centuries before had been German and had been weaned away from their loyalty by the specious, superficial Gauls, but who now were returning to their own kindred and their best traditions. Bismarck assured the Reichstag in 1871, "I feel myself called to be the advocate [of the annexed people] in the new state they are entering": and von Sybel, the court historian, announced his certainty that his new fellow burghers of the Empire would soon feel the blessedness of their change. "They will have lighter taxes," he wrote, "greater religious freedom, and in the army will meet the sons of the educated classes." [2]

---

[1] "Conversations with Prince Bismarck," collected by Von Poschinger, English Translation, p. 86.

[2] A sneer at conditions in the French army which seems to have been without the slightest justification.

Unfortunately the conquerors had never learned the sage proverb: "The more haste, the less speed." If loyal subjects of the Kaiser could have been made by ministerial edicts from Berlin, the Alsatians would have been instantly contented and happy: but they were not Brandenburgers. Their lands had been trampled over by invading armies: their homes had often been desolated: Strassburg had been ruthlessly bombarded: while up and down the whole land they were still mourning their dead. On the 30th of September, 1872, the new government, however, enforced its edict compelling all the people to decide whether they wished to be Germans or Frenchmen. If Germans they must submit to the new régime. If Frenchmen they must prepare speedily to quit the land of their fathers wherein they were now counted as alien interlopers. As a result, at the very least 45,000 persons (in the main among the most intelligent and promising young men in the land) deliberately took the sorrowful road to exile. In 1914 these men, gray-headed now, were to see visions, dream dreams, and say moving things to the soldiers of France. Almost simultaneously the teaching of the French language in elementary schools was forbidden. In the city of Strassburg, where the *Marseillaise* had first been flung upon the air, it was prohibited to learn its language, save as a "foreign tongue" for advanced pupils, like English, Italian and Russian. Under French occupation a certain mongrel type of German had always been spoken in the Alsatian villages.[1] The French had never troubled about this. It had not prevented the Alsatians from being zealous patriots. Now, by a natural reaction, many a Teuton-speaking Alsatian prided himself on chattering also a little bad French.

But what drove the annexed population to peculiar wrath, was the almost instant enforcement of the German military conscription. Their slain brethren in the French uniform were hardly cold and buried before the youth of the two provinces were commanded to don the spiked helmet and follow the Prussian drill-sergeant. Vain were protests. In

[1] This was true especially in Alsace. Lorraine had been pretty strictly French in speech as well as in sympathies.

1871 a deputation of citizens went up to Berlin to expostulate. Bismarck told them brusquely, "Prussia had an immense experience of the results produced by wearing the Prussian uniform. Get the King's coat on a man's back and let him wear it for three years, and you have made not only a good soldier but a good 'burgher' [for Germany] out of him." "Yes," retorted Klein, leader of the deputation, "but you must get the coat on first and *that* is what you can never do!" Twelve thousand Alsatian young men at that time fled from their homeland merely to escape the kaiser's livery, and entered the French army. The rest submitted outwardly, but with a sullen spirit that made them of most dubious value as soldiers. The new régime might introduce an admirable legal system and build many new railroads,—all this counted for nothing beside the tyranny of the drill-master.

The conquerors had in fact adopted a relentless policy of "thorough," and held to it with native tenacity. Under the French régime, whatever the Paris government, the Alsatians had enjoyed pretty complete local autonomy. The French prefect had usually been a lax, good-natured functionary, only meddling in serious cases. The government had no doubt been haphazard, unscientific, somewhat inefficient—and popular. Now everything was changed. A swarm of officials with all the Prussian characteristics, plus even greater rigidity —thanks to feeling themselves on the defensive and to being charged with the propagation of *Kultur*—was turned loose on the land with autocratic powers. Down to 1879 the two provinces were ruled practically by a military dictator sent from Berlin. In that year an attempt was made to set up a simulacrum of constitutional rule. The provinces were henceforth to be a "Reichsland," a dominion held by all the Empire in common, not by Prussia merely, but with the Kaiser appointing the governor-general and otherwise exercising pretty complete sway. There was to be a local elective diet and other forms of political "freedom," but the powers of the governor-general and his council (appointed by the crown) were such that the voters could do little more than register public protests by their ballots at one governmental act after another. The Berlin rulers did indeed make a serious attempt to conciliate local opinion by sending down for once a really humane and enlightened governor, Baron von Manteuffel. His intentions were good, and he tried sincerely to let the Alsatians preserve their self-respect. "I do not ask for your sympathy," he declared, "but I advise you to look on the union of Alsace-Lorraine to the German Empire as definitive."

Von Manteuffel won the personal good will of the people he was sent to govern. But his very condescension raised against him enemies at home. He was accused by his fellow Germans of "negotiating with the enemy" because he adopted mild measures; and the horde of lesser officials who had swarmed into the new province, greedy adventurers ("carpetbaggers" Americans would call them), anxious only to seize on every public post, tyrannize and grow fat, denounced him as little better than a traitor. In 1887 he died. The Alsatians mourned him, but he had not convinced them their new masters were anything but despots. At many an election the deputies Alsace-Lorraine sent up to the Reichstag were violent "protesters" against the new régime, and the friction grew rather than diminished. It was under Manteuffel that the Bishop of Metz was awarded the Prussian Order of the Crown, which he repaid by expressing his regret at this unwelcome honor in a public letter to the governor.

When Manteuffel died, the small-fry officials felt that their time was come. Kindness had failed; "proper severity" should now teach these returned but ungrateful sons of the Fatherland, the provincials, to appreciate their blessings. What happened soon after is thus summed up by Paul Hymans, a native Alsatian,—born in 1874 after the annexation, and witness to many things. "Within a few months Alsace was subjected to every kind of German brutality. Deputies were expelled and Alsatian societies were dissolved. Political prosecutions took place on every side, for offenses such as seditious cries or emblems, membership in the 'League of Patriots,' high treason, etc. To guard the Alsatians against 'intimidation' by their French relatives, intercourse with persons beyond the frontier was made impossible by a regulation prescribing the use of passports." There was even a report that Bismarck wished there would be an insurrection in the hope of crushing disaffection once for all in blood.

The natives were too wise for such folly. They offered the passive resistance which is always so exasperating to a government which demands inward submission as well as external obedience. Of course all important government offices were retained by Germans from across the Rhine. Emigrants were sent in from Prussia to take the farms of the exiles who had gone to France, just as other colonists had been sent into the Polish lands. The newcomers naturally were treated as pariahs by the natives. Their social relations were miserable. A Prussian came to Alsace as a stationmaster. Being a domestic soul he desired a wife; no Alsatian girl would marry him. He was obliged to send to Berlin for a consort to share his home and responsibilities. In all about 300,000 Germans thus settled in the Reichsland; but they remained a mere army of occupation among the 1,550,000 odd natives who longed to see them go. They were only so many untactful provocatives to friction and a new disloyalty.

After William II had ousted Bismarck, there was a partial relaxation of the worst of the régime of petty officials that had followed Manteuffel. William, however, by his speeches gave small encouragement to the hopes of the Alsatians for a revocation of the deed of 1871. "We would rather," said he in an oration, "sacrifice our eighteen army corps and our 42,000,000 inhabitants on the field of battle than surrender a single stone my father and [his generals] . . . have gained."

A new generation was growing up in Alsace-Lorraine: young men and women to whom French days were a story for their elders, but the new generation was not being won for the German régime. Unfortunately for their loyalty the Alsatians as a race had a keen sense of humor. It was not always possible for them to take their Prussian preceptors with sufficient seriousness. In 1895 occurred a typical incident at Detwiller, a village near Zabern. A certain peasant

had a fine white cock with a lordly red crest. The owner
most treasonably dyed the bird's tail blue—making him the
veritable emblem and colors of France. This overt act was
promptly denounced by the emperor's loyal police. They
ordered the peasant to slaughter his sedition-teaching fowl.
The man refused. The police saber then avenged the outraged fatherland: and so the feathered traitor perished. The
Paris papers made merry over the tale: and diplomats more
gravely observed that the incident had completely effaced all
the efforts of the Kaiser to cultivate "good relations" with
France at the opening of the Kiel Canal and the visit there of
some French warships.[1]

From the beginning of the third emperor's reign down to
the eve of the great conflict matters did not better themselves. Sometimes it was a case of petty persecution, sometimes of grievous invasion of ordinary human rights. The
police played a kind of game with the French press of the
two provinces, suppressing it on every pretext possible. By
passport regulations they did their uttermost to prevent
Frenchmen from visiting Alsace and Alsatians from visiting
France. When a historical drama was offered in Strassburg
which required a display of the tricolor in one scene, the government forbade the use of the offending banner and then
comically compromised the issue by allowing the use of the
Dutch flag, wherein the red, white and blue strips run horizon-
tally instead of vertically. The great Sarah Bernhardt was
invited to play in Strassburg. The government refused her
license to appear unless she would bury her memories of 1870
and appear in Berlin likewise. The famous actress haughtily

[1] German self-seriousness and lack of humor produced weird results
sometimes in Alsace. A German Protestant clergyman visited an Alsatian pastor's family. He tried hard to persuade his clerical friend
to speak German in his household. The other replied that "his wife
insisted on speaking French." The visiting cleric vainly argued that
it was weak and cowardly to be thus dominated by a woman. Finding
his efforts unsuccessful, he sent his friend a treatise "On the Biological
Imbecility of Woman" (*"Über den biologischen-Schwachsinn des
Weibes"*). The Pan-German congress, to which he formally reported
this deplorable case of demi-treason, duly applauded his patriotic endeavors.

consented, for she had set her heart on meeting an Alsatian audience, but after her enforced performance in Berlin she revenged herself by using her enormous influence to create disgust for Germany, not merely in France, but in many other lands, notably in America.

Finally in 1911 the German authorities conferred on their Reichsland a moderately complete autonomy with a real local constitution, putting it somewhat on a par with the other German states, although the governor-general was still sent down from Berlin and there were other unpleasant evidences of servitude. This long-delayed benevolence produced no lucky results. The newly elected "Landtag" promptly showed its disaffection by cutting down the governor-general's salary, and refusing to vote the annual allowance for the Emperor's hunting trips to Alsace, when he had deigned to chase a few stags and flush some partridges in the game preserves of this part of his dominions. The Prussians promptly retaliated in 1912 by canceling the orders for locomotives for their state railways which had been given to an Alsatian concern. That same year the "All-Highest" visited Strassburg and flung his imperial warning at the Mayor. "Listen! Up to now you have only known the good side of me; you might be able to learn the other side of me. Things cannot continue as they are: if this situation lasts, *we will suppress your Constitution and annex you to Prussia!*"

The Social Democrats all over the empire of course danced with glee at this threat. Their spokesman in the Reichstag declared that here was a confession, on the very highest authority, "that annexation to Prussia is the heaviest punishment one can threaten to impose upon a people for resistance against Germany. It is punishment like hard labor in the penitentiary, with loss of civil rights!" The Landtag, however, was not suitably intimidated. It answered the Kaiser by two resolutions: (1) that their new constitution was not to be altered save by the will of the Alsatians themselves; (2) that the Reichsland should have a national flag. Neither of these suggestions of course was acceptable at Berlin, and so the stress continued.

In 1913 came the notorious Zabern incident (see p. 219), which served formal notice on all the world that the German civilian was under the heel of the German militarist. This was peculiarly exasperating and outrageous to Alsace because the specific acts of tyranny took place within its borders, and the brutality of the officers was probably accentuated because the perpetrators suspected their victims were French sympathizers. In that same year the situation became so bad that Alsatian conscripts who had lately, as a special favor, been allowed to render their army service near their home towns as were the rest of their fellow citizens, were now ordered to perform their terms in the army at a distance from their native state.[1]

Nineteen hundred and fourteen saw increased friction, with the poet-artist Jacob Waltz, one of the most distinguished literary men in Alsace, under prosecution for treason because of satires upon the German administration in the form of books for children. For this crime he was tried before the Imperial Supreme Court at Leipzig, acquitted on the more serious charge, but sentenced to one year's imprisonment "for insulting the police and inciting to disorder." He fled to France, and very soon thereafter the Great War began, at the outbreak of which several prominent Alsatians either escaped over the border, or were imprisoned for the attempt.

When the European conflict commenced it was clear enough that the German attempt to assimilate Alsace had failed utterly. "In Alsace-Lorraine we are in an enemy's country," a Prussian statesman is quoted as saying: and the Kaiser's forces were sent through the country with a healthy anxiety lest the first defeat make the whole region blaze up in revolt behind them. Many of the "needful severities" the Germans inflicted on Belgium were explained as being absolutely unavoidable, because the experience of Alsace-Lorraine had demonstrated that a policy of "leniency" was useless for a con-

[1] During three sojourns in Germany the author of this chapter was assured that the Alsatian conscripts could not be trusted in battle on the Western front. In 1914 I understand they were actually mobilized against Russia.

quered population. The fact of course was, as an American writer has well put it, that "begotten as the Prussian system had been under conditions where iron discipline was a requisite for success, thoroughly convinced of its own efficiency, it knew no law but that of force, and failed in those peaceful contests where victory must be won by conciliation." [1]

However, the issue of the lost provinces had still larger bearings, important for all the world. A calm-minded Frenchman stated the issue as seen by his nation thus: "It is produced by *an irreconcilable opposition between two conflicting conceptions of right;* sovereignty of government by right of conquest—the principle of the German monarchy; sovereignty of the people, whence arises the right of every population to determine its nationality—the principle of French democracy." [2]

In 1884 the "International Peace League," one of those multifarious and pathetically ineffective peace societies which were covering the earth, met at Geneva and passed this resolution: "The conquest and forcible annexation of Alsace-Lorraine constitutes the chief obstacle to [lasting] peace, and the true cause of the enormous armaments." This statement was still true with only a slight exaggeration in 1914. If Germany had been sure of the loyalty of her Reichsland and on reasonably good terms with France, Armageddon could hardly have come to pass as it actually did.

---

[1] Fife, "The German Empire between Two Wars," p. 227. Professor Fife, writing in 1916, while America was still neutral, makes a peculiarly fortunate attempt to interpret German conditions with penetration and perfect fairness.

[2] Seignobos, "Europe since 1814": (English Edit.) p. 831.

CHAPTER XII

AFTER the ink had dried on the signatures to the Treaty of Berlin, the several diplomats of the great powers went home, England and Russia disarmed, the world breathed easier and the chart-makers prepared a new map for the Balkans. Roumania and Serbia speedily signalized their new independence by causing their rulers to be proclaimed "kings": but Nicholas of Montenegro contented himself with the more modest status of "prince" for some decades longer. For quite a while none of these countries had more than occasional mention in the western newspapers, although Montenegro had much friction with Turkey before she secured the boundaries assigned her by the Berlin settlement. Rumania's problems were mainly those of internal development, save for a standing difficulty with Bulgaria over the unsatisfactory frontier given Rumania in the Dobrudja. Serbia watched the appearance of a Christian neighbor on her eastern flank with ill-disguised concern. She had expected to be the reversionary heir to a large part of the Balkans as the Ottomans perished—and lo! here was Bulgaria, a certain rival crowding up against her. Nevertheless, for many years it was not on Belgrade or Bucharest that European eyes were turning. They gave a fleeting glance upon Bosnia:—which was not occupied and "pacified" by Austria until after bitter resistance by the Moslem element among the natives, and some really desperate fighting: but they were soon steadily fixed upon Bulgaria. Here was a new state, an unknown nation intruded into Balkan politics, and an unknown quantity is always perplexing and interesting. In 1870 hardly any western European knew where the district of Bulgaria was.

In 1880 its affairs were discussed even in obscure journals in distant America.

Bulgaria had been kept small and subdivided because Disraeli had expected that the new country would be almost as completely under the czar's influence as Finland or Turkestan. But Britain and Austria had not been able to deny to Russia the task of organizing the country preparatory to setting up its new government. The Bulgar peasants were at first grateful to their liberators from Muscovy, but soon began to complain how Prince Dondukov-Korsakov, the czar's commissioner, filled up all the public positions with Russians and otherwise showed that he felt that he was over a kind of subject province. His intention was to tie Bulgaria to her great protector in the closest possible manner, and for that reason (although a devoted friend of autocracy at home) he helped to draft a constitution at once ultra-democratic and ultra-conservative, "which was so devised that the prince could be checkmated by the people, and the people by the prince, while the *real* power would remain with the czar." [1] A parliament, elected by the people, was set up, and this *Sobranje* was endowed with very great power, although the prince was permitted decided latitude in interfering with its workings. His Excellency the commissioner firmly anticipated that the prince and the Sobranje would be perpetually quarreling, and that the prince would have to lean steadily upon the advice of the czar in order to keep down his subjects. What the Russian never reckoned upon was that the new prince and the new popular parliament, refusing to quarrel, might unite against their over-zealous "protector" in the North. And this was precisely what was to happen.

Under these auspices, and with decided Russian concurrence, the Bulgarians found themselves selecting Prince Alexander of Battenberg, a son of the Prince of Hesse, and a nephew of the czar, as their first ruler (1879). He was only 22 years old when proclaimed, but he had already served

[1] Miller, "The Ottoman Empire," p. 412.

as a cadet at Plevna, and still later as a Prussian lieutenant. He was erect, military and gallant, but he lacked a good education in political problems He could not speak the Bulgar language, and although obstinate and prone to quarrel with his advisers, did not in the least understand the tortuous methods of a semi-oriental land, although he honestly desired the prosperity of Bulgaria. It was not an entirely fortunate selection.

Alexander began by governing with the aid of the extreme pro-Russian element among his subjects. He soon found himself at odds with the Sobranje, wherein the so-called "nationalists" (anti-Russians) were in the majority. In 1881 he forced a suspension of the constitution, under threat of quitting the country and leaving everything in chaos, and thus secured dictatorial authority for a term of seven years. But the prince was soon disgusted at the way the czar's generals thrust themselves into Sofia, monopolized the ministries and treated the prince not as their master, but their tool. Alexander was a German and he did not mix well with the Russians. In 1883 he suddenly restored the suspended constitution and sent the two chief Russian ministers out of the country. From that moment it was evident that Bulgaria was *not* about to become a Muscovite satrapy, and there was a great revolution in European opinion. Czar Alexander II was now dead. Czar Alexander III branded Prince Alexander as an "ingrate" and quasi-traitor to Russia to whom he owed his crown, and began at once to undermine his authority. But in England the feeling soon developed that Bulgaria was not likely to be such a peril to British interests as had been feared. She was henceforth a principality to be encouraged, not crushed.

Meantime that purely artificial segment of Bulgaria, Eastern Rumelia, which had been set off as an "autonomous province of the Turkish Empire," had naturally used its partial freedom to develop hopes for a complete union under its true government at Sofia. The first Turkish governor-general, Aleko Pasha, a smooth Greek, had been fairly popular, but in 1885 the sultan appointed the far less tactful and worthy

Gavril Pasha to the office, and the blow soon followed this provocation. On September 18th, 1885, at Philippopolis, the Eastern Roumelian capital, a band of Christian officers forced their way into the pasha's palace and informed him that his rule was at an end. The bewildered governor-general was hustled into a carriage and paraded around the city with a Bulgarian school mistress flourishing a naked saber at his side, and was then shipped off to Constantinople. The Sultan, taken by surprise for an instant, did nothing. All eyes were turned towards Prince Alexander at Sofia. The prince hesitated to defy Turkey and very likely Russia, but his ministers gave him the choice of advancing to Philippopolis or retiring to Darmstadt. Bulgarian opinion wanted the union with Eastern Roumelia, and woe to the ruler that withstood! The prince went straight to Philippopolis, and the Sobranje at once approved the union. Europe was thus confronted by that most disagreeable thing to explain away—an accomplished deed.

Then followed a strange event. In 1878 England had been willing to fight Russia to prevent Bulgaria from being made united and strong, and Russia had complained bitterly because Bulgaria was to be left dismembered. In 1885, however, such was Czar Alexander III's personal hatred of Prince Alexander (the "Battenberg," as St. Petersburg circles called him), that solemn instructions were sent to Russian officials from the imperial foreign office: "remember that the union [of the two Bulgarias] *must not* take place until after the abdication of Prince Alexander." On the other hand, English influence was all in favor now of undoing the act of 1878. "If you can help to build up these [Balkan] peoples into a bulwark of independent states, and thus screen the 'Sick Man' from the fury of the northern blast, for God's sake do it!" Thus wrote the British ambassador to Russia (Morier) to the British ambassador at Constantinople (White). English diplomacy realized that a strong barrier state between Russia and the remnant of Turkey-in-Europe would be a great hindrance to the Czar, and the latter had played straight into the hands of London by alienating the Bulgars. Acting mainly under British pressure, Sultan Abdul Hamid did not resist the union of Eastern Rumelia with Bulgaria. A notable change seemed to have taken place on the map of the Balkans, without a shot being fired.

Alexander of Russia had feared to coerce Bulgaria directly. That might have started a world war. But there was a much weaker ruler than he who was jealous, angry and irresponsible. King Milan of Serbia was a clever, dissipated man who followed a policy which had made his little country exceedingly dependent on Austria. Very persistent rumor had it, that it was by such subserviency to Vienna that he got the funds for gay visits to Paris, for expensive friendships with actresses, and similar royal pleasures. Very probably Austria now egged him on. Bulgaria must not grow powerful. Doubtless personal ambition impelled him also. In any case it was easy to tell the Serbians that "the balance of power in the Balkans" had been destroyed, and that they must expand their boundaries at the expense of Bulgaria which was waxing too fast. On November 14, 1885, Serbia suddenly declared war on Bulgaria. All the cards seemed in Milan's favor. The Bulgar army was a wholly new creation, untested in battle. The czar suddenly recalled all the numerous Russian officers who had acted as its instructors, and military Europe imagined Prince Alexander as left utterly in the lurch, for the Serbians were experienced veterans of the wars with Turkey.

Milan quitted Belgrade acclaimed with cheers as "King of Serbia *and Macedonia*," but his glory was short-lived. On the 16th of November, the Serbs met the Bulgars at Slivnitza, a village on the road to Sofia. There was a desperate three-day battle. The raw Bulgar levies under their young officers did not break and run away. They fought heroically, and in the end the Serbs were flung back into their own country with the foemen at their heels. Milan's troops were disgracefully routed.[1] Prince Alexander saw the

[1] The defeat of the Serbians was so complete that it became the subject for a comic opera, "The Chocolate Soldier," well-known in Europe and America.

road to Belgrade open before him, when Austria intervened in the name of peace and informed the victors that if they continued their march they must face the troops of Franz Josef.

The Bulgars were obliged to halt, make an armistice, and presently (1886) a definite peace with Serbia. The war had lasted only fourteen days. "Bulgaria had gained from Serbia neither territory nor money; neither Pirot [a disputed town] nor pigs," but she *did* gain recognition of her right to Eastern Rumelia, and better still a consciousness of her own strength and powers of achievement. The battle of Slivnitza was a decisive battle inasmuch as it taught the world that Bulgaria was an effective fighting nation, not lightly to be put off the map. Milan returned to his dissipations at Belgrade or sometimes at Paris, while Alexander returned with better grace to Sofia.

One might have imagined that this victory would have assured Alexander of his throne, but in a very few months he was actually to lose it. It seemed intolerable to the whole vast Russian interest in the Balkans that a man who had proved so intractable to the czar should boast himself and prosper. After the battle of Slivnitza the prince failed to reward certain officers according to the deserts which they themselves considered their due. These discontented men speedily became conspirators under Russian influence. After some preliminary intrigues, on the night of August 21, 1886, a regiment of disloyal troops suddenly mutinied at Sofia and surrounded the princely palace, and the arch-conspirators forced their way into Alexander's bedroom. The prince escaped into the garden, but was chased back with bayonets. The leading rebels tore a sheet out of a visitor's book on the table, scrawled a few words announcing an abdication and forced Alexander to sign. He was then hustled into a carriage, and driven at full speed to the Danube, on reaching which he was thrust upon his own yacht and her bows pointed towards Russia.

As a first stroke the deed had seemed prosperous, but the after-clap was quite otherwise. There was a celebration by

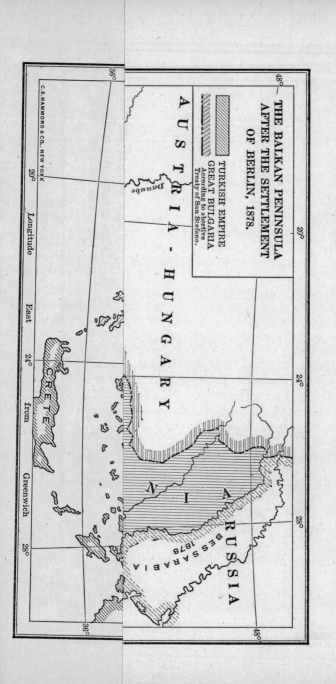

THE BALKAN PENINSULA
AFTER THE SETTLEMENT
OF BERLIN, 1878.

TURKISH EMPIRE
GREAT BULGARIA
According to abortive
Treaty of San Stefano.

C.S.HAMMOND & CO., NEW YORK

AUSTRIA - HUNGARY

Danube

CRETE

RUSSIA

BESSARABIA
1878

Longitude   East   from   Greenwich

36°   20°   24°   28°   36°

48°   20°   24°   28°   48°

the mutineers in Sofia and even a Te Deum in the cathedral over "the liberation of Bulgaria from Prince Battenberg." But from the outset many officers in the garrison had held aloof. Above all Stambulov, the most powerful of the ministers, set his face against the conspiracy. In an amazingly short time a revulsion of popular feeling swept the mutineers out of power, and enabled Stamboulov to telegraph to Alexander to return to his people.

The prince had been landed in Russia, but the czar's government had not dared actually to detain him. He now returned in triumph amid the plaudits of all Bulgaria. Had luck favored him he could have resumed his government amid great popularity and the sympathy of nearly all non-Muscovite Europe. But he ruined his position by a grievous blunder. While returning to Bulgaria he telegraphed to the czar in a vain attempt to propitiate his mighty protector, "Russia having given me my crown, I am ready to give it back to its sovereign." Magnanimity, however, was no quality of the cold and ungenerous Alexander III. He took his unlucky namesake at his word. Instantly the czar published in the official paper at St. Petersburg, "I cannot approve your return to Bulgaria, as I foresee the sinister consequences that it may bring on that country, already so much tried . . . your Highness will understand what you must do." [1]

The prince was received with frantic joy at Tirnova, Sofia, and elsewhere in Bulgaria. He entered his capital on September 3, barely twelve days after he had been kidnapped, but to the great grief of his subjects he at once called his faithful officers around him and announced that he must again abdicate. Many of the soldiers burst into tears, crying out, "Without Your Highness there is no Bulgaria." But Alexander persisted. His word was pledged to the czar; besides, he felt the whole safety of the new Bulgarian state would be compromised if he endeavored to hold his position in the face of the enmity of his mighty neighbor. The de-

[1] There were rumors, seemingly well founded, that the prince was deliberately tricked by Russian diplomats, as to the real attitude of the czar, and inveigled into a position where he could be forced to abdicate.

cisive factor may well have been the attitude of Germany. Bismarck was throwing all his influence against the prince, not because of personal dislike, but because he feared an attempt by Russia to eject him by force would precipitate a general European war;—since 1870 Bismarck (after his lights) had become a zealous friend of peace. It was best for the prince to go quietly, and he went.

Alexander left Bulgaria on September 7, 1886, amid the open lamentations of his people. But it was a pyrrhic victory for the czar. Austria and England alike practically served notice on him that he would not be allowed to compromise the freedom of Bulgaria or to dictate its internal affairs. The principality was overrun with pro-Russian spies and intriguers. The czar's rubles supplied a great corruption fund. Stambulov, as head of the Bulgarian regents, flatly refused, however, to be bullied by the insolent threats of General Kaulbars, sent on as the Russian high commissioner "to restore order." At the election to the Sobranje there were elected 30 pro-Russians, 20 neutral deputies, and 470 friends of Stambulov and supporters of national independence. The Russian yoke had been thrown off indeed, and since Alexander III did not dare to intervene by force and fight Austria and England, the last chance of Bulgaria becoming a vassal state of Muscovy had vanished.

For the next eight years Stambulov, the son of a poor inn-keeper, was the uncrowned ruler of the principality. He was a "strong man" of the Porfirio Diaz type, which Americans have seen in countries like Mexico. The majority of the nation had rallied around him, and the minority he eliminated or silenced by the arbitrary imprisonment or even the arbitrary execution of unwelcome agitators. The Russophiles intrigued incessantly against him, but he had taken their measure—the czar would threaten, but he dared not fight—and so Stambulov went on his way.

For six months after the exit of Prince Alexander the Bulgarian crown was being hawked around Europe for some eligible prince to accept. So long as the czar refused to recognize the candidate elected by Stambulov's government the princely crown had only a very uncertain value. But in December, 1886, a man of hardihood was found—Prince Ferdinand of Saxe-Coburg, a German prince who, however, had also the advantage of descent from Louis-Philippe, onetime king of the French. He was, in addition, a relative of Queen Victoria. Dynastically it was a lucky choice from every standpoint save that of Russia, and Bismarck gave this young man of twenty-six very sage advice: "Let yourself be driven gently by the stream . . . your greatest ally is time, force of habit. Avoid everything that might irritate your enemies. Unless you give them provocation they cannot do you much harm, and in the course of time the world will become accustomed to see you on the throne of Bulgaria." [1]

The new prince who now "mounted the throne of the glorious Bulgarian kings" had of course to face from the outset the formal protest of Russia at his accession, but no great harm was done by this save that the czar had as a consequence no diplomatic representative at Sofia. For a long time the government was conducted by Stambulov while Ferdinand slowly learned the situation and felt his way. The great minister did a notable work for Bulgaria—railroads, schools, industrial awakening, improved methods of agriculture, all these he brought to a hitherto benighted and backward land. But in the end he overplayed his part with "strong arm" methods. The passions of his enemies rose. One of his associates in power was murdered in Sofia; one of his lesser agents was stabbed while in Constantinople. At length the relations of Ferdinand and Stambulov became strained. The prince, who had been cannily gathering the reins into his own hands, and who was now sure of his position, was able to dispense with his too formidable vice-regent. In 1894 he forced Stambulov to resign, and all the fallen minister's enemies rejoiced over him. They were not content merely to drive him from power; in 1895 he was set

[1] S. Whitman, "Personal Reminiscences of Prince Bismarck," p. 179.

upon by three assassins and murdered under circumstances
of great brutality, while the government hardly lifted a
finger to avenge him.[1]

These methods certainly were "Levantine" if not Oriental,
but Prince Ferdinand was at length ruler in his own house.
In 1896 he made his pact with Russia. Alexander III was
dead and Nicholas II had partly forgotten the old feud.
Besides, was not the death of Stambulov a kind of peace
offering? Ferdinand himself was a Catholic, but his people
were "Orthodox," even as were the Russians, and now the
ruler's infant son Boris was solemnly "converted" to the
Greek form of Christianity and at his baptism Nicholas II
acted (by proxy of course) as godfather. Ferdinand was
thus formally recognized by Russia, and instated in the good
social graces of the czar and his court. For the next ten
odd years the western world heard comparatively little of
Bulgaria. Stories were told of the steady economic development of the country, and of the creation of a formidable
army. The native race gained too a very fair name for its
love of political liberty and its lack of aristocratic traditions.[2]
Nevertheless under the terms of the constitution the sovereign
was left with almost complete control of foreign affairs and
of the army. It was impossible, despite the outward reconciliation, for Ferdinand of Bulgaria ever to be very friendly
to the Russia of the czars. Russian dominance in the
Balkans implied death to the hopes, ever developing more
clearly, that Bulgaria should become the preponderant
Balkan state. Besides, the relations of Germany and Russia
grew steadily less cordial and Ferdinand was after all a German prince, sent on his adventure with the good wishes of
Berlin. Not until 1908, however, was he to begin to show
his hand; then the "prince" proclaimed himself to all the
world the independent and sovereign "Tsar of Bulgaria."[3]

[1] Only one of the murderers was tardily brought to trial, and then
was merely sentenced to fifteen years' imprisonment.
[2] There is, of course, the oft-repeated tale of the American visitor in
Sofia, who was asked by a shoe-black in the public square, "Did you
wish to meet my uncle the Prime Minister?"
[3] For convenience the rulers of Russia are here called "czars," and

While Bulgaria thus seemed to be developing a solid and advancing prosperity, and was receding from the unwelcome limelight, her western neighbor was far less fortunate. The annals of Serbia are almost as gory and troublous as those of medieval Scotland. Serbia was indeed an essentially primitive land, with the institutions of peaceful parliamentary life more a name than a reality. The country was small, poor and often unmanageable; nor can outsiders studying the strife of its parties easily tell where patriotism ended and sordid selfishness began. Yet through it all, it was evident that a naturally gifted, intelligent people were struggling upward to the light—although handicapped earlier by the direct tyranny of the Turks, and hindered in great measure later by the absence of any seaport and by their complete dependence on Austria for every kind of commercial outlet.[1]

No nation can become wise, pacific and free until it is allowed to breathe, and Serbia could only breathe through Austrian lungs. As long as this continued the South Slavs had to remain a people of turbulent pig-raisers.

King Milan was no man to free his country from this bondage. A throne to him was not a trust but an opportunity. He was quite content to remain the satrap of Vienna, taking his private orders from Franz Josef's ministers, probably in return for a steady pension. His queen Natalie, however, was a Russian lady of strong anti-Austrian tendencies. This split the court asunder, and upon these national antipathies came personal scandals and finally a divorce, which horrified all the prudes in Europe. The defeat by Bulgaria in 1885 of course undermined Milan's popularity. He granted a liberal constitution in 1888, but could not make the people love him. In 1889, disgusted with the burdens of his inglorious royalty, Milan abdicated. He spent much of the

those of the Balkan kingdoms "tsars." Both words are, of course, transliterations of essentially the same Slavic title.

[1] There is the story of how when protest was made, in the Belgrade parliament, against a very unfavorable commercial treaty with Austria, the Prime Minister declared, "You *must* vote this, gentlemen, or we are a ruined nation!"

remainder of his life very "unconventionally" at Paris. He
was an intelligent man but absolutely without principle, and
he brought little but sorrow to his country.

In his stead ruled his son Alexander, only 13 years old
when he began his reign, and consequently at first represented
by three regents. But the tone of Belgrade public life did
not mend. The ex-king and ex-queen insisted on revisiting
their son, and aired their differences by means of bloody
scuffles between their partisans. Natalie had to be escorted
to the station by the police and told to leave Belgrade; Milan
more peaceably took the express back to Paris. At last in
1893 Alexander suddenly threw off the restraints of boy-
hood and invited his three regents to a dinner party, where
he smilingly arrested them; then he issued a proclamation declaring himself of age, and assumed the actual government.
In 1894, by another stroke, he defied the "Radicals" by abolishing the liberal Constitution of 1889 and restoring the far
more autocratic one of 1869; and for the next six years he
ruled with a high hand.

A woman undid this "tsar of the Serbians." The rulers
of Belgrade did not have the status among western princes
to allow them to aspire to wed German "highnesses" or Austrian "arch-duchesses"; therefore, in 1900, Alexander proceeded to marry a waiting lady of his mother, a certain
Madame Draga Mashin, "the widow of a Bohemian engineer"
and herself of "Bohemian tendencies," which Belgrade gossip at once exaggerated. No heir was born to this union, and
quickly rumors spread that the new queen was busy arrang-
ing that one of her own brothers should be declared successor
to the throne. The king and queen became intensely unpopular. All the cafés and officers' messes in the Serbian
capital developed into hotbeds of intrigue. Alexander felt
that his position was becoming undermined and made vain
efforts to save himself. He restored the suspended liberal
institutions; then, seeing this brought no love from radicals,
suspended them, then restored them again, with drastic re-
visions, however, in favor of autocracy, "in order to secure
order, unity and peace."

By 1903 all Belgrade was on edge, knowing that a great faction hated Queen Draga and was making capital out of her gross personal irregularities, and that "action" was in the air. There was a plot rumored to poison the royal couple by the aid of a traitorous palace cook. There was another plot to shoot the king at the door of the Cathedral on Palm Sunday. But the real deed was done on the night of June 10, 1903, just thirty-five years after Prince Michael, the king's predecessor, had been assassinated,—a proper anniversary! The band of officers was led by Colonel Mashin, the brother of the queen's first husband and her violent ill-wisher. A malcontent regiment seized the approaches to the palace. Dynamite bombs burst in the doors of the residence, and waving their revolvers the murderers ranged through the palace hunting for their prey. Alexander, the last of the line of Obrenovich, was shot down, clasping his wife in his arms; Draga was stabbed and the two mangled corpses flung out the window.[1] It was a truly "Balkan" deed; duly completed by the murder of the queen's brothers, who were prime minister and minister of war.

The act may be justly described as "brutal but not unprovoked." Alexander and Draga had been fast becoming irresponsible tyrants, and it is one of the miseries of autocracy that it is highly difficult to end bad government without ending also the bad ruler. In the morning Belgrade openly rejoiced. The city was hung with flags; church bells rang; bands played; young people danced in the streets. A national assembly was promptly convened by the politicians who had sagely closed their eyes to the preparations for murder. All the papers of Europe might rage, every great power threaten its condign displeasure, the British minister might quit the city; but everybody knew that the last of the line of Obrenovich was dead and that unless the exiled house

[1] When the writer of this chapter was in Belgrade in 1905, local guides would proudly indicate the precise chimney on the roof of the palace, behind which the wretched pair were found concealed when they were shot down. The ordinary printed evidence, however, states that the deed was done in the Queen's clothes-closet, where she and the King were hiding.

of Karageorgevich were recalled, Serbia would fall into anarchy. A national assembly therefore convened and proclaimed Prince Peter Karageorgevich, an elderly gentlemen, who had spent most of his life in Geneva in exile. Whether the new "tsar" had been cognizant of all of the conspiracy is not quite certain; assuredly he was quite innocent of the murder. However, King Peter had to face his bitter troubles. He was at first the mere puppet of the regicides and dared not punish them. The great powers all eyed him with utter suspicion. Indeed the only two of them that at first recognized him were Austria and Russia. Franz Josef denounced the murder as "a heinous and universally reprobated crime." But since he feared that if he refused recognition the Russian influence would become all-powerful in Serbia, the Austrian minister did not depart; and little by little King Peter won back the good graces of Europe. He took oath to rule as a liberal "constitutional" monarch, and he held to his promise, while he gradually developed firmness enough to remove the regicides from power (1906). From that time till the outbreak of the Balkan wars, unlucky Serbia entered upon a period of comparatively peaceful economic development, and the little country receded from the public eye. It was only a calm before a fiercer gale, however; speedily Austria was to annex Bosnia and thereby drive every South Slav into a frenzy; and after that was to come the whole chain of intrigues and deeds leading up to the tragedies of the Balkan wars. Finally, in 1914, Serbia was to be the occasion and center for the outbreak of the mightiest armed struggle the world has ever seen.

While Bulgaria was thus defying the czar, and Serbia scandalizing Europe by the strange deeds in its royal palace, their neighbor Greece was showing the world the melancholy example of a small nation carried away by the memories of a great past and by a keen ambition for the instant realization of its just hopes, thereby launching upon a military task to which it was entirely unequal, and consequently meeting with humiliation and overthrow.

Greece had been grievously disappointed that she had not been awarded a greater part of Thessaly and Epirus, following the Berlin Congress. She had kept quiet during the Russo-Turkish War on the strength of repeated assurances from the powers that she could get more by keeping still and trusting to their generosity than by drawing the sword. These promises had been very poorly kept. Especially Crete, a large island close to Greece, and with the majority of its inhabitants strongly Christian and "Hellenic" in their sympathies, had been left to the misrule of the sultan. Between the Christian majority and the Moslem minority of the Cretan population there had been almost chronic civil war with the Turkish governors and garrisons giving their fellow Mohammedans just enough military aid to make the fighting odds well balanced and the misery of the island therefore perpetual. The "reform of Crete" had been one of those standing demands by the powers upon the sultan, like the "reform of Macedonia" and the "reform of Armenia." The sultan had always smoothly promised the reforms—and the devil's dance had continued.

In 1868 an "organic statute" of liberties had been promised the Cretans. In 1878 this had been improved and amplified. In 1889 Abdul Hamid had recalled his promises, and thereby of course provoked a new insurrection, which could not be stamped out. In 1896 the insurgents were more than ordinarily active and their kinsmen in Greece seethed with anxiety to rescue them and to annex the island. There were many other ticklish matters then at issue in the diplomatic world. Most of the great powers, especially England, sympathized platonically with the Greek demand for the ending of Turkdom in Crete, but Germany, already drawing nigh to her Ottoman friends on the Bosphorus, set her face like flint against any scheme to dismember the Turkish Empire, and there was no unity among the other powers as to the program to be pursued in case they attempted a redistribution of Abdul Hamid's unhappy realm. Therefore with united voice the foreign ministries warned King George of Greece to restrain his people, and to wait before drawing the sword on Turkey,—none of the great powers would aid him.

Unfortunately it was not in the power of King George (a very moderate and intelligent man) to wait. In Athens ardent patriots utterly despised the fighting power of the Turks, and courageously ignored the feebleness and lack of organization of the Greek army. The king's hand was forced. He had to choose between yielding to popular clamor or losing his throne; and he preferred to keep the latter. In February, 1897, a Greek torpedo flotilla and a small body of troops were sent to Crete. The war-ships of the great powers prevented them from expelling the Turkish garrisons, but this only made national feeling burn the hotter. King George understood the situation perfectly, but his people had not drawn the sword since 1829 and were arrogant in their confidence of victory. Their intense love of democracy led the private soldiers to give very scant respect to their officers, and they forgot that all their successes in the old "War for Independence" had been won in strictly guerilla fighting, and that now they must measure arms in open battle. Checked in Crete, these over-zealous patriots therefore began raids in Macedonia. Soon there was brisk fighting on the Greek northern frontier. Abdul Hamid could restrain himself no more. He knew that his army was superior, and that Germany would befriend him in case of any mishap, and accordingly the "Thirty Days' War" followed.

Turkey declared war April 17, 1897. Instantly the Greek bubble burst. Edhem Pasha promptly broke the Greek lines in Northern Thessaly, and sent the army of Crown Prince Constantine [1] back in headlong rout to Larissa which they were fain to evacuate. The defeated Hellenes rallied and fought again, more stoutly but equally vainly, at Pharsalos. A third defeat at Domokos forced the defenders to retire still further south, and take their last stand at the classic Pass of Thermopylæ. If Edhem forced this he could march into

[1] This prince later, as King Constantine of Greece, was to play a notable if unenviable part in the Balkan phase of the great war, 1915–1917.

Athens. It was believed in many quarters that Kaiser Wilhelm II was contemplating such an event with satisfaction. The pasha had been accompanied by German officers. Not a word of sympathy for the Greeks came from the Berlin official press. The representative of the German minister at Athens made an ostentatious visit to the confinement camp of the few Turkish prisoners "to inquire for their welfare." Although Kaiser Wilhelm was the brother-in-law of the same Prince Constantine who had fled the field in Thessaly, his unconcealed friendship for the Turks went to the very limits of neutrality. It was all part of the fixed German policy of strengthening the Turkish alliance at any cost.

When the news of Domokos reached Athens there was panic in that capital. Popular clamor accused the innocent king of betraying the national cause. The royal family durst not drive out on the street. Yet there was nothing for it but to confess that the case was desperate and ask for an armistice. On May 20, 1897, the Turks were compelled to give one. Even Germany could not risk the complications if Abdul Hamid seemed too triumphant; besides, if the war continued, even with Turkish victories, so many of the Sultan's troops would be diverted that Bulgaria might strike to enlarge her southern boundaries. The powers, however, compelled the Greeks to pay for this gallant but ill-advised attempt to rescue their Christian brethren in Crete by tasting all the dregs of defeat. Certain strategically located villages in Thessaly were ceded back to Turkey by the final treaty of peace, and Greece had to submit to a war idemnity of about $20,000,000, a heavy burden for so small a nation. To discharge it, she had to place her finances under the control of commissioners from the great powers, and to undergo grievous taxation. Thus disastrously ended a brave but reckless adventure.

Nevertheless, the efforts of the Greek patriots were not wholly vain. The conditions in Crete were intolerable. Germany and her satellite Austria openly washed their hands of the business and declared they could do nothing that might displease the Sultan, but the other four great powers were less squeamish. Actually eject the Turks from Crete they would not—*that* might have precipitated more fighting, but in 1898 they set up what amounted to an autonomous government in the island, with all the preponderance granted to the Christian majority, confined the Turkish garrison to an islet in Suda Bay, where alone the sultan's crescent flag was to be kept flying, and, last but not least, appointed Prince George of Greece [1] to the post of "High Commissioner of the Powers, under the suzerainty of the sultan." The mere selection of such a governor-general was of course tacit admission that the claims of Greece to the island were well-founded.

The results of the change were soon evident. An efficient gendarmerie under Italian officers restored peace to the afflicted island. Many of the Mohammedans (now they had ceased to be the governing class) emigrated quietly to Asia Minor, thus simplifying the religious situation. Crete became a reasonably prosperous and well-ordered petty republic, although the desires for final annexation to Greece never died away, and on the eve of the Balkan wars were to blow up again to white heat.

During the few years preceding 1908, the date which heralded a great change, Balkan affairs were comparatively quiet. Serbia, Bulgaria and Greece, as well as Montenegro and Rumania, had recovered from their various spasms and were not intruding in the western newspapers. Germany and Austria had not yet developed their full ambitious policies. Everybody knew that Turkish misrule was creating a grievous problem in Macedonia, but that was a danger that had been many times postponed. Then suddenly there came a most curious revolution in Constantinople (1908). At first it shook only the sultan's palace; then the whole Turkish Empire; then the Balkan kingdoms; then the great powers of Western Europe,—and behold the face of all things was changed! From 1908 onward, the Near East beheld

---

[1] A younger brother of Prince Constantine.

event follow on event, and crisis on crisis, with a startling rapidity until the catastrophe of 1914.

To understand how this sinister process could originate in Constantinople and not elsewhere, one must examine the reign and evil doings of Abdul Hamid II, "the red sultan."

CHAPTER XIII

ABDUL HAMID, "THE RED SULTAN"—HIS DEEDS AND DOWNFALL

WHILE the new Balkan kingdoms were painfully wrestling with their several problems, their old oppressor the Turk was being thrown wearily back upon himself and was trying for a new lease of life.

In Europe the Treaty of Berlin left the sultan the mere shadow of his former dominions,—some 65,000 square miles, divided with rough equality between Thrace (or Roumelia proper), Macedonia and Albania. About 6,000,000 people lived in this long, narrow, ill-compacted "Turkey in Europe," and outside of Constantinople and the Albanian uplands the majority of them were Christians. "Turkey in Asia," however, was still a truly huge empire, embracing some 700,000 square miles, without reckoning uncertain claims to suzerainty over the tribes of Arabia and of Tripoli in Africa. These Asiatic dominions possessed little unity save that of a common oppression. It was utterly beyond the ability of the Ottomans, although they had been in Asia Minor since well before 1300, to weld even the Mohammedan portion of their subjects into a single nation. The population of Asiatic Turkey was about 17,000,000. Of this possibly 6,000,000 were actual Turks. The remainder was rather equally divided between non-Ottoman Mohammedans, Arabs and Kurds (the latter mainly in the Caucasus Mountains), and various kinds of Christians,—Greeks, Armenians and Syrians. The Christians were the leaders of the merchant and artisan classes and probably represented at least ninety per cent. of the intelligence and hope of progress in the entire empire. The Turks were settled pretty solidly in Asia Minor and their lower elements were hard working though very unprogressive peasants: of course they also furnished most of the civil officials and the officers for the army. The Arabs in Syria and Mesopotamia were on very cold terms with their Ottoman fellow believers. They represented an older and worthier type of Moslem civilization, and regarded the Turks as oppressive interlopers. As for the Kurds, they were such crude, unruly mountaineers that the sultans counted themselves lucky if they were not in constant uproar and rebellion. On the whole, the Asiatic Christians and Mohammedans lived together in tolerable harmony; but the least unlucky incident would touch off the Moslem fanatics to go on a Jihdad—a "holy war" to kill infidels—and then massacre would become the order of the day. It is needless to remark that in 1878 Asia Minor, Syria and Mesopotamia had practically no railroads and very few decent highroads, and that a great part of the sultan's Asiatic dominions represented the true unspoiled Orient,—a certain amount of tawdry luxury and glitter almost hidden under a much vaster amount of squalor, sordidness, primitiveness in all economic and cultural conditions, with here and there black patches of even grosser barbarism. If the conditions in Turkey in Europe were bad, conditions in Turkey in Asia were still worse. And Europe had hardly given them the slightest serious attention.

Abdul Hamid II had come to the throne in 1876, after two palace revolutions, which gave him warning to tread warily. Almost immediately after his succession came the disastrous Russo-Turkish War with the loss of Bulgaria, and the virtual loss of Bosnia and Cyprus.[1] This was no glorious beginning for a reign, but everybody knew that Abdul Hamid was not responsible for the misrule and bad generalship which led to the catastrophe. It was easy to exile or to bowstring certain unfortunate pashas; and the world at first looked on the new sultan as a man likely to bring a real regeneration to Turkey.

Even with great abilities the task of a reformer in the Ottoman empire would have been an almost impossible one; and

[1] Theoretically these lands were held only temporarily by the sultan's good friends Austria and England; practically all the world knew they were lost forever.

Abdul Hamid had no ambitions as a reformer. He was a man of much capacity, but his antipathy for things Christian and western was intense. Christendom had torn from him some of his fairest provinces, and to the best of his ability he would make Christendom pay the price. As he watched events not unshrewdly from his gilded chambers in the Yildiz-Kiosk by the Bosphorus, two things became increasingly clear to him: first, that the Great Powers of Europe were intensely jealous of one another, that under scarcely any circumstances would the other nations allow Russia a second time to punish the sultans for their sins, and that although the "concert of Europe" might present "joint-notes" and threaten him, it could almost never act decisively. Secondly, that there was developing in Central Europe a powerful friend for the Ottomans. The German Empire did not touch Turkey territorially. It disclaimed any ambition to make annexations. It did not pose as a champion of the "Orthodox" Christians of the Sultan's empire as did Russia; or of the "Catholic" Christians as did France.[1] The Hohenzollern kaiser merely seemed to desire "friendly relations" with Constantinople and a proper chance for the commercial expansion of his subjects. Abdul Hamid was presently led to believe that the great military machine created and led to victory by von Moltke would be at his service in case the czar again undertook to make the Crescent retreat before the Cross, or England translated her admonitions to "reform" into harsh deeds. The sultan doubtless realized that his "brother" at Berlin was scarcely hinting of this protection out of disinterested love; but this troubled him little. The future could care for the future. The important thing was that for the moment he had a free hand for revenge and reaction.

From 1880 to 1908 Turkey was governed under a stark tyranny worthy rather of the ninth than of the nineteenth century. The few pashas who dared to hint of genuine reform, or of an attempt to galvanize the institutions of the empire, were imprisoned or obliged to flee into exile. The

[1] This was true of France down to the disestablishment of the Catholic Church in that country, early in this century.

grand viziers became simply the first ministers of despotism. Liberty of press became such a farce that virtually no one would read a Turkish newspaper because everything of the least interest, even on non-political subjects, was carefully excised by the vigilant censor. A distinguished American, traveling through Turkey, was invited to address a religious meeting of native Christians. He chanced to use the word "freedom." The interpreter dared not translate the phrase containing it—the act might have landed him in a dungeon. Indeed a certain side of Abdul Hamid's government seemed as if taken from plain farce comedy. An American mission college imported some elementary chemistry text-books from England. The consignment was held up in the customs office and the professor in charge was informed that the volumes were "highly seditious." When he expressed surprise, he was told a dangerous cipher against the sultan had been discovered, and he was shown the familiar formula for water, H_2O. It was gravely explained to him that "H" undoubtedly indicated [Abdul] Hamid, and "2" even more clearly connoted "Second"; while "O" was a palpable covering for "nothing." The cipher therefore obviously read "Abdul Hamid Second equals, or is good for, nothing"—a deliberate incitement to treason!

Another sage deduction of the sultan affected the entire city of Constantinople. Long after the use of electric light was common elsewhere, the city of the padishahs was illuminated by gas. The reason for this was that Abdul Hamid lived in perpetual fear of death by dynamite, and the difference between a "dynamo" (needful for electricity) and "dynamite" never became clear in the mind of the "Commander of the Faithful." He prudently prohibited them *both* to be on the safe side.

Only one act of real benefit came from this ruler's intense timorousness. A sacred Mollah (Mohammedan holy-man) had predicted that the sultan would perish of the plague. To give this prophecy the lie, the sultan caused divers precautions to be taken for the cleansing and sanitation of Constantinople, and for the establishment of a strict quarantine. This policy is said to have saved the lives of some thousands of his subjects, but it was almost the only deed for which they could ever bless him.

And yet with all this, Abdul Hamid, according to his lights, possessed a certain fearful intelligence. He detested every suggestion that the Western civilization was superior to the Oriental; his words indeed dropped honey to every distinguished Occidental visitor who was invited for coffee and sherbet to the palace, but every attempt to introduce changes into the "unchanging East" was met with almost masterly obstruction. The sultan was frightfully extravagant in his court and harem. The revenues wrung out of the Armenian merchants and the toiling rayahs of Asia Minor were spent, even as in the palmy days of Solyman the Magnificent, on the odalisques, the fat Circassian beauties and the infamous boy favorites who were marshaled by the chief of the eunuchs. Every kind of public service was neglected. The Ottomans had possessed a fairly formidable fleet in the seventies. The iron-clads were now moored along the water-front at Constantinople and allowed to become land-locked by the growth of sea-weeds and barnacles, while their decks and turrets were covered with flower-gardens grown by their idling care-takers. Meanwhile the "captains" and "admirals," favored satellites of the padishah, idled ashore, squandering the upkeep money of the navy. Much of the army was miserably equipped and fed and still worse paid. The sultan, nevertheless, knew how to keep himself in power. Trusted and devoted myrmidons were seldom asked what they took from the treasury, and an adequate number of picked regiments were kept at Constantinople, their loyalty being assured by prompt and high pay and very tender discipline. For long Abdul Hamid's grip on the throne seemed so firm that no one ventured to shake it.

After 1878 the old influence of England at Constantinople waned. By exacting Cyprus she had destroyed any claims to gratitude for upsetting the treaty of San Stefano. By her occupation of Egypt (1882), a country still nominally under Turkish sway, that gratitude had been still more diminished. The English had become ashamed of the countenance they had given to Ottoman iniquities in the past, and Gladstone and Lord Salisbury sent too much scolding advice through their ambassadors to make their words very welcome. Russian influence also waned. Bulgaria was growing into a solid state and her relations with Russia were not cordial. She would hardly let the czar's troops cross her willingly, and if her neutrality were violated by the Russians, Austria would have much to say. England and Russia (now allied with France) were still on very bad terms. A combination of these powers against Turkey seemed the last thing possible. Abdul Hamid was thus growing more confident as the eighties advanced and the nineteenth century entered its last decade.

In 1888 died William I of Germany, likewise his son, the short-reigning Emperor Frederick. A new master was in power in Berlin, a master who would not hesitate to depart abruptly from old diplomatic paths, who had soaring ambitions for his monarchy, and who was to prove not over-nice in his methods. On November 1, 1889, the German imperial yacht, the *Hohenzollern,* steamed through the Dardanelles, between the saluting forts. On board were William II and his Empress. It was their first visit of ceremony to any great European sovereign, and it is worthy of notice that they selected for this high honor no Christian monarch but the Kalif of Islam. They received an ovation at Constantinople, tricked out with all the pageantry and obsequiousness of the East. Prussian *Kultur* and Ottoman medievalism met happily together. Abdul Hamid went to extravagant lengths to do his friends full honor. "Rarely has a ceremonial visit been productive of consequences more important."

William II was on the eve of breaking with the great chancellor he had inherited from his grandfather. Bismarck had been cordial indeed with the sultan, and willing enough to have him look hopefully to Berlin, rather than London for comfort and counsel, but he had never approved of ambitious schemes for imperial expansion. William II, however, belonged to a younger and bolder generation. Soon he was to dismiss his aging servant and do that which was right in his own eyes. The chancellor's conservatism was to become a discredited tradition. "Bismarck," wrote one of the German authors of that younger school in whom the kaiser delighted, "merely led us to the threshold of German regeneration." The past belonged to the minister, the future to the emperor; and the latter willed the rapprochement of Germany and the Turk.

Abdul Hamid probably did not enquire the price his redoubtable new friend would ultimately ask for his protection. Possibly his Oriental cunning made him believe that if ever Berlin in turn became too domineering he could seek defenders again from St. Petersburg or London. The important thing was that for the moment this informal but very real alliance with Germany made him quite independent of the dictation of both of those capitals. He could hardly have known that as early as 1886 the distinguished German Orientalist Dr. Spenger had stated, "Asia Minor is the only territory of the world which has not yet been monopolized by a Great Power; and yet it is the finest field for colonization. If Germany does not miss the opportunity, and if she seizes it before the Cossacks clutch hold, she will have secured the best part in the division of the world." But Abdul Hamid *ought* to have known that the Hohenzollerns never ruined themselves by acts of disinterested kindness. The immediate prospects, however, were wholly satisfactory. We need not examine here what hopes and projects William II and his kindred spirits in Germany were entertaining touching Turkey, but only what the Sultan speedily did himself.

In the mountains, near the southeastern coasts of the Black Sea and in the eastern part of Asia Minor, with scattered colonies elsewhere, especially in Constantinople, lay the Armenians. A fraction of this people was across the border in Russian Transcaucasia, but the great majority (some 2,000,000) lay under the power of Abdul Hamid. These Armenians were an ancient and much-tried race. On the sculptured slabs of hoary Nineveh the Assyrian kings had vaunted their bloody triumphs over the men of "Uratu"— the dwellers in the Armenian hill-country. Conquerors had come and gone; the Armenians still were there. They seldom

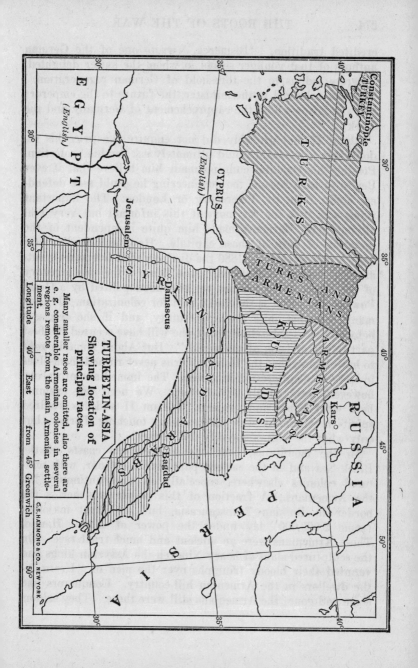

TURKEY-IN-ASIA
Showing location of
principal races.

Many smaller races are omitted, also there are e. g. considerable Armenian colonies in several regions remote from the main Armenian settlement.

Longitude   40°   East   from 45° Greenwich

C. S. HAMMOND & CO., NEW YORK

succeeded as soldiers. Roman, Persian, Arab and Turk all oppressed them, but they retained tenaciously their native language and customs, and their oft-persecuted Christian faith. Very many of them of course were peasants, but their upper classes had come to provide much of the brains of the Turkish Empire. These "Christian Jews" were bankers and merchants in their upper social strata; money-changers and hucksters in their lower. The Ottomans often hated them because they were richer, cleverer and more progressive than their masters. Still, for decades there had been no grievous friction. Then suddenly, towards the end of the nineteenth century, "Armenia" became a word unwelcomely familiar to Western ears.

The Armenians had been impartially mistreated, of course, along with the rest of the sultan's subjects, and since they were Christians the great powers inserted a special clause in the Berlin treaty making the Turkish government pledge the Armenian districts "improvements and reforms" and guarantees of "security against the Circassians and Kurds." Besides, by the "Cyprus Convention" Turkey had very specifically promised England "to introduce the necessary reforms . . . for the protection of the Christians . . . in these (Asiatic) territories." (See p. 94.) The position of the Armenians, therefore, after 1878, ought to have been considerably improved.

But Abdul Hamid soon willed otherwise. Into his heart there had entered the tyrant's demon, fear. He had seen Serbia, Bosnia, Bulgaria and Rumania all slip from Turkish suzerainty or direct lordship. He knew too that among the Armenians there was a wide circle of those who were encouraged by the success of their fellow-bondsmen in the Balkans, and who were ready to start an agitation for Armenian freedom also. They could adduce plenty of typically Turkish acts of oppression. The "reforms" were still merely pious wishes, and about 1890 they organized a political society called "The Bell," and began an agitation in Western Europe for Armenian liberty.

It was not a fortunate time. Apart from the attitude of

Germany, Czar Alexander III was very unwilling to encourage a "free Armenia," fearing the liberated folk would prove as ungrateful to Russia as in Bulgaria, and halt the Muscovite advance southward with another barrier state. The Russian policy was clearly at that time to wait until a lucky turn in European affairs left them free to strike the Sultan boldly and to absorb his whole dominion. This Armenian agitation, however, filled Abdul Hamid with terror. He must kill the serpent of rebellion, ere it could raise its head. Likewise he was very angry at the perpetual nagging advice and threats of intervention by certain of the great powers, especially by England. Also, as intimated, he was now grown bold to risk the immediate consequences of action, by the pledges of good will from Wilhelm II. He struck, struck ruthlessly, and gained a name along with Zhengis-Khan and Alva in universal history.

In 1893 there were some slight agitations in the Armenian mountain villages. This gave Abdul Hamid his pretext for "restoring order." In 1894 he let loose on many Armenian districts, not at first the Turks, but the even more ferocious and fanatical Kurds of the Caucasus uplands. When these did not suffice, they were duly helped out by Turkish regular troops. The story is one catalog of horrors that seemed unsurpassed until in 1915 the Armenians were the victims of a yet greater massacre, with the Prussian this time the avowed and not the silent partner of the butchers.

The massacre began in August, 1894, in the villages of the Sassoun district in the province of Bitlis. Nine hundred Armenians there were slain in cold blood with every possible barbarity. Zekki Pasha, in charge of this worthy work, was decorated by the Sultan for his public "services." The ambassadors of the great powers were horrified. Great Britain demanded a commission of inquiry. The Sultan blandly answered by ordering a commission "to inquire into the criminal conduct of the *Armenian* brigands." Nothing was done to punish the guilty. Village after village blazed to heaven, while the victims poured out their blood. Schemes of "reform" were amicably discussed at Constantinople between the ambassadors and the grand vizier—and still came in the tales of massacre accompanied by deeds of "the foulest outrage and the most devilish cruelty."[1] All through 1895 the systematic demons continued their work, moving from district to district. In 1896, goaded beyond endurance, a band of frenzied Armenians rose at Constantinople and seized the Ottoman bank. Of course their attempt instantly failed, and the angry sultan retaliated by having 6,000 Armenians hunted down and clubbed to death in the very streets of the capital, and under the very noses of their Excellencies, the protesting ambassadors.

It was patent to all the world that Abdul Hamid cared nothing for moral appeals, nothing for ordinary threats.[2] Only an overwhelming show of force with an obvious intention to use it would make him confess his sins and render what justice was possible. Fifty thousand Armenians, according to an English, 75,000 by an American estimate, had perished. The consciences of very many Englishmen were terribly stirred. There were great meetings for protest in London and Liverpool. Mr. Gladstone, now a very old man, raised his voice in angered protest, branding Abdul Hamid as *"the Great Assassin,"* while others as pithily styled the padishah *"Abdul the Damned."* In France too there was fury and indignation. *"The red sultan,"* the Parisian journals called him. But France was still hesitant to play a bold hand for herself in foreign affairs: Russian ministers were cynically declaring that "they did not want another Bulgaria in Asia Minor." Austria was already dancing to Germany's pipe, and although

---

[1] The words are those of the calm and responsible British statesman, the Duke of Argyle.

[2] The writer recalls being present as a lad, at a meeting in an American city to protest against these Armenian atrocities. A distinguished judge declaimed against the Sultan, but asserted that soon the "moral indignation of the world" would force him to mend his ways. Even at that time I pondered confusedly on the question, "But what if Abdul-Hamid cares nothing for the 'moral indignation of the world'?" —The excellent judge merely exhibited that Anglo-American ignorance of militarism and its logic that was to breed us all the miseries subsequently caused by pacifism.

William II in no wise promised to take up arms for Abdul
Hamid, all the tremendous diplomatic influence of Berlin was
thrown in favor of ignoring the tragedies and doing nothing.
The Prussian official press explained away the deeds which
cried to God, and the kaiser's ambassador was often at the
Yildiz-Kiosk—assuredly not to threaten.

No nation was more responsible at that day, however, for
the existence of Turkey and for her chance to work iniquity
than England. England had forced through the Treaty of
Berlin and the Cyprus Convention. Her honor was plighted
to secure reforms for Armenia. The best instincts of England
were in favor of a bold stroke worthy of a mighty nation. A
great fleet lay off the Dardanelles: and those were before the
days of drifting mines and the huge howitzers which closed
the straits in 1915. The prime minister of Britain was Lord
Salisbury, a man of ability, personal honor and considerable
statesmanship. But he was a "Conservative" of the Disraeli
school, full of dread of Russia and with a surviving partiality
for the Turks, although admitting their sins. He was weighed
down by the many great cares of the world-wide British
Empire. He had no firm ally, if he attacked the sultan, save
possibly Italy—the weakest of the great powers. It was the
time when courage urged a bold stroke; but the prudence
which tapers off into cowardice urged procrastination. Salisbury issued solemn admonitions to the sultan that misgovernment would earn calamity: he urged the other powers to join
in common action—he met stolid ears at Berlin and St. Petersburg. *And then he did nothing.* The technical excuse was
good. The fate of Turkey was an affair for "the Concert of
Powers": and no one power had the right to disturb the general peace of the world by individual action to which the rest
did not consent. But technical excuses avail not at the
judgment bar of history. In 1896 not merely Abdul Hamid
but wiser men than he believed that they had taken the
measure of Great Britain, and that despite her proud navy
and spreading empire, save for the most sordid reasons she
would not fight.[1] And of course from this time British diplo-

[1] In 1906 the author, while in Berlin, was assured by a prominent

matic influence in many oriental quarters waned, and German influence increased.

At that time, and subsequently, Englishmen felt and expressed keen humiliation at this failure of their government to discharge a very specific moral obligation. The incident deepened that most unfortunate belief in the inherent pacifism of the British Empire which was one of the direct causes of the calamity of 1914; and in 1915 myriads of Englishmen were to perish on that peninsula of Gallipoli, before which, in 1896, their fleet strained on its moorings, to attack and to pass on to Constantinople. The cowardice and flinching was that of Robert Arthur Cecil, Marquis of Salisbury, and his cabinet. The penalty was paid by the whole British Empire within nineteen years.

Abdul Hamid, "the red sultan," cared little for the scoldings in the London and Paris papers. He had discovered his friend. He had taken the measure of his enemies. He had "quieted" the remnant of the wretched Armenians for yet a while. In 1897 came the brief war with Greece over Crete, and the Turkish army, disciplined by Von der Goltz and other German officers, was able to give its master all the joys of a conqueror. Even so, many monarchs of Europe looked askance at Abdul the Damned. There was one ruler, however, who did not share their qualms—William II.

Barely was the Greek war out of the way when the German Kaiser again hastened to visit his august Mohammedan friend who had just so happily resisted "malice domestic and foreign levy." Bismarck was out of power now, and dying. The Emperor was fain to show his full hand. The "red sultan" was delighted at the cordiality of his guest: "the imperial visitor kissed him and called him brother." There were many cordial *tête-à-têtes:* "it was then that the proposals for the Bagdad railroad [to be built by German cap-

professor, who became one of the leading spirits in the Pan-German movement and who was close to the circle of William II, that he was convinced that "England would never go to war provided her soil was not invaded nor her commerce directly molested." He cited this failure to make good her threats against Turkey in 1896 as proof positive of his contention.

ital] were negotiated: and privileges were secured which have developed into a stupendous mortgage over the whole Turkish Empire. French prerogatives and concessions were arbitrarily revoked. British and French influences were reduced to naught."[1] William II, however, traveled far beyond his comrade's palace by the Bosphorus and its rose gardens. Like a crusader of old he must go on to Jerusalem. It was a crusade under strictly modern auspices. Not Peter the Hermit but "Messrs. Thomas Cook & Co., Tourist Agents," personally conducted the new champion of Western civilization from Jaffa up to Jerusalem and then on to Damascus. In Berlin the kaiser had passed for a zealous Protestant, and indeed at the Holy City William II did show an approving interest in various Lutheran missions. He also displayed a truly impartial zeal for the prosperity of the German Catholics in Palestine: but it is to be feared his main interests in Syria were hardly the direct propagation of the Gospel. As a witty Frenchman who wrote up this pilgrimage observed: "The emperor varied his parts as quickly as he changed his uniforms." Within fourteen days of having offered his "profound homage" at the Holy Sepulcher at Jerusalem and the manger at Bethlehem, he found himself in Damascus—a distinctly Moslem city. The blood of the slaughtered Armenians had hardly sunk into the ground. In the corps of smiling dark-mustachioed Turkish officers that salaamed to the great ally of their master, were many very probably who had slain the babe, and more than slain the mother; but all was cordial and charming even for the polite East. The kaiser delivered an address on the 8th of November, 1898, before these servants of the second Herod. One of its sentences stuck in the minds of Western statesmen: "His Majesty the sultan Abdul Hamid, and the three hundred million Mohammedans who reverence him as Kalif,[2] may rest

1 Bracq, "The Provocation of France," p. 69.

2 This implied not merely the Turkish Moslems, but all the other followers of the Prophet who considered the sultan as "kalif"—a kind of Islamic pope and head of their religion whatever their political allegiance.

assured that at all times the German Emperor will be their friend." That meant, if words mean anything, that the emperor was to constitute himself the general champion of all the millions of Mohammedans under British, French and Russian rule, and even of the Sulu Isles of the Philippines, which had just been seized by the United States. Of course William II did not translate his ideas more clearly or put them into instant action, but from this time onward the chances of Germany yoking all Islam to its chariot wheel and making Mohammedanism an agent for Teutonic propaganda were recognized by responsible men.[1]

From this time onward it was recognized that the German ambassador at Constantinople exercised more real power in Turkish affairs than the average grand vizier. As a fruit of the emperor's visit, the negotiations for the construction of the Bagdad railway, which was to connect Constantinople with the Tigris River and then with the Persian Gulf, went forward to a climax fortunate for Germany. In fairness it must be said English commercial interests about 1880 could probably have won a similar opportunity, but the chance was ignored because the eyes and expectations of all Britons were

[1] The writer was informed by American missionaries in Asiatic Turkey that they had heard Ulemas solemnly explain to the faithful that the Lutheranism of the Kaiser was really only a slight modification of the true teachings of the Prophet, and that Germans ought not to be reckoned infidels: also they tell that William II has been often prayed for in mosques as "His *Islamic* Majesty." In 1899 a German Protestant pastor, a keen observer of Teutonic policy in the East, wrote as follows: "We must be politically indifferent to the sufferings of the Christian peoples of the Ottoman Empire. . . . As Christians we welcome the expansion of the faith, but our politics have no occasion to be concerned with Christian missions. . . . When we have made our choice we must never turn back. William II has made his choice. He is the friend of the Padishah, because his faith is in a greater Germany." (Friedrich Naumann, "Asia," p. 148.)

German policy was not always so indifferent to the cause of missions, however: witness the seizure of Kiau-Chau in China, almost at the time the above words were written, on the avowed grounds that the murder of two German missionaries must be avenged. Evidently His Imperial and Royal Majesty felt a greater obligation to enforce the blessings of Christianity upon the Chinese than upon the Turks.

centered on the route to India via Suez, and they were not anxious to develop a rival highway. Now in 1902 a convention was signed for the construction of this railway under distinctly German auspices. It was all part of the grand scheme that was to yoke Hamburg, Vienna, Belgrade, Constantinople, Bagdad and finally Basra on the Persian Gulf in one magnificent steel trunk-line controlled end to end from Berlin. "A great conception, worthy of a scientific and systematic people," admitted an Englishman frankly. "Should it materialize, it will turn the flank of the great Sea-Empire [of Britain]."[1] Of course the scheme was still imperfect. German control over the essential link in Serbia was far from established: and English influence was quite strong enough to halt the building of the link from Bagdad to Basra which gave the ocean outlet at the doors of India. However, the work now gradually went forward, conducted by skillful German engineers, and the completion of the vast project could await the fortunate turn of events. Serbia in her day must succumb, and there would be a method of handling even England.

Abdul Hamid sat contentedly in the Yildiz-Kiosk and found the world going pleasantly around him. He had snapped his fingers at England. In 1904–5 Russia became involved in an unlucky war with Japan: she had no strength left for another Balkan venture. Austria was acting only at her best friend's suggestions, and France was soon too embroiled with Germany over Morocco to have any plans for reforming the Levant. The Armenian villages were "peaceful." In Macedonia indeed Greeks, Bulgars and Serbs were reciprocally cutting throats, and the ambassadors were reminding the padishah of the need of drastic innovations. But he no longer feared any ambassador but the German, and the Macedonian problem for decades had been very serious but never acute. The padishah, now aging, still lived however in constant terror of assassination, and absurd precautions were taken at the palace to prevent his contact with any dangerous visitor: but fear for one's life is a regular perquisite of an Oriental monarch. A horde of dancing girls worthy of Solomon comforted

[1] Marriot, "The Eastern Question," p. 359.

his declining days: and countless black eunuchs and ministers of pleasure assured him that he was the terror of the Christians, the hope of the Moslems and the admiration of the entire world. Then suddenly the ground opened at Abdul Hamid's feet. First he found his power jeopardized; then he was abruptly flung from the throne.

If the "Red Sultan" had been the only tyrant in Turkey he might have kept his position, but men like William II's imperial "brother" cannot maintain their sway without a whole train of ministering spirits, each making the most of his own field of power. There were Turkish begs and pashas who were relatively high-minded, humane and honest men, but such persons Abdul the Damned could not trust and seldom placed in office. To fill his vizierates, ministries and pasha-liks he had to summon Levantine adventurers, slippery scoundrels of the most depraved type who loved their master only because he let half the public money stick in their fingers. Since to report a "conspiracy" was about the surest method of winning imperial favor, espionage, false charges, arbitrary imprisonment, and even secret executions were every-day perils even for the most aristocratic and loyal Ottomans. The methods of some of Abdul Hamid's chief myrmidons were as remarkable as their master's. It is reported that a certain high pasha required suddenly 200,000 francs ($40,000). He therefore invited a wealthy Constantinople Greek merchant to visit him in his palace. The poor man came, innocently expecting to be consulted about a government loan. Once in the building the pasha informed his amazed guest that he expected a gift of the money, and that the Christian would not leave the palace alive unless the sum were paid. The pasha's servants, with leveled revolvers, forced the Greek to write out a check on his bank, and held him prisoner until a messenger brought back the cash. These were very primitive financial expedients, and while this particular Christian was perhaps helpless, many Turkish victims of similar deeds were not so ·impotent. They had no foreign power to plead in their behalf; therefore they turned the more briskly to conspiracy.

For a long time there had been a party of Ottomans known

commonly as the "Young Turks." This band had been considered by the diplomats as rather harmless dreamers. They
believed that Abdul Hamid's misrule was ruining the empire,
and paving the way for a final conquest by Russia. They
wished for the revival of the still-born "Constitution of
1876," and for the introduction of various Western reforms
and innovations as the last hope of saving their native land
from ruin. In the time of their propaganda they announced
many high-sounding humanitarian propositions which, in the
days of their power, they were never to execute. The "Young
Turk" movement was, however, in its first stages a genuinely
liberal movement, grafted upon the Orient by men who often
mistook program for performance.

Abdul Hamid of course detested and dreaded these "Young
Turks," some of whose leaders came from the highest Ottoman families. Those whom he could not arrest fled to Geneva,
Berlin and Paris where, as exiles, they imbibed atheism and
absinthe, and acquired a little thicker veneer of West
European notions. They published a small paper, issued
petitions to the courts of Europe and made the "Red Sultan"
spend a great deal of money keeping spies after them. But
while the spies were busy in Paris, the Young Turks were busy
in Saloniki. They understood perfectly that no petty bomb
outrages nor flash-in-the-pan demonstrations would overthrow
the tyrant. The misrule of the sultan was disgusting wider
and wider circles of Ottomans, but he still kept around him
some regiments of highly paid troops who guaranteed him
against any ordinary outbreak in the capital. At Saloniki,
however, lay the powerful Third Army Corps:—ill-paid, restless and very good material for conspiracy. Upon this force
the Young Turks' "Committee of Union and Progress"
worked from 1906 to 1908, and then, with very few prelimi-
naries, at Saloniki in July, 1908, they suddenly proclaimed
again the Constitution of 1876, and started for Constantinople
with the Third and also the Second Army Corps at their backs.

Abdul Hamid had been caught completely unawares. His
force at Constantinople was inadequate. He was not sure of
the troops in Asia. With astounding promptitude he seemed

to throw up the struggle and transform himself into a liberal, constitutional monarch. The censorship of the press was abolished, the constitution put in full force, and a chamber of 280 deputies was ordered convened, to be elected by all the male citizens (whatever their faith) of the entire Ottoman empire.

For a moment it seemed as if the age of miracles had returned. In the regions of the recent massacres Moslem ulemas publicly embraced and proclaimed their brotherhood with Christian priests and Jewish rabbis. Delegations of citizens called on American missionaries to request a precise meaning of the thing called "liberty," which they were about to put into effect. The Young Turks were delighted. "Henceforth," cried Enver Bey,[1] one of their leaders, "we are all brothers! There are no longer Bulgars, Greeks, Rumanians, Jews, Moslems; under the blue sky we are all equal: we glory in the name of being Ottomans!"

The victorious party of course seized at once all the government offices. The favorites of Abdul Hamid were justly obliged to disgorge. One of his ministers, who had been in power only 18 months, was found to have secreted in his house $850,000 of the public money. The new parliament was elected with a great show of zeal for liberty and equality; but of course the assembly was composed of men utterly without political experience, and despite the talk of treating all races alike, the Christians complained that the districts had been gerrymandered in the Moslem interest. The Young Turkish managing committee was the real power behind the throne. It dictated the acts of the ministers and the bills laid before the parliament. For the moment its decisions seemed law.

But Abdul Hamid, crafty spider, had only made concessions that he might bide his time.[2] Against the Young Turks

[1] This same chieftain later seems to have been largely responsible for the slaughter or miserable deaths of over 1,000,000 Armenians in 1915–16. .

[2] The new Parliament had been assembled December 10, 1908. In his speech at the opening the sultan blandly said that he had dissolved the original parliament temporarily "until the education of the people had

were rallying all the noxious elements that had battened on the fallen régime. Also the fires of Ottoman conservatism were being awakened—were not Enver Bey and his peers ruining the faithful with strange doctrines learned among the giaours, and by practices utterly strange to the Prophet and all the holy imams? The "Red Sultan" had still an ample privy purse, and he used it. A serious massacre of the Armenians took place at Adana in Cilicia, probably in order to kindle the fanaticism of the faithful. The eunuchs and pages of the Yildiz-Kiosk did their master's bidding, spreading disaffection for the new régime through Constantinople. On April 13, 1909, a counter revolution shook the capital. The sultan's troops seized the parliament house; the liberal grand vizier resigned to save his life; the minister of justice was murdered, and Abdul Hamid magnanimously issued a "pardon" for all the acts of his zealous soldiery.

Those of the Young Turks who still lived fled the city for their lives, but they were not long absent. The "Committee of Union and Progress" at Saloniki promptly took charge of the situation, and the whole European army, save the "Red Sultan's" corrupted regiments, obeyed its orders to march on the capital.

On April 25, the Saloniki army entered Constantinople. Some of the mutineers pleaded for mercy. "Have you brought us the old man's head?" sternly demanded the attacking general,—a demand, however, which was not finally insisted upon. Five hours of fierce fighting were required before the rebel troops in some of the barracks could be bombarded into submission. Abdul the Damned had played his game and the dice had fallen against him. To save his power no hand was openly raised by the German ambassador nor by the war-lord in Berlin. The moment the sultan had lost his grip on the situation and his ability to serve them, Prussian interest in his cause had waned. "Our relations with Turkey are not of a sentimental nature," Prince von Bülow, the kaiser's chancellor, asserted a little later, most pithily. Pos-

been brought to a sufficiently high level by the extension of instruction throughout the empire."

sibly, however, German influence was exercised to keep the sultan from the executioner. All through the attack and the bombardment, the padishah is said to have sat on his divan, pale and biting his nails, with bevies of terrified slave girls cowering and shrieking around him. Now the Young Turks were determined to take no chance of a second counter-revolution. On April 27th, the parliament met again to consider the question of the throne. The fetvah (solemn opinion) of the Sheikh-ul-Islam, declaring Abdul Hamid unworthy to rule, was read. The parliament unanimously voted him deposed, and his younger brother, Mohammed V, was "girt with the sword of Osman" and summoned to reign.

The "Red Sultan" for hours had been in keen animal terror. Now he was greatly relieved when told he might keep his life, and depart to Saloniki to a comfortable villa, still solaced by a considerable number of his harem ladies. On the 28th of April he was so transferred. Had he stayed in Constantinople he might have seen some forty of his instruments— breeders of the recent mutiny, powerful eunuchs or extortionate ministers, dangling from nooses as they were hanged in full view on the bridges and streets of the capital. William II's "brother" had ceased to be a useful ally.

The new sultan was amiable and harmless. Being the presumptive heir to the throne, he had been kept in gilded imprisonment through the whole of his brother's reign, and he declared that "he had not read a newspaper for twenty years." [1]

The Young Turks, however, had found in Mohammed V precisely what they wanted—a figurehead, without force or wit to govern, and who owed everything to their intervention.

Enver Bey and his associates now had grasped the entire government. It seemed as if the German alliance with Turkey had been dissolved with the downfall of Abdul Hamid. Speedily the Young Turks were to discover that it is easier to draw up abstract programs for making an Oriental Empire

[1] Doubtless Abdul Hamid prided himself on not having had his brother strangled, as had been the frequent Ottoman usage to stop all possible competition for the throne.

into a modern parliamentary state, than to execute those programs smoothly and happily; and as their difficulties increased they were to discover again the need for the friendship of Berlin. For the instant, however, the prospects opened fair before them, and all the more trustful liberals in Europe echoed the applause that followed the new sultan's announcement: ''The safety and happiness of the country depend on the constant and serious application of the constitutional régime, which is in conformity with the sacred law, as well as with the principles of civilization.''

Noble sentiments—but the subjects of Mohammed V were to see greater wars and woes than the subjects of Abdul the Great Assassin.

CHAPTER XIV

THE HAPSBURG EMPIRE AND ITS DISCORDANT SUBJECTS

THE very first fact with which any student of Austria-Hungary is confronted is that he is *dealing with a state and not with a nation*. Nationalities are plentiful within the limits of the empire—more nationalities and more languages than in any other European state except Russia—but there is no Austro-Hungarian nation. When the emperor wishes to address a manifesto to his subjects it is not "to my people" that he speaks, but "to my peoples." Nor have these nationalities anything in common except their government. Race, religion, all that tends to make nationalities different from one another are present. And so whether we apply to it the terms of one of its severe critics,[1] "a ramshackle empire," or describe it, as its friends do, as an exceedingly hopeful experiment in racial federalization, we are necessarily brought back to the conclusion that the Austria of to-day is not a nation but a government functioning over a group of struggling nationalities each differing from the other in race, religion and methods of life.

Nor does the Austrian difficulty end there. In their struggle with each other the nationalities look not merely to their own strength for aid but also to their brothers outside the borders of Austria-Hungary. The German looks to Germany, the Slav to Serbia and Russia for assistance in their hopes of strengthening their position within the Dual Empire.[2] The result is that this question has been too often regarded by the Austrian statesmen as a question of foreign policy to be settled with these outside powers rather than an internal question to be settled within the empire. Moreover, the Austro-Hungarian Empire has been constantly endeavoring to expand

[1] Mr. David Lloyd George.
[2] The term commonly applied to the Austro-Hungarian Empire.

either its territory or its influence, at first in Italy and Germany, and more lately in the Balkan peninsula. And these attempts at expansion have brought it into acute conflict: in the first case with Italy, France and Prussia: in the second case with Russia. So the Dual Empire, whether on the defensive or offensive, has always made foreign policy its chief aim, and has given far too little attention to the pressing questions at home. There are some nations which suffer from too little attention to foreign policy; Austria seems to have suffered from giving it too much.

Finally the Austro-Hungarian Empire shares the fate of all empires on the borderland between two civilizations. "Asia," says a Viennese proverb, "begins on the Ringstrasse," [1] and there seems to be an element of truth in the saying. The traveller who goes from the Tyrol to Bosnia or to northwestern Hungary passes into a different world. One is European, the other is Oriental, and all the efforts of the rulers to Europeanize their subjects and to mitigate this difference have only partially succeeded. And this difference has increased still further the dissension within the Dual Empire and prevented the formation of a united nation.

This is Austria, a state, a foreign policy, an army, a ruler, but never a nation. How did such a state come to be formed? To answer this question we must go back into the late Middle Ages, to the period when the old Holy Roman Empire of the Germans was struggling with the non-German races on its borders, Slavs and Magyars. To provide for defence against these races was formed the so-called East March—the kernel of modern Austria. Originally purely German, it extended to the south to take in the Slavs along the northern Adriatic. But the genesis of modern Austria begins with a certain Ferdinand, brother of Charles V, whom Luther faced at Worms in 1521. By a fortunate marriage and by equally fortunate deaths he acquired Hungary and Bohemia.

But he acquired something in addition to these territories, he acquired a Turkish war among his possessions in Hungary.

[1] The principal street of Vienna.

And for the next two centuries Austria waged almost unceasing war against the Turks. At first the struggle went rather against them; in 1529 and again in 1683, the Turks nearly captured Vienna and settled the problem of Austria in a Turkish sense. But after 1683 the war went steadily in Austria's favor. She gradually extended down the Danube and into the Balkans, taking under her dominion large numbers of Slavs who welcomed her armies as deliverers from the hated oppression of the Turk.

In 1914 they were singing in the streets of Vienna a song commemorating the exploits of the great Austrian general, Prince Eugene of Savoy, who had led the Austrian armies during one of the most successful periods of these wars. Formerly many a Slav has joined in this song because he realized that it was this Prince Eugene who had delivered his race from the Turk. But these voices have long been still. Because they have discovered that they have merely exchanged one set of bonds for another, the cramping rule of the Ottoman for the equally cramping rule of the German and the Magyar, they have ceased to celebrate these Austrian victories over the Turk. All the opportunity that Austria has enjoyed, all the tragedy of her failure to realize it, lies in this situation.

And thus was formed a state which never was the expression of a nation, a mere machine, a *thing* in which the breath of national life has never really stirred. It was given the great opportunity to reconcile Slav and Magyar and German, East and West, and, on the whole, it has failed. Opportunities countless it has had; some it has utilized—enough to tantalize yet not to satisfy; but the great majority it has left unutilized. It has, at best, but partially fulfilled its destiny and now it comes for its accounting before the judgment-bar of the nations.

The Austrian problem, then, is, at bottom, a problem of nationalities. What are these nationalities, their characteristics and their location in the Empire? Roughly speaking, they are comprised in five grand divisions, the German, the

Magyar, the Slav, the Roumanian and the Italian. Of Slavs there are numerous subdivisions, Czechs, Poles, Ruthenians, Slovaks, Slovenes, Croats and Serbs. But the fundamental characteristics of them all are the same, and for introductory purposes we may group them together.

First of all in our study of the nationalities is the German, the original Austrian. They settled mainly in the upper basin of the Danube along the north and west borders of Bohemia. There is also a little island of Teutondom in western Hungary formed from the descendants of sturdy German settlers sent during the Middle Ages to hold this region against the Slav, but today lost in the surrounding sea of Hungarians and Roumanians. These Germans are not the Germans of Prussia. They view life with a less serious eye, love the good things of this world, and are in many ways more charming and less efficient than their racial brethren to the north. In the past they have done much for music and art; even today they are contributing their share, and they have made Vienna a place of great charm to the casual visitor. But they appear to have abandoned commerce and industry to the Jew; statesmanship they have left far too often to the Pole and the Magyar. Children of this world, they are today probably the best embodiment of real German *"gemüth-lichkeit."* Many a critic of the Dual Monarchy has been softened by an hour in the charming society of an Austrian officer. And yet their easy-going ways seem to have proved their ruin. In the last fifty years they have undoubtedly lost the direction of the internal affairs of the Empire to the Magyar, and the control of foreign policy to their more ruthless and efficient brothers of the German Empire. Likeable though they may be, it is to be feared that their faults will greatly hinder them in taking the control of a new and regenerated Austria.

If you travel by the Danube steamer from Vienna to Budapest you pass, about half way, the citadel of Pressburg. This old frontier fortress of the Hungarian kingdom may be taken as the boundary where one passes from the land of the Germans into that of the Magyars. From that point on this race inhabits the great Hungarian plain, until, in its western part, it gives way to the Roumanian. Descendants of a wild, nomadic race which dashed itself against western Europe in the tenth century and then recoiled into the Danube plain, the Hungarian people have retained some of the fire and energy and some of the wildness, as well, of their youth. Probably they have never been completely Europeanized. And perhaps in their exoticism lies the charm they always seem to possess for the native of west Europe and America. Their nobility, widely-travelled and often widely-read, simple in their tastes, gentlemen of the world in the best sense of the term, seem a survival of the old feudal and patriarchal days. The peasants are energetic, and in the main good farmers and householders. With his brilliancy and charm, and with an almost oriental suppleness of mind, the Magyar seems a born politician, as the other nationalities in the Empire have found to their cost. Proud of his nationality and of its traditions, determined that it shall be the directing force in the kingdom, he has carried on a policy toward the other nationalities—a policy to be treated in detail later—which has been one of the causes of the present war. Rarely passive, active and aggressive, the Magyars have fought their way to their present position in the Dual Empire and they mean to maintain it at all costs.

From the two ruling nationalities, German and Magyar, we pass to the ruled nationalities, the Slav, the Roumanian and the Italian. To link together the Slavs as one nationality involves a certain stretching of the term, for, even yet, it is doubtful if the Czechs of Bohemia feel their kinship with the Croats or Serbs in Hungary, and in at least one case, that of the Poles and Ruthenians, the feeling is still decidedly antagonistic. But it is notable during the last few years that all these Slav races in the empire have been uniting in their common grievances, feeling more and more their racial kinship and more and more inclining to work together for common ends. The Czech banks of Prague have subsidized the common enterprises of the Croat and Serb in Dalmatia, and

the people of Prague contributed heavily to the Serbian Red
Cross during the period of the two Balkan Wars, considering
the Serbian victories as those of the Slav race as a whole.
This is that movement called Pan-Slavism, which will be
discussed at greater length presently. Here it may be cited
merely as a proof of increasing Slav solidarity.

Who are these Slavs and whence came they? History
tells us but little, for they pushed into Europe unheralded
and unsung in the centuries immediately following the fall
of Rome. They were evidently of a low grade of civilization,
hunters and fishermen, wanderers on the face of the earth,
with few if any political bonds to confine them, individualists
by choice. They always seem to have lacked, to some extent, the ability to organize, although it may be said that this
defect has been somewhat exaggerated by those who write
concerning this race. Dreamy, rather impractical, they may
have contributed less than their share to the material side
of life—although this may very likely be due to the economic
circumstances in which they have been placed, for, when given
the opportunity, some of them have attained eminence in these
very fields. On the other hand they have probably contributed more than their share to music and art. Generally they
appear as an undeveloped race of great possibilities, but what
these possibilities are and what their future will be is hard
to prophesy.

Geographically the Slavs form a fringe along the northern
and southern borders of the empire, although they have
pushed many outposts into the central portion as well.
Numerically they are the leading race in the empire, having
a larger population than the two ruling races, German and
Magyar, taken together. The majority are Roman Catholics.

The eastern part of Hungary is occupied, in the main,
by Roumanians. They seeped in across the Carpathians some
time during the later Middle Ages, and ever since the thir-
teenth century seem to have made up the peasant class in
this district,[1] "first as serfs, later as political helots"—to
quote the characterization of Mr. Seton Watson. They claim

[1] Seton Watson, "Roumania and the War," p. 35.

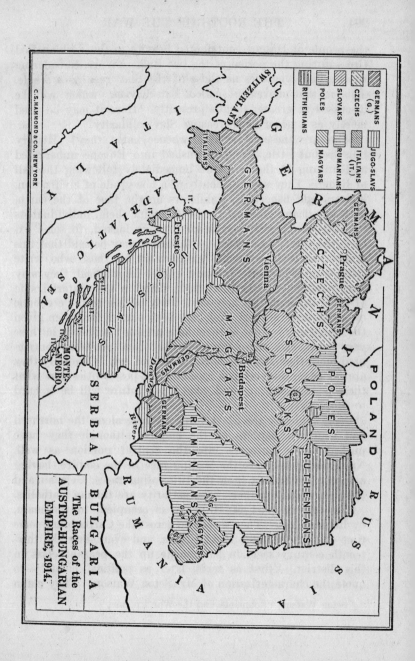

C.S.HAMMOND & CO., NEW YORK

The Races of the AUSTRO-HUNGARIAN EMPIRE, 1914.

GERMANS (G.)
JUGO-SLAVS
POLES
ITALIANS (IT.)
SLOVAKS
RUMANIANS
CZECHS
MAGYARS
RUTHENIANS

SWITZERLAND

ITALY

GERMANS

POLAND

RUSSIA

Vienna

Prague CZECHS
GERMANS

GERMANS

SLOVAKS

POLES

MAGYARS

Budapest

RUTHENIANS

GERMANS

GERMANS

Danube River

RUMANIANS

MAGYARS

RUMANIA

BULGARIA

SERBIA

MONTENEGRO

ADRIATIC SEA

Trieste

JUGO-SLAVS

ITALIANS

to be the descendants of the Latin colonists left by Trajan in the Roman province of Dacia; actually they are probably a mixed race from many origins and their Roman antecedents are much more certain as to their language than their blood. They are still agriculturists for the most part, and, although greatly hindered in their development, have done much through organized self-help.

Last among the nationalities come the Italians, who are almost entirely found in the coast cities along the northern and eastern shores of the Adriatic. Originally they came as colonists, sometimes under the control of Venice, sometimes independent, in order to trade with the people of the back country, and they brought with them an Italian culture that has never died out, even though the Italians today are a minority among the population. Traders and culture-bearers they are still, these lost children of Italy, living, for the most part, in the cities which are little Italian fortresses in the surrounding hosts of Slavdom. But one after another these fortresses have been falling, and it appears that now the Italians must undergo the melancholy fate of those who, in a strange land, give it their culture and then are swallowed up. On the northern shore things are better for the Italians, but in Dalamatia the future appears to belong to the Slav.[1]

Such are the nationalities in this polyglot empire. Every manner of race, every manner of religion are represented. The task of welding these discordant peoples into one organism might well defy the abilities of a statesman. Let us see how the Austro-Hungarian statesmen have solved it.

The present government of Austria-Hungary is based on the so-called *Ausgleich*, drawn up in 1867. By it Austria and Hungary were united together in a loose federation which left each of the parties practically independent in their internal affairs. Outside of the fact that the emperor of Austria is also King of Hungary, the bonds of union between

[1] Those who read Italian may find these conclusions stated at greater length and with attendant proof in V. Gayda, "L'Italia d'oitre Contine." For other discussion of these Italians see p. 157.

the two dominions consist of the joint ministries of Foreign
Affairs, Finance and War and the so-called "Delegations."
The latter are elected bodies, one from the Parliament of
Austria and one from that of Hungary which convene in
Vienna and Budapest alternately, confer with each other
in writing, and only meet together after three exchanges
in writing have proved unavailing and then only to vote,
not to debate. All in all they leave the impressions of two
independent powers negotiating with each other and not
that of a common parliament for two parts of the same state.
Economic matters, such as railways, tariffs, etc., are settled
by treaties, having life for only ten years, and each renewal
has been accompanied by no little strife.

It is easy to see then that such internal questions as economic reform, treatment of the nationalities and so forth will
not be dealt with directly by the Austro-Hungarian state but
will be left to the separate action of the two parts, Austria
and Hungary. It is true that every now and then Franz
Josef intervened in the question of nationalities, and in Austria he succeeded, to some extent, in bringing in a more healthy
spirit in the treatment of this question. But in Hungary this
intervention has been mostly a rapping of the table to bring
the dominant Magyar party into line on other questions.
"Constitutional to the point of injustice,"[1] Franz Josef
left the Hungarians the settlement of their own internal problems, within the limits laid down by the Ausgleich. And so
the study of the treatment in Austria-Hungary of the problem
of nationalities falls into two divisions: the treatment of
the problem in Austria and the treatment in Hungary.

In Austria the problem has mainly centered in the treatment to be accorded to the Czechs of Bohemia. When the
Magyars were given favored treatment in 1867 these Slavs
of Bohemia confidently expected that they would receive
the same, and that a practically autonomous Czech government would be set up in Bohemia. Four things appear to
have prevented this. First of all was the dislike on the
part of the Austrian government to split up further the em-

[1] Skeed, "The Hapsburg Monarchy," p. 30.

pire unless it was necessary. Second was the refusal of the German minority in Bohemia to allow the erection of what would be a predominantly Slav state in which they would have to play a secondary rôle. These same Germans, who view with the utmost complacency the crushing out of Slav majorities in Austria and in Hungary, wax exceedingly eloquent over the nationalistic wrongs the German minority in Bohemia would undergo if the Czechs were given control there. The Berlin government appears to share this feeling to the utmost, and in 1867 and later it seems to have used all its influence and even threats to secure the defeat of this scheme. Third in the list of reasons was the attitude of the Magyars. Having won for themselves a privileged position in the empire they had no intention of sharing it with the Czechs. And so they joined with the Germans in opposition. Finally the Czechs, at this period, appear to have lacked the statesmanship shown by the Magyars. The latter, led by Deak and Andrassy, were able to seize every opportunity for gain, while the Czechs seemed unable to do this. Thus, while the Czechs were far better entitled to the control in Bohemia than were the Magyars in Hungary, they failed in securing the desired position and were left under the control of the Germans of Austria.

But they had no intention of remaining in this subordinate position. Instinctively they seem to have felt their needs, better education, and a stronger economic position within the empire. And these two things they set out to secure. Schools were established throughout Bohemia, a Czech literature was encouraged, and an organized system of mutual help did much to better their economic position. Prague, once German, became a purely Czech city. German, formerly the language of culture, was more and more replaced by the use of the native language. In brief, Bohemia has witnessed during the last forty years a tremendous Czech renaissance that has left that race socially, economically and culturally the master of Bohemia.

Politically, however, this was not true. For the state was still a power in the hands of the Germans and they used it

ruthlessly to hold this Slav movement in check. The Slav-
Czech language was not placed on an equality with German
in the courts and in government business, and when an attempt was made to do this by Count Badeni in 1897 it broke
down, owing to German opposition and, it would appear,
to threats from Berlin.

The question, however, did not end there. Rebuffed in
their attempts to secure their ends by legal means, the Czechs
took refuge in systematic parliamentary obstruction. Several deputies gained great proficiency in speaking twelve hours
or so at a stretch; others became experts in hurling ink-
bottles and other missiles at their opponents. The Germans
retorted in kind and the sessions of the Austrian Parliament
were one continuous uproar. Finally, in sheer desperation,
the government decided to bring in a bill conferring universal
suffrage throughout Austria. Up to this time the suffrage
in Austria had practically been limited to the property-hold-
ing classes. In 1906 it was agreed to throw all seats open
to manhood suffrage and it was hoped that, by this method,
the nationalities other than German would be satisfied by the
added power their numbers would bring them, and also that
social and economic questions, hitherto untreated in an assembly elected by property holders, would come to the fore
and throw the nationalistic question into the background.

In this hope the Austrian government does not appear to
have been wholly deceived; while the non-German nationalities had some grievances with the districting in the new
Parliament, they seem to have been willing to drop these and
give manhood suffrage a fair trial. And so the nationalistic
question faded, at least relatively, into the background. On
the other hand, social and economic questions received far
better treatment and much useful work was done. The
Austrian half of the Empire appeared to have at least started
on the road to recovery.

But the nationalistic question was not dead in Austria.
Old memories continued to fan the flames of racial strife and
many years would have been necessary before a complete
racial truce could have been established. The Czechs, con-

scious of their power, were agitating for a privileged and even an autonomous position for Bohemia, and intended to secure it. The Germans were discontented and threatening separation from Austria and union with Germany. Time and patience were necessary,—and instead Austria-Hungary plunged into war.

While Austria was slowly progressing toward a better treatment of the problem of nationalities, the treatment of this problem in Hungary is one long, sordid series of acts of oppression committed by the Magyars against the other nationalities of the kingdom. A minority in the land they govern, but proud of their past and determined to remain the ruling caste, the Magyar has systematically refused to the other nationalities any right of expression except through Magyar channels. "Magyarization," they call the policy adopted, and the word sums up a series of measures taken to stifle the language and literature of the other races for the benefit of the Magyars, and to cripple their economic prosperity in order to contribute to Magyar comfort and Magyar wealth.

In 1867 it had been agreed in the "Ausgleich" that the non-Magyar nationalities should be protected in all their rights. Deak, the ablest and the noblest of the Hungarian statesmen, was determined that this so-called "Law of Nationalities" should be carried out. But he was in ill-health and soon was forced to relinquish his hold on affairs, and other men, able but unscrupulous and aflame with the pride of race, took up his work. In their hands, the "Law of Nationalities" soon became a dead letter, "Magyarization" replaced the racial federation Deak had hoped for, and the long series of acts of racial oppression, which were to contribute so much to the present war, was started, and continued without a break down to 1914.

The story has been often told and here needs to be indicated only in its main lines. Magyarization strikes the traveler at every turn in the Hungarian kingdom. Street-names are posted in Magyar, place-names are at least officially Magyar-

ized, time-tables are in Magyar, as are the tickets you buy,
and Magyar is the language used by the railroad staff, who
luckily also know French and a little English, sometimes, as
well. Magyar is the language of the courts and though
interpreters are allowed they must be paid for at the private
expense of the client, a grievous burden on poor litigants.
A petition may be handed in in some non-Magyar language,
but the reply will always come back in the tongue of the
dominant nationality.[1]

And just as Magyar is insisted on as the language of the
state and society, so is every effort made to stamp out all
non-Magyar education and culture. The schools of the other
nationalities in Hungary have been rigorously dealt with.
In 1868 the Slovaks possessed three upper schools, founded
and supported by their own efforts, in 1875 these were closed
and have never been re-opened. Their elementary schools
have been reduced from 1921 in 1869 to 440 in 1911, despite
a growth in population.[2] Indeed had schools been allotted
in proportion to population the non-Magyar nationalities
should have 48 per cent., while, as a matter of fact, they
now possess 19 per cent. of the elementary schools and between 7 and 8 per cent. of the upper schools. Naturally the
non-Magyar population is uneducated, a prey to Magyar
wiles and Magyar intimidation.

Pass from schools to the press. Any paper which raises
its voice against the present state of things is silenced.
Journalists are imprisoned and fined, and journals suppressed.
Between April 1906 and August 1908 sentences were passed
on non-Magyars for press offences totaling 181 years, 3 months
imprisonment and fines of 99,000 crowns.[3] A free press is
difficult in such a land.

Yet, it may be asked, why do these nationalities not unite
to use their numbers in gaining control of the Parliament?

[1] Even tombstones in Budapest may bear no inscriptions save in
Magyar.

[2] For these and the following figures I am indebted to Seton-Watson,
"German, Slav and Magyar," pages 40, 41.

[3] Ibid., p. 44.

In the first place the franchise is mediaeval, giving undue weight to property and education, of which the Magyars have by far the greater share. Again the districting, originally bad, has been made worse by systematic gerrymandering. Finally corruption, intimidation and even the use of troops at the polls has been carried on to such an extent that a fair election is an impossibility. Out of the 413 deputies in the Hungarian parliament, the non-Magyar nationalities are entitled, through their population, to 198: actually they have never held over 25. Under these circumstances there is little hope in political action.

Also, if any political leader or any political party rises to challenge the present system, woe betide them in a land where *habeas corpus* is unknown and "conspiracy" is a flexible term on which to find an indictment. The vengeance of the government follows them even beyond the tomb, for monuments to non-Magyar leaders have been often prohibited and funds collected for that purpose confiscated. Even funeral processions of such leaders have been interfered with if, in the opinion of the government, they are being made the occasion of nationalistic demonstrations.

The whole Magyar racial policy may be summed up in the words of two of the leading Magyar statesmen. The first is the former Premier, Koloman Szell. Speaking in 1908, he declared that "this country must first be preserved as a Magyar country, and then it must be cultured, rich, enlightened and progressive." The second is from Count Stephen Tisza, premier when the war broke out. "A cardinal condition," he stated, "of the enjoyment of rights by other nationalities is that the citizens of other nationalities should recognize unreservedly that this state is the Magyar state." Such are the principles of Magyar government.

Such a situation of affairs could not last. For many years the Slav and Roumanian nationalities, poor, because of the denial of economic advantages, uneducated, because their schools had been closed, were held down by the iron hand of Budapest. But gradually they began to emancipate themselves. Many of them went to America, made their little "pile" and returned to buy out the estates of the magnates and work for the emancipation of their nationality. Better educated, they have formed the leaders in this recovery, teaching and inspiring the masses to hope for better things. Sooner or later trouble was bound to occur, and the Magyars seem to have dimly realized this. In the face of this movement and under pressure from Vienna a new franchise law was brought in in 1908 which, although granting but few concessions, was at least an opening wedge. Time might have alleviated the difficulties, but it was too late. In 1912 came the Balkan wars which aroused the entire Slav race, and in 1914 followed the world-struggle.

But it was in one corner of Hungary that the torch was kindled that was to set the world aflame. Croatia-Slavonia—the land of the South Slavs—had always possessed a local government of its own and this government had been confirmed to it by the agreement with Hungary in 1868. This compromise, originally not ungenerous, was twisted and distorted at Budapest until it became a tool for oppression. According to the agreement railways were to be built jointly by the two parts of the "Crown of St. Stephen" and to be their common property. But while Hungary has a thick network of railroads, Croatia-Slavonia is forced to be content with one poor line which has never been extended by a single branch. Railway tariffs have been shamelessly manipulated to the benefit of Hungary and the detriment of Croatia-Slavonia. Finally by the compromise it was agreed that the governor or *ban* of Croatia should be appointed by Budapest, and the Hungarians made use of this opportunity to endow Croatia-Slavonia with a gentleman who could teach much to the most corrupt of American politicians, Count Khuen-Hedervary. For twenty years (1883–1903) the ban made use of every variety of electoral corruption and fraud, official pressure, and intimidation. And for the time being he was aided by one very important factor in the problem.

Croatia-Slavonia was inhabited by two branches of the South Slav race, the Croats, the original settlers, and the Serbs, who had come in from Serbia during the eighteenth century. The former were Roman Catholic, the latter Greek Catholic, and thus racial and religious differences prevented a united front on the part of the population towards the exploitation and misgovernment of Budapest. And Khuen-Hedervary seized on this situation and used it to the utmost. But even before his corrupt rule was over, it was becoming evident that this difference was dying out and that the two parts of the South-Slav nationality were beginning to draw together for common defence.

Let us pass from Croatia-Slavonia for the moment to another unhappy country to the south. The diplomacy of Andrassy had given Austria the administration of Bosnia and Herzegovina, two provinces formerly Turkish, but almost entirely occupied by South Slavs. The occupation commenced with a revolt of the population, and it is hardly too much to say that this revolt has never really ceased since 1878. Not that the rule of the Austrians has been a bad one: for it has provided schools, and railways, has cleaned and ornamented the cities, has provided industries for the people and, in general, has done much to better the material and bodily welfare of the people of Bosnia and Herzegovina. But the situation was much the same as that of Italy in the early 1850's: a situation that was summed up by Daniele Manin in the words: *"We do not want Austria to reform, we want Austria to get out."* For these inhabitants are, almost to a man, Serbs and, as Serbs, they desire to be united with Serbia and not with Austria even though, in a material sense, the Austrian rule may be better for them. And they have expressed the faith that is in them by seizing their rifles and taking to the mountains, there to wage unceasing war against all things Austrian, good as well as bad. They are the soldiers of nationality, protesting, dying for a principle, for the right of a people to dispose of itself. Never has Austria completely subdued this revolt. Suppressed in one locality it appears in another: it inspires plots which have planned the death of Austrian governors and which finally claimed the heir to the Austrian throne.

To return to Croatia-Slavonia, Khuen-Hedervary had been

a failure; all his corruption, his gerrymandering, his intimidation had not helped matters, indeed it had made them worse. Daily the religious and racial differences between the Croats and the Serbs were losing their importance, daily the two nationalities were becoming more united in their resistance to Budapest. In 1907 the Hungarian parliament began to extend its policy of ''Magyarization'' to Croatia-Slavonia by insisting on the use of Magyar as a language on the railways of the province. At once Croats and Serbs united in opposition and the next year, despite every form of corruption and intimidation, their united party won a majority in the diet of Croatia-Slavonia.

In 1908 occurred the Austrian annexation of Bosnia and Herzegovina. The disastrous results of this act on the foreign policy of the Austro-Hungarian Empire have been described elsewhere, but the results on the internal situation in the empire were equally bad. It inflamed the population of the annexed provinces to a revolt of despair, for it seemed to end, for ever, their dream of union to Serbia, while in Croatia-Slavonia the humiliation of a Slav state was a blow at pride of race. And this feeling of hatred was greatly deepened by certain events in the latter part of 1908 and during 1909.

In the summer of 1908 the official press of Croatia-Slavonia worked up a ''Pan-Serb conspiracy,'' aiming at rebellion and the union of the province with Servia. By the early part of 1909, 58 persons, mostly obscure, were in prison, but the real aim of the whole business, the implication of members of the Croat-Serb party in the diet, proved a failure: no evidence could be found against them. And so the trial opened in March, 1909, and dragged its weary course until October, when 31 of these wretches were sentenced to varying prison terms.

More sensational matter, however, followed. In March, 1909, the ''Neue Freie Presse,'' a newspaper of Vienna, published, over the signature of Professor Friedjung, the famous Austrian historian, charges against the leaders of this Croat-Serb party, backing up his charges with certain written documents. The Croat-Serb leaders retorted by bringing a libel action against Professor Friedjung and in the trial it was proved that these documents, which had been supplied by Aerenthal, the Austrian Foreign Minister, had been forged in the Austro-Hungarian legation at Belgrade.[1] The matter was hastily hushed up, but not before it had terribly damaged the reputation of Austro-Hungarian diplomacy and Austro-Hungarian government.

In this fashion—amid constant quarrels and deadlocks between the diet of Croatia-Slavonia which was now controlled by the Croat-Serb party, and the government of Budapest, things went on for three years. In the fall of 1912 the Balkan wars broke out, and the situation at once became critical. Hitherto the Slavs in the empire had but one great Slav power to appeal to, Russia, and this power they dreaded. But with the victories of Serbia there came to all the Slavs of the empire the feeling that they were no longer members of a mean and despised race, but of a race which could fight and could conquer. The Slavs of the empire gave their all to the Serbian Red Cross, and rejoiced in the Serbian victories as though they had won them themselves. The Slav sailors on the Austrian flagship, blockading Montenegro in 1913, decorated their ship on the news of the fall of Scutari: the very event they were there, if possible, to prevent. After the Balkan wars the Slav race had apparently "found its Piedmont," like a new Italy.

"Serbian and Russian intrigues" thus the Austrian statesmen described these events, for they failed to see that the real difficulty lay within their own borders, that these Slav nationalities had turned to Serbia and to Russia only because every attempt they had made to approach the Austro-Hungarian Empire had been rebuffed. One does not need to hold a brief for either the Russian or Serbian policy in the Balkans in order to condemn the shortsightedness of the Austro-Hungarian government. Yet that government refused

---

[1] The minister to Serbia, Count Forgach, after a period of "retirement," returned to office, and as assistant minister of foreign affairs, aided in the Serbian ultimatum.

to see the light. From the summer of 1913 to the summer of 1914 their whole endeavor was to find a way to crush the Serbian state, whose intrigues, they claimed, were destroying the empire. Not a word of internal reform, although at the last moment, that might have saved the situation. For, argued the Austrian statesmen, if Serbia be crushed we can exploit our Slav subjects at our will. And so they delivered themselves, German, Slav, and Magyar, to be exploited by the Prussian.

It is easy to point out the defects in the Austro-Hungarian Empire, but it was not all darkness. No one would, probably, deny the conscientious devotion to duty of Franz Josef. Franz Ferdinand, his heir, seems to have harbored plans that might have redeemed the empire.[1] The present emperor appears to have good intentions and, possibly, the ability, also, to execute them. Not as an able dynasty appear these Hapsburgs, but, on the whole, a conscientious one. The army, too, has been a force for unity. Far more democratic than that of Germany, it has been the education of many a peasant of Austria and Hungary in the primal duties of order, cleanliness and self-control. Finally economic factors, an industrial Austria, an agricultural Hungary, make for unity. But a dynasty, however good, an army, however democratic and efficient, and even economic ties do not make a nation. That can only be formed by the union of free peoples, in common endeavor in a common cause. No Austro-Hungarian nation can be based on the rule of German and Magyar over Slav and Roumanian and Italian. So long as this continues there will be a ''question of Austria,'' internal troubles and, probably, European wars. Dissolution of the empire is a far better solution than the continuance of the present situation.

Yet may there not arise in Austria a statesman who will solve the problem and unite these nationalities into one nation? We in American who see men of every race taking their part in our national life, calling themselves Americans,

---

[1] And the Austro-Hungarian court camarilla appear to have broken into his papers and even searched his pockets after his murder in Serajevo.

living as Americans, know that nationalities *can* be fused. Even now, at this eleventh hour of the night, it may not be too late for this statesman to arise. The future has nothing too good for the Austria-Hungary he will create.

CHAPTER XV

AFTER the smoke of the Franco-Prussian War had rolled away, Europe found herself facing a new diplomatic situation. France was fallen from her old post as the pre-eminent power. Germany had taken her place, and for long statesmen hardly knew what to make of it. The power of the new Hohenzollern empire was obviously so great that any blundering attack upon it was likely to be resented with fearful results. Bismarck, however, did nothing to make the powers which had stood neutral in 1870 repent of their inaction. With Russia for some time he was friendly, with England and Italy reasonably cordial, with Austria at least correct. He realized keenly, perhaps too keenly, that by taking Alsace-Lorraine he had relegated any genuine reconciliation with France to a distant future. Henceforth, whenever Germany found herself in difficulties, right across the Vosges lay a nation of ill-wishers whom Teutons at least believed to be always ready to stab or strike. In view of this "French mortgage" Bismarck's policy therefore seemed dictated along rather simple lines. He worked on three plausible hypotheses:

I. That after the lessons of 1870–71 it was not likely France, without allies, would attack Germany, unless Germany foolishly reduced her armaments. Therefore the new Hohenzollern empire must remain armed to the teeth.

II. A Republican system of government in France was likely to keep the "Grand Nation" faction-rent and divided, and on bad terms with the various great monarchies (especially Russia) which might possibly help her. Therefore to keep France weak and isolated Bismarck deliberately discouraged attempts (very natural for Prussian monarchists) to undermine the Third Republic. When Von Arnim, the German ambassador at Paris in the early seventies, seemed coquetting with the French royalists, Bismarck had him recalled and disgraced.

III. To prevent any other power from giving comfort to France, the Iron Chancellor studiously avoided all incidents that might give them offense. England was treated with marked consideration by him. "Cousin Land-rat and Cousin Water-rat," as Bismarck said, ought to be the best of friends. Italy was praised and cajoled. As for Russia and Austria the great minister soon went much further.

England, Italy and France had each, after their manner, liberal constitutions. In Germany, Austria and Russia, although the first two empires had the forms of constitutions, the personal influence of the monarchs was still—to state it mildly—tremendous. These three empires were therefore the bulwarks of militarism, autocracy, and anti-liberalism against all the rest of the civilized world. Their rulers had very many interests in common, and every season to work together. Austria had been beaten roundly by Prussia in 1866, but she was already getting over the effects of a defeat which Bismarck had taken pains should not be humiliating. The relations of William I and Czar Alexander II were excellent.

The chancellor was speedily to turn this community of interest into something tangible. In Austria in 1871 the old, violently anti-German foreign minister Beust had been replaced by the Hungarian Andrassy, who was on far better personal terms with Bismarck. The results of this change manifested themselves in the early days of September, 1872, when Franz Josef the Hapsburg, Alexander II the Romanoff and their gold-braided suites simultaneously visited Berlin to be received by their Hohenzollern friend and rival, and to congratulate him in turn upon his new imperial honors. Of course behind the elaborate state-banquets, reviews, fêtes and spectacular ceremonies the ministers of the three greatest conservative monarchies in the world were mapping out a programme. Naturally the Austrian representatives were

somewhat reserved, in view of the happenings of 1866, but
they were practical men who did not cry too much over the
spilled milk of the past. As a consequence, the "League of
the Three Emperors" was admitted before Europe. It was
not a formal alliance. The three monarchs simply agreed not
to attack one another, and to work for the common peace
with good comradeship and harmony. It was, as Englishmen or Americans would say, merely "a gentleman's agreement." But Bismarck desired nothing more. He knew that
France would hardly attack Germany single-handed, and as
for England or Italy turning upon the expanded Hohenzollern empire, the thing was almost out of the reckoning.

In 1873 Bismarck accompanied William I and Von Moltke
to St. Petersburg. The chancellor was lionized in the most
distinguished Russian society. No one could compliment
him enough; and in return he made profuse acknowledgment
of the great debt Germany owed to Russia by her attitude
in 1870. "If I should admit merely *the thought*," said Bismarck, "of ever being hostile to the czar and to Russia, I
should consider myself as a traitor!" All through 1874 this
spirit of happy unity among the three empires seemed to
continue. Then in 1875 came the first rift.

France had recovered from her humiliation with a most
disconcerting ease. The skill of her financiers and the patriotism of her people in subscribing for a vast issue of government bonds, had enabled her to discharge the war indemnity which German experts had expected would prove
crushing. She was setting up an orderly system of government, and was reorganizing her army on a strictly scientific
basis. There were plenty of angry spirits in the officers'
messes at Berlin to rail at the chancellor for not having
exacted a more pitiless ransom, and for not driving home
the original blow so as to prevent forever a war for "revenge." There was also a feeling akin to alarm and anger
in influential German circles at the rapid rehabilitation of
their old enemy. It was freely alleged that the new French
army was not, as announced in Paris, "purely defensive,"
but had a deliberately aggressive intention.

Then followed a serious "war scare." The exact details are still vague. "The whole incident remains mysterious," says a very competent American writer.[1] But a "scare" certainly there was. On April 8th, the influential "Post" of Berlin published an ominous article headed "War in Sight!" Three days later the "North German Gazette" (practically a semi-official organ) republished the article without comments. The French government, made anxious already by several happenings, now began to feel real alarm. Its ambassador sent word to Paris that at a banquet Von Radowitz, one of Bismarck's prime lieutenants, had talked ominously of "preventive wars" and of how Germany would be justified "on the grounds of humanity" in attacking France, instead of waiting for the latter to recover further from the effects of 1870. There were stories too of threats in military circles from Moltke and others; and on May 5th, the German ambassador at Paris told the French ministry formally that "his government was not entirely convinced of the inoffensive character of the French armaments"; and that "the German general staff considers war against Germany as the ultimate object of those armaments, and so looks forward to their consequences."

France, however, had no intention of being dragged into a hopeless quarrel without serious reasons. Her envoys at London and St. Petersburg sought and obtained sympathetic hearings. Blowitz,[2] the famous continental correspondent of the London "Times," published a sensation article. Lord Derby, the British foreign minister, sent very direct remonstrances to Berlin. Queen Victoria, whose personal influence with all monarchs was incalculable, wrote direct to William I in the interest of peace. Most serious of all (from Bismarck's point of view), Alexander II bestirred himself. No longer

[1] Coolidge, "Origins of the Triple Alliance," p. 60.

[2] Blowitz was the very prince of newspaper correspondents. He enjoyed the secrets of great statesmen. At Berlin Congress (1878) he kept making such revelations that at the beginning of a certain session Bismarck was seen solemnly looking under the table. Some one asked if His Excellency could explain his actions. "I am looking for Blowitz," gravely retorted the chancellor.

passive as in 1870, he made it clear that he would not wait to see France ruined a second time. On May 10th the czar and his great minister Gortschakov arrived on a friendly visit in Berlin. Instantly William I, a genuine lover of moderation, assured them he had no desire for war. Gortschakov thereupon grandiloquently issued a public statement, "peace is now assured." Bismarck did not enjoy being thus openly lectured by Gortschakov, nor did he like having all the nations know that France had somehow turned a trick on Germany. Henceforth he and the Russian minister became personal enemies, and could no longer co-operate for the weal of Europe.

What exactly had happened behind the scenes is as yet a decided puzzle. Bismarck declared that Radowitz had taken too much wine at the banquet, and had chattered nonsense. All the rest, he said, was newspaper irresponsibility. But it was not simply that. The military clique around Moltke had been assuredly ready for a blow, and Bismarck had not seemed very ready to prevent them. There is no reasonable doubt that a deadly stroke had been almost directed at France. The afterclap of course was to demonstrate that England and Russia (and presumably other powers also) were not willing to have France eliminated for all time from the list of great nations, and to have Germany shatter to bits the much cherished "balance of power in Europe." Henceforth Germany must talk at least courteously, and not brandish the sword merely because France claimed the right to self-respecting existence.

This was the first and the immediate result of the famous "war scare" of 1875. The next was to teach Bismarck that he could not reckon on the steadfast support of Russia. In 1878 he was to revenge himself by helping to smash up the Treaty of San Stefano (pp. 92–3) for the benefit indeed of England, but still more for that of Austria on whom he had decided to lean in preference to the czar.

By 1878 it was therefore pretty clear: (a) that France had pulled herself together and was again a real power in the world; and (b) that since both Austria and Russia were

conferred with the astute Austrian prime-minister Andrassy.
The Austrian statesman indeed refused to make the pact as
elaborate as the German desired; particularly he declined to
make a general treaty of alliance, saying Austria had no
quarrel with France; but that did not trouble Bismarck, for
he knew that France without an ally was helpless against
Germany. By September 24, the treaty had been drafted, and
Bismarck undertook to induce Kaiser Wilhelm to give it his
signature.

The German emperor, however, hesitated long. He considered himself personally beholden to Alexander. To silence
his objections Bismarck induced the king of Bavaria, Moltke,
the whole military staff, and other high officials to join in
urging William to ratify. Reluctantly he did so; and on
October 7, 1879, the final treaty was perfected.

This treaty seemed of a wholly defensive character. It
was aimed clearly enough at Russia, the one power that then
seemed strong enough to menace the safety of either Austria
or Germany. In brief, it was provided that if either the
Vienna or Berlin kaiser got into war with any government
save the czar's, "the high ally" of the party engaged should
preserve a "benevolent neutrality"; but if the czar took up
arms, either alone, or as the confederate of some other power,
then both Austria and Germany were to unite against him.
When the pact became known in England, Lord Beaconsfield's
foreign minister, Lord Salisbury, hailed the issue as "good
tiding of great joy." In France there was much apprehension; but Bismarck assured his old enemy there was no danger
of a new attack. The Russians, realizing the treaty was aimed
directly at them, were resentful, indeed, but bided their time.
William I wrote to Alexander II, trying to explain that the
treaty implied nothing unfriendly. The czar wrote back
ironically: "I like to see in it the return to that perfect
understanding between the three emperors which you [praise
so highly]."

Very soon after this Alexander II was murdered by nihilists
(1881). In his stead ruled Alexander III, an arbitrary, narrow-minded despot, who was however a real lover of peace,

importunate seekers for the same Balkan booty fr
Turks, the Germans could not have the hearty alli
both. Yet Bismarck needed at least one sure ally; otl
he might have to face a hostile coalition created by F
He could still have had Russia by giving the czar
support in his Balkan adventure. The chancellor, hov
preferred Austria. It is doubtful whether he had al
caught the Pan-Germanists' vision of an Austrian er
rendered economically and politically obedient to the sup
genius of Prussia, and with the Hapsburg emperor only
highest satrap of the kaiser at Berlin. But even bar
that, he knew that Austria needed a reliable protector aga
Russia and would consequently repay faithfulness with fai
fulness; and also that the czar was so masterful a soverei
with such a mighty realm, that it would be useless to e
pect of *him* any prompt obedience to the suggestions of h
ally. In other words, if Germany made league with Russi
she made alliance with a proud equal; if with Austria wit
a useful subordinate. Bismarck's choice was thus marked ou
for him.

At the Berlin Congress, it is reasonably clear that Bismarck tried to keep on fairly friendly terms with Russia, while
at the same time playing the game of Austria; but even his
adroitness failed when it came thus to carrying water on
both shoulders. The Russian newspapers in the winter of
1878–79 were full of violent anti-German articles, and even
spoke favorably of an alliance with France; and Russian newspapers (in that land of the censor) were not permitted to say
things unwelcome to the government. The Iron Chancellor
was the more ready therefore to go over to Austria. Still,
he had a hard fight with his own sovereign, William I, who
was very intimate personally with his nephew Alexander II,
and the czar was using his influence to warn the Kaiser not
to let a mere quarrel between Bismarck and Gortschakov
(for so he saw the issue) be the means of embroiling two
mighty empires. Nevertheless, Bismarck as usual beat down
the objections of his rather simple-minded lord and master.
On September 21, 1879, the chancellor went to Vienna and

and who was so busy crushing down revolutions at home that he had no time for foreign adventures. Russia, in fact, for a while, relaxed part of her interests in the Balkan lands towards which Austria was extending eager hands; she even allowed Austria to make the profligate Milan of Serbia so completely her pensioner that while he reigned Serbia was only in name an independent kingdom. But although the new alliance of Germany and Austria had seemed thus to have a most quieting effect on Europe, Bismarck intended to make it still stronger. The Dual Alliance reached out its hand to Italy.

Italy had no special love for the Hohenzollerns, and no love at all for Austria. The desires for *Italia irredenta,* for the lands about Trieste and Trent, were still ardent; but there seemed no prospects of recovering them speedily. On the other hand the relations between France and Italy were cold. French troops had been of great service in 1859 in partially clearing Italy of the Austrians, but Napoleon III had won the poor esteem of the Italians by failing to discharge his complete promise to Cavour to deliver Venetia although exacting Nice and Savoy, the lands promised France in return for her complete aid, and finally by sustaining the temporal power of the papacy. On the other hand, for a long time after 1870, it seemed possible that France would fall under a party very friendly to the Church and that at any moment a French army might be marching on Rome to restore the temporal power of the pope. There was, besides, some little commercial and industrial rivalry and friction between Italy and her Gallic neighbor. Italy wished to be treated as a great power and to have her interests consulted on most world-questions; she was extremely sensitive to slights, and extremely angry when she was not taken quite seriously. At the Congress of Berlin Italy was invited to send a delegate to occupy a chair at the conference table and to look important when Beaconsfield was speaking, but he brought back nothing except, as he boasted, "clean hands." His French colleague had been rather more lucky.

In the southern Mediterranean only one hundred miles of

dancing blue water sundered Italian Sicily from Moorish Tunis. Here, in the country of the ancient and mighty Carthage, stagnated a wretched little Moslem principality which had declined steadily since its one industry of piracy had been frowned upon. This principality Italy was now marking for her own. In 1871, the great patriot Mazzini had written, "Tunis, the key to the central Mediterranean, . . . distant but twenty-five leagues from Sicily, obviously turns toward Italy. . . . Today the French are making eyes at it, and will soon possess it, if we do not."

Mazzini was entirely right in his surmise. The French had now a firm grip on Algeria, next to Tunis, and were not at all averse to considering taking over that country. Besides, two great powers were egging them on. Bismarck deliberately gave the French to understand that he would not oppose their seeking a group of colonies. "Stop gazing always at that gap in the Vosges," he once admonished the French ambassador, in that frank tone of the gruff uncle which he often liked to assume. He really believed, it seems, that the joys of a great colonial domain would make the French less pensive about Alsace-Lorraine, and that the petty wars and troubles of colonies would certainly head off schemes for "revenge." At the Berlin Congress he dropped very broad hints to Waddington, the French envoy, that Germany would not oppose France if she went into Tunis. Waddington received another authoritative hint:—this time from Lord Salisbury, to the effect that England recognized the position of France in Algeria and would be glad to see her in Tunis also. Such intimations were not lost upon the Paris colonial office, and it shaped its policy accordingly.[1]

---

[1] Bismarck was later blamed severely by the Pan-Germans for thus letting France build up a colonial empire,—the very thing Germany needed. Representative Germans have told me that it was a misfortune that in 1870 the victors had not demanded the French colonies, especially Algeria (the loss of which then would have cost France few pangs) instead of Alsace-Lorraine and its heritage of hatred.

England probably did not want to see Italy control simultaneously Sicily and Tunis, and thus dominate both sides of the Mediterranean at one of its narrowest points.

The Italians had an inkling of French intentions and their consul at Tunis, Signore Maccio, at once commenced a vigorous course of intrigue to get the main influence over the native bey, and to wean him away from French predilections. But after some hesitation the French resolved to strike. In 1881, 30,000 reliable troops, avowedly in pursuit of an unruly Moorish tribe, crossed the frontiers from Algeria and marched straight on Tunis. Italy stood helpless. She could not resist France unaided, and no other power arose to champion her. The French general calmly entered Tunis and dictated in the palace a treaty to the distracted bey, which in name indeed left to His Highness his throne, but which consigned to his French "adviser" practically all the final authority. Italy had lost Tunis entirely. It had become a Paris protectorate.

There was wrath in Rome and vain mutterings, but in Berlin a sage old statesman was smiling and taking comfort. It would take twenty years at least for Italy and France really to become friends again. The great foe of Germany was more isolated among the powers of Europe than ever.

King Humbert of Italy and his ministers had only one effective way in which to show their ill-will to France. They would make friends with Germany and Austria. In October, 1881, King Humbert deliberately went on a visit to Vienna to the old oppressor of the House of Savoy, Franz Josef. This trip of ceremony was followed by the real business among the diplomats. Italy was only too ready for an alliance provided she could henceforth feel secure against the insults of France. She was so eager for the pact that she waived all question of *Italia irredenta* and even of the support of her ambitions in the Mediterranean. The most that she really obtained was a pledge for the defense of her territories against invasion. The actual terms of this treaty of the "Triple Alliance" were secret. They have never been published in full, but the general impression is that Italy was promised very little except the integrity of her own homeland and in return had to pledge herself to maintain a huge army, far beyond her wealth, and to come to the rescue of

Germany and Austria if they should be attacked [1] by "two foreign powers" (i.e., Russia and France) even if the quarrel was one that concerned Italy not the slightest.

On May 22, 1882, the pact was signed at Vienna, although it was some months before the existence of the great alliance was admitted to the world.

"The formation of the Triple Alliance was another triumph for Bismarck. He paid almost nothing for it" in what he gave Italy, and he obtained "an important addition to the forces of the Austro-German alliance in case of a conflict with France and Russia." France was of course more isolated, helpless, and angry at the European situation than ever. Russia likewise disliked the whole case. But for the hour Bismarck seemed to have achieved another master-stroke in diplomacy. So long as England remained neutral he had created one of the most powerful international combinations conceivable, and "for better or for worse the Triple Alliance was destined to last for a whole generation, during which it was to be one of the dominant forces in the European world." [2]

The Triple Alliance seemed to stand without a rival for several years. France was too perplexed with her own sore problems and her government seemed too unstable to make her a useful ally for Russia, even if the alliance of a liberal republic and a despotic empire did not seem almost an absurdity. As long as Russia and France stood apart Germany was not in the slightest real danger, and that was the guar-

---

[1] It should be observed that Italy was only bound to aid in a *defensive* war: not in an *offensive* war, as she considered the one begun by her nominal allies in 1914.

[2] Coolidge, "Origins of the Triple Alliance," pp. 213–218. Bismarck had only a slight esteem for the Italian army, although he considered King Humbert's fleet as a power in the Mediterranean. What he *did* wish to be sure about was that the French should have to divert troops to guard their south-eastern frontier. A threat there would produce great weakening elsewhere. "It was enough," he said, "that an Italian corporal with an Italian flag and a drummer beside him should array himself against the West (France) and not against the East (Austria)."

antee which Bismarck wanted. But after the fall of Boulanger in 1889, it was reasonably evident that the Third Republic would enjoy a long lease of life, and circumstances
were making Russia more and more in need of a powerful
ally. France was recovering the respect of the world. She
no longer appeared to be inhabited by "a gay people, fond
of dancing,"[1] nor by a set of hopeless "red revolutionaries."
French thrift had accumulated a great deal of loanable capital, and Russia needed the same for factories, railroads, new
artillery and what-not else.

As a result the two powers drew together. It was clearly
a "marriage of interest," not of affection. There was little
inherently in common between the land of Latin republicans
and the then land of the czar, the Cossacks, the knout and the
road to Siberia. But both nations feared and distrusted
Germany, and both nations, at this time, were on no good
terms with England. France was grieved at the way she had
been elbowed out of Egypt (see Chapter VI), even if her
troubles there had been partly of her own making. Russia
remembered the voided pact of San Stefano and the way in
which England had halted her advance to India via Afghanistan. In fact, as things seemed then, it was physically possible
that England should make an alliance with Germany, Britain
to rule the seas and Prussia to dominate the continent, and
thus leave both the Third Republic and the czar in peril of
their independence.

In 1887, at a time when Bismarck was blustering against
France, in order to get the Reichstag to vote more money for
the army, Czar Alexander II wrote on the margin of a confidential report from his foreign minister, "We must not
let France be diminished." Speedily afterwards there came
on the scene a M. Hoskier, a banker of Danish birth but
French connection, who undertook to float a large Russian
loan in the Paris money markets. In December, 1888, a
great loan, subscribed to by over 100,000 persons and for

---

[1] This characterization of the French appeared in a geography very
familiar in American schools a generation ago. Such damnations of a
great nation by a phrase have done the French infinite harm.

500,000,000 francs ($100,000,000) was thus placed in France for the benefit of the czar. This was only the beginning. There were more loans, and still greater ones, in 1889, 1890, 1891, 1894, 1896, 1901, 1904 and 1906. By that time France had loaned Russia for one purpose or another (governmental, municipal and industrial) at least 12,000,000,000 francs ($2,400,000,000) ; and too late the Berlin bankers were lamenting the blindness of their diplomats in angering the czar to the extent that had opened this vast field of exploitation to their rivals.

Enormous loans like this, however, were not to be had in Paris for nothing but the bond certificates and the interest. French diplomats knew how to insinuate this point delicately but clearly at St. Petersburg. Besides, in 1890, M. Constans, the French minister of the interior, rendered Alexander III an invaluable personal service by clapping in jail a band of nihilist exiles in Paris who were in the act of manufacturing a whole arsenal of bombs intended for the Russian imperial family. Russians found the great French munition plants always at their disposal, and speedily the results of all this by-play were evident. In 1891 Admiral Cervais led a French fleet proudly under the guns of the mighty fortress of Kronstadt. There was elaborate ''fraternization'' by the sailors of the two navies. The czar visited the French flagship and stood with uncovered head under the shadow of the tri-color flag of the great Revolution, while the naval band played the ''Marseillaise,'' the fighting hymn of democracy. It was not until 1896 that there was official announcement of the treaty of alliance, but everybody knew that it existed. The Triple Alliance was opposed now by the Dual Alliance.

The exact terms of the new pact were not published, any more than were those of its older rival. It was soon understood, however, that it did not contemplate any war of aggression or any scheme to tear up the Treaty of Frankfort and win back Alsace-Lorraine. On the other hand, it did undoubtedly guarantee France against a new attack from Germany unless provoked by France herself.

The world did not fail to notice that the Dual Alliance had come into being just about a year after William II had "dropped the pilot," Bismarck, and begun to steer the German ship of state himself. From his retreat the ex-chancellor covered with bitter ridicule the new rulers who had failed to stave off this dreaded combination. It may be a fair question, however, whether Bismarck with all his genius could have kept Russia and France asunder much longer, unless he had been willing to give the czar a free hand in the Balkans at the expense of Austria, or to cede back Alsace-Lorraine. The new combination, furthermore, seemed at first more anti-British than anti-German. Britain was still shivering at the idea of seeing French regiments ferrying across the Channel to Dover and of seeing Cossacks riding simultaneously into Egypt and India. The combined navies of France and Russia figured up, on paper, dangerously close to the navy of Britain. In short, at the new alliance Berlin was piqued but in no wise alarmed. Although the great population of Russia made the number of bayonets in the new "Dual Alliance" seem about as many as those in the Triple Alliance, military students knew that the two leagues were hardly equal in land-strength. The czar's legions lacked suitable railroads for complete mobilization, their officers were of less technical ability than their possible opponents, and the Muscovite infantryman, brave though he might be, lacked the education and probable intelligence to make him match man for man his Western rivals. In addition to all else the Triple Alliance had the great advantage of continuous boundaries and inner military lines. In short, the Dual Alliance hardly equalled the Triple Alliance as a military combination.[1]

Nevertheless, France plus Russia constituted a mighty power, the destruction whereof would test all the strength of Moltke's war-machine and its allies. There was nothing for Berlin to do but to make the best of the facts:—to treat France with greater consideration than formerly, and to be exceed-

[1] This was of course amply demonstrated in 1914 when the Teutonic powers, even without Italy, very possibly would have won a pretty speedy victory had England stayed neutral.

ingly gracious to Russia. This latter policy was made easy by
the death of Alexander III in 1894 and the accession of Nicholas II. The character of this unfortunate prince is discussed
elsewhere (see page 506); it is enough to say that he was subject to the personal hypnotism which William II was able to
throw over very many men whom he desired to win: the
Kaiser easily played on his imperial "brother" and kinsman's personal weaknesses. The extremely practical considerations which had impelled both Russia and France to
enter the Dual Alliance prevented either side from being at
all anxious to draw the sword in behalf of its ally save in a
clear-cut case of wanton aggression. In 1898, France had
a grievous collision with England over the Fashoda affair
in Africa (see page 112). Russian statesmen merely shrugged
their shoulders, however, when it was suggested that they
should go to war over the right of France to plant her flag
upon the Upper Nile. In 1904–05, Russia in her turn fell
into war with Japan. France showed herself a very friendly
neutral towards Russia, but was not required to fight in a
purely Asiatic quarrel. In 1904 also came the famous Dog-
gerbank incident that almost embroiled England with Russia.[1] France did her best to get the quarrel composed by
arbitration. Whether she would have gone to war then if
England had come to blows with Russia is an open question.

The Dual Alliance, therefore, like the Triple Alliance, was
only a defensive pact, and not a serious menace to the world's
peace. However, that fact for a long time made it all the
more valuable. Both alliances promised little help to their
members if individual powers went off on schemes for bloody
exploitation; but both alliances promised honest defense in
case any member was attacked in its home territories and real
integrity. So long as there was no single nation in Europe
that felt so confident of its own might that it could safely dis-
regard the wishes of its nominal allies, the two alliances pro-

---

[1] When a Russian fleet en route through the North Sea for the Pacific
fired upon a number of English fishing craft, imagining them to be Japanese torpedo boats.

vided excellent safety-valves for the occasional blasts of war-steam. This state of equilibrium, unstable indeed but fairly secure, lasted from 1891 to 1905. During that time there were, on the whole, fewer "war-scares" and capital problems for the diplomats than in any like period earlier or later. German statesmen were still believed when they talked "peace"; the Balkans and Turkey were not more than ordinarily vexed, despite the Armenian and Cretan issues; England was still content with her "splendid isolation." Confident in her fleet, engrossed in her home and colonial problems, she still jauntily despised the jealousy of France, faced down the aggressions of Russia in the East and reared up Japan as a counterpoise to the Muscovite, while treating Germany as at the worst a land of learned professors with execrable table manners. Thus Albion went on her way—little disturbed for long when warning voices told her that many nations hated her and that, especially in Berlin, statesmen with shoulder-straps were preparing trouble for her.

The one great gainer by the balance of alliances was France. "By means of the Russian alliance, she had broken the circle of solitude in which Bismarck had confined her" (Tardieu). Certain now that the czar would shield her from her worst nightmare, an unprovoked attack by the whole power of Germany, her statesmen recovered their poise and their self-confidence. In 1898, she had obtained a remarkable foreign minister, Theophile Delcassé, who, before 1904, had with great success cleared up old outstanding diplomatic problems with Italy, with Spain, and, more important still, with England. France, by the test of years of firm government and by patient economic expansion, had won back her place in the world. The nations respected her; her influence was increasing; and yet all Europe seemed at peace. Then in 1904 upon her Russian ally came the Japanese war. The czar was obviously involved on a disastrous foreign venture. He could give no real aid to his confederate in Europe. Hardly, in 1905, had the news spread of the serious defeat of the Russians at Mukden, when the Berlin foreign office manifested a sudden and amazing interest in the relation of France to Morocco, a question whereof earlier the Kaiser's minister had hardly breathed a word.

The year 1905 marked the opening of nine years of intrigue, threats, "war scares," tension and growing national hatred leading steadily towards Armageddon.

CHAPTER XVI

THE PROMISE AND FAILURE OF THE HAGUE
PEACE CONFERENCES

INTERNATIONAL law is that branch of law which has
to do with the relations of states to each other. Because
it has not been made by a supreme law-giver, and because no
impartial authority has been set up definitely to enforce it,
some men insist that it is not law at all. This may be the
case, but at least all must admit that there is a branch of
human relations which is covered by a code of what we call
"international law."

The two great problems of international relations are war
and peace. The two conditions are opposed to each other.
Peace is that state of affairs between nations in which the governments conduct all common business without resort to force,
by what we call peaceful negotiations. War is the reverse
of this: it is the prosecution of claims by one state against
another by *force*. Instead of persuading the spirit and con-
vincing the mind of its neighbor, the state in war uses material forces, men and munitions, to destroy and weaken its
opponent until the latter sees that it is useless to resist. Destruction is not an end in itself. War has absolutely no other
object except to convince a state that, whatever may be its
ideas as to the right or wrong or the fundamental justice,
of the demands put upon it, it is not possible to resist them.
Then it sues for peace; the victorious state takes what it
wants; and the condition of peace is supposed to prevail again
between them.

Since international law has to do with the relations of states
to each other, it falls naturally under two heads: the law of
peace, and the law of war. All international law can be
put under the one or the other caption.

The ancient Greeks, perhaps even the Babylonians and the Persians, had customs regulating the relations between groups of people,—villages, tribes, and city-states,—which may be considered as having constituted the international law of their day. Rome, too, at first acknowledged such customs, but as she towered upward to world empire, she recognized outside tribes and nations only as inferiors and enemies, to whom she owed nothing but contemptuous tolerance or hard blows. It was not, indeed, until after the rise of the modern state system out of a decadent feudalism that international law came into its own. The Thirty Years' War, which raged on the continent of Europe during the first half of the seventeenth century, and the treaties of Westphalia which concluded it in 1648, first brought into clear light the existence in Europe of many national states. It was Hugo Grotius's masterpiece, "The Law of War and of Peace," written while this savage war was being waged, which laid the foundations of the modern study of international law (1625).

Since the days of Grotius two important things have happened to international law. In the first place, it has come to be recognized by states as more or less binding upon them. Developing at first all unconsciously, it had grown until it became noticeable to scholars, above all to Grotius. They took the facts as they found them, spun their theories, and presented the results to the world in treatises. Scoffed at a little at first, the new learning summoned up also its supporters, and soon found itself woven into the very life of the nations as their law. Young men aspiring to places in the departments of foreign affairs either at home or abroad are now required to have a knowledge of international law. The mere fact that this requirement is made shows that all states intend to recognize this law, though some may study it as lawyers often study ordinary law, in order to discover its loop-holes. There is probably not a state on the planet which would not confess that international law is more or less binding upon it, even to-day in the crisis of the world.

The second important thing that has happened to international law since Grotius's times is that it has developed and expanded tremendously, and that methods have been devised of developing it *consciously*. International law develops from two independent but complementary sources,—custom and convention. A word ought to be said as to each. *Custom* is a source of both municipal and international law. When there is no written law as to the rights of the parties under certain conditions, or as to the method of procedure, given a set of facts calling for action, the judge or the parties find a convenient and just way around the difficulty. If a second case of the same type arises soon, it is likely to be settled according to the precedent in the first, or if that worked out badly, then a different decision is reached. In time an habitual method of settlement is reached, and when a thing has become customary it is very nearly law.

Thus it is in international law, as a single case will show. In the eighteenth century and earlier, it was the custom for *all* states to take part, more or less directly, in a war between any two. The conception that a state could be neutral, though existent, was vague. In 1793, when France and Great Britain were at war, France desired us to enter the war on her side. Washington, confronting this grave problem for the first time, called together his cabinet, and together they decided to issue a proclamation of neutrality. The step was a novel one, but its results were extremely important in the history of international law. Neutrality became a definite status, and the issue of neutrality proclamations at the commencement of wars between other states, became a regular and soon an expected practice. It seems impossible to talk of "starting a custom," but that is just what Washington's administration did in issuing the neutrality proclamation of 1793. The importance of this custom in the limitation of wars to the few actual participants cannot be overestimated. Wars thereafter were limited definitely to a few parties, and, to speak in metaphor, there ceased to be any reason why every local fire should become a conflagration.

The other source of international law is *convention* or *agreement*. International agreements are of many kinds, but two can be easily distinguished. Treaties, in the ordinary sense, are generally limited to two parties. Moreover, the contents of simple treaties are usually not declarative of international law. On the other hand, there are conventions, drawn up and adopted by two or more, usually more, states, and very often declarative of some new principle of action to be binding among them in the future. Such conventions are especially important sources of international law. Many such have been drawn up in the course of the nineteenth and early twentieth centuries, for the purpose of expanding or developing international law. Up to 1914, statesmen were relying more and more upon this method of improving the relations existing between states, especially in the direction of limiting war and its awful consequences. This action was conscious and statesmanlike. It built upon the prevalent state system and the existing principles of international law. It was evolutionary, and therefore it accorded well with the natural human material of which states are, after all, composed.

It is in pursuance of this method of developing international law that there have been held in Europe from time to time conferences of the official representatives of leading states. Thus, at the close of the Crimean War there was held at Paris (1856) the Congress of Paris, in which England, France, Sardinia, Austria, Prussia, and Russia were represented, as well as Turkey, which was then admitted to the circle of nations. This conference issued the Declaration of Paris, abolishing privateering forever, and laying down the fundamental rules concerning the capture of goods and ships at sea, including therein a clear definition of lawful blockade. In 1864 the representatives of the chief powers on the continent of Europe met at Geneva and adopted a convention for the amelioration of the condition of wounded soldiers, the convention which gave to the Red Cross an international status. In 1868 the delegates of practically the same powers drew up the Declaration of St. Petersburg, which laid down ''that the only legitimate object which states should endeavor to accomplish during war is to weaken the

military forces of the enemy,"[1] and that any weapon or
missile which not only put the wounded man *hors de combat*
but uselessly aggravated his sufferings or made his death
inevitable would "be contrary to the laws of humanity."
In 1874 the powers again met in conference, this time at
Brussels, and drew up the draft of a declaration concerning the laws and customs of land warfare. This declaration was never ratified.

The beginnings here enumerated were pregnant with the
possibility of good results. It is notable that in all these
great conferences of the nations, steps were taken to make
war less brutal, and to protect the neutral as far as possible
from suffering. It is also to be remarked that the method
followed was the same in all: a conscious international agreement to fix and to improve the principles of international
law. The conferences were practically limited to European
powers, Japan, the United States, and other distant nations
not being represented, though they later accepted the results in one way or another.

While these great steps were being taken by statesmen in
the direction of making war less brutal, there was parallel
progress in the way of substituting peaceful for warlike
means of settling international disputes. In the so-called
Jay Treaty, drawn up in 1794 between England and the
United States to settle some outstanding differences as to
boundaries and debts, provision was made for the creation of
several boards of arbitrators, one to ascertain the northeastern
boundary of the United States, another to adjudicate upon
debts owed by Americans to British merchants, and a third
to pass upon the amount of damages inflicted upon peaceful
American commerce by British ships in the war then raging
between France and England. This plan of submitting disputes to arbitrators was a revival of a very ancient principle
in international law well known to the Greeks and the
Romans, and its results were extremely beneficent. The
practice thus begun in 1794 grew steadily, almost rapidly.

[1] See end of chapter, note on "German War Practices."

From 1794 to 1872 history records the peaceful settlement of over ninety international disputes by the arbitration method. The last, and most important up to that time, the settlement of the *Alabama* Claims at Geneva in 1872, though it angered the British because they had to pay what they considered excessive damages, proved that this method could be successfully used in cases of first-rate importance. Naturally, people of pacific leanings looked with ever more favor on arbitration as a possible means of averting war entirely.

The two lines of development which have here been indicated came at about the same time. One aimed to debrutalize war; the other had the effect of making wars less frequent. Naturally enough, the progress toward peace and humanity roused in some breasts hopes of a coming millennium. The impression it made upon others was quite the reverse.

Three entirely different classes of thinkers should here be distinguished. In the first place there are those who deplore war, and emphasize the importance of trying to settle all things peacefully, but who believe, nevertheless, that war is in some cases inevitable. They argue that war is in itself always wasteful, and because of the antagonisms it arouses it is never so successful as a peaceful solution of a problem. Most of the statesmen of the past century, responsible for the lives of millions of people, have taken this conservative attitude. They have not, in most cases, risked lightly the lives of thousands of their fellow-citizens, but have recoiled from war until it appeared to be absolutely impossible to avoid it. Of this class we may mention a few American statesmen: Washington, who, though seriously provoked to war both by England and by France, refrained; Madison, who felt himself finally compelled to advocate a war against Great Britain; and Wilson, who was at last forced by an unusually arrogant violation of the rights of humanity to call us to war upon Germany.

In recent years there has developed a group of thinkers, not themselves statesmen, who go much farther than the class just mentioned. These men, who have styled themselves pacifists, have argued that war is never justified and is to be avoided in all cases, without exception. Their arguments are various. They consider the life of a single soldier worth more than was ever gained by any war. Some say that war never pays; that states know that it does not pay; therefore, states will never go to war. The trumpet call to Armageddon in 1914 was a sad awakening for men of this persuasion. Many were convinced that they had been "thinking with their hearts" instead of with their heads.[1] A few have, unfortunately, remained absolutely unconvinced.[1]

On the extreme opposite wing of the great class first mentioned are the militarists who glorify war as desirable. They fall into various groups. Some of them argue that the modern national state is the highest product of civilization, worthy beyond all things else to be preserved. War, they say further, is one of the functions of the state, the army an essential institution. Therefore, they idealize war as a splendid necessity. Others say that man deteriorates, loses his virility, becomes a lover of money and the weakening pleasures of society, a distinctly lower type of man, unless he has wars occasionally to rouse him, purify him, force him to make sacrifices, and thus raise his ideals. These classes constantly incite to war, preaching and glorifying it on all possible occasions. When you mention the decrease of armaments, they say the military equipment should be increased rather than decreased. If you dwell upon the suffering of men and women in war, they retort that it is better that a man die for his country than that he die a haberdasher, counting over his wares and telling his cash,—a degraded money-grubber. Tell him that Christianity is a religion of peace and that the Nazarene was a man of peace, and he replies that the Master said that "He came to bring not peace, but the sword," and that He himself used force to drive the money-changers from the Temple. *Force—*

[1] See Chapter XXII for a discussion of the predictions and theorizings of pacifism.

that is the thing to which the war-worshipper pins his faith. This man, put at the head of a state, makes war on the slightest pretext, and sometimes without a pretext. After he has done the deed, he says, he will find preachers and college professors aplenty to justify all he has done and more. He considers that state weak and contemptible which, instead of making war at once, tries first to reason with another state and does not make war until it is compelled to.

Of the preachers of the doctrines of pacifism, there are some in every country, and they are to be found in every class of society. The socialist parties in every country, the so-called International, are of this faith. To them the State itself is unjustified, and had better be abolished, together with all its paraphernalia of armies, patriotism, and all, in favor of international government. The world-wide struggle between working classes and capitalists is the only important contest they recognize. There are also, in every country, those who believe in the doctrine of force and militarism, but as the result of historical processes their number is extremely small, especially in the small nations, but also in England, France, Italy, the United States, and, strange to say, in Russia. There has been a great concentration of believers in the theory of force in Germany. It is there especially that they have been developed in recent times, and there in recent years they have been able to get control of the government as nowhere else in the world. These German thinkers,—rulers, bureaucrats, army officers, preachers, university professors,— have shown a great contempt for the developments of international law which tend to limit war, and not a little apprehension that the heresy would spread among Germans too, making them less warlike, less amenable to military control. To them war is a "part of the divine order," "the sole arbiter" in the affairs of men.[1] We quote but a few passages from the excellent compilation here referred to, passages drawn from Nietzsche, Treitschke, famous professors, army men, and the emperor himself. War is "a biological necessity, . . . an

[1] See Notestein, Wallace and Stoll, Elmer E., "Conquest and Kultur," especially chapters 3–5.

indispensable regulator, because without war there could be neither racial nor cultural progress." "War is a holy thing, the holiest thing on earth." "Arbitration treaties must be peculiarly detrimental to an aspiring people which has not yet reached its political and national zenith and is bent on expanding in order to play its part honorably in the civilized world." "Between states regarded as intelligent beings disputes can be settled only by material force." "War is the fundamental phenomenon in the life of a state, and preparation for it assumes a preponderant place in the national life." "We must strenuously combat the peace propaganda. War must regain its moral justification and its political significance in the eyes of the public." "War is justified because the great national personalities can suffer no compelling force superior to themselves, and because history must always be in constant flux; war, therefore, must be taken as part of the divinely appointed order."

Thinkers of this class, detesting the very thought of peace and revolting against anything which will limit the sovereign state, naturally looked upon the progressive development of international law in the direction of peace and humanity as particularly subversive. Instead of encouraging the growth of international law, they felt it their duty to stop it, to "combat the peace propaganda."

The pacifists, at the other extreme, looked upon the progress of international law as entirely too slow. Pacifists in all ages have been utopians, from Dante (1265–1321) who spun his fine theory of a federal world-state under a single monarch or president, down through Kant who, in 1795, philosophized about "perpetual peace," even to our own day, in which we are being deluged with talk about the "federation of the world." While the law was making slow and steady progress up to about 1875, in limiting the use of force, the international socialists and the peace societies and agitators clamored for the quick adoption of treaties to abolish all war.

Meanwhile, the statesmen of the world, backed by the great middle class of thinkers, were making haste slowly, some holding back and desiring even slower progress. With sure steps, however, they went forward, building nothing on the sands if possible, but founding every advance upon solid achievements of the past. So they were progressing, when in 1874 the movement received a serious check.

The failure of the European powers to ratify the Brussels draft declaration concerning the laws of war on land was a hard blow to the international conference idea. Germany saw in this declaration various articles which retrospectively condemned her methods in the recent Franco-Prussian War. Other powers did not like certain innovations introduced by the declaration. It went unratified, and there followed a period in the development of international law which is worthy of study because it represents the arrest of this development. In the twenty-five years between 1874 and 1899, the number of general international conferences to define the principles of law binding the nations was almost nil. There were minor special conferences galore for the protection of trade-marks, copyrights, and so on. In distant America there began the Pan-American Congresses, but Europe knew them not.

The main reason, it appears, why no general conferences were held during this quarter-century was that a feeling of profound uneasiness and distrust had fallen upon Europe after the Franco-Prussian War. At one sharp blow, France had been deposed from her place as the first power on the Continent. A new state, Germany, had forcefully taken her place, a nation which came preaching and practicing the gospel of "blood and iron." *Europe was to be ruled during the succeeding decades not by peaceful international agreements, but by fear.* The alliances and the balance of power were in the making as long as Bismarck, the man of Blood and Iron, was dominant in Europe,—and his preëminence was admitted even after his fall from power. There was but one thing for Europe to do: *prepare for war.* In the face of the new situation to prate of peace was to be foolish.

Then it was that the competition in armaments between the European nations began in earnest. What had gone before seemed child's play by comparison. America, far removed from the danger, could get along with a few regiments, but France, Russia, Austria, and Italy, in direct contact with the peril, prepared on a scale never before known in history. Compulsory military service became the rule everywhere on the Continent. The nations of Europe transformed themselves into great armed camps. Army leaders, soldiers, and people watched the annual army manœuvers of their neighbors with apprehension. Newspapers succeeded in concocting "war scares," especially between France and Germany, with distressing frequency. The consequent state of armed peace was more burdensome than some wars of earlier days. To the people at large as well as to statesmen it brought much of the sacrifice, the anxiety, the depression, of real war, without war's compensating glory and excitement.

Into this deplorable situation shot a sudden ray of hope. It was the unheralded call issued late in August, 1898, by the young Czar Nicholas, summoning the nations to a conference to consider the means of preserving peace and of reducing armaments. The moment was favorable, said the summons; it neglected to say that Prince Bismarck had died but a few weeks before, after having been already some years out of office, and that the new captain of state, Emperor William II, though he leaned strongly on his army, also preached peace. It neglected also to observe that practically all the states of Europe had been looking with grave suspicion, not to say a little fear, on the war conducted by the United States against Spain.

The ground of public opinion had long been under preparation by the pacifists, already well organized, who looked on with increasing dread as the annual military budgets rose steadily and rapidly. Their great fear was that, when the nations some day reached the maximum possible military preparation, the whole world would suddenly burst into the flames of destructive war. With all their resources they had been bringing the dreaded facts before the people in both Europe and America, but it needed the official utterance of some one high in authority adequately to emphasize the portentousness of the situation. This result the czar accomplished as perhaps no one else could have done. Some of his words may well be quoted.[1]

He said that peace, everywhere desired, was everywhere far from realization. The method of preserving peace which the nations were all following, namely, that of steadily increasing their military forces, was not attaining the wished-for end. Indeed, this ever-growing militarism was having very bad results. "The intellectual and physical strength of the nations, labor and capital, are for the major part diverted from their natural application, and unproductively consumed. . . . National culture, economic progress, and the production of wealth are paralyzed or checked in their development. Moreover, in proportion as the armaments of each power increase, so do they less and less fulfil the object which the governments have set before themselves. The economic crises, due in great part to the system of armaments *à l'outrance,* and the continual danger which lies in this massing of war material, are transforming the armed peace of our days into a crushing burden, which the peoples have more and more difficulty in bearing. It appears evident, then, that if this state of things were prolonged, it would inevitably lead to the very cataclysm which it is desired to avert, and the horrors of which make every thinking man shudder in advance. To put an end to these incessant armaments and to seek the means of warding off the calamities which are threatening the whole world—such is the supreme duty which is to-day imposed on all states."

The thing could hardly have been better stated. Everywhere the solemnity of the warning was understood. Everywhere men began to talk, and the newspapers and magazines to be filled with articles, about the coming "Disarmament Conference." The idea of disarmament, long current among pacifist thinkers, was seized upon as the final solution of the

---

[1] Of course, Nicholas II himself did not prepare the summons, for which Count Mouravieff, then Russian minister of Foreign Affairs, is perhaps chiefly responsible.

difficulty. Even some military men accepted the proposition as sound and feasible. Nevertheless, it is true the czar did not himself propose complete disarmament, nor did he dare to hope for so much. Perhaps he would not even have wished it. What he did propose was that the conference should seek "without delay *means for putting a limit to the progressive increase of military and naval armaments,*" and to this end he suggested "an understanding not to increase for a fixed period the present effectives of the armed military and naval forces, and at the same time not to increase the budgets pertaining thereto; and a preliminary examination of the means by which a reduction might even be effected in future in the forces and budgets above mentioned."

The conference met in May, 1899, at The Hague. All the great nations were represented and also many smaller ones. The tensity of the international situation among the large powers even at that time may be judged from the fact that the capital of no first-rate nation was considered a fit place for holding the conference. Indeed, even while the call to the conference was under consideration, several of the large states of Europe proceeded to increase their military forces.

The czar had proposed a very definite program for the consideration of the conference. It fell naturally into three parts, and was accordingly divided among three commissions. The first dealt exclusively with the question of limitation of armaments, the second with various proposals to change the laws of war both on land and sea, and the third with the peaceful settlement of international disputes.[1]

It depended largely upon the first commission whether or not the conference was truly to become a "Disarmament Conference." The discussions began with an address by the president, M. Beernaert of Belgium, who was followed by

---

[1] The Second Hague Conference met in the same place in 1907, and dealt with a similar but larger program of proposals. The work of this second conference will be discussed in connection with that of the first. The holding of a third conference was prevented by the outbreak of war in 1914.

M. de Staal for Russia.   Both emphasized the extreme seriousness of the problem, yet believed that progress could be made.
Soon thereafter the official Russian proposals were presented,
which can be summed up in one word: non-augmentation.   In
itself, the suggestion was certainly modest enough.   Unfortunately, it was known even before the propositions could be
discussed that certain powers, and especially Germany, were
opposed not only to their adoption but even to consideration.
General Gross von Schwarzhoff rose early in the meetings
of the first commission, and after making a light jibe at a member from the Netherlands "who made himself a warm defender of these propositions even before they had been submitted to us," he said:

"I can hardly believe that among my honored colleagues
there is a single one ready to state that his sovereign, his government, is engaged in working for the inevitable ruin, the
slow but sure annihilation, of his country.   I have no mandate
to speak for my honored colleagues, but so far as Germany is
concerned, I am able to completely reassure her friends and
to relieve all well-meant anxiety.   The German people is not
crushed under the weight of charges and taxes,—it is not hang-
ing on the brink of an abyss; it is not approaching exhaustion
and ruin.   Quite the contrary; public and private wealth is
increasing, the general welfare and standard of life is being
raised from one year to another.   So far as compulsory military service is concerned, which is so closely connected with
those questions, the German does not regard this as a heavy
burden, but as a sacred and patriotic duty to which he owes
his country's existence, its prosperity, and its future."   The
fine sarcasm in this speech can be appreciated only by one who
knows the international situation as it existed at the time; but
the assumption of Germany's superiority over any nation that
would care to suggest limitation of armaments no one can fail
to feel as he reads these words.

It is probably true that, even without this open opposition
on the part of Germany, the czar's proposals would not have
been adopted in full at the conference of 1899.   Technically
the problem proved to be of extreme difficulty.   It is proper

to point out, however, that it was Germany which was constantly leading the way during these years in increasing armaments, that the other nations were arming in defense against her, and that *if Germany refused to agree to non-augmentation, no other nation dared to adopt that policy.* It was finally on the motion of a French delegate that the proposal was saved from complete defeat, and held open for further discussion by a resolution, adopted by the conference, "that the restriction of military charges . . . is extremely desirable for the increase of the material and moral welfare of mankind."

It is not amiss here to look forward eight years to the *Second Conference* which met in the same place and under the same auspices. The Russian government had in the meantime suffered a severe defeat at the hands of the Japanese, and was hardly inclined to think of nonaugmentation of armaments, far less of disarmament. Owing to the objections of other powers also, including Germany, the limitation of armaments was left out of the 1907 official program entirely. Nevertheless, the English and the American representatives insisted upon bringing the question forward, and in this they were supported by France, and also by a Russian delegate, M. de Nelidow. The result was the adoption once more of the pious resolution of 1899, and there the matter rested!

The Russian circular outlining a program of work for the First Hague Conference put the proposals for the peaceful settlement of disputes between nations at the bottom of the list. The results of these proposals were, however, so much better than those in other directions, that the question of improving the arbitration conventions was put first in the program of the 1907 conference.

At the first conference the delegates were confronted by the very brief Russian preliminary proposal, and a Russian draft convention covering mediation, good offices, and arbitration. The general tenor of the proposal was that a permanent court of arbitration should be created to which all powers could have recourse when disputes of a nature that could be arbitrated might arise. To this plan, the American delegation and the representatives of other countries wanted to add a provision that, within definite classes of cases, the recourse to arbitration should be compulsory.

That the majority of the nations represented at the conference earnestly desired the consummation of this desirable end was clearly evident in the speeches made to the conference. In May it appeared that the German delegates, though not enthusiastic, were not entirely opposed to the plan. As the year advanced into June, however, and the Third Commission proceeded with its discussions, the attitude of Germany became clearly that of opposition. Count Münster, head of the German delegation, had already stated to Mr. Andrew D. White, head of the American delegation, *"that arbitration must be injurious to Germany;* that Germany is prepared for war as no other country is or can be; that she can mobilize her army in ten days; and that neither France, Russia, nor any other power can do this. Arbitration, he said, would simply give rival powers time to put themselves in readiness, and would therefore be a great disadvantage to Germany." [1]

The rest of the nations were talking peace and arbitration. Germany's attitude stood out in sharp contrast, for she was unconsciously, and therefore naturally, showing that her trust lay wholly in force. But more disquieting news than this was yet to come. On June 9th it became known to members of the Third Commission that Emperor William was "determined to oppose the whole scheme of arbitration," as Mr. White records, and a little later that he would insist that his chief allies, Austria and Italy, should stand with him in opposition. On the 16th came the time of greatest tension. The German delegation received on that day—the very day when the sub-committee was to meet to settle the matter—"a despatch from Berlin in which the German Government—which, of course, means the Emperor—had strongly and finally declared against everything like an arbitration tribunal."

---

[1] Andrew D. White, Autobiography of, 1905, II, 265. For his account of the First Hague Conference, see generally II, pp. 250–354.

Germany insisted that a permanent court of arbitration would be impracticable and dangerous to Germany, and that it would derogate from her sovereignty as a nation. There was apparent consternation in the German delegation. The meeting of the sub-committee was postponed, while Professor Zorn, a representative of Germany, and Mr. Holls of the American delegation, were sent posthaste to Berlin by the heads of their respective delegations. Mr. Holls bore with him a careful and cogent letter from Mr. White to his good friend Baron von Bülow, then German minister for foreign affairs, a letter which argued that it was *good policy* for Germany to accept the idea of creating the permanent court of arbitration.

The German foreign office was at the last moment convinced that its opposition to the permanent tribunal would be very detrimental to Germany's standing in the world. New instructions were issued which soon cleared the atmosphere. The relief which this news brought to the tense situation at The Hague was appreciated by no one more than by the American delegates. Had Germany continued its opposition to the permanent court, the Conference would have ended almost in complete failure. Its only result would have been to emphasize a common belief that Germany did not wish peace.

The adherence of the Teutonic empire was dearly bought. The draft convention then under consideration contained a clause making recourse to arbitration *compulsory* on the signatory powers *in a few specified cases*. This point Germany would not yield, and it was in the interest of harmony that the American delegation and others backed up Germany on this matter, and caused the clause to be stricken out.

In the few cases settled by arbitration between 1899 and 1907, certain defects in the convention of 1899 appeared; but on the whole it worked well. Germany herself had tried the method, with success, and had negotiated several arbitration treaties. Her argument of 1899 that it was impracticable seemed, therefore, to have been disproved by her own policy and experience. Indeed, there was growing up in Germany a body of opinion strongly in favor of arbitration. There seemed to be, therefore, no longer any reason why Germany should oppose.

It was now time, in 1907, to take the second step to make arbitration compulsory in those cases where there were no questions of "vital interests" or "honor" involved. Several proposals were made to this effect in the Second Hague Conference, among them the American. This provided that with certain liberal reservations legal questions and those involving the interpretation of treaties, where they did not involve the independence, vital interests, and honor of the parties, were always to be submitted to arbitration. This was thought to be a reasonable minimum requirement, that nations should agree not to go to war over questions entirely trivial in themselves.

Certain early speeches by the German delegates roused the hopes of the conference that Germany had begun to see the light. The language of her representatives was certainly not that of opposition. Indeed, it aroused instead the enthusiasm and the highest hopes of the exponents of arbitration. But in 1907, as in 1899, these hopes were dashed to the ground. Germany accepted the idea of compulsory arbitration "in principle," but was unable to find any way around the difficulties "in practice." She could not find a "formula" which could be put into a general treaty for compulsory arbitration which would not be open to objections. Because she could not find such a "formula," therefore Germany had to reject the idea of a general treaty, and would content herself with making special treaties with particular countries. As a distinguished South American delegate put it, *this was "the death of arbitration."* [1]

It is hard to make a summary of the progress which has resulted from the two peace conferences at The Hague. It is perhaps harder to give due credit to all the nations which were represented in those conferences of splendid conception; it has also been said that you cannot indict a nation.

[1] James Brown Scott, "The Hague Peace Conferences of 1899 and 1907, 1909," vol. i, 124–131, 319–385, *passim.*

But if the rulers of any nation did more than those of Germany to block the beneficent works which these conferences might have accomplished, it does not appear in the record. England being still the mistress of the seas, and likely to control the seas in case of war, Germany was not unwilling to propose, with the United States, complete immunity from capture for private property at sea. That would have worked in favor of Germany, and against England. To the voice of peace by understanding, however, the German Imperial Government would not listen. It refused to consider a limitation of armaments, even in the mild form of non-augmentation, and in 1907 declined even to discuss the matter.[1] When a permanent arbitration court was proposed, it at first rejected the idea *in toto*, being won over in the end only by compromises and with the greatest difficulty. Later when it was proposed to make arbitration compulsory in a few classes of cases, the German refusal was absolute. Thus did the rulers of Germany purpose to keep their hands free to use diplomacy *or force* as they saw best. The world must judge from what has since occurred on which of these forms of persuasion they were already planning to rely.

GERMAN WAR PRACTICES

The principle of sparing non-combatants so far as possible in warfare had been slowly evolved since far back in the Middle Ages, but had not before 1864 been finally formulated. It has often been violated, but never so flagrantly and withal so methodically as in the present war. German generals have scoffed at the weak sentimentality of the rule. The great General von Moltke declared in 1881, *"I cannot, in any way, agree with the Declaration of St. Petersburg* when it pretends that 'the weakening of the military forces of the enemy' constitutes the only legitimate method of procedure in war. No! One must attack all the resources of the enemy government, his finances, his railroads, his stock of provisions and even his prestige." Three years earlier General von Hartmann wrote that "whenever a national war breaks out, terrorism becomes a necessary military principle." "It is a gratuitous illusion to

---

[1] England twice proposed directly to Germany a mutual reduction of naval armaments, once in 1906 and once at a later date. In both cases Germany answered by voting increases Cf. the speech of Dr. Eduard David, a German Social Democrat, quoted in Notestein and Stoll's "Conquest and Kultur," 1917, p. 49–50.

suppose that modern war does not demand far more brutality, far more violence, and an action far more general than was formerly the case." "When international war has burst upon us, terrorism becomes a principle made necessary by military considerations." A year after the first Hague Peace Conference, Kaiser Wilhelm, in bidding farewell to his troops bound for China, said, "As soon as you come to blows with the enemy he will be beaten. No mercy will be shown! No prisoners will be taken! As the Huns, under King Attila, made a name for themselves, which is still mighty in traditions and legends to-day, may the name of German be so fixed in China by your deeds, that no Chinese shall ever again dare even to look at a German askance. . . . Open the way for Kultur once for all." The "German War Book" itself advises officers against the "sentimentality and flabby emotion" of humanitarian considerations in time of war, and teaches that "certain severities are indispensable in war, nay more, that the only true humanity very often lies in a ruthless application of them." Therefore, war should be made against the entire "moral and material resources" of the enemy. An especially good treatment of this question will be found in "German War Practices," by Dana C. Munro, George C. Sellery, and August C. Krey, a pamphlet issued by the Committe on Public Information, Washington, D. C., 1917.

It should also be mentioned that in the Hague Peace Conferences, Germany stood out against certain changes in the laws of war which would have made war more humane, and refused to ratify various provisions of the laws of war embodied in the conventions drawn up by those conferences.

CHAPTER XVII

WHILE Bismarck the Old and then William the Young were building the strong new Germany, were increasing her army, welding her alliances, multiplying her commerce, and rendering her nobles, bankers, and university professors the loud champions of this autocracy made modern and efficient, two far less distinguished personages were unconsciously doing their share to bring nearer the day of Armageddon. One of these was a philosopher who died in 1900, after having suffered from a disordered intellect since about 1890. The other was an historian who with less shaken powers continued a leader until close to his end in 1896. The first was Friedrich Wilhelm Nietzsche; the second was Heinrich von Treitschke. The influence of these two men, even in militarized Prussia, went far to justify the well-worn saying that "the pen is mightier than the sword."

Nietzsche was anything but an admirer of the Prussian system. But he supplied abstract philosophy which was to give convenient justification to the ideas and purposes that were seething in the brains of ambitious men who dominated the new German empire. He couched in terse, aphoristic language precepts worthy of an ultra-militarist. He treated all the old moral laws and humane conventions that had seemed to tie down the unlimited ambitions of men, as a remnant of "Christian superstition," and as representing merely the virtues of the weak, not of the strong, progressive and vic-

[1] The abundant evidence as to the ideas, ambitions and general methods of Pan-Germanism has been excellently assembled and translated in Notestein and Stoll's "Conquest and Kultur" (Committee of Public Information, Washington, D. C., 1917). The present chapter represents the merest skimming of a great subject.

torious.[1] His ideal of the "superman" was to be developed
by giving unbridled freedom in the struggle for existence, and
he was to be a ruthless spirit who would seek only his own
power and pleasure, and would know not pity.

Here are some of the aphorisms in Nietzsche's famous book,
"Thus Spake Zarathustra," wherein the modern philosopher
couched his doctrines in the language of an ancient sage:

> "Ye shall love peace as a means to new wars,—and a short peace
> more than a long."
>
> "Ye say it is the good cause which halloweth even war? I say
> unto you, 'It is the good war which halloweth every cause. War
> and courage have done more great things than charity.'"
>
> "'Thou shalt not rob! Thou shalt not slay!'—such precepts were
> once called holy. . . . Is not all life robbing and slaying?
>
> "This new table, O my brethren, put I up over you,—'Become
> hard!'"

Terribly was the world to see some of these sayings translated into practice in 1914.

Nietzsche did not create Pan-Germanism nor all the bellicose
things that went with it. He *did* supply it, however, with a
philosophic stimulus and semblance of intellectual authority
which were to fertilize its soil. The poor lunatic who died at
the dawn of the twentieth century thus was to be one of the
unconscious producers of the World War.

Mightier by far in his influence was Treitschke. He was
a native of Saxony, but in 1866 withdrew to Prussia and
gave his whole sympathies and energies heartily to upholding

[1] Despite their *practical* acceptance of the ethical teachings of
Nietsche, the Pan-German leaders were by no means atheistical in
their formal professions of faith. Bernhardi, and the less extreme
Rohrbach, both indicate their complete sympathy with Protestant
Christianity as they understand it They are quite critical of Catholicism. It is not quite clear, however, whether they object to the Catholics on theological grounds, or rather because they hold that it is impossible to be obedient to the Pope and to remain really good Germans
There are some reasons for saying the Pan-German schemings included
ultimately the idea of a strictly national Teutonic church, into which all
true sons of the expanded Fatherland were to be induced to enter.

the Bismarckian régime. He became official historian upon the rise of the Hohenzollern power,[1] and from 1874 to 1896 he was the most distinguished professor of history in the University of Berlin. No ordinary lecture room was his. His lectures on German history attracted not merely his colleagues but officials, administrative officers, and often extremely distinguished men. The fascination of his eloquence was such that he cast a spell over all his hearers. Young men of family, the leaders of the next generation, left his presence in a glow of enthusiasm. He wielded an influence equal to that of many of the Kaiser's ministers. The government did well to honor him—for he defended the cause of military monarchy with remarkable adroitness, proving to all who fell under the spell of his argument that for Germany and for Prussia the rule of the Hohenzollern meant the highest blessing and destiny.

Much that Treitschke taught was pure and noble. He kindled in his hearers a keen patriotic ardor, and an intense longing to do or die for native land. "Patriotism," he would tell them earnestly, "is the highest and holiest of passions." He would also tell his students that war might come at any moment and they must live in constant readiness for the unavoidable summons. To a large extent, therefore, considering the chronically dangerous state of Europe, Treitschke was only saying impressively what any professor in England or France might have stated to warn his audience.

But Treitschke used his eloquence to preach a political philosophy which not merely extolled the Hohenzollern régime in Germany, not merely taught general lessons in self-sacrificing patriotism, but made the young men, who sat at his feet, go from the lecture hall with their heads buzzing with notions which menaced the future peace of the world.[2]

[1] His "History of Germany in the Nineteenth Century" is a remarkable achievement, though broken off (because of his death) with the year 1847.

[2] It must be remembered that Treitschke's lectures were attended by the scions of the upper classes, young noblemen, future generals and

Treitschke in substance taught that the state was the center and acme of all human existence; that men could not live without it, that its necessities exceeded the necessities of any one of its members, and that *it was not governed by the moral laws or lines of conduct binding upon mere individuals.* The state was all-powerful, or it ceased to be a real state. In dealing with other states its policy was merely one of expediency. "A state cannot bind its will for the future as against another state. A state has no superior judge over itself and it will conclude all its treaties with this tacit reservation." In other words, a treaty was a mere convention to be repudiated when it became convenient to the government which had sworn to it. Between the various states there was inevitably a constant struggle for existence with only the strongest permitted to survive. "Empires rise and grow strong, and little commonwealths and principalities cease to be states." As for such an "abnormal" country as neutralized Belgium, Treitschke wrote: "Belgium is neutral, it is [therefore] mutilated by its very nature"—i. e., it has not the power of ordinary states to assert itself. Wars are terrible to the individual but very necessary to the true life of the state. "The establishment of an international court of arbitration as a permanent institution is irreconcilable with the nature of the state. . . . To the end of history weapons will maintain their right; and precisely herein lies the sanctity of war." Or again: "We have learned to recognize the moral majesty of war precisely in those of its characteristics which seem to superficial observers brutal and inhuman." Or still more grimly: "The living God will take care that war shall always return as a terrible medicine for the human race."

As to the duty of Germany to expand her power by force of arms Treitschke had not the least doubt. "In the division of the non-European world among the European powers Germany has hitherto failed to get its share; and the question whether we can become an oversea power involves our very

diplomats and many others who by 1900 were helping to shape the policy of Germany. His essays and histories (very readable) also had enormous circulation and carried the same potent message.

existence as a power of the first rank.'' Or in another place: ''The result of our *next* victorious war must, if possible, be the acquisition of something in the way of a colony.'' [1]

But this redoubtable professor did more than preach pagan generalities to his audience of German leaders for the twentieth century. He was a man of sharp, hard international prejudices which he voiced continually. When he began to lecture at Berlin the relations of England and Germany were correct, friendly, at times even cordial. When he died they had become much worse. After his death, while the seeds he had sown germinated in the intellectual life of his nation, Britain and the Prussianized empire passed from one stage of hostility to another until the day of great darkness. Von Treitschke was by no means the sole cause of this enmity, but upon him rests a fearfully large fraction of the responsibility. He devoted his ''rhetoric, invective and ridicule to making Britain odious in the eyes of the generation which heard him with enthusiasm and read his book as a gospel.'' In a long series of lectures and writings he dwelt on the undoubted shortcomings of England, exaggerated them, and made them appear a direct menace to Germany. He denounced the action of British sea-power as ''organized piracy.'' He treated British expressions of love of humanity and fair play as a smug hypocrisy that covered sheer commercialism. In his history he wrote of England: ''That last indispensable bulwark of society—the duel—went out of fashion; the riding-whip supplanted the sword and pistol, and this triumph of vulgarity was celebrated as a triumph of enlightenment.'' All British foreign policy was directed merely to keep other nations divided and weak in order that British merchants might bleed and plunder them. He denied to the English soldiers and sailors even the common attribute of valor, as the prime factor in building the British empire.

---

[1] These quotations are all from his "Politik." There are good examples of the political opinions of Treitschke in the collection of German sentiments, "Out of Their Own Mouths," pp. 41–48, (N. Y. 1917), as well as in Notestein and Stoll's excellent "Conquest and Kultur," Washington, D. C., 1917.

That fabric, he taught, was created by the geographical position of the British Isles, by the supineness of other nations, by the measureless duplicity of British ministers and by the natural and innate hypocrisy of their people as a whole. Built, however, out of such rotten materials, without a worthy national life behind it, the dominions of the London government were vast and pretentious indeed but easy to overthrow by a power possessed of true valor. And Treitschke was sure that all the world would join in one rejoicing pæan when the British colossus crumbled.

Touching other nations, France, Austria, Russia, etc., his opinion was sufficiently disparaging. Of America he knew little and cared less. He ridiculed certain unlovely phases of our democracy as the reports of our political inefficiency and corruption came to him; [1] but America (in his day) had no outlying colonies to excite his cupidity. England was the true child of his hate; and concerning her, he uttered a famous and ominous word: "With Austria, with France, with Russia *we have already squared accounts;* [2] the last settlement—with England—seems likely to be the longest and hardest."

Such a dictum coming from the most influential professor in the most influential German university spelled calamity for the human race.

It is a rule in history that at certain recurring intervals some particular nation feels itself summoned by a high, as it were divine, destiny to extend its dominion over all other nations by the sword, and to *establish something approximating a world empire.* And when such an attempt is made there is no real peace for the earth until the attempt has failed after perhaps generations of fire, blood, and human agony. As-

[1] It must be remembered that in the eighties and nineties America presented certain abuses in her public life which have been, in part at least, remedied today.

[2] Note this necessity of "squaring accounts," i.e., of humiliating and dismembering by warfare. Treitschke and all the Pan-German writers after him seem to treat this as an inevitable part of successful national existence—to aim a great stroke at each neighboring state in turn.

syria was vexed by this "world-empire microbe" until Nineveh, the wicked capital of her pitiless and despoiling kings, vanished amid smoke and flame. Persia had it likewise, until Xerxes's arrogant hopes went down amid the crash of the ships at Salamis. Rome had it; and being, on the whole, the worthiest nation that ever made the attempt at dominion, achieved for a while a great success; yet in the end the Roman Empire perished—and great was the fall thereof. The Arabs in the early Middle Ages had it, going forth at Mohammed's summons to their fanaticism to win all the earth for the one Allah and his prophet—so threatening the life of Christian Europe till they broke their lances on the iron wall of Charles Martel's Franks at Tours. The Spaniards had it in the day of Philip II, until William the Silent, Queen Elizabeth and Henry of Navarre between them blasted their ambitions. Then twice, under differing circumstances, France was possessed by this hunger for unbounded power. It required an alliance of practically all Europe through at least four great wars to keep Louis XIV from establishing a lordship over all contemporaneous kings. It required a still mightier exertion by all Europe to prevent Napoleon I from founding a more extensive empire than the Cæsars. All these attempts (save temporarily that of Rome) failed, and left the aggressor broken and bleeding; but until they had failed there was anxiety in almost every palace and hovel throughout civilization. Early in the twentieth century there began to be ominous signs that yet another great nation was being possessed by this most malific of demons,—that it was being induced, as one of the prime champions of this terrible gospel frankly confessed, to follow the path which leads to *"world power or downfall."*

By 1900 the new German empire seemed an astounding success in almost every respect save that of developing political liberty for its subjects. It is not amazing that its patriotic admirers looked confidently from a glorious past to a yet more glorious future. Many of the things they hoped for no honest non-German had a right to ask that they should disavow. Surely no Englishman, Frenchman, or American had a right to tell his fellow in Germany that the Fatherland ought not to seek for greater commerce, industries, riches, general prosperity, honorable prestige in diplomacy and national influence; nor to desire seasonably a great marine, a colonial empire and all the other things which in a physical sense causes a nation to be reckoned "great." In the past indeed the achievements of Germany had been in the cultural field rather than in the material, but if later the Teutons chose e. g., to develop their steel industry rather than their poetry, that was their own affair. There was bound to be a certain amount of friction and pettiness all around, as the older nations were elbowed aside to make room in the world for the lusty new empire; but this empire itself was admittedly so powerful that there was little danger of its being refused a high position unless its manners should be very brusk. In short, considering the population, intelligence, potential wealth and actual armed strength of the Bismarckian empire there would have seemed little chance of its failing to win a *reasonable* "place in the sun," provided its rulers were diplomatic, its policies moderate and its patriots able to learn that hard word for the ardent—"wait."

Of course, from the founding of the Empire at Versailles, there had been millions of voices ready to acclaim Germany as the "greatest nation in the world." There was no menace to the peace of mankind in *that*. Frenchmen, Britons and Americans were always saying the same about their own lands—with contemptuous pity for the non-favored remainder of humanity which did not happen to be governed from Paris, London or Washington respectively. But now that France was chastened, her neighbors did not fear wanton aggression from her. Queen Victoria's vast dominions held almost no civilized white men under a galling subjection, save the eternally baffling Irish, and the conquest of European lands by Englishmen was unthinkable. As for American boasts, before 1898 the United States army and navy had been insignificant, and even after the war with Spain the army continued so small as to be incapable of invading the smallest European state. Nobody, save possibly certain ill-mannered South American dictators, quailed at the thought of American aggression. But as Germans repeated their self-confident boasts, the world began to grow uneasy, and with reason.

It is a law, almost as certain as that of gravitation, that great and growing nations attract unto themselves new power and influence by no very deliberate effort but simply because they are great and are growing. No country could have become at once the factory and the school-house of the world as Germany was becoming and not have likewise come to exercise a simply incalculable power, not by pushing any aggressive designs, but merely by making it clear that it would defend its recognized and reasonable rights. In 1914 the admitted strength of the German empire was so vast that only a nation whose statesmen were fools would have deliberately sought a quarrel with it. By the mere influence of economic attraction, the Scandinavian lands, Holland, Belgium and Switzerland were being led half-consciously and not very unwillingly into the circle of Berlin influence. The same was even true of Austria, Italy and to a great extent Russia. The ties, racial, intellectual and commercial, which Germany was extending around America were to become patent to all men in 1914. *Everything* seemed coming the Germans' way. Their government had only to conciliate foreign opinion, create a reputation for fair and friendly dealing, make it clear that commercial relations did not have behind them political scheming, keep a firm front in England, France or Russia, the only possible military rivals really menacing,—and the empire would have invariably advanced from glory to glory. It might have been predicted that by 1940, let one say, Germany would reach a position of such wealth, such influence, such prestige, that by a magnet-attraction the lesser nations of northern Europe would have been drawn into her federal system upon terms honorable for all parties, and no nation outside the Teutonic pale would have had the courage to command them nay.[1]

[1] I know that shortly before 1914, as well as earlier, there was much complaint in commercial circles in Amsterdam as to the limitations imposed on Dutch enterprise by being confined to so small a country, and considerable discussion of the great advantages of a proper fed-

Such a placid waiting for almost inevitable results was not to satisfy the generation that had fed on the glories of Moltke and spent its days admiring the magnificent edifice of Bismarck. Not honorable leadership in very many forms of cultural endeavor; not a position as a nation which no coalition would lightly provoke or menace; not a hegemony, even, in the brotherhood of friendly empires working for the common betterment of man—not these were the ambitions of the framers of high policy for the new Germany. Ever more clearly developed their keen intention to *found a Teutonic world empire and to found it immediately*—and to do this preferably with the sword.

Therefore, in the language of the ancient mystic, instead of friendliness and peace there came forth the "pale horse, and his name that sat on him was Death, and Hell followed with him."

It is a difficult and dangerous matter to assume what are the determining motives and intentions of a great people, before a historical issue passes from words to deeds. England, France, America and every other mighty nation had its irresponsible talkers and writers, and by a careful selection of their utterances it would have been possible to fasten upon their respective countries every kind of criminal intention. Before 1914 it was well known that there were a great number of noisy fire-eaters and advocates of unscrupulous expansion in Germany, but not many took them very seriously. As the American President, who was also a professional historian and teacher of political science, declared in 1917, "The statesmen of other nations, to whom that purpose [of the Pan-Germans] was incredible, paid little attention; [they] regarded what German professors expounded in their classrooms and German writers set forth to the world as the goal of German policy as rather the dreams of minds detached from

eration with Germany. These sentiments would not have been diminished if Berlin had played its cards well. The Dutch East Indies would have been a colonial acquisition amply fitted to satisfy the appetite of a Treitschke.

practical affairs, as preposterous private conceptions of German destiny, than as the actual plans of responsible rulers.'' [1] Only after the terrific events which began late in July, 1914, did men realize, as this same statesman added, ''what concrete plans, what well advanced intrigues, lay back of what the professors and writers were saying, and [that the rulers of Germany] were glad [to have these plans] go forward unmolested.''

Between the fall of Bismarck and the outbreak of the great war twenty-four years later, there was a constant current of literature in Germany which forms the evidences of what has been styled the ''Pan-Germanic movement,'' i.e., the movement that aimed to make the world *All*-German, just as rapidly as possible.[2] This literature illustrates the state of mind and the developing intentions of the men who controlled the destinies of the Hohenzollern empire. It emanates mainly from three classes of people who were now in close working alliance—the Prussian military aristocrats, the university professors (favored by the government and in turn its convenient mouthpieces and defenders [3]), and the great manufacturers and merchants who were hungering and thirsting for new fields of trade to be opened and for new colonies to exploit. It was a movement on the whole much stronger in Prussia than in South Germany; somewhat more favored by Lutherans than by Catholics; and shared in feebly, or partially opposed, by

[1] President Wilson, "Flag Day Address," June 14, 1917.

[2] In its more limited form Pan-Germanism aimed for the "recovery" of the "lost Teutonic lands," i. e., Switzerland, Holland, Austria, Kurland, Scandinavia, etc. This local ambition of course fitted in well with the more grandiose schemes for world empire.

[3] Despite much proud talk of "academic freedom," it was practically impossible for a German professor to get preferment in the universities unless he made himself agreeable, or better still, zealously useful to the governing powers. An "ordinary" (i. e., permanently appointed and full rank) professor was free to exploit bizarre theories as to the atomic theory or the date of the battle of Marathon, but he was never suffered to carry with impunity his playing with academic quiddities over into systematic undermining attacks upon the government.

The universities were prime agents in the preaching of militarism and of the doctrine of governmental infallibility.

the lower middle classes, the artisans and of course the socialists. Its patrons were from the first men on the very footsteps of the throne. The wealth of the huge Krupp artillery
works and of the other great corporations gave it the control
of influential newspapers. In the later stages of its propaganda it certainly received almost open approval from the government. The crown prince of Germany practically avowed
himself its champion; the emperor, although compelled to
remain formally aloof, unless he would give mortal offense to
foreign powers, gave it encouragement by countless broad
hints and speeches. Finally, in 1914, the condition of Europe
being ripe, in the opinion of these titled propagandists, to
pass from theorizing to performance, and the public opinion
of Germany now being worked up to a suitable pitch, they
very abruptly stopped the printing press and drew the sword.
The rest of the story is military history.

The literature of Pan-Germanism is vast: books, pamphlets,
editorials without number. To summarize it fairly is hardly
possible. The most that can be done is to indicate what
seem to have been the best established parts in the Pan-German program and to select the writings of one or two arch-
prophets of this fiery gospel as fair examples of the arguments
of its lesser devotees.

Treitschke and Nietzsche had blazed the way clearly. The
world was to be inherited by a race of supermen and those
supermen were the Germans. Grave professors explained
that Dante, Shakespeare, Galileo, Michael Angelo, Voltaire
and other intellectual paladins owed their greatness to the
fact that they were really of pure or at least of mixed Teutonic blood. "The numerous busts of Julius Cæsar show a
thoroughly Teutonic type of skull and face," wrote an authority on anthropology, and he went on to claim the like race
traits for Alexander the Great.[1] This same professor asserted: "The Teutons are the aristocracy of humanity; the
Latins, on the contrary, belong to the degenerate mob"; and
again, "whosoever has the characteristics of the Teutonic
race is superior. . . . All dark people are mentally inferior,

[1] Ludwig Woltmann, "Politische Anthropologie" (1903).

because they belong to the *passive* races. . . . The cultural value of a nation is measured by the quantity of Teutonism it contains.'' So convinced were these experts of the superiority of the Teutonic peoples that to that great dominant branch of the white race ordinarily known as ''Aryan'' or ''Indo-European'' the ethnologists of Germany regularly gave the name ''Indo-Germanic'': implying that of all the members of that race which had settled in Europe only the German part need be reckoned with seriously—Greeks, Romans, Celts, Slavs, etc., being too insignificant to count!

A typical instance of German self-sufficiency was illustrated to the author when a few years ago he interrogated some intelligent friends in Leipzig as to the German love of Shakespere, and chanced to remark that ''Shakespere was an Englishman.'' He was at once assured that Shakespere was ''truly German'' in everything but the accident of his birth. As for his foreign language, so excellent were the translations by Schlegel, and others, that the translations were actually improvements upon the original, many new shades of meaning, etc., being developed. Besides Shakespere's English was hopelessly archaic for a modern British or American audience, while the German translations were strictly up-to-date, and could be understood by everybody. Therefore *it were better, if possible, to read Shakespere in German than in the original.* All this was advanced quite seriously!

Not merely however were the Teutonic peoples incomparably the superior race in all civilization but, being thus gifted, it was incumbent upon them to carry the blessings of their *Kultur* (i. e., general civilization, national pose and philosophy of life) out to the remainder of the planet. The clearest statements of this self-assurance came indeed after the great war began in 1914, when it was necessary to preach a very robust doctrine to demonstrate to the world that German victory was essential for the salvation of the race; but the idea was developed broadly enough earlier. An author whose influence and work will be discussed presently, wrote in 1911 these terse words, after speaking of the admirable patriotism of Japan: ''We Germans have a far greater and more urgent duty towards civilization than the Great Asiatic power. We . . . can fulfill it only by the sword.'' [1]

[1] Bernhardi, ''Germany and the Next War,'' p. 258.

This duty of Germanizing the world was of course all the more justifiable because the Teutonic race was only at the beginning of its unlimited capacity for achievement. It was not "degenerate" and "effeminate" like the French, "savage" like the Russian, "commercialized," "sordid" and "sodden in repose" like the English: nor for that matter "undisciplined," "lawless," and "miserably governed" like the people of the United States. As early as 1897 Fritz Bley, a writer of considerable influence, put the case thus: "We are the most capable nation in every field of science and in every branch of the fine arts. We are the best colonists, the best mariners and even the best merchants. And yet we do not enter into our share of the heritage of the world. . . . That the German empire is *not the close but the beginning of our national development* is an obvious truth [as yet grasped only] . . . by a small body of cultured men." [1]

As Germans looked about the world they found, nevertheless, that the other nations were hardly as yet prepared to make that ungrudging admission of Teutonic superiority which the sons of the Fatherland were anxious to demand. They lamented the fact that some millions of their fellow-countrymen had emigrated, especially to America and Brazil, and were, for the time being at least, "lost" to kaiser and country. It is true there were schemes for linking up some kind of connection with America and more definite schemes for downright absorption of southern Brazil; nevertheless, the situation was unsatisfactory. The development of commercial and industrial life in Germany did indeed stop the emigration, but it did not stop the desire for foreign fields of exploitation. "We have shown already," declared an extremely moderate writer, "that the German labor at home is fully capable of feeding our people despite their increase. It is therefore no longer the thought for his daily bread which sends a German forth, but the love of enterprise and the desire of shaping his life along broader and freer lines than is possible at home." [2] Or, as less delicate pamphleteers made it evident,

[1] Fritz Bley, "Die Weltstellung des Deutschtums," pp. 21, 22.
[2] Rohrback, "German World Policies" (translation, p. 138). Rohr-

*colonies were still needed—not for the sake of surplus popula-
tion but for exploitation.* The young Prussian officers and
money-kings filled their heads with visions of great pro-
consulships, lording it over millions of trembling Asiatics or
negroes. The Belgian possession of the Congo was frankly
coveted, and influential hints were thrown out as to its acquisition by trade or "purchase." What use had a petty
kingdom like Belgium for a vast tropical realm worthy the
best attention of a mighty empire? It is true that the African
colonies Germany already possessed brought her much expense, a considerable number of scandals and very little profit:
as well as in Southwest Africa, a rather serious war with the
natives. However that was merely because unkind destiny
had forced Germany to enter the lists as a partitioner of
Africa among the last.

Since the Dark Continent already had been divided among
the Europeans it was obvious that for the Kaiser's government to extend its share must be at someone else's expense.
This, however, was discussed calmly. Belgian Congo was
within the dreams of acquisition; so were the colonies of weak
Portugal: and for a while it seemed as if the British grip on
South Africa was very feeble. The resistance of the Boers
awakened all manner of Pan-Germanic hopes. Public opinion
ran almost irresistibly in their favor when from 1898 to 1902,
they struggled bravely if vainly against British over-lordship.
If Germany had possessed a strong navy at the time, probably
popular clamor in favor of the Boers would have forced some
action destructive to the peace of Europe. The sympathy for
the Boers was not all of it chivalrous feeling for the "under
dog." It sprang also out of a keen expectation that a weak
Boer republic could exist only under the protecting ægis of
the Fatherland.[1] But if British lands were not to be won,
there also were the ample colonies of decadent, defeated, and

bach is a very moderate writer, who did not sympathize with the more
rabid type of Pan-Germanism.

[1] I remember well how bitterly at the time intelligent Germans deplored their inability to help the Boers "and quite honorably to get a
grip for ourselves on South Africa."

despised France. The Third Republic had no need of her great chain of African colonies; her population was stationary and her commerce unaggressive. The great empire she was flinging out across Algeria and the deserts clear to the Sahara was an abortion of nature: something she did not need, and something her German rival desired sorely. In 1914 it was sufficiently clear that Ahab had been looking eagerly upon Naboth's vineyard when the German Chancellor was quite willing to assure England that in event of war his government would respect the European territories of France, but that he could give no assurances about the French colonies.

Outside of Africa there were the hopes as to north China, where in 1897 an available harbor (Kiau-Chau) and a large circuit of hinterland had been forcibly "leased" from a very feeble native government. But here also the barriers of diplomacy hemmed in the hopes for Teutonic expansion. British, American and Japanese pressure made it impossible for Germany to grow peaceably at the expense of China, and William II consented with outward cheerfulness to the John Hay doctrine of the "Open Door."

Africa was thus closed to peaceful annexation: so was China. The few isles that could be snapped up in Oceania,— the Carolines, part of Samoa, the Solomon group, etc.,—were mere mouthfuls for a giant's appetite. There remained the possibility of South American colonies. Here the natives, "Indians with a veneer of Spanish pseudo-culture," were indeed somewhat beneath contempt, but the Monroe Doctrine was an inconvenient barrier. In 1902, an attempt had been made by Germany, after picking a quarrel with Venezuela, to make some headway towards the "temporary occupation" of a desirable harbor. Instantly it had been evident that President Roosevelt was prepared to thwart such an undertaking with the full strength of the United States fleet. William II was in no condition then for a sudden attack on America. The proposition therefore had to be dropped.[1]

[1] In 1902, the year that President Roosevelt concentrated the American fleet in the West Indies, and then served what amounted to an informal ultimatum upon Germany to desist in her schemes to secure

Then finally Germany made an attempt to elbow France out of Morocco, the one part of Africa not hitherto pre-empted, and which was fairly available for white settlement. This attempt, as will be elsewhere described (see p. 409), ended in diplomatic failure, and won for the Kaiser's government not much beyond the black looks of France and England and a little extra land in Central Africa. The German appetite for colonies seemed unlikely to be sated by any peaceful means.

Whether colonies were really essential to the industrial and commercial life of Germany or whether, when its trade with such lands as England and America was advancing with leaps and bounds, their economic happiness and the national future demanded expansion beyond seas, the Pan-Germans waited not to ask. Despite their unconcealed dislike and scorn for things English, the junker lords of the new generation never concealed their covetous admiration for the British colonial empire. Why should a young nobleman of Pomerania or Brandenburg spend his days in the petty routine

a naval base in Venezuela, there occurred this incident. Two American gentlemen, on whose accuracy and judgment I implicitly rely, were at an open-air restaurant in a small German city. They had been on a long tour, had purchased many articles of clothing of German manufacture and did not probably, at first glance, betray themselves as American excursionists. At the other end of their table two German naval officers of the junior grades seated themselves. These men fell presently into a violent discussion as to some point in naval strategy and tactics. Presently the Americans were startled to hear such names as "Long Island," "Block Island," "Sandy Hook," "Connecticut," etc. Suddenly the two officers realized that they were being followed with intense interest and that their table-companions were Americans who understood German. The officers abruptly rose, called the waiter and paid their bill, whereupon the older officer said in excellent English, "You must not take our professional argument too seriously: we have only good will for your great and very interesting country." —The "professional argument" had been as to whether the best method for a naval attack on New York was via Sandy Hook or Long Island Sound.

Very soon after that the German government sent Prince Henry to America with his lips dropping honey and friendship. The German fleet at that time was manifestly unequal to a contest in American waters, especially in view of the complete absence of coaling stations.

of home army life, working up to be colonel or even general in a little garrison city, when his contemporary at Oxford or Cambridge was training himself to go possibly to India with a great "presidency" over millions of natives as the reasonable goal for his ambition? The British empire fascinated the second generation in the new German empire, even while they execrated all traits British.

There was one other possible line for expansion. Austria was falling more and more under German influence. Franz Josef was almost in his dotage. The Vienna statesmen were mediocre and pliable. The Magyar leaders, needing German help against their Slavic fellow-citizens, were quite open to suggestions from Berlin. Working through Austria, Germany could strengthen her influence on the Balkan states; already German influence was dominant at Constantinople. The Balkans, and still more the whole weak Turkish Empire, might become Teutonic domain-lands: and once possessed of the Tigro-Euphrates valley German influence could spread around the Persian Gulf and turn the flank of the British road to India and the Far East. But here again there was nothing for it but to wait. William II could stiffen up Abdul Hamid to defy alternately England and Russia: but neither of these powers was disposed to see Germany change herself from the mere ally of the Sultan into the actual possessor and mistress of his lands. Once more there was no new soil for Teutonism without fighting. The German had become a candidate for colonial empire very late.

Under these circumstances a public opinion, fed upon the traditions of Bismarck, the lectures of Treitschke and the military history of Frederick the Great and of Moltke, was ready enough with its concrete philosophy. The State constituting the highest of all possible human interests, and being bound by none of the ordinary moral laws, must advance these interests by whatever means were possible. Peaceable means of course were ordinarily the best: but not merely was war useful as a final expedient, it was sometimes preferable to peace, even when peace could win its end.

Never since the days of Sennacherib, unless possibly in the

tents of Attila the Hun or Timour the Tartar, was the duty of living by the sword more exultantly taught. "Perpetual peace is a dream, and it is not even a beautiful dream. War is part of the eternal order instituted by God," the great Moltke had written in 1880, and a generation of ardent officers, eager to translate their science into practice, had gladly echoed the saying. The good end of the armed struggle of course justified the means. "A nation's field of labor, its land, must satisfy its people as to character, quality and extent. If it is not satisfactory, the nation must stretch itself, extend itself over the territory of others and gain new land in the selective struggle. . . . It would be unjust and immoral if a noble nation were to restrict its increase of population because of lack of room, while lower races have room to spare." So wrote Klaus Wagner in 1906, and went on to argue that the Darwinian law of the struggle for existence made wars of conquest mere proper fulfillments of the laws of nature, and to add the corollary that if one nation seems possessed of territory another *may need later*, to attack this overwealthy neighbor "is a struggle for the national future, for unity, independence and free soil." [1]

Such doctrines could not have been uttered in any other great country in the twentieth century by responsible leaders of public opinion. But for the two decades preceding Armageddon they were being hammered into the German mind until they became a part of the national gospel. In 1911 appeared a remarkable book, "Germany and the Next War," by Lieutenant-General Friedrich von Bernhardi. It did not differ materially in philosophy and program from a num-

---

[1] It was freely argued that the British empire having reached such a size, Britain owed a certain "compensation" to Germany if she was to be a decent neighbor. Either England should give part of her empire up to Germany or she should at least let the latter take what she required of the colonies of France, Portugal, Belgium and Holland. In June, 1913, Rohrbach (too moderate for most Pan-Germans), wrote bluntly, "Germany could not content herself with the rôle of registering increases of England's power, and must take up the very self-evident position that the principle of compensation should be given *a certain retroactive force.*"

ber of other books which enjoyed equal or greater popularity in the author's own country, but the excellence of its literary workmanship and the high military rank of its writer, caused it to receive serious attention abroad. Almost the instant the war began in 1914, it became so apparent that the German general staff was putting into effect almost all the propositions advanced by Bernhardi, that the author was accepted throughout the world as having been permitted to utter inspired prophecy—to express the aspirations, purposes and high policy of the men who had come to control the government of William II;[1] and Bernhardi's doctrines and their prompt fulfillment showed clearly enough that the Pan-Germans were driving the Prussian war-chariot.

Bernhardi's main proposition and deductions were these: The future was full of perils for Germany, other nations hated her, yet her people failed to realize their danger because of their unfortunate love of peace. The true fortune of the nation, however, was not to be made by peace but by war. "War is the father of all things," to quote a Greek philosopher, and among nations "right is respected so far only as it is compatible with advantage." War itself is a blessing when properly used and understood: and since growing nations need more territory, this must "as a rule be obtained at the cost of its possessors—that is to say, by conquest, which thus becomes a law of necessity." Again, His Excellency, the author, observes that "Might is at once the supreme right, and the dispute as to what is right is decided by the arbitrament of war. War gives a biologically just decision: since its decisions rest on the very nature of things."

Arguments for peace are usually based on sordid self-interest: e.g., the United States has urged arbitration, etc., "in order to be able to devote its undisturbed attention to money-making and the enjoyment of wealth, and to save the

[1] Bernhardi did not indeed claim to speak with official authority: he was on the retired list of the army. But Prussian lieutenant-generals were not ordinarily expected to utter sentiments on ticklish subjects unwelcome to the "All-Highest."

three hundred million dollars which it spends on its army and navy." This is a grievous mistake for America, not merely because of the risk she runs from England or Japan, but because she "avoids the stress of great political emotions [stirred by a war] without which the moral development of the national character is impossible." (pp. 28–29.)

The Christian precept of love clearly does not apply to the affairs of nations. Christian morality is merely personal. Jesus himself said, "I came not to send peace on earth, but a sword." If we understand Christianity properly, "we cannot disapprove of war in itself, but must admit that it is justified morally and historically." [1]

Arbitration treaties "must be peculiarly detrimental to an aspiring people which has not yet reached its political and national zenith, and is bent on expanding its power in order to play its part honorably in the civilized world"; and Bethmann-Hollweg was entirely right when in a speech in the Reichstag (March 30, 1911) he declared them to be practically useless. Various Americans, like Elihu Root, seemed enamored with them, but that was because they imagined "public opinion must represent the view which American plutocrats think most useful to themselves." Of course many of the most profitable annexations of Prussia, e.g., Silesia, seized by Frederick the Great, would never have come by arbitration, and if they had so come it would have been without the vast moral gain which accrued to Prussia by winning them in war. Besides, courts of arbitration would have to treat all nations alike, and it is outrageous to establish that "a weak nation is to have in short the same right to live as a powerful and vigorous nation." "Our [German] people must learn to see that *the maintenance of peace never can or may be the goal of a [national] policy.*" (Italics Bernhardi's own.) "The inevitablness, the idealism and the blessedness of war, as an indispensable and stimulating law of development, must be repeatedly emphasized."

War therefore is often a most desirable, as well as righteous

[1] The context clearly shows Bernhardi here means *offensive* wars, not defensive merely.

and holy thing. Often also it is the duty to make it, even if it can be honorably avoided. Frederick the Great set an admirable example: "None of his wars were forced upon him; none of them did he postpone as long as possible. He had always determined to be the aggressor, to anticipate his opponents, and to secure for himself favorable prospects of success."[1]

Treitschke was very right, thinks Bernhardi, when he said that the morality of the state must be.judged by the nature of the state and not of the individual citizen; and again when he said that "among all political sins the sin of feebleness is the most contemptible:—it is the political sin against the Holy Ghost!"

Germany must recognize that she has long been weak and oppressed; that she is now powerful and must for the sake of the rest of the world expand still further. "To no nation except the German has it been given to enjoy in its inner self 'that which has been given to mankind as a whole.' " Other peoples may have special talents but none others have "the capacity for generalization and absorption. It is this quality which especially fits us for leadership in the intellectual world and imposes on us the obligation to maintain that position." Furthermore, a great many real Germans unfortunately are not yet in the empire. The mouths of the "German Rhine lie in non-German lands"; also "the overflow of the strength of the German nation has poured into foreign countries." "Obviously this is not a condition which can satisfy a powerful nation, or which corresponds to the greatness of the German nation and its intellectual importance." "All that which other nations attained in centuries of national development—political union, colonial possessions, naval power, international trade—were denied to our nation until quite recently. What we now wish to attain must be *fought for* [Bernhardi's italics] and won against a superior force of hostile interests and powers."

[1]This was written in 1911. In 1914 the German war council evidently felt required to act fully on this interpretation of the Fredrician precedents.

land must not allow Germany to wax too strong. "If England is forced to fight America, the German fleet must not be in a position to help the Americans. Therefore it must be destroyed." "All facts considered, a pacific agreement with England is, after all, a will-o'-the-wisp which no serious German statesman would trouble to follow." As for protests of certain "English politicians, publicists and Utopians," they "cannot alter the real basis of affairs."

Of one other thing Bernhardi was very sure. "In one way or another *we must square our account with France* [his italics], if we wish for a free hand in our international policy. . . . France must be so crushed that she can never again come across our path." [1]

As for treaties, questions of neutrality and international compacts, "it is essential that we do not allow ourselves to be cramped in our freedom of action by considerations, devoid of any inherent political necessity, which depend only on political expediency, and are not binding on us." "No man," to quote Frederick the Great, "if he has a grain of sense, will give his enemies leisure to make all prepara-

[1] Bernhardi here evidently means that because France cannot forget Alsace-Lorraine, and submit herself as a convenient tool of German ambition, she must therefore be crushed so utterly that she can never cross the Teutons' path again.— "The injured can forgive a wrong; the injurer never."

The practical annihilation of France was a fixed part of the Pan-Germanic programme, partly because the ruin of France would be a great step to the ruin of England. The failure of Bismarck to take much greater territories in 1871, as well as to "bleed France white" by a simply crushing war-indemnity was deplored at many Pan-Germanic conferences. In 1911 Herr Class, President of the Pan-German League, wrote openly advocating the annexation of all Northern France from Nancy to the mouth of the Somme so that Germany could possess Boulogne, Calais and Dunkirk as a means to getting at England. David Fryman, a kindred spirit, wrote, "The victorious German nation will be able to insist that an end shall be put once for all to the *threats* of France. Therefore France must be crushed. We shall also insist upon the cession of so much French territory as will ensure our security for evermore. Such territory will have to be evacuated by its inhabitants. Then we shall take whichever of the French colonies will best suit Germany's requirements."

The most famous of Bernhardi's chapters was his
bearing the significant title "World Power or Downf
He argues that the time has come when Germany must
world empire by one great stroke or fall ruinously in the
tempt. It will not be enough to stand simply ready to w
off attack. That is the bane of the old Triple Alliance:
offers a certain security against hostile aggression, but c
not consider the necessary development of events, and d
not guarantee to any of its members help in the prosecut
of essential interests." Germany must try to make it wo
while for Austria and Italy [1] to support her by herself pu
ing their pet projects, but of course German interests mi
come first. Russia, France and England can never fail to
obstacles in the Fatherland's way. With them there can
no real peace; only an armistice. It is true Russia may l
kept quiet for a while because "her present political attitud
depends considerably on the person of the present emperor
[Nicholas II], who believes in the need of leaning upon a
strong monarchical state, such as Germany is, and also upon
the character of the internal development of the mighty
empire"; although of course the "revolutionary and moral
infection" which has tainted Russia may produce a change
in her policy which can upset all calculations. "But in any
case we shall always find her on the side of those who try
to cross our political paths."

English policy also can never permit true friendship for
Germany. English leaders "committed the unpardonable
blunder, from their point of view" of not supporting the
Southern Confederacy in the American Civil War, and so
crippling Britain's great transatlantic rival. Germany car
possibly hope for a war between America and England, bu
as things are, it is unsafe to count definitely upon it, al
though friction over Canadian issues may easily "strain rela
tions to a dangerous point." England realizes, however, tha
Canada, South Africa and Australia are none too loyal; an
that Moslem India may revolt. With these facts in view En

[1] Bernhardi expresses Platonic hopes that Italy will stand by t
Teutonic powers, but makes it plain that he does not really count on h

tions in order to destroy him; he will rather take advantage of his start to put himself in a favorable position." And the good general pauses at this point somewhat significantly to consider whether, by acquiring the Congo State, Belgium had not destroyed her status of neutrality, saying that in any case "the conception of permanent neutrality is entirely contrary to the essential nature of the state." "No one stands above the state; it is sovereign, and must itself decide whether the internal conditions of another state menace its own existence or interests."

Bernhardi's final gospel may be said to be summed up in two significant paragraphs. "No people is so little qualified as the German to direct its own destinies, whether in a parliamentary or republican constitution; to no people is the customary liberal pattern so inappropriate as to us." Therefore the country requires "the leadership of powerful personalities" who can "force conflicting aspirations into concentration and union" and to win world empire the German nation must sacrifice not merely lives and property but "private views and preferences, in the interests of the common welfare."

This must be done, for the stake in the impending war will be tremendous: "We have fought the last great wars for our national union among the powers of *Europe;* we must now decide whether we wish to develop into and maintain a *World-Empire"*—Bernhardi's italics—"and procure for the German spirit and German ideas that fit recognition which has hitherto been withheld from them."

The remainder of this book was taken up with an acute analysis of the military reforms needful in Germany to make this victory sure—reforms almost completely accomplished between 1911 and 1914.[1]

[1] In discussing the European armies Bernhardi rates the "tactical value" of the French troops as "very high," but thinks "the French army lacks the subordination under a single commander, the united spirit which characterizes the German army, the tenacious spirit of the German race and the *ésprit de corps* of the officers."

England he thinks will never enter heartily into anything but a naval war. Her generals are probably poor, and her army small. In any

In 1914 practically everything (so far as it lay in the control of the German General Staff) came true even as Bernhardi predicted. His book therefore enjoys an almost unique value as being the interpretation of a great state policy and an accurate prediction of the things which were to be. Bernhardi, however, was only *one* among the many influential Pan-Germanist prophets. After the outbreak of the great war Teutonic apologists denied that his book had had influence or circulation. This is in no wise the case. It had gone through six editions within sixteen months after publication. Enthusiastic reviews commended it as "engaging the serious attention of our own political—and it need hardly be added, military circles," and deplored the fact that its high price prevented a still wider distribution. To very many thoughtful Germans of the dominant classes it seemed a welcome declaration of the nation's hopes and policy. It was mentioned for praise or blame in Reichstag debates and the newspapers. Outside of Germany it surely increased the distrust in which the Fatherland was being held; but no Frenchman, Englishman, or American could discover its true importance until the beginning of Armageddon.

It is a fact, nevertheless, that by himself Bernhardi would have been only a voice in the wilderness. He only contributed the most readable, pungent and logical book of the whole great Pan-Germanist literature. Other books were cheaper and had probably equal influence and greater direct popularity. Their burden was always the same:—the superiority and holy mission of the Teutons; the need for expansion territorially both in Europe and across the seas; the blessedness of war; the inevitability of a great struggle with France, England and Russia, with America in the background; and the certainty of being able by one great heroic stroke to achieve world-empire.

Almost simultaneously with Bernhardi another writer, Tannenberg, stated the problem even more bluntly than he.

case, "it is very questionable whether the English army is capable of effectively acting on the offensive against continental European troops."

"Our fathers have left us much to do. The German people
is so situated in Europe that it needs only to run and take
whatever it requires. . . . Today it is for Germany to rise
from the position of a [merely] European to that of a world
power. The German nation holds a position among European
powers which permits it to reach its goal by a single rapid
rush. . . . Public policy prompted by the emotions is stupid-
ity. Humanitarian dreams are imbecility. Diplomatic charity begins at home. Statesmanship is business. Right and
wrong are notions indispensable only in private life. *The
German people are always right because they number 87,000,-
000 souls.* Our fathers have left us much to do." [1]

While this philosophy was mastering the souls of a great
civilized people, what was the attitude of their rulers—the
princes who were clinging to their "God-sent" political
power, and the ministers who were the agents of these princes?
The ministers were indeed speaking frequently of "peace"!
for had they spoken otherwise and openly endorsed the Pan-
German program the much belauded war would have blazed
forth spontaneously,[2] but they were using none of those round
measures of repression for an unwelcome propaganda to which
the Social Democrats were well accustomed; and they were
faithfully delivering their annual sermons in the Reichstag,
as to how the nation was ringed around with jealous enemies
and must therefore increase her mighty army and build a
correspondingly mighty fleet.

The heir to the throne, the Crown Prince Frederick William,
was openly consorting with the extreme militarist, pro-war

[1] "Gross-Deutschland," pp. 230–231, Tannenberg is probably a
pseudonym, possibly for some exalted personage.

[2] The extreme bluntness of the Pan-German doctrines was of course
disconcerting to the ministers who hoped to keep the peace at least
until the proper time for "The Day" was at hand. A former French
ambassador to Berlin wrote, in 1907, that it was lucky Germany was
not a democratic country, otherwise public pressure would have already
rushed it into war. The Kaiser's government had to restrain constant
expressions of "disgust and anger" against foreign powers. "Anything
the government would do to bother France or England is sure to be
applauded by the people."

party, applauding violent jingoist speeches in the Reichstag, and evidently going to the extreme limit permissible without provoking extreme foreign disquietude. In 1913 he wrote an introduction to a volume, "Germany in Arms," in which he said, "It is only by relying upon our good German sword that we can hope to conquer that place in the sun which rightly belongs to us, and which the world does not seem willing to accord us. . . . Till the world shall come to an end, the ultimate decision must rest with the sword."

The emperor, his august father, could not indeed use quite such unveiled language. His position forbade him to announce a program of conquest until he was actually ready to draw the sword. Probably in his professions of love of peace he was not consciously hypocritical: but was not the peace he claimed to desire a peace in which no rash power should oppose "the legitimate aspirations of Germany"? The kaiser's speeches abounded in talk of "sharpening the sword," of wearing "shining armor," of the brave military deeds of his "glorified ancestors," and of the need of being ready for an instant summons to arms. We shall see how he built a great navy, useless for defense against France and Russia, and directly provocative of Germany's old neighbor and comrade-in-arms, England. What precise things were always stirring in the mind of this brilliant, aggressive, irresponsible and wholly erratic man who may wisely say?

Yet at times William II almost lifted the veil over his inmost projects and ambitions. In 1900 he used a phrase whereof the world might well have taken anxious notice. "I hope to Germany it will be granted . . . to become in the future as closely united, *as powerful, and as authoritative as was once the Roman empire,* and that just as in the olden times they said, 'I am a Roman citizen' (*Civis Romanus sum*), hereafter, at some time in the future, they will say, 'I am a German citizen!' "[1]

Here then was the vision—the dream of world-empire which

[1] Speech at the opening of a museum of Roman Antiquities, at the Saalburg, October 11, 1900. The Emperor was of course speaking in-

had lured the hosts of Xerxes, Alexander, Julius Cæsar and Napoleon on the greatest of human adventures.

formally. He would hardly have dared to use such words in a formal state document on account of foreign complications.

A few years later at Bremen, he said, "God has called us to civilize the world: we are the missionaries of human progress."

CHAPTER XVIII

THE GROWING ENMITY OF BRITAIN AND GERMANY

IN the opening years of the twentieth century one great fact stood out in ever-blackening relief to every student of international affairs and lover of his fellow men—the growing enmity of Britain and Germany. Much energy was expended in denying it. The mere fact that such energy seemed called for proved that the hatred existed. It is possible to argue away a concrete incident; it is impossible to argue away a great mass of national ill-feeling. This was what made the whole situation so hopeless. No arbitration tribunal, no majestic peace conference, could ordain that Britons and Teutons should love one another and then see to it that its mandate was obeyed. Shortly before 1914 an American familiar with Germany declared that the great majority of the kaiser's subjects undoubtedly "dreaded the Russians,[1] despised the French, but *hated* the English." He was quite justified in his statement.

In fairness it should be added that English dislike of Germany was also extreme. Books, plays and newspapers taught King George's subjects that between Prussianized Saxon and Anglo-Saxon there was little more than an armed

[1] There is little doubt that the Germans lived in genuine dread of the great mass of Slavs stretching from their eastern border to the Pacific. "We can never defeat Russia," they would say, meaning that no momentary military victories would ever turn back the great Russian peril. The Germans undoubtedly over-estimated the ability of the Russians to translate their great potential resources into actual military action. The fears of a Russian invasion were probably stimulated by the Prussian militarists to get political and financial favors for the army, and the dread of being overrun by "Slavic hordes" went far to reconcile the peace-lovers in Germany in 1914 to the need of a "war for defence."

truce possible, and that it was high time for Britons to drop their old grudges against Frenchmen and Russians and recognize their true enemy. On both sides of the North Sea, therefore, there existed a body of public opinion ready for any spark in the magazine of international combustibles. How had this most sorrowful situation come about?

The two nations had many points of superficial similarity. Both used a Teutonic language. In both the majority of the population were Protestants, not Catholics. In both there was a certain seriousness, if not heaviness, of the national temper not found in the Latinized South. The royal houses of England and Germany were closely interrelated. History linked Englishmen and Germans as brothers-in-arms on many honorable battlefields: and Blücher and Wellington had shared jointly in the glories of Waterloo.[1] The two nations had never been opposed in any very serious war. They carried on a thriving commerce one with another. There had been a constant influx of British students to Berlin, and of waiters, commercial travellers and more pretentious merchants from Germany to London. The policy of Bismarck had always been to stand well with the great island empire. "England is more important to us than Zanzibar and the whole East African coast," he had exclaimed angrily to a delegation when urged to get into a quarrel over some wretched tropical colonies. The British on their part were grateful for the good turn the chancellor had done them at the Berlin Congress. In short, down to 1900, or thereabouts, the relations of the two powers seemed excellent because, as Bismarck at another time had said: "As regards England we are in the happy situation of having no conflict of interests, except commercial rivalry and [mere] passing differences . . . *but there is nothing that can bring about a war between two pacific and hardworking nations.*" And yet in 1914 this war had been brought about. Which power had changed— England or Germany?

[1] It may be added that disputes as to which army, British or Prussian, really did the most to win that battle, contributed not a little to the international hard-feeling.

In the earlier stages of the great European conflict it was usual to allege that "at bottom this is merely a war of commercial interests." Such a statement is folly. It is perfectly true that there was grievous commercial competition. Before the rise of the new German empire, England had been the workshop of the world, exporting incomparably a greater quantity of manufactured articles than any other nation. Her nearest rival, France, had, in a former generation, only maintained a certain preëminence in the elegant articles of fashion and luxury: silks, toilet articles, furnishings for the parlor, the wardrobe and the boudoir, choice wines and champagnes, etc. Such French competition never sent real fear down the spines of Birmingham and Manchester. It is true, on the other hand, that the intrusion of the products of German industry, whether woollen-goods, pianos, pocket knives or artillery, supported as these products were by an admirable commercial system which studied the foreign markets and gave long credit, often produced anger and consternation in many a British factory. "Made in Germany" was undoubtedly the text for many unscriptural anathemas. Nevertheless, it assuredly took more than counting-room fury to make Briton and German fly at one another's throats. Certainly German commercial prosperity was increasing by such leaps and bounds that Teutons had no right to grudge their English cousins their trade. On the other hand, in the decade before the outbreak of the great war, British commerce was by no means so decadent as to justify gloomy prognostications and a resort to desperate remedies to check competition. *Both* nations were genuinely prosperous, and it was becoming very evident that the world contained ample opportunities alike for Sheffield and for Essen, for Leeds and for Leipzig.[1]

[1] The evidence to show that England was not commercially decadent is admirably assembled in Schmidt, "England and Germany," pp. 111-115. As he wisely observes, "If sheer profit had been the only consideration, England would never have risked her very existence in a struggle which must cost infinitely more than the sum total of Germany's foreign trade for many, many years."

There is better proof, however, that England and Germany did not fall out merely over commercial issues. They were not the only super-great trading and industrial nations of the world. There was also the United States.

America did not indeed possess the merchant marine which Germany was developing. A large percentage of our products were natural and not manufactured. Nevertheless, by 1914 American commercial competition was pressing the two European leaders hard in almost every market of the word. Trade rivalry sometimes produced for us real international friction. It accounted for many of the flashes of unfriendliness which occasionally flared up between the United States and Britain. It was hard for Americans quite to forgive England for the way she had let our merchant marine be ruined at the time of our Civil War. "The lion's tail" was often "twisted" by blustering speeches in Congress, provoked by questions of free trade, protection, fishery rights, etc. Nevertheless, despite this extremely keen competition, despite these exchanges of very unamiable candor, the relations of the United States and Britain were growing steadily better, ever since the so-called "Venezuela incident" of 1896, which had ended in the virtual acceptance by England of the Monroe Doctrine. In 1914 a war between America and Britain had become almost impossible,[1] despite a commercial rivalry which threatened to become more acute as the United States reformed her financial policy and developed her enormous resources.

Englishmen and Americans were thus becoming simultaneously commercial rivals, and friends at the same time. Englishmen and Germans were becoming commercial rivals and increasingly bitter enemies. What was the reason for this?

[1] Germans persistently imagined that Americans had retained all their old feuds with Great Britain. In Germany the writer has been repeatedly assured, "The English are of course your natural enemies." There is much reason to believe that part of the Pan-German propaganda included a systematic fostering in the United States of the ancient prejudices against all things British. In 1914 transatlantic sympathy with England was, to many Germans at least, a great surprise as well as a corresponding disappointment.

The answer briefly is that the Germans were becoming very much more than commercial rivals.

Long before Britons, in their insular pride and self-concentration, began to realize that they were cordially hated from the Rhine to the Memel, their race and its representatives had become generally unpopular everywhere save along the familiar lines of tourist travel. Doubtless the lordly condescension and brusque manners of English travellers were no more enjoyed in Saxony than in France or Italy. But Englishmen were not unpopular merely because they had blunt manners and failed to take off their hats when they entered a shop. The low opinion of Britain entertained by Treitschke has already been noted (p. 349). The famous lecturer was not alone in his opinion. Bismarck himself, despite his studious official cordiality for England, privately used to express an ardent detestation of many things British. His relations with the Empress Victoria (wife of Frederick II and mother of William II) were very bad, and he is alleged to have arranged the marriage of the future William II with a Holstein princess not simply to propitiate a princely dynasty which the Hohenzollerns were claimed to have ousted from their duchy, but also, as the chancellor is said to have put it, "to get less of that cursed English blood" in the next generation of the imperial house.

In truth, even in the upper classes, between the British aristocracy with their magnificent country estates, their refined Oxford education, their careers as civilian administrators and governors-general of great colonies, or their cabinet ministries under a strictly constitutional government, and the Prussian junkers with their ancient schlosses, cubbish breeding in military schools, followed by barrack-room life or unexciting existence in the grubbing routine of provincial civil offices there could not be a great deal in common. The English aristocrats had long since emerged from the squirarchy stage: very many of the junkers were still in it. As touching the rest of the British nation, the great democratic element, the liberals who held bishops and dukes at bay, the mighty parties which had reduced the king to a personified social function and which ever constantly whittled down the power of the lords—all these of course seemed distressing in the eyes of the Bismarckians. It was impossible to understand a land where army officers were forbidden to fight duels and had to go to law, where base-born men frequently ejected noblemen of pedigree from public power by means of the ballot box, and above all, where the army was small, generally distrusted, and not allowed the slightest political influence.[1] All this was true before the two countries began to have any official quarrels.

Englishmen vaguely felt that Germans disliked them, but in the nineties they treated this possibility with their characteristic disdain. The interests of the great land and the great sea empires seemed to clash at few points. In 1890 Britain actually ceded to Germany Helgoland, in return indeed for concessions in East Africa, but it was an island, which, minute though it seemed, formed a veritable pistol in the North Sea pointed at Hamburg and Bremen. That by ceding this small isle, British statesmen were actually striking a blow at their own naval safety was the last thing that then crossed the mind of Lord Salisbury and his astute fellow ministers. It may in fairness, however, be stated that this ill-feeling of the Prussian junker class for England was no menace to the world's happiness until it came into sinister combination with the darling policies and ambitions of William II.

The young kaiser from the outset spoke much of peace; he was a frequent visitor at the court of his grandmother, the puissant old lady of Windsor; he professed (probably not insincerely) a keen admiration for many things British, but he also, from the outset of his reign, manifested a tendency to make innovations in German policy which spelled collision with England if pushed beyond a certain point. By a long

[1] German military men even objected that British (and American) army officers did not have the true military spirit and were "hopelessly subject to the cowardly civilian power" because unlike German officers, who wore their uniforms on all occasions, British officers, in peace times, frequently wore civilian clothes when off duty.

series of acts and speeches he also played into the hands of the great elements among his subjects who were coming to teach that war was a blessing, and that war with England was most blessed of all.

Kaiser Wilhelm took pride not merely in being the head of the Prussian war-machine. He speedily indicated his ambition to be the head of an extremely formidable naval machine also. Germany, or the parts thereof, formerly had never made boasts upon the high seas. In 1870 the French had blockaded North German ports and done considerable damage to their commerce. When the new emperor took power he found that he possessed a naval establishment of a few efficient cruisers, a few iron-clads of the coast defence type and a fairly large torpedo flotilla—enough to make blockading perilous, hardly more. In 1889 the German navy had been so weak for offensive purposes that Bismarck had been fain to come to an understanding with the United States over the possession of the Samoa Islands, despite the fact that the issue had been serious, and that the American navy then barely reckoned a small squadron of modern steel vessels. William's ambitions made this situation seem intolerable. *"Our future is upon the sea,"* he announced in a famous prophecy.

In 1896 the kaiser sent a telegram to President Krüger of the Boer Republic of the Transvaal congratulating him on having repelled a raid of English filibusterers. For a variety of reasons this message was peculiarly obnoxious to the English people, especially as the Transvaal was supposed to have all its foreign relations pretty strictly through Britain, and the Emperor had expressed his glee that Krüger had avoided his danger "without appealing to the help of friendly powers." This seemed to imply that Germany was ready in case of need to stand behind the Transvaal against England. The latter answered by mobilizing a "flying squadron" of battle-ships and cruisers so superior to anything William could send to Africa that the helplessness of the kaiser to make good his bold suggestion became absurd.

In 1898 occurred the Spanish-American War, and the

Dewey-Diedrichs incident at Manila. The rising Pan-German party saw the democratic Yankee republic carrying off a whole string of tropical islands (the very thing good Teutons lusted after) before their very eyes. Their first jealousy was aimed at America: had the German fleet been only a little stronger how many interesting things might have happened! But it was clear that England regarded American success with profound complacency. She had given us very effective help at Manila. The wrath of the Pan-Germans was directed against England too.

In 1899 the Boer War was begun in Africa. Germans as a nation sympathized intensely with the Dutch farmers struggling against a mighty empire. It was not merely natural partiality for the under-dog. In crushing the Boers the British were putting an end to a dream very many Germans had half consciously cherished of a South Africa that should be controlled or at least "protected" by the Hohenzollern eagle. Nowhere in Europe was England popular, but in Germany least of all. If the Emperor had been willing to make the least official move to support the Boers he would have had enthusiastic popular support. The German press exaggerated every British defeat. It was gravely stated that the English regiments regularly ran at the first volley or surrendered in droves.[1] The failure of the British generals to cope with perplexing questions of guerilla warfare was hailed as proof positive that here was a doomed and degenerate nation. Grossly vile caricatures of Queen Victoria had an abundant sale in all the little "post-card" shops wherein the Fatherland abounded:[2] and no story of British misconduct or inhumanity was too improbable to be believed. In short, the Boer War for the first time taught the British that they

[1] The writer was repeatedly assured of this fact, by very intelligent persons, while he was in Germany during the Boer War.

[2] I have had many of these coarse "souvenir cards" thrust upon me on the supposition that as an American I must needs enjoy every fling at Britain.— It is worth observing that the very worst atrocities charged by the German press against the British in 1899–1902 did not constitute one tithe of the outrages committed undoubtedly by the German troops in Belgium and France in 1914 and subsequently.

were very unpopular on the continent, but that they were most unpopular of all in Germany.

Nevertheless, while the newspapers and public meetings raged, the Emperor and the responsible statesmen kept their heads. British regiments might run away—possibly?—but nothing at least had happened to show that the British navy was not as terrible as ever. William II preserved a studiously correct attitude towards England until the Boers had surrendered (1902). He used the situation, however, to preach a very plain sermon to his subjects: he must have a greatly enlarged fleet.

Already in 1898 the Reichstag had been induced to vote a considerable naval program. Now the emperor and his very efficient and adroit High-Admiral Von Tirpitz came forward with a very much more elaborate proposition. William II struck when the iron was hot, when the Pan-German element was smarting under the sense of impotence at seeing first the Spanish-American and then the Boer wars being fought to a finish, and they utterly unable to get into the game. In 1897 the emperor had really disclosed his program by saying: "The trident of Neptune must be in our hands." In 1899 he spoke out more fiercely, "We are in bitter need of a strong German navy. If the increases demanded early in my reign had not been refused in spite of my warnings and my continued entreaties, how differently should we be able to further our flourishing commerce and our interests overseas." What interests of Germany had suffered save that she had not been able to bear help to Spain and the Boers is hard to say: but the emperor certainly knew how to work on the purse-strings of his subjects. In 1900 a great naval program was laid before the Reichstag.

Germany's need of a mighty navy was not solely based on the idea of reckoning with England. Von Bülow, as imperial spokesman, stated the case concisely late in 1899. Two of the three instances which he cited as proving the necessity of a powerful fleet are of more interest to Americans than to Britons. He said a need of naval increase was urgent because "first the Spanish-American War, then the disturbance in

Samoa,[1] and then the war in South Africa put our overseas interests at such different points in serious embarrassment: and fate proved it [this requirement of a strong navy] before our eyes." . . . "*You will understand, gentlemen, that in my official position I cannot say much, and that I cannot dot all my i's.*" It is quite likely, then, that if at the close of the nineteenth century Germany had possessed a powerful fleet, America and not England might have first tested Teutonic naval valor. Nevertheless, the main uses of a great fleet would have been against England. The nation that could cripple Britain upon her chosen element could obviously give the law to any lesser maritime power.[2] In submitting the 1900 naval program, Von Tirpitz therefore announced frankly, "Germany must have a battle-fleet so strong that with the greatest of the sea powers for adversary, a war against it would involve such dangers as would imperil his own position in the world."

Von Tirpitz and his associates did not indeed propose to build a navy of the same nominal strength as that of Britain. They believed that the latter could never be able to concentrate her whole armada in home-waters for defence against an attack across the North Sea; or, if she did so, her great outlying interests would probably go to ruin. They also argued that by superior training and discipline a smaller number of ships (German) could defeat a greater number (English),

[1] In 1898–99 there had been renewed friction in Samoa, which had ended in the partition of those islands between Germany and the United States.

[2] Without entirely endorsing the statement that the British fleet has been for recent years the sole genuine protection of the United States against Germany, it seems fair to point out that Germans clearly realized that any attack upon America, until the absolute neutrality or helplessness of Britain had been assured, would be extremely hazardous. In any case Britain would gain commercially and economically while German energies were preëmpted by the Trans-Atlantic struggle, and at the end the English might step in with overwhelming naval might and rob the Germans of the fruits of any victory. "In a war at present between Germany and the United States *the victor may be England!*" is the way I have heard the case stated.

It was therefore necessary to pull down English sea-power *first*, after which America could be handled according to the pleasure of Berlin.

likewise that "careful preparation permitting rapid mobilization can ensure a momentary superiority." [1]

Faced with these arguments the Reichstag in 1900 passed a new law providing for the gradual increase of the fleet until, in 1920, it should contain 38 battleships, 14 large cruisers, 38 light cruisers and appropriate small craft. This was a long time in which to create a great navy and Britain was not seriously alarmed. Prussian policy however often knew how to speed up authorized programs and the German fleet was not destined to grow at this very moderate pace. It was still a difficult matter, however, for the government to get money for ships. As a class the junker leaders were landsmen. Their joy was in the army wherein their sons held commissions, and Germany was still a sufficiently poor country to make it seem very hard to keep up a great army and a great navy simultaneously. The Kaiser and Von Tirpitz however were temporarily satisfied. The entering wedge had been driven.

On January 22nd, 1901, died the mighty Queen Victoria. Not quite sixty-four years had reigned this good as well as great sovereign. Her direct political influence in England had not seemed very large: her indirect social influence in every monarchy of Europe had been tremendous. Kings and emperors had recognized her moral priority and her right to lecture them privately in behalf of peace and of fair international dealing. Even the Hohenzollern had stood in respectful awe of her. But now in her place reigned her son Edward VII. The relations of the new monarch and William II, his nephew, were not cordial. The later reasons alleged for their coldness were various, but coldness undoubtedly there was.[2] Great monarchies do not go to war today merely

1 Statement on Naval Strategy, published at this time by Admiral von der Goltz, former chief of staff of the German navy.

2 The story as told the writer, by ordinarily well-informed Germans, was that while still Prince of Wales, Edward had borrowed money of his imperial nephew: after he became king, William asked for a loan in his turn but was refused. These tales are mere rumor: it is notorious however that Edward had his serious money difficulties, and that the Hohenzollern dynasty was—as royal families go—not well provided in its private fortune. The present Crown Princess is said to have been

because their rulers are personally unfriendly, but the public peace is not strengthened when two kings mistrust one another. Edward VII was sixty years old when he began to reign. All his life he had been over-shadowed by his august mother. His chief duty for long had been to represent the queen at many court ceremonials and public functions, when a royal presence and a few smooth, non-committal words were in order. People did not take Edward VII very seriously, but he had served a long apprenticeship in the school of the world. He knew all the capitals of Europe and was on especially good terms with the French. The political power of an English king, he knew, was slight; his indirect opportunities, especially in diplomacy, enormous. Edward was a very patriotic Englishman. His father had been a German prince, his nephew and many other kinsmen were German rulers: to German courts the English royal family had gone for many of the wives and husbands of its scions: and Edward himself is said to have spoken the tongue of his own subjects with a marked Teutonic accent: nevertheless he was (apart even from any disagreement with William II) no great admirer of Teutonic traits and tendencies. Much earlier than most Englishmen, he seems to have grasped the serious consequences of the growing spirit of Pan-Germanism—and how it was likely to focus all its antipathies and ambitions against Britain. He realized too that other nations than Germany, notably France and Russia, had disliked England extremely: but he considered that their hostility was not so serious and could be readily placated. With great skill he devoted himself to this end—to show the non-Teutonic nations whither Pan-Germanism and its high-placed sponsors were leading: and how there was no advantage anywhere in keeping up the old feuds with Britain.

In 1903 Edward VII began a deliberate cultivation of friends for Great Britain. He commenced by visiting Italy, with which indeed England had excellent relations, and the king whereof (Victor Emmanuel III) had been a very welcome

an acceptable bride especially because her Mecklenburg family was decidedly wealthy.

visitor while a young prince at the court of Queen Victoria.[1] It was easy and natural to return from Rome by rail, and to be received in Paris by President Loubet. It was only five years since the Fashoda incident and the great humiliation of France (p. 113), but Parisians were always courteous and French statesmen were beginning to discover that if the Pan-German scheme menaced the British empire, an indispensable preliminary to the scheme involved the crushing of France. Edward, therefore, was cordially received in Paris. He welcomed President Loubet to England on a return visit a little later. People observed that with the king there usually travelled an English under-secretary of foreign affairs. This was true on other visits to Spain, Portugal, Austria and Russia. While the monarchs exchanged congratulations and asked after the health of their "good friend's" or "brother's" families, the practical diplomats were busy with boundary questions, "spheres of influence," trade agreements and the like. In 1904, the first direct consequence of Edward's policy became known: on April 8th, Lord Lansdowne, the British foreign minister, and M. Paul Cambon, the French ambassador at London, signed a series of conventions that ended practically *all* the outstanding questions between England and France. There were of course many other points settled: but the main decision was this—France agreed to cease to make difficulties about the English occupation of Egypt: and on the other hand England was to pull no wry faces if France found it needful to stretch her hands over Morocco. *Thus was born the famous "Entente Cordiale":* an informal agreement for good fellowship and harmony that should have spelled happiness for the world.

The immediate consequences of the entente with France were of course to precipitate a crisis with Germany. The Morocco question was thrown into European politics by the sudden discovery of the Teutonic rulers that here was a nefarious attempt by the despised Gaul and the obstreperous

[1] The story is that Queen Victoria, after shrewdly observing the young Italian, declared he was the most promising crown prince who had ever visited Windsor.

naval despot to settle an international problem without consulting Berlin. What followed in the Morocco issue receives separate treatment in this book (see chapter XIX). But the curious point in question, when once the case had gone beyond its first stages, was this—namely, the frantic anxiety of the Germans not merely to win their way in Northwest Africa but also to drive a wedge between France and England: as if the healing of the old feud between those nations could spell only disaster for the fatherland. Early in the discussions, it had seemed likely enough that the English would give only diplomatic help to France in event of a crisis, and it was with a forsaken consciousness of this fact in 1905 that France had sacrificed Delcassé, because friendly state letters would never have stopped a Teutonic march on Paris (see p. 411). But in 1912, in the Agadir crisis, things were different. Germany learned well enough then that much water had run through the mill, and that if France had to fight she would not fight without a mighty naval ally.

Not to particularize all his travels, Edward VII, working informally with the British foreign office, visited from time to time all the major powers of Europe, and nowhere—in German opinion—wrought the kaiser's policies any good. Nicholas II of Russia was a weak, pliable man. In 1917 there was published a correspondence betwixt the czar and William II showing clearly that in 1905 the German kaiser, taking advantage of the Czar's anger at English support of Japan, had almost induced Nicholas to conclude a secret alliance with him against England. France was to be cudgelled into joining the combination by her Russian ally. The great powers of Europe were thus to be lined up for a deliberate assault on the naval empire, which would have to defend herself unaided. Denmark was to be seized (as Belgium was in 1914) to prevent the British fleet from entering the Baltic. This cheerful scheme, duly thrust upon "Nicky" by "Willy," proceeded a considerable distance towards maturity, and then for obscure reasons came suddenly to grief. It may be surmised that not merely did an anti-German faction at the Russian court get the ear of Nicholas, but that Edward VII, tactful and energetic, knew how to throw a counter personal influence over the none too resolute czar. This project of William II in any case failed ignominiously. Russia was not caught in the net of Pan-German intrigue; and what was worse still, in 1907 Sir Edward Grey, the British foreign minister (aided one cannot tell how much by his astute sovereign) executed a masterly counter-stroke. Russia and England in turn swore off all their old feuds. Questions of influence in Afghanistan and Thibet were cleared up: and chief matter of all, Persia, a distracted empire over the "protection" of which there had been vast wrangling, was to be divided into three spheres of influence; a Russian one in the North, an English one in the South, and a neutral zone between. Not a single German interest was menaced by this agreement. The two signatories did not make any kind of an alliance. They only agreed to cease quarreling and to live together in harmony, and yet the Berlin newspapers were soon full of solemn if not inflammatory editorials:—another case of Edward's nefarious policy of "isolating Germany," of "hemming her in," and forming a great barrier against her which only the sword could cleave away.

The ill relations between Germany and England became so manifest indeed that to prevent too open scandal the king and emperor exchanged visits. At least twice in his reign, Edward VII rode along Unter den Linden with the outriders of his imperial nephew ahead of him, the imperial cuirassiers at his side and all the buildings up to the Hohenzollern's schloss hung with gala bunting. The visits were outwardly cordial and perfectly correct; presumably good stories were told over the emperor's champagne; then the effect of the "reconciliations" ended instantly. Everybody knew it.

Everybody knew, too, that without having a single great direct point of quarrel—for the Morocco friction had been primarily with France—two great empires were getting into relations of increasing hatred. In truth England was at last becoming seriously alarmed for her safety. German commercial competition could be met or borne. German threats

against France, however disturbing, were not a direct menace
to England. But two things were putting fear into Britons:
first the increasingly hostile tone of the German press,
especially that part known to reëcho the thoughts of the governing class, which preached rancor against England at every
possible turn: [1] and secondly the rapid, nay, almost frantic,
increase of the German fleet.

Sensible German writers, even ardent advocates of Teutonic expansion, deplored the irresponsible utterances of their
journalists: e. g., Rohrbach lectured his countrymen upon the
bad manners of their press which had "wrought the greatest
damage to Anglo-German relations," and suggested that
Germans had given Englishmen too much reason to believe
that they "were thinking of attacking England at a favorable
opportunity and enriching themselves at her expense." But
assuredly the ill-feeling grew apace. The idea that England
was a decrepit nation, gripping in some miserly fashion upon
a maritime power which in justice belonged to the virile Teutonia—this idea was fostered in literally a myriad ways. In
1906 a cheap volume in paper covers lay on almost every book-
stall in the Fatherland. It sold by huge editions. Very possibly it was not published without high inspiration. Its title
was literally "Sea-Storm," and told of how the nations of
Europe, headed by Germany, attacked Britain and cast her
from her naval throne. The last chapter gleefully described
the entrance of Prussian regiments into London, and how the
United States, taking advantage of the plight of her old
enemy, annexed Canada and all other British possessions in
America.

The great "Navy League" of Germany with its 1,000,000
members, its staff of eloquent lecturers, its periodicals and its
huge mass meetings, although avowedly directed against no

[1] These anti-British sentiments seemed all the more alarming because
of the influence of the government upon the press in Germany, and the
likelihood that it could have silenced the worst offending organs if it
had really possessed the desire to do so. The socialist press was mostly
pacific: the "semi-official" papers often offended the worst.

one foreign nation in particular, was a perfect forcing-house
for anti-British propaganda. Other fleets Germany was soon
to outvie, but until she had driven that of Britain to bay there
was no real outlet to Teutonic aspirations. Indeed the tone of
some of the arguments implied that England was committing
an iniquity when she refused to scale down her naval appropriations in order to let Germany catch up with her. The
weaker sides of English life, the smug commercialism, the af-
fectations of indolence, the short hours of labor, the excessive
fondness for outdoor sports, the refusal to assume military
obligations, even the predilection for afternoon tea in lieu of
coffee or beer,—all these made many a German writer or lecturer imitate Jugurtha, the ancient Numidian king, when he
cried on quitting degenerate Rome: "O venal city, and soon to
perish—if but a purchaser be found!" Millions in the
Fatherland were willing to name the purchaser—provided the
price were not in gold but in iron.[1]

The effect of all this in Britain was of course to produce
wrath, distrust, and considerable counter-reviling. A great
part of the Pan-German literature luckily was never indeed
put into English, but quite enough was translated to produce
a most disagreeable impression. England in turn had a fair
supply of her jingoes, pamphleteers and mud-slingers: and
naturally her responsible statesmen were obliged to take serious notice of undeniable facts. As was written in 1911, "If
a nation constantly proclaims that it is the strongest and
greatest people on earth, that its destiny is to dominate the
world, that it will do so by the use of the mightiest armaments
the world has ever seen, and that it will use them instantly
and mercilessly against those who thwart its will, what wonder
that its neighbors take it at its word and insure one another's
prosperity and safety by *ententes* and understandings?"[2]

The above is certainly true. It was, however, not merely
the angry disparagement of Britain that led to this tension
with Germany, but the continual growth of the German fleet.
With a civil-speaking Germany, Englishmen might not have

[1] See note at end of chapter.
[2] "The Round Table," December, 1911.

been so anxious: but new threats and the clamorous forging
of new armor went on together. The result was the constant
tightening of the diplomatic bow.

So long as Germany was merely a military power, Englishmen could regard its disesteem with relative indifference.
Great armies could not swim the North Sea. It was when
Germany, without in the least reducing her land armaments,
began to add battleship to battleship until the naval experts
could play with the question whether the English fleet was
equal to stopping a great convoy of transports over to the
east coast of Britain, that a situation arose promising infinite
trouble. For her naval policy the kaiser's government could
indeed advance excellent arguments, at least for Germans.
The dignity of the Empire required that it should be powerful
on the seas as well as on the land. The multiplication of German foreign commerce required a corresponding protection
which only a fleet could give. A blockade of German ports
would be ruinous to industry even if Holland and Scandinavia remained open. It was even alleged that since Italy
and Austria were allies they must be aided by the German
navy in the Mediterranean against the large southern squad-
rons of France.

None of these arguments went to the base of the matter.
Germany could punish France or Russia, if they molested her
commerce, by a swift march upon their capitals. A much
smaller fleet than was projected would have effectively discouraged America or Japan from any outrages on Germany's
maritime rights. Nor had Germany anything real to dread
from England. British "navalism" was a bogey, useful
mainly to frighten money out of the purses of Teutonic tax-
payers. In times of peace German traders competed with
Englishmen in every British colony, and North German Lloyd
steamers actually cut into the profits of the British lines carrying passengers and freight from England herself to India,
Australia and John Bull's other colonies. The islanders
grumbled, but there was not a single instance of a British
warship being employed to diminish a German's just gains
by a pfenning.

In case of war, indeed, Britain might have blockaded Hamburg and Bremen and seized much German shipping; but she could have inflicted no direct harm upon the Kaiser's empire. If German diplomacy had been able to keep on decent terms with its land neighbors, food and every other necessity would have flowed in from France and Russia. Before the opening of the Morocco question England was cordially disliked both at Paris and St. Petersburg. The enmeshing of her power in a prolonged indecisive war with Germany would have been a direct invitation to France to ask her to move out of Egypt and to Russia to push home every darling project in Afghanistan and the far East. Indeed, had the successors of Bismarck really known how to extend the olive branch to the Third Republic and to the Czar, they might have gotten the navies of the Dual Alliance (as we see William II unskillfully attempted in 1905) to help them to pull down the power of that "perfidious Albion" which every French lad up to 1870 had been taught was "the natural enemy." Finally a war with Germany provoked by England would have been a direct present to her other great commercial rival, America, of an opportunity to gobble up a large part of the trade of the world.[1]   In short, any attempt by Britain to use her great navy to sweep German commerce and shipping from the seas would have been tremendously costly and run the risk of all kinds of failure. No serious English statesman (however bellicose) would have advocated it save under the most grievous kind of provocation.

Nevertheless, for better or for worse the building of the new German navy went on. So long as only the old style four-gun battleships were in vogue,[2] the initial superiority of England was so great that it seemed hopeless for Teutonic ambition to attempt to rival it. But in 1905, in an excess of cleverness, the British admiralty committed a serious blunder. To show their competitors that they were mere tyros in naval architecture, the royal shipyards suddenly produced

[1] An opportunity of course duly used by Americans between 1914 and 1917.

[2] Vessels like the American *Wisconsin* or *Missouri*.

the famous "Dreadnaught," the original "all-big-gun battle-ship"—with cruiser speed and ten 12-inch guns.[1] For the moment British sailors snapped their fingers gleefully. Here was the type of a ship whereof not one craft flew the pennon of the Kaiser. But High Admiral Von Tirpitz and his august master quickly grasped what had happened. The "dreadnaught" had rendered all the other battleships obsolete: ergo,—the great British fleet of pre-dreadnaughts was of only waning value. Britain had one new style vessel and Germany none: but if the latter seized her opportunity there was nothing to prevent her from building dreadnaughts almost as rapidly as England. By a prompt effort the supremacy of "Britannia" would become at least an open question.

Imperial influence and the great skill of Von Tirpitz in wheedling for votes in the Reichstag won their way. The recurring tension over Morocco served to loosen German purse-strings. The naval programs slid through the Reichstag with constantly weakening opposition. Even the socialists used the great building projects more as an opportunity to get concessions in other matters than as things to oppose. It was not until 1910 that the first German "dreadnaught" was commissioned. England already had ten vessels of the type. But with his program once legally voted and the money in hand, Von Tirpitz built rapidly. The industrial efficiency of the new Germany was admirably displayed. Early in 1914 she had ready for action 17 all-big-gun battleships or battle cruisers. England had then indeed 29: but considering her vast imperial interests and the great difficulty the British would have in concentrating all their capital ships for a single action in the North Sea, one may wisely assert that could the gap have been made a little narrower Germany might have risked a decisive naval battle. If she had lost the battle England

[1] It may be said that America was preparing to build a similar ship, but Congress delayed making the appropriation our architects desired.

The German navy department showed little spontaneity in its designs. Most of its best ships were pretty complete imitations of British or American models. Certain vessels (e. g., the old *Kaiser* class), in which some originality was attempted by using a great number of small guns, turned out most disappointingly.

at worst could only have blockaded her: had she won the battle, the British empire would have crumbled like a house of cards and almost every Pan-Germanist dream would have been instantly fulfilled.

Under these circumstances what wonder that Englishmen took alarm?

The situation was not eased by the intervention of William II. Did the Emperor realize that some day his correspondence with Nicholas II would see the light, and the world would know that he had endeavored to confront Britain, unfriended, with an enormous European coalition? Possibly having failed in 1905 to make a bargain with the Czar, and realizing that Edward VII was circumventing his attempts to get allies for some great adventure, the Emperor, with whom consistency was never an abiding virtue, decided to attempt to placate English opinion. In 1907 he wrote somewhat privately to Lord Tweedmouth, British first lord of the admiralty, protesting against "this perpetual quoting of the German danger" as "utterly unworthy of the great British nation, with its world-wide Empire and mighty commerce." His lordship replied to His Majesty by communicating the naval estimates for the coming year 1908–9, providing for only two battleships, the smallest number England had laid down since 1898. Evidently the emperor made good use of his knowledge. If the then Liberal government of England, intent as it was on strictly internal reforms, did not care to build very many war-ships this was no reason why *he* should imitate them. In March, 1908, a new navy law was passed at Berlin, providing for a general speeding up of the whole German naval program. In that year 4 new battleships were to be laid down, and between 1906 and 1908 9 German battleships were actually authorized as against only 8 British. Whatever his nephew's motives, Edward VII was no fool, and in the summer of 1908 he had an interview with William at Cronberg, in which he explained the suspicions and fears which his naval policy was awakening. William abruptly refused to discuss with any foreign government his right to build war-ships and is said to have "avowed his intention of going to war rather than submit to such a thing.'' Edward returned home, presumably with private warnings to British statesmen. Then the kaiser delivered himself of an astonishing interview with an English diplomatist, which was published in the ''London Telegraph,'' October 28, 1908.

''You English,'' said the Emperor, ''are mad, mad, mad as March hares. What has come over you that you are given over to suspicions that are quite unworthy of a great nation? I have declared . . . that it is one of the dearest wishes of my life to live on the best terms with England. *Have I ever been false to my word? Falsehood and prevarication are alien to my nature.* . . . This [suspicion] is a personal insult which I resent. . . . The prevailing sentiment of large sections of the middle and lower classes of my own people is not friendly to England. I am therefore, so to speak, in the minority in my own land, but it is a minority of the best element, just as it is in England respecting Germany.''

Here was a statement from an unimpeachable source that the majority of Germans hated England, and that the emperor (at least so he said) was at variance with his own people. But this ruler had just declined to make the slightest concession in the way of halting the naval program in which a great part of the unfriendliness focused. The result was an unheaval of British opinion that could not be ignored. A highly educational and popular play, ''An Englishman's Home,'' taught the unimaginative middle class public what it would mean to have Teutonic invaders suddenly landing on their East Coast. There was a bitter fight in the Liberal cabinet:—so many demands for money for old-age pensions, and many another state philanthropy, and a corresponding desire to reduce taxes! Certain of the ministers, e. g., John Burns, Lord Morley, etc., seem to have refused to see the hole through the ladder, to realize that a great war was in any sense possible. But the majority were convinced, albeit sorely against their wills. Money was diverted to the fleet. Mr. Asquith, the premier, announced in 1909 the intention of the Liberal government to maintain the ''unassailable supremacy'' of Britain upon the seas. From that time until 1914 the distance between the two fleets was never allowed to close quite up to the point of danger for the islanders.

During that interval matters did not really mend. The Agadir incident (1911) was treated by many Germans—including many who were anything but extremists—as a national humiliation that could never have come to pass save that England had put her navy at the disposal of France, and that the German fleet was still unequal to its task. After the Morocco trouble had been at last disposed of, however, the Kaiser invited Lord Haldane, a prominent Liberal minister, to visit Berlin. Haldane was peculiarly welcome in Germany: he had been educated there and spoke of it as his "spiritual country": he was therefore well qualified to bring the two nations together. His visit nevertheless was utterly fruitless.

Haldane arrived in February, 1912. Two days before his arrival the emperor's ministers had introduced an increased army and navy budget in the Reichstag. This was not a promising beginning for negotiations: but the chancellor Bethmann-Hollweg desired "conversations" and they took place. Haldane was authorized to assure Bethmann-Hollweg that England had no secret treaty with Russia and France, although she would have supported France in the Agadir case because she had herself a great interest in the result. The Chancellor proposed thereupon a treaty which provided that neither England nor Germany should enter into any project or combination for the purpose of attacking the other. This sounded fair upon its surface, but obviously left the way open for Germany to attack France or Russia on her own terms, with England standing helplessly by. The upshot might have been to leave Germany supreme on the Continent, and with England isolated and exposed to the second leap of the now colossal Teutonic empire. Haldane balked at the terms. England, he thought, could only promise to oppose any "aggressive or unprovoked attack upon Germany."

"How can you define what is meant by 'aggressive and unprovoked attack'?" asked the chancellor.

"How many grains make a heap?" responded his guest. "But one knows a heap when one sees one."

The real issue, however, was over the steady increase of the German fleet. There was a solemn luncheon at which the Emperor, Admiral von Tirpitz and again Bethmann-Hollweg all conferred with Haldane. The Englishman put it bluntly that there was no good in an agreement if Germany was going to increase her battleships and then have England do the same, and he made it clear England intended to lay down two keels for her rival's one. The Emperor and Von Tirpitz were "visibly disturbed" at the suggestion that no political agreement could be made without a curtailment of the imperial naval program. They argued that the naval scheme for Germany was fixed in advance by law and that it was impossible to change it. The most that could be promised was a "retardation" of the new ships. In minor matters, e. g., the control by Britain of the Eastern outlet of the Bagdad railway, Haldane's hosts were ready to make concessions. He departed, however, with nothing really accomplished. It was evident Germany wished England to promise to stay neutral in case she herself undertook to crush France:—and this England would not do. It was equally evident that England wished Germany to pare down her battleship program as being aimed directly at her—and this Germany would not do. Nothing therefore resulted from the imperial luncheon party save a clear understanding by certain British statesmen at least, that they had sent their most acceptable emissary to Berlin to heal the feud, and lo! he had not healed it.

Bethmann-Hollweg later stated in the Reichstag that when Haldane asked him for some guarantee (provided England promised to remain neutral) that Germany would not fall on France and destroy her, "I replied that the policy of peace which Germany had pursued for more than forty years ought to save us from such a question."[1] It is to be wondered whether His Excellency, the chancellor, imagined that English public men had no idea of the main teachings of Pan-Germanism?

There were some more negotiations at London, but they all came to nothing. Germany would not modify her naval pol-

[1] Bethmann-Hollweg speaking in the Reichstag, August 19th, 1915.

icy, which seemed directed straight at England:[1] and she
would not sign any agreement which did not seem to give her
carte blanche to overrun the rest of the world with England
looking on in dumb neutrality. This was practically the end
of attempts at a formal agreement. In 1912 and again in 1913
Mr. Winston Churchill, then first lord of the admiralty, did
indeed make public proposals for a "naval holiday"—i. e.,
in whatever year Germany decided not to build any new war-
ships England would refrain likewise: and in this way "without any negotiations, bargaining, or the slightest restriction
upon the sovereign freedom of either power," relief might be
obtained.[2] Churchill's suggestion fell on very stony ground.
Von Tirpitz, full of pride in his growing battle-fleet, would
have none of it. The Pan-Germans at once pounced on the
First Lord's 'statement as an official admission that England
was wearying in her purpose to keep up a supreme navy.
A little more exertion on their own part and the Mistress of
the Seas would be mistress no longer. There was never a
sign of a naval holiday. England continued to build new
ships, practically on the ratio of eight for Germany's five,
down to the catastrophe of 1914.

The events since 1900 had sufficiently convinced Englishmen of all but the extreme radical wing that a great navy was
the only reasonable life insurance for the nation. Had they
been persuaded otherwise, undoubtedly the outbreak of Armageddon would have been followed in a few months by so com-

[1] Germans sometimes complained that Englishmen. saw the United
States building a navy nearly as strong as that of the kaiser, and yet
took no umbrage. Why, if there was not gross partiality, were there not
complaints addressed to Washington as well as to Berlin? The complete answer was that behind the American fleet there was practically
no army whatever. Behind the German fleet there was a vast army,
the landing of a fraction whereof on British shores meant the ruin of
the British Empire. The German fleet was not unwisely likened to
"the head of the lance" for the conquest of England. The battleships
were to clear the way for the transports and the many army corps of
the invasion.

[2] Churchill used very plain speaking, however, in describing the naval
rivalry. He called England's navy a "necessity," Germany's a "luxury"
—to the great wrath of the Pan-Germans.

plete a victory for Teutonia as would have realized the Pan-Germans' wildest dreams. But Englishmen of the predominant Liberal party utterly refused to listen to the proposition that not merely a great navy, but also a great army were needful if their presumptive enemies were to be held at bay. The most they would consider was sending a modest expeditionary force from their limited old-style professional army to give France a little friendly aid, while their navy swept the seas and kept London snug and warm whatever the fate of Paris. The blindness of otherwise highly able English leaders to the fact that the life of their empire could be menaced by a land-drive upon the Channel ports, or upon Egypt or the Persian Gulf, would seem today inconceivable to retrospective Americans did we not find so many among our own wise and good who, long after 1914, continued to asseverate that the United States needed neither army nor fleet and that our own participation in the European war was merely a wicked, disordered dream.

There were indeed many Englishmen of rank and influence who declared that the storm would blow by land as well as by sea, and that something more than "territorials"—a kind of glorified volunteer militia—must be ready to meet it. But these men were for the most part members of the Conservative party, out of sympathy with the Liberal ministry, and cordially hated by the Liberal voters because of many bitter domestic questions. King Edward VII had died in 1910, after accomplishing a great work in creating the Triple Entente—the informal but genuine "cordial understanding" with France and Russia. Had he lived, he might have done something to persuade his countrymen to increase their army:—but his son George V was relatively young, inexperienced and fain to keep clear of even indirect political action.

One great voice was indeed raised strenuously for some form of compulsory military service: that of Lord Roberts, the doughty old conqueror of South Africa. A clear-headed, practical man, able to take the Pan-Germans from their own point of view, he strove earnestly to tell the truth to his countrymen and shake them out of their smug self-confidence. In

October, 1912, he delivered a tremendous speech at Manchester warning Englishmen that Germans were planning a speedy war against Great Britain, that this war would come the moment the Teutonic forces were ready, that the policy of a ruthless stroke applied by Bismarck in 1866 and 1870 would be used over again, and that *"Germany strikes when Germany's hour has struck."* He therefore urged universal military service.

The rejection of his plea by the Liberal leaders of England was furious and disdainful. "The Nation," their chief weekly, carried a fiery article on "A Diabolical Speech," describing Roberts as speaking merely according to the "crude lusts and fears which haunt the unimaginative soldier's brain." "The Manchester Guardian," their chief daily, flatly denied Roberts' facts and premises, and declared that Germany was never accused with justice "of breaking her word, of disloyalty to her engagements, or of insincerity." And so they laughed him to scorn.[1]

And thus through 1913 and into 1914 events moved forward —outwardly calm, but within the fires of international hatred burning: England utterly distrustful of Germany but only half girded for the worst: Germany looking on England as the chief element which held her back from her ever-strengthening ambition—a land empire across Europe and Asia, a sea empire with innumerable colonies, and a great dominion in South America easily acquired by smashing the Monroe Doctrine[2] after the United States had been left isolated by the

[1] To make my own position clear, I would say that the program for internal reforms, urged by the English Liberals during the last decade, seems on the whole admirable. It was the misfortune of the Liberals, however, that most of them became so intent on distracting and violent domestic problems, that they failed to take proper heed of the growing foreign danger. Like the ancient Greek philosopher, intent on studying the heavens they almost walked into a well.

[2] Germans have repeatedly stated in my presence that without British help America could never uphold the Monroe Doctrine, which was really entirely to British advantage, that we ought to welcome a German protectorate in Southern Brazil, etc. Whether the United States could have defended the Monroe Doctrine unaided is, of course, a question not to be settled here.

ruin of the British fleet,—in short, a greater Roman Empire.
In 1911 Rohrbach, the distinguished German publicist,
summed up a formidable political theory in four words:
"*Germany's fate is England.*"

GERMAN HATRED OF BRITAIN

The antipathy and the contempt for the English which prevailed in
Germany in the dozen years preceding Armageddon is of course known
to every visitor to the country who went off the common beat of tourist travel. I well recall being obliged at sundry small inns, eating-
houses and the like, to have to explain that I was an American in
order to get civil treatment from some of the guests and waiters.

In 1905 I vividly remember being thrown in company with two
Bavarian soldiers upon a furlough. They were men evidently from
good middle class families and were not ordinary conscripts but "one
year volunteers" (i. e., thanks to superior education, they had been
allowed to reduce their time in the army). At first they were positively insulting because they deemed their travelling companions to be
English. When they realized they had to deal with Americans, "who
had fought the English just as we want to," their manner changed,
and with artless candor they described with many details their ardent
hopes of how they could in their time fight the British, "very much
more gladly we assure you than the French," how after a few volleys
the foe would surely run "howling like cowards for mercy," how then
the Germans would use their bayonets, give no quarter, etc., etc., adding to this recital many things their lieutenant had told them about
the certainty of war with Britain, and the need for instant readiness.
All this of course was nearly nine years before the actual coming of
Armageddon.

Several years ago circulars describing the English naval programme
were distributed to all the students of Berlin university, and they were
urged to attend a mass meeting to petition the government to take
effective counter-measures against this "menace." The circulars were
placed in class-rooms and buildings where by no chance political propaganda could have been permitted save by high university authority.
At the subsequent meeting the speeches against Great Britain were as
violent and inflammatory as if there had been a serious diplomatic issue
then with England, and war immediately in the air. As a matter of
fact there were for the nonce almost no grave issues pending with England or even with France or Russia.

CHAPTER XIX

THE STORM CENTER IN MOROCCO

DURING the later years of his life Otto von Bismarck was surveying the possible causes for war which might arise in the world. And the danger spot he selected was a country little known at the time and which had not then been in any way a source of dispute: Morocco. Bismarck, in this, was a true prophet. For while the Moroccan difficulty did not cause the European war it undoubtedly contributed to bringing it about. It left the nations of Europe in a state of feverish tension and of hostility, a situation out of which a war may easily proceed.

What was this country of Morocco and why did it become a European problem? It was the last independent state on the north coast of Africa, occupying the north-west corner of the continent, with an area of about 219,000 square miles and a population somewhat exceeding five million. Formerly it had been a stronghold of fanatical Mohammedanism and the home of daring pirates—the Salee rovers—who had been the terror of mariners as far north as the English Channel. But of late it had greatly fallen from its high estate. The sultans had grown weaker and weaker, the last able representative of the line, Mulai Hassan, died in 1894, although his policy had been continued with some success by an able minister, Ben Hamed, up to 1901.

· But it was not the previous strength or the present weakness of the country that made Morocco a European problem: it was the great national resources of the land. Morocco was, with the possible exception of Asia Minor, the last "white man's country" left unoccupied by the European nations. The land was rich in minerals of every sort, iron especially—

that great necessity of modern industry. Its agricultural resources were immense and it had a rich soil, which the Moroccan native had barely scratched. The climate, especially in the uplands of southern Morocco, was entirely suitable for Europeans, and the small number of inhabitants in proportion to the area permitted of large immigration. No wonder that the European peoples rushed forward to gain the chance to exploit such a prize.

But, unfortunately, they did not come forward singly or confine their attention each to certain localities. They pushed their interests all over Morocco, and as each group of nationals felt the competition from a group from some other nation they appealed to their home government for aid and protection, thus making of their economic quarrels international questions. The diplomacy of Europe was busily occupied with the economic squabbles of different national groups desiring to exploit the mines, work the lands or build the railroads of Morocco.

Such, then, were the roots of the Moroccan problem.

But this was not all of the difficulty. The people of Morocco, in whose land these European groups wished to build railroads and work mines, were fanatical Mohammedans and as such bitterly opposed to the entry of Europeans into Morocco. Nor did they manifest their displeasure merely passively; whenever possible they endeavored to put an end to these activities by violence. But, again, these activities were being carried on as a result of concessions granted by the Moroccan government, and it was, therefore, the duty of that government to give them protection. This duty, however, the Moroccan government seemed unable to fulfill.

This brings us to what is, perhaps, the real crux of the Moroccan difficulty, the weakening of the government of the sultan. I have already mentioned the fact that the government of Morocco had sadly fallen from its former glory; that the last man capable of really dealing with the situation, Ben Hamed, had died in 1901. Since that day it is hardly too much to state that anarchy had been the rule in the sultan's dominions. The government was a feudal one. The country was divided among various tribes, each with its caïd, or chief, some of whom had more real power than the sultan himself. The control of the sultan over these was dependent on the amount of military force he could bring against them, and as this military force was by no means strong, each caïd was generally left to do what was right in his own eyes except during the rare moments when the sultan and his army were in the neighborhood. Therefore, if a caïd, either for personal reasons or because of pressure from his followers, decided to oppose the European influx, it was exceedingly hard for the sultan to bring him to book or to protect the endangered Europeans.

In addition, the character of the sultan introduced a new complication. It seems, unfortunately, only too often true that a mixture of Eastern manners and Western civilization produces, in a character, the vices of both and few of the virtues of either.[1] Such a character was the then sultan, Abdul-Aziz. He had heard enough of the civilization of the West to long for it and not enough to acquire a discriminating taste. Photography, billiard-tables, automobiles, even an American bar were shipped, at great expense, to Morocco to gratify the tastes of the Sultan. The religious feelings of the Moroccan people were horrified by the spectacle of the ladies of the harem, with unveiled countenances, riding, in the Palace grounds, on bicycles provided by the kindly generosity of Abdul-Aziz. Of the palace orgies, or of the wild extravagance of the sultan it is unnecessary to speak, but their effect on his people may be easily imagined. It turned their hearts from him and contributed in no small degree to the increase of the disorder.

For the extravagance of the sultan Europe can hardly be held responsible. But when it brought him into debt, when he was obliged to search Europe for those who would take his loans, the credit and stability and general character of the Moroccan government were forced anew on European attention. If money was to be loaned to Abdul-Aziz some care

[1] Another instance of this can be found in the career of the extravagant Khedive Ismaïl of Egypt. See p. 100.

must be taken not only that it should be paid but also that it should be expended with some degree of wisdom. This and the prevalent disorder practically forced Europe to consider some form of intervention in Moroccan affairs.

What form was this intervention to take? Was it to be entrusted to a single power? Or to a group of powers—which would mean the internationalization of Morocco? One thing appeared certain: this intervention must be backed up by an armed force capable of maintaining order, and, secondly, a firm hand must be placed on the Moroccan government. What power or group of powers, however, was willing to go to this trouble and expense? And, if they did, ought they not to be rewarded to an especial extent in the returns from the exploitation of the country? Finally, if this intervention took place, with the intervening power or powers holding a strong army in the country, could Morocco be said to be an independent state? Would it not go the way of Egypt and Tunis and become a dependency?

On the fact that some intervention in Morocco was needed the European powers seem to have been agreed, but no agreement was reached as to the power or powers to which this intervention was to be entrusted. The prize was too great and each power was too jealous of the others to allow anyone to secure it without a struggle. Moreover those powers which had vested national interests in Morocco feared that the state which was then allowed supremacy, would use this opportunity to make Morocco a closed field for its own nationals. From this question and from the international economic disputes arose the Moroccan problem.

What claims had the various European powers for the position of restoring order in Morocco?

First of all, let us consider England. She had probably been the first to secure interests in Morocco—the story of McLean and Harris, the two supporters of England in Morocco, reads like a page from English eighteenth century colonial expansion. At the opening of the twentieth century she had by far the largest share of the Moroccan trade, and this leading position she managed to keep during the next ten years, although she was rapidly losing it to France. But England seems to have been unwilling to undertake the responsibility—the restoration and maintenance of order—which this privileged position placed on her. She was too much occupied elsewhere—in South Africa and in India. And so, gradually, Englishmen—McLean and Harris as well as the government—came to the conclusion that this position of supremacy must be allowed to pass to France, provided that France allowed full economic opportunity to all in Morocco. They were unwilling that a strong military and naval power like France should control that part of Morocco opposite Gibraltar, but here certain claims of Spain—to be mentioned later—came to British aid. But it is to be noted that England in a period when she was in relations in no way friendly to France—for it was in the years of colonial quarrels between 1895 and 1902—came to the conclusion that France was the best power on which to confer the control of Morocco. And at this time England was distinctly friendly to Germany!

These claims of France to the supreme control in Morocco rested on various grounds. In the first place, geographical. The possessions of France surrounded Morocco on two sides, east and south, and, with the exception of a small strip bordering on the Spanish colony of Reo del Oro, the entire land frontiers of the sultan bordered on French colonies. France therefore was better fitted than any other power with bases from which such military forces as were necessary for the maintenance of order might operate. Moreover, to France, a state of order in Morocco was far more necessary than to any other state, for disorder in the sultan's dominions might easily affect the neighboring French colonies. And in case of war an independent and disorderly Morocco would form a convenient base from which irregular expeditions might be made on French colonies. In the second place, there were economic bases for this claim. Although French trade was not in the lead in Morocco it was fast taking that position, aided by the favorable geographical situation. Indeed, Algeria and Morocco economically belonged together and could best be developed together.

But these French claims were zealously contested by Germany. Germany's trade was still a very poor competitor with that of France and England, but it was growing, being organized in the true Teutonic fashion. It may be doubted, however, if it could ever overcome the advantages which geographical position had conferred on France and take the first position. And yet it is only fair to point out that Germany had certain rights and interests in Morocco which they were entitled to protect, and that reasonable German action taken to this end is justifiable.

The German position, however, seems to have been based on broader considerations. She had entered late into the race for colonies, and had been, or thought she had been, left behind in the rewards. And here was the last "white man's country" obtainable, passing into the hands of France! This consideration, alone, seems to have been the factor which moved the German colonial party and the Pan-Germans to make every effort to prevent such a result. The real Moroccan question was lost, in German minds, in the larger question of the division of the pleasant and profitable places of the earth—a division in which they claimed France and England had secured an undue share. At bottom, then, it appears to have been a question of prestige.

Spain had certain claims, rather shadowy, but none the less earnestly insisted on, to the northern part of Morocco. But beyond that her interests did not go. Her trade in the rest of Morocco was almost nil, her resources in men and money for the preservation of order in the entire country were insufficient. Her claim to northern Morocco, however, as a "sphere of influence" happened to coincide with the wishes of Great Britain. For the latter power wished to prevent France from acquiring the control of the Moroccan coast across from Gibraltar and so it urged the claims of Spain in this region.

Thus every one of the four powers mentioned had claims in Morocco which they were justified in protecting. And one of them, France, was by its position peculiarly fitted to take the task of maintaining order and directing the future of

Morocco. But another of the powers, Germany, was unwilling to acquiesce in such an arrangement, and her constant efforts to prevent it are the chief feature of the Moroccan problem of the first eleven years of the twentieth century.

The modern phase of the problem opens with the Anglo-French agreement of 1904. By this arrangement England agreed to allow the predominant position of France in Morocco provided that English trade were protected and that Spanish claims were satisfied. In return France agreed to admit England's predominant position in Egypt. Up to this period France and England had been rivals in the colonial field, a rivalry so keen that six years earlier it had nearly brought the two countries to war. In April, 1904, however, they came to an agreement on the points in dispute in a series of treaties of which the Moroccan-Egyptian agreement was one. In October of the same year this agreement was completed by a treaty between France and Spain by which the Moroccan situation of the two was regulated. In both treaties the maintainance of the independence of Morocco was assured.

Both treaties also contained secret annexes by which, in "the event of either government being constrained, by force or circumstance" to alter the existing situation, mutual aid was promised, and the French-Spanish secret annex laid down the bases for a partition of Morocco between France and Spain. It is possible to consider these secret annexes as destroying all the effect of the public declarations and as indicating the covert intention of proceeding, as soon as possible, to a Franco-Spanish absorption of Morocco by English aid. It does not seem as if this reasoning is necessarily true. Conditions in Morocco were subject to rapid change and any government embarking on a policy of maintaining order and of directing the sultan's government ought to be prepared for all contingencies. And we do know that the great majority of Frenchmen, even members of the Colonial party, were then and later inclined to oppose any commitment of France in Morocco further than was absolutely necessary. Secret diplomacy is always dangerous, but, under the circumstances, it may not have been unwise to keep in reserve and unknown an arrangement looking to a possible future contingency. The exact intention of the French government at this time is hard to discover; possibly it was not sure itself; but this line of reasoning toward the secret treaties appears to be, at least, not impossible.

Germany's first attitude toward these agreements was not hostile. Von Bülow, the German Chancellor, stated that Germany's interests in Morocco were entirely economic, and as long as these interests were not endangered, she would offer no opposition. But as time went on this earlier position was modified. Many reasons contributed to this. First was the rather discourteous attitude of M. Delcassé, the French foreign minister, in declining to give to Germany official notice of the Agreements of 1904. Then, too, the secret agreements may have leaked out to such an extent as to give Germany the idea that some arrangement detrimental to her interests was under consideration. But the real reason for her actions in 1905 appears to lie in factors far greater than the mere problems of Morocco.

In the days of Bismarck, Germany had been content to wait in calm confidence in her strength and had refused to waste her energies and to make enemies in raising barren questions of prestige. But with the more feverish days under William II the idea seems to have developed that Germany ought to insist on her rights and demand that in every problem raised in Europe or in the world she be consulted. If such a settlement was made without German co-operation it was looked on as a blow to German position and German prestige. But these arrangements of 1904 had been drawn up without any consultation with Berlin, indeed, as has been said, without any official notification to the German government. And so an increasing group in Germany demanded that, in the name of the prestige of the imperial government, these agreements should be questioned and brought under the purview of German diplomacy.

Gradually this group seems to have secured control of the imperial government, although it is doubtful if they ever secured the complete adherence of the Emperor, who seems, at this time, to have disliked violent measures against France. But the German chancellor, Prince von Bülow, was in a difficult political situation at home and needed the support of the conservatives, which could only be gained by a more spirited foreign policy. And the moment for this display of strength was most propitious, while Russia, France's continental ally, was undergoing defeat in the war against Japan and the European position of France was thereby weakened. It was therefore decided in Berlin to challenge this new Anglo-French agreement, to "rap the table," in order to show that Germany still existed in the world and that she had claims which must be satisfied.

The emperor, William II, was cruising in the Mediterranean in the early spring of 1905. Suddenly on March 31 he appeared at Tangier and replied to the greetings addressed to him with a speech which at once produced a serious diplomatic situation. "It is to the sultan in his position as an independent sovereign that I am paying my visit today. I hope that under the sovereignty of the sultan a free Morocco will remain, open to the peaceful rivalry of all nations, without monopoly or annexation, on the basis of absolute equality. The object of my visit to Tangier is to make it known that I am determined to do all that is in my power to safeguard efficaciously the interests of Germany in Morocco, for I look on the sultan as an absolutely independent sovereign." [1]

It was a direct challenge to the Anglo-French treaty in which the paramount interests of France in Morocco had been admitted, and to the entire foreign policy of friendship with England as directed by M. Delcassé. And when this speech was backed by an ultimatum that Morocco should be placed under an international control, the whole foundation of the agreement of 1904 was attacked. [2] But France was in no

[1] There is good evidence for the belief that the whole visit and speech was arranged by Von Bülow and that William II played an unwilling part in the affair.

[2] Delcassé appears to have allowed his policy to run ahead of the military support which might have given it weight. This was shown in the

position to fight even though England appears to have promised armed aid in case she so elected.[1] Delcassé resigned and France agreed to submit the whole Moroccan question to an international conference to meet at Algeciras in 1906.

There is something, as has been already admitted, to be said for the German claims in the matter. Germany had certain interests which would be destroyed if France were allowed to make Morocco a closed preserve for her capitalists. But England was in the same position and had Germany decided to open diplomatic negotiations with England she could probably have secured the latter's aid against such a contingency without this undue exhibition of table-thumping. Indeed the whole affair left an impression which cost Germany many possible friends at the conference. Moreover it was not the secret, but the *public* clauses of the Moroccan treaty which Germany attacked, clauses which she had hitherto accepted, and this conduct left a feeling of insecurity in Europe. What international agreement would Germany decide to attack next!

Indeed the whole German aim in this affair seems to have been to gain prestige and not to protect her interests in Morocco. We are far from those days when Bismarck, in the calm confidency of Germany's strength, was able to declare in the Reichstag that "we Germans fear God and nothing else in the world and it is the fear of God that makes us seek peace and ensue it." Calm confidence gave way to a sort of nervous irritability that saw a danger to German prestige at every turn and appeared to feel that, unless the sabre was rattled every now and then, Germany would be forgotten.

cabinet before his resignation, when the secretaries of war and the navy declared hostilities with Germany were impossible.

[1] A personal representative of William II, Prince Henckel von Donnersmarck, was sent to warn the people of France that Declassé was *persona non grata* to Germany. This he did in an interview published in the "Gaulois" in June, 1905. In October following Delcassé retorted by publishing in the "Matin" the English offer of assistance. This statement was never denied by English statesmen.

Indeed Germany had spoiled her case—which was not altogether a bad one at the start—by her bullying methods, and
when the conference met at Algeciras, a little Spanish town
near Gibraltar, French diplomacy had arrayed against Germany almost all of the powers.   To this conference had come
delegates from the United States—called thither, it is said,
by the German government in the hope of securing their aid—
but these neutral delegates decided to uphold, in the main,
the French contentions.   Indeed the claim of France was
based on the very nature of the situation: France alone was
really well situated to keep order and to guide the Moroccan
government and these two were necessities in handling the
problem.   Even Italy, Germany's ally, deserted her and
Austria-Hungary, her most devoted friend, at times showed
signs of independent action.   So a compromise was made—
a compromise which merely covered the German defeat,
sketched out in its main outlines, it is said, by President
Roosevelt in reply to an appeal for aid from the German
emperor.   This act of Algeciras contained in its one hundred
and twenty-three articles many principles dear to Americans,
for example, that of the Open Door.   It declared the sovereignty and independence of the sultan and the integrity of
his dominions and made the control, in form, international.
All these were concessions to Germany.   On the other hand
it admitted the French claim of paramount interests in the
land and confided to France and Spain the direction and the
greatest share in this international control.   In itself it was
a splendid document, full of hope for the future.   But would
it work?

It soon became evident that it would not.   The other powers involved in the international control, after having asserted their claims in Morocco, promptly withdrew to their
own affairs and left France and Spain to grapple with the
Moroccan anarchy and to try to manage the sultan.   They
were willing to take the trade and exploit the resources of
the country but they shrank from the attendant responsibilities.   England was content to let France control the situa-

tion as had been agreed in 1904; Germany, feeling that her prestige had been satisfied, turned back to Turkey and the Bagdad railway. France and Spain struggled on with the growing anarchy, the incompetence of the Sultan, the bankrupt treasury, and the hostile land.

Under these circumstances the act of Algeciras was unworkable. A strong control over Morocco was needed. This control could be international, but if the other powers refused to assist France and Spain, then the control had to be vested in these two. And so, in the five years following Algeciras, Morocco drifted more and more into the status of a Franco-Spanish protectorate or a division between the two. Not that this result was greatly desired in either France or Spain: both seem to have shrunk from the expense in men and money that this obligation would involve, and yet the facts of the situation drove them on. Affairs could not continue as they were.

Almost all the European powers were reconciled to the protectorate as the ultimate solution: the exception was Germany. In the first place, her trade in Morocco was growing and she feared that it would be destroyed if the protectorate was allowed. In the second place, her prestige was bound up in the Act of Algeciras. She endeavored in every way, therefore, to check French efforts, intriguing with the Sultan and raising questions. Abdul-Aziz, the incompetent, had lost his throne to his abler brother Mulai-Hafid, and Germany hoped that she could secure the new sultan. In vain, for he gradually gravitated toward France. Finally Germany in 1909 made a swift volte-face. In an agreement with France she recognized the paramount interests of the latter in Morocco and in return obtained the chance for her subjects to associate with the French in all the economic development of Morocco.

Now this agreement practically destroyed the open door in Morocco which had been, all along, the great German contribution. For it set up an economic joint-control in Morocco in favor of France and Germany and to the detriment of the other interested powers. For this reason England protested against it, but without avail. Again, in it, Germany admitted the paramount political interests of France in Morocco, a thing which hitherto she had refused to do. The agreement was regarded in France as giving her a free hand to deal with the sultan in return for economic concessions to Germany. Unfortunately the wording of the agreement was so loose as to allow two different interpretations by the two parties to it and, instead of peace, it led to strife.[1]

It is idle to go into the whole history of the 1909 agreement—misunderstandings, inability of each government to deal with its subjects interested in Morocco, delay on the part of France, threats on the part of Germany. Suffice it to say that almost immediately after the agreement was signed it proved as unworkable as the Algeciras Agreement. Probably the most difficult question arose out of the building of two military railroads. Since Germany could not be associated in the construction of French military railroads, she demanded, as compensation, the prohibition of all outside competition with the "Society of Public Works"—an international company for the development of Morocco in which France and Germany controlled eighty per cent. of the stock. Such an arrangement would make Morocco an almost closed field for France and Germany and shut out England to a large extent, and this latter power naturally protested. France then decided to drop the question of compensation despite the fact that M. Cambon, her ambassador in Germany, urged the danger of such a proceeding. On this and on other questions disagreement became rife and trouble was evidently brewing.

It was at this inopportune moment that news came to Paris of a bad situation at Fez, the capital of Morocco. Anarchy was said to be increasing, the power of the sultan gone, the lives of Europeans endangered. How far this information was correct seems never to have been entirely settled, but, at any rate, it was enough to cause the French government

---

[1] One of the obvious aims of German diplomacy in this agreement was to bind France to Germany and separate her from England.

to send a strong force inland to Fez to restore order. This action, however, in such a critical time was full of danger. Germany was disgruntled and would surely seize the opportunity to declare that the Act of Algeciras was violated and a new situation had arisen. And, in this view, they would have some justification, for a French force once in Fez would probably never withdraw—in fact, it never did—and in such a situation it was idle to talk of the independence of Morocco. Spain promptly took a hand in the game by seizing the territory allotted to her by the secret treaty of 1904. A new situation had indeed arisen: the Act of Algeciras was dead.

Probably it would have been better for France to have openly avowed this fact and to have asked the price of Germany's consent. Such seems to have been the advice of M. Cambon, the sagacious French ambassador to Germany, and to such a course France would probably have come in time. But unfortunately there had been two quick changes of ministry in Paris, and French policy at this time was rather weak and uncertain. Therefore it lost precious time while Germany became more and more angry and threatening.

When one army is attacking another, it selects a position to assault, not because that position is important in itself so much as that it is the weakest spot in the opposing line and that defeat there will endanger the entire plan of the enemy. Morocco was France's weakest position in world-policy and Germany attacked it, not because Morocco in itself was so important to her—although some Pan-Germans insisted that it was—but because a defeat for France *here* might force her to come to terms elsewhere. And so the story of the events of 1911 passes outside the boundaries of the Moroccan problem into the wider limits of world policy. These wider limits lie somewhat outside the scope of this chapter but they must be briefly indicated in order that the final act of the Moroccan drama may be clearly understood.

If we examine the map of Africa, as it was in 1911, between the Niger and the Congo rivers, we find two colonies, one of

Germany—Kamerun—and one of France—the French Congo. Both these colonies were typical tropical dependencies—not white man's countries—and yet very valuable in the economic sense. Each had been farmed out by the respective governments to various trading companies of which the leading French example was the so-called N'Goko-Sangha Company. Unfortunately for world peace the boundary between the two colonies was uncertain, border disputes were frequent [1] and it appears that a more enterprising Germany company had encroached on the land of the French company. Despairing of any settlement, the French government decided to form a co-partnership in the Congo such as had been formed in Morocco. But in return for granting this arrangement the N'Goko-Sangha Company demanded an indemnity for losses sustained to the Germans, and when the French Chamber of Deputies refused to vote the indemnity the whole plan fell through much to the disgust of the Germans, who had hoped to gain much from such an arrangement.

In the spring of 1911, however, M. Caillaux, at first foreign minister, then premier, took up the negotiations again. This new negotiation seems to have had a much wider scope. Carried on in secret—French diplomacy seems to have known nothing of it—Caillaux's negotiations seem to have aimed at a general exchange of territories in central Africa, and even the cession of French Congo in return for German allowance of a French protectorate in Morocco. In addition, it appears that the French purse was to be opened to the support of German economic plans in Turkey and elsewhere. A splendid colonial empire in Central Africa, French funds for the completion of the Bagdad railway—such was the vision opened before the Germans. It is not to be wondered at that they seized it.

Speed was above all necessary. France had taken her share —her army was at Fez—and now Germany wished her compensation. Germany was grumbling, there was talk [2] of "lost

---

[1] If the evidence given by Tardieu, *Le Mystere d'Agadir*, be accepted, this was admitted by the German company itself. pp. 175–6.

[2] In the Reichstag and the newspapers.

prestige.'' France might be merely delaying and so Germany decided to call for a show-down. Unfortunately for her, this violence ruined her cause.

On July 1, the German ambassador notified the French government that Germany had decided to send [1] a warship to Agadir, a port in Southern Morocco. This act showed that Germany placed herself on an equality with France in Morocco, denied all that had gone before, and reopened the whole Moroccan problem. Her ostensible reason—protection of Germans and prevention of unrest around Agadir—was frivolous, for neither Germans nor unrest were present in the region. It was merely another gesture with the fist on the table, another warning to the world that Germany and German prestige must be considered. It was a mistake because it solidified France and ruined any chance the Caillaux schemes might have had. It was a crime because it nearly plunged Europe into war.

The new situation was received in France with great calm. In England there was more tension, and this was increased by the obstinate refusal of Germany, at the start, to give to England any statement of her intentions, an action which seemed to show a design to exclude England from the negotiations and treat the Anglo-French Entente as a thing of naught. Probably Germany had no such intention, but it was felt in England that this matter must be cleared up speedily. And so on July 21st [2] Mr. Lloyd George, speaking for the British government, declared at a Guild-hall dinner that England could not and would not be disregarded, that England's interests in Morocco and treaty relations with France must be taken into account. Probably it would have been wiser to wait, for the German government had, a day or so be-

[1] The vessel actually sent was the insignificant gun-boat, *The Panther*, but any vessel flying the Hohenzollern naval flag and ordered under the given circumstances to Agadir carried the chances of war in its magazines. A few shots would have sufficed.

[2] The effect of the Lloyd George speech was increased by the fact that the speaker then passed as one of the leading pacifist ministers. He took an attitude studiously friendly to Germany up to the end in 1914.

fore, decided to give England a frank statement denying that they had any intentions of seizing territory in Morocco. And in this they were undoubtedly sincere, for if in the days immediately following July 1st they had dreamed of a German South Morocco, they had soon changed their demands to compensations elsewhere.

But the Lloyd George speech changed matters. Germany assumed a tone of injured dignity and war was not far off. But neither side seemed anxious to press the matter and on July 27th friendly relations were again resumed. The German government stated its ends in the negotiations with France, and the English government agreed not to interfere.

These negotiations between France and Germany had been dragging on since July 1st. On July 7th the German government agreed, in principle, to a French protectorate in Morocco—although they wished to limit this—but in return demanded heavy compensations in the French Congo. At times the Germans showed a desire to take all and give little or nothing, and in the second week of September it seemed as if the negotiations would be broken off. A panic set in on the Berlin bourse, and war was generally expected. But good sense finally prevailed and the negotiations were carried on to a final settlement in the Treaty of November 4th, 1911. By this the French protectorate in Morocco was admitted, although France agreed to maintain the open door for the trade of outside nations. And in return France ceded to Germany a large section in French Congo.

Thus ended the Moroccan question. Not entirely, for it continued to grow for months in the Reichstag and in the Pan-German newspapers. The Colonial minister resigned in disgust and the German colonial party declared that the Fatherland had suffered an intolerable humiliation. These men, in their rage, were now ready for desperate measures; but official Germany was not—as yet. And so the whole question slowly sank below the horizon, its departure luridly illuminated by the flames of Pan-German oratory. On the whole its history is a rather sordid story of intrigue and of violence. Twice it nearly plunged Europe in war and its legacy was an increased mistrust between England and France on one side and Germany on the other. It did not cause the world war of 1914 but it greatly contributed to the spirit of hostility out of which the war came.

CHAPTER XX

THE Treaty of Berlin had long been unsatisfactory to all
its signers. Yet it stood for decades, save only in respect to Eastern Roumelia, because of the grievous fear that
any attempt to alter it might precipitate a disastrous general
war. However the effect of this dread gradually wore off.
This was partly because Germany and her understudy, Austria, were coming to count a great war not always a bane but
sometimes a blessing: because England and Russia were no
longer so much at feud as formerly over Balkan questions:
because the little Balkan nations were becoming conscious of
their own strength and were willing to take a chance at defying the Western Powers, and finally and chiefly because the
situation created by the Berlin settlement was in many respects so outrageous that men grew willing to run great risks
to cure great evils.

Ever since about 1900 a dangerous explosion in the Balkans
was increasingly possible. The magazine became ever more
full of dynamite—but whence would come the detonating
spark? In 1908 that spark was to be supplied by the first
Young Turk revolution in Constantinople.

The crippling and later the downfall of Abdul Hamid certainly were not welcomed by Germany, although there is evidence that the Hohenzollern régime was ceasing to find him a
useful instrument and was getting ready to change its Ottoman friendships. But the upheaval by the Bosporus was
very welcome to Austria and Bulgaria. It meant that Turkey
would be so torn by civil strife that she could not risk a war
if things happened contrary to her liking. The letter of the
Berlin treaty weighed as nothing against their darling pro-

jects to Kaiser Franz Josef and Prince Ferdinand. Their only considerations were those of expediency.

On July 24, 1908, Abdul Hamid, with a bitter grimace, had accepted the revived Turkish constitution. On October 5th, Ferdinand of Bulgaria proclaimed his complete independence and took the lofty title of "tsar." On October 7th, Franz Josef's government announced that Bosnia was annexed outright to the Austro-Hungarian monarchy.

These last two acts produced instant wrath in four capitals —Constantinople, Belgrade, St. Petersburg and London. Of course there was far more anger against Austria than Bulgaria. The latter had been independent already in everything but name. It merely implied now that Ferdinand, calling himself not "prince" but "tsar," could claim all the diplomatic honors of a recognized monarch, and could stop sending tribute to Constantinople. Outside of Turkey there was only informal protest at his action, and even the Ottomans showed that they were not very resentful. After much negotiation, when Bulgaria showed her willingness to shoulder a small share of the Turkish debt, the sultan formally recognized Ferdinand as a royal equal. Bulgaria thus entered the status of a completely independent country (April 19, 1909).

But with Bosnia things were very different. The annexation of the country was an actual, and not merely a formal, violation of the Berlin treaty, and an aggrandizement of Austria to the obvious detriment of her neighbors. The case was somewhat as follows:

I. The Turks had regularly considered Bosnia as part of their old empire, albeit for administrative purposes "occupied" by Austria. Its permanent loss to them was an open blow at the Young Turks then striving to grasp the Ottoman government. At Constantinople therefore there was wrath, with protests and a fierce boycott of Austrian wares. The Turks were helpless, nevertheless, before the Hapsburg military power. They were at length induced to remain quiet and not to enter upon a hopeless struggle, the more especially as European opinion would never have consented to let a partially Christian land lapse again to Moslem tyranny.

II. England was very angry:—not so much because Austria, the ally of Germany, was increased in might, as because
here the Treaty of Berlin (the triumph of British statesmen)
was being torn up before her face. If great international
compacts could be violated with impunity, what guarantee was
there that some day British interests might not be most dire-
fully affected?

When the news of the seizure of Bosnia "came to King
Edward VII at Balmoral, no one can forget how terribly he
was upset. . . . The king was indignant. . . . His forecast
of the danger which he communicated to me [Lord Redesdale]
at the time showed him to be possessed of the prevision which
marks the statesman. Every word he uttered that day has
come true." [1]

But it was soon evident that Austria intended to stand her
ground. Behind her was Germany. The British foreign
office fumed, but British public opinion was totally unwilling
to risk a great war over an issue in which the immediate harm
done to English interests was very slight. London therefore
confined herself to protests and, seeing these were disregarded,
presently put the best face on the matter possible. England
did nothing more.

III. Serbia, the home of the independent South Slavs, was
quite willing to do a great deal: even to risk a life and death
war. The Bosnians had been counted the blood brethren of
the Serbs. At Belgrade there had been plenty of dreams
and visions of a "Great Serbia" which should embrace Serbia
proper, Montenegro, Bosnia and a large amount of Macedonian
land still to be reclaimed from Turkey. Bosnia had been
held by Austria, indeed, but her occupation had been
technically "provisional." When she retired—as by the letter of the law she would some day do—it was unthinkable that
Bosnia should relapse to Ottoman bondage. Serbia would
surely then proceed to annex her own. Besides the Serbs
were more conscious than ever of their grievous need of a
seaport. In 1905–6 they had been subjected to the economic

[1] Lord Redesdale's "Memories": 1.   178–9.

friction and famous "Pig-war" with Austria,[1] which taught them that they could never amount to anything until they possessed a good outlet that was not in Austrian hands. Now all this hope was blighted, and Austria was also building a road for herself half-way across the Balkan peninsula, clearly aiming for the great haven of Saloniki, the seizure of which would render Serbia, even more than Bulgaria and Greece, her helpless vassal. In desperation and anger at the prospect Serbia was ready to rush to arms if only she had a little encouragement from her "great brother" Slavs at St. Petersburg.

IV. To Russia the seizure of Bosnia was hardly less unwelcome. Russia had just been defeated by Japan in the far East. She had signed the Treaty of Portsmouth in 1905. All her grandiose projects for forming a mighty empire on the Pacific had been thwarted. For that very reason therefore she had been thrown back on her old hopes of a warm-water port on the Mediterranean and if possible of Constantinople itself. The pressure of Austria southward was a direct menace to those hopes: and besides, the Russian ruling classes, now that Bulgaria had disappointed them, had a strong sympathy for the Serbs, as fellow Slavs, struggling against Austrian pressure and entitled to the warmest kind of support from Muscovy. If Nicholas II had taken up arms in 1908 he would have been enthusiastically supported by at least a great fraction of his people. However, the moment it seemed possible that St. Petersburg would encourage the belligerency of Belgrade there came an ominous sword rattling from Berlin. "In melodramatic phrase the German emperor

[1] The chief export of Serbia was pigs. In 1905, when the little kingdom tried to pursue an independent economic policy, Austria coerced her by a delightfully simple process. A few veterinary surgeons on the frontier inspected the Serbian swine, found them suffering from sundry maladies, and forbade their export across Austrian territories. The quarantine soon made the Serbs face commercial ruin and they adjusted their financial policies according to the mandate of Vienna. A dozen veterinaries had accomplished more than three army corps! —The moment the economic treaty was signed, the learned veterinaries suddenly discovered that the Serbian swine were again quite healthy.

announced that if his 'august ally' were compelled to draw the sword, a knight 'in shining armor' would be found at her side.'' [1] In simpler words, Germany was avowedly ready to fight Russia as Austria's ally.

The pill was bitter for the Czar but he had to accept it. His army was still demoralized after the disasters in Manchuria. The projected strategic railroads to the German frontiers had not been built. It was clear that England would not fight as an ally. It was even doubtful whether France would be an active ally, considering that the Teutonic powers were not making a direct attack upon either Serbia or Russia. There was nothing for Nicholas' expert advisers to do but to tell him that the case was virtually hopeless from a military standpoint, and that he must keep the peace. The czar most gloomily consented. Belgrade was informed that Russia could not fight for Serbia, and that Bosnia must be left to its fate. In anguish of soul the Serbs (March 31, 1909) sent a formal statement to Vienna that they would cease to protest about the annexation of their brethren and would "live in the future on good neighborly terms with Austria."

So the Hapsburgs and their Hohenzollern backers bore off the bloodless victory. Serbia and Russia once eliminated, it was easy to compound with the Turks. In April 1909 for about $11,000,000, and the recession of the small district euphoniously known as the "Sanjak of Novi-Bazar," the Ottomans agreed to waive their old claims to Bosnia. But it was a victory that caused very bitter feelings. It left many English statesmen irritated and regretful that their countrymen had not let them speak in sterner accents. It left Russia deeply humilated. The czar's prestige in the Balkans had suffered a deadly blow. Another such humiliation would almost have taken Russia off the list of great powers: and to avoid a second humiliation there were plenty of people at St. Petersburg and Moscow quite ready to say, "better a bloody and even a disastrous war." As for the feelings of Belgrade, they were indescribable. If Bosnia seemed for the moment lost, all the more reason for looking

[1] Marriott, "The Eastern Question," p. 381.

on Austria as the implacable foe of the South Slavs, and for
subordinating everything else to winning some other outlet
upon blue water before she could hem Serbia in completely.

Thus the annexation of Bosnia in 1908 was a direct sowing
of dragon's teeth—but for the nonce in Vienna and in Berlin
the Excellencies and generalissimos were very happy. The
two Kaisers had rattled the Teutonic swords—and England
and Russia had alike declined to fight.[1]

This Bosnian menace to the world's peace faded however.
Abdul Hamid was driven from his throne (see p. 287) : his
army of 40,000 spies was sent about its business, and the
Young Turks showed great zeal in all kinds of modernizing
reforms. Liberal journals in France, England and America
contained articles by well-meaning people extolling the new
régime that was giving a new lease of life to the miscalled
Sick Man of Europe. After a little, however, the Young
Turks began to show their hand. Their sultan, Mohammed V,
was indeed a puppet. The government was in the hands of
the all-powerful "Committee of Union and Progress" which
drafted the bills for the obsequious parliament and made
and unmade ministers. Nevertheless, while the new régime
was less mediaeval than the old rule by eunuchs, parasites and
dancers, it was not more humane or more tolerant. The
Young Turks recognized the serious difficulty of governing
the Ottoman Empire—because of the great diversity of races,
religious and legal systems, but they were totally incapable
of hitting upon any scheme for enlightened tolerance whereby
Turk, Kurd, Arab, Jew, Greek, Armenian and Syrian could
even exist happily together on the principles of live and
let live. They deliberately undertook to force all the non-
Turkish races to become, in language, habits, laws and almost
everything else, "Ottomans." The Christians were contemptuously told they might for the present keep their re-

[1] German support of Austria at this time was very shrewd. Besides
putting Austria under a debt of gratitude, it taught the Young Turks
that they were helpless without German support. England (with whom
they had at first coquetted) was shown as unwilling to strike a blow to
prevent Austria from putting through her program.

ligion: in all other matters they must prepare to become
Turks. Arab officers and sheiks (devout Mohammedans, of
course) were also informed that they could get no government favor unless they showed zeal themselves for this
"Turkification." The empire, in short, was to be strengthened and consolidated by a wholesale suppression of a thousand prejudices and customs in order to create a purely
artificial uniformity.

In many of their strait-jacket schemes no doubt Enver
Bey and his associates had the model of Prussia before them:
but they had only the Prussian ramrod discipline without
the Prussian scientific intelligence and efficiency. The results were, naturally, first, disorders, then revolts, then two
very disastrous wars. In Asia Minor there were very serious
massacres of Armenians, probably to teach that afflicted people the advantages of prompt submission. In Macedonia, the
cockpit of the races, Greeks, Serbs and Bulgarians were persecuted impartially—probably again to make them all live
in happy harmony as "Turks." "They treat us," said the
Greek patriarch of Constantinople to an American visitor,
"like dogs. Never under Abdul Hamid or any sultan have
my people suffered as they are suffering now. But we are
too strong for them. We refuse to be exterminated." [1]

The Young Turk policy was riding straight to some kind
of a fall, unless the new leaders demonstrated that whatever
else they had failed to accomplish, they had at least put
fighting strength and scientifically trained energy into the
Ottoman army. This, quickly enough, it was discovered that
they had failed to do. The bubble of Turkish military prow-
ess was pricked first by Italy, then by Albania, and finally
by the new Balkan League.

The news of the annexation of Bosnia had not been very
pleasant reading at Rome. It meant that Austria was tightening her grip upon those Adriatic lands which ambitious
Italians had not wished to go to Serbia because, to speak
plainly, some day they might go to Italy. But the seizure
of Bosnia showed also that Kaiser Wilhelm was quite willing

[1] Gibbons, "The New Map of Europe," p. 189.

to permit his Turkish friends sometimes to be stripped of outlying dominions. He could not well object if Italy now walked in the footsteps of Austria. The Triple Alliance was becoming weak, but the Berlin leaders were not anxious deliberately to wreck it. Now, therefore, with a suddenness that left little chance for palavers or protests, Italy struck a blow to seize Tripoli.

Tripoli was the last relic of the old Turkish possessions in North Africa, for Egypt of course was really held by England. It was a strip of coast with some fairly fertile districts containing a few towns with a certain trade and beginnings of civilization, and then stretching away from the coast a land of palm oases, camel caravans, swarthy Moorish nomads and finally the parching Sahara desert: not a very desirable country but the last unpreëmpted piece of North Africa, and a region which by general consent had been reserved for Italian influence. In 1901, France had agreed to let Italy have a free hand in Tripoli, and at Algeciras in 1906 these Italian claims had been generally confirmed. However, it was understood that King Victor Emmanuel's government was content with "peaceful penetration," and as long as the Young Turks' régime let Italian economic interests alone, nothing seemed likely to happen. But now the new "Turkifying" process was applied to Tripoli also, to the great detriment of many Italian claims and interests. At Rome again there was grave distrust as to whether their "beloved allies" at Berlin might not develop some day the same interest in Tripoli they had shown in Morocco. In any case on September 27, 1911, the Italian ambassador at Constantinople suddenly presented a demand on the sultan, that within forty-eight hours he consent to an Italian occupation of Tripoli, "under the sovereignty of the Sultan and subject to the payment of an annual tribute."

One need not praise the moderation of this document. The Italian statesmen doubtless had studied the life of Bismarck, and the more recent example of how Austria had suddenly demolished the Berlin Treaty without squeamishness or apology. Italy wanted Tripoli. She could legitimately allege various infringements on the rights of her subjects. She was pretty sure she could get the country without precipitating a general war. Therefore she went straight ahead. The Young Turks tried to make a mollifying reply. It was bluntly rejected, and on September 29, 1911, Italy declared war on the sultan. The whole thing had been done so quickly that the neutral diplomats had simply lost their breath. Now they could do nothing but try to localize the war.

Italy promised not to do anything to upset the Balkan situation. This reassured Germany and Austria. With her superior navy Italy could make it virtually impossible for the Turks to reënforce their garrisons in this isolated province.[1] In one sense therefore the case of the Young Turks was hopeless, but with courage if not with wisdom they determined to make a hard struggle to save their last African dominions. Army officers in civilian disguise smuggled themselves across Egypt to Tripoli, and there were some attempts at blockade-running to get munitions to the hard-pressed garrisons. The case, however, was desperate from the Ottoman standpoint unless some great power undertook to thwart Italy, but despite the scoldings of the Berlin and Vienna press, no Christian nation stirred. The Turks were left to their fate.

The Turko-Italian War has few dramatic chapters. On September 30th, Italian battleships bombarded the town of Tripoli and in a few days silenced the decrepit forts and landed a force to hold the city. On the 8th of October, the coast town of Derna surrendered. On the 19th, Benghazi fell. After that it was simply a case of ferrying across a large Italian army to hold these towns and gradually to conquer the interior. The Turks fell back into the hinterland and rallied the Moorish tribes by telling them that their religion was at stake, and sometimes they pressed the Italians hard with raids, sudden attacks and guerrilla warfare. The invaders slowly wore down this resistance and began to sub-

[1] Service in Tripoli had been hated by Turkish officers. It had been a kind of punishment and exile to be detailed to serve in the garrisons there.

due the oases. But although Turkey could do nothing really to save the province, she stubbornly refused to make peace by ceding the same. Things became very awkward for King Victor Emmanuel's government. It was forbidden by Austria [1] to make any attack upon the Ottoman possessions in the Adriatic, the war was very expensive, and the Young Turks, knowing that little could happen to them beyond the loss of Tripoli (lost anyway!) were in no mood to make peace.

Finally, in the face of north European displeasure, the Italians began to strike their foe nearer home. Italian warships bombarded Beyrut in Syria and exchanged shots with the Dardanelles forts, and at last the Rome government seized Rhodes and sundry other small islands in the Ægean. This at length produced the desired effect. The neutral powers grew anxious and began urging "peace" at Constantinople. There were signs of revolt also in Albania and a clear rumor of an impending Balkan war. In June, 1912, Turkish and Italian diplomats began parleying in Switzerland. The Orientals held out stubbornly all summer, but in the autumn the Balkan situation was such that the Turks yielded. They agreed to withdraw their forces from Tripoli. Nothing was said about Italian annexation, but it was plain enough the Italians would stay if the Ottomans went. The islands around Rhodes were to be held until the Italians were satisfied the Turks had executed their part of the bargain.[2] This treaty of Lausanne then, signed October 15, 1912, registered a successful act of the sword. One more member had been ampu-

---

[1] The anomalous relations of Italy and Austria were well illustrated by a cartoon in a German comic paper of this time, representing an Austrian general at military manœuvers opening the envelope containing his orders. *"Problem:* An army of our dear Italian allies is advancing on Trieste, another corps of our beloved comrades-in-arms is threatening Trent. *Required:* Utterly to rout and repulse our admirable brothers-in-a-common-cause, and drive them headlong back upon Verona."

[2] The Italians still retained these Ægean islands at the time this chapter was written. Soon after the end of this war the Balkan War broke out, and then the Turks did not press for the restoration of the islands, realizing that Greece was likely to seize them if the Italians departed.

tated from the body politic which the Young Turks were trying to revivify.

The Italian war had come upon the Young Turks like a cloud from a clear sky. They had had little warning of their danger. Not so with their troubles in Albania. That country was so close to Saloniki, their old headquarters, that they should have understood clearly that in trying to "Ottomanize" the Albanian uplands they were playing with fire. Yet this thing was precisely what they attempted. They endeavored to introduce into that untamed hill-country the full régime of taxation, army conscription and a unified legal system which they were inflicting simultaneously on Arabs, Kurds and Armenians. The answer was a violent revolt in the spring of 1912, which the Constantinople government was unable to quell. Worse still, in June, 1912, the Turkish garrison at Monastir made common cause with the insurgents and demanded the overthrow of the Young Turk ministry. All over Macedonia and Albania there were skirmishes, outrages and sudden death, which Mohammed V's administrators seemed powerless to terminate. The result of this was not merely ominous for the future stability of the Young Turkish régime, but it gave admirable opportunity for the Christian Balkan nations to strike with every possible advantage. They used the opportunity.

The "Macedonian problem" had been the greatest single question left over from the inadequate and unsatisfactory Berlin "settlement." Into this unlucky territory, wedged between Greece, Albania, Serbia, Bulgaria and Thrace, with the great city of Saloniki giving an admirable frontage upon the sea, had been thrust sections of practically *all* the peoples of the Balkan peninsula. *"Macedonia,"* wrote an Italian, *"has for two thousand years been the dumping ground of different peoples* and forms, indeed, a perfect ethnographic museum."

Naturally the regions nearest Greece had contained many Greeks, those nearest Bulgaria many Bulgars, etc., but unfortunately Serb, Greek, Bulgar, Turkish and often even Roumanian villages were scattered all over the picturesque hill country without it being possible to advance the boundaries of *any* of the neighboring states, unless by the inclusion of many Christian communities alien to the conqueror and Christians that might prefer the old Turkish master, for instance, to a new Serbian one. At Saloniki there was a huge colony of Jews. Austria had set her eyes upon the country —its absorption was for her the next logical step after the annexation of Bosnia: but this ambition was of course jealously checked by St. Petersburg. Nearer at hand Greeks, Serbs and Bulgars alike maintained an unofficial propaganda among the people of their race and faith, endeavoring, nominally by "educational" and "religious" enterprises, to make the land just as thoroughly theirs as possible, against the time when the Turk should depart and the ablest claimant come to his own. These three species of Christians hated one another, sometimes, it seemed, more than they did the infidel oppressor. Raids, feuds of village against village, wholesale banditage, abduction of travellers for ransom,[1] and downright massacres of whole communities made Macedonia a land of romance and bloody anarchy. The European powers had addressed numerous remonstrances to Constantinople on the subject, and received rather more than the usual number of promises to "reform." There were even half-hearted attempts toward establishing a financial control and a gendarmerie under western direction. But to the only solution that would really have profited—namely, the setting up of Macedonia as an autonomous province under a Christian governor—the Turks, "Old" or "Young," would never consent. Therefore they frittered away their last opportunities. In 1912, with an amazing suddenness they lost Macedonia outright.

It had been an axiom of the diplomats, oriental and western, that the Christian Balkan states hated one another far too cordially ever to unite for any common purpose. Serbs hated Bulgars, Greeks hated Bulgars, and Bulgars hated impartially Greeks and Serbs.[2] On this reciprocal hate Turks, Austrians,

---

[1] Thus not long before the end of Turkish rule an American woman, a missionary, was carried off for purposes of extortion.

[2] In 1902, when in Athens, I recall noticing very many troops drilling,

and Germans had implicitly counted. But recent events were working a miracle. The Balkan nations were coming to realize their grievous physical limitations: that their boundaries were not to be expanded by brave hopes, fiery oratory and patriotic pamphlets: and that to win even *part* of the coveted lands of the Turks was a major military undertaking. A number of things also conjoined in 1912 to make Serbia, Bulgaria and Greece simultaneously willing to drop their feuds and fight in a common cause.

I. The success of Austria in annexing Bosnia had put fear in Bulgaria and Greece as well as in Serbia that she was next about to seize Macedonia and ruin them all three. What must be done must therefore be done quickly.

II. The success of the Albanians in resisting the Turks was showing that the Turkish army was not everything it was claimed to be. A well-conceived attack upon the Sultan did not seem hopeless. Besides the Albanian revolt was likely to give Austria a good pretext for intervening in the south— another reason for haste.

III. The Italian attack on Tripoli was demonstrating that the great powers were very unwilling to take drastic action to prevent small-scale local wars, lest they precipitate a world war. This circumstance of course made the Balkan Christians bolder.

IV. The gross outrages committed by the Turks and Albanians (during their own disorders) upon the Christian population in Macedonia filled the neighboring kingdoms with fury. They all, and especially Bulgaria, grew more ready to forget old grudges and to unite in a common effort against the Moslem oppressor.

V. It is a very reasonable inference that Russian diplomacy, although nominally urging peace, was entirely willing to have something happen that would kill abruptly the well-known Austrian schemes for Macedonia. The humiliation in 1908 over Bosnia had not been forgotten at St. Petersburg:

and asking a Greek friend if these men expected to fight the Turks. "Not Turks but Bulgars," was the reply: "all Greeks consider them our coming enemies." .

and the fact that the Muscovite agents had smiled in the days following, did not prove that their counsels had always been pacific.

Nevertheless the formation of a firm Balkan confederacy for a joint attack upon the Turks seemed so improbable that up to the very last German and Austrian diplomats, friendly to Ottoman interests, refused to become excited. True, it was known that Serbia and Bulgaria had reached an alliance (March 13, 1912), and that a little later there was a Greco-Bulgarian treaty (May 10, 1912) : followed still later by pacts binding Greece to Serbia, and little Montenegro to her three greater Balkan companions.[1] It is not quite clear to whom the main credit for organizing this military confederacy is due. Probably a large part should be assigned to M. Gueshoff, prime minister of Bulgaria, and to M. Milanovanic, prime minister of Serbia: but common report gives a great share of the glory to M. Venizelos, the astute and statesmanly prime minister of King George of Greece. On August 26, 1912, the final convention was signed. Bulgaria agreed with the other powers that if Turkey did not consent to certain demands, war should be declared on the Sultan in October.

In September the four "allies" made a formal appeal to the great powers to join with them in requiring Turkey to institute very drastic reforms in Macedonia—especially a Christian governor, a local legislature and a militia recruited exclusively inside the province. Now at last their Excellencies the ambassadors at Constantinople began to write out long telegrams to wire to their chancellories, and the newspapers in the great capitals to issue special editions. The impossible seemed about to be accomplished. The four Balkan states had forgotten their enmities and were girding for a common war.

The exhortations of "peace, peace" from London, Paris, Berlin, Vienna and St. Petersburg fell on wholly deafened ears. The promises that the Powers would presently get reforms for Macedonia, if only her free neighbors would sit

[1] Montenegro, throughout, loyally stuck by Serbia. The hope of these two branches of the South Slavs was to effect some kind of a union on terms honorable to both.

quiet, touched a familiar but unresponsive chord. The Turks on their part acted with an arrogance which made hard the lot of the peace-makers. They began mobilizing a large army "for manœuvres" near Adrianople, convenient for a stroke against Bulgaria, and when the Balkan states answered with a counter mobilization, they seized all the Greek merchant-ships at Constantinople. The grand vizier and his colleagues gave little hope of any real changes in Macedonia. Manifestly the whole region was headed straight towards conflict, but the western chancellories with pompous pride made one last formal effort to order away the war god. On the morning of October 8th, 1912, the Austrian and Russian ministers (acting for the other four great Powers) handed in at each of the Balkan courts a solemn warning that, while the Powers would take in hand most seriously the better ordering of Macedonia, if, despite their wishes, "war did break out, they (the Powers) would not admit at the end of a conflict any modification of the territorial *status quo* in European Turkey."

Very possibly the shoulders of the Russian ministers shrugged when these communiqués were delivered. They could at least tell their Austrian colleagues that *they* had done everything in their power to avert a war very unwelcome at Vienna. The direct reward of these peace-makers surely was not large! Probably they merely helped to precipitate the war. One hour after the delivery of this note the Montenegrin chargé was asking for his passports at Constantinople—as if the Balkan kingdoms had wished to indicate their contempt for the Sultan by having his smallest enemy be the first to declare war. There were still a few more demands and refusals passed between the other Balkan kingdoms and Constantinople, but nothing now could avert a conflict. The great Powers looked on helplessly. The Montenegrin chargé, on his way home to Cettinje, said bluntly at Bucharest, "Montenegro wants territorial increase and will not give back whatever conquests she makes. We do not fear to cross the will of the great powers, for they do not worry us." These were grim, raw sentiments worthy of a Bernhardi. Balkan diplomacy certainly was more honest than much of that imported from the west. The only way to argue with it was at the cannon's mouth.

So the "Concert of Europe" saw itself flouted. Nevertheless, the high diplomats refused to get excited as they smoked twisted Russian cigars and read the dispatches. The consensus of military opinion, especially in Teutonic lands, was that the Turkish army excelled infinitely the ill-organized confederate forces that could be led against it. The Ottoman army had been organized by the great Prussian general Von der Goltz and a corps of fellow-experts. Its artillery was from the Krupp works at Essen. The excellent fighting quality of the Turkish rank and file was justly extolled. On the other hand, the Serbs and Greeks were treated as lacking alike organization and valor. The Bulgars were a little better, but they were heavily outnumbered and their artillery was French. The Young Turkish régime had been of course unable to fight the Italians because it lacked a good navy, but now it would assert its full might. The Vienna and Berlin war offices looked forward to the results with some complacency.[1] The only fear was that the Turks might prove so completely victorious there would be some trouble to restrain them before they committed "atrocities" which would revolt queasy stomachs in France, Russia and England.

On the 18th of October, 1912, all sides had completed mobilization and fighting began. The Montenegrins attacked and besieged Scutari, the strong fortress close to their frontier. The Serbs struck southward towards Uskub in Macedonia, intending to get ultimately in touch with the

[1] The Young Turks, after a hesitant interval following the deposition of Abdul Hamid, had fallen as completely under German influence as their deposed master. The accomplishment of this was a triumph for Berlin diplomacy, but the details of the achievement of this success are still a closed book. The English diplomatic service unquestionably missed a great opportunity when it failed to get on intimate terms with the Young Turks soon after they seized power. It is claimed Great Britain changed ambassadors at this time and that it was some years before the new envoy correctly grasped the situation. Meanwhile the new Ottoman leaders had been captured by Germany.

Greeks who were fighting their way northward from Thessaly to Saloniki. The Bulgars, who had the most serious task, flung themselves straight into Thrace, headed for Adrianople and Constantinople. The war thus had four distinct theaters. The Bulgars had about 300,000 men in action:[1] the Serbs and Greeks about 150,000 each: the Montenegrins about 50,000. The Turks theoretically should have assembled far more than 500,000. As a matter of fact, they probably never sent 400,000 men into action. Almost immediately, the discrepancy between their boastful confidence and the hard facts of the case were patent to the world. As M. Gueshoff, the Bulgarian premier, wrote with exultation: "A miracle took place. . . . Within a brief space of one month the Balkan alliance demolished the Ottoman empire; four tiny countries with the population of some 10,000,000 souls defeating a great power whose inhabitants numbered 25,000,000."

For a few weeks the Christian races of the Balkans forgot their miserable jealousies with their neighbors. In the spirit of true Crusaders they turned unitedly upon the infidel enemy that had oppressed them all so long. Christian fanaticism struck Moslem fanaticism as in the days of Godfrey of Bouillon—and the Christian prevailed.

The Turkish mobilization scheme (devised as it had been by Prussian experts) worked on the whole excellently: a very large army of conscripts and reservists was sent over from Asia Minor into Thrace. But from the outset the Turks were handicapped in their communications. They could send no reënforcements by water to Saloniki or elsewhere, for the Greek navy was in control of the Ægean,[2] and this threw them back upon their miserable roads and wholly inadequate railroads. Their first line troops (nizams), to the number

[1] Bulgaria mobilized so great a fraction of her male population at the outset of the war that in Sofia all the newspapers suspended for lack of printers, and the electric cars for lack of motor-men.

[2] There was only one large armored cruiser in the Greek navy, but this was admirably manned, giving the Hellenes an incalculable advantage over foes who did not possess a single warship that was competently handled. The Greeks had also a number of excellent smaller craft.

of about 80,000, were fairly well officered, equipped and disciplined: but the reservists (*redifs*) lacked shoes, tents,
blankets, almost everything in short but rifles, and there were
hardly any competent officers to lead them. As for the com-
missariat, it absolutely broke down. No proper arrangements
had been made to feed a vast host. Most of the troops were
gaunt and weak with starvation when they went into battle.
And yet such was the arrogance of the Turkish commanders
that they packed their dress uniforms in their baggage-kits
in order that they might make a fine appearance when they
rode into conquered Sofia!

In less time than it took Moltke to prick the bubble of the
French Second Empire in 1870, the Balkan allies displayed
the absurdity of the Turkish boasts. War practically began
October 18th, 1912. On the 19th the Bulgars were hemming
in Adrianople. On the 20th, there was outpost fighting with
the main Turkish army. On the 23rd, the Bulgars under
General Dimitrieff struck the Turkish hosts near Kirk Kilissé
in Thrace. Position after position the raging Christians
stormed with the bayonet. As night came on the Turks fled
the field in panic-stricken rout. The victory was so complete the Bulgars did not realize their success soon enough
to make proper pursuit.

Their next move was to leave an army to invest Adrianople
and with their remaining hosts to head straight for Constantinople. On October 28th began the battle of Lulé Burgas
with about 175,000 men on each side. There had been very
few struggles like it, prior to 1914. The Turks fought better
this time. For two days they flung back nearly every attack, fighting like the sons of the terrible Ottomans who had
once menaced all Europe. But the French-made artillery
of the Bulgars at last got in its deadly work. The Turkish
soldiers were starving and had lost their strength to make
counter-charges. At last on the 31st their right wing gave
way and by the next morning the whole great army of the
sultan was fleeing in a rabble from the field of disaster: artil-
erymen forsaking cannon to ride off on the horses: infantrymen dropping rifles that they might run the faster. The

flight ceased not until the Turks were behind the Tchatalja forts just beyond which lay Constantinople. It was a mighty victory.

Had the Bulgars possessed a reserve of cavalry to hurry the pursuit, they might have entered Constantinople on the heels of the fugitives. As it was, they were themselves almost spent by their exertions. When at last on the 17th of November they came up to the "Tchatalja lines," which extended from the Sea of Marmora to the Black Sea across the peninsula where the capital lies, they found that the Turks had rallied, mounted heavy cannon and used sundry old ironclads as floating batteries to cover either flank of their fortifications. The Bulgars attacked on the 17th and the 18th, and sustained repulses and losses. Then they suddenly discontinued their attacks. There is still uncertainty why General Savoff, their commander, did not press the case home. Was he discouraged at the first repulses, was he short of ammunition, was he fearful of the cholera in the city, did he dread lest the great powers never permit Bulgaria to enjoy the fruits of so fair a conquest? Or was his government more anxious now about its allies, the Greeks and Serbs, than about its foe the Turks? Certain it is only that Savoff did not renew his main attack, and that on December 3rd an armistice was signed, preliminary to peace negotiations. Lulé Burgas had been only the center of the Turkish tragedy. Victory had come also to the Greeks and to the Serbs.

The Turkish armies in Macedonia and Albania had been weaker than those in Thrace, but on paper they were formidable forces. They were, however, no better commanded or organized than their companions near the capital. When the Serbs struck southward to take Uskub in Macedonia there was a fierce battle at Kumanova, but it ended in the ignominious defeat of Zekki Pasha who had tried to bar the invaders' way. The Turks fled towards Monastir. The Serbs were hot after them. Monastir surrendered on November 18th, and 40,000 Turks became Serbian prisoners. It was another Lulé Burgas.

The Greeks had remembered with shame their defeats in

1897. Since then they had been disciplined by skillful French officers: and now the Turks could hardly recognize their once inefficient foes. At Yanitza (November 3rd) they won a locally decisive battle over Tahsin Pasha and opened the way to Saloniki—their heart's desire. The courage oozed out of the Ottoman officers holding the city. They had still 30,000 men and plenty of munitions, but they knew things were going miserably in Thrace: the Serbs were coming down, and there was no relief in sight. On November 9th they surrendered abjectly to the Greek Crown Prince Constantine—and so ended their grip on a city which they had possessed before they took Constantinople.

Meantime the Greek fleet was busy in the Ægean islands. With their inefficient warships cowering behind the Dardanelles forts, the Turks could do nothing to relieve Lesbos, which yielded in November, or Chios, which held out until January. Samos expelled the Turks by a local uprising. The lesser islands were easily taken. The Turkish flag soon floated nowhere by the Ægean save from the forts on the Asiatic mainland.

The "impossible" of the Teutonic military men had happened. Turkey had been utterly beaten. Nowhere in Europe did Mohammed V keep his hold, save on Constantinople itself, the Dardanelles forts and the three isolated and besieged fortresses of Adrianople, Janina and Scutari, the last two in far Albania. To ask for an armistice and to send delegates to a peace conference in London was something the haughty Ottomans dared not court destruction to avoid. It was clear enough now that the Great Powers had not the slightest intention of forcing the Balkan Allies to disgorge their conquests. England and France were watching the situation with complacency. The Russian bear was hardly concealing his grin. Even the Teutonic powers and Italy were not prepared to interfere for the Turk, provided a proper arrangement was made about Albania. Therefore in December the peace conferences began in London, the Turks offering haggling small concessions: their foes requiring that they should practically retire from Europe save for a narrow strip

in Thrace between Constantinople and the Dardanelles. The
sultan's situation was desperate; the treasury empty, the
army virtually starving, and at length the more reasonable
Ottoman ministers decided to accept the offered terms, grievous as they were. But the Young Turk leaders, especially
Enver Bey, were enraged at the idea of throwing up the fight
without one more effort to save a better remnant of the once
great Mohammedan dominion in Europe. Their methods
were on the standard Levantine model. Nizam Pasha, the
leading "peace" minister, was shot dead. The weak Mohammed V was then induced to make up a new Cabinet of
fire-eaters. The peace conferences ceased and the war was
begun again.

Enver Bey, however, found it impossible to put life into a
corpse by brave speeches. The fighting spirit of the Turkish
army was dead. The Bulgars were still camped at the very
outskirts of Constantinople and could not be dislodged. The
three isolated fortresses, Janina, Adrianople and Scutari were,
one by one, starved out. On April 22nd, 1913, the last-named
fortress, the longest to resist, surrendered to the Montenegrins, who had devoted practically their entire energies
through the war to the investment of the stronghold. Already, chastened by new adversity, the Turkish envoys had
resumed their conferences with the Balkan delegates. On
May 1, 1913, the Treaty of London was signed. The sultan
ceded Crete to Greece, leaving the other Ægean islands "to
the decision of the great powers" (i. e. practically all of them
to Greece), and he ceded also to his foes all his dominions in
Europe beyond the "Enos-Midia" line west of Constantinople.

The Turk had been almost expelled from Europe. The four
Balkan allies had won a simply astonishing victory. If they
were able to make moderate use of the same, if they avoided
dissensions among themselves and the western powers played
them fair, their triumph meant nothing but good for the
world. The Sick Man of Europe had been nearly relegated
to Asia where alone he belonged. The Macedonian problem
seemed settled. Montenegro, Serbia, Bulgaria and Greece

had all received extensions of boundary which they sorely
needed. The Balkan War had appeared to justify itself by
promising blessings to mankind.

This happiness was not to be. Long before the final treaty
of London, there had been all too many tokens that the
Balkan allies were sorely divided among themselves. These
dissensions had been partly suppressed so long as the war with
Turkey lasted; but the instant this pressure was removed
a situation was disclosed which was very ugly, promising
not peace but a second war. And this second war was being
encouraged by the attitude of a great Christian power, Austria.

In one sense the allies had been the victims of the very
magnitude of their victory. They had hoped to win a few
square miles apiece and to force a Christian governor on
Macedonia after a hard wavering war. And lo, they had almost exterminated Turkey in Europe! But they did not find
themselves at liberty after their victory to distribute their
spoils according to the division compacts which they had
made before commencing the joint campaign. Now, one of
the prime objects of the war had been to get some kind of a
fair outlet for Serbia, preferably upon salt water. The
Serbs soon after their first successes had struck into Albania,
forced their way over the mountains, and for a few proud,
hopeful days their flag had floated at Durazzo beside the blue
Adriatic. But Austria instantly showed her hand, and Austria was naturally supported by Germany, and by Italy also
—which had its own ambitions in Adriatic countries. Serbia
must not extend her sway over Albania, otherwise a clear
belt of South Slav country would be drawn from the Danube
to the Adriatic to the vast detriment of all Austria's darling
schemes for expansion. As a corollary to this policy, Montenegro was to be forced to relinquish Scutari, an Albanian fortress, on which she had set her heart and done everything to
win. Since the Turks were now gone, an independent "principality of Albania" was to be set up under the protection of
the powers, who were to provide it with a respectable sover-

eign and to aid him to get started as the head of a quasi-
civilized state.[1] This arrangement was of course outwardly
satisfactory to the Albanians who detested their Serbian
neighbors, but the real author and finisher of this newly
created "state" was obviously Austria, whose politicians were
in acute anxiety at the threatened growth in power of the
once despised South Slavs.

It was evident enough that the whole Triple Alliance was
opposed to any serious control of Albania by the Serbs or
Montenegrins. England and France were not anxious to
fight over the question. Russia, once more isolated, gave way
before the Teutons. In great bitterness of spirit the forsaken Serbs evacuated Albania, and the Montenegrins
marched out of their gallantly won Scutari. Naturally both
of these ambitious little countries looked for recompense elsewhere.

The situation therefore was as follows. Bulgaria had seized
most of Thrace and by its location neither Greece nor Serbia
could have that territory. But the Bulgars were also intensely interested in getting a great part of Macedonia.
Here were the "unredeemed" lands of their people, and it
was primarily for them that King Ferdinand's armies had
rushed to war. By the compacts made before the struggle
began, Bulgaria was certainly to be given a great extension
in Macedonia. Serbia and Greece could not deny this letter
of the bond. But they could argue with much moral em-
phasis that conditions had utterly changed. *They* had expected (Greece indeed less than Serbia) to get their reward
in Albania. From Albania they had been excluded by the
fiat of the great powers. Was it just that with Serbia denied

1 The Powers elected as prince of Albania, William of Wied. One of
the prime qualifications of this titled gentleman was that he was a
Protestant, and so could hold the scales impartially for the Moslems,
Catholics and Greek Orthodox that made up his subjects, with never a
single Protestant among them! The prince was only perfunctorily
obeyed by the lawless hill tribes, during his year of troubled and very
nominal "power," and in 1914, soon after the outbreak of the Great
War, was fain to abdicate and go home to Germany. Albania lapsed
at once to her unspoiled barbarism.

nearly all her expected gains, and Greece also a part of them,[1] Bulgaria should continue to exact her pound of flesh in Macedonia? The net result of that would have been to give Bulgaria most of *both* Thrace and Macedonia and her allies very little new land anywhere. Obviously here was a case very ticklish to be handled by the "grim, raw" methods of Balkan diplomacy.

Had the Balkan kingdoms been let alone to adjust the problem they might have worked it out peaceably, albeit their case was difficult. The Bulgars were swelled with pride at their victories over the main Turkish armies. They treated their allies with insulting condescension. Their officers were swaggeringly confident that in a new war they could teach Serbs and Greeks simultaneously which race was the true master of the Balkans. They had already quarreled with the Greeks over the possession of Saloniki, insisting on thrusting in a garrison there to share control of the city, although the Greeks had won the place unaided. As early as April, 1913, the "allies" were grievously at loggerheads. As soon as the Treaty of London was signed they let their feuds be seen more clearly. On May 28th Serbia demanded that Bulgaria should revise the treaty of partition in view of the creation of an autonomous Albania. On June 8th the case had gone so far that the Russian czar issued a solemn appeal to the kings of Bulgaria and Serbia begging them not to "dim the glory they had earned in common by a fratricidal war," offering himself as a friendly and impartial arbiter, and warning them "that the State which begins war will be held responsible before the cause of Slavdom" and that he reserved "all liberty as to the attitude which Russia will adopt in regard to the results of such a criminal struggle."

Nicholas II and his advisers were honestly, this time at least, on the side of peace. The Russian secret service would have grievously failed in its duty had it been unable to inform St. Petersburg whence came the chief pressure on the Bulgars to draw the sword,—in short, to expel the Serbs from

---

[1] The Greeks had had great projects for large annexations in Southern Albania: of course they would also in any case gain many islands.

Macedonia and the Greeks from Saloniki while of course retaining themselves a firm clutch on Thrace. The favorable prophets of war were now manifestly in Vienna and in Berlin.

To break up the Balkan League had seemed indispensable to Teutonic diplomacy. Were the four allies to compose this feud, and to distribute their conquests amicably, the next step would be to organize something like a permanent Balkan federation,—"Balkania," as certain newspapers were already hopefully calling it. Such a federation would have been a formidable military power. It would promptly have taken advantage of the next display of weakness in Turkey to push new annexations. Being "Orthodox" and partially Slavic it would have been peculiarly friendly to Russia. It would have lain like a stone wall across that road to the east which was always part of the Pan-Germanic schemes. In short, to Austria and Germany alike this Balkan confederation spelled nothing but calamity.

Under these circumstances the politicians of the school of Bismarck felt themselves well justified in desperate expedients. "Bulgaria's exasperation was Germany's opportunity. To fan the fires of Bulgarian jealousy against her allies was not difficult, but Germany spared no effort in the performance of this sinister task." [1] The Greeks and Serbs were quite aware of the intrigues, and drew together in the face of a common danger. On June 2nd, they concluded an alliance against any Bulgarian attack. All through that month, despite the czar's fervent appeal, the situation continued dark and lowering. Serbia accepted the Russian offer of arbitration. Bulgaria did not refuse it flatly, but made so many conditions and delays that it was little more than declination. Meanwhile Vienna and Berlin were watching the situation with ill-concealed glee. Gueshoff, the Bulgar prime minister, a sincere lover of peace, found himself being overborne by

[1] Marriott, "The Eastern Question," p. 408. To stir up wars that might be of advantage to Germany has been of course an accepted expedient in Hohenzollern diplomacy: e.g. the famous "Zimmermann note" to Mexico in January, 1917, with its effort to embroil America with Mexico and Japan.

the violent pro-war militarist party which, backed by German influence, had gained the ear of King Ferdinand and was heading straight towards bloodshed. In disgust Gueshoff resigned and in his place came Daneff, a violent advocate of "action." Under these dark circumstances it is rather remarkable that war did not begin sooner. The great powers again looked on helplessly. At Austro-German instigation they had agreed on a policy of "disinterestedness" and non-intervention, no matter which side won. This seemed very satisfactory to the Teutons, because their experts had this time selected Bulgaria as the certain winner.

On the evening of June 29, 1913, however, war had not broken out. At a certain boundary-point Bulgarian and Serbian outposts were cooking their suppers and fraternizing amicably, but that same night, without the slightest warning, the Bulgar general, Savoff, ordered a general attack along the whole Greek and Serbian lines. It was a cold-blooded piece of deviltry, devised by King Ferdinand's general staff, and ordered (so M. Gueshoff afterwards confessed) without the knowledge of his late colleagues in the civil cabinet. Savoff and his lieutenants were confident that by one crude, faithless blow they could break the power of both of their enemies at once. Never were men more egregiously self-deceived. The brief "Second Balkan War" which followed was terrible for its ferocity. All the old race hatreds of the afflicted peninsula were traded out. Each side charged the other with gross cruelties, and with massacres of the civil population of Macedonia: and both sides were probably right. In any case, however, the struggle was mercifully brief. On the 29th of June it began: on the 30th of July came the concluding armistice. Bulgaria had been utterly and dramatically defeated.

The Serbs and Greeks had alike been infuriated by the suggestion that they had not done their full share against the Turks. Their exasperation with their obstreperous "allies" was unspeakable. Each little nation flung itself into the new struggle with explosive energy.[1] The Serbs fought to avenge

[1] Montenegro gave loyal help to Serbia.

Slivnitza: the Greeks to show that they did not owe Saloniki
to any borrowed valor. From July 2nd to July 6th, Greeks
and Bulgars wrestled in a hideously bloody battle near the
Vardar. Then the Bulgars broke and retreated hastily. The
Greeks pursued and when the final armistice came had forced
their way over the mountains and were penetrating Bulgaria.
The Serbs in turn showed themselves anything but comic-
opera fighters. Rallying from the first treacherous attack
they fought back steadily, and by the 8th of July they had
their enemy hopelessly on the defensive.

So Bulgaria stood in a parlous way had the war been prolonged, but fortunately for humanity's sake it was not. Like
an apparition from the north there suddenly intervened
Roumania.

That country had remained steadily neutral during the first
war, although urging on Bulgaria a rectification of her very
unsatisfactory frontier in the Dobrudja, as "compensation"
for the great increase in power which King Ferdinand's people were getting at the expense of Turkey. With ill-grace
Bulgaria had agreed in April to make a very small and (to
Roumania) inadequate concession. King Carol's government cannily bided its time. The North Balkan kingdom
waited with masterly inactivity until Bulgaria was hopelessly
committed to a war on her old allies. Then on July 3rd,
Roumania mobilized. On July 10th, she declared war and
sent her army pouring over the Danube. It was again a cold,
non-moral proceeding, but the Balkan rulers had learned that
nice scrupulosity seemingly paid no dividends in the greater
capitals of Europe; and when would a like opportunity come
again?[1] Besides, it is more than a shrewd guess that if
earlier there had come a broad hint from Berlin to Sofia, now
there came one to Bucharest from St. Petersburg. Roumania's intervention of course sealed the fate of Bulgaria.

The "war" was little more than a holiday march for the
Roumanians. Their foes were already so completely at grips

[1] Ferdinand of Bulgaria is alleged to have laid it down as his personal doctrine "that if the Balkan countries were governed by brigands,
he intended to have the brigands on his side!"

with the Serbs and Greeks that the Roumanians could advance straight on Sofia. The military odds against King Ferdinand were so overwhelming that he and his generals soon gave up an utterly hopeless struggle. On July 30th came the armistice which was to be followed by a peace conference at Bucharest, where the Bulgarian delegates were obliged to take the law humbly from their conquerors.

However, the cup of Bulgarian sorrows was not yet full. Adrianople had been one of the fairest prizes just wrested from the Turk. But now, almost before the new Christian administration had settled to its task and while the Bulgars were struggling with their Christian foes, a rehabilitated Ottoman army marched down from Constantinople and without resistance reoccupied the city. There were no means for King Ferdinand to get it back. He could not risk singlehanded a new war with Turkey. Adrianople and the regions around went back to their old possessor.

At Bucharest the peace delegates deliberated until August 10, 1913, when the treaty was signed which once more, for a little while, was to indicate the "final" map of the Balkans. The Bulgars had been hopelessly beaten. The Serbs and Greeks accused them of bad faith and extreme cruelty, and were in no tender mood. The Teutonic nations, chagrined over the outcome of this war they had provoked, could do nothing to aid their unlucky protégés, thanks to the nonintervention agreement they had urged on the other Great Powers. Only the moderating influence of Roumania saved Bulgaria from a worse fate than befell her. As it was, she had to cede to Roumania a large strip of the Dobrudja with the fortress city of Silistria, and she was almost expelled from Macedonia, losing besides her extreme claims many regions that would have been surely assigned her by the arbitration of the czar. All the rest of the original conquests from Turkey, minus of course Albania, were divided between Greece, Serbia and Montenegro, save only some districts of Thrace which were contemptuously left to King Ferdinand. And so the diplomats went home, the Bulgarian delegates dejectedly, the others joyously; and for a little while the blessing of peace seemed to rest on the blood-soaked Balkan peninsula.

In these two wars about 348,000 men were killed or wounded, and about $1,200,000,000 in treasure expended by all the combatants together: figures small indeed compared with the awful sacrifices of Armageddon, but compared with previous wars no trifling price to pay even for very great changes upon the maps. Turkey in Europe had almost disappeared. It had shrunk from 65,300 square miles with 6,130,000 people, to 10,880 square miles with about 1,900,000. Roumania had gained at the expense of Bulgaria 2,687 square miles with 286,000 inhabitants. Montenegro had gained 2,125 square miles and 230,000 inhabitants. Bulgaria had been allowed to make a net gain of 9,660 square miles, but with only 125,500 inhabitants. Serbia had nearly doubled her territory by annexing some 15,000 square miles with about 1,500,000 inhabitants. Greece (thanks to getting Crete, with many islands, Saloniki, etc.) had been the greatest direct gainer of all. She had won nearly 18,000 square miles and about 1,700,000 inhabitants. Thus it was the Balkan powers made their answer to the "solemn warning" of the Powers on October 8th, 1912, that they would "not admit, at the end of the conflict, any modification in the *status quo* in European Turkey." European Turkey had been whittled to a vanishing-point, and not one of the six great powers had stirred. Such were the resources of twentieth century diplomacy!

The Peace of Bucharest had settled that the Turk should be relegated to the barest corner of Europe. Any intelligent man, however, knew that it did not settle anything else. It was decidedly unfair to Bulgaria, which had been treated after the sins of her rulers and of the German influences behind them, and not according to her inherent rights as a progressive nation. It did not give the Serbs an outlet on the ocean, although it brought to them pride and confidence and willingness to form violent schemes for Bosnia. It left Germany and Austria angry and resentful because their protégés, first the Turks and then the Bulgars, had been utterly beaten; they had been unable to rescue them, and all men knew how grievously Teutonic military experts had miscalculated. It also left these same statesmen at Berlin and Vienna terror-stricken lest Russia make some new attempt to placate Bulgaria and revive the almost successful scheme of a permanent Balkan League, closing the German "road to the east." In short, the Treaty of Bucharest spelled not lasting peace but new collisions, and not indistinctly were the battles of the first and still more of the miserable second Balkan wars the bloody prologues to the greater tragedy of 1914. Twelve months after the signing of the Treaty of Bucharest, the five greatest powers of Europe were struggling in the agony of a mighty conflict.

CHAPTER XXI

RUSSIAN POLICY AND THE GREAT WAR

THE history of Russia since 1871 may be looked at in two ways: first as a phase in European international history, and secondly as a chapter in the political emancipation of the human race, in the development of democracy. The first is almost entirely a story of foreign policy and the conditions influencing it, the second is a study of the internal history of Russia. In the history of the causes of the war of 1914 the first is of primary importance, while the second has only an indirect part. And as this book deals with the causes of the war it is necessary to confine ourselves almost entirely to the foreign policy of Russia and to omit the struggle for liberalism except in so far as it affects the international position of the Empire.

And yet this account can only be of historical importance, for the causes which led Russia to war in 1914 are of little value in the study of the Russia of to-day. All the factors which were of importance in 1914 have been swept away in the events which have followed the revolution of March, 1917, and other factors have taken their place. Therefore it is only fair to warn the reader that if he expects to find in this chapter anything that will directly help him to understand the Russia of 1918, its probable policy and its effect on the war, he will certainly be disappointed. The task of the writer is a simpler one: to sum up the causes which led the Russian government of 1914 to enter the war and to place these causes in their historical background. [1]

[1] It will of course be realized that in 1914 the foreign policy of Russia was in control of an absolutely different class of men from those who seized it in 1917-18. Many of the leaders of the moderate liberal movement, who deposed the Czar in 1917 and who were then quickly forced out of power by the rising flood of ultra-radicalism, were perhaps

Three causes probably led Russia to break with Germany. The first was the age-long search for an ice-free port as an outlet for Russian commerce. The second was the industrial development of Russia, the growth of a capitalist class and the demands which this class made on the Russian government and on Russian policy. The third is the force of Pan-Slavism, the idea of the union of the entire Slav race under the protection of Holy Russia. These three causes taken together will probably explain the entry of Russia into the war.

Take a map of Russia. It will soon be seen that she has no outlet for her commerce which is not controlled to some extent by another power, or, if free in this respect, is not icebound for several months in the year. On the north is the port of Archangel, ice-bound during the greater part of the winter, and whose railway connections to the south are also frequently ice-bound as well. Her Baltic commerce must pass through seas controlled by Germany, and her Black Sea commerce must pass through the Bosporus and the Dardanelles, controlled by Turkey. On the east she has never been able to get further south than Vladivostok, ice-bound for three months in the year. And so it is a natural result of this situation that Russia should strive to find a free outlet, either by pushing into China or else down to Constantinople, or possibly by a third route down through Persia to the Persian Gulf. Any of these solutions would be acceptable to the Russian government, and yet, up to 1914, she had failed in all three directions.

The reason is easy to see. Take the case of Constantinople. Of course the presence of Russia at Constantinople is of vital interest to the Turks, for it would probably mean the destruction of their Empire. But behind Turkey stood other powers, interested in keeping things as they are and in preventing any Russian acquisition of the Bosporus and the Dardanelles. In short, wherever she turned, Russia found across her path certain powers, or combination of powers, that were strong enough to check her policy. A somewhat more

more heartily in favor of an aggressive foreign policy than many of the old-line absolutists. [W. S. D.]

detailed study of these various efforts will, perhaps, bring out more clearly the difficulties with which Russia has had to contend.

Russia has tried these various solutions separately. The historic solution has always been the acquisition of Constantinople. Peter the Great, the founder of modern Russia, in the early eighteenth century directed Russian arms towards this solution. Gradually in the next century and a quarter Russia pushed her hold around the Black Sea toward the Danube and Constantinople. But in this forward progress she found two adversaries. The first was Austria, which objected to the extension of the Russian empire in the Balkans because in the first place it would unduly strengthen the Russian Empire; and in the second place she wished to exploit the Balkans for herself. The second enemy was even more determined to prevent a Russian possession of Constantinople. Ever since she gained India in the eighteenth century, England has dreaded the great power of Russia placed on the flank of her line of communications with this dependency, and it has been one of the standing features of her policy to prevent Russia from gaining a position from which this line of communication could be broken. That Constantinople was such a position was clear to almost all the English statesmen of the middle of the last century. Add to this the fact that England had large commercial interests in Turkey which would be destroyed by a Russian Constantinople and it is easy to see why England was a determined enemy to the Russian plan.

There were other allies for England and Austria in their effort to stop Russian development, but as these allies changed constantly and were moved by opportunistic motives it is not necessary to give their policies in detail. Suffice it to say that England and, to a less extent, Austria always formed the kernel of these combinations. The result was that Russia was balked by force of arms in the Crimean War of 1854–56 and again by diplomacy after the successful war with Turkey in 1877–78. Constantinople seemed for the time being unattainable, and Russia turned her attention elsewhere.

Her next effort was less consistently followed and may have

been only a diversion to draw the attention of Europe from the Balkans. But it would appear that in the eighties Russia took up with some seriousness the idea of pushing south to the Persian Gulf and finding there her ice-free port. Turkestan was overrun by Russian forces, and Russian outposts were pushed far into Afghanistan and south into Persia. Such a solution of Russian difficulties was as distasteful and dangerous to England as was the Constantinople solution, for a Russian stronghold on the Persian Gulf was quite as dangerous to India as a Russian Constantinople. And so when Russia occupied the city of Merv in 1885 on the northern border of Afghanistan, the English public had an attack of what was wittily described as "Mervousness" and war with Russia was freely discussed. But the expected war did not take place because Russia, for some reason, declined to push her progress further. Merv was retained, but the progress to the Persian Gulf seemed to have stopped.

Perhaps the reason for this change in policy was that Russia felt that she had a better solution at hand for her difficulties. For many years Siberia had been to Russia practically an unoccupied territory. A handful of roving Cossacks, miners, prospectors of every sort and kind, fur hunters and traders had wandered into the land, but it was still mainly left to the tribes of native Indians.[1] But in the years immediately before 1890, the plan was developed of a settlement of the Siberian Plains by Russian colonists and of an outlet to the warm water on the Pacific. Finally in 1891 the Trans-Siberian railway was started and the intention was to make its terminus at some ice-free Pacific port. But such a port could only be found within the territory of China, which led to the Russian encroachment on that country.

This encroachment on China, however, brought into the field a number of opponents for Russia. In the first place, England and the United States were pledged to support the integ-

[1] The term is a bit confusing but seems customarily used to describe the native races of Siberia. They are on a low scale of civilization, not utterly unlike that of the Indians of Alaska to whom they are, perhaps, related.

rity of China. In 1900, as the Russian plan was becoming more and more evident, Mr. John Hay, the secretary of state of the United States, asserted the principle of the "Open Door" by which was laid down the integrity of China against any attack whatsoever. But inasmuch as this doctrine was not defended by any measure stronger than expostulation, and as England did not appear to desire to act alone, Russia might have attained her ends had it not been for another power, more vitally interested and more determined to maintain her aims. This was Japan.

Korea and Manchuria were vital to the Nippones, because they produced much of the food necessary to Japan. And it was through these districts that Russia had decided to pass on her way to the warm water port, Port Arthur, which was made the terminus of the Siberian Railway. Japan was determined that no strong power like Russia should be entrenched across the narrow straits a short voyage from her own shores. And so that Empire began a determined resistance to Russian encroachment, and in 1902 England joined with the Japanese in a defensive alliance. Strengthened by this new support the Japanese resisted every effort of the Russians, and when it finally came to war in 1905 utterly defeated them, to the great surprise of most of the world.

Thus ended the Russian dream of an ice-free port on the Pacific. But the fact that Russia was balked in one direction did not mean that she was to give up the game: it merely meant that she was to revert to another solution. Within two years after the Russo-Japanese War, Russia had "liquidated" her claims in the Far East—to use the phrase of M. Isvolski, the then Russian secretary of foreign affairs, and had reverted to her old policy in the Near East and to her efforts to secure Constantinople as her ice-free port. But before we take up this last phase of Russian policy in detail it might be worth while to compare the two policies of expansion, in the Near East and the Far East, as to their effect, first on Russian opinion and secondly on international affairs.

In the first place the policy of securing Constantinople was the historic policy of Russia. For a century and three-quarters it had been inflexibly carried on through weal and woe and the Russian people could not understand its abandonment. Then, too it was to them the natural goal of Russian ambition. Remember that from Constantinople had come to Russia not only religion but civilization, and the eyes of the great majority of the Russian people turned toward it as the center of the world. Just as in the Middle Ages Rome was the religious and cultural center of the world for the men of western Europe, so *Tsarigrad*—the city of the czars, as they termed Constantinople,—was the religious and cultural center of the world for the Russian peasant. To place that city in its natural position under the "Little Father," to plant the cross on Sancta Sophia, he would gladly sacrifice his all. And so any move toward Constantinople would secure the willing support of the Russian people.

But it was far different with the Far Eastern venture. Vladivostok and Port Arthur were too far away to be more than dimly known to the average Russian. In them centered none of the tradition, none of the sentiment with which Constantinople was surrounded. And so the Russian peasant trooped off to the war against Japan, not willingly, but simply because the czar had ordered it; to his mind, the word of the czar was still law. But there was none of the popular enthusiasm with which the wars against Turkey had been proclaimed: it was not a popular war with the masses. Indeed, it seems to have been more than anything else a capitalists' war, a war to secure rights for a railroad company, a timber monopoly, and the Siberian capitalists. And over all these projects was thrown the camouflage of the desire for an ice-free port for Russian development: a real need, but a need not met best by a Russian Port Arthur, but by a Russian Constantinople. And so when Russia oscillated, between 1906 and 1908, from her Far Eastern venture back to her historic policy of expansion toward Constantinople, it was to put again in force a policy much more ancient and much more popular than that which had led to the battlefields of Manchuria and to the Peace of Portsmouth.

It meant, however, more than a change to a policy more popular with the Russian people; it meant a complete revolution in the international position of Russia. So long as Russia pursued her Far Eastern policy, England was her enemy and Germany her friend; when she oscillated back to the Near East, England became her friend and Germany her enemy. The reason for this is easy to see. A Russia encroaching on China was sure to arouse the enmity of England which had pledged herself to the integrity of the Celestial Empire, while on the other hand as long as Russia was occupied in the Far East Germany had her hands free to pursue her own policy in the Near East: she therefore favored Russia's designs and urged her on. Anything that would at the same time keep Russia occupied in distant parts and on bad terms with England was so much grist to the German and Austrian mill. And, free from danger from this quarter, Germany busied herself with the control of Turkey and with the Bagdad railway while Austria busied herself with plans for the economic control of the Balkans. And Russia made a very feeble resistance to these schemes: her attention lay elsewhere.

But with the orientation of Russian attention back to the Near East the whole situation was changed. It was a direct threat to all the plans of Germany and Austria. No longer could Austria peacefully exploit the Balkans, and Germany the Turkish Empire; they must now count on Russian demands and Russian opposition. Moreover, this change made possible the friendship of England for Russia. If the latter was no longer a danger to China and to India, England could easily form a friendship with her, especially since the new Russian policy seemed likely to bring her into hostility with the arch-enemy of England, Germany. And so in 1907 England and Russia agreed to wipe the slate clean of any difficulties between them and to pursue parallel policies in international affairs. Even a Russian Constantinople had ceased to be a bug-bear to English statesmen, for between that and a *German* Constantinople the choice in favor of the former was easy.

Another power, for many years a nominal ally, found aid and comfort in this change of Russian policy. France, allied to Russia since 1893, had gained little from Russian support in the years when Russia was involved in the Far East. For France the alliance was intended as a protection against Germany, but during the Far Eastern years Russia was too much occupied to think of her lonely ally in the west. Indeed during these years she was fully as much the ally of Germany as of France. But with the change and its attendant hostility to Germany, Russia and France were drawn closer together. The Triple Entente, France, England and Russia, really dates from 1908.

Such were the results of this change of front on the part of the Russian Empire. Renewal of the friendship with France, a new friendship with England, hostility, on the other hand, with Austria and Germany. It completed the formation of alliances out of which was to spring the war of 1914.

But the return of Russia to a desire for Constantinople was not the sole reason for this new interest in the Near East. It may have been the main reason with the Russian government, and it probably was a strong factor in the popular mind. But there was another reason for the change, very strong with the Russian people and not without its influence on the government. This may be summed up in one word: *Pan-Slavism.*

Pan-Slavism is a very difficult movement to define because it undoubtedly meant different things to different men. Originally it was merely a movement to organize, protect and assist Slavonic culture: music, literature, art. But gradually it took on a political meaning: the union, so far as possible, of all the Slavonic peoples into one political whole. And as it was expressed by the Russian government, it almost certainly meant the extension of Russian power and influence over all the Slavonic race. In its hands it became a tool of Russian imperialism, a movement to be utilized if it served Russian ends, if not, to be abandoned. But it is very doubtful if it meant this to the Russian peasant. To him all Slavs were brothers, the sorrows of one were the sorrows of all, the advantages of one should be the advantages of all. Were these Slavs groaning in captivity to Mohammedan Turk or heretic Austrian or German? Then it was the duty of the Slavs everywhere to unite to deliver them from their yoke. From the standpoint of the Russian peasant, Pan-Slavism was not unlike the spirit of the men of the French Revolution who having voted liberty to all mankind, rushed to the frontier, arms in their hands, to deliver subject peoples from the yoke and to endow them with the advantages of liberty they themselves had won.

But it is easy to see the distrust this movement was apt to bring to neighboring peoples. Turkey up to 1912, Austria and Germany in 1914, had Slav peoples among their subjects and in no case were they well treated. Especially did Austria appear threatened by this movement (see pp. 329ff), for the majority of the population of the Austro-Hungarian empire was Slav and was misgoverned and oppressed. Such a movement as this meant in the minds of the Austrian statesmen the disintegration of the Austro-Hungarian empire, and ought, therefore, to be opposed in every possible way. Especially dangerous was the governmental theory of Pan-Slavism, for that meant the absorption of the greater part of Austria, and of the Balkans by Russia, and the destruction of the balance of power in Europe. And so they denounced Pan-Slavism as an international danger.

What, however, they did not see or did not care to see was that the remedy lay in their own hands. The history of Bulgaria or Serbia could have taught them that the Balkan or Austrian Slavs had no intention of escaping from one yoke only to fall under another—that of Russia. The only reason that these Slavs were willing to listen to Russia was that Russia offered them a way to freedom from oppression: were the oppression removed, the voices from Russia would call in vain. And yet because they refused to see this, they made of Pan-Slavism a danger, and left a fertile ground for the emissaries of the Russian government to exploit. The Pan-Slavism of the Russian peasant was a spiritual union of all the Slavs, the Pan-Slavism of the Russian intellectuals was a cultural union: both were not without danger for either Austria or Europe. The Pan-Slavism of the Russian government indeed was such a danger, but this danger was vastly increased by the stupid attitude of Austria toward the movement.

Whoever may be to blame, there can be little doubt that Pan-Slavism tended greatly to embitter the relations between Russia and Teutonic Europe in the years immediately preceding the war. The movement was very popular in Russia and the tales of oppression of the Slavs in Austria-Hungary fanned Russian popular resentment to a white heat. The annexation of Bosnia-Herzgovina in 1908 and the humiliation of Serbia were blows at Slavdom that the Russian popular mind did not easily forget. The pitcher that goes too often to the well is generally broken, and the constant measures taken by Austria against the Slavs in her own dominion and in Serbia greatly increased the flood of resentment against the Austro-Hungarian government. And when the final blow came in 1914 it can hardly be doubted that the great majority of the Russian people joined the czar in his feeling that this state of affairs had been endured long enough and that the time for patience had passed.

There is one other feature of Pan-Slavism, less important in its effects on the war than the features just mentioned, but yet not without its effects. The new Russian culture, started by Peter the Great, was not Russian at base, but West European and imposed on Russia by the will of the czar. Naturally, then, the men who assisted the czar in this cultural and administrative work would be drawn in from outside. Finally the ruling family of Romanoff had intermarried so frequently into German houses as to become almost more German than Russian. And so the czars tended to call on Germans to carry on the government of Russia. The court circles of St. Petersburg, once cosmopolitan, became more and more German. Bismarck was nearly prevailed on to enter the Russian service—it is interesting to speculate on what would have been the results had he accepted the czar's offer—

and many others were approached with better results.[1] A register of the bureaucracy and of the army gave a preponderance of German names. Against this the Pan-Slavs protested. They desired that the government should be in the hands of Russians, not Germans; and that Russian not German tradition should control it. But to Germany this was a vital matter. So long as there were a number of Germans in the government service it would be hard for the government to take an anti-German course; were these men dismissed Germany would lose a strong hold on Russian affairs. Germany therefore opposed Pan-Slavism on this account as well, and urged on the czar the necessity of German friendship and the value of Germans as officials. And in this it appears to have been, in the main, successful. Germans retained their grip on government offices up to 1914, as Russia was to learn to her sorrow in the war.

There was a third cause that moved Russia to the war against Germany, which was somewhat apart from a desire for Constantinople, and entirely apart from a desire to help oppressed Slavs. This was the desire of the new industrial class, which had been rising in Russia for the twenty years preceding 1914, for economic nationalism and economic independence from Germany. The influence of this desire on the Russian government and the Russian people is not so easy to see as the influence of Pan-Slavism and the desire for Constantinople, and yet it was almost certainly a strong one. It remains, then, to trace out this cause for the war in its historic development and to show its connection with the outbreak of hostilities.

Russia, in 1871, was almost entirely an agricultural country, a land of estates on which was produced almost everything that the simple needs of the people required. Luxuries were imported from outside, but they were comparatively few. Fifteen years afterwards, however, a change began to take place. Manufactories began to spring up all over Russia and their growth was almost American in its swiftness.

[1] Some of the worst agents of Russian autocracy were of German extraction, notably Von Plehve.

Within twenty years (1887–1907) the number of factory operatives in Russia had grown from one and a quarter million to over three million; an increase of over one hundred and fifty per cent. Cities grew up at mushroom speed, expanding from a few thousands to over two hundred thousand. At the beginning of the twenty-year period ten per cent. of the Russian population dwelt in cities; at the end of the period it had increased to fifteen per cent. The production of iron, of coal, of textile fabrics increased by leaps and bounds. Railway construction was enormously increased during these years; in the period 1885–1913 the mileage increased from sixteen thousand to fifty-one thousand, or over three times. By 1914 Russia was no longer purely an agricultural country; it was rapidly becoming an industrial one.

Much of the capital which had produced these changes came in from foreign countries, but a goodly share of it was Russian. And the result was the development of an urban capitalist class anxious to protect Russian industry against outside competition. But the outside competition had become, by 1914, almost entirely German. The German empire was glad to allow Russian grain a free entry because it wished to provide cheap food for its industrial population, but it wished to pay for this grain by providing Russia with the products of German manufactories. Any change in the tariff regulations between the two countries was bound to work to the detriment of Germany, because it could only retort to a Russian protective tariff on German manufactures by a tariff on Russian grain: and this duty would be paid, not by the Russian farmer, but by the German consumer, to whom this grain was a necessity.

The tariff in force between the two states dated from 1905. It had been extorted from the Russian government at the time when Russia was in difficulties in the Far East and needed German support. But in 1915 the treaty would run out and the Russian industrial classes were determined that it should not be renewed without great concessions on the part of Germany. As a result the industrial classes in the latter country were resolved, if possible, to force Russia to renew the treaty as it stood. In the spring of 1914, threats were freely published in the German newspapers and replied to in those of Russia: newspapers were inspired by the rival groups of capitalists that did much to add fuel to the flames of resentment between the two countries. If this was not one of the great causes of war, at least it appears to have reconciled the industrial classes of Russia and Germany to its possibility.

These three causes then made impossible the continuance of good relations between Russia and Germany. (I) First, the renewal of the idea of gaining Constantinople as an ice-free port for the export of Russian goods, to which was joined the desire of the Russian people to possess the place which was, to them, the center of the world. This plan inevitably collided with the plans of Germany and Austria to exploit the Balkans and Turkey for themselves, and rendered a conflict certain unless one side changed its policy. (II) Second, was the movement of Pan-Slavism: the idea of the union of all the Slavs, which made every Russian sensitive to the oppression of their racial brothers by Austria and Germany and, on the other hand, made these states apprehensive of a movement which would disrupt the one and curtail the territory of the other. (III) Lastly was the growth of an industrial class in Russia which wished to protect Russian manufactories against German competition and to change a tariff arrangement which allowed the German manufacturer to flood Russia with his goods. To this pile of inflammable material the Austrian demands on Serbia were the match which started the conflagration.

Conditions in Russia in 1914 were distinctly chaotic. An autocratic government is entirely dependent on the character and personality of the autocrat: if he be a strong man he will rule, otherwise he will be controlled by the men who surround him. Nicholas II was not a strong man. Amiable, well-intentioned, he seemed incapable of a strong consistent policy but was swayed by the feelings of the moment or by the influence of the changing groups who surrounded him. He seems to have regarded William II as a bulwark against the rising flood of democracy in his dominions, and yet he appears not to have been insensible to the demands of Russian patriotism. His foreign minister, Sazonof, seems to have been an upright, conscientious gentleman, although he was without great knowledge of European affairs or a very fixed and certain policy. Many of the court were strongly German in sympathy, partly because of value received, partly because they felt that only through friendship with Germany could autocracy be upheld. The attitude of Russian diplomats abroad was uncertain and even contradictory. A well-informed observer sums up the Russian diplomacy of this period as follows:[1] "It is difficult, even after the event, to get any clear idea of the purpose and proceedings of Russian diplomacy, further than that it has been going to and fro in the earth and walking up and down in it; for, even when it plays providence, it moves in a mysterious way." Uncertainty, confusion, contradiction marked the Russian policy in the summer of 1914.

The anti-German party was led by the Grand Duke Nicholas, married to a daughter of the king of Montenegro. Practically commander-in-chief of the army, he had been working on the problem of preparedness and waiting for the day when his army could try conclusions with Germany. He was the unofficial leader of the Pan-Slavist movement, and his emissaries filled the Balkans with intrigue. Whether he wanted war in 1914 is doubtful; he would almost certainly have liked to wait for several years until the army was in better shape. But, in his mind, the war seems to have been regarded as inevitable, and he intended that Russia should be ready when it came. Such were the plans of the Grand Duke Nicholas and his following,—the war party in Russia.

Opposed to him was a group of men not by nature pro-Germans, but whose policy was favorable to German plans. This was the so-called party of the "Easterners." This group had never accepted the abandonment of Russia's designs in the Far East, and it now urged that they be taken up again and that the Pan-Slavist and Constantinople policy be

[1] "Nationalism and the War in the Near East, by "A Diplomat."

abandoned. Russia, it declared, had nothing to gain in the Balkans, and had no interest in opposing Germany. In the East could the real Russian empire be found, not in the direction of Constantinople. Such was the theme of the celebrated "Secret Memoir" of Baron Rosen, handed in some time in early 1914, and such was the advice of General Kuropatkin and others. The stroke of the Pan-Germans against Serbia cut the ground from underneath this party.

But behind all these parties was the Russian people. And there can be little doubt that after the Austrian demands on Serbia, the vast majority of the thinking Russian people was united in the feeling that Serbia should be protected at all costs. And so, at bottom, it was a peoples' war that Russia declared in 1914, even though the uneducated parts of the Russian population understood it not. But their views on the subject are of later formation: all that can be done in this chapter is to point out the situation as it existed in 1914 and to leave to other hands the account of the further course of events.

CHAPTER XXII

THE LAST YEARS IN THE FOOL'S PARADISE

THE five or six years preceding Armageddon seemed to show the world as an increasingly calm and happy place. This was true despite the shock of Agadir and of the Balkan wars. Great "crises" had come and gone, but the Western powers had never joined battle save in the newspapers. Responsible statesmen had apparently suppressed the jingoes. Kaiser Wilhelm and Bethmann-Hollweg seemed to be treating the Pan-Germanists with contempt. As for a general European war, widespread opinion was that it would be so unsettling economically, as well as so inhumanely destructive, that the money kings of the world, more powerful by far than their "crowned puppets," would never suffer it. If their potent influence failed, confident predictions had it that the socialists of Europe, by some kind of a general strike, would render the wicked schemes of capitalistic rulers hopeless: and this opinion was comfortably adhered to, notwithstanding the firm refusals of the German socialists to join in pledges to their non-German "comrades" to support a policy of extreme nonresistance, and the clear announcement by German socialist leaders that in a *defensive* war they and their followers would shoulder guns as bravely as the junkers.[1] But even apart from this alleged but certainly peculiar

[1] Of course there has never been an admittedly "offensive" war in all modern history. Every nation avowedly has taken up arms because it was actually "attacked" or because its dearest rival was "violating its rights" so wantonly as to constitute an attack. By making this exception the German socialists practically gave away the entire case.

Considering the inordinate hopes which non-German pacifists placed on the socialist influences in Germany, it is not unfair to suggest that here again was a part of the general German peace-propaganda, to lull

alliance of the toilers and the money kings in the blessed cause of peace, there were thousands of other reasons which made supposedly wise men declare wars impossible, and armies and navies increasingly useless. "I do not believe there ever will be another serious war," asserted a distinguished French lecturer touring the United States in 1912, "and I will tell you why—because *we have out-grown wars, they are too silly.*" And vast audiences had applauded. It was a period of innumerable "peace conferences," conciliation proposals, enrollment of women and school-children in peace-leagues, cut-and-dried infallible schemes for substituting courts of arbitration for shrapnel, and for ending the questions of Alsace-Lorraine, Poland, the Balkans, and the desires of the Pan-Germans for a new Roman empire, by applying a few delightfully simple principles for international conduct as worked out by self-constituted reformers, men who knew little of the concrete problems they so jauntily attacked.

American millionaires endowed costly peace institutes with well-salaried staffs of excellent gentlemen, without special diplomatic training, to go up and down the world explaining how foolish it was to dream of aggressive schemes on the part of one's neighbors. This peace propaganda had of course been seized upon especially in America with the customary Yankee enthusiasm for "something new": and no doubt it attracted its largest lecture audiences and circulated the greatest multitude of its tracts in the United States where whole cities were ready as a unit to assent to the cheerful dictum, e. g., that it was absurd for Alsace-Lorraine to

to rest the fears of other nations until the right hour struck. The complete docility of the German socialists in event of a crisis was assuredly one of the most important things the General Staff made certain of before preparing its blow. Of course there were plenty of German socialists who were sincere lovers of peace (as the earnest protests against the Serbian note demonstrated), and who deplored the militaristic tendencies of their country, but the General Staff knew their action would be strictly vocal, and that "conscientious objectors" would be a negligible factor the instant martial law was proclaimed. The German socialists seem to have obeyed the summons to arms with the docility of cattle.

keep France and Germany asunder. But American pacifism, although possibly the best financed, was hardly more aggressive and outwardly successful than that of France and England.[1] In France pacifism took the form of a violent agitation against the army and its discipline, with the clear suggestion that there was no need of trying to prepare against a German attack which could never possibly happen. In England pacifism made such an impression upon the somewhat stodgy, unimaginative and essentially peace-loving "lower-middle" and laboring classes, that any attempt to introduce general military service became extra difficult. In Italy the propaganda also made hopeful headway, as of course it did in all the small non-Balkan countries of Europe, where consciousness of military impotence easily convinced even the foreign ministers that arbitration was far better than artillery. Russia was of course sodden in her medievalism, and admittedly conditions in Germany and Austria were less favorable to the cause than elsewhere,[2] although enough persons were found to write encouraging letters to the pacifist leaders of France, England and America to make the latter certain that the good leaven was working, and that if only their own countries would refrain from irritating the Teutonic "extremists" by insisting on maintaining considerable armies and fleets themselves, the happy day would soon dawn when a

[1] In England the "Gorton Foundation" seems to have done its best to persuade the nation that the German menace was an evil imagining.

[2] It is worthy of note that although the very considerable band of peripatetic pacifist apostles, English and American, seem to have gained limited hearings and cold courtesy, when they visited Germany, and even sometimes hootings and "unpleasant incidents," *outside of* Germany, Teutonic influence seems to have been very decidedly on their side. E.g., the most vigorous champion in the Congress of the United States of "peace movements," and an equally vigorous opponent of increase of the American army and navy, for long seems to have been a congressman from a western state with a predominantly German constituency and himself of German antecedents, habits and sympathies, although undoubtedly loyal to America. Probably like instances could be found in other lands wherever the Hohenzollern influence extended. It is alleged that a part of the English peace movement was financed by men of demonstrably German connection.

fortunate humanity, released from the bare imaginings of war, would find itself unitedly beating its spears into pruning-hooks.

The detailed history of the "peace-movement" between 1900 and 1914, the story of how men and women of apparent sanity and in many cases at least of perfect purity of motive, hypnotized themselves as well as deluded millions of others who accepted their opinions as facts into believing that a great war had become impossible—this story will constitute one of the most interesting as well as one of the most melancholy in all human annals. Had the propaganda had only a little greater shade of success; had it been able to drug England into curtailing her fleet and France into curtailing her army, the Pan-German dream might have enjoyed almost instantaneous fulfillment.

Such a movement, "prophesying smooth things," and providing a philosophic justification for believing what every honest Englishman, Frenchman and American was fain to believe if his intelligence permitted, required of course a literary prophet: and such a prophet was at hand. Mr. Ralph N. A. Lane's "The Great Illusion"[1] seems at this writing as ancient and withal as discredited a volume as the Egyptian "Book of the Dead": and yet it was actually published as recently as 1910. Its issuance was considered by its author (who preferred the pen-name of "Norman Angell") and his backers as an international event. Not merely did it appear simultaneously in London and New York, but also in Paris, Leipzig, Copenhagen, Madrid, Leyden, Börga (Finland), Stockholm, Turin and Tokio. Some of the great incorporated peace agencies with their enormous financial resources, seem to have given "Norman Angell's" ideas their peculiar favor and benediction. The writer took himself with the colossal seriousness worthy of a new apostle from Mecca proclaiming a new Koran. In his preface he explained carefully what were the "key chapters" of a book which had in its first draft "provoked discussion throughout Europe." A synopsis was provided for the unlucky mortals who could not

[1] See note 1 at end of chapter, on Ralph Norman Angell Lane.

tarry to study the complete gospel, although the author, overwhelmed by the greatness of his mission earnestly assured them, "those who desire to understand thoroughly the significance of the thesis with which the book deals—and it is worth understanding—had better read every line of it." ("Great Illusion," p. iv.)

"Norman Angell" was not always lucky indeed in his choice of authorities. For example,—he repeatedly quoted as an "acute American observer," useful to prove several of his most essential points, a person whose name seems identical with an American journalist who received most unpleasant notoriety in 1917 for alleged pro-German sympathies and propaganda. (G. I., p. 324 and p. 332.[1])

This author also took pains to advertise the fact that "within three months of the appearance (of his preliminary pamphlet) the German ambassador in London had made the principles outlined the basis of a diplomatic pronouncement" (G. I., p. 348). None of these things troubled Mr. Lane or anybody else in 1910. His book had an enormous vogue on both sides of the Atlantic and was accepted by its author and his friends as of epoch-making importance:—and important it was, as aiding to mark not the beginning, as they imagined, but the close of an era.

Mr. Lane attacked the old methods of the peace-advocates who had argued against war merely because it was very cruel. Perhaps this is true, but it will never convince the world, because in private affairs men are often very cruel likewise. Mr. Lane knew a far better reason for abolishing war —because it did not pay. First of all, armaments were of little use in protecting "weak" unaggressive states against aggressive ones. Why does one know this? Because little states, barely able to struggle if attacked, today (1910) are far happier and more prosperous than strong military ones. They are not liable to conquest because *"conquest becomes*

[1] These references are to the first edition of "The Great Illusion," 1910: in which the author stated most bluntly what appear to have been his real convictions. In later editions some portions of his gospel seem to have been prudently modified.

economically futile." (G. I., p. viii.) Trade is an infinitely complex thing and all human prosperity depends on trade. The least military knock will disturb it. Thus it does no real good, e. g. for Germany to over-run one of her minor neighbors. "When Germany annexed Schleswig-Holstein and Alsace, not a single ordinary Germany citizen was one pfenning the richer." (G. I., p. 37.)[1] Then why assume that the conquerors will be so stupid as to blunder for another time and seize something that will breed them only trouble? "The conqueror is thus reduced to economic impotence. . . . Armies and navies cannot destroy the trade of rivals nor can they capture it. The great nations of Europe do not destroy the trade of small nations to their benefit because they cannot." (G. I., p. 37.)

In proof of the above assertion Mr. Lane looked at the higher security of the government bonds of the little countries rather than of the big, and surely the financiers know the cold facts:—"Thus the three per cents. of powerless Belgium are quoted at 96 and the three per cents. of powerful Germany at 82 . . . all of which carries with it the paradox that the more a nation's wealth is protected the less secure does it become." (p. 38.) Of course "Norman Angell's" powers of vision did not reach forward the scant four years when Belgium was to be systematically looted after the manner of a Sennacherib or a Nebuchadnezzar.

Trade, credit, the prompt exchange of commodities and the steady processes of banking have become so indispensable to the world that it was really a silly speculation to imagine the capture of London by a host of invading Germans would do any special harm to London. What if the Teutons *did* seize the Bank of England? Of course every other British bank would suspend payment. That would hit all the German banks and their correspondents and "German finance would present a condition of chaos hardly less terrible than

[1] "Norman Angell" apparently was entirely ignorant of the great economic gain to Germany from the seizure of the Alsace-Lorraine iron mines. In 1918 Germans were declaring it would spell industrial ruin to their empire to release the annexed ore districts.

that of England." The German general who ordered the deed would himself find "that his own balance in the Bank of Berlin would have vanished in thin air . . . and for the sake of loot, amounting to a few sovereigns a-piece among his soldiers, he would have sacrificed the greater part of his own personal fortnue." (G. I., p. 55.) Even if the German army were guilty of such "economic vandalism," Teutonic banking interests would raise such an outcry that the war would probably stop, and as for the German jingoes, "an elementary lesson in international finance, which the occasion afforded would do more than the greatness of the British navy to cool their blood." (G. I., p. 56.)[1]

And so through an elaborate argument! Much of the discussion and logic was undoubtedly clever, and many of the points worthy of serious consideration, but the whole book was charged with a Sadducean materialism, with half-truths, and with evasions of patent spiritual facts which made it one of the most unhappy documents of its age. A great English thinker and critic, Frederic Harrison, in March, 1914, stated thus the whole impression which this widely disseminated book produced upon him: "I have long ago described the policy of 'The Great Illusion' . . . not only as a childish absurdity but a mischievous and immoral sophism. . . . To preach a doctrine of Peace as if its main principle were finan-

---

[1] There seem to have been various other Englishmen willing to play with the cheerful idea that military conquest by the Teutons would have nothing very distressing about it. A Mr. Brailsford, in his book, "The War of Steel and Gold," published early in 1914, argued that even if Germany did conquer all armed opposition, nobody would be really one penny the worse. He added his measured and solemn opinion, however, that "there will be no more wars among the six great powers."

As Sir Gilbert Murray observed a little later, "I think we may assume that the author's opinion of the comparative harmlessness of being conquered by Germany has been as much changed as his belief that there would be no more European wars." Presumably a like change took place in the mind of the excellent Mr. Lane.

Pacifists in general seem to have expected that German generals would wage war with about all the amenities of medieval tournaments in silken Languedoc, and not after the robust manner developed in 1914.

'cial and material interest is rank falsehood to all the lessons of history . . . but it is also a degrading distortion of the genuine sources of patriotic enthusiasm.''

Indemnities would not pay; annexations would not pay; colonies would not pay. It would be very silly for Germany to try to get any British colonies. She would be sorely disappointed if she seized them, and as for England it would be no great loss if they disappeared. ''How grossly erroneous . . . (is) the common jargon . . . that the 'loss' of her colonies is going to involve Great Britain in ruin, and that the 'conquest' of her colonies is going to achieve for the conqueror some mysterious advantage which the present owner has never been able to secure!'' [1] (G. I., p. 129.)

Equally futile and non-profitable is the idea that there are moral heroisms or any other compensating non-material advantages through war. Theodore Roosevelt had spoken in favor of ''the stern strife of actual life'' for nations as well as for individuals, when a righteous case called for it. Charles Kingsley had praised ''a just war against tyrants and oppressors.'' Ernest Renan (quite a different genius!) had written that ''man is only sustained by effort and struggle [in national no less than individual affairs].'' (G. I., pp. 153–55.) ''Norman Angell'' is under no such ''grave misconception.'' The author drew his analogy for the qualities of soldiers from those which made good vikings and pirates.

''We owe a great deal to the viking,'' wrote this Englishman (p. 275), four years only before the best and bravest of his countrymen with their comrades of France were going forth to give their lives that London and Paris might not suffer the fate of Liége and Louvain, but the race was outgrowing that juvenile stage when vikings and pirates could

[1] In his 1910 English edition Mr. Lane kindly informed his British readers that in his German editions he had entered into this point at greater length than for them, because Germans somehow labored under the delusion that colonies were sometimes worth while.—I have not seen this German edition. Did the author tell an intelligent Teutonic audience that the possession of India had been of no economic advantage to England, or of Java to Holland?

be heroes. Therefore we are "quite prepared to give the soldier his due place in poetry and legend and romance," but we "are nevertheless *inquiring whether the time has not come to place him* [*the soldier*], or a good portion of him, *gently on the poetic shelf with the viking; or at least find other fields for those activities . . . which have in their present form little place in the world.*" (G. I., pp. 277–78.)[1]

The above are samples of the philosophy and conclusions of a book that in its hour was read as a new evangel by amiable women, and concerning which spectacled professors wagged their heads respectfully in their lectures as demonstrating great discoveries as of a new economic Columbus.

With these opinions, it is not strange that Mr. Lane makes short and bitter work of those who fail to believe that nations should live by bread alone. The American Admiral Mahan had written: "Like individuals, nations and empires have souls as well as bodies. Great and beneficent achievements minister to worthier contentment than the filling of the pocket." This sentiment the Englishman quotes, to make the retort: "Have we not come to realize that this is all moonshine and very mischievous moonshine?" (G. I., p. 309) and more in like strain.[2] One of his own countrymen, Mr. Blatchford, had written a clear opinion about certain things

---

[1] At this moment, when the writer is bidding God-speed to very many stalwart, high-souled young men, his students, sending them forth from their studies to the training camps and to the more immediate armed service of embattled America, it is impossible to resist the statement that the above sentence, putting the soldier in a just cause on a level with the freebooter, represents one of the most unhappy and perverted sentiments ever expressed in the English language.

"Norman Angell" seems to have stood to these outrageous opinions in 1914 even after the outbreak of the Great War (Prussianism and Its Destruction, pp. 230–31).

[2] When I was in Germany a few weeks before the outbreak of hostilities in 1914, intelligent Germans asked me about the acceptance of "Angell's" books in England,—did they represent the point of view of most Englishmen, were many copies sold, how far were they received in America, etc., etc.? It may be honestly stated that "The Great Illusion" probably aided to create *one* "great illusion"—namely, the belief which very many responsible Germans hugged up to the end—*that England would not fight!*

as he saw them: "Germany is deliberately preparing to destroy the British empire. . . . The German nation is homogeneous, organized. Their imperial policy is continuous, their rulers work strenuously, sleeplessly, silently. Their principle is the theory of blood and iron." Upon which Mr. "Angell" freed himself thus—"It would be difficult to pack a more dangerous untruth into so few lines. What are the facts?" etc., etc., (p. 301). He was indeed willing to reach the grudging conclusion that under existing conditions it was useless to plead for immediate disarmament, but some of his confident assertions make marvellous reading a few years after they were penned, as e. g. his statement:—"Take the case of what is reputed, quite wrongly incidentally, to be the most military nation in Europe,—Germany. The immense majority of adult Germans,—speaking practically, all who make up what we know as Germany—have never seen a battle, and in all human probability never will." (G. I., p. 190.) Apparently he little reckoned on living to see the day when current reports would declare that 5,000,000 of those non-military Teutons were then mobilized under arms, and that 4,500,000 of them had already been killed or wounded in battle.

And so he proceeded spinning his pleasant arguments, and hiding himself in Merlin's "House of Dreams."

"Angell" rejoiced in the lime-light of a vast deal of correspondence and criticism. It made him and his backers very happy when distinguished Englishmen like Mr. Frederic Harrison ran a tilt with him in public letters. But the excellent gentleman never heard (until much later) of the comment made upon his book by the most distinguished critic of them all. About six months before the outbreak of the Great War, a prominent American lady met His Imperial and Royal Highness the Crown Prince Frederick William of Germany and Prussia at Naples. She had discovered a certain bellicose vein in His Highness and an excessive admiration for the deeds of Napoleon I.[1] As an antidote she

[1] The Napoleon cult was almost an essential part of Pan-Germanism. He had indeed been a foe to Prussia, but he had given the Pan-Ger-

presented the prince with a copy of Norman Angell's "The Great Illusion," which seeks to prove that war is unprofitable." His Highness' answer was brief and pointed. "He said that *'whether war was profitable or not, when he came to the throne there would be war, if not before, just for the fun of it.'* "[1] It is only just to record that the prince had a great advantage over the worthy Mr. Lane in his opportunities to translate his ambitions into action.

Mr. Lane and his fellow-spirits whose name was legion continued their brisk activities up to the coming of Armageddon. On the 31st of July, 1914, when, as will be explained (p. 525), English diplomats were making frantic endeavors to discover whether Germany would respect the neutrality of Belgium and thus save the world from being completely changed from an Eden to Gehenna, Mr. Lane could see nothing in all the Teutonic schemes that should make Englishmen turn in their sleep. In a letter to the London "Times" he solemnly pooh-poohed at "the trouble Germany would pile up for herself should she attempt the absorption of a Belgium, a Holland and a Normandy." To enter the impending war would be merely for the promoting of the growth of autocratic Russia. "We can best serve civilization, Europe—including France and ourselves,—by remaining the one power in Europe that has not yielded to the war madness. This, I believe, will be found to be the firm conviction of the overwhelming majority of the English people."[2]

The British chancellory, however, did not feel required to ask this gentleman to draft its state papers. Probably Sir

mans an admirable example of how to discard moral law and to found a colossal empire.

[1] Gerard's "My Four Years in Germany," p. 96. See note 2, at end of chapter: Bernhardi and the Pacifists.

[2] "Norman Angell's" assumption that he understood completely the temper of the English people and the egregious misstatements contained in this letter are typical of the whole pacifist propaganda. He may not have known all the confidential facts as to Belgium, but in that case he was making sweeping public assertions without possessing any proper knowledge.

Edward Grey and others in the Foreign Office felt that Mr. Lane and his numerous compeers had already done the cause of peace a disservice simply incalculable. Besides hinting to the Pan-Germans that the British people were open to *the most callow species of arguments, and subordinated national security and honor to strictly materialistic considerations,* such presentations naturally tended to increase the assurance of the Prussian militarists that in confronting Britain they were dealing with a society incapable of large sacrifices and sure to knuckle under, the moment it was smitten by another nation animated by the spirit of do or die.[1] Mr. Lane then could comfort himself that he had at least contributed not insignificantly to the bringing to pass of the greatest war that ever afflicted the planet,—a fame certainly sufficient for many private citizens.[2]

While great peace societies in England and America were spending large sums persuading non-Teutonic nations that arbitration treaties were cheap and complete substitutes for rifles and battle-ships, the government of the French republic was spending money also. This money was not being spent on peace lectures, but on secret service. It was not spent in vain. The German spy system may have been the most complete in Europe, but it was not without efficient rivals. On April 2, 1913, the French minister of war transmitted to his colleague the minister for foreign affairs an "official secret report received from a reliable source" of the scheme for increasing the German army and the political reasons for the same. Neither the men who drafted this report nor the men who read it lived in the "House of Dreams."

The secret report was dated Berlin, March 19, 1913. It set forth that France, England and Russia had obviously formed an *entente* to hem in Germany. The new Balkan

[1] And to England must be added France and America: because the same pacifist influences seemed at work in those countries also, using similar arguments and seemingly producing similar results.

[2] See note 3 at end of chapter: Mr. Lane in America, and American Pacifism.

situation "had lessened the value of the help our ally [Austria] could give us." Germany, however, must now make a marked increase in her army for "properly ensuring her influence in the world. . . . Neither the ridiculous shriekings for revenge by French chauvinists, nor the Englishmen's gnashing of teeth, nor the wild gestures of the Slavs will turn us from our aim of protecting and extending *Deutschtum* [German influence] all the world over." German public opinion therefore must be carefully schooled. "We must accustom them to think that an offensive war on our part is a necessity, in order to combat the provocations of our adversaries. We must act with prudence so as not to arouse suspicion, and to avoid the crises which might injure our economic existence. We must so manage matters that under the heavy weight of powerful armaments, considerable sacrifices and strained political relations, an outbreak [of war] would be considered a relief, because after it would come decades of peace and prosperity, as after 1870. We must prepare for war from the financial point of view; there is much to be done in this direction. We must not arouse the distrust of our financiers, but there are many things which cannot be concealed." [1]

To win the war, native Mohammedan factions must be stirred up against the French in Tunis, Algeria, and Morocco, and especially against the English in India. The small European states must also be looked to: "it will be necessary that the small states should be forced to follow us or be subdued." The Scandinavian lands could perhaps be ignored, but a careful policy must be formed as to Holland and especially Belgium. If the attitude of Belgium gave "advantages to our adversary in the west, we could in no circumstances offer Belgium a guarantee for the security of her neutrality." Germany must accordingly get ready a strong army to take

[1] One gets the decided impression that it was because this financial mobilization was incomplete that Germany did not support Austria in her more extreme Balkan demands in 1913, and so precipitate a crisis in 1913, instead of a year later. The great increase in the German gold reserve between 1913 and 1914 would go far to justify this opinion.

the offensive promptly on the Lower Rhine (opposite Belgium). "An ultimatum with a short time limit, to be followed immediately by invasion, would allow a sufficient justification for our action in international law." If war comes, "we will then remember that the provinces of the ancient German Empire, the county of Burgundy and a large part of Lorraine are still in the hands of the French: and that thousands of brother-Germans in the Baltic provinces of Russia are groaning under the Slavic yoke."[1]

A little later (May 6, 1913), M. Jules Cambon, French ambassador to Berlin, wrote to his government quoting some remarks General von Moltke had made at a German military gathering. "We must put aside," said this high general, "all commonplaces as to the responsibility of the aggressor. When war has become necessary it is essential to carry it on in such a way as to place all the chances in one's own favor. Success alone justifies war." Therefore to defeat France before Russia could mobilize, "we must anticipate our principal adversary as soon as there are nine chances to one of going to war, and begin it without delay in order ruthlessly to crush all resistance."[2]

M. Cambon was a thoroughly reliable diplomat of high integrity, who knew what he was reporting. Upon this question of anticipatory wars, Moltke might have seen Bismarck's opinion rising up against him; although Bismarck himself had not practised strictly his own dictum. In his "Reflections and Recollections" (II, 101), the Iron Chancellor said, "[I have always been of the] conviction that *even victorious wars cannot be justified unless they are forced upon one,* and that one cannot see the cards of Providence far enough ahead to anticipate historical development according to one's own calculations." He adds that it was very risky to let young military men, in their anxiety to put their troops into action, get control so as to menace the nation's peace.

"But it [the military power] only becomes dangerous *under a monarch whose policy lacks sense of proportion and power to resist one-sided and constitutionally unjustifiable influences.*"

The Pan-Germans, however, had long come to consider Bismarck as somewhat of an old fogey, who would have been unable to adapt himself to the up-to-date demands of the twentieth century.

[1] French Official Correspondence on Outbreak of War; Sec. 2.
[2] Ibid, Sec. 3.

The bellicose sentiments did not diminish during 1913. We have already seen what M. Cambon later reported to Paris about the visit to Berlin of the King of Belgium. (p. 223.)

In the face of these warnings France, not without reluctance, but convinced by her military men that refusal would menace the national safety, reënacted her law making three years, instead of two, the normal term in the army. The republic consented to this with a heavy heart, for the declining French birth-rate was throwing her sadly behind in competition with Germany, and this long diversion of the young men to the colors increased the drain on the national economic prosperity; but despite pacifist protests and syndicalist threats, the "three year law" went through parliament and into the statute book. Also Russia was taking warning. Her army was being steadily reorganized after the Japanese fiasco. Money borrowed from France was being wisely spread out on strategic railways. The handicap in munitions manufactories promised to be overcome. By 1917 it seemed likely that the Russian army would be in a state of efficiency partially corresponding at least to its pretensions and its numbers. As for England, the Liberal ministers were giving no sign of building up a formidable army, but they were at least taking pains with the fleet. The Liberal ministry, also, by the end of 1913 seemed to be not very firm in its saddle. The Irish question was threatening its existence. If it was driven from power, the Conservatives were considerably more likely than their rivals to do something looking toward universal military service as well as being, by the traditions of their party, somewhat more ready to go to war. The Teutons therefore felt constrained to take cognizance of this situation which was not all to their benefit.

During 1913 and the early part of 1914, German diplomacy, however, was markedly more pacific than in the past. There was real coöperation between Berlin and London in the efforts to keep Austria and Russia from shaking down the world during several ticklish turns of the Balkan situation. England helped the Teutons to create their precious Albania;

the Teutons consented to see Serbia get a great territorial expansion by the Treaty of Bucharest. It is therefore reasonable to assume that *part* at least of the German statesmen had taken honest alarm at the position to which the Pan-Germanist propaganda had led them; that on the brink of precipitating an incalculable calamity they not unnaturally hesitated, and that, too, some of them realized that it was the height of blundering to pursue a policy by which nations hitherto so discordant as England, France, and, above all, Russia should be arrayed as common foes to the Central Powers. There is to-day hardly formal evidence but there are abundant grounds for assured inference that the Pan-Germanists were told by those in high authority that if they would conquer the world they must not try to conquer it all at one stroke, and that until the German fleet had reached it fullest projected development, say by 1920, there was no wisdom in deliberately picking a quarrel with England. On the contrary, it seemed quite possible to create a Balkan situation in which British public opinion would not sustain its government for interfering, and a quarrel might be pushed home with Russia in which that empire, defeated and humiliated probably along with France, would be compelled to gaze hopelessly at a later "reckoning" in which Britain must fight without an ally against victorious and invigorated Teutonia. This project was eminently feasible according to German diplomatic and military standards. It was a scheme in which Berlin could count on the most hearty coöperation of Vienna and probably of Turkey, but it was one that would have to be executed quickly before the new army reforms in Russia and France could be completed. There is cumulative and indubitable evidence, in short, that by the beginning of 1914 Germany had made up her mind to risk precipitating a capital war: but all the circumstances of the case indicated that she preferred to become mistress of continental Europe before aiming to become mistress of the seas. Not on England, but on Russia and devoted France was the first bolt to fall.

It should be recalled that until well after the beginning of the war in 1914 the German navy had developed its submarine service relatively little, and was undertaking to stake naval issues almost entirely on its dreadnaughts.

Had Bismarck lived and been in control, he would have arranged the quarrel, assuming he were determined to have one, so that infallably:

(I) England would have been isolated from France and Russia and in no mood to interfere in a struggle of which the formal rights, under international law, Bismarck would have surely secured for the German side.

(II) Italy would have been made to feel it both her duty and her opportunity to fight with her Teutonic "allies."

But only Bismarck's office, not his mantle of genius, descended on Bethmann-Hollweg, Jagow and the other urbane gentlemen in the Berlin foreign ministry, who arranged the diplomatic stage in 1914.

In 1913, without waiting for similar movements in France and Russia, a notable increase was authorized by the Reichstag in the German army.[1] The standing peace-army was to be raised from about 720,000 to about 860,000, with a corresponding increase in the reserves. There were to be startling additions to the new motor-tractor and aircraft services, also (as a jealously guarded secret) sundry great mobile howitzers were to be manufactured, which could beat the best forts to powder. To pay for the huge amount of extra equipment needful for this addition, an extraordinary tax was levied on capital, the tax being made the more popular by being laid upon noble and princely personages no less than on the commonalty. This additional armament was to be ready by the fall of 1914, at a time when the new Russian

[1] The German government alleged that the new quotas for the army were simply to match corresponding increases in France and Russia. As a matter of fact the German increases were first formulated in November, 1912, openly discussed in January, 1913, and became a law June 30, 1914. The French increases were formulated in February, 1913 (after great alarm over the situation in Germany) and only became a law July 19, of that year. The Russian increases were not even formulated until March, 1913, when the new German programme was patent to all the world.

The "defensive" character of the German measures can be judged from the statement on June 28, 1913, in the semi-official "Kölnische Zeitung": "This security gives us a free road to a profitable world policy. We are as yet but at the starting-point. Long roads, full of promise, open before us in Asia and in Africa."

preparations at least would be toiling far behind. The new strategic railways parallel with the Belgian and Polish frontiers were in good order: and Prussian card-catalog efficiency had worked out every possible detail for a military effort beside which that of Moltke and Roon in 1870 would seem but as children's play.—What sane militarist would wait, while the Fatherland declined from this top-notch of efficiency, while Russia and France completed their deliberate reforms, and while England at last listened to Lord Roberts?

The completeness of the German preparation has thus been summed up admirably by a distinguished French writer (Louis Madelin, "The Victory of the Marne," English trans., p. 11):

"For forty-three years the conquerors of Sadowa and Sedan had concentrated all their time and efforts upon the forging of the most formidable weapons that a nation ever used against her enemies. They possessed everything that science and wealth had at the disposal of war, the largest mortars and the most deadly gases, Zeppelins for war in the air, armorclads and submarines for war on the seas, every possible weapon, known or unknown, legitimate or otherwise, perfected and in huge quantities. They had secretly accumulated a treasure for war. They thought that they alone possessed the secrets of strategy and tactics, for the rawest German captain fancied himself a past master in all those arts far more than our greatest generals. And above all they could depend on the iron discipline of their army and the grim patriotism of a military nation."

When after the return of peace and the calming of passions the official papers are all printed, the "lives and letters" of prominent statesmen are written and the "confidential" instructions become confidential no longer, ten thousand interesting things will see the light: but among the most interesting will be the exchange of opinions between Berlin and Vienna during the year before the great catastrophe. Austria had no great interest in a war for Germany's benefit against England or even France, but she was intensely anxious to extend her grip upon the Balkans and hold back Russia and especially to break up the new power of Serbia. On August 9th, 1913, the day before the signing of the Treaty of Bucharest, Austria had informed Italy and Germany of her "intention of taking action against Serbia" and her hopes that her allies would support her in a "defensive" war. Italy promptly negatived the proposition, and the scheme was as promptly dropped.[1] Surely not only because Italy objected. Austria undoubtedly was told also by her major ally that Germany was not yet quite ready to have her throw down the gauntlet to Russia. But Austria did not abandon her intentions, nor did Germany ask her to do this. "Serbia had committed two unpardonable crimes: she had strengthened the barrier between Austria and Saloniki, and she had enormously enhanced her own prestige as the representative of South Slav aspirations. Serbia must be annihilated."[2] The field was therefore open for all those violent schemes, intrigues and dark doings which men of Southeastern Europe love so well.

Truth to tell, the Serbs gave plenty of formal provocation to their enemies. There was a constant infiltration of anti-Austrian propaganda and propagandists over the boundary from Serbia into Bosnia. The Bosniaks were incited to resist Austrian officialdom at every possible turn, and officialdom reacted with "police measures" which easily degenerated into plain tyranny. Bosnia was full of turmoil and passive

[1] Speech by Signor Giolitti, in the Italian Chamber of Deputies, Dec. 5, 1914, quoting a telegram to him from the Marquis di San Giuliano, Italian foreign minister in 1913.

[2] Marriott's "The Eastern Question," p. 418. In January, 1918, the Berlin "Tageblatt" carried a statement by Prince Lichnowsky, ambassador to England in 1914, which practically destroys any claim that Teutonism did not force the war over Serbia. The Prince bluntly admitted that "a wide interpretation of the alliance with Austria permitted our Austro-Magyar friends, with our [German] help to combat Serbian strivings for unity which were supported by Russia." . . . Austria felt it very needful to prevent Serbia from reaching the sea, even by merely a friendly understanding with Greece as to the use of Saloniki. "When finally Count Berchtold [Austrian foreign minister], who had never really recognized the peace of Bucharest, was proceeding, supported by Germany, to revise the Bucharest treaty, the world war developed out of the resistance offered by Russia " . . . After this authoritative statement what use of pretending that the murder of the Archduke caused the war?

(or active!) resistance over school questions, press questions, language questions, taxation questions, and almost everything else. A powerful Pan-Serbian society, the "Narodna Odbrana," with its headquarters in Belgrade, devoted its concentrated energies to make the Bosniaks hate the Austrians and to make the Serbs gird their loins for the hour when a sudden blow would dissolve the Austrian conglomerate, and Bosnia would join itself to its own kinsmen in Serbia, now also to be united with Montenegro. The Serbian press, violent and irresponsible, teemed with offensive anti-Austrian articles. In short, Serbian methods, the methods of a small, imperfectly civilized people which had been grievously oppressed, were not nice, and thus gave the more polished gentlemen at Vienna plenty of formal reasons for writing notes and talking of drastic action.

And then from clear heaven came a gift of the gods! An outrageous crime, which shocked the world, which gave the Austrians ample excuse in their own eyes for picking a quarrel with Serbia: which gave the Pan-Germans equal excuse also to their own people for supporting Austria in case the quarrel should take in Russia. So singularly fortunate a happening could hardly have been imagined by the war-lords around the Hohenzollern and the Hapsburg.

Serajevo, the capital of Bosnia, was a picturesque, semi-oriental city of about 37,700 people, mostly Serbs or Croatians, with a colony of Jews. It was a very interesting place to tourists with its Turkish bazaar, numerous mosques,[1] wooden houses and cypress groves. "Howling" and "dancing" Moslem dervishes still gesticulated in their monastery, and there were numerous oriental baths and cafés. There were pretentious Catholic and Orthodox cathedrals, and the "three religions" dwelt together in this little city in reasonable harmony. The sympathies of many of the Christian Slavs were strongly "Pan-Serbian" however. It was, in short, a place which the Austrian government felt required to keep under careful watch and ward.

Hither on June 28, 1914, came His Imperial Highness the

[1] Very many of the Bosniak Serbs were of course Mohammedans.

Archduke Franz Ferdinand, Crown Prince of Austria, along with his consort the Duchess of Hohenburg,[1] upon a visit of state and ceremony. The archduke was not popular with many elements in the Austrian empire. He was alleged to have entertained a scheme for raising the Slavs among his subjects to a kind of federalized equality with the Germans and the Magyars—a proposition that earned him the wrath of the leaders of those two predominant races. He was, however, extremely unpopular with the Pan-Serbists: mainly because his project would have put an end to any idea of ever ruling Bosnia from Belgrade. There is some reason for feeling that certain influential personages in Austria realized that the archduke's visit to Serajevo was likely to be perilous, and that they did not nevertheless order any very efficient police measure to protect him. The dark skeins in Balkan history are innumerable and to-day it is impossible to untangle this one.[2] One fact, however, is certain. The news of the death of Franz Ferdinand did not leave certain influential politicians at Vienna and Buda-Pesth bowed with anguish: all other surmises are unsafe.

Whoever was ultimately to blame, General Potiorek, the local governor and army commandant, provided neither proper police nor military escort for the archduke's automobile as it went through the streets of Serajevo. As the imperial visitors proceeded from the station a bomb was unsuccessfully thrown at the car by the son of an Austrian police official. On arriving at the Town Hall the archduke is said to have exclaimed, "Now I know why Count Tisza advised me to postpone my journey." Still police precautions were not redoubled. The princely couple now left the Town Hall to pass through the city. On the way the archduke and his wife were mortally wounded in broad daylight by three

[1] The archduke had married beneath his station by taking the hand of the Countess Sophie Chotek. She had been refused elevation to the rank of "Imperial Highness" by the irate old Kaiser Franz Josef. It was said, however, that the archduke was full of schemes whereby the two sons she bore him could be placed in succession to the throne.

[2] For a discussion of all that can be reasonably guessed on the subject, see Evans Lewin, "The German Road to the East," pp. 223–230.

pistol shots from a second assassin. The murderer was a wretched Bosniak youth of South Slav blood but a subject of Austria and not a Serbian citizen. The archduke in his last moments is reported to have had his fearful surmises as to why he had been left unguarded. "The fellow," he gasped, "will get the Golden Cross of Merit" (a high Austrian order) "for this." The mystery will probably never be cleared up. It is a fact, however, that no high officials were demoted or punished for at best criminal carelessness in failing to guard the archduke, in a city where it was notorious that thousands of Bosniaks and Pan-Serbists hated him. It is also a fact that his funeral was extraordinarily hurried, mean, and without the pomp worthy of the heir of the Hapsburgs.

Of course the crime was execrated throughout Europe. The British parliament passed resolutions of sympathy for the aged and bereaved emperor of Austria. The feeling was general that Serbia had failed to curb a criminal agitation within her borders, and that Austria would be justified in bringing her roundly to time and forcing her to halt various Pan-Serbist societies as well, of course, as to bring to justice any possible Serbian instigators of the Bosniak criminals. In diplomatic circles this was believed to be likely to be accomplished in a moderate and decent way. There seemed no menace to the peace of Europe. Britain was desperately absorbed in her eternal Irish question, which now at last appeared about to blaze out in civil war. France was racked by a sordid personal scandal and a public trial centering around one of her most prominent politicians. Russia seemed also preoccupied by various industrial troubles. Kaiser Wilhelm departed upon a yachting trip among his favorite Norwegian fjords. Most of the various ambassadors left the capitals to go on vacations. The Austrian newspapers, denunciatory of Serbia at first, soon became admirably calm. The Rhinelands, Switzerland, Belgium, Holland and Italy were overrun with more than the ordinary number of American and English tourists, snapping cameras and buying post-cards. The guides at The Hague did a thriving business exhibiting the famous "Peace Palace," which was no doubt putting all the munition factories out of business.

Then came the 23rd of July.

RALPH NORMAN ANGELL LANE AND HIS BOOK IN INDIA

The original name of this gentleman seems to have been Mr. Ralph Norman Angell Lane, but after the fashion of sundry fiction-mongers and actresses he apparently desired to change his name, and he usually appeared in print and on the lecture platform as "Norman Angell." He was an Englishman, who had spent part of his younger days in America, and he claimed American citizenship: he seems nevertheless to have liked to present himself impartially and alternately as a Briton and an American according to the country in which he was proffering gratuitous counsel upon its foreign questions. His standing address however appears to have been London.

Besides the numerous European cities in which the "Great Illusion" was caused to "appear simultaneously" with great flourish of trumpets, editions seem to have been published in Japan, China, and in *five British Indian dialects*. "Norman Angell" was of course a perfectly sincere pacifist who would have been horrified at the suggestion of giving even the most indirect assistance to Pan-German schemes. It is a fact however that his book, by creating an impression that representative Englishmen regarded colonies of little value, and therefore to be easily relinquished, was well calculated to promote that unrest and disaffection towards Britain in India, which there is evidence enough the Pan-Germans regarded with profound complacency. One becomes a bit curious as to the original financial sources for the publication of these Hindu editions. Of course Mr. Lane was wholly innocent of any distasteful uses to which this book might be put.

Recent neutrality trials in America have shown the great interest the German propagandists took in Indian affairs and their willingness to resort to even the most far-fetched and indirect weapons.

BERNHARDI AND THE PACIFISTS

One cannot read through "The Great Illusion" and then Bernhardi's "Germany and the Next War" without feeling that, in everything save bloodless humanitarianism, the German is, as a practical philosopher, superior,—more candid with himself, more willing to face disagreeable facts as he sees them, more willing to accept the logical consequences of his philosophy, more willing to uphold a heroic and non-sordid standard for his countrymen, more willing to tell them plainly that they must be ready for great material and spiritual sacrifices in behalf of those things which mighty nations are wont to hold dear.

To-day one rises from reading a mass of antebellum Pan-Germanist tracts with sentiments of wrath, but from a similar volume of Anglo-American pacifist literature simply with disgust.

The Pan-German had all the crude, headlong valor of the desert lion. His contemporary, the professional pacifist, exhibited all the traits of the desert ostrich. The latter animal, with his head in the sand, has never been counted the king of beasts.

MR. LANE IN AMERICA, AND AMERICAN PACIFISM

After the outbreak of the war Mr. Lane, finding his countrymen becoming chilly to his preachments, withdrew to America. During the earlier stages of our "preparedness" movement he is alleged to have done yeoman service in haggling at the effort for a better American army and navy:—e.g. at the "Lake Mohonk Conference," May 20, 1915, two weeks after the sinking of the *Lusitania* he is reported to have taken violent issue with the views of Secretary of War Garrison and other responsible officials of the United States Government. "Mr. Angell [Lane] fairly ran to the speaker's stand to make his reply," stated the New York "Times."

Later in 1915, having caught the stride of American opinion, he apparently modified his opposition to preparedness. On November 11, 1915, he is alleged to have predicted that we would "probably" have war with Japan. (N. Y. "Times," Nov. 12, 1915.) At last, having seemingly exhausted the round of the uplift societies and the patronage of the peace propagandists, he took himself back to the land of his birth. He was, it would seem, in England when in 1917 America no less than Britain repudiated his materialistic gospel of 1910 and entered the great war, not to win sordid profits but to redeem her soul.

When crossing the Atlantic in the spring of 1914 the present writer found on his steamer an estimable clergyman from a small city in Ohio. The good man was on his way to attend an unofficial peace-conference to be held, as I recall, in Brussels.

"We have seen our last war," my excellent friend liked to declare, and when we passed a British cruiser he denounced the vessel as "one of the most absolutely useless things in the world"! All ideas of armed conflict were merely "wicked imaginings, for it was impossible to believe that Providence could allow such fearful things to happen again."

In his steamer chair my friend read not light novels, but Mr. Lane's "The Great Illusion" and sundry writings by American pacifists which squared the international circle with equal erudition, but which are now of merely archæological interest.

In conversation, this gentleman exhibited a complete ignorance of the most ordinary events and problems of European history, but he was entirely ready to offer panaceas for all the international ills of the old world and the new. He was, of course, an American and had the American privilege of snap judgments on perfectly strange questions, but many of his English contemporaries were hardly better. I well recall in 1912 a crowded parlor in a large hotel at Ilfracombe, England, where, to a typical "middle class" audience, a popular lecturer for the peace interests demonstrated with mathematical certainty that war between England and Germany was an absolute impossibility, and that those who made serious preparation for it were fools as well as knaves. This particular worthy commended the diffusion of "Esperanto" as the cure-all for international ills.

I have not the slightest doubt of the sincerity of these two gentlemen nor of most of their fellow-workers, but the service such good souls unconsciously rendered to Pan-Germanism is not to be computed in dollars, pounds,—or marks.

CHAPTER XXIII

SOWING THE WIND—THE SERBIAN NOTE [1]

ON July 25, 1914, the London "Spectator," a periodical by no means pacifistic, and one that frequently spoke of the "German danger," began its front-page news summary thus: "The news of the week which eclipses all others in interest and importance is the meeting of the Conference of political leaders which assembled [to consider the Irish question] at Buckingham palace on Thursday, and is sitting as we write." On the third page there was a vague statement that a serious situation existed between Serbia and Austria, and that Austria had sent a note "whereof the language was exceedingly emphatic." On the fifth page was a somewhat perfunctory editorial which said that the tension between Austria and Serbia appeared extreme, but "even if things look blacker than they do now . . . we cannot believe Franz Josef will let his government go to war," and scoffed at the idea of any but a peaceful solution to the crisis.

Two weeks later this same periodical was telling its readers that the great European war, "so often predicted," had come to pass, and was discussing the strategy and tactics of the generals and admirals.

As a matter of fact, the war cloud first really gathered on July 23rd. It broke with complete fury on August 4th. What had happened in the interval? These twelve days comprise one of the most fearful and memorable fortnights in universal history.

---

[1] The numerous quotations in this and the following chapter are nearly all from the various official "books" of diplomatic correspondence published by the belligerent governments at the outbreak of the war. These "books" are so well known that specific references have seemed pedantic and superfluous.

Until the German government shall open its private archives, it is impossible to trace the details of events between June 29th and July 23rd, 1914. But there seems to be absolutely reliable evidence that early in July a great state council was held at which it was determined to precipitate war just as soon as possible, or else to inflict upon Russia such a diplomatic humiliation as would shake her whole prestige and position as a great power, and as a result establish the Teutonic empires as the resistless dominators of the Balkans. Shortly after the outbreak of actual hostilities, Baron Wangenheim, the German ambassador at Constantinople, in an outburst of enthusiasm over the early successes of his country, made a statement to his colleague, Mr. Morgenthau, the American ambassador to Turkey: "The German ambassador informed me [Morgenthau] that a conference had been held in the early part of July [1914] at which the date of the war was fixed. This conference was presided over by the Kaiser: Baron Wangenheim was present to report on conditions in Turkey. Moltke, the Chief of Staff, was there, and so was Grand Admiral von Tirpitz. With them were the leaders of German finance, the directors of the railroads, and the captains of industry. . . . Each was asked if he were ready for the war. All replied in the affirmative, except the financiers, who insisted that they must have two weeks in which to sell foreign securities and arrange their loans." His Excellency the Baron seems to have told the same story also to his colleague the Italian ambassador to Constantinople. There is not the least reason to doubt that this tale is substantially true.[1]

After the Great War began, all the governments interested issued collections of "papers," diplomatic correspondence between foreign ministers and envoys, setting forth how the disaster came about and of course absolving the country issuing the particular "book" from guilt or blame. These "papers" possess enormous interest and importance. The fullest of them are incomplete. Even the ones that seem

[1] See end of chapter: note on The Precipitation of the War by Germany.

most straightforward contain obvious omissions. They of course give only a minor fraction of the whole vast story. But taken in the aggregate (and they fill in all two large volumes), they constitute an interlocking record of these terrible Twelve Days, such as makes quite sufficient evidence for the jury "in the court of civilization." Men go to the gallows every day from competent criminal courts on testimony far less complete than that in the ponderous "Diplomatic Documents relating to the Outbreak of the European War." [1] One does not therefore feel obliged to wait half a century before calling a spade a spade. From the outset of the great struggle in Europe, the analysis of this official evidence has been keen and ardent: and the conclusion has already been accepted in almost every civilized land save those dominated by Teutonism, as proving that Germany and Austria between them, prime-mover and supple accomplice, precipitated Armageddon to serve their own aggressive ends.

It is superfluity therefore to give a new analysis of the documents, when to have any original probative value, that analysis ought to be very searching and complete. There is some value, however, in giving a bald recital of the principal happenings on each one of these terrible days, that one may see precisely how the torch was finally applied to the magazine. This cursory treatment becomes all the more justifiable if the earlier part of this book has carried any conviction as to its main thesis—that the Pan-Germanists had gained control of the wills and purposes of the disposing personages in the Teutonic empires and had already prepared the magazines of explosives which now took fire. Woe unto the reckless fool who willfully kindles the flame that will cause the indescribable explosion. Greater woe unto the supposedly sane man who deliberately prepares the combustibles where he well knows the spark may fall. Greatest woe

[1] The most complete edition is in two large volumes issued by the "Carnegie Endowment for International Peace, Division of International Law": 1916. This arm of the peace movement kept itself honorably clear of certain pacifist proceedings which seem to have fitted in well with Pan-German policy.

of all to the offender if he who has cheerfully prepared the powder as cheerfully also brings near the spark!

July 23, 1914, announced the approach of "The Day." Upon it was unmasked the first deliberate step in the attempt to found a second "Roman" Empire.

At six o'clock on the balmy summer evening of "The Day," when the cafés of Belgrade were full of peaceful citizens over their sugar-water and syrupy Turkish coffee, when the market had broken up and the Serbian peasant women were trudging back to the villages with the gains from their chickens and cabbages, and when the band was playing in the beautiful gardens overlooking the Danube, His Excellency, Freiherr von Giesl, the minister of Austria, presented himself at the office of M. Patchóu, the Serbian minister of finance. He did not go to the Serbian foreign ministry because M. Pashitch, the premier, who also handled foreign matters, was absent from the little capital: and the Austrian minister's business seemed urgent: so urgent indeed that he could not wait although nearly all the Serbian cabinet was away from Belgrade electioneering in view of the coming choice of a new chamber of deputies. Freiherr von Giesl presented an official document and added verbally that he was under orders that "if the note was not accepted integrally within forty-eight hours, he was to leave Belgrade with the staff of the legation."

M. Patchou was so agitated when he read the document that he at once telegraphed for all his colleagues to come back to Belgrade, and also got in touch with the Russian chargé d'affaires. He informed the latter "that he solicited the help of Russia, for no Serbian government could accept the demands of Austria." The next morning the wires not merely from Belgrade but from Berlin, Vienna, St. Petersburg, Paris, London and Rome were overladen with the messages of excited diplomats, and M. Sazonof, the czar's minister for foreign affairs, was issuing a frantic appeal for moderating counsels whereby "to prevent consequences, incalculable and equally fatal for all the powers." Obviously the good

Von Giesl had had the honor of delivering a somewhat momentous document. The "Serbian note" had been thrust upon the world.[1]

The Austrian note to Serbia will remain a famous document hundreds of years after the millions who first read it have mouldered in their graves. It marks the end of one era in the world's history, the beginning of yet another. The French Revolution is commonly held to fairly begin with the fall of the Bastile. A revolution in the polity and economy of the entire world was undoubtedly to begin with the delivery of that typewritten paper by the peaceful-looking Freiherr von Giesl.

The document was instantly recognized as charged with dynamite. It recited the sins of the Serbian government in failing to check the unfriendly and obnoxious Pan-Serbist agitation, called on the Serbian government to make formal repudiation of the same in its "official journal," then added ten categorical demands whereof the substance was that King Peter's ministers forthwith promise to suppress every paper "inciting to hatred and contempt" of Austria, to dissolve the Pan-Serbist society, the Narodna Odbrana, and all similar

---

[1] The question arises,—why, if Germany and her Austrian accomplice were bent on war, they went to any trouble to fish up a pretext, and indulge in twelve days of diplomatic stress? The answer is that dominant as were Pan-German influences around William II, they were by no means so strong in the empire at large, that the conscience of the German nation would have supported heartily the necessary sacrifices of a war which the dullest minds could perceive had been wantonly provoked, and in which the whole empire was asked to bleed for the selfish aggrandizement of the not always popular junker class. The nation had been sufficiently drugged so that a flimsy pretext might suffice, more flimsy than in almost any other great country: but a certain pretext there had to be. Besides, a sop had also to be cast to neutral opinion, especially to England, if she was expected to keep out of the struggle.

It may also be added that around the Kaiser were doubtless influential men of a somewhat moderate caste, who sincerely preferred a great diplomatic advantage for Teutonic influence in the Balkans (as the humiliation of Serbia would have been) to the more perilous joys of a capital war, certainly involving Russia and France. They were willing to take great risks of war, but they accepted peace if they could reap enormous advantages.

societies, to dismiss from the Serbian public service all military and civil officers "guilty of propaganda against Austria whose names and deeds the Austrian government reserved to itself the right of communicating" (i. e. without letting Serbia satisfy itself of their guilt), "to accept the collaboration *in Serbia* of representatives of the Austrian government" to help put down the anti-Austrian propaganda, to prosecute the accessories in Serbia to the plot against the archduke, in the investigation of which delegates of the Austrian government will take part, to arrest two Serbian officials who had been implicated by the trial at Serajevo, and to put a stop to the smuggling of arms from Serbia into Bosnia.

But the most deadly sting of this scorpion was in the tail. "The Austrian government expects the reply of the royal [Serbian] government at the latest by 6 o'clock on Saturday evening, the 25th of July."

Any person with a smattering of international law knew that Serbia could not assent to the demands that Austrian officials should enter the country to sit in judgment on Serbian subjects (whose guilt seemed assumed in advance) without withdrawing King Peter's kingdom automatically from the list of self-respecting and independent countries. From the outset the diplomats who read this note knew one or two things to be true: either the Vienna foreign office assumed the Serbians to be veritable rabbits ready to barter soul and honor for safety, or Vienna wished for nothing but war. *And only forty-eight hours were left to Serbia to decide either to sign away her national independence, or engage in a deadly struggle against hopeless odds;*—unless Russia stirred. Then the South Slav cried to the North Slav, and he did not cry in vain.

During the terrible Twelve Days which were to follow a large number of diplomats were to sign dispatches that will live long in history, but of course certain figures played the greater parts. In St. Petersburg it was M. Sazonof, the reasonable and moderate foreign minister, one of the really capable men whom Nicholas II, with all his faults, contrived to enroll in his service. In Vienna it was Count

Berchtold, Franz Josef's foreign minister, bent on a snug little war with Serbia at almost all hazards, but perhaps not so anxious as his compeers at Berlin to bring to pass the universal "Day." At Berlin it was (on the surface) the Chancellor Bethmann-Hollweg and his smooth foreign secretary Von Jagow, speaking "peace" with their lips and yet somehow always rejecting any effective proposition for ensuring it. At Paris there was at first merely an acting foreign minister, because President Poincaré and Premier and Foreign Minister Viviani were on a battleship returning from a visit to Russia, and then it was those gentlemen themselves. At London it was above all else the secretary of state for foreign affairs, Sir Edward Grey, one of the ablest members of the Liberal cabinet, accounted an honest lover of peace through fair dealing, and a high-minded gentleman of the best British type, who refused down to the last minute to account the case desperate so long as an honorable expedient remained untested. And at every one of the capitals there were of course also the care-laden ambassadors, haunting the anterooms of the foreign ministers, and keeping the wires hot with their hourly messages homeward.

One great European power plays only a minor part amid all this mounting in hot haste. Italy was nominally the ally of Austria and of Germany. But the Teutonic empires had not deigned to notify her in advance of their intentions, nor to take her in the least into their confidence. She was left to guess at their intentions with the rest. Her statesmen raised their voices for peace along with those of the Triple Entente, but for the nonce they were helpless witnesses, not participants, of the mighty things coming to pass.[1]

On the morning of July 24th, the various Austrian embassies communicated the instantly famous "note" to the foreign offices of the other powers and cheerfully awaited results. The delivery of the note at Belgrade had been devil-

[1] The moment Germany delivered her ultimatum to Russia and France, Italy announced that she considered German intentions aggressive not defensive, and that consequently she was not bound by the Triple Alliance and would stand neutral. (Aug. 1, 1914.)

ishly well-timed. Nominally forty-eight hours of grace were given. Actually by delivering the document at 6 P. M., it was the next morning before the various foreign ministers would have real opportunity to digest the same. It was well on toward noon of the 24th before the forces interested in preserving peace could begin their activities: of the "forty-eight" hours graciously provided, seventeen or even eighteen were thus gone.

One of Sir Edward Grey's first comments was: "I had never seen one state address to another independent state a document of so formidable a character": he added that the demand to send Austrian officials into Serbia was subversive of Serbian independence. At St. Petersburg, M. Sazonof met in haste with the French and English ambassadors. His diagnosis of the case was expert and speedy. "Austria's conduct was both provocative and immoral. She would never have taken such action unless Germany had first been consulted." Sazonof now begged of Great Britain that she declare that in case of war she would fight beside Russia and France. The latter was bound by firm treaty to Russia in any case, but England only by an informal "entente" for diplomatic coöperation. If the Teutons, however, were sure they would have to fight England also they might recede. The British ambassador and Grey in London could not, however, give a binding engagement as to this. English public opinion would never sanction a war which seemed primarily to defend Serbia and Russia. All that London could then promise was to put pressure on Berlin and Vienna to keep the peace: and this pledge was most vigorously fulfilled.

Meantime in Austria the Russian ambassador was hastening back from his vacation by fast train to Vienna. In his stead the Russian chargé was presenting an urgent request that Austria extend her forty-eight hour time limit for Serbia, to see if some outlet could not be arranged from a black situation. "He was very coldly received," the Vienna and Berlin papers reported gleefully: and in fact his request was absolutely disregarded. And so night fell upon the world with the telegraphers still pounding their keys with countless "urgent" diplomatic dispatches.

On July 25th Sazonof announced that Serbia might evacuate Belgrade and allow Austria to seize it without fighting. Such a move ought to satisfy the pride of Vienna. After that, "Russia would be quite willing to stand aside and leave the question in the hands of England, France, Germany and Italy." He said, however, that if worst came to worst, "Russia could not allow Austria to crush Serbia and become the predominant power in the Balkan. . . . He did not wish to precipitate a conflict, but unless Germany could restrain Austria the situation could be regarded as desperate."

Thus at St. Petersburg; while in Belgrade the pressure was extreme from all the non-Teutonic powers upon King Peter's cabinet to do everything possible to meet the demands of Austria. The Serbs were terror-stricken. They knew that part of the Austrian demands were justifiable; that the Pan-Serbist propaganda had been undeniably unfriendly; and that there had been unseemly rejoicings in Belgrade at the news of the murder of the archduke. Besides, Serbia had been in bad odor in Europe ever since the killing of King Alexander. Russia was not anxious for war, and France very loath to pour out blood and treasure purely over a Balkan squabble. England was still more unwilling. As a result the Serbs almost literally fell on their knees. They did everything but pawn their national independence. For practical purposes they assented to every one of the drastic Austrian demands save only those requiring that Austrian officials should conduct investigations and trials on Serbian soil, and they would accept this so far as it "agrees with the principle of international law, with criminal procedure, and with good neighborly relations." If Austria was not satisfied with this reply Serbia would be glad to refer all mooted questions "to the decision of the international tribunal of The Hague." [1]

[1] It took an amazingly long time for professional pacifists in America and elsewhere to discover how completely this suggestion was ignored by the Teutons: it did not even receive the poor honor of abusive comment.

It was 5:45 P. M. when this formal humiliation of a weak nation before a strong one was placed in the hands of Von Giesl, the Austrian minister. That noble gentleman evidently did not feel required to waste much time studying its clauses, to see whether under their "evasive" and "unsatisfactory" phrases (so the Vienna papers soon announced) there might not be terms admitting of accommodation and peace. Also little time was wasted telegraphing the document to Vienna and weighing its terms in Franz Josef's cabinet: for practical purposes the Serbs might just as well have flung back brave defiance. *At 6:30 P. M.* Freiherr von Giesl handed in a note at Belgrade "that *not having received a satisfactory answer* within the time limit set, he was leaving Belgrade with the entire staff of the legation." The train containing this "high-born" Austrian soon rumbled over the Danube into his own empire. Diplomatic relations were broken, and the mobilization of troops opposite the Serbian capital and the approach of Austrian river monitors indicated that bullets would soon supersede protocols. In Buda-Pesth and Vienna there was parading and huzzaing in the streets. Serbia was weak and very much hated. It was generally felt that Russia would not dare to stir in the face of Germany. The short easy war seemed very popular. The invasion of Serbia would be merely a promenade. Such was the morning and the evening of the second day.

On the 26th the diplomats somewhat anxiously waited for the next move. Breaking friendly relations was not quite the same as declaring war. Would it not be possible to limit the case to a little harmless "punishment" of Serbia for certain unquestioned sins? Sir Edward Grey began moving heaven and earth to convene a conference of the ambassadors of the four "disinterested" powers (France, Germany, Italy and England) at London to find some outlet for the case honorable both to Russia and to Austria. Serbia might be chastised but surely her national life and honor must be spared. To this English proposition Italy and France agreed promptly and gladly: but Von Jagow at Berlin at once raised difficulties. Russia and Austria had better fail to reach a direct understanding, so he thought, before others intervened. So another day was lost.

That night the German Kaiser suddenly returned from Norway. His foreign officials said that he came back on his own initiative and they feared lest His Majesty's "return cause speculation and excitement." The Berlin foreign office was undoubtedly the calmest chancellory in Europe. Good Herr von Jagow talked placidly of taking "a more hopeful view of the general situation." Such was the morning and the evening of the third day.

On the 27th the British ambassador at Vienna telegraphed that "the country has gone wild with joy at the prospect of war with Serbia: and its postponement or prevention would undoubtedly be a great disappointment." Meanwhile Von Jagow was still giving smooth words about being willing to coöperate with England to get peace, but he was becoming painfully vague when it passed to details: in London, however, Sir Edward Grey was *not* vague when he talked with the Austrian ambassador. That personage was told clearly that his government was taking a terrible risk if it imagined it could attack Serbia and still satisfy Russia. If they failed in this last "the consequences would be incalculable." The case was becoming so bad that the British had not been able to disperse their fleet after manœuvres, and as for Serbia, that country had already submitted to "the greatest humiliation I had ever seen a country undergo"; and it was utterly disappointing to have her grovelling answer treated like "a blank negative." At St. Petersburg, Sazonof was again saying that Russia was very willing to let the four "disinterested powers" get together and decide on what was just under the premises. From Berlin there came almost no decisive sign. Such was the morning and the evening of the fourth day.

On the 28th the situation, which had been drifting from hour to hour, with the diplomats hoping that so long as actual fighting did not begin there might be an exit, showed signs of reaching an issue—but not a peaceful one. Austria formally declared war on Serbia. This meant that the situa tion could not be put back into its old state without formal negotiations and a solemn treaty. Soon cannon shots were flying across the Danube. Austria was now mobilizing vast armies, avowedly to crush feeble Serbia, but on so general a scale that it was plain she was getting ready for anything. As a natural answer Russia began to mobilize also—not the entire hosts of the Czar, but only in the South—a partial mobilization to prevent herself from being hamstrung by a sudden blow in case it should turn out Austria was *not* mobilizing against Serbia only, and also, it should be fairly added, to lend weight to her urgent representations that Serbia ought not to be blotted from the list of independent nations whatever the justice of her cause. Russia took pains to inform Germany that her mobilization was merely partial and facing Austria only: and that she did not intend war. In fact, the Russian ambassador had orders still to remain at Vienna and to work for peace. Meanwhile at Berlin Bethmann-Hollweg was telling the English ambassador that he could not consent to a general conference of the powers to put pressure on Austria. Russia ought to keep out of the quarrel. ''From Austria's standpoint, and in this he agreed, her quarrel with Serbia was a purely Austrian concern with which Russia had nothing to do.'' If peace was to be kept, it was to be by a direct agreement between Vienna and St. Petersburg. Almost simultaneous with this interview was another at Vienna between Franz Josef's foreign minister and the Russian ambassador. The latter was told that no accommodation with Russia as to Serbia was possible. The ambassador therefore wired St. Petersburg that the only hope of healing the breach was by a conference of the powers: which conference was the very thing Bethmann-Hollweg at Berlin had just rejected. Such was the morning and the evening of the fifth day.

On July 29th a great change came over the whole situation. Hitherto the quarrel had been between Austria and Russia as to the right of the latter to interpose in behalf of Serbia. Berlin had simply sat back quietly, folded its hands and rejected every practical suggestion—especially from England—for averting dire disaster. "The contest must be localized": i. e., Austria must be allowed to treat Serbia unhindered in her own stern way,—that had been the substance of a dozen "conversations" permitted by Von Jagow and his superior the Chancellor.[1] Now suddenly Berlin began an amazing activity. Was this because William of Hohenzollern was constitutionally unable to be the spectator of any drama when he might personally be an actor? Was it because the precise point had been reached when by prearrangement Germany was to intervene? Both things are very likely and by no means incompatible. While France and England were still endeavoring frantically to find some decent outlet that would save Austria's interests, Serbia's life and Russia's honor, while Sir Edward Grey was telegraphing Berlin that if the proposed schemes for conciliation did not suit, Germany "should suggest *any* method by which the influence of the 'four powers' could be used to prevent war between Austria and Russia"; and that England, France and Italy would put the scheme into effect "if mine was not acceptable"—while all these things were going on, Bethmann-Hollweg had been not at his office on the Wilhelmstrasse but with his imperial master at Potsdam sixteen miles away.

There at the old seat of the Hohenzollerns was being held

[1] I decline, at this late date, to enter into the question whether Germany had cognizance of the precise text of the Serbian note by Austria. The denial by the magnates of the Berlin foreign office that they had had advance knowledge of its precise tenor or wording is the denial of men concerning whose personal veracity Americans have formed a very clear-cut opinion. But in any case the evidence is plain that the German government knew perfectly well that Austria intended to precipitate a crisis menacing to the peace of Europe, and that it egged on its dupe and ally to accomplish its purpose. This is bluntly admitted in the German "White Book" issued officially at Berlin at the outbreak of the war. "*We were perfectly well aware* that a possible warlike attitude of Austria against Serbia might bring Russia into the field, and that we might therefore be involved in a war, in accordance with our duty as allies. We could not however . . . advise our ally to adopt a conciliatory attitude incompatible with her dignity."

Such a statement is enough for the densest jury!

a great war council. The heir of William I and of Frederick the Great was there, his captains, his admirals, his master financiers: all the controlling spirits who had perfected the huge Hohenzollern war machine in expectation of precisely this moment. Doubtless views were exchanged with the uttermost frankness and all possibilities discussed in perfect cold blood and the precise moves by which millions of lives might be snuffed out in the war-game arranged and everything made ready for the last grim decision. Of course the details were kept carefully hidden, but there is no reason for doubting the substantial accuracy of what the well-informed Berlin correspondent of the London "Times" telegraphed the next day: "No secret, I understand, is made at the foreign office this morning of the fact that the military authorities were pressing for immediate mobilization, and that a decision must be reached within a day or two. . . . Imminence of mobilization is so obvious that there is little secret about the preliminary preparations that are being made."[1]

When the conclave broke up Bethmann-Hollweg returned with precipitancy, presumably by fast motor-car, to Berlin and telephoned the British embassy. He wished to see Sir Edward Goschen. The ambassador at once called on the chancellor. Their interview was memorable. Hitherto nearly all their talk had been about Russia and Austria. Now suddenly Bethmann-Hollweg spoke openly of Germany entering a general war "owing to her obligations as Austria's ally." But the chancellor "made a strong bid for British neutrality." Let England only stand clear and Germany would promise not to crush France too severely, and especially would not annex any of her home territories, although he was very vague as to what might happen to her colonies. "And Belgium?" asked the Englishman. "It depended upon the action of France," came the answer, "what operations Germany might be forced to enter upon in Belgium, but

[1] There was as yet no censorship on telegrams from Germany, and that country was as yet, officially, on good terms with England. The correspondent had every chance to get the gist of events.

when the war was over her integrity would be respected if she had not sided against Germany.''

There was more pleasant talk about a permanent ''understanding with England,'' on which Bethmann-Hollweg had set his peaceful heart. The ambassador, however, received his words very coldly, said he did not think his government cared to make any pledges based on such propositions, and made haste to put his momentous tidings on the wires to London. That night Sir Edward Grey and his associates at least knew that Germany was plotting war against France and Russia, and that she wished to see England sit calmly by while Germany stripped France of her colonies, and otherwise so crippled her (e. g., by a bleeding indemnity) that even if her home territories were left intact, France would be eliminated from the list of great nations.

This was the offer subsequently described by Mr. Asquith in the House of Commons as Germany's ''infamous proposal.'' Its answer, however, had to wait till the morning following. Perhaps the Chancellor would have been less blunt and tactless in his suggestion had he known almost that very minute Sir Edward Grey had been saying to the German ambassador at London that England was not pledged to fight beside France and Russia, but that if war *did* come British interests and honor might draw her in, and in that case England must not ''be open to any reproach . . . that his [German] government had been misled [by the friendly tone of the conversation] into supposing that we would not take action, and that if they had not been so misled the course of things might have been different.''

That night, when wearied diplomats turned in to snatch a little troubled sleep, they knew that the world was facing the greatest military crisis in human history, and that Germany was forcing the issue. Such was the morning and the evening of the sixth day.

On July 30th, Sir Edward Grey answered, with the bluntness of an honest man deeply stirred, to the proposal sent the night before by Bethmann-Hollweg through the British ambassador. ''His Majesty's government cannot for an instant entertain the Chancellor's proposal that they should bind themselves to neutrality on such terms." England is being asked "to make this bargain with Germany at the expense of France." To do so would hurt British interests, but still more "it would be a disgrace to us from which the good name of this country [England] would never recover." Nor was it possible to bargain away "whatever obligation or interest we have as regards the neutrality of Belgium"— England therefore must "preserve her full freedom to act as circumstances require" in case things should come to a head as Bethmann-Hollweg contemplated. But Grey added an earnest and friendly promise—that, if the peace of Europe could be preserved, he would do his uttermost to get some arrangement by which *Germany "could be assured that no aggressive or hostile policy would be pursued against her or her allies by France, Russia or ourselves, jointly or separately."* Grey was not a man to make such a promise lightly. It would be unfair possibly to say that Bethmann-Hollweg brushed this suggestion thoughtlessly aside. The probability was rather that the Prussian war-party was then in such complete control of the German situation that nothing England could have said, short of a promise to attack France— to prevent her from being true to her alliance to Russia, would have had any effect on the crisis.

Neither at Berlin nor at London, however, were all the prime actors in the drama. For several days now St. Petersburg had been terribly stirred. The brutality of the Austrian attack on Serbia had seemed a direct insult to Russian prestige, honor and self-respect. Nicholas II was assuredly no genius and some of his intimates were strongly pro-German in their sympathies, but he was not an absolute weakling and he bitterly resented being displayed now before his own people as the shivering puppet of the Hohenzollern and the Hapsburg. The Russian aristocracy was not full of schemes for world empire like their Prussian compeers but they were proud of their national honor, of the claims of Holy Russia to be the protector of the lesser Slavic people, and of the right of Russia to be treated with decent consideration in every question of the Balkans: and for once the grand dukes and the generals were sustained by their old foes, the "Constitutional Democrats" and all the other more intelligent champions of a more liberal régime.

Around Nicholas were now scores of powerful men repeating the dread words "mobilize" and "fight"—and behind them was the voice of all the intelligence of the nation. It was realized that the empire was not well prepared for a life and death struggle, but this was a case where national honor demanded even a disastrous defeat rather than an ignominious peace which would show that the dearest Russian interests could be trampled upon with impunity. On the 29th the czar had written personally to Kaiser Wilhelm: "A disgraceful war has been declared on a weak nation: the indignation, which I fully share, is immense in Russia." The czar therefore begged the kaiser "in the name of our old friendship" to do his uttermost to avert the danger. The kaiser had offered to mediate, but had denied that "Austria's action was 'disgraceful war'": and then at 1 A. M. on the morning of the 30th he had wired Nicholas that Russia's mobilization against Austria would have "danger and serious consequences": adding ominously, "The whole weight of the decision rests upon your shoulders,—they must bear the responsibility for war or peace."

The telegraphic service between these imperial gentlemen was rapid. Twenty minutes later Nicholas was wiring back that the military measures Russia was taking "were decided upon five days ago for defensive purposes against Austria's preparations. . . . We need your strong pressure on Austria in order that an understanding may be brought about with us." Thus Nicholas, in the simplicity of his heart, made answer, imagining that "Willy" (as he addressed his august friend) was in good faith working for peace. But to sit with folded hands and without stirring a soldier while Austria assembled her myriads to trample over Serbia, was a thing not to be asked of the heir of Peter the Great: that is, not if a czar of all the Russias was to keep his throne. There is no autocracy strong enough to defy public opinion beyond a certain point, and every barrack room, every military club in the huge Muscovite empire was seething with impatience and martial fury. If Nicholas had done nothing but write protests in this crisis he would soon have written also his abdication, in 1914 instead of in 1917. But after all he was a man and a Russian. By July 30th he was being goaded into action—a fact which the Potsdam war-lords had of course complacently discounted.

While the kaiser and the czar were exchanging telegrams, the kaiser's ambassador at St. Petersburg was making a frantic visit at 2 A. M. on the 30th to the Russian foreign office. This ambassador (Count Pourtalès) was personally an honorable man who, now that the ground was opening at his feet, began to realize how horrible was the danger. M. Sazonof met him to point out that "war was inevitable." How could it be otherwise when the Teutonic powers were unyielding, and authentic information was coming in that Germany was making elaborate military and naval preparations against Russia, doing everything in short except to decree formal mobilization: "There would be a revolution in Russia if she were to tolerate such a state of affairs." At this interview the unhappy Pourtalès, overwhelmed by the crisis, "completely broke down on seeing that war was inevitable." He made a fervent appeal to Sazonof to give him something to telegraph to Berlin as "a last hope." The Russian (doubtless also greatly moved) drew up this formula which went the very limit of possible concession and should have ended all controversy unless the Teutonic powers were bent on war at any price: "If Austria, recognizing that her conflict with Serbia has assumed the character of a question of European interest, declares herself ready to eliminate from her ultimatum points which violate the principle of the sovereignty of Serbia, Russia engages to stop all military preparations." More than that no Russian could say, unless he were prepared to urge his country to sit down as helpless as China before the greatest insult that had ever threatened a great European power.

Nevertheless, the day wore on without any developments

much more threatening. The truth seems to have been that at last at Vienna leaders were coming to realize the terrible nature of the tempest they had almost unchained, and that possibly they were being made the dupes and tools of their "loyal allies" at Berlin. Even Cæsar hesitated at the Rubicon, and Count Berchtold and his noble associates were very puny Cæsars. They told the ambassadors that since Russia was mobilizing they must of course hasten their own preparations, but "this should not be regarded as a threat." Their own ambassador at St. Petersburg could hold "conversations" with Sazonof, although they did not specify just what concessions were possible. The situation was still complex and clouded, but the Russian ambassador at Vienna grew more hopeful "that something may yet be done to prevent war with Austria." He does not seem to have realized that it mattered little whether Vienna stood on the brink of the stream and hesitated, or dashed across, provided Potsdam had no chilly scruples. Such was the morning and evening of the seventh day.

On July 31 the morning seemed brighter at Vienna, London and St. Petersburg. Grey sent his last hopeful suggestion: "If Germany will get any reasonable proposition put forward, which made it clear that Germany and Austria were striving to preserve European peace and that Russia and France would be unreasonable if they rejected it, I will support it at St. Petersburg and Paris, and go to the length of saying that if Russia and France will not accept it, I will have nothing to do with the consequences. Otherwise, if France is drawn in, we shall be drawn in." If the words that had been coming from Berlin about "peace" were not those of brazen hypocrisy, here surely was something for German diplomats to work upon: and if they felt that "their duty to their ally" made them hesitant, their ticklish honor might have been appeased by the knowledge that *Austria was actually agreeing to talk terms of accommodation with Russia.* Austria showed a willingness to agree to halt her march into Serbian territory, while Russia "undertook to preserve her waiting attitude," and the six great powers were to "examine how Serbia can give satisfaction to Austria without impairing her sovereign rights or independence.''

This compliant attitude of Austria was undoubtedly the very last thing welcomed at Potsdam. It deprived the war party of its best pretext for striking home—namely, its claim that as a loyal ally Germany must stand by Austria, come what might. There had been much excitement in Germany during these days of tension: patriotic demonstrations, preliminary warnings to the reservists to get ready, everything in short, save actual mobilization; but although the junker newspapers had been fiery from the outset, the attitude of the more moderate press had been at first very hesitant to accept the Austrian ultimatum as a thing for unqualified German endorsement. The Social Democrats (who had cast over 4,000,000 votes at the last election) failed to see any reason why their own country should intervene. The "Vorwaerts," their great Berlin organ, had said bluntly on July 25th, that the demands on Serbia "are more brutal than have been ever put to an independent state in the world's history, and can only be intended deliberately to provoke war." On the 29th it had declared that "the camarilla of war-lords is working with absolutely unscrupulous means . . . to start a world-wide fire to devastate Europe." On that day also there had been several great mass meetings in Berlin to denounce the war, and one of these was said to have been attended by 70,000 men. If therefore war in behalf of Austria was unpopular with a great mass of the folk of Germany, what chance of a fortunate "Day" if Austria should ungratefully slink back at the end and refuse to force the situation? Something must be done, and done quickly. There was no Ems telegram ready with Bismarck as the genial "editor," but press and electricity could nevertheless be put to other purposes. Was it the crown prince himself who knew how to force the issue, or Von Moltke the Chief of Staff, or Von Tirpitz the admiral, or some other less prominent Highness or Excellency? The personal memoirs will one day tell. There is little doubt that some noble gentleman felt the impulse of genius and acted upon it. He presumably lived to be amply satisfied by the magnitude of his achievement.

Hitherto Russia had only mobilized partially. She had called out a certain number of corps of her huge reserves to concentrate against Austria. But Austria and Russia had repeatedly mobilized on a pretty large scale during earlier Balkan crises, and then had looked on placidly while the diplomats disentangled the snarls. Austria seemed quite willing to let Russia mobilize partially again, and to confine her own military energies entirely to Serbia. But so far Russia had not mobilized the remainder of her army in a way spelling any menace to Germany. If she did so, the Prussian war-lords could demand the mobilization of their own host and after that—the rest would be inevitable.

Everybody in Berlin was expecting a mobilization order. Young men were making their farewells to sweethearts and families; factory managers were preparing to operate with reduced help; bankers were taking precautions against "runs" and panics. Still, on the 30th, no order had come: although beyond a doubt the military chiefs were clamoring for it. Why this delay? Because, according to all reasonable inference, the chancellor was feeling great uncertainty as to what he had earlier reckoned upon—the neutrality of England. The German ambassador at London and all his astute assistants had probably sent messages earlier as to the growth of pacifism in Britain, of the absorption of the great labor elements in schemes for social betterment, of the influence in the cabinet of John Burns and Lord Morley, devoted peace-at-any-price men, and of the alacrity with which divers Englishmen had swallowed doctrines like those of the comfortable "Norman Angell." Better still had been the news that Britain was about to be entangled in a civil war in Ireland over the miserable contentions between the Catholic Home Rulers and Protestant Ulstermen. It had seemed incredible that selfish and pacifist Britain could ever draw the sword over a "Balkan question." But there were increasing signs that Britain did not consider this crisis strictly a "Balkan question," that if the Pan-German plot had not been unmasked it had been seen through a pretty thin veil, and that

England was not prepared to watch Russia's ally France trampled over and stricken from the list of great powers. And if England entered the war Bethmann-Hollweg, and it may well be also his astute if not squeamish master, probably had clear suspicions that the "Day" might not close upon a prompt and easy victory. Therefore mobilization had been delayed. Irrevocable words had not been spoken. All of which was highly irritating to the "high-born" Excellencies of the Great General Staff. England or no England, they would go ahead.

About mid-day on the 30th of July Berlin newsvenders began hawking in the central part of the city a special edition of the "Lokal-Anzeiger" announcing that general mobilization for Germany had been ordered. This paper was reputed to be in close touch with the German government bureaus. It was also alleged to have been financed by junker capital. Its reputation as a quasi-government organ was high. There had been a "leak," or had there been an inspiration? The police at length were hard after the newsvenders, confiscating their copies, and an official contradiction was also ordered. But there had been an appreciable length of time between the hawking of the paper and the contradiction. The moment the paper had appeared, the Russian ambassador and also the St. Petersburg press agents had wired the tidings home. The Prussian war-lords (if they knew in advance of this newspaper "enterprise") knew well what the effect these tidings would have in Muscovy.

Already Nicholas II was being beset with frantic appeals from *his* men of action to order complete mobilization, because, as was being justly said, the (1) Russian mobilization was in any case very much slower than the German, and might be too late at best: (2) Germany had already gone so far with her "advance preparations" that final mobilization was in part a formality. And now came the news that Germany had ordered complete mobilization, which meant (as everybody knew) that she would soon be ready to strike with terrible effectiveness. Nicholas II would have been more than human had he refused to give way: especially as a very awkward interval occurred before the tidings of German mobilization were contradicted. When the contradiction did come, the Russian men of action could wisely say that the tale would never have been printed had not mobilization been imminent, and what with German secret methods that it was probably taking place *sub rosa*. To hesitate longer was to imperil the life of Russia.

Nicholas was won over. Early on the morning of the 31st the Russian wires were carrying the summons of the "little father" to all his battle-worthy subjects. The "Lokal Anzeiger" edition had supplied precisely the needful impetus to produce Russian mobilization. If it was an "accident," it was one of those accidents which makes one believe that the devil directs the laws of chance.[1]

And now the Prussian war-lords could work their will. The instant the news came back that Russia was mobilizing, they could cry in turn "the fatherland is in danger," and that, whatever England did, radical measures must be taken to fend off invasion. At noon on the 31st, "Imminence of War" was proclaimed throughout Germany, with consequent martial law and the complete squelching of socialistic demonstrations and protests. On top of this home proclamation went the ultimatum to Russia—couched in terms no proud empire could possibly accept, and reducing all the protesting talk about peace to monkey's chatter.

Alleging that Russian mobilization put Germany in peril, Bethmann-Hollweg telegraphed his ambassador in St. Petersburg to serve notice on Sazonof that Germany would mobilize "unless Russia stops every measure of war against us *and Austria*[2] within twelve hours and notifies us definitely to this effect." Simultaneously another message went over the

---

[1] The Russian judgments as to this "accident" are dark and specific. They allege that not merely was the edition carefully concocted by those in high authority, but that by a suddenly imposed "censorship," dispatches contradicting the alleged news were held up for hours ere they could go on to St. Petersburg.

[2] Why "Austria," unless Germany was bound on forcing the war at any price, inasmuch as Austria had already indicated she did not consider Russian mobilization unfriendly?

wires to Paris. France had remained helpless and hoping against hope through all this terrible week. The quarrel was not the least of her making. Her diplomats had exhausted themselves seeking an honorable issue for Austria and Russia alike: but she was bound by the firmest kind of treaty to help Russia if Russia should be attacked. Were she to break this pledge her pleasant villages would lie unscathed for the moment, but at the cost of the last shreds of French honor. Betraying her own ally, she could expect no succor from any nation, and she would remain isolated and helpless—as well as sullied—before Teutonia. To President Poincaré's cabinet the chancellor now sent word that twelve hours' grace had been given Russia to demobilize: and did the French government "intend to remain neutral in a Russo-German war? Reply must be made within eighteen hours." [1]

In Berlin that day there were tumultuous demonstrations,—cheers and huzzas from the brave young officers who saw visions of battle, glory, quick promotion, amid the transforming into splendid reality of all the strategic and tactical theories they had evolved in study or peaceful manœuvre. *The Day*, THE DAY for which they and every other loyal Pan-German had wearily waited, was about to dawn. There were great crowds in Unter den Linden, and deep cries, "To Paris!" "To St. Petersburg!" The multitude swarmed down the famous avenue to the huge grey palace of the Hohenzollerns, acclaiming the master of a greater army than ever Xerxes had led to battle. From the balcony of the palace William II sent his powerful voice over the sea of heads of his upward-gazing subjects:

"A fateful hour has fallen for Germany," proclaimed the Emperor. "Envious peoples everywhere are compelling us to our just defence. *The sword is being forced into our hand.* I hope that if my efforts at the last hour do not succeed in bringing our opponents to see eye to eye with us and in main-

[1] Reliable evidence, published in 1918, indicated that if France had pledged neutrality, Germany would next have demanded occupation for the war of Verdun and Toul as pledges of good-faith. The Potsdam leaders were anxious to pick a quarrel with France at any cost.

taining peace we shall with God's help so wield the sword that we shall restore it to its sheath again with honor. War would demand enormous sacrifices of blood and property from the German people, but we should show our enemies what it means to provoke Germany. And now I commend you to God. Go to church. Kneel down before God and pray for His help for our gallant army.''

Did the Emperor realize the verdict the world would pass on his cry, "The sword is being forced into our hand"? Had he prepared this dramatic call to battle some days in advance, or did he speak with true spontaneity? One thing is certain, that on this July 31, the last faint chance of peace was gone. The military men at Potsdam and Berlin knew well enough what they were doing when they sent threats with a time limit to St. Petersburg and Paris. Neither Russia nor France could have cringed to them *then* and have continued to hold up its head as a self-respecting nation. So their Excellencies, Serenities and Highnesses waited while the fateful hours went by: and thus passed the morning and the evening of the eighth day.

The German ultimatum had not been presented in St. Petersburg until close to midnight on the 31st. The 1st of August saw from the outset the signs of the inevitable climax. It is true, Germany had only threatened Russia with countermobilization if the czar would not demobilize: and in theory, negotiations could still continue merrily with each party armed but not fighting. Austria seemed quite willing to let this be the case: but not Germany. If there was one archmaxim, however, in the Prussian military program it was that German mobilization, being extremely rapid, must be followed by an instantaneous and deadly blow before the slower mobilization of probable enemies could be completed and the initial weaknesses in their war machine repaired. To sit passively across the frontier while Nicholas II brought up troops from Manchuria was to the Great General Staff an act not of folly but of suicide. As early as July 26, Count Pourtalès had stated the certainty of this deduction plainly to Sazonof. If mobilization once took place, he had said, "the military considerations of the General Staff will be supreme, and the situation will become irrevocable once 'the button has been pressed' by the Chief of Staff in Germany.'' Everybody knew then that for the land of the Hohenzollerns mobilization meant the same as war.[1]

On this fateful August 1st, there went out the imperial order for general mobilization and all the German Empire rang with the clang of arms. From Paris a similar summons went out to the French Republic, although up to the last Premier Viviani was assuring the German ambassador that ''mobilization did not necessarily entail war,'' and that there was no need for a rupture of diplomatic relations. The position of France needed no pronunciamentos. ''I have no intention of making any statement [to the German ambassador] on the subject of his demands,'' declared Premier Viviani dryly, ''and I shall confine myself to telling him that France will have regard to her own interests.''

The final move on the chess board was clearly Germany's and her rulers had no hesitancy about making it. At 7:10 A. M. on August 1st, Count Pourtalès again went his familiar way to the office of Sazonof. He had a communication which, by the errors and duplication of words in the copy presented, had obviously been prepared in great haste and apparently with the intention of declaring war on Russia whether she gave no answer to the ultimatum at all, or any kind of answer except one of servile compliance. After reciting the good intentions of Kaiser Wilhelm as peacemaker with Austria, and the ruin of all these efforts by the Russian mo-

[1] Americans will recall the fact that Germany had refused a little earlier to sign with us one of the so-called Bryan "cooling off" treaties, providing for a year of negotiations ere declaring war, in-as-much as she could not sign similar treaties with France, England or Russia because then "Germany would be deprived of her greatest asset in war—namely her readiness for a sudden and overpowering attack." (Mr. Gerard's "My Four Years in Germany," p. 61.)

The statement about the German Staff policy, quoted in the text, does not appear in any German report of Count Pourtalès' doings, but is less discreetly published in a dispatch of the *Austrian* ambassador at St. Petersburg to his government. (Austrian "Red Book, No. 28.")

bilization, the ambassador closed the document with these fateful words: *"His Majesty, the Emperor, my august sovereign,
in the name of the German empire, accepts the challenge and
considers himself at war with Russia."*

So the dream of the crown prince, of Bernhardi, of all the
exultant Pan-Germans up and down the Fatherland, was
about to be realized. The war-machine that had stood silent
but not rusting for forty-three years was to resume its appointed and glorious task. Yet the world still waited. The
picture of embattled Europe was not yet complete. In Germany, in Austria, in Russia and still more in agonizing
France, on whom all knew the first bolt was to fall, there was
one all-important question:

"What would England do?"

THE PRECIPITATION OF THE WAR BY GERMANY

Mr. Morgenthau recorded in his diary that the conversation with
the German ambassador took place August 26th, 1914. See New York
"World," October 14, 1917. His statement was received as having official
accuracy by the United States Government Committee of Public Information which reprinted his statement in its official pamphlet, "Conquest and Kultur" (December, 1917), pp. 144-5.

There is a good deal more cumulative evidence as to the nature of this
conference early in July. On July 28, 1917, the London "Times" published a circumstantial account of the reports current in well-informed
circles in Germany about the matter. The council was held, according
to this story, on July 5th, at Potsdam, and high Austrian dignitaries
were present. The meeting "decided upon the principal points in the
Austrian ultimatum which was to be dispatched to Serbia eighteen
days later. It was recognized that Russia would probably refuse to
submit and that war would result." The Kaiser then departed for
Norway to throw dust in the eyes of the French and Russian governments.

The German foreign office was quite confident that England would
not fight, and this was part of the working hypothesis of the high-born
conspirators. "Three weeks later, when it became known that England
would not remain neutral, Bethmann-Hollweg wished to withdraw, but
it was too late. The decision of July 5th was crucial and irrevocable."
The denials which came from Berlin of this story were perfunctory and
pro forma.

After the outbreak of the war it was easy to recall circumstances
which seemed to indicate that the German army was getting ready for
action some weeks before the dispatch of the Serbian note. As a minor

example, the writer can state that he was in Trier (Treves) on the Mosel around July 10th, 1914. At that time the quaint old frontier city was very full of troops, there was a large encampment in the suburbs, the hotels were over-run with officers, and in the little villages round about there was the constant sound of rifle firing,—evidently of target practice on the ranges.

There is abundant evidence that in the two weeks preceding the "twelve days" the stock markets of the world witnessed a selling movement which was afterward amply explained as being engineered by the German banking interests seeking cover. The gold reserve of the empire had already been practically doubled over that of 1913.

In passing, it may be observed that throughout all these adventures, down to the final catastrophe, the Austrian leaders and politicians showed themselves servile puppets of their infinitely more masterful and intelligent "allies." For a mess of pottage of increased local influence in the Balkans they were willing to commit their empire to a bloody scheme that promised, in any case, to deliver it over hand and foot to an enormously powerful Germany.

The more the plot of July, 1914, is examined the more fixed becomes the conviction that the Pan-Germans had adopted a somewhat deliberate project for achieving world-dominion by means of three separate but not remotely connected stages:

1. The defeat and reduction to impotence of Russia and still more of France, with the establishment of Teutonic influence across the Balkans and Turkey to the Persian Gulf.

2. The defeat of Great Britain, the seizure of all or most of the British colonies, and the substitution of German sea-power for English.

3. The violation of the Monroe Doctrine to permit German dominance in Latin America and the seizure of the Panama canal, and the penetration and breaking-down of the independence of the United States by an admixture of outward force and internal German-American "influence."

If however England had been willing to stand clear, the attack on America might well have come second, or even first on the list.

CHAPTER XXIV

ENGLAND was in a position of terrible difficulty. If the crisis had come a week later Ulster and the rest of Ireland would probably have been at each other's throats in civil war. Several members of the cabinet up to the last minute refused to see the ground opening at the nation's feet, and threatened to disrupt the Liberal party in event of Grey and others pressing for action. Mr. Asquith, the premier, seems to have realized that what Germany was forcing was not merely a "Balkan question" but an issue of world power in which England was enormously interested, but he was very loath to anticipate public opinion, very loath to see all the fine Liberal program of domestic reform shipped overboard in the face of a foreign tempest, and very loath (so his critics insisted) to let matters come to a point where the Liberals might be pushed from power and their Conservative rivals seize the helm of state. Englishmen generally were decidedly unwilling to pour out blood and treasure merely to save the independence of Serbia, and although they did not love the German kaiser they had very little enthusiasm for defending the despotism of Nicholas II, many phases whereof they not unjustly hated.

Nevertheless the case was very different about France. Very many Englishmen realized that to have France trampled over again by German armies, to have Paris taken, to have France bled white by a tremendous indemnity (even if there were no more annexations) meant striking France from the list of great powers, and meant an inordinate growth of the new Teutonic colossus. The ruin of France was the immediate preliminary to a direct stroke at England; and the majority of intelligent Englishmen knew it.

But not all Englishmen were intelligent. The laboring

and the rural classes and the small tradespeople were probably
the least military and the least imaginative folk in Europe.
That any summons from across the Channel to march forth
to battle could take them away from their firesides and their
toast and tea seemed one of the most improbable things in the
world. And among Englishmen who should have known
better divers had been temporarily infected with the pale
pacifism of the Angel Lane type and its gospel of crass materialism—a gospel that agreed well with the hopes of regular
dividends and undisturbed vacations. Never was there a
people less prepared for a horrid crisis than the good people
of England.[1] They had even been better prepared two years
before at the time of the Agadir tension, for since then countless voices and pens had assured them that "relations with
Germany were steadily improving," and various home issues,
especially that of Ireland, had assumed an almost overpowering gravity.

Since July 23rd Sir Edward Grey had been placed in a
dilemma indescribably difficult. He had been besought by
France and Russia to tell Germany that if war *did* come, then
England would surely fight against her. He knew that if he
made this threat the chances of keeping peace were probably
greatly increased—Germany did not want too many foes at
once. But he also knew that then, if Germany despite everything drew the sword, England was involved in a war as to
the wisdom of which her cabinet was divided, and her people
wholly uninstructed, and which very likely they would
refuse to conduct with the sacrifice and energy without which

[1] The writer passed from the continent to England the day of Russian mobilization, and he stopped in the small cathedral city of Canter-
bury. The town was decorated with bunting in honor of an approaching athletic carnival. Anything like a great war and its confusion and
danger seemed utterly unthinkable in that slumberous town under the
shadow of its august minster. There was not the least excitement, and
only a rather languid sale for the London "extras" sent up that evening,
although their headlines were lurid.

The attitude of the good citizens seemed admirably summarized by
the remark of the worthy keeper of the hotel: "I hope to goodness, sir,
this accursed war-talk will soon come to nothing: *otherwise cricket week
will be a dead failure!*"

no great war can be waged. The most he could do was to warn Germany that England reserved "complete liberty of action"; to assure France and Russia that she would take an extremely friendly attitude in case worst came to worst; and finally on August 2nd, when it was clear that peace between Russia and Germany was broken, to inform France—after a British cabinet meeting—that subject to approval of parliament, "I am authorized to give assurance that if the German fleet comes into the channel or through the North Sea to undertake hostile operations against French coasts or shipping, the British fleet will give all the protection in its power." That was all for the moment, although great interests and parties in London called for more radical action, and action was in the air. Then while England shook herself from her dream of peace, while the rumblings of the mobilizations drifted across the channel, came one word "Belgium"—and the pacifists slunk to their caves.[1]

Belgium was one of the most happy and prosperous countries in the world. Its people had been counted fortunate among their neighbors. Its dense and thrifty population lived mostly by peaceful industry. Its elegant capital, Brussels, was accounted a "little Paris." Antwerp vied with Hamburg as one of the chief ports of the continent. The quaint cities of Flanders were a delight to visitors alike for their reminiscences of the past and their thriving present. Confident in her peace, unafflicted by vast imperial ambitions, without a single serious outstanding diplomatic problem with the great Powers, Belgium seemed to face nothing but a placid and fortunate future. She was without the slightest Balkan interests; and was the member of no alliances. Theoretically the clash over Serbia should have left her as unaffected as a contest between Argentina and Chile—it was something very far away.

Belgium also was not merely neutral, but she was especially *neutralized* in Europe. In the olden days the "Low Countries" had been the cock-pit of the nations, and England in

[1] See note at end of chapter: Attitude of England, August 1, 1914.

particular had fought bitter wars to prevent them from falling into the hands of some great unfriendly power—the
aggressor usually having been France. It was long recognized that the naval power which held Antwerp held one of the
doors for invading England. Hence the English had, in self-
protection, insisted that France should not control Belgium,
and the French in turn had disliked to see this country controlled by one of their national enemies. In 1815 the Congress of Vienna had annexed Belgium to the kingdom of Holland, but this arrangement had not worked well. In 1830 the
Belgians revolted against the Dutch. In 1831 the great Powers recognized the independence of Belgium, and at the same
time determined that Belgium should form "a perpetually
neutral State" and that they should guarantee to her "perpetual neutrality and also the integrity and inviolability of
her territory." This pledge was signed by England, Austria,
Russia, France and Prussia, Italy not having yet come into
national existence.

In 1839 this treaty was reaffirmed by the Powers in a still
clearer treaty: "Belgium . . . shall form an independent and
perpetually neutral state. It shall be bound to observe such
neutrality towards all other states." It was well understood
that one of the prime points in this "neutrality" was that no
foreign armies were to be allowed to cross Belgium for any
warlike purpose. To enable Belgium to discharge this duty
she was allowed to maintain an army and to fortify certain
strategic points, notably Antwerp, Namur and Liége. Seemingly the position of Belgium, however, was very secure. The
five greatest nations in Europe had pledged themselves to
protect her provided she discharged her own obligations, for,
as King Leopold I wrote to Queen Victoria in 1856, "Belgium's very existence is based upon [her] neutrality, which
the other powers have guaranteed and are bound to maintain
if Belgium keeps her engagements."

The resistance of any violation of her territories was thus
a part of the duty of Belgium, and ought not to have involved
her in any general war. In 1907 the Hague Conference de-

cided that "the resistance, even by force, of a neutral Power
to attempts against its neutrality cannot be considered as acts
of hostility."

During the earlier part of Belgium's existence as a kingdom
the general fear had been of an attack by France. In 1866
Bismarck had even tempted Napoleon III to dally with a
treacherous attempt to annex Belgium to France; an attempt
which Bismarck duly exploited in 1870 in order to win hatred
for his enemy. England became anxious in that year lest
France try to seize Belgium in event of her victory over Prussia, and caused both France and Prussia to sign special compacts for the occasion reaffirming "their settled determination to maintain the independence and neutrality of Belgium
as established by the . . . treaty of 1839." In Prussia's case
this precaution was hardly necessary, for two weeks before this
pact was signed Bismarck gave firm assurances at Brussels
that Prussia "and its allies will respect the neutrality of Belgium, provided that it is respected by the other belligerent
party." So the case had rested, being strengthened of course
by the Hague proviso of 1907 that belligerents should not send
troops or supply trains across any neutral country.

Belgium thus seemed doubly protected: I. By the clear
sanctions which that once reverenced thing called international law afforded to *all* self-respecting neutral countries in
general; II. By the special compact of 1839 which gave Belgium a peculiar and privileged place among the nations.

After 1870 it was clear enough that France would not for a
long day be in a position to over-run Belgium. If there was
any aggression it would be from Germany. That a German
invasion was possible military men long knew. Years before
the crisis the case had been stated pithily in 1882 in a quasi-
official German newspaper,[1] "Germany has no political motive
to violate the neutrality of Belgium, but the military advantages which might result may force her to do so." The reason
for this military opinion is clearly explained in the "Deutsche
Krieger Zeitung"[2] just one month after the great war actu-

[1] "Norddeutsche Allgemeine Zeitung"; March 4th, 1882.
[2] Official organ of the German Military Union; Sept. 2nd, 1914.

ally began; "*The plan for the invasion of France had been clearly settled for a long time*. It had to be pursued with success in the north through Belgium: thus avoiding the strong line of delaying forts which the enemy [France] had made to defend its frontiers towards Germany, and which would have been extremely difficult to break through." [1] Military books had discussed this desirability of "the Belgian route to Paris" with the uttermost frankness. Everybody knew that in case of war the Germans would throw away a great martial advantage if they respected the treaties and tried to advance on the direct road from Lorraine via Verdun or Nancy. What, of course, the Pan-Germans thought about respecting these treaties was no enigma.

Nevertheless the government of William II did not denounce the treaties, despite dark suspicions. On the contrary it used every effort, apparently, to stifle unfriendly surmises in Belgium and England without actually making a cast-iron statement that the neutrality pledge was in all cases to be respected. In 1904 the constant building of "strategic railways" near the Belgian frontier began to make Brussels anxious, but nothing actually came to pass until 1911, when the Belgians inquired of Bethmann-Hollweg whether something could not be done to dispel their growing anxiety. Upon this, the latter "declared that Germany had no intention of violating Belgian neutrality," but he could not make a public declaration to that effect because then France would know she had nothing to guard against on that part of her frontier. However, in April, 1914, during a Reichstag debate a Socialist deputy asked Von Jagow, the foreign minister, about the fears in Belgium lest her neutrality be not respected. Von Jagow replied, "Belgian neutrality is provided for by international conventions, and Germany is determined

---

[1] After the loss of Alsace-Lorraine the French had manfully constructed an artificial line of barrier forts to replace the lost line of the Rhine. The chief of these great fortresses were Verdun, Toul, Epinal and Belfort. The Germans were quite justified in not desiring to break their teeth upon them. The military road to Paris via Belgium was much smoother, with better roads, fewer hills and fewer formidable fortresses.

to respect those conventions." Von Heering, the minister of war, added, "Germany will not lose sight of the fact that the neutrality of Belgium is guaranteed by international treaty."

Such statements might lull the thoughtless and delight the pacifist, but they were not likely to satisfy responsible statesmen. In 1906 and again in 1912 there seem to have been conversations between British and Belgian officers as to the kind of military aid England might send Belgium in event of a wanton attack from Germany. Nothing definite was arranged; no unfriendly unneutral move was planned against Germany—the first move must be hers. Unfortunately, however, the Belgians were decidedly too confident in their forts at Liége and Namur to hold up the invader, for they never dreamed of the new mobile howitzers; they also were too slow in reorganizing their army. Nominally they had enforced universal military service; actually the number of youths exempted was large and the training of part of the remainder imperfect. Laws were duly passed to stiffen the army but they were not to be in full effect until 1918. There was a complete lack of heavy artillery. The guns had been ordered (from Krupps!) and when the crisis came most had been unaccountably "delayed." Most of the remainder of the new Belgian military material was "awaited" from other German munition plants. From a population of 7,000,000 Belgium ought to have mobilized 700,000 men to defend hearth and home. Actually in the first crisis a field army of only 110,000 seems to have been mobilized. Of course this condition was well known to the German General Staff, which probably had more spies in Belgium than in any other one country, and this entered into the plan of campaign which the staff relentlessly followed.[1]

[1] The tale is that William II, when asked as to the time required to force his way across Belgium, answered by swinging his hand violently from right to left, exclaiming, "I shall go through her like that!" There is no doubt that the German authorities held the Belgian army in the uttermost contempt, and considered the little kingdom protected only by a sentimental barrier.

Shortly before the outbreak of the war a German colonel is reported by Baron Beyens, Belgian minister to Berlin, as remonstrating thus

When the crisis broke over Europe, the Belgians made haste to assure all the jangling powers of their perfect neutrality and began taking military precautions to protect their frontiers. Naturally they drew near diplomatically to England, which was obviously the one power, fairly disinterested, that could give them real protection, and England had already stirred in their behalf. Her honor was deeply committed to seeing that the Belgian compacts were observed, and besides her honor it is not unfair to add that her national safety would be obviously jeopardized if a great rival empire, under the guise of attacking France, were actually to seize upon Antwerp and Ostend. As soon as the chances of a general war became serious, Grey began giving plain hints to Berlin that assurances as to Belgium were in order. The answers he obtained only strengthened rising suspicions. At last on the 31st of July he sent identical questions to Paris and Berlin. Would France and Germany respectively "engage to respect the neutrality of Belgium, so long as no other power violates it?"

The answer from Paris was a clear and satisfactory affirmative. Not so that from Berlin. Von Jagow told the British ambassador that "he must consult the emperor and the chancellor before he could possibly answer. I [the envoy] gathered from what he said that he thought any reply they might give could not but disclose a certain amount of their plan of campaign in the event of war ensuing, and *he was therefore very doubtful whether they would return any answer at all.*"

Such a reply of course confirmed Grey's worst suspicions.

with him upon reports of the increase in the Belgian army: "What is the good of enlarging the number of your troops? With the small number that you had before, you would never dream of barring the way to us in a Franco-German war. The increase of your effectives might inspire you with the idea of resisting us. If a single shot were fired on us, Heaven knows what would become of Belgium!" Beyens answered, "We should be rated still lower than at present, if we were craven enough not to defend ourselves." He repeated this opinion several times to other Germans, but "they listened with smiles, they did not believe me."

The next morning (August 1) he took up the matter directly with the German ambassador at London. If Germany could give some assurance about Belgium "it would materially contribute to relieve anxiety and tension here [in England]." Prince Lichnowsky blandly replied with the counter question: If Germany gave such a promise would England engage to remain neutral? Grey could only tell him the future must decide British policy, only it was true that respect for Belgium would appeal very strongly to the peace element in England. Nothing therefore came from this thrust and counter thrust. It was perfectly plain that England might be selling her neutrality for a mess of pottage, if she undertook to bargain with Germany as to the conditions under which that power would keep her plighted word and perform her most obvious international obligations: [1] and so through that fatal Sunday on which the kaiser had sent defiance to Russia the case drifted, and then shifted abruptly to yet another capital.

During these days of clamor in Europe Belgium had mobilized her small army indeed and taken precautions. She had sent very solemn assurances of her neutrality to all the great powers. Her statesmen of course were extremely anxious, and yet the danger did not seem imminent. On the morning of the 31st of July the German minister at Brussels had assured the Belgian foreign office that "he was certain the sentiments expressed [in 1911 by Bethmann-Hollweg, to the effect that Belgium was not to be violated] had not been changed." From Berlin the reports were not as clear as could be desired, but as M. Davignon, the Belgian foreign minister, said, "a declaration from the German government might appear superfluous in view of existing treaties."

On August 1st, it appeared that the Germans had seized the small, independent and neutralized Grand Duchy of Luxemburg. This caused a shock at Brussels, yet the cases of Luxemburg and Belgium were not quite parallel. [2] The good folk

[1] Of course all question as to England's attitude was mere quibbling on the part of Germany. So long as Belgium was neutral Germany had no right to enter the country whatever England did.

[2] The seizure of Luxemburg was a high-handed and illegal act; but

of Brabant and Flanders refused to take alarm. "Every one thought," wrote a Belgian, looking back on the causes of his exile, " 'they will not fight here. It will be just as in 1870.' " The German minister to King Albert's court was indefatigable with reassuring interviews. He delivered himself to a Brussels journalist, "you may perhaps see your neighbor's roof in flames, but your own house will not catch fire." And Captain Brinckman, the military attaché of the German legation, on the very day that war was declared on Russia, telephoned to "Le XXᵉ Siècle" (a great Brussels newspaper) to deny "in your largest type" that Belgians had anything to dread.

"And Luxemburg?" asked the anxious editor.

"It would not be surprising if certain precautions were taken, but you must not deduce any conclusions about Belgium from that."

The Luxemburg affair however made King Albert's ministers still more anxious. When on the morning of the 2nd of August, Herr von Below, the German minister, called on M. Davignon, the latter said they had received a very firm promise of inviolability from France, and yet nothing had come from Germany. His Excellency the minister replied that nothing indeed had come from Germany yet, but "we [Belgians] knew his personal opinion as to the feelings of security which we had a right to entertain towards our eastern neighbors." Thus the day glided by. There was still contentment and peaceful confidence in Brussels. Crowds of burghers and artisans crowded the narrow streets in family promenading, or went out toward the park of the "woods" toward Tervueren and all the other pleasure resorts in happy parties of picnicers. The afternoon also passed in peace. It was about seven o'clock. Various "musical societies" were returning to the city after country excursions, making the air cheerful and noisy with their instruments. The picnicers with their empty baskets and romping children were coming back from the

the treaties securing the little country were by no means so inclusive in their nature as those for Belgium, and the Germans could claim a direct interest in the Luxemburg railways and customs system.

"woods," when Herr von Below, Minister to King Albert from the German emperor, appeared again at M. Davignon's door at the Belgian foreign office. At last the desired official communiqué from Berlin—a long document, solemnly headed "very confidential!"

The Belgians had asked for an assurance of peace and inviolability in a conflict in which they had not the slightest interest or concern. They received instead—an ultimatum.

The sum of the document was that Germany had learned that French forces "intend to march through Belgium against Germany." [1] Since it was unlikely Belgium could repel such an invasion Germany would have to "anticipate any such hostile attack." However, if Belgium interposed no resistance to the passage of German hosts, Belgian independence would be graciously preserved, the whole country evacuated at the end of the war, and payment made for any supplies taken or damage done. If Belgium should make the least resistance, however, "Germany will to her regret be compelled to consider Belgium as an enemy"; and in that event also

---

[1] At this day there is no need of saying more of this alleged French design in Belgium than that it appears nothing but an impertinent lie. Possibly one of the numerous German spies had concocted some gossip on this point to curry favor with his masters. More likely it was manufactured out of the whole cloth. The proof that the story is a lie is easily obtained by the fact that the original French mobilization was towards the eastern frontier only, and entirely failed to concentrate towards Belgium in time to protect against invasion thence, much less to enter Belgium in any real force.

On August 8th, 1914, William II telegraphed personally to President Wilson that Belgium *"had to be violated by Germany on strategical grounds,"* news having been received that France was already preparing to enter Belgium."

Neither William II nor Bethmann-Hollweg (speech in Reichstag, August 4th, 1914) nor any other German leader ever deigned to produce serious evidence, worthy of consideration for ten minutes in a self-respecting court, that France had any such designs; although it would have been of enormous value to Germany to introduce such testimony. The only reasonable conclusion is that German diplomats and leaders, including the very highest, had different standards of personal honor and veracity than those of the nations of inferior "Kultur" they affected to despise. The real reasons for the invasion have been already given.

Germany could give no guarantee as to the future of Belgium when "left to the decision of arms." Twelve hours were granted in which to answer this ultimatum—until 7 A. M. the next morning, i. e., not enough time to hold any real consultation as to what to do in a most awful crisis, much less sufficient time to consult with the only efficient adviser Belgium could have—England.

It is recorded that the moment the Belgian Royal Council could gather at the palace, there was not one voice upraised for submission. The only questions were about the forms of answer and the organization of resistance. From time to time as the minister and councillors rose from their chairs and paced feverishly before the lighted windows, it is told how they heard the voices of belated city-folk drifting back from their excursions in the fine summer evening,—the fresh laughter of young girls, the trolling of popular songs, the wailing of sleepy children and even now and then the tremulous shouting of a drunken man. Within, until early dawn, King Albert and his council were facing like brave men the impending tragedy of an unmilitary nation of 7,000,000 people against whom was about to be launched the most formidable war machine known to recorded history. It was 4 A. M. when the council dissolved. King Albert and his ministers could not know all the hideous future, but they did know that they had met an awful crisis worthily and had redeemed their souls.

That morning (August 3rd) the Belgian reply was in the hands of the German minister. It recited the outrageousness of violating Belgian neutrality which France had given not the least sign of infringing; and then threw down the gauntlet, "[the Belgians] refuse to believe that the independence of Belgium can only be preserved at the price of the violation of her neutrality. If this hope is disappointed, the Belgian government is firmly resolved to repel with all the means in its power every attack upon its rights." King Albert sent a personal telegram at the same time to King George beseeching the "diplomatic" intervention of England —Belgian pride forbidding a direct appeal for military aid.

When this telegram reached London on the 3rd the British cabinet was still sitting. The pacifists within and without it were still busy. John Burns and Lord Morley were still wagging their tongues that the continent might blaze, France be crushed, Germany become ruler of Europe, and yet nothing must touch their precious schemes for land tenure reforms, poor relief and the reform of this and amelioration of that. In Hyde Park "popular" orators were cursing a war "in behalf of the Czar" and deriding all suggestions that William II was not full of benignity towards England. Pacifists caught by "The Great Illusion," were said to be frantically organizing processions with banners, and (it is alleged) endevoring to hire gutter loafers by the scores to tramp the streets with "sandwiches" advertising the blessings of peace and the follies of war. So the witless sparrows twittered amid the ivy, but the thunder storm drew nigh.

The appeal of the Belgians came now as the last decisive argument, to aid the men in the cabinet council who said that under the circumstances peace for England meant alike utter dishonor and equally certain physical ruin. To have sat still *now* while Belgium, trusting that England would live up to the treaty and would help her, was trampled over by Teutonic armies would have made the name "Briton" another name for craven the wide-world round. Sir Edward Grey received the appeal of the king of the Belgians just as he was about to leave the cabinet and speak in the House of Commons. The speech he delivered there on August 3rd really left no question in the minds of all decent Englishmen as to what their government should do. It was no longer a case, Grey plainly showed, of Serbia, or of Russia, or even of protecting France against the aggrandizement of Germany. All those things might be important, but they were swallowed up in the one obvious duty of redeeming the Belgian treaty. When Grey rose to speak in Parliament there were still many pacifists in England, ready to argue for peace at *almost* any price. When he finished a plain recital of how Germany had shuffled, twisted and evaded on the Belgian question, with this her ultimatum to King Albert as her finale, the pacifists were beaten men. Most of them were no longer pacifists, the remnant were a dazed, helpless minority, silenced or whimpering witnesses of events over which they had not the slightest control.

With the conscience and high consent of the British Empire back of him, on August 4th, Grey sent another telegram to Berlin. It was to be almost the last of a long series.

Sir Edward Goschen went to the German foreign office on the afternoon of the 4th,[1] and fulfilled his instructions. He inquired of Jagow "in the name of His Majesty's government whether the Imperial German government would refrain from violating Belgian neutrality. Herr von Jagow at once replied he was sorry to say that his answer must be 'no,' as in consequence of the German troops having crossed the frontier that morning Belgian neutrality had already been violated."

The German added the already standardized excuses that it was a "matter of life and death" to them to get into France by the best roads and by the least defended way. Therefore, to his great regret, "it was impossible for them to draw back."

Goschen had to wait until this answer could go on the wires to London and he could get his reply, although he knew what the reply would be. Almost at the moment the ambassador and Jagow had been in conference, Bethmann-Hollweg had been addressing the Reichstag, called in special, hasty session. Concerning Belgium he used words, already quoted at this present time of writing until they have grown threadbare, yet destined assuredly to be quoted in many another history a thousand years from today. Speedily the chancellor was to regret his frankness, but his statement could never be recalled: "Gentlemen, we are now in a state of necessity and necessity knows no law. Our troops have occupied Luxemburg, perhaps already they have entered Belgian territory. Gentlemen, this is in contradiction to the rules of international law. . . . France could wait, but we could not wait. . . .[2] So we were forced to set aside the just protests

[1] See end of chapter, note: Beyens, Von Jagow and Belgian Neutrality.

[2] The chancellor repeated some assertions that although France had

of the Luxemburg and Belgian governments. The wrong—I speak openly—the wrong which we do now, we will try to make good again as soon as our military ends have been reached. When one is threatened as we are, and all is at stake, he can only think how he can hack his way through."

Meantime the telegraph wires had been working. Sir Edward Goschen received his final message from London so that he could deliver it about 7 P. M. It was fitting that the last of the series of ultimata should be delivered in Berlin. If Sir Edward went along Unter den Linden, on his errand, he must needs turn off upon the Wilhelmstrasse, and then go to a long one-story building built in the style of the early years of the nineteenth century. It was very bare and unpretentious, but within it, fifty years ago, had been planned the mighty changes which the Hohenzollerns had wrought with their swords in the map of Europe. Here in his long days of power Bismarck had had his seat; for this was the ministry for foreign affairs of the German empire. The visitor on entering went up a marble staircase, catching the musty smell of the masses of papers and documents in the huge ill-ventilated archives as he passed down the upper corridor. Then an attendant would politely escort him to a small room where he would meet the foreign secretary. Thus Goschen proceeded and thus he met Jagow. His instructions were clear and he delivered them. "I informed the secretary of state that unless the imperial government could give assurance by 12 o'clock that night that they would proceed no further with their violation of the Belgian frontier, and stop their advance, I had been instructed to demand my passports and to inform the imperial government that his Majesty's government would have to take all steps in their power to uphold the neutrality of Belgium and the observance of a treaty to which Germany was as much a party as themselves."

Jagow regretfully replied that no reconsideration was pos-

indeed promised to respect Belgian neutrality, "we knew that France stood prepared for an inroad." In other words he charged that France, besides intending to invade Belgium, intended to break a solemn pledge just given. Such assertions need not now be refuted. See p. 528, note 1.

sible. Goschen asked then if he might take farewell of the chancellor. Jagow begged him to do so. Bethmann-Hollweg received his visitor "very much agitated." The plain truth seems to have been that up to the last instant Berlin had cherished *the hope that,* for all her threats and fury, *England would not fight.* No nations were ever psychologically further apart than the two "cousins," the German and the Anglo-Saxon. The apparent commercialism of much British life, the affectation of ease, the distaste for military discipline, the playing and dawdling with pacifism, the interruption of "trade as usual" which a great war would inevitably cost,—these and a thousand alleged similar traits or factors had been hopelessly misinterpreted at the Berlin foreign office and by the great General Staff. The superb German spy system could tell its masters how many guns there were in the British arsenals and what were the plans of the newest dreadnaught, but it could not answer truthfully such a fundamental question as "Will Britain fight?" Seemingly as things drew to a climax Bethmann-Hollweg had realized all was not well at London and had tried to put on the brakes, but the war-party was now in complete control in Berlin and had thrust him aside. Now the last hope was shattered. Instead of humiliating Russia without a war, instead of fighting Russia and France simply, the war was bound to assume simply incalculable proportions. No wonder the chancellor lost self-control and "began a harangue which lasted for about twenty minutes."

England was going to war for "neutrality; 'neutrality,' a word which in war-time had been so often disregarded;—*just for a scrap of paper* Great Britain was going to make war!" So Bethmann-Hollweg continued, his grey-bearded face doubtless purple with passion, his tall form leaning toward the British ambassador, whilst the other, with pale countenance, maintaining the habitual coolness of his race, answered that if Germany wished to talk of "life and death interests," he also "wished him to understand that it was so to speak a matter of 'life and death' for the honor of Great Britain that she should keep her solemn engagement to do her uttermost to defend Belgium. . . . That solemn compact simply *had* to be kept, or what confidence could any one have in engagements given by Great Britain in the future." "But at what a price will that compact have been kept!" groaned the chancellor. Clearly he was "so excited, so overcome by the news of our action, and so little disposed to hear reason that I [Goschen] refrained from adding fuel to the flame by further argument," and speedily went away.

That night a cursing, roaring crowd, brushing aside the usually over-watchful police, cast cobble-stones and lumps of coal into the front windows of the British embassy, where excited attachés were busily packing their portmanteaus. The next morning all the world was reading the dispatch from London that Great Britain had declared war on Germany the preceding midnight. *England had gone in.* Hereafter, for a period infinitely longer and more terrible than any man in 1914 could have imagined, the history of the world was to be written not by the diplomat but by the soldier, while "the boundaries of Europe were being retraced in blood."

On the night of August 4th, the last of the terrible "Twelve Days," came the end of that era in European history which began that fateful night in 1870 when Otto von Bismarck re-wrote the Ems dispatch from King William. This epoch had been ushered in by a deed which, if it had failed, would have been branded as an act of outrageous depravity: but which, since it succeeded, was to be lauded as the master stroke of genius. It was to end with the chancellor of the German empire calling a most solemn international treaty a "scrap of paper," when the ambassador of a great power talked of truth, justice and faithfulness between nation and nation. The dawn of this epoch had seen the consolidation of the German states under the domination of Prussia into the formidable German empire. It found its sunset when, disregarding all established sanctions, covenants and moral processes, the rulers of this new empire surrendered themselves to schemes of world conquest which would take them straight along the paths of imperial Rome. Manifestly, therefore, for years there could be no more peace in the world.

In the London "Times," on the morning of August 6th,

1914, appeared this sonnet by William Watson. It spoke the sentiments not merely of England and France, but with increasing clearness those of almost every non-Teutonized folk throughout the wide earth.

TO THE TROUBLER OF THE WORLD

"At last we know you, War-Lord. You, that flung
  The gauntlet down, fling down the mask you wore,
  Publish your heart, and let its pent hate pour,
You that had God forever on your tongue.
We are old in war, and if in guile we are young,
  Young also is the spirit that evermore
  Burns in our bosom even as heretofore,
Nor are these thews unbraced, these nerves unstrung.
We do not with God's name make wanton play:
  We are not on such easy terms with Heaven:
But in Earth's hearing we can verily say,
  'Our hands are pure; for peace, for peace we have striven;
  And not by earth shall soon he be forgiven,
Who lit the fire accursed that flames to-day!' "

ATTITUDE OF ENGLAND, AUGUST 1, 1914

The writer may register a personal opinion, having been in England at the outbreak of hostilities, with a reasonable opportunity to observe events and opinions, that if Belgium had been left intact, England would not have entered the war during its opening stages, although her "neutrality" might have been very unbenevolent to Germany. Probably after a little, the pressure of her more intelligent classes would have compelled her to go into a contest which, if Germany had won promptly, would have left England in ruinous isolation facing aggrandized Teutonia. Whether however England would have entered soon enough to save France from complete overthrow, I dare not state.

From the outset nearly all Englishmen accustomed to study foreign affairs believed it their clear duty to "go in"; but the apathy and bewilderment of the less educated classes was pathetic. For some days after war was declared they could not realize anything serious had really happened. August 9th, in a small English city, I attended the regular Sunday morning service in the Wesleyan church. A typical, respectably dressed, but not aristocratic audience was present. Neither in prayer, sermon, nor less formal remarks was there the slightest reference to the outbreak of war. No patriotic hymn was sung. All the announcements were of a routine order, and the only appeal made was for a liberal contribution for a mission in Africa. No one present at that service would have imagined that Great Britain was at war.

Many Church of England circles were no more enkindled. I know specifically of a church where the day before war was declared the vicar explained to his flock that it was impossible for them to have any prayers suitable for the dread occasion because "the bishop had not enjoined any," and he (the vicar) "did not feel the case serious enough to read any unusual prayers upon his own unauthorized initiative."

BEYENS, VON JAGOW AND BELGIAN NEUTRALITY

At 9 A. M. on this day Baron Beyens had already called on Von Jagow to tell him of the final determination of the Belgian government to resist to the uttermost. He asked Jagow what the Germans would have said of Belgium if before French threats she had yielded a passage though against Germany. "You would have said . . . that we were cowards, incapable of defending our neutrality and unworthy of an independent existence." To this Jagow made no reply.

After some further argument by Beyens, the envoy said that it was impossible for Belgium to consent to the German demands when "In recognition of our loyalty [to neutrality] you wish to make our country the battlefield for your struggle with France, and we know what devastation modern warfare brings with it. . . . You must recognize that no other reply [to your demands] was possible."

Jagow was silent or evasive, but in the face of Beyens' persistence replied at last, "I recognize it, I understand your reply. I understand it as a private individual but as a secretary of state I have no opinion to express." He then reiterated the old argument that "a rapid march through Belgium was a question of life or death," for Germany, and every other consideration had to give way to that.

There is little doubt that the German General Staff committed at the outset of the war the grievous blunder of underestimating the tenacity and resistance of the French, and the no less serious blunder of underestimating the ability of the Russians to effect fairly rapid mobilization. I may give as a civilian, non-military opinion the judgment that if the Germans had stood on the strict defensive against France, had let Belgium alone, and had concentrated all their main energies upon a sudden drive against Russia, the war would have ended in a comparatively short time with the utter defeat of the czar. England probably would have stood neutral or at most only fought Germany in a naval way, and the French would soon have been glad to make peace after a few brave but unsuccessful offensives into Lorraine, which could not have been pushed home desperately as soon as the French people were convinced that Germany's quarrel was with Russia, and that William II did not intend a new invasion of France.

RULERS OF EUROPE, PRIME MINISTERS OF GREAT BRITAIN AND CHANCELLORS OF GERMANY, SINCE 1870

GREAT BRITAIN

Queen and Kings:

Victoria,	1837–1901
Edward VII,	1901–1910
George V,	1910–

Prime Ministers:

Gladstone (L),	1868–1874
Disraeli (C),	1874–1880
Gladstone (L),	1880–1885
Salisbury (C),	1885–1886
Gladstone (L),	1886
Salisbury (C),	1886–1892
Gladstone (L),	1892–1894
Rosebery (L),	1894–1895
Salisbury (C),	1895–1902
Balfour (C),	1902–1905
Campbell-Bannerman (L),	1905–1908
Asquith (L),	1908–1916
Lloyd George (L),	1916–

L = Liberal.
C = Conservative

GERMANY

Emperors:

William I,	1871–1888
Frederick III,	1888
William II,	1888–

Chancellors:

Bismarck	1871–1890
Caprivi,	1890–1894
Hohenlohe,	1894–1900
Bülow,	1900–1909
Bethmann-Hollweg,	1909–1917
Michaelis,	1917
Hertling,	1917–

FRANCE

Presidents:

Thiers,	1871–1873
MacMahon,	1873–1879
Grevy,	1879–1887
Carnot,	1887–1894
Casimir-Perier,	1894–1895
Faure,	1895–1899
Loubet,	1899–1906
Fallières,	1906–1913
Poincaré,	1913–

AUSTRIA

Emperors:

Franz Josef I,	1848–1916
Charles I,	1916–

RUSSIA

Czars:

Alexander II,	1855–1881
Alexander III,	1881–1894
Nicholas II,	1894–1917

ITALY

Kings:

Victor Emmanuel II,	1861–1878
Humbert,	1878–1900
Victor Emmanuel III,	1900–

ROUMANIA

Prince Carol I,	1866–1914
(As "Tsar"),	1908–
King Ferdinand,	1914–

TURKEY

Sultans:

Abdul Aziz	1861–1876

Murad V,	1876	SERBIA	
Abdul Hamid II,	1876–1909	*Kings:*	
Mohammed V,	1909–	Milan IV,	1868–1889
GREECE		Alexander,	1889–1903
Kings:		Peter,	1903–
George I,	1862–1913	BULGARIA	
Constantine,	1913–1917	Prince Alexander,	1879–1887
Alexander,	1917–	" Ferdinand,	1887–
		(As "Tsar"),	1908–

GROWTH OF THE BRITISH, GERMAN, AND FRENCH COLONIAL EMPIRES, SINCE 1870

BRITISH COLONIES, ACQUIRED SINCE 1870 WITH APPROXIMATE AREA AND POPULATION OF EACH

Pacific and East Indies:

	Area (Sq. Miles)	Population
Fiji	7,435	139,541
Tonga	390	23,000
Federated Malay States	27,506	1,036,999
Other Malay States:		
Kelantan	5,500	286,750
Trengganu	6,000	154,037
Kedal	3,800	245,986
Perlis	300	32,746
State of Johore	9,000	180,412
Brunei (in Borneo)	4,000	30,000
North Borneo	31,106	208,183
Sarawak (in Borneo)	42,000	500,000
Papua (Brit. New Guinea)	90,540	269,900

Africa:

Nigeria	336,080	17,000,000
Somaliland	68,000	310,000
Bechuanaland	275,000	125,350
Zululand	10,424	185,000
British East Africa	246,822	4,038,000
Rhodesia	438,575	1,744,559
Zanzibar	640	114,069
Uganda	121,437	2,893,494
Nyasaland	39,315	1,000,000
Ashanti		287,814

	Area (Sq. Miles)	Population
Orange Free State	50,389	528,174
Transvaal	110,426	1,686,212
Swaziland	6,536	99,959

Added to India:

	Area (Sq. Miles)	Population
Northwest Frontier Province	13,418	2,196,933
British Baluchistan (1854–1876)	54,228	414,412

GERMAN COLONIES, ACQUIRED SINCE 1870

In Africa:

	Area (Sq. Miles)	Population
Togo	33,700	1,031,978
Kamerun	191,130	2,648,720
German South-west Africa	322,450	79,556
German East Africa	384,180	7,645,770

In Asia:

Kiauchau (from China)	200	168,900

In the Pacific:

German New Guinea	95,160	600,000
Samoan Islands, etc.	1,000	34,579

FRENCH COLONIES, ACQUIRED SINCE 1870

In Asia:

Annam ⎫ with Cambodia Tonking ⎬ and Cochin- Laos ⎭ China	309,980	14,500,000

In Africa:

	Area (Sq. Miles)	Population
Algeria	222,067	5,563,828
Sahara	1,544,000	800,000
Tunis	45,779	1,878,620
Senegal ⎫ with Upper Senegal ⎪ Guinea and Niger ⎬ and Dahomey ⎪ Ivory (inclusive area) Mauritania ⎭ Coast	1,585,810	(total pop.) 7,500,000
Congo	553,030	3,900,000
Madagascar	226,015	3,257,895

In Oceania:

New Caledonia (protectorate earlier)	7,200	50,500
Tahiti, etc. " "	1,544	30,600

POPULATIONS OF THE GREAT EUROPEAN POWERS IN THE GENERATION BEFORE 1914

	1875	1885	1905	1914
Great Britain	33,110,167	36,707,418	43,221,123	46,089,249
Germany	42,727,360	46,844,926	60,641,278	67,812,000
France	36,905,788	38,218,903	39,252,267	39,602,258
Italy	27,482,174	29,361,032	33,733,198	35,597,784
Austria-Hungary, (excluding Bosnia)	35,901,435	39,224,511	45,405,267	49,882,331
Russian Empire, (including Siberia)	86,450,751	104,785,761	146,796,600	178,378,800

MERCHANT SHIPPING OF BRITAIN, GERMANY, AND FRANCE

(Net tonnage of steam and sailing vessels registered.)*

	1875	1885	1905	1914
Great Britain	6,152,000	7,387,000	10,735,582	12,415,204
Germany	1,258,381	1,294,288	2,352,575	3,320,071
France	1,028,228	1,033,829	1,349,327	1,582,416

* The "gross tonnage," by which vessels are often measured, would would make each of these figures rather more than 50% greater.

USEFUL BOOKS FOR
GENERAL STUDIES OF EUROPEAN DIPLOMACY

Prepared by MASON W. TYLER, PH.D.

I

A SUMMARIES OF POLICY TO 1914.

1. Seymour, "The Diplomatic Background of the War," New Haven, Yale University Press.

   Covers in broad outline the period 1870–1914.

   Confined to European diplomatic history.

2. Schmitt, "England and Germany," Princeton, Princeton Univ. Press.

   Deals with relations of England and Germany merely.

   Covers period from about 1900 to 1914.

3. Lemonon, "L'Europe et la Politique Britannique 1882–1911," Paris, Alcan.

   In French. Covers relations of England and the Continental powers within the dates given.

4. Pinon, "France et Allemagne," Paris, Perrin.

   A brief study of the relations of the two powers, 1870–1914.

5. Reventlow, "Deutschlands auswärtige Politik," Berlin, Mittler and Son.

   The foreign policy of Germany 1890–1914. Interest somewhat concentrated on naval affairs.

6. Fullerton, "Problems of Power," New York, Scribners.

   A study of economic questions and of the growth of public opinion, 1880–1912.

7. Reinsch, "World Politics," New York, Macmillan.

   Economic imperialism, especially in the Far East.

8. Gibbons, "The New Map of Europe," New York, Century.

   Brief introduction, followed by detailed study of the Balkans, 1908–1914. Excellent.

9. Tardieu, "France and the Alliances," New York, Macmillan.

   France's foreign policy in the early years of the twentieth century.

B COMMENTARIES ON DIPLOMATIC METHODS.

    1. Lippman, "The Stakes of Diplomacy," New York, Heubsch.

        Argues for a world federation for the exploitation of territories. Keen and thoughtful criticism on the relation of public opinion to foreign policy.

    2. Weyl, "American World Policies," New York, Macmillan.

        American policy considered in relation to the new situation. A thoughtful commentary.

    3. Brailsford, "The War of Steel and Gold," New York, Macmillan.

        Traces the present situation back to capitalistic imperialism. A Liberal's criticism of the pre-war diplomacy. [Honest pacifism. W. S. D.]

C AMERICA AND THE WAR.

    1. Roosevelt, "America and the World War," New York, Scribners.

        Published in the early days of the war. The American nationalist position eloquently stated.

    2. "The War Peril," Princeton, Princeton Univ. Press.

        Essays on various phases of the war in their relation to America.

II

ENGLAND

1. Gretton, "A Modern History of the English People" (2 volumes), London, Richards, Ltd.

    A breezy journalistic history of England from 1880 to about 1912.

2. Slater, "The Making of Modern England," Boston, Houghton Mifflin.

    Especial emphasis on economic questions. Covers the period 1815–1912. [Largely ignores foreign questions. Not a continuous history. Ultra-radical. W. S. D.]

3. Morley, "Gladstone" (3 volumes), New York, Macmillan.

    The best introduction to liberal England 1850–1900.

4. Lowell, "The Government of England," New York, Macmillan.

    The classic account of English government.

5. Lucas, "The British Empire," London, Macmillan.

    Historical account of the British Empire.

6. Curtis, "The Problems of the Commonwealth," Toronto, Macmillan.

 An analysis of the bases for Imperial Federation.

III

FRANCE

1. Wright, "France under the Third Republic," Boston, Houghton, Mifflin.

 A good brief account.

2. Guérard, "French Civilization in the Nineteenth Century," London, Fisher Unwin.

 A study of the tendencies in France since 1815. A little inclined to be radical and anti-clerical. Should be read in connection with the following:

3. Dimnet, "France Herself Again," London, Chatto and Windus.

 Also a study of tendencies in France since about 1870. Rather clerical and conservative in tone.

4. Sabatier, "France Today," New York, Dutton.

 A clear and broad-minded study of the French religious situation.

5. Poincairé, "How France Is Governed," London, Fisher Unwin.

 A good account of French government under the Third Republic by the present President.

IV

GERMANY

1. Fife, "The German Empire Between Two Wars," New York, Macmillan.

 Covers the history of Germany 1870–1914 in its broadest relations.

2. Dawson, "The Evolution of Modern Germany," New York, Scribners.

 More confined to economic questions and politics. Penetrating analysis.

3. Bülow, "Imperial Germany," New York, Henry Holt.

 The German official apologia by the former Chancellor.

4. Naumann, "Central Europe," New York, Knopf.

 Moderate pan-Germanism, urges a federation of central Europe under German hegemony.

5. Rohrbach, "Germany's Isolation," Chicago, McClurg.
   Moderate pan-Germanism in the colonial field.
6. "Conquest and Kultur," United States Government (Red, White
   and Blue Series).
   Extracts from the more extreme pro-Germans, as well as the
   moderates, to show the world-policy of this group.

V
AUSTRIA-HUNGARY

1. Steed, "The Hapsburg Monarchy," New York, Scribner.
   A penetrating study of modern Austria. Little consideration
   of the question of nationalities.
2. von Schierbrand, "Austria-Hungary," New York, Stokes.
   A somewhat favorable view of the future of Austria.
3. Seton-Watson, "German, Slav and Magyar," London, Williams
   and Norgate.
4. Seton-Watson, "The Southern Slav Question and the Hapsburg
   Monarchy," London, Constable.
   Both are rather unfavorable but scholarly accounts of the
   question of nationalities in Austria.

VI
THE NEAR EAST

1. Miller, "The Ottoman Empire," Cambridge, Cambridge Univ.
   Press.
   Really a history of the Near East in the nineteenth century
   (1815–1913).
2. Marriott, "The Near East," Oxford, Clarendon Press.
   Same subject but broader in scope. Covers period from Middle Ages to 1914.
3. Pinon, "L'Europe et L'Empire Ottoman," Paris, Perrin.
4. Pinon, "L'Europe et la Jeune Turquie," Paris, Perrin.
   Two valuable commentaries on the Near East covering the
   period from 1900 to the Balkan Wars.
5. "A Diplomat," "War and Nationalism in the Near East," Oxford,
   Clarendon Press.
   More a commentary than a history. Extremely suggestive.
6. Lewin, "The German Road to the East," London, Heinemann.
   Violently anti-German accounts of German policy in the Near
   East.

VII

MOROCCO

1. Tardieu, "Le Conference d'Algeciras," Paris, Calmann-Levy.
2. Tardieu, "Le Prince de Bülow," Paris, Calmann-Levy.
3. Tardieu, "Le Mystère d'Agadir," Paris, Calmann-Levy.
    Together they constitute the best apology for French policy in Morocco 1905–1912.
4. More, "Ten Years of Secret Diplomacy," London, Labor Press.
    An attack on English and French policy in Morocco.

For extensive critical bibliography on "War Causes" see *History Teachers' Magazine*, March, 1918.   Excellent.

INDEX